EARLY TRAVELS
IN PALESTINE

EARLY TRAVELS
IN PALESTINE

EDITED BY
THOMAS WRIGHT

DOVER PUBLICATIONS, INC.
MINEOLA, NEW YORK

Bibliographical Note

This Dover edition, first published in 2003, is an unabridged republication of the work originally published by Henry G. Bohn, London, in 1848.

Library of Congress Cataloging-in-Publication Data

Early travels in Palestine / edited by Thomas Wright.
    p. cm.
    An unabridged republication of the work originally published by Henry G. Bohn, London, in 1848.
    Includes bibliographical references and index.
    ISBN 0-486-42871-0 (pbk.)
    1. Palestine—Description and travel—Early works to 1800. 2. Middle East—Description and travel—Early works to 1800. I. Wright, Thomas, 1810–1877.

DS105.E37 2003
915.69404'3—dc21
                                2003046072

Manufactured in the United States of America
Dover Publications, Inc., 31 East 2nd Street, Mineola, N.Y. 11501

TO HIS GRACE

THE LORD ARCHBISHOP OF YORK,

THIS VOLUME

IS VERY RESPECTFULLY DEDICATED

BY

THE EDITOR.

CONTENTS.

REFERENCES TO PLAN OF JERUSALEM,

REDUCED FROM A LARGE PLAN, CONSTRUCTED BY SCHULTZ, PRUSSIAN CONSUL AT JERUSALEM.

1. Chapel of Scourging.
2. Scala Sancta.
3. Pilate's House.
4. Chapel of Crowning with Thorns.
5. Arch of '*Ecce Homo.*'
6. First place where Simon carried the Cross.
7. Second do.   do.
8. Gate of Judgment (Porta Judiciaria).
9. House of Urias.
10. Bath of Bathsheba.
11. House of the High Priest Zacharias.
12.   „   St. Marcus.
13.   „   St. Thomas.
14.   „   High Priest Annas.
15.   „   „   Caiphas.
16. Room in which the Last Supper was instituted.
17. House of the Virgin Mary.
18. Place where St. Peter wept.
19. House of Sta. Anna.
20.   „   the Pharisee Simon.
21. Place where Stephen was stoned.
22.   „   Jesus sweated blood.
23.   „   the Disciples slept.
24.   „   Judas kissed Christ.
25.   „   Jesus taught the Lord's Prayer.
26.   „   „   wept over Jerusalem.
27.   „   the Apostles learned the Creed.
28.   Judas hanged himself.
29. Tomb of Jehoshaphat.
30.   „   Absolom.
31.   „   Jacob.
32.   „   Zacharias.

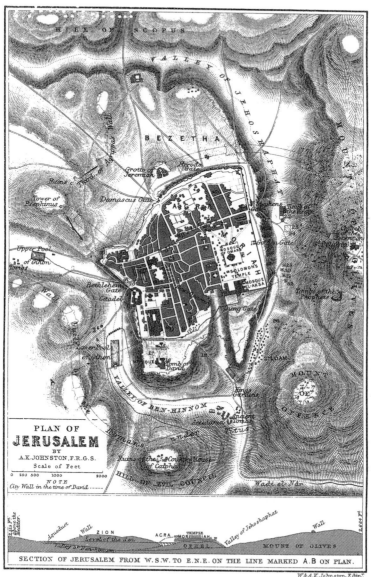

PLAN OF
JERUSALEM
BY
A.K.JOHNSTON,F.R.G.S.
Scale of Feet

0   250 500   1000   2000

NOTE
City Wall in the time of David ....

SECTION OF JERUSALEM FROM W.S.W. TO E.N.E. ON THE LINE MARKED A.B ON PLAN.

W.&A.K.Johnston.Edin.ʳ

INTRODUCTION.

THE attentive reader of history cannot fail to remark how often, in the confusion of the middle ages, the very movements or principles which seem in themselves most barbarous, or are most strongly tinctured with the darkest shades of superstition, have been those which, in the sequel, gave the strongest impulse to the advancing spirit of civilization which has at length changed that dark past into this bright present It is in the contemplation of this oft-recurring fact, that we trace, more distinctly, perhaps, than in any other, the inscrutable but unerring ways of that higher Providence to whose rule all things are subjected. Few of those duties enjoined by the ancient Romish Church were accompanied with, and seemed to lead to, more abuses and scandals than the pilgrimages to the Holy Land, so natural an attraction to every Christian ; few were attended with so much bigotry, and blindness, and uncharitableness, or ended in observances and convictions so grossly superstitious and so degrading to the intelligence of mankind. Yet it was this throwing of people upon the wide and distant scene, on which they were forced into continual intercourse, hostile or friendly, according to the circumstances of the moment, with people of different manners, creed, sentiment, and knowledge, that gradually softened down all prejudices, and paved the way for the entire destruction of that system to which it seemed intended to give support. If the seeds of civilization ever existed in the cloister, they were seeds cast upon the barren rock, and it was not until they were transplanted to another and richer soil, that they began to sprout and give promise of fruit.

Even in this point of view the narrative of those early pilgrimages must possess no ordinary degree of interest, and it gives us no little insight into the history of the march of intellectual improvement to accompany these early travellers in their wanderings, as they have themselves described them to us, and to watch their feelings and hear their opinions. The human mind is one of those important objects of study that we can never look upon from too many standing-places. But there is another point of view in which the narratives of the early pilgrims, of which so many have been preserved, are perhaps still more interesting. That favoured land to which they relate, the scene of so many events of deep import to our happiness in this world and in the future, has never lost its attractions, and more steps, as well as more eyes, are now turned towards it, than in those so-called ages of faith, when every mile on the road was believed to count in heaven for so much towards the redemption of the past crimes and offences, however great, of the traveller. Pilgrims innumerable still visit the holy places, with a purer faith and a less prejudiced understanding, yet with the desire of knowing what others in past ages saw, which is now not to be seen, or which is seen under different circumstances; to know what they thought of objects which still offer themselves to view; and to trace in their successive observations and reflections the gradual development of a thirst for discovery and knowledge which has at length given them the power of being so much wiser than their forefathers. It was the interest created by the objects these pilgrims visited personally, and the curiosity excited by the vague information obtained from intercourse with men who came from parts still more distant, that laid the first foundation of geographical science, and that first gave the impulse to geographical discovery.

A comparison of the numerous narratives to which we allude, places before our eyes the most distinct view we can possibly have of the various changes which have swept over the land of Palestine since it was snatched from the power of the Roman emperors. The more ancient are, of course, the most interesting, because they relate to a period when a far greater number of monuments of still earlier antiquity remained in existence than it has been the lot of any modern pilgrims to visit, and the traditions of the locality were then much more deserving of attention, because they were so much nearer to the time of the events to which they related. It can hardly be supposed that the Christian inhabitants of Jerusalem and its neighbourhood, under the Romans, did not preserve some authentic traditions concerning the localities of the more important events of Gospel history.

We have fortunately one document of a very remarkable character, which has preserved to us the local traditions of the Christians of Syria under the Romans. It was first brought to light by the celebrated French antiquary, Pierre Pithou, who printed it, in 1588, from a manuscript in his own library, under the title of "*Itinerarium a Burdigala Hierusalem usque;*" and it was afterwards inserted in the editions of the "*Antonine Itinerary,*" by Schott and Wesseling. The author of this Itinerary was a Christian of Bordeaux, who visited the Holy Land in the year 333*, and it was evidently compiled for the use of his countrymen. This visit took place two years before the consecration of the Church of the Holy Sepulchre, built by the emperor Constantine and his mother Helena. The compiler of this Itinerary, who is the first traveller to the East who has left us an account of his journey, departed from Bordeaux, then one of the chief cities of Gaul, passed by Arles and other towns, and crossed the Alps into Italy, which country he traversed, passing through Turin, Pavia, Milan, Brescia, Verona, &c., to the then magnificent city of Aquileia; thence he crossed the Julian Alps, and passed through Noricum, Pannonia, Illyria, Dacia, and Thrace, to Constantinople, and thence, after crossing the Bosphorus, he continued his route through Asia Minor to Syria. Hitherto the Itinerary is a mere recapitulation of names and distances, but, after his arrival in Syria, he continually interrupts his bare list of names, to mention some holy site, or other object which attracted his attention. On his arrival at Jerusalem, he gives us a long description of that city and its neighbourhood. From Jerusalem he returns to Constantinople, varying a little his route, and thence he retraces his steps as far as Heraclea in Thrace, where he leaves his former road, passing through Macedonia to Thessalonica, and thence to Italy, where he visited Brundusium, Capua, and Rome, and thence returned to Milan.

---

* This date is fixed by a statement of the writer of the Itinerary:— " Item ambulavimus Dalmatio et Dalmaticei Zenophilo cons. iii. Kal. Jun. a Kalcidonia, et reversi sumus ad Constantinopolim vii. Kalend. Jan. consule suprascripto." We know from the historians that Flavius Valerius Dalmatius (brother of the emperor Constantine) and Marcus Aurelius Zenophilus were consuls together in 333.

Although this Itinerary has come down to us as a solitary narrative, we learn from the writings of some of the Greek fathers, that pilgrimages to the Holy Land had already, at that period, become so frequent as to lead to many abuses; and the early saints' lives have been the means of preserving to us brief notices of some of the adventures of the pilgrims, which are obscured by the incredible miracles with which those narratives abound. St. Porphyry, a Greek ecclesiastic of the end of the fourth century, after living five years as a hermit in the Thebaid of Egypt, went with his disciple Marcus to Jerusalem, visited the holy places, settled there, and finally became bishop of Gaza. St. Eusebius of Cremona, and his friend St. Jerome, embarked at Porto, in Italy, in June 385, in company with a great number of other pilgrims, and in the midst of tempests passed the Ionian Sea and the Cyclades to Cyprus, where they were received by St. Epiphanius. They went thence to Antioch, where they were welcomed by St. Paulinus, who was bishop of that city, and from thence they proceeded to Jerusalem. After passing some time in the holy city, and visiting the surrounding country, they went to Egypt, to visit the hermits of the Thebaid, and then returning, they took up their abode at Bethlehem, where they founded a monastery. Nearly at the same time, St. Paula, with her daughter, left Rome for Syria, and landed at Sidon, where she visited the tower of Elijah. At Cæsarea she saw the house of the centurion Cornelius, which was changed into a church, and the house of St. Philip, with the chambers of his four daughters. Near Jerusalem she beheld the tomb of Helena, queen of Adiabene. The governor of Palestine, who was acquainted with the family of St. Paula, prepared to receive her in Jerusalem with due honours, but she preferred taking up her abode in a small cell, and she hastened to visit all the holy objects with which she was now surrounded. She went first to the church of the Holy Sepulchre, where she prostrated herself before the true cross, and entered the sepulchre itself, after having kissed the stone which the angels had taken from the entrance. On Mount Sion, she was shown the column to which Christ was bound when scourged, and which then sustained the gallery of a church. She saw also the spot where the Holy Ghost had descended on the Apostles on the day of Pentecost. She thence went to Bethlehem, visiting on the way the sepulchre of

Rachel. At Bethlehem she descended into the grotto of the Nativity. She next visited the tower of Ader of the Flocks. At Bethphage, she saw the sepulchre of Lazarus, and the house of Martha and Mary; on Mount Ephraim, she was shown the sepulchre of Joshua, and of the high priest Eleazar; at Sichem, she entered the church built over the well of Jacob, where our Saviour spoke to the Samaritan woman; she next visited the sepulchres of the twelve patriarchs; and, at Sebaste, or Samaria, she saw those of Elisha and Abdias, as well as that of St. John the Baptist. To the latter were brought, from all parts, people possessed with demons, to be cured. St. Paula went subsequently to Egypt, to visit the hermits of the desert, whence she returned to Bethlehem, where she built cells and hospitals for pilgrims, and there she lived in retirement till her death*. St. Antoninus visited the Holy Land early in the seventh century; his life contains some absurd legendary stories relating to the cross, which he saw in the church of Golgotha; and he tells that there stood on one part of Mount Sion an " idol of the Saracens," made of very white marble (no doubt an ancient sepulchre), which, at the time of the festival of that idol, suddenly became black as pitch, and after the festival was restored to its original colour. At Nazareth, St. Antoninus praises the beauty of the Jewish women who resided there; and he tells us that the land round that place was prodigiously fertile, and that it produced excellent wine, oil, and honey. The millet grew there to a greater height than elsewhere, and the straw was stronger. After visiting all the holy places, St. Antoninus, like all the other pilgrims who went to the east before the conquests of the Saracens, repaired to Egypt, to visit the hermits of the Thebaid. He landed at Alexandria, a very fine city, the people of which were light in disposition, but friendly to the travellers who came thither. He saw there, in the Nile, a multitude of crocodiles, a great number of which were collected together in a pond. Perhaps this was some remnant of the ancient worship of the Egyptians. On his return to Jerusalem, St. Antoninus fell sick, and was received into a

---

* St. Jerome, in one of his Epistles, has given us the history of the adventures of St. Paula. The lives of the other saints mentioned here will be found in the large collection of the Bollandists. The abstract given here is taken from the Essay on Early Pilgrimages, by the Baron Walckenaer, inserted in Michaud's History of the Crusades.

hospital destined for poor pilgrims; he then went into Mesopotamia, and returned by sea to Italy, his native country.

Soon after this period, the circumstances of the pilgrims
who arrived in the Holy Land were entirely changed, in consequence of the conquests of the Saracens, who, under Omar,
obtained possession of Jerusalem in 637, by a capitulation,
however, which allowed them the use of their churches on
payment of a tribute, but forbade them to build new ones.
This interdiction could not be in itself a great grievance, for
the whole of Palestine must have been literally covered with
churches when it passed under the Mohammedan yoke. The
conquerors soon saw that greater advantages would be reaped
by preserving the holy places, and encouraging pilgrimage,
than by destroying them; many of them, indeed their own
creed taught them, were to be considered as objects of reverence; and thus for two or three centuries the Christians of
the west continued to flock to the Holy Sepulchre as numerously as before, subject, perhaps, to not much greater taxation
at the holy places than in former times, but exposed on their
way to more or less insult and oppression, according to the
political or local circumstances of the moment.

Not many years after it had thus fallen under the power of
the Arabs, the Holy Land was visited by a French bishop
named ARCULF, whose narrative stands at the head of the
present volume. The French antiquaries have not been
able to discover of what see Arculf was bishop, or when he
lived; and all that is known of him is the statement of
Adamnan, who wrote down his narrative, that on his return
from the east he was carried by contrary winds to the shores
of Britain, and that he was received at Iona. We learn
from Bede*, that Adamnan visited the court of the Northum-
brian king Aldfrid, and that he then presented to the king
his book on the Holy Places, which he had taken down from
the dictation of bishop Arculf. The visit to king Aldfrid is
generally placed in 703, but by an apparent misunderstanding
of the words of Bede, and it is probable that it occurred at
least as early as 701†. The pilgrimage of Arculf must thus
have taken place in the latter part of the seventh century.
In relating a miracle concerning the *sudarium* or napkin
taken from the head of our Saviour (which has not been

* Bede, Hist. Eccl. v. 15.
† See my Biographia Britannica Literaria, Anglo-Saxon period, p. 202.

thought worth retaining in the present translation), Arculf is made to speak of "Majuvias, king of the Saracens," as having lived in his time*, and the character of the story leaves no doubt that the king referred to was Moawiyah, the first khalif of the dynasty of the Ommiades, who reigned from 661 to 679. I am inclined to think that Arculf's visit to Jerusalem must be placed not long after this khalif's death.

Arculf's travels, having been reduced to a sort of treatise by Adamnan, do not always present the exact form of a personal narrative, and we cannot trace his course from his native land as we do those of most subsequent travellers. He seems to have followed in the steps of the more ancient pilgrims, and his visit to Egypt, with the avowal of his voyages up the Nile, can only be explained on the supposition that he also went to visit the Coptic monks of the Desert, who had been allowed to remain there, tributary to their Arabian conquerors. He either derived little satisfaction from this visit, or Adamnan considered it as having no interest for his countrymen; and we find no allusion to the Egyptian monks in the later pilgrimages. Arculf speaks of no difficulties he had to encounter, and his narrative is of especial interest, from the circumstance of his visiting the country when all the buildings of the Roman age were still standing.

The narrative of bishop Arculf, besides its intrinsic value as a minute and accurate description of localities and monuments at this interesting period, is of especial importance to us, because, through the abridgment made by Bede, it became the text book on this subject among the Anglo-Saxons, and led to that passion for pilgrimages with which they were soon afterwards seized, and which was not uncongenial to the character of that people whose adventurous steps have since been carried into every corner of the world.

Among the Anglo-Saxons who followed the example of Arculf, one of the most remarkable, and the earliest of whose adventures we have any account, was WILLIBALD, a kinsman, it is said, of the great Boniface, and a native of the kingdom of Wessex, probably of Hampshire. His father, who appears to have been of high rank, was honoured with a place in the Roman calendar, under the title of St. Richard. He, with his two sons, Willibald and Wunibald, and a daughter,

* Majuvias, Saracenorum rex, qui nostra ætate fuit, judex postulatus.

afterwards so celebrated under the name of St. Walpurgis, left England probably in the year 718, and travelled through the land of the Franks on their way to Italy. At Lucca, Willibald's father sickened and died; and, having buried him, the three children reached Rome in safety, but there they were seized with a severe fever, on their recovery from which Willibald determined to make a pilgrimage to Jerusalem. I have fixed the date of his departure to the year 721, because that would place his departure from Tyre on his way to Constantinople, in 724; and I have stated on another occasion *, that it is in the highest degree probable that the difficulties Willibald and his companions experienced in obtaining a passport, and the troubles they met with in their departure from Syria, were coincident with the persecution of the Christian churches in that country in the year just alluded to, when the khalif Yezid II., at the end of his reign, had been instigated by the Jews to publish an edict against the paintings in the churches of his Christian subjects, in consequence of which many of the latter fled their homes. After the death of Yezid, hostilities recommenced between the Greeks and the Arabs, and continued during many years; and it is evident that the two countries were not yet at war when the pilgrims left. At the same time, the whole tenor of the narrative shows that they quitted Syria on account of some sudden change in the internal state of the country, and that they were anxious to get away, for they came to Tyre at the wrong season of the year for making the voyage to Constantinople, and they sailed in rough and tempestuous weather. In 740 or 741, Willibald was consecrated bishop of Eichstadt, being then forty-one years of age. He died, it is supposed, in the year 786. His life was written before his death, by a nun of Heidenheim, of whose name we are ignorant, but who was his kinswoman, and who took down the account of his travels, as she avows, from his own mouth.

The war with the Greeks did not, however, put a stop to pilgrimages from the west, but the travellers now seem to have been obliged to pass by way of Egypt. The geographer, Dicuil, in his treatise *De Mensura Orbis Terræ*, which he wrote at a very advanced age, in 825, tells us, when speaking of Egypt, that when a youth at school in France, he heard a monk named Fidelis give an account of his travels in Egypt

* See the Biographia Britannica Literaria, Anglo-Saxon period, p. 341, 342.

and the Holy Land, to his master, Suibneus, and, from the accuracy with which he cites it, he must have taken notes at the time. He says, that Fidelis went with a party of pilgrims, clerks and laymen, who sailed direct to the mouth of the Nile, no doubt to Alexandria. Proceeding up the Nile a long way, they were struck with astonishment at the sight of the seven " barns " (*horrea*), built by Joseph, according to the number of the years of abundance, which looked at a distance like mountains, four in one place, and three in another. Curiosity led them to visit the group of three, and near them they found a lion, and eight men and women, all lying dead; "the lion had slain them by its strength, and they had killed the lion with their spears and swords, for the places occupied by both these groups of barns are deserts." They found that these buildings, in their whole elevation, were of stone; at the bottom they were square, in the upper part round, and twisted at the summit in a spire. Fidelis measured the side of one from one angle to the other, and found it to be four hundred feet. Then, entering their ships in the river Nile, they navigated direct to the entrance of the Red Sea, where they entered a port, not far to the east of which was the spot where Moses passed on dry land. Fidelis wished to go to this place, where he expected to see the traces of Pharaoh's chariot wheels, but he could not prevail with the sailors to turn away from their own course. He observed, however, that the sea appeared there to be about six miles across. They sailed thence, without loss of time, along the western part of the Red Sea, or that part which extends itself in a gulf or bay far to the north. From thence we are left to suppose that they proceeded to Palestine*. The barns of Joseph were of course the pyramids, with respect to the form of the upper part of which the pilgrim might easily have been deceived; but it will be at once evident to any one acquainted with the geography of Egypt, that the channel by which he passed in a ship from the Nile to the Red Sea, was the ancient canal of Hadrian. This canal is said to have been repaired, and rendered navigable by the Arabs, not long after they had rendered themselves masters of Egypt, but we know that it was finally blocked up by the khalif Abu Giafar Almansor, in 767, to hinder provisions from being sent to the people of Mecca and Medina, who had

* Dicuil, De Mensura Orbis, vi. 3, ed. Letronne.

revolted against his authority. It was therefore previous to this date that Fidelis visited Egypt.

Peace, broken immediately after the departure of Willibald, was not restored till the learned reign of the magnificent Haroun-er-Raschid (786–809), whose name, and his friendship and intercourse with the no less splendid monarch of the west, Charlemagne, have been so often celebrated in history and romance. Their friendship led to the opening of Palestine to the Christian pilgrims on much more liberal terms, and various privileges and comforts were secured for them in the holy city. Pilgrimages now became more frequent, and several are mentioned during the latter part of the eighth and the course of the ninth centuries.

The only one of these pilgrims whose own account of his adventures has been preserved, was a Breton monk, evidently of the celebrated monastery of Mount St. Michel, named BERNARD, who is distinguished in the manuscripts by the title of *Bernardus Sapiens*, or Bernard the Wise, although we have no other testimony to his wisdom except the account of his pilgrimage. This very curious narrative was discovered by Mabillon, in a manuscript of the library of Rheims, and printed in the *Acta Sanctorum Ordinis Benedictini*. Bernard has given, at the commencement of this narrative, the date of the year in which he started. In Mabillon's text, and in a manuscript of the Cottonian Library, now lost, it is 870; while in another manuscript of the Cottonian Library, still existing, it is given as 970. Internal evidence at once fixes the date of Bernard's pilgrimage to the ninth century, and not to the tenth; and as it is evident that he was at Bari before the siege by Louis II., we can have little hesitation in considering both the dates given by the manuscripts as errors of the scribes, and in fixing Bernard's departure to the year 867.

Bernard left Europe at a time when the Saracens of the west were engaged in hostility with the Christians, and he was obliged to furnish himself with a variety of protections. Although he points at the disadvantageous contrast between the barbarity and turbulence of the western Christians and the well regulated government of the Arabs in the east, it is quite evident that a change had taken place in the condition of the Christians in Syria, and that the pilgrims no longer enjoyed the immunities obtained for them by the emperor Charlemagne. They now, on the contrary, seem to have been subjected to extortions on every side. Bernard, like Fidelis, went by way of Egypt, and proceeded thence into Palestine by land. He is the first traveller who mentions the afterwards celebrated miracle of the holy fire. At Jerusalem Bernard lodged in the hostle which had been founded by Charlemagne, and which was still appropriated to its original destination.

Somewhere near this period a noble Breton of the name of Frotmond, who, with his brother, had committed one of those deeds of blood which so often stain the history of the middle ages, was condemned by the church to a penance, not uncommon in those times. A chain was close riveted round his body and his arms; and in this condition, covered only with a coarse garment, his head sprinkled with ashes, he was to visit, bare-foot, the holy places, and wander about until God should deign to relieve him of his burthen. In the fourth year of his wanderings he returned to France, and went to the monastery of Redon, where he was miraculously delivered from his chains, which had already eaten deep into his flesh, at the tomb of St. Marcellinus. The account of his pilgrimage was collected from the traditions of the monastery long after Frotmond's death, by one of the monks. It is said that he and his brethren went direct to the coast of Syria, and made some stay at Jerusalem, practising there all kinds of austerities. They next went into Egypt, and took up their abode among the monks of the Thebaid, and then went to pray at the tomb of St. Cyprian, on the sea-coast, two leagues from Carthage. They then returned to Rome; but still not obtaining pardon of the pope (Benedict III.), they again passed the sea to Jerusalem, from whence they went to Cana, in Galilee, and then they directed their course to the Red Sea. They next proceeded to the mountains of Armenia, and visited the spot where Noah's ark rested after the deluge. On their way they suffered all kinds of outrages from the infidels, who stripped them naked and scourged them cruelly. This, however, did not turn them from their purpose, and they went subsequently to Mount Sinai, where they remained three years, and so returned to Italy, and thence to France. Frotmond started on his wanderings in the year 868.

Other pilgrimages are mentioned as having taken place before the end of the ninth century, at which time new wars broke out between the Greeks and the Saracens, in the course of which the whole of Judea was taken from the Mohammedans by the emperor John Zimisces, and the holy places were again thrown open to pilgrims from all parts. On the death of Zimisces, in 976, the Greek empire again sunk into weakness, and Palestine was snatched from them by the Fatimite khalifs of Egypt, whose policy it was at first to treat the Christians with lenity, seek commercial relations with the Franks, and encourage the pilgrimages to the holy places. But all these fair prospects were soon cut short by the accession to the throne of Hakem, the third khalif of the Fatimite dynasty, who threw his kingdom into confusion by his cruel despotism, and who made the unfortunate Christians feel the whole weight of his fury. They were everywhere oppressed and massacred, their churches were taken from them, profaned, and destroyed, and the holy places were deserted. During the whole of the eleventh century the Christians of Syria were thus treated with every kind of indignity. Pilgrims still made their way to Jerusalem, and a great number of brief notices of their adventures are preserved by the numerous writers of the age; but they brought back with them little more than complaints of the profanations to which the holy places were exposed, and of the wretched condition to which their brothers in faith had been reduced. The celebrated Gerbert, afterwards pope, under the name of Sylvestre II., was one of the first who made the pilgrimage during the persecutions of Hakem; and on his return, in 986, he published a letter, in which he made Jerusalem deplore her misfortunes, and supplicated the whole Christian world to come to her aid. The French and the Italians were excited to vengeance, and they began to make pilgrimages in armed bodies, and even to attack the coasts of Syria. This only served to exasperate their enemies, who interdicted the Christians in their dominions from the exercise of their religion, took from them their churches, which they profaned by turning them into stables and to still more degrading purposes, and threw down the church of the Sepulchre, and the other sacred places in Jerusalem, in 1008. According to the best authorities the church of the Holy Sepulchre was rebuilt by Hakem's grandson, Al-Mostanser-Billah, between 1046 and 1048, in consequence of a treaty with the Byzantine emperor.

The news of these events threw all Christian Europe into consternation, and excited every where the desire for vengeance on the infidels; but it increased the eagerness for pilgrimage, and, in spite of all the insults and perils to which they were exposed, devotees of all ranks and conditions made their way to Jerusalem in crowds. New revolutions were, however, taking place there; for another people, the Seldjouk Turks, having rendered themselves masters of Persia, and established there a new dynasty of monarchs, the Abassides, passed forwards into Mesopotamia, and then conquered Syria from the Fatimites. The Seldjouks took Jerusalem in 1071, massacred both Saracens and Christians, and delivered up to pillagers the mosques as well as the churches. The fate of the pilgrims under the new rulers of Palestine was more deplorable than ever. They were not allowed to enter the gates of Jerusalem without payment of a very heavy tax; and, as most of them had been plundered on the way, if they had anything to tempt the merciless rapacity of the infidels, the greater part remained outside, to perish by hunger or by the sword. Those who gained admission into the city only entered to suffer new outrages, and, which was still worse, to see everything they held most sacred trodden under foot and defiled by unbelievers.

The Turks, in their turn, became divided and enfeebled; and the Fatimites made a successful effort to recover their power in Syria. In 1096 Jerusalem was delivered, by capitulation, to the general of the khalif Al-Mostaali-Billeh; but the change of masters seems to have ameliorated in no degree the condition of the Christians.

The cry of the eastern Christians had, however, already made itself effectually heard throughout Europe. The voice of Peter the Hermit was first raised in 1095, in the November of which year he stood by the pope, Urban II., at the council of Clermont, and the first crusade was proclaimed. The vast army of invaders assembled in the autumn of 1096, traversed Europe and Asia Minor, and those who escaped from the terrible sufferings and losses it experienced on the road reached Palestine in 1099, and took Jerusalem by assault on the 15th of June. Ten days after the conquerors elected Godfrey of Boulogne king of Jerusalem.

The first pilgrim who followed the crusaders, who has left us a personal narrative, was an Anglo-Saxon named SÆWULF. Our only information relating to this personage, beyond what is found in his own relation, occurs in a passage of William of Malmesbury which appears to relate to him. This writer, in his History of the English Bishops *, tells us that Sæwulf was a merchant who frequently repaired to bishop Wulstan, of Worcester, to confess his sins, and as frequently, when his fit of penitence was over, returned to his old courses. Wulstan advised him to quit the profession in which he met with so many temptations, and embrace a monastic life ; and, on his refusal, the bishop prophesied that the time would arrive when he would take the habit which he now so obstinately refused. William of Malmesbury says that he himself witnessed the fulfilment of this prediction, when in his old age the merchant Sæwulf became a monk in the abbey of Malmesbury. It is fair to suppose that, in a moment of penitence, the merchant sought to appease the divine wrath by undertaking the pilgrimage to Jerusalem, the road to which had then been laid open by the first successes of the crusaders. Nothing in the narrative proves that our traveller was a monk.

The date of Sæwulf's voyage has been fixed by his learned editor, M. D'Avezac, from internal evidence of the most satisfactory kind. Sæwulf makes two or three allusions to historical personages in the course of his adventures. Thus, on his arrival at Cephalonia, he informs us that Robert Guiscard died there. This celebrated warrior, the first duke of the Normans in Italy, the father of the celebrated crusader Bohemond, prince of Tarentum, was meditating the conquest of Greece, when he died, according to some poisoned, in July 1085 †. Further on Sæwulf mentions two Christian princes, distinguished by their activity in the first crusade, as still living ; Baldwin, king of Jerusalem, and Raymond, duke of Toulouse. The first was made king on the 25th of December, 1100, and the latter died on the 28th of February, 1105. Sæwulf mentions further, that when he returned from Syria Tortosa was in the possession of duke Raymond, while Acre still remained in the hands of the Saracens. The latter place was captured on the 12th of March, 1102, while Acre did not fall into the hands of the Christians till the 15th of May, 1104. Now he informs us further that he embarked at Joppa, on his re-

---

* W. Malmesbury de Gest. Pontif., p. 282. See also my Biographia Britannica Literaria, Anglo-Norman Period, p. 38.

† See, on Robert Guiscard, W. Malmesbury, Hist. book iii. pp. 294, 295. (Bohn's Antiquarian Library.)

turn on the day of Pentecost, which day in the year 1104 fell on the 5th of June, and, as Acre had then been taken, this could not be the year; and we have only to choose between 1102 and 1103. To remove all doubt on the subject, M. D'Avezac points out an element of calculation contained in Sæwulf's text, which enables us to fix the exact date of his departure from Italy, after having brought it within so small a compass from the historical allusions. Sæwulf says that he set sail from Monopoli on Sunday, the feast of St. Mildred. St. Mildred's day is the 13th of July, and that day fell on a Sunday in the year 1102. It was, he says, an unlucky day—*dies Ægyptiaca*, and they fell in with a storm which drove them along the coast to Brindisi, whence, after a short stay to refit, they sailed again on an unlucky day. Now the ordinary formula to find the unlucky or Egyptiac days, composed by the medieval calculators, give us the 13th and 22nd of July, as falling under this character. It was, therefore, the 13th of July, 1102, when Sæwulf sailed from Monopoli, and the 22nd of the same month when he left Brindisi; and it was the day of Pentecost, 1103, when he embarked at Joppa, on his return. These dates will agree very well with the age of the Sæwulf mentioned by William of Malmesbury.

The events preceding, and connected with the crusades, had considerably modified the route followed by the pilgrims in their way to Jerusalem. They had previously gone by way of Egypt, because it was no doubt safer to pass in ships employed in commerce with the Saracens, or to go with Saracenic passports from the west, than to encounter the hostile feelings with which people were received who came into Syria from the neighbouring territory of the Greeks. But now they might proceed with greater security through the Christian states on the northern shores of the Mediterranean, either visiting Constantinople before they proceeded to Jerusalem, or, if their eagerness to see the holy city overcame all other considerations, sailing along the coast of Greece and through the islands of the Archipelago. The latter course was taken by Sæwulf; he sailed from Italy to the Ionian islands; proceeded overland to Negropont, where he embarked in another ship, and, after touching at several of the islands, proceeded along the coast of Asia Minor to Jaffa, whence he travelled by land to Jerusalem, reserving his visit to the metropolis of the Grecian empire for his return. The narrative appears to be truncated, which has deprived us of Sæ owulf'sbservations of Constantinople.

Sæwulf's account of the disastrous storm which attended their arrival at Jaffa shows us what multitudes of pilgrims now crowded to the Holy Land. Among these were people of all classes, rich and poor, noble and ignoble, laymen equally with monks and clergy. Some went in humility and meekness to visit the scene of their salvation, while others, embarking with crews of desperate marauders, although they went to the Holy City with the same professions, proceeded as privateers, or rather as pirates, plundering and devastating on their way. Among this latter class the descendants of the sea-kings of the north appear to have been especially distinguished, and the Scandinavian sagas have preserved more than one narrative, half authentic and half romantic, of their adventures. It has been thought advisable to give, as a specimen of these, the story of SIGURD THE CRUSADER, a northern prince, whose presence at the capture of Beyrout, in 1110, is mentioned by William of Tyre.

The land of Palestine was at this time beginning to attract, in an unusual degree, the attention of another class of travellers from western Europe—learned men of the Jewish nation—who were anxious to discover and to make known to their brethren the condition of the various synagogues in the East, after so many sanguinary revolutions, as well as to visit the burial-places of the eminent Hebrews of former days. Several of their relations, written in Hebrew, are still preserved in manuscript, and a few have been printed *. The earliest of these of any importance is that of BENJAMIN OF TUDELA. We have an "Itinerary of Palestine" made by Samuel bar Simson in 1210; a "Description of the Sacred Tombs" by a Jew of Paris named Jacob, in 1258; and several tracts of the same kind in the fourteenth and fifteenth centuries.

Mr. Asher, to whom we owe the best edition of Benjamin of Tudela, has fixed the date of Benjamin's travels from his own narrative with great acuteness. It appears from different circumstances to which he alludes, that his visit to Rome must

---

* An interesting volume of these narratives, translated into French, and accompanied with valuable notes, has recently been published under the title, " Itineraires de la Terre Sainte des xiii, xive, xve, xvie, and xviie siècles, traduits de l' Hébreu, par E. Carmoly," Brussels, 1847.

have taken place subsequent to 1159, that he was at Constantinople probably in December 1161, and that his account of Egypt, which almost concludes the work, must have been written prior to 1171*. "If we add to these dates," Mr. Asher observes, " that of his return, as given in the preface, we shall find that the narrative refers to a period of about fourteen years, viz. from 1159 or 1160, to 1173." To these dates pointed out by Mr. Asher, it may be added, that he appears to have been at Antioch immediately after the accession of Bohemond III. in 1163; and that he probably reached Sicily, on his way back, early in 1169. By comparing these dates with the general course of the narrative, I have endeavoured to arrange with tolerable accuracy the successive years of Benjamin's wanderings; the dates of which are given at the heads of the pages.

Rabbi Benjamin is the first European traveller whom we find taking a wider circuit in his travels than that which would have been restricted by the limits of Christian or Jewish pilgrimage. As Mr. Asher observes, he appears evidently to have been a merchant, and hence, though the object most at his heart seems to have been to note the number and condition of the Jews in the different countries he visited, he has preserved some valuable information relating to their trade and commerce at that period, and, in spite of some credulity, and an evident love of the marvellous, he describes what he saw with more good sense and accuracy than the Christian travellers of the same age. Benjamin, who was a Jew of Spain, began his travels from Saragossa, and proceeded through Italy and Greece to Constantinople, which city he describes at considerable length. He proceeded thence, by the Greek Islands, to Antioch, and thence through Syria, by Acre and Nablous, to Jerusalem. From Jerusalem he went to Damascus, and from thence to Bagdad, but his route here and elsewhere appears to have been far from direct, as we often trace him moving backwards and forwards, to obtain information, or visit districts that lay out of the ordinary road. The actual extent of his wanderings towards the East appears doubtful; but it is certain he remained at Bagdad and in Persia two or three years, and he returned by way of Arabia and

* For these dates see the notes on pp. 67, 75, and 119 of the present volume. See the notes on pp. 78, 124.

Nubia to Egypt. From Egypt he returned to Sicily, and he then made a tour in Germany before his final return home. Mr. Asher observes that there is "one very peculiar feature" in this work, by which its contents are divided into *what he saw*, and *what he heard*. "In many towns, on the route from Saragossa to Bagdad, rabbi Benjamin mentions the names of the principal Jews, elders, and wardens of the congregations he met with. That a great number of the persons enumerated by rabbi Benjamin really were his contemporaries; and that the particulars he incidentally mentions of them are corroborated by other authorities, has been proved in the biographical notes furnished by Dr. Zunz. We therefore do not hesitate to assert that rabbi Benjamin visited all those towns of which he names the elders and principals, and that the first portion of his narrative comprises an account of *what he saw*. But with Gihiagin, the very first stage beyond Bagdad, all such notices cease, and except those of two princes and of two rabbis, we look in vain for any other *names*. So very remarkable a difference between this and the preceding part of the work leads us to assert that rabbi Benjamin's travels did not extend beyond Bagdad, and that he there wrote down the second portion of our work, consisting of *what he heard*. Bagdad, at his time the seat of the prince of the Captivity, must have attracted numerous Jewish pilgrims from all regions, and, beyond doubt, was the fittest place for gathering those notices of the Jews and of trade in different parts of the world, the collecting of which was the aim of rabbi Benjamin's labours." It may be observed, further, that the information he thus collected agrees in general with that furnished by the contemporary Arabian geographers.

The travels of rabbi Benjamin had little, if any, influence on the state of geographical science amongst the Christians of the west; but a variety of causes—the thirst for novelty in science excited by the educational movement of the twelfth century, scattered information, gleaned from an increased intercourse with the Arabs, and the adventurous spirit raised by a hundred years of crusades—were now combining to render them every day more eager for information relating to distant lands, and this spirit received a new impulse from the astonishment and terror excited by the incursions of the Tartars in the earlier half of the thirteenth century. Shrewd and intelligent men were sent out by the monarchs of the west, nominally as ambassadors, but really as spies, to ascertain who these dreaded invaders were, and whence they came, and to report on their strength and character. These envoys met at the court of the khan men of distant, and, to them, unknown countries, from whom they collected information relating to the central and eastern parts of Asia. Among the first of these envoys was John du Plan de Carpin, an Italian friar of the order of St. Francis, sent out by Pope Innocent IV., in the spring of 1245. He was followed immediately by Simon de St. Quentin, a Dominican monk, also sent by the pope; and a year or two later, in 1253, by William de Rubruk, another Franciscan, sent on an embassy to the Tartars by St. Louis. These, as well as other missionaries of the same century, have left behind them interesting narratives, several of which are preserved, and some of them are well known. Merchants, led by the hope of gain, followed in the steps of, and even preceded, the political or religious missionaries, and their objects being less restricted, they often penetrated into the remotest regions of Asia, where they sometimes settled, and rose to rank and wealth. One of these, an Italian named Marco Polo, on his return, after a long residence in Asia, in the middle of the thirteenth century, published the well known narrative, which conduced, more than any other work, to the development of geographical science, and which first gave the grand impulse to geographical research, that led to the more extensive and substantial knowledge which began to dawn in the following century.

From this time, although short descriptions of the Holy Land became more numerous than ever, travellers who published their personal narratives were seldom contented with the old limits of the subject, but they either visited themselves, or described from the information of others, some at least of the surrounding countries. This was carried at times almost to the extreme of affectation. A remarkable example is furnished to us in the book of SIR JOHN MAUNDEVILLE. This singular writer, more credulous than the most bigotted monk, appears to have visited the east with the double object of performing the pilgrimage to the Holy Sepulchre, and of seeking military service in foreign lands. Professedly a guide to pilgrims to Jerusalem, to which a large portion of the book is devoted, it contains, nevertheless, the description of nearly the whole of Asia, and of some parts of Africa and Europe, and extends to countries which its author visited and to many others which he certainly did not visit. From the rather equivocal light in which he exhibits himself, and the peculiar form of his work, it is impossible to trace the course of his travels, but he assures us that he set out from England in 1322, and that he returned home and compiled his book in 1356. It appears clear, from evidence furnished by the book itself, that Maundeville was in Egypt for some time previous to the year 1342 *, and a closer examination would probably fix the date of his presence in some other countries. But there can be no doubt that his book is partly a compilation, for we find him not only borrowing from ancient writers, like Solinus and Pliny, but it is quite evident that he made large use of the previous narratives of Marco Polo and of the Franciscan Oderic, who had travelled over a great part of Asia in the earlier years of the fourteenth century, and had published his account during Maundeville's absence in the east. It would not be difficult to analyze a great portion of Maundeville's book, and show from whence it was compiled.

It is now generally agreed that Marco Polo originally wrote the account of his travels in the French language, from which it was subsequently translated into Latin and Italian. French had now, indeed, become the general language of popular treatises, and it seems to be equally well established that in it was written the original text of Maundeville, who states expressly in the French copies preserved in manuscript, that he chose French in preference to Latin, as a language more generally understood, " especially by lords and knights, and others who understand not Latin."† We learn, from the colophon to some of the Latin copies, that he was at this time residing at Liege, where he is said to have ended his days, and that he soon afterwards translated his own book into Latin. An English version, said to be also from the pen of Maundeville himself, appeared soon afterwards, and the three versions must have become extremely popular within

---

* See the note, p. 146 of the present volume.

† " Et sachiez que je eusse mis ce livre en Latin pour plus briefment deviser ; mais pour ce que plusieurs entendent mieux Français que Latin, l'ai-je mis en Rommant à celle fin que chascun l'entende, et les seigneurs et chevaliers et aultres qui n'entendent pas le Latin." See on this subject, and on Maundeville's narrative, M. D'Avezac's preface to his edition of " Plan de Carpin," pp. 29—33.

a few years after their publication, from the number of early copies that are still found among our various collections of manuscripts. The travels of Sir John Maundeville form, perhaps, the most popular work of the fourteenth and fifteenth centuries, and it continued long afterwards to be read eagerly in a variety of forms. Yet all we know of him with any certainty is his own statement that he was a native of St. Albans,—the rest of his biography, as commonly given, is a mere tissue of errors. Bale tells us that he died at Liege, on the 17th of November, 1371, and that he was buried there in the abbey of the Guillamites. Abraham Orbelius, in his "Itinerarium Belgiæ," gives an epitaph from that abbey, which appears to be a comparatively recent fabrication. One of the manuscripts, written in the fifteenth century, (MS. Harl. 3989,) says that Maundeville died at Liege in 1382.

Contemporary with Maundeville lived a German named variously Boldensel, Boldensle, and Boldenslave, who visited the east in 1336, and, on his return, published a description of the Holy Land, of which there is an early printed edition. It had been preceded by the description of the Holy Land by Brochard, published in 1332. From this time the narratives of travels in Palestine became much more numerous and more detailed, and I shall not attempt even a bare enumeration. The majority of them consist of little more than a repetition of the same facts and the same legends. Some, however, are far superior to the rest, by the interest of the narrative, and the novelty of the information gathered by the traveller. Two,·belonging to the fifteenth and sixteenth centuries, stand pre-eminent in this respect, the narratives of Breydenbach and Rauwulf, which merit separate publication. I have selected to follow sir John Maundeville, the travels of BERTRANDON DE LA BROCQUIÈRE, on account of their peculiar character.

The Turks, who were gradually overthrowing the empire of the Arabs in the east, were becoming formidable to the Christians also towards the end of the fourteenth century. Since the time of Brochard, who had written expressly to show how the east lay open to an attack from the Christians, several attempts had been made to raise a new crusade. La Brocquière, like Maundeville, was a knight, and he held the high position of counsellor and first esquire carver to the duke of

Burgundy. As was the case with so many others of his own
class, his pilgrimage to Jerusalem was the result of a vow, but
the curiosity and ardour of the man-at-arms were perhaps
more powerful in him than the mere calls of religion. He
left Burgundy in the February of 1432, in company with other
great lords of that country, passed through Italy by way of
Rome to Venice, and there embarked and proceeded by sea
to Jaffa. But when this holy pilgrimage was completed, as
far as lay in his power to perform it, he undertook a pilgrimage
of another kind, and in order to observe the manners and condition of the Turks, who were already threatening Constantinople, he formed the bold scheme of returning to France
overland, which would lead him to traverse the western part
of Asia and eastern Europe. The notices he has given us of
the countries through which he passed, some of them but im-
perfectly known even at present, combined with the interesting period at which the journey was made, give an especial
importance to this narrative, which is marked by the accuracy
and good sense of its writer, and exhibits none of the credulity of previous travellers. On his return to the court of
Burgundy, La Brocquière's appearance excited great interest,
and duke Philip began to talk loudly of his intention to lead
a crusade against the Infidels. It was probably to further
his object that La Brocquière compiled his narrative, which
was published in French, soon after the year 1438, to which
date he alludes in his text. The state of Europe, however,
was not now favourable to a crusade, and the duke's designs
never went further than a few empty proclamations, and some
equally fruitless feasting and pageantry. The Turks were allowed to pursue their conquests, and the victorious Mohammed II. became master of Constantinople in the May of
1453.

Our notices of the medieval travellers would properly conclude
here. A new era was opening upon the west as well as upon the
east, and the last breath of the spirit of the crusades died, as
the system which had nourished it sunk before the great religious Reformation of the sixteenth century. Instead of monks
and soldiers, Europe, more enlightened, began soon afterwards to send merchants, and consuls, and ambassadors. A
clearer and more satisfactory light was now thrown on the
geography of the Holy Land. The English traveller in

Palestine of most authority in the seventeenth century was
Sandys, who, however, often erred on the side of credulity.
Before the end of the century came the well known HENRY
MAUNDRELL, who, on account of the brevity of his narrative
and the extreme accuracy of his descriptions, has been selected
to conclude the present volume. We know little more of
Maundrell than that he was a fellow of Exeter College, Ox-
ford, which he left to take the appointment of chaplain to the
English factory at Aleppo. It is not within our province to
notice the works of subsequent travellers.

It will be necessary to make some statement to our readers
of the manner in which the present volume has been edited,
and of the sources from which the different works it contains
have been derived.

The travels of bishop Arculf, (as compiled by Adamnan,) as
well as those of Bernard the Wise, and the life of Willibald,
were printed in the Acta Sanctorum Ordinis S. Benedicti, Sæc.
III., Part II., in 1672. A previous edition of Arculf had been
published in a small quarto volume, Ingoldstadt, 1619, which
also contained the abridgment by Bede. The latter, under
the title of *Libellus de Locis Sanctis*, is included in the different
editions of Bede's works, and will be found in the recent
edition by Dr. Giles, accompanied with an English translation. Another edition of the narrative of Bernard was published from a manuscript in the Cottonian Library in the
British Museum by M. Francisque Michel, in the Memoirs of
the Society of Geography at Paris. M. Michel's text is in
many respects inferior to that of Mabillon, but it contains the
concluding paragraphs relating to the state of society in
Egypt, Italy, and France, which were wanting in the manuscript from which Mabillon printed. But the new editor,
M. Michel, has fallen into a very grave error; for the treatise
of Bede, *De Locis Sanctis*, following in the Cottonian manuscript the tract of Bernard, he has mistaken them for one
continued treatise, and printed them as such, accusing Mabillon of having printed only one half of his author. The
narrative of Sæwulf, the only manuscript of which is preserved in the library of Corpus Christi College, Cambridge,
was published in the collection of the French Geographical
Society by M. D'Avezac, from a transcript furnished by the
editor of the present volume. M. D'Avezac has executed his

task of editing with remarkable care and discrimination, but I fear that the transcript was in two or three instances inaccurate, and at the time of publication it was unfortunately not in the power of M. D'Avezac to have it collated with the original. One omission of some importance for the architectural history of the church of the Holy Sepulchre was very kindly pointed out to me by Professor Willis, and has been corrected in the translation. In describing this church, the text as printed by M. D'Avezac contains the words, " Ista oratoria sanctissima continentur in atrio Dominici sepulchri ad orientalem plagam. In lateribus autem ipsius ecclesiæ suæ capellæ sibi adhærent præclarissimæ hinc inde, sicut ipsi participes Dominicæ passionis sibi in lateribus constiterunt hinc inde." In the original manuscript the passage stands thus, and is rendered intelligible—" Ista oratoria sanctissima continentur in atrio Dominici sepulchri ad orientalem plagam. In lateribus vero ipsius ecclesiæ *duæ* capellæ sibi adhærent præclarissimæ hinc inde, *Sanctæ Mariæ scilicet Sanctique Johannis in honore*, sicut ipsi participes Dominicæ passionis sibi in lateribus constiterunt hinc inde."

These four narratives are here translated for the first time. In translating Bernard, the text of Mabillon has been compared with that of Michel. The narrative of Arculf has been somewhat abridged, and relieved of some miracles and theological observations that are totally without interest. It may be right to observe, also, that in the original manuscript this narrative is accompanied with plans of churches, copies of which are given in the edition of Mabillon, and in the editions of Bede's abridgement.

The translation of the Saga of Sigurd the Crusader, is taken, by the obliging permission of Mr. Laing, from his recently published "Hemskringla," or "Chronicle of the Kings of Norway."

A number of editions, and several translations, of the travels of Benjamin of Tudela, have appeared, but the only strictly correct one is that published by Mr. A. Asher, Berlin, 1840. The translation published in the present volume is a mere revision of the English version by Mr. Asher, altered a little in the language, to make it more suitable for the popular English reader. My notes are chiefly abridged from the valuable volume of notes published by Mr. Asher in 184.

The only edition of the English text of the book of Sir John Maundeville which correctly represents an original manuscript, is that published from the Cottonian Library in 1725, of which a reprint appeared in 1839, with an introduction, and some additional notes by Mr. Halliwell. The language of this edition has been modernized for the present volume. The travels of Bertrandon de la Brocquière are preserved in a manuscript preserved in the Royal Library in Paris, from which they were published, with some abridgment and in modernized French, in the fifth volume of the Mémoires of the Institute of France, by Legrand d'Aussy. They were thence translated into English by Mr. Johns, and printed at his private press at Hafod, in 1807. This translation, which has become a rare book, has been here slightly revised, and a few illustrative notes have been added. Maundrell's journey is reprinted from the original edition.

Brompton, Aug. 28, 1848.

THE TRAVELS OF BISHOP ARCULF
IN THE HOLY LAND.

TOWARDS A.D. 700.

WRITTEN FROM HIS DICTATION, BY ADAMNAN, ABBOT OF IONA.

ARCULF, the holy bishop, a native of Gaul, after visiting many remote countries, resided nine months at Jerusalem, and made daily visits to the surrounding districts. He counted in the circuit of the walls of the holy city eighty-four towers and six gates, the latter being distributed in the following order:— the gate of David on the west of Mount Sion, the gate of the valley of the Fuller, St. Stephen's gate, Benjamin's gate, the little gate leading by a flight of steps to the valley of Jehoshaphat, and the gate called Tecuitis; of which, the three most frequented are, one to the west, another to the north, and a third to the east. That part of the wall which, with its towers, extends from the gate of David over the northern brow of Mount Sion, which overlooks the city from the south, to the precipitous brow of the same mountain which looks to the east, has no gates.

The city itself begins from the northern brow of Mount Sion, and declines with a gentle slope towards the walls on the north and east, where it is lower; so that the rain which falls on the city runs in streams through the eastern gates, carrying with it all the filth of the streets into the brook Cedron, in the valley of Jehoshaphat. On the 15th of September, annually, an immense multitude of people of different nations are used to meet in Jerusalem for the purpose of commerce, and the streets are so clogged with the dung of camels, horses, mules, and oxen, that they become almost impassable, and the smell would be a nuisance to the whole town. But, by a miraculous providence, which exhibits God's peculiar attachment to this place, no sooner has the multitude left Jerusalem than a heavy fall of rain begins on the night following, and ceases only when the city has been perfectly cleansed.

On the spot where the Temple once stood, near the eastern wall, the Saracens have now erected a square house of prayer, in a rough manner, by raising beams and planks upon some remains of old ruins; this is their place of worship, and it is said that it will hold about three thousand men *. Arculf also observed many large and handsome houses of stone in all parts of the city, but his attention was more especially attracted by the holy places.

The church of the Holy Sepulchre is very large and round, encompassed with three walls, with a broad space between each, and containing three altars of wonderful workmanship, in the middle wall, at three different points; on the south, the north, and the west. It is supported by twelve stone columns of extraordinary magnitude; and it has eight doors or entrances through the three opposite walls, four fronting the north-east, and four to the south-east. In the middle space of the inner circle is a round grotto cut in the solid rock, the interior of which is large enough to allow nine men to pray, standing, and the roof of which is about a foot and a half higher than a man of ordinary stature. The entrance is from the east side, and the whole of the exterior is covered with choice marble to the very top of the roof, which is adorned with gold, and supports a large golden cross. Within, on the north side, is the tomb of our Lord, hewn out of the same rock, seven feet in length, and rising three palms above the floor. These measurements were taken by Arculf with his own hand. This tomb is broad enough to hold one man lying on his back, and has a raised division in the stone to separate his legs. The entrance is on the south side, and there are twelve lamps burning day and night, according to the number of the twelve apostles; four within at the foot, and the other eight above, on the right-hand side. Internally, the stone of the rock remains in its original state, and still exhibits the marks of the workman's tools; its colour is not uniform, but appears to be a mixture of white and red. The stone that was laid at the entrance to the monument is now broken in two; the

---

* Jerusalem was first captured by the Saracens, under the khalif Omar, in 637, about sixty years before it was visited by Arculf. The patriarch Sophronius, when requested by Omar to point out a place for the erection of a mosque, is said to have taken him to the ruins on the site of Solomon's Temple, which had been deserted by the Christians, and where the building known as the Mosque of Omar was subsequently built. Until Arculf's time, the Mohammedans appear, however, to have had but a rough and temporary erection, unless the worthy bishop's pious zeal would not allow him to speak of the mosque otherwise than disrespectfully.

lesser portion standing as a square altar, before the entrance, while the greater forms another square altar in the east part of the same church, covered with linen cloths.

To the right of this round church (which is called the Anastasis, or Resurrection,) adjoins the square church of the Virgin Mary, and to the east of this another large church is built on the spot called in Hebrew Golgotha, from the ceiling of which hangs a brazen wheel with lamps, beneath which a large silver cross is fixed in the very place where stood the wooden cross on which the Saviour of the human race suffered. Under the place of our Lord's cross, a cave is hewn in the rock, in which sacrifice is offered on an altar for the souls of certain honoured persons deceased, their bodies remaining meanwhile in the way or street between this church and the round church. Adjoining the church of Golgotha, to the east, is the basilica, or church, erected with so much magnificence by the emperor Constantine, and called the Martyrdom, built, it is said, in the place where the cross of our Lord with the other two crosses were found by divine revelation, two hundred and thirty-three years after they had been buried. Between these two last-mentioned churches, is the place where Abraham raised the altar for the sacrifice of his son Isaac, where there is now a small wooden table, on which the alms for the poor are offered. Between the Anastasis, or round church, and the basilica of Constantine, a certain open space extends to the church of Golgotha, in which are lamps burning day and night. In the same space between the Martyrdom and the Golgotha, is a seat, in which is the cup of our Lord, concealed in a little shrine, which Arculf touched and kissed through a hole in the covering. It is made of silver, of the capacity of about a French quart, and has two handles, one on each side. In it also is the sponge which was held up to our Lord's mouth. The soldier's lance, with which he pierced our Lord's side, which has been broken into two pieces, is also kept in the portico of the Martyrdom, inserted in a wooden cross. Arculf saw some other relics, and he observed a lofty column in the holy places to the north, in the middle of the city, which, at mid-day at the summer solstice, casts no shadow, which shows that this is the centre of the earth *.

* It was a very old article of popular belief, founded on a literal interpretation of the words of Ps. lxxiv. 12, that Jerusalem was the centre, or, as it

Arculf next visited the holy places in the immediate neighbourhood of Jerusalem.   In the valley of Jehoshaphat he saw
the round church of St. Mary, divided into two stories by slabs
of stone; in the upper part are four altars; on the eastern side
below there is another, and to the right of it an empty tomb
of stone, in which the Virgin Mary is said to have been buried;
but who moved her body, or when this took place, no one can
say.   On entering this chamber, you see on the right-hand side
a stone inserted in the wall, on which Christ knelt when he
prayed on the night in which he was betrayed; and the
marks of his knees are still seen in the stone, as if it had
been as soft as wax.   In the same valley, not far from the
church of St. Mary, is shown the tower of Jehoshaphat, in
which his tomb is seen; adjoining to which little tower, on
the right, is a separate chamber cut out of the rock of Mount
Olivet, containing two hollow sepulchres, one, that of the aged
Simeon the Just, who held the child Jesus in the temple, and
prophesied of him; the other of Joseph, the husband of Mary.
On the side of Mount Olivet there is a cave, not far from the
church of St. Mary, on an eminence looking towards the
valley of Jehoshaphat, in which are two very deep pits.   One
of these extends under the mountain to a vast depth; the other
is sunk straight down from the pavement of the cavern, and is
said to be of great extent.   These pits are always closed above.
In this cavern are four stone tables; one, near the entrance, is
that of our Lord Jesus, whose seat is attached to it, and who,
doubtless, rested himself here while his twelve apostles sat at
the other tables.   There is a wooden door to the cave, which
was often visited by Arculf*.
   After passing through the gate of David, which is adjacent
to Mount Sion, we come to a stone bridge, raised on arches,
and pointing straight across the valley to the south; half-way
along which, a little to the west of it, is the spot where Judas
Iscariot hanged himself; and there is still shown a large fig-
tree, from the top of which he is said to have suspended
himself, according to the words of the poet Juvencus,—

"Informem rapuit ficus de vertice mortem."

was often expressed, the navel, of the world; and it is so exhibited in nearly
all the medieval maps.
   * Dr. Clarke is the only modern traveller who has given any notice of
these subterranean chambers or pits, which he supposes to have been ancient
places of idolatrous worship.

On Mount Sion, Arculf saw a square church, which included the site of our Lord's Supper, the place where the Holy Ghost descended upon the apostles, the marble column to which our Lord was bound when he was scourged, and the spot where the Virgin Mary died. Here also is shown the site of the martyrdom of St. Stephen. He saw on the south of Mount Sion a small field (Aceldama) covered with a heap of stones, where the bodies of many pilgrims are carefully buried, while others are left to rot on the surface.

The ground to the north of Jerusalem, as far as the city of Samuel, which is called Ramatha, is at intervals rough and stony. There are open valleys, covered with thorns, extending all the way to the region of Tamnitis; but, on the other side, from Ælia (Jerusalem) and Mount Sion to Cæsarea of Palestine, though some narrow and craggy places are found, yet the principal part of the way is a level plain interspersed with olive-yards. Arculf states that few trees are found on Mount Olivet, except vines and olive trees, but wheat and barley flourish exceedingly; the nature of the soil, which is not adapted to trees, is favourable to grass and flowers. The height of this hill appears to be equal to that of Mount Sion, although it is much more extensive in length and breadth: the two mountains are separated by the valley of Jehoshaphat. On the highest point of Mount Olivet, where our Lord ascended into heaven, is a large round church, having around it three vaulted porticoes. The inner apartment is not vaulted and covered, because of the passage of our Lord's body; but it has an altar on the east side, covered with a narrow roof. On the ground, in the midst of it, are to be seen the last prints in the dust of our Lord's feet, and the roof appears open above, where he ascended; and although the earth is daily carried away by believers, yet still it remains as before, and retains the same impression of the feet. Near this is a brazen wheel, as high as a man's neck, having an entrance towards the west, with a great lamp hanging above it on a pulley, and burning night and day. In the western part of the same church are eight windows; and eight lamps, hanging by cords opposite them, cast their light through the glass as far as Jerusalem; which light, Arculf said, strikes the hearts of the beholders with a mixture of joy and divine fear. Every year, on the day of the Ascension, when mass is ended, a strong blast of wind comes down, and casts to the ground all who are in the church. All that night, lanterns are kept burning there, so that the mountain appears not only lighted up, but actually on fire, and all that side of the city is illuminated by it.

Arculf visited at Bethany a field in the middle of a large grove of olives, where there is a great monastery, and a church built over the cave where our Lord raised Lazarus from the dead. There is also a much frequented church to the north of Bethany, on that part of Mount Olivet where our Lord is said to have preached to his disciples.

From Jerusalem Arculf went to Bethlehem, which is situated on a narrow ridge, surrounded on all sides by valleys. The ridge is about a mile long, from west to east; and a low wall, without towers, surrounds the brow of the hill, and overlooks the valley. The houses of the inhabitants are scattered here and there over the space within the wall. At the extreme eastern angle there is a sort of natural half cave, the outer part of which is said to have been the place of our Lord's birth; the inside is called our Lord's Manger. The whole of this cave is covered within with precious marble. Over the place where more especially our Lord is said to have been born, stands the great church of St. Mary. Near the wall is a hollow stone, which received back from the wall the water in which our Lord's body was washed, and has ever since been full of the purest water, without any diminution. If by any accident or service it has been emptied, it quickly becomes as full as before. In the valley to the north of Bethlehem, Arculf saw the tomb of David, in the middle of a church, covered with a low pyramidal stone, unadorned, with a lamp placed above it. In another church, on the slope of the hill to the south, is the tomb of St. Jerome, equally without ornament. About a mile to the east of Bethlehem, by the tower of Ader, that is, of the Flock, is a church containing monuments of the three Shepherds, to whom, on this spot, the angel announced the birth of our Lord.

There is a highway, according to Arculf, leading southward from Jerusalem to Hebron, to the east of which Bethlehem is situated, six miles from Jerusalem. At the extremity of this road, on the west side, is the tomb of Rachel, rudely built of stones, without any ornament, presenting externally the form of a pyramid. Her name, placed there by her husband Jacob, is still shown upon it.

Hebron, which is also called Mamre, has no walls, and exhibits only the ruins of the ancient city; but there are some ill-built villages and hamlets scattered over the plain, and inhabited by a multitude of people.   To the east is a double cave, looking towards Mamre, where are the tombs of the four patriarchs, Abram, Isaac, Jacob, and Adam the first man.   Contrary to the usual custom, they are placed with the feet to the south, and the heads to the north; and they are inclosed by a square low wall.   Each of the tombs is covered with a single stone, worked somewhat in form of a church, and of a light colour for those of the three patriarchs, which are together.   The tomb of Adam, which is of meaner workmanship, lies not far from them, at the furthest extremity to the north.   Arculf also saw poorer and smaller monuments of the three women, Sarah, Rebecca, and Leah, who were here buried in the earth.   The hill of Mamre is a mile to the south-west of these monuments, and is covered with grass and flowers, with a flat plain at the summit; on the north side of which is a church, in which is still seen, rooted in the ground, the stump of the oak of Mamre, called also the oak of Abraham, because under it he received the angels.   St. Jerome says that this oak had stood there from the beginning of the world.   Passing from Hebron towards the north, a hill of no great size is seen to the left, covered with fir-trees, about three miles from Hebron.   Fir-wood, for fuel, is carried hence to Jerusalem on camels, for, as Arculf observed, carriages or waggons are very seldom met with throughout the whole of Judæa.

In another excursion, Arculf proceeded to Jericho, where, although the city had been three times built, and as many times utterly destroyed, yet the walls of the house of Rahab still stand, although without a roof.   The whole site of the city is covered with corn-fields and vineyards, without any habitations.   Between it and the Jordan are large groves of palm trees, interspersed with open spaces, in which are almost innumerable houses, inhabited by a diminutive sort of men of the race of Canaan.   A large church stands on the site of Galgalis, where the children of Israel first encamped after passing the Jordan   It is five miles from Jericho. Within the church are the twelve stones which Joshua ordered to be taken out of the Jordan; six on the south side of the church floor, and six on the north.   They are so heavy, that two strong men, at the present day, could hardly lift one of them; one has been accidentally broken in two, but the pieces have been reunited by means of iron.

A wooden cross stands in the Jordan, on the spot where our Lord was baptized, the depth of which, when the water is highest, reaches to the neck of a tall man, and, when lowest, to the breast. The river is here about as broad as a man can throw a stone with a sling. A stone bridge, raised on arches, reaches from the bank of the river to the cross, where people bathe. Arculf swam backwards and forwards in the water. A little church stands at the brink of the water, on the spot where our Lord is said to have laid his clothes when he entered the river. On the higher ground is a large monastery of monks, and a church dedicated to St. John. Arculf found the waters of the Jordan of a yellowish milky colour, and observed that they preserved this colour to a considerable distance, after they flowed into the Dead Sea, where he also witnessed the way in which salt was obtained from the waters of the latter.

In another excursion, Arculf visited the spot at the foot of Mount Libanus where the Jordan has its rise from two fountains, which are named Jor and Dan, the waters of which uniting, take the name of Jordan; and he went round the greater part of the Sea of Galilee, called also the Lake of Gennesareth, and the Sea of Tiberias, which is surrounded by thick woods, and is a hundred and forty stadia in length. The waters are sweet, and fit to drink; for it receives no mud, or other coarse substance, from any marshy pools, but is surrounded on all sides by a sandy shore. Arculf also travelled over the country of Samaria, and visited the town called in Hebrew Sichem, but by the Greeks and Latins Sicima, and now more usually Sichar. Here, without the walls, he saw a cruciform church, in the centre of which is the well of Jacob, where our Saviour met the Samaritan woman. Arculf, who drank of the water, estimated its depth at forty cubits. He also saw in the wilderness a clear fountain, protected with a covering of masonry, at which it is reported John the Baptist used to drink. He likewise saw a very small species of locust, the bodies of which are slender and short, about the size of a finger; and, because they make short leaps like frogs, they are easily caught among the grass. When boiled in oil, they form a poor sort of food. In the same desert he saw trees with broad round leaves of a milky colour, with the savour of honey, which are naturally fragile, and, after being bruised with the hand, are eaten ; and this is the wild honey found in the woods. He further saw, on this side of the Sea of Galilee, to the north of the city of Tiberias, the place where our Lord blessed the loaves and fishes, a grassy and level plain, which has never been ploughed since that event, and shows no traces of buildings, except a few columns round the fountain where, as they say, those persons drank after they had eaten their fill.

Those who wish to go from Jerusalem to Capernaum, take the direct way by Tiberias, and from thence, along the Sea of Gennesareth, to the place where the loaves were blessed, from which Capernaum is at no great distance. Arculf saw this place from a neighbouring hill, and observed that it has no walls, but lies on a narrow piece of ground between the mountain and the lake. On the shore, towards the east, it extends a long way, having the mountain on the north and the water on the south. Arculf remained two days and two nights at Nazareth, which is on a hill, and is also without walls, but it has large houses of stone, and two very large churches. One of these is raised upon mounds and arches connecting them, and under it, between the mounds, is a clear fountain, from which all the citizens draw water in vessels, which they raise up into the church by means of pulleys. On this site stood formerly the house in which our Lord was nursed when an infant. The other church was built on the site of the house in which the archangel Gabriel came to the blessed Mary.

Mount Tabor, in Galilee, is three miles from the Lake of Gennesareth, of a remarkably round shape, and covered in an extraordinary manner with grass and flowers. At the top is a pleasant and extensive meadow, surrounded by a thick wood, and in the middle of the meadow a great monastery, with numerous cells of monks. The meadow is about twenty-four stadia in breadth, and the height of the mountain about thirty stadia. There are also three handsome churches on the top, according to the number of tabernacles described by Peter *. The monastery and churches are inclosed by a stone wall.

From Mount Tabor, Arculf went to the royal city of

---

* Matth. xvii. 4.

Damascus, eight days' journey, and remained there some days. It is situated in a plain, surrounded by a broad and ample circuit of walls, with numerous towers, and is intersected by four great rivers. On all sides beyond the walls are numerous groves of olives. The king of the Saracens has obtained possession of this city, and reigns in it*. It contains a large church of St. John the Baptist, frequented by the Christians. The unbelieving Saracens have built themselves a large mosque here. From hence Arculf repaired to Tyre, and thence (as it appears) he returned to Jerusalem. He went subsequently from Jerusalem to Joppa, and thence sailed, in forty days, to Alexandria in Egypt, a city famous throughout the whole world. It extends to a great length from east to west, so that Arculf, who began to enter the city at nine o'clock in the morning (*hora tertia*), in the month of October, and proceeding through the whole length of the city, hardly reached the other side before dark†. On the south it is bounded by the mouths of the Nile, and on the north by the Lake Mareotis. Its port is difficult of access, and bears some resemblance to the human body; for in its head it is sufficiently ample, but at its entrance it is very narrow, where it admits the tide of the sea, together with such ships as run into the port to take shelter and refit. But when you have passed the narrow neck and mouth of the harbour, the sea, like the human body, stretches out far and wide. On the right hand side is a small port, in which is the Pharos, a large tower, which is every night lighted up with torches, lest mariners might mistake their way in the dark, and be dashed against the rocks in their attempt to find the entrance, particularly as this is much impeded and disturbed by the waves dashing to and fro. The port, however, is always calm, and in magnitude about thirty stadia. The precautions alluded to are necessary for a port which is, in a manner, the emporium of the whole world; for innumerable people from all parts go there for commerce, and the sur

---

* Damascus was taken by the Arabs in 634. By the capitulation, the Christians were to have seven churches; but one of the Arabian leaders having broken into the city before the capitulation was completed, it was only very partially observed.

† Alexandria fell into the power of the Arabs in 640. The account given of the city by Arculf would lead us to believe that its prosperity and importance were not so suddenly reduced by that event as is generally believed.

rounding region is extremely fruitful. Although the country is destitute of rain, the Nile serves both as a cultivator of the land, and as the means of transferring its products from one place to another. Here you see people sowing, there navigating, which are their chief occupations. The Nile is navigable to the place they call the town of Elephants *; beyond that the cataracts hinder a ship from proceeding, not from want of water, but because all the waters of the river run in a sort of wild ruin down a steep descent. Towards Egypt, as we enter the city, there is a large church on the right, in which St. Mark the Evangelist is interred. The body is buried in the eastern part of the church, before the altar, with a monument of squared marble over it. Along the Nile, the Egyptians are in the habit of constructing numerous embankments, to prevent the irruption of the water, which, if these mounds were broken down by the neglect of their keepers, would rather inundate and destroy than irrigate the lands below. The Egyptians who inhabit the plains, as Arculf, who frequently passed backward and forward along the Nile, observed, make their houses over canals by laying planks across. Arculf relates further, that the river Nile is haunted by crocodiles, aquatic beasts, not so large as they are ravenous, and so strong, that if one of them see by chance a horse or an ass, or even an ox, feeding near the bank of the river, he suddenly rushes out to attack it, and seizing it perhaps by the foot, drags it under the water, and devours the whole.

On his return from Alexandria, Arculf went to Constantinople, which is bounded on all sides, except the north, by the sea. The circuit of the walls, which are angular, according to the line of the sea, is about twelve miles. Constantine was at first disposed to build it in Cilicia, near the sea which separates Europe and Asia; but on a certain night all the iron tools were carried away, and when men were sent to seek them, they were found on the European side; for there it was God's will that the city should be built. In this

---

* *Urbs Elephantorum.* The town of Elephantina, famous for its interesting monuments, situate on the Nile, just below the cataracts. It is to be presumed that Arculf had visited this place; and perhaps he had here seen the crocodiles subsequently described, as those animals are said not to be found in Lower Egypt. It must, however, be observed, that St. Antoninus, who visited Egypt in the seventh century, appears to have seen crocodiles in Lower Egypt. See his Life, in the Act. Sanct. of the Bollandists.

city is a church of wonderful workmanship, called the Church of St. Sophia, built circular from its foundation, domed in, and surrounded by three walls. It is supported to a great height on columns and arches, and has, in its inmost part, on the north side, a large and beautiful closet, wherein is a wooden chest with a wooden lid, containing three pieces of our Lord's cross *; that is to say, the long timber cut in two, and the transverse part of the same holy cross. These pieces are exhibited for the adoration of the people three times only in the year; namely, on the day of our Lord's Supper, the day of the Preparation, and on Holy Saturday. On the first of these, the chest, which is two cubits long and one broad, is set out on a golden altar, with the holy cross exposed to view: the Emperor first approaches, and, after him, all the different ranks of laymen in order kiss and worship it; on the following day, the Empress and all the married women and virgins do the same; on the third day, the bishops and different orders of the clergy observe the same ceremonies; and then the chest is shut, and carried back to the closet before mentioned.

Arculf saw other sacred relics in Constantinople, and then sailed for his own country. About twelve miles from Sicily he saw the isle of Vulcano, whence constantly issued smoke by day and fire by night, with a noise like thunder, but with more intensity on Fridays and Saturdays. The noise is heard in Sicily, where Arculf made a short stay; and afterwards, on his way home, he was carried by contrary winds to the shores of Britain, and at length came to me, Adamnan, who by diligent inquiry obtained from him the above particulars, which I have carefully committed to writing.

* The subsequent history of the supposed real cross, or rather the supposed fragments of it, which were scattered as relics over Christian Europe, would fill a volume. It was pretended that it was brought to France by Charlemagne.

THE TRAVELS OF WILLIBALD.

A.D. 721—727.

WRITTEN FROM HIS OWN RECITAL BY A NUN OF HEIDENHEIM.

AFTER the ceremonies of Easter were ended, the active cham
pion (of Christ) prepared for his voyage with his two companions,
and left Rome. They first went eastward to the town of Date-
rina *, where they remained two days; and thence to Cajeta, on
the coast, where they went on board a ship and sailed over to
Nebule †. They here left the ship, and remained a fortnight.
These are cities belonging to the Romans; they are in the
territory of Beneventum, but subject to Rome. There, after
waiting anxiously, in constant prayer that their desires might
be agreeable to heaven, they found a ship bound for Egypt, in
which they took their passage, and sailed to the land of Calabria, to the town which is called Rhegia ‡, and there remained
two days; and then proceeded to the island of Sicily, in which
is the town of Catania, where the body of St. Agatha, the
virgin, reposes. And there is Mount Etna; in case of an
eruption of which, the inhabitants of Catania take the veil of
St. Agatha, and hold it up towards the fire, which immediately ceases. They made a stay of three weeks at this place,
and then sailed to the isle of Samos, and thence to the town
of Ephesus, in Asia, which is one mile from the sea. They
walked thence to the place where the seven sleepers repose;
and onward thence to John the Evangelist, in a beautiful
locality by Ephesus. They next walked two miles along the
sea-side to a large village which is called Figila §, where
they remained one day, and, having begged bread, they went
to a fountain in the middle of the town, and, sitting on the
edge, they dipped their bread in the water, and so made their
meal. They next walked along the sea-shore to the town of

---

* Probably Terracina.
† Probably this is a corruption of Neapolis, or Naples.
‡ Now Reggio.
§ This evidently corresponds to the Πυγελα (or Pygela) of Strabo, which
he calls πολίχνιον, a little town. Stephanus and Pomponius Mela also write
Pygela, but Pliny has it *Phygala*. The site is now, according to Hamilton,
(Trav. vol. ii. p. 28,) covered with fragments of Roman tiles and pottery;
and near the road is the foundation of a large marble building, apparently a
temple.

Strobole *, seated on a lofty hill, and thence to the place
called Patera, where they remained till the rigour of winter
was past.

After this, going on ship-board, they came to the town
which is called Melitena †, which had been nearly destroyed by
an inundation; and two hermits lived there on a rock, secured
by walls, so that the water could not reach them. And there
they suffered much from hunger, from which they were only
relieved by God's providential mercy ‡. They sailed thence to
the isle of Cyprus, which is between the Greeks and the
Saracens, to the town of Papho, where they passed the first
week in the year. And thence they went to the town of Con-
stantia, where St. Epiphanius reposes, and there they remained
till after the Nativity of St. John the Baptist §. They then
put to sea again and came into the region of the Saracens to
the town of Tharratas ‖, by the sea; and thence they walked a
distance of nine to twelve miles to a castle called Archæ ¶, where
there was a Greek bishop; and there they had divine service
according to the Greek custom. Thence they walked twelve
miles to the town which is called Emessa, where there is a large
church built by St. Helena, in honour of John the Baptist,
whose head was long preserved there. This is in Syria.

Willibald's party had now increased to eight in number,
and they became an object of suspicion to the Saracens, who,
seeing that they were strangers, seized them and threw them

* Mr. Ainsworth, with whom I have consulted on this name, observes,
"I can only suppose that we must read Trogilium for Strobolem, or that the
latter was the native corruption of Trogilium, the name, according to Ptolemy,
of the promontory which lies between Ephesus and the Meander, and which
is opposite the island of Samos." In the Acts of the Apostles, xx. 15, it is
written, "And we sailed thence, (Mitylena,) and came the next day over
against Chios; and the next day we arrived at Samos, and tarried at
Trogyllium; and the next day we came to Miletus."

† *i. e.* Miletus.

‡ The passage in the original is rather obscure. The later anonymous life
of St. Willibald says that they came to the mount of the Galani, which
having been ravaged by war, they were distressed for want of provisions.
"Navim demum ingressi, ad montem Galanorum transfretarunt; quo bellorum
tempestate tunc temporis depilato sævam passi sunt inediam."

§ June 24, 722.

‖ Tortosa, now called Tartus.

¶ The Arca of Ptolemy, placed in the Antonine Itinerary, 18 M.P. from
Tripolis, and 32 M.P. from Antaradon. Josephus (De Bel. Jud., lib. vii. c. 13)
says the Gentiles called this Phœnician town Arcæa or Arcena. It is now
called Tele Arka.

into prison, because they knew not of what country they were, and supposed them to be spies. They carried them as prisoners before a certain rich old man, that he might examine them; and he inquired whence they came and the object of their mission; whereupon they related to him the true cause of their journey. The old man replied, " I have often seen men of the parts of the earth whence these come, travelling hither; they seek no harm, but desire to fulfil their law." And upon that they went to the palace, to obtain leave to proceed to Jerusalem.

While they were in prison it happened, by a manifest intervention of Divine Providence, that a merchant residing there was desirous, as an act of charity, and for the salvation of his soul, to purchase their deliverance, that they might pursue their way, but he was not allowed to carry his generous design into effect; nevertheless he sent them daily their meals, and on Wednesdays and Saturdays sent his son to them in prison, who took them out to the bath, and brought them back again. And on Sunday he took them to church through the market, that they might see the shops, and whatever they seemed to take a liking to he afterwards bought for them at his own expense. The townsmen used then to come there to look at them, because they were young and handsome, and clad in good garments.

Then, while they were still remaining in prison, a man, who was a native of Spain, came and spoke with them, and inquired earnestly who they were and from whence they came, and they told him the object of their pilgrimage. This Spaniard had a brother in the king's palace, who was chamberlain to the king of the Saracens; and when the governor who had thrown them into prison came to the palace, the captain in whose ship they had sailed from Cyprus, and the Spaniard who had spoken to them in prison, went together before the king of the Saracens, whose title is Emir-al-Mumenin *, and, when their cause came on, the Spaniard spoke to his brother, and begged him to intercede with the king for them. After this, when all three came before the king, and told him the

---

* *i. e.* Emir, or commander of the faithful. Willibald, not understanding the language, translated the title of the khalif into the name of a king, whom the biographer calls *Mirmumni*. In a similar manner the old Spanish and English historians frequently turned the same title into the name Miramomelin. The khalif here alluded to was Yézid II.

case, he asked whence the prisoners came. And they said,
" These men come from the west country, where the sun sets;
and we know of no land beyond them, but water only."
And the king replied, " Why ought we to punish them?
they have not sinned against us :—give them leave, and let
them go." And even the fine of four deniers, which the
other prisoners had to pay, was remitted to them. The
Cyprians were then situated between the Greeks and the
Saracens, and were not in arms : for there was great peace
and friendship between the Greeks and Saracens. It was a
great and extensive region, and had twelve bishops.

As soon as they had obtained leave, the travellers went
direct to Damascus, a distance of a hundred miles. St. Ananias reposes there, and it is in the land of Syria. They remained there one week. And at two miles from the city was
a church, on the spot where St. Paul was first converted, and
the Lord said to him, " Saul, Saul, why persecutest thou me?"
&c. And after praying there, they went into Galilee, to the
place where Gabriel first came to St. Mary, and said, " Hail,
full of grace, ' &c. A church now stands there, and the
village which contains the church is Nazareth. The Christians repeatedly bought that church of the pagans, when
the latter were about to destroy it. And having there recommended themselves to the Lord, they proceeded to the town
of Cana, where our Lord turned water into wine. A large
church stands there, and near the altar is still preserved one
of the six vessels which our Lord commanded to fill with water
to be turned into wine ; and the travellers drunk wine out of
it. They remained there one day, and then continued their
journey to Mount Tabor, the scene of our Lord's tranfigura-
tion, where there is now a monastery and a church consecrated to our Lord, and Moses, and Elijah. And those who
dwell there call it Hagemon (the Holy Mount). After praying there, they proceeded to the town of Tiberias, which
stands on the shore of the sea on which our Lord walked with
dry feet, and on which Peter tried to walk but sank. Here
are many churches, and a synagogue of the Jews. They remained there some days, and observed where the Jordan
passes through the midst of the sea. And thence they went
round the sea, and by the village of Magdalum to the village
of Capernaum, where our Lord raised the prince's daughter.
Here was a house and a great wall, which the people of the

place told them was the residence of Zebedæus with his sons John and James. And thence they went to Bethsaida, the residence of Peter and Andrew, where there is now a church on the site of their house. They remained there that night, and next morning went to Chorazin, where our Lord healed the demoniacs, and sent the devil into a herd of swine. Here was a church of the Christians.

Having performed their devotions there, they went to the place where the two fountains, Jor and Dan, issue from the earth, and flowing down from the mountain are collected into one, and form the Jordan. And there they passed the night between the two fountains, and the shepherds gave them sour ewes' milk to drink. The sheep are of an extraordinary kind, with a long back, short legs, large upright horns, and all of one colour. There are deep marshes in the neighbourhood, and when the heat of the sun, in summer, is oppressive, the sheep go to the marsh, and immerse themselves in the water all but the head. Thence they proceeded to Casarea, where there was a church and a multitude of Christians. They next went to the monastery of St. John the Baptist *, where there were about twenty monks, and remained one night there, and next day went the distance of a mile to the spot in the river Jordan where our Lord was baptized. Here is now a church raised upon stone columns, and under the church it is now dry land where our Lord was baptized. They still continue to baptize in this place ; and a wooden cross stands in the middle of the river, where there is small depth of water, and a rope is extended to it over the Jordan. At the feast of the Epiphany, the infirm and sick come thither, and, holding by the rope, dip in the water. And women who are barren come thither also, and thus obtain God's grace. Willibald here bathed in the Jordan, and they remained at this place one day.

Thence they went to Galgala, a journey of five miles, where is a moderate-sized wooden church, in which are the twelve stones which the children of Israel carried out of the Jordan to Galgala, and placed there as a memorial of their passage. Here also they performed their devotions, and then proceeded to Jericho, above seven miles from the Jordan, and saw there the fountain which was blessed by the prophet

---

* In the desert of Quarantania.

Elisha, and hence to the monastery of St. Eustochium, which stands in the middle of the plain between Jericho and Jeru-salem.

On their arrival at Jerusalem, they first visited the spot where the holy cross was found, where there is now a church which is called the Place of Calvary, and which was formerly outside of Jerusalem; but when St. Helena found the cross, the place was taken into the circuit of the city. Three wooden crosses stand in this place, on the outside of the wall of the church, in memory of our Lord's cross and of those of the other persons crucified at the same time They are without the church, but under a roof. And near at hand is the garden in which was the sepulchre of our Saviour, which was cut in the rock. That rock is now above ground, square at the bottom, but tapering above, with a cross on the summit. And over it there is now built a wonderful edifice. And on the east side of the rock of the sepulchre there is a door, by which men enter the sepulchre to pray. And there is a bed within, on which our Lord's body lay; and on the bed stand fifteen golden cups with oil burning day and night. The bed on which our Lord's body rested stands within the rock of the sepulchre on the north side, to the right of a man entering the sepulchre to pray. And before the door of the sepulchre lies a great square stone, in the likeness of the former stone which the angel rolled from the mouth of the monu-ment. Our bishop arrived here on the feast of St. Martin*, and was suddenly seized with sickness, and lay sick until the week before the Nativity of our Lord. And then, being a little recovered, he rose and went to the church called St. Sion, which is in the middle of Jerusalem, and, after performing his devotions, he went to the porch of Solomon, where is the pool where the infirm wait for the motion of the water, when the angel comes to move it; and then he who first enters it is healed. Here our Lord said to the paralytic, " Rise, take up thy bed, and walk!"† St. Mary expired in the middle of Jerusalem, in the place called St. Sion; and as the twelve apostles were carrying her body, the angels came and took her from their hands and carried her to paradise.

Bishop Willibald next descended to the valley of Jehoshaphat, which is close to the city of Jerusalem, on the east side. And

* Nov. 11, 722.   † John, v. 8.

in that valley is the church of St. Mary, which contains her sepulchre, not because her body rests there, but in memory of it.   And having prayed there, he ascended Mount Olivet, which is on the east side of the valley, and where there is now a church, where our Lord prayed before his passion, and said to his disciples, "Watch and pray, that ye enter not into temptation."*   And thence he came to the church on the mountain itself, where our Lord ascended to heaven.   In the middle of the church is a square receptacle, beautifully sculptured in brass, on the spot of the Ascension, and there is on it a small lamp in a glass case, closed on every side, that the lamp may burn always, in rain or in fair weather, for the church is open above, without a roof; and two columns stand within the church, against the north wall and the south wall, in memory of the two men who said, "Men of Galilee, why stand ye gazing up into heaven?"†   And the man who can creep between the wall and the columns will have remission of his sins.

He next came to the place where the angel appeared to the shepherds, and thence to Bethlehem, where our Lord was born, distant seven miles from Jerusalem.   The place where Christ was born was once a cave under the earth, but it is now a square house cut in the rock, and the earth is dug up and thrown from it all round, and a church is now built above it, and an altar is placed over the site of the birth.   There is another smaller altar, in order that when they desire to celebrate mass in the cave, they may carry in the smaller altar for the occasion.   This church is a glorious building, in the form of a cross.   After prayers here, Willibald came to a large town called Thecua, where the children were slain by Herod, and where there is now a church; here rests one of the prophets. And then he came to the valley of Laura, where there is a large monastery; here the abbot resides in the monastery, and he is porter of the church, with many other monks who belong to the monastery, and have their cells round the valley on the slope of the mountain.   The mountain is in a circle round the valley, in which the monastery is built.   Here rests St. Saba.   He next arrived at the place where Philip baptized the eunuch, where there is a small church, in an extensive valley between Bethlehem and Gaza, where the travel-

---

* Matth., xxvi. 41.   † Acts, i. 11.

lers prayed, Thence they went to St. Matthew, where there is great glory on the Sunday. And while our bishop Willibald was standing at mass in this church, he suddenly lost his sight, and was blind for two months. And thence they went to St. Zacharias, the prophet, not the father of John, but another prophet. They next went to the castle of Aframia, where the three patriarchs, Abraham, Isaac, and Jacob, repose, with their wives, and thence he returned to Jerusalem, and there, entering the church where the holy cross of our Lord was found, he recovered his sight.

After remaining some time at Jerusalem, Willibald set out on another journey, and came first to St. George, at Diospolis, which is ten miles from Jerusalem, and then to a town where there is a church of St. Peter the apostle, who here restored to life the widow named Dorcas. He went thence to the coast, far away from Jerusalem, to Tyre and Sidon, which stand on the sea-shore six miles from each other; after which he passed over Mount Libanus, to Damascus, and so again to Cæsarea, and a third time to Jerusalem, where he passed the following winter. And then he went to the town of Ptolemais, on the extreme bounds of Syria, and was obliged by sickness to remain there all Lent. His companions went forward to the king of the Saracens, named Emir-al-Mumenin, with the hope of obtaining letters of safe conduct; but they could not find the king, because he had fled out of his kingdom. Upon this, they came back, and remained together at Ptolemais until the week before Easter.

Then they went again to Emessa, and asked the governor there to give them letters, and he gave them a letter for each two, because they could not travel in a company, but only two and two, on account of the difficulty of obtaining food. And then they went to Damascus, and returned a fourth time to Jerusalem, where they remained a short period.

They now left Jerusalem by another route, and came to the town of Sebaste, which was formerly called Samaria, and they call the castle Sebastia. Here repose St. John the Baptist, and the prophets Abdiah and Elisha; and near the castle is the well at which our Lord asked for water of the Samaritan woman, and over which well there is now a church. And near is the mountain on which the Samaritans worshipped; for the woman said to our Lord, " Our fathers worshipped in this mountain, and ye say that in Jerusalem is the place where men ought to worship."* Here the travellers performed their devotions, and then they proceeded to a large town on the farthest borders of Samaria, where they reposed that night. And thence they continued their journey over an extensive plain covered with olive trees, and they were accompanied by a black with two camels and a mule, who was conducting a woman through the wood. And on their way they were met by a lion†, which threatened them much with fearful roaring; but the black encouraged them, and told them to go forwards; and when they approached it, the lion, as God willed, hurried off in another direction, and they soon heard his roaring in the distance. They supposed he came there to devour people who went into the wood to gather olives. At length they arrived at a town called Thalamartha, on the sea-coast; and they proceeded onwards to the head of Mount Libanus, where it forms a promontory in the sea, and where stands the tower of Libanus. Nobody is allowed to pass this place without letters of safe conduct, for there is a guard in it; those who are without such letters, are seized and sent to Tyre. That mountain is between Tyre and Thalamartha. And so the bishop arrived again at Tyre.

Willibald had formerly, when at Jerusalem, bought balsam, and filled a gourd with it; and he took a gourd that was hollow, and had flax, and filled it with rock oil‡; and poured some in the other gourd, and cut the small stalk, so that it fitted exactly and closed up the mouth of the gourd. So, when they came to Tyre, the citizens stopped them, and examined their burthens to see if they had any thing concealed; for if they had found any thing, they would immediately have put them to death. But they found nothing but Willibald's gourd, which they opened, and, smelling the rock oil in the stalk, they did not discover the balsam that was within. So they let them go. They remained here many days waiting for a ship, and when they had obtained one they were at sea all the winter, from the day of St. Andrew the apostle§ till a week before Easter, when they reached Constantinople.

* John, iv. 20.

† Lions were ever of very rare occurrence in Syria: perhaps it was some other wild animal peculiar to the country that Willibald saw. It may, however, be pointed out as a curious illustration of the words of Jeremiah (xlix. 19, and l. 44), "He shall come up like a *lion* from the swelling of Jordan."

‡ *Petræ oleum.* No doubt the writer means naphtha, bitumen, or asphaltum.

§ Nov. 30, 724.

Here repose in one altar the three saints, Andrew, Timothy, and Luke the evangelist; and the sepulchre of John Chrysostom is before the altar where the priest stands when he performs mass. Willibald remained there two years, and was lodged in the church, so that he might behold daily where the saints reposed. And then he came to the town of Nice, where the emperor Constantine held a synod, at which three hundred and eighteen bishops were present. The church here resembles the church on Mount Olivet, where our Lord ascended to heaven, and in it are the pictures of the bishops who were at the synod. Willibald went thither from Constantinople, that he might see how that church was built, and then returned to Constantinople.

At the end of the two years they sailed, in company with the envoys of the pope and the emperor, to the isle of Sicily, to the town of Syracuse, and thence to Catania, and so to the city of Regia, in Calabria; and thence to the isle of Vulcano, where is Theodoric's Hell *. And when they arrived there, they went on shore to see what sort of a hell it was; and Willibald especially, who was curious to see the interior, was wishful to ascend to the summit of the mountain where the opening was ; but he was unable to accomplish his wish, on account of the cinders which were thrown up from the gulf, and settled in heaps round the brim, as snow settles on the ground when it falls from heaven. But though Willibald was defeated in his attempt to reach the summit, he had a near view of the column of flame and smoke which was projected upwards from the pit with a noise like thunder. And he saw how the pumice-stone, which writers use †, was thrown with the flame from the hell, and fell into the sea, and was thence cast on the shore, where men gathered it and carried it away. After having witnessed this spectacle, they sailed to the church of St. Bartholomew the apostle, which stands on the sea-shore, and came to the mountains which are called Didymi. Thence they went by sea to Naples.

* *Infernus Theodorici.* In the legends of this age, the craters of volcanoes were believed to be entrances to hell. A hermit, who resided on the Isle of Lipari, told a friend of pope Gregory the Great that he had seen the soul of the Gothic king, Theodoric, thrown into the crater of the Isle of Vulcano (Gregor. Magn. Dialog., lib. iv. c. 30). Hence the name given to it in Willibald's narrative.

† The medieval scribes made constant use of the pumice-stone, for smoothening their vellum and for making erasures.

THE VOYAGE OF BERNARD THE WISE.

A.D. 867.

In the year from the incarnation of our Lord Jesus Christ 867, in the name of the Lord wishing to visit the holy places at Jerusalem, I, Bernard, having taken for my companions two brother monks, one of whom was of the monastery of St. Vincent at Beneventum, and named Theudemund, and the other a Spaniard, named Stephen, we went to Rome, to Pope Nicholas, and obtained the desired licence to go, along with his benediction and assistance.

Thence we went to Mount Gargano, in which is the Church of St. Michael, under one stone, covered above with oak trees; which church is said to have been dedicated by the archangel himself. Its entrance is from the north, and it is capable of containing sixty men. In the interior, on the east side, is the image of the angel; to the south is an altar on which sacrifice is offered, and no other gift is placed there. But there is suspended before the altar a vessel in which gifts are deposited, which also has near it other altars. Benignatus is abbot of this place, and presides over a numerous brotherhood.

Leaving Mount Gargano, we travelled a hundred and fifty miles, to a city in the power of the Saracens, named Bari*, which was formerly subject to Beneventum. It is seated on the sea, and is fortified to the south by two very wide walls; but to the north it stands exposed to the sea. Here we obtained from the prince of the city, called the sultan, the necessary arrangements for our voyage, with two letters of safe conduct, describing our persons and the object of our

---

* The Saracens had established themselves at Bari in the early part of the century, and it was now the head seat of their power on the coast of Italy. Their predatory excursions into the territory of Beneventum caused the emperor Louis II. to prepare an expedition against them, and he took Bari after a siege of four years, and returned to Beneventum in 871, while his troops laid siege to Tarentum, which, however, was not taken from the Saracens till a somewhat later period. The Christian captives mentioned by Bernard, as carried in such numbers into slavery in Africa and Egypt, had been carried off in the incursions into the territory of Beneventum. To judge from the numbers embarked in one ship, they must have been packed up almost as close as negroes in a slave-ship.

journey, to the prince of Alexandria, and to the prince of
Babylonia *. These princes are under the jurisdiction of the
Emir-al-Mumenin, who rules over all the Saracens, and re-
sides in Bagada and Axinarri, which are beyond Jerusalem.

From Bari we proceeded to the port of the city of Tarentum, a distance of ninety miles, where we found six ships,
having on board nine thousand captives of the Christians of
Beneventum. In the two ships which sailed first, and which
were bound for Africa, were three thousand captives ; and in
the two which followed them, and which went to Tunis, there
were also three thousand. The two others, which likewise
contained the same number of Christian captives, carried us to
the port of Alexandria, after a voyage of thirty days. Here
we were prohibited from landing by the captain of the sailors,
who had sixty under his command, until we had given six
aurei for our leave. Thence we went to the prince of Alexandria, and showed him the letter which the sultan had given
us, to which, however, he paid no attention, but obliged each
of us to pay thirteen deniers, and then gave us letters to the
prince of Babylonia. It is the custom of these people to take
in weight only what can be weighed ; and six of our sols
and six deniers make three sols and three deniers of their
money.

The city of Alexandria is adjacent to the sea. It was
here that St. Mark, preaching the gospel, bore the episcopal
dignity ; and outside the eastern gate of the city is the monastery of the saint, with the church in which he formerly
reposed. But the Venetians coming there obtained his body
by stealth, and carrying it on shipboard, sailed home with it.
Without the western gate is a monastery called The Forty
Saints, in which, as well as in the former, there are a number of monks. The port is to the north of the city ; on the
south is the entrance to the Gyon, or Nile, which waters
Egypt, and, running through the middle of the city, empties
itself into the sea in the aforesaid port. We entered the
river, and sailed to the south six days, and came to the city
of Babylon of Egypt, where once reigned king Pharaoh,
under whom Joseph built the seven granaries still remaining.

---

* This is the Egyptian Babylon, now Fostat, or, as it is often called, Old
Cairo. Bagdad (Bagada) was, for many ages, the capital of the Saracen
empire, and residence of the khalifs. It is doubtful what place is meant
by *Axinarri*, which, in Mabillon's text, is called *Axiam*.

When we went on shore at Babylon, the guards of the city
carried us before the prince, a Saracen named Adalhacham,
who inquired of us the object of our journey, and asked us
from what princes we had letters.   Whereupon we showed
him the letters of the aforesaid sultan, and those of the
prince of Alexandria; but they were of no service to us, for
he sent us to prison, where we remained six days, and then,
having consulted together, we obtained our liberty by giving
more money.   He then gave us letters, which effectually protected us from any further exactions, for he was second in
command to the Emir-al-Mumenin aforesaid.   Nevertheless,
when we entered the cities mentioned in the following narrative, we were never allowed to leave them until we had
received a paper or impression of a seal, for which we had to
pay one or two deniers.

There is in this city a patriarch, by name Michael*, who by
the grace of God rules over the bishops, monks, and other
Christians throughout Egypt.   These Christians are tolerated
by the pagans, on condition of paying for each person an
annual tribute to the aforesaid prince, and they live in security and freedom.   This tribute is three, or two, or one aureus,
or for a meaner person thirteen deniers.   But he who cannot pay
thirteen deniers, whether he be a native or a stranger, is thrown
into prison, until God or some good Christian redeem him.

We now returned by the river Gyon, and came to the city
of Sitinulh, and thence proceeded to Malla; and from Malla
we sailed across to Damietta, which has the sea to the north,
and on all other sides the river Nile, with the exception of a
small strip of land.   We sailed thence to the city of Tamnis,
in which the Christians are very pious, and exceedingly hospitable.   This city possesses no land, except where the
churches stand; and there is shown the field of Thanis,
where lie, in the manner of three walls, the bodies of those
who died in the time of Moses†.   From Tamnis we came to

---

* This was the patriarch Michael I., who ruled over the Melchite portion
of the Coptic Christians from 859 to 871.   There was at this time a schism
among the Christians of Egypt.

† Of the places here visited by Bernard, Sitinulh is perhaps Menuph; Malla
is Mahalleh; and Tamnis is Tennis, or Tennesus, the field of Thanis, answering
to "the field of Zoan," Psal. lxxviii. 12.   Faramea (in the next page), is Farama
or Pelusium. The caravanserais are perhaps *al-bir* (the well) and *al-bákara* (the
pulley), both common names given to wells; but it is uncertain now what were
the particular spots alluded to by Bernard.   Alariza would seem to be Al-arish,

the city of Faramea, where is a church of St. Mary, on the
spot to which, by the admonition of the angel, Joseph fled
with the child and its mother.   In this city there is a multitude of camels, which are hired from the natives by travellers
to carry their baggage across the desert, which is a journey
of six days.   At this city the desert begins; and it may well
be called a desert, for it bears neither grass nor fruit of any
kind, with the exception of palm-trees, and it is white, like a
plain covered with snow.   In the middle of the route there
are two caravanserais, one called Albara, the other Albacara,
in which the Christians and pagans traffic for the things
necessary on the journey.   But around them the earth is as
barren as in the rest of the desert.   After Albacara the earth
becomes fruitful, and continues so to the city of Gaza, which
was the city of Samson, and is very rich in all things.   Then
we came to Alariza, and thence we went to Ramula, near which
is the monastery of St. George the Martyr, in which he rests.
From Ramula we hastened to the castle of Emaus; and thence
we went to the holy city of Jerusalem, where we were received in the hostel founded there by the glorious emperor
Charles *, in which are received all the pilgrims who speak
the Roman tongue; to which adjoins a church in honour of St.
Mary, with a most noble library, founded by the same emperor,
with twelve mansions, fields, vineyards, and a garden in the
Valley of Jehoshaphat.   In front of the hospital is a market,
for which every one trading there pays yearly to him who
provides it two aurei.

Within this city, besides others, there are four principal
churches, connected with each other by walls; one to the
east, which contains the Mount of Calvary, and the place
in which the cross of our Lord was found, and is called the
Basilica of Constantine; another to the south; a third to the
west, in the middle of which is the sepulchre of our Lord,
having nine columns in its circuit, between which are walls
made of the most excellent stones; of which nine columns,

---

* Charlemagne. We have no other account of Charlemagne's foundations
at Jerusalem; but the khalif Haroun-er-Raschid is said to have shown great
favour to the Christian pilgrims from respect for the Frankish emperor,
and even to have sent him the keys of the Holy Sepulchre and of Jerusalem.
A legend prevalent in the twelfth century made the emperor visit Jerusalem
in person; and an Anglo-Norman poem on Charlemagne's pretended voyage
to the Holy Land, composed in that century, was printed by M. Fr. Michel
in 1836.

four are in front of the monument itself; which, with their walls, include the stone placed before the sepulchre, which the angel rolled away, and on which he sat after our Lord's resurrection.   It is not necessary to say more of this sepulchre, since Bede has given a full description of it in his history*.   I must not, however, omit to state, that on Holy Saturday, which is the eve of Easter, the office is begun in the morning in this church, and after it is ended the *Kyrie Eleison* is chanted, until an angel comes and lights the lamps which hang over the aforesaid sepulchre†; of which light the patriarch gives their shares to the bishops and to the rest of the people, that each may illuminate his own house.   The present patriarch is called Theodosius‡, and was brought to this place on account of his piety from his monastery, which is fifteen miles from Jerusalem, and was made patriarch over all the Christians in the Land of Promise. Between the aforesaid four churches is a parvis without roof, the walls of which shine with gold, and the pavement is laid with very precious stone; and in the middle four chains, coming from each of the four churches, join in a point which is said to be the middle of the world.

There is, moreover, in the city, another church on Mount

---

* See "Bede's Ecclesiastical History," book v. chaps. 16 and 17. Bede professedly takes his account from Adamnan's narrative of the travels of bishop Arculf, and the description referred to will be found at p. 2 of the present volume.

† This was a very celebrated miracle in the middle ages, and will be remembered as the cause of the persecution of the Christians in the Holy City, and of the destruction of the Church of the Holy Sepulchre, by the khalif Hakem, in A.D. 1008 or 1010.   An eastern Christian writer, Abulfaragius, tells us that "the author of this persecution was some enemy of the Christians, who told Hakem that, when the Christians assembled in their temple at Jerusalem, to celebrate Easter, the chaplains of the church, making use of a pious fraud, greased the chain of iron that held the lamp over the tomb with oil of balsam; and that, when the Arab officer had sealed up the door which led to the tomb, they applied a match, through the roof, to the other extremity of the chain, and the fire descended immediately to the wick of the lamp and lighted it.   Then the worshippers burst into tears, and cried out *kyrie eleison*, supposing it was fire which fell from heaven upon the tomb; and they were thus strengthened in their faith."   This miracle was probably instituted after the time when so much encouragement was given to the pilgrims under the reign of Charlemagne.   It is not mentioned in the works that preceded Bernard, but it is often alluded to in subsequent writers, and continues still to be practised by the Greeks.

‡ Theodosius was patriarch of Jerusalem from 863 to 879.

Sion, which is called the Church of St. Simeon, where our
Lord washed the feet of his disciples, and in which is suspended our Lord's crown of thorns.   St. Mary is said to have
died in this church.   Near it, towards the east, is a church
in honour of St. Stephen, on the spot where he is believed
to have been stoned.   And, indirectly to the east, is a church
in honour of St. Peter, in the place where he denied our
Lord.   To the north is the Temple of Solomon, having a
synagogue of the Saracens *.   To the south of it are the iron
gates through which the angel of the Lord led Peter out of
prison, and which were never opened afterwards.

Leaving Jerusalem, we descended into the Valley of Jehoshaphat, which is a mile from the city, containing the village of Gethsemane, with the place of the nativity of St.
Mary.   In it is a round church of St. Mary, containing her
sepulchre, on which the rain never falls, although there is no
roof above it.   There is also a church on the spot where our
Lord was betrayed, containing the four round tables of his
Supper.   In the Valley of Jehoshaphat there is also a church
of St. Leon, in which it is said that our Lord will come at
the Last Judgment.   Thence we went to Mount Olivet, on
the declivity of which is shown the place of our Lord's
prayer to the Father.   On the side of the same mountain is
shown the place where the Pharisees brought to our Lord the
woman taken in adultery, where there is a church in honour
of St. John, in which is preserved the writing in marble
which our Lord wrote on the ground†.   At the summit of the
mountain, a mile from the Valley of Jehoshaphat, is the place
of our Lord's ascension, in the middle of which, on the spot
from which he ascended, is an altar open to the sky, on
which mass is celebrated.   Thence we proceeded to Bethany,
which is to the south, on the ascent of the mountain, one
mile from the top ; there is here a monastery, with a church

* *i. e.* the Mosque of Omar.

† The event alluded to occurred in the Temple, and not on the Mount of
Olives.   The notion mentioned in the text must have arisen from a wrong
reading of the first verses of John, viii.   It is stated in the Gospel, John,
viii. 6, "But Jesus stooped down, and with his finger wrote on the ground,
as though he heard them not."   This writing on the ground was worked up
into a popular legend in the middle ages, according to which Christ is represented as writing on the ground the secret sins of all the persons assembled
to condemn the woman ; and this, we are told, was the cause that they all
slunk away ashamed.

containing the sepulchre of Lazarus; near which, to the north, is a pool in which, by our Lord's command, Lazarus washed himself after he had been raised from the dead: and he is said to have been subsequently bishop in Ephesus forty years. On the western declivity of Mount Olivet is shown the marble from which the Lord descended on the foal of an ass. Between these, to the south, in the Valley of Jehoshaphat, is the pool of Siloah.

When we left Jerusalem on the way to Bethlehem, the place of our Lord's nativity, distant six miles, we were shown the field in which Habakkuk was at work when the angel of the Lord ordered him to carry his meal to Daniel in Babylon, which is to the south, where Nebuchadnezzar reigned, but which is now the haunt of serpents and wild beasts. At Bethlehem there is a very large church in honour of St. Mary, in the middle of which is a crypt under a stone, the entrance of which is from the south, and the egress from the east, in which is shown the manger of our Lord, on the west side of the crypt. But the place in which our Lord cried, is to the east, having an altar where masses are celebrated. Near this church, to the south, is a church of the Blessed Innocents, the martyrs. One mile from Bethlehem, is the monastery of the Holy Shepherds, to whom the angel appeared at our Lord's nativity. Lastly, thirty miles to the east of Jerusalem is the river Jordan, on which is the monastery of St. John; in which space there are also many other monasteries. Among them, one mile to the south of the city of Jerusalem, is the church of St. Mamilla, in which are many bodies of martyrs slain by the Saracens, and diligently buried there by her.

We returned from the holy city of Jerusalem direct to the sea, where we took ship, and sailed sixty days in very great peril, from the violence of the wind. At length we landed at *Mons Aureus*, where is a crypt containing seven altars, and having above it a great forest; which crypt is so dark, that none can enter it without lamps. The abbot there is Dom Valentine. Thence we went to Rome, within which city, to the east, in a place called Lateran, is a well-built church in honour of St. John the Baptist, where is the special see of the popes; and there, every year, the keys are carried to the pope from every part of the city. On the west side of Rome is the church of St. Peter, the chief of the Apostles, where he rests; the magnitude of which is unequalled by any church in the whole world, and it contains a variety of ornaments. In which city repose innumerable bodies of saints.

Here I separated from my companions; I myself proceeded thence to St. Michael *ad Duas Tumbas**, which is a place situated on a mountain that runs out two leagues into the sea. At the summit of this mountain is a church in honour of St. Michael; the mountain is surrounded by the tide twice every day, at morning and evening, and men cannot go to the mountain until the sea retires. But on the Feast of St. Michael the sea does not join round the mountain when the tide comes in, but stands like walls to the right and left, so that on that day all who wish to perform their devotions there can pass to the mountain any hour of the day, which they cannot do on other days. There Phinimontius, a Breton, is abbot.

Now I will tell you how the Christians keep God's law both at Jerusalem and in Egypt. The Christians and Pagans have there such a peace between them, that if I should go a journey, and in the journey my camel or ass which carries my baggage should die, and I should leave everything there without a guard, and go to the next town to get another, on my return I should find all my property untouched. The law of public safety is there such, that if they find in a city, or on the sea, or on the road, any man journeying by night or by day, without a letter, or some mark of a king or prince of that land, he is immediately thrown into prison, till the time he can give a good account whether he be a spy or not.

The people of Beneventum, in their pride, slew their prince, Sichard, and did great injury to the Christian faith; then they had quarrels and contentions among themselves, until Louis, the brother of Lothaire and Charles†, obtained

* Mount St. Michel, on the coast of Brittany, which was commonly called St. Michel *ad tumbam* or *ad tumbas*, and was a place of great celebrity in the romantic, as well as in the religious, legends of the middle ages. It is more than probable that, before the foundation of the monastery, the top of the mount was occupied by a cromlech, like so many of the islands on this coast.

† Sichard was a cruel and oppressive tyrant, and was deservedly hated by his subjects. At length, having attempted to violate the wife of one of his nobles, the latter excited the people of Beneventum to revolt; and they burst into his palace, and slaughtered him, towards the end of the year 839. This act of popular vengeance was succeeded by a period of domestic troubles,

the empire over them. And in Romania many crimes are committed, and there are bad people there, banditti and thieves, and so men cannot go to Rome to visit St. Peter, unless they join together in troops, and go armed. In Lombardy, under the reign of the aforesaid Louis, there is tolerably good peace. The Bretons also have peace among themselves; and it is there the custom that if any one injure another, a third immediately comes, whoever he may be who witnesses it, and takes up the cause of the injured man as though he were his neighbour. And if any one is proved to have stolen more than four deniers, they slay him, or hang him on a gallows *.

I will add, in conclusion, that we saw in the village of Gethsemane squared marble stones of that fineness that a man might see any thing he liked in them, as in a looking-glass.

THE TRAVELS OF SÆWULF.

A.D. 1102 AND 1103.

I, SÆWULF, though conscious of my own unworthiness, went to offer up my prayers at the Holy Sepulchre; but, owing to my sins, or to the badness of the ship, being unable to proceed thither by the direct course on the open sea, I will commence with an enumeration of the different islands at which we touched.

Some pilgrims embark at Bari, others at Barlo (Barletta?), some at Siponte, or at Trani; while others take ship at Otranto, the entrance port of Apulia. We set sail from Monopoli, one day's journey from Bari, on Sunday, being the feast of St. Mildred †. But starting at an unlucky hour, as happened to us again on a subsequent occasion, we had not proceeded more

which favoured the designs of the Saracens, and ultimately brought Beneventum under the power or protection of the emperor Louis II., or the Germanic, (the brother of Lothaire and Charles the Bald, and grandson of Charlemagne,) who was emperor and king of Germany from 840 to 876.

* Salomon III. was count of Brittany at this time; but history hardly bears out Bernard's boasts of the peace and good government of the country under his rule.

† July 13, 1102.

than three miles, when the mercy of God alone saved us from perishing; for the same day the violence of the waves wrecked our vessel, but with God's help we all reached the shore in safety. We then went to Brandia*, and again our ship, being refitted, set sail on an unlucky day†, and reached the town of Corfu, on the eve of St. James the Apostle‡. From thence we were driven by a tempest to the island of Cephalonia, which we reached on the 1st of August. Here Robert Guiscard died§; we also lost some of our party, which was the cause of sadness to us. We next touched at Polipolis||; after which we came to the celebrated island of Patras, the city of which we entered for the sake of praying to St. Andrew the Apostle, who suffered martyrdom and was buried here, but was afterwards translated to Constantinople. From Patras we went to Corinth, which we reached on the eve of St. Lawrence¶. St. Paul preached the word of God here, and wrote an epistle to the citizens. In this place we suffered many contrarieties. Thence we sailed to the port of Hosta**; from which place we proceeded, some on foot, others on asses, to the city of Thebes, vulgarly called Stivas. On the eve of St. Bartholomew the Apostle††, we came to Nigropont, where we hired another ship. Athens, where the Apostle Paul preached, is two days' journey from Corinth; St. Dionysius was born and taught there, and was afterwards converted by St. Paul. Here is a church of the blessed Virgin Mary, which has a lamp that burns always and never wants oil.

We went afterwards to the island of Petalion‡‡; thence to Andros, where are made rich sindals and samits and other stuffs of silk. We then touched successively at Tinos, Syra,

* The modern Brindisi (*Brundusium* of the ancients).

† *Die Ægyptiaca, hora Ægyptiaca.* The superstitious belief in unlucky, or, as they were commonly termed, Egyptian days, was universally prevalent in the middle ages; and the days of the month believed to have this character, and on which it was unpropitious to begin or undertake any thing, are often marked in the early calendars and other manuscripts.

‡ July 24.

§ See our Introduction.

|| M. D'Avezac conjectures this to be merely some *palæopolis*, or ancient site. No such name as Polipolis can be traced in the maps.

¶ Aug. 9.

** This appears to be the place formerly called Liva d'Osta, now corrupted into Livadostro.

†† Aug. 23.

‡‡ The modern Spili.

Miconi, and Naxia, near which is the famous island of Crete.
Next we came to Carea (Khero), Amorgo, Samos, Scio, and
Meteline.   We then proceeded to Pathmos, where St. John
the Apostle and Evangelist, banished by Domitian Cæsar,
wrote the Revelations.   On the side towards Smyrna, a
day's journey distant, is Ephesus, where he afterwards entered the sepulchre living; the apostle Paul, moreover,
wrote an Epistle to the Ephesians.   Then we came to the
isles of Lero and Calimno, and afterwards to Ancho*, where
Galen, the physician most celebrated among the Greeks,
was born.   Thence we passed over to the port of Lido†, a
city destroyed, where Titus, the disciple of St. Paul, preached.
Next, to Asus, which is interpreted silvery.

Our next station was the famous island of Rhodes, which is
said to have possessed one of the seven wonders of the world,
the idol called Colossus, which was a hundred and twenty feet
high, and was destroyed by the Persians, with nearly all the
province of Romania, when they were on their way to Spain.
These are the Colossians, to whom St. Paul the Apostle wrote
his epistle‡.   Hence, it is a distance of one day to the city
of Patera, where St. Nicholas the archbishop was born, and
where we arrived in the evening, after escaping a violent
storm.   Next morning we sailed to an entirely desolate town
called Mogronissi of St. Mary, which means Long Island,
which it would appear by the churches and other buildings
had been inhabited by the Christians, after they had been
driven by the Turks from Alexandria§.   Then we came to
the city of Myra, where St. Nicholas was archbishop, and

---

* Stancho, the ancient Cos; Hippocrates, and not Galen, was born there.

† M. D'Avezac is probably right in his conjecture that the Lido of Sæwulf
represents the ruins of Cnidus, near Cape Crio; and that Asus, which immediately follows, is the little island of Syme (Συμὴ), which lies off Cnidus.
It is likely enough that the local pronunciation of Cnido may have
been taken by the monkish traveller for something like Lido.   No detailed
legend of St. Titus is preserved.   What is known of him will be found in
the Acta Sanctorum of the Bollandists, vol. i. p. 163.

‡ This is a remarkable blunder, arising from a strange confusion of words
and ideas.   The Colossians were the inhabitants of Colossus, in Phrygia.
The *Persians* of Sæwulf were the Saracens, who captured Rhodes in A.D.
651.   It had been taken by the Persians in 616.

§ Mogronissi, or Macronisi, is supposed by M. D'Avezac to be the island
of Kakava, on the western point of which are still traced the ruins of a town
and church.   The Alexandria here alluded to is of course Alexandretta, or
Iskenderoon.

which is the port of the Adriatic Sea, as Constantinople is the port óf the Ægean Sea. After having worshipped at the sepulchre of the saint, we sailed to the island which is called Xindacopo *, which means sixty oars, on account of the force of the sea; near it is the port and district of Finica. Thence we sailed over the broad part of the Adriatic Sea†, to the city of Paffus (Baffo), which is in the isle of Cyprus, where all the Apostles met after the ascension of our Lord, and held a council for the arrangement of the affairs of the gospel, on which occasion they sent forth St. Barnabas to preach; after whose death St. Peter went thence to Joppa, and sowed the seed of God's word there, before he ascended the episcopal see of Antioch.

After leaving the isle of Cyprus, we were tossed about by tempestuous weather for seven days and seven nights, being forced back one night almost to the spot from which we sailed; but after much suffering, by divine mercy, at sun-rise on the eighth day, we saw before us the coast of the port of Joppa, which filled us with an unexpected and extraordinary joy. Thus, after a course of thirteen weeks, as we took ship at Monopoli, on a Sunday, having dwelt constantly on the waves of the sea, or in islands, or in deserted cots and sheds (for the Greeks are not hospitable), we put into the port of Joppa, with great rejoicings and thanksgivings, on a Sunday‡.

And now, my dear friends, all join with me in thanking God for his mercy shown to me through this long voyage; blessed be his name now and evermore! Listen now to a new instance of his mercy shown to me, although the lowest of his servants, and to my companions. The very day we came in sight of the port, one said to me (I believe by divine inspiration), "Sir, go on shore to-day, lest a storm come on in the night, which will render it impossible to land to-morrow." When I heard this, I was suddenly seized with a great desire of landing, and, having hired a boat, went into it, with all my companions; but, before I had reached the shore, the sea was troubled, and became continually more tempestuous. We landed, however, with God's grace, without hurt, and entering the city weary and hungry, we secured a lodging, and reposed ourselves that night. But next morning, as we

* This is evidently Khelidonia.
† This term was then applied to all the eastern part of the Mediterranean.
‡ Sunday, Oct. 12, 1102.

were returning from church, we heard the roaring of the sea, and the shouts of the people, and saw that every body was in confusion and astonishment. We were also dragged along with the crowd to the shore, where we saw the waves swelling higher than mountains, and innumerable bodies of drowned persons of both sexes scattered over the beach, while the fragments of ships were floating on every side. Nothing was to be heard but the roaring of the sea and the dashing together of the ships, which drowned entirely the shouts and clamour of the people. Our own ship, which was a very large and strong one, and many others laden with corn and merchandise, as well as with pilgrims coming and returning, still held by their anchors, but how they were tossed by the waves! how their crews were filled with terror! how they cast overboard their merchandise! what eye of those who were looking on could be so hard and stony as to refrain from tears? We had not looked at them long before the ships were driven from their anchors by the violence of the waves, which threw them now up aloft, and now down, until they were run aground or upon the rocks, and there they were beaten backwards and forwards until they were crushed to pieces. For the violence of the wind would not allow them to put out to sea, and the character of the coast would not allow them to put into shore with safety. Of the sailors and pilgrims who had lost all hope of escape, some remained on the ships, others laid hold of the masts or beams of wood; many remained in a state of stupor, and were drowned in that condition without any attempt to save themselves; some (although it may appear incredible) had in my sight their heads knocked off by the very timbers of the ships to which they had attached themselves for safety; others were carried out to sea on the beams, instead of being brought to land; even those who knew how to swim had not strength to struggle with the waves, and very few thus trusting to their own strength reached the shore alive. Thus, out of thirty very large ships, of which some were what are commonly called dromunds, some gulafres, and others cats *, all laden

---

* These were the names of ships in the middle ages, of large dimensions, but for which it would be difficult to assign any thing like equivalents from our modern naval nomenclature. The title of palmer (*palmarius*) was given, from an early period, to the pilgrims to the Holy Land; it is said, on account of the palm branches or leaves which they usually brought back with them as signs that they had performed the pilgrimage.

with palmers and with merchandise, scarcely seven remained
safe when we left the shore. Of persons of both sexes, there
perished more than a thousand that day. Indeed, no eye
ever beheld a greater misfortune in the space of a single day,
from all which God snatched us by his grace; to whom be
honour and glory for ever. Amen.

We went up from Joppa to the city of Jerusalem, a journey
of two days, by a mountainous road, very rough, and dangerous on account of the Saracens, who lie in wait in the caves
of the mountains to surprise the Christians, watching both
day and night to surprise those less capable of resisting by
the smallness of their company, or the weary, who may
chance to lag behind their companions. At one moment, you
see them on every side; at another, they are altogether invisible, as may be witnessed by any body travelling there.
Numbers of human bodies lie scattered in the way, and by the
way-side, torn to pieces by wild beasts. Some may, perhaps,
wonder that the bodies of Christians are allowed to remain
unburied, but it is not surprising when we consider that there
is not much earth on the hard rock to dig a grave; and if
earth were not wanting, who would be so simple as to leave
his company, and go alone to dig a grave for a companion?
Indeed, if he did so, he would rather be digging a grave for
himself than for the dead man. For on that road, not only
the poor and weak, but the rich and strong, are surrounded
with perils; many are cut off by the Saracens, but more by
heat and thirst; many perish by the want of drink, but more
by too much drinking. We, however, with all our company,
reached the end of our journey in safety. Blessed be the
Lord, who did not turn away my prayer, and hath not turned
his mercy from me. Amen.

The entrance to the city of Jerusalem is from the west,
under the citadel of king David, by the gate which is called
the gate of David. The first place to be visited is the church
of the Holy Sepulchre, which is called the Martyrdom, not
only because the streets lead most directly to it, but because
it is more celebrated than all the other churches; and that
rightly and justly, for all the things which were foretold and
forewritten by the holy prophets of our Saviour Jesus Christ
were there actually fulfilled. The church itself was royally
and magnificently built, after the discovery of our Lord's
cross, by the archbishop Maximus, with the patronage of the

emperor Constantine, and his mother Helena. In the middle of this church is our Lord's Sepulchre, surrounded by a very strong wall and roof, lest the rain should fall upon the Holy Sepulchre, for the church above is open to the sky. This church is situated, like the city, on the declivity of Mount Sion. The Roman emperors Titus and Vespasian, to revenge our Lord, entirely destroyed the city of Jerusalem, that our Lord's prophecy might be fulfilled, which, as he approached Jerusalem, seeing the city, he pronounced, weeping over it, "If thou hadst known, even thou, for the day shall come upon thee, that thine enemies shall cast a trench about thee, and compass thee round, and keep thee in on every side, and shall lay thee even with the ground, and thy children with thee; and they shall not leave in thee one stone upon another."* We know that our Lord suffered without the gate. But the emperor Hadrian, who was called Ælius, rebuilt the city of Jerusalem, and the Temple of the Lord, and added to the city as far as the Tower of David, which was previously a considerable distance from the city, for any one may see from the Mount of Olivet where the extreme western walls of the city stood originally, and how much it is since increased. And the emperor called the city after his own name Ælia, which is interpreted the House of God. Some, however, say that the city was rebuilt by the emperor Justinian, and also the Temple of the Lord as it is now; but they say that according to supposition, and not according to truth. For the Assyrians†, whose fathers dwelt in that country from the first persecution, say that the city was taken and destroyed many times after our Lord's Passion, along with all the churches, but not entirely defaced.

In the court of the church of our Lord's sepulchre are seen some very holy places, namely, the prison in which our Lord Jesus Christ was confined after he was betrayed, according to the testimony of the Assyrians; then, a little above, appears the place where the holy cross and the other crosses were found, where afterwards a large church was built in honour of queen Helena, but which has since been utterly destroyed by the Pagans; and below, not far from the prison, stands the marble column to which our Lord Jesus Christ was bound in the common

* Luke, xix. 42-44.

† By the Assyrians, who are subsequently mentioned more than once, we are to understand the Syrian Christians, as distinguished from the Greeks.

hall, and scourged with most cruel stripes. Near this is the spot where our Lord was stripped of his garments by the soldiers; and next, the place where he was clad in a purple vest by the soldiers, and crowned with the crown of thorns, and they cast lots for his garments. Next we ascend Mount Calvary, where the patriarch Abraham raised an altar, and prepared, by God's command, to sacrifice his own son; there afterwards the Son of God, whom he prefigured, was offered up as a sacrifice to God the Father for the redemption of the world. The rock of that mountain remains a witness of our Lord's passion, being much cracked near the foss in which our Lord's cross was fixed, because it could not suffer the death of its Maker without splitting, as we read in the Passion, "and the rocks rent."* Below is the place called Golgotha,where Adam is said to have been raised to life by the blood of our Lord which fell upon him, as is said in the Passion, "And many bodies of the saints which slept arose."† But in the Sentences of St. Augustine, we read that he was buried in Hebron, where also the three patriarchs were afterwards buried with their wives; Abraham with Sarah, Isaac with Rebecca, and Jacob with Leah; as well as the bones of Joseph, which the Children of Israel carried with them from Egypt. Near the place of Calvary is the church of St. Mary, on the spot where the body of our Lord, after having been taken down from the cross, was anointed before it was buried, and wrapped in a linen cloth or shroud.

At the head of the church of the Holy Sepulchre, in the wall outside, not far from the place of Calvary, is the place called Compas, which our Lord Jesus Christ himself signified and measured with his own hand as the middle of the world, according to the words of the Psalmist, "For God is my king of old, working salvation in the midst of the earth."‡ But some say that that is the place where our Lord Jesus Christ first appeared to Mary Magdalene, while she sought him weeping, and thought he had been a gardener, as is related in the Gospel. These most holy places of prayer are contained in the court of our Lord's Sepulchre, on the east side. In the sides of the church itself are attached, on one side and the other, two most beautiful chapels in honour of St. Mary and St. John, as they, participating in our Lord's sufferings, stationed themselves be-

---

* Matth. xxvii. 51.　　　† Ib. 52.　　　‡ Psal. lxxiv. 12.

side him here and there.   On the west wall of the chapel of St. Mary is seen the picture of our Lord's Mother, painted externally, who once, by speaking wonderfully through the Holy Spirit, in the form in which she is here painted, comforted Mary the Egyptian, when she repented with her whole heart, and sought the help of the Mother of our Lord, as we read in her life.   On the other side of the church of St. John is a very fair monastery of the Holy Trinity, in which is the place of the baptistery, to which adjoins the chapel of St. John the Apostle, who first filled the pontifical see at Jerusalem.   These are all so composed and arranged, that any one standing in the furthest church may clearly perceive the five churches from door to door.

Without the gate of the Holy Sepulchre, to the south, is the church of St. Mary, called the Latin, because the monks there perform divine service in the Latin tongue; and the Assyrians say that the blessed Mother of our Lord, at the crucifixion of her Son, stood on the spot now occupied by the altar of this church.   Adjoining to this church is another church of St. Mary, called the Little, occupied by nuns who serve devoutly the Virgin and her Son.   Near which is the Hospital, where is a celebrated monastery founded in honour of St. John the Baptist.

We descend from our Lord's sepulchre, about the distance of two arbalist-shots, to the Temple of the Lord, which is to the east of the Holy Sepulchre, the court of which is of great length and breadth, having many gates; but the principal gate, which is in front of the Temple, is called the Beautiful, on account of its elaborate workmanship and variety of colours, and is the spot where Peter healed Claudius, when he and John went up into the Temple at the ninth hour of prayer, as we read in the Acts of the Apostles.   The place where Solomon built the Temple was called anciently Bethel; whither Jacob repaired by God's command, and where he dwelt, and saw the ladder whose summit touched heaven, and the angels ascending and descending, and said, " Truly this place is holy," as we read in Genesis.   There he raised a stone as a memorial, and constructed an altar, and poured oil upon it; and in the same place afterwards, by God's will, Solomon built a temple to the Lord of magnificent and incomparable work, and decorated it wonderfully with every ornament, as we read in the Book of Kings.   It exceeded all the

mountains around in height, and all walls and buildings in
brilliancy and glory. In the middle of which temple is seen
a high and large rock, hollowed beneath, in which was the
Holy of Holies. In this place Solomon placed the Ark of the
Covenant, having the Manna and the Rod of Aaron, which
flourished and budded there and produced almonds, and
the two Tables of the Testament; here our Lord Jesus Christ,
wearied with the insolence of the Jews, was accustomed to
repose; here was the place of confession, where his disciples
confessed themselves to him; here the angel Gabriel appeared to Zacharias, saying, "Thou shalt receive a child in
thy old age;" here Zacharias, the son of Barachias, was slain
between the temple and the altar; here the child Jesus was
circumcised on the eighth day, and named Jesus, which is in
terpreted Saviour; here the Lord Jesus was offered by his
parents, with the Virgin Mary, on the day of her purification,
and received by the aged Simeon; here, also, when Jesus
was twelve years of age, he was found sitting in the midst of
the doctors, hearing and interrogating them, as we read in the
Gospel; here afterwards he cast out the oxen, and sheep, and
pigeons, saying, "My house shall be a house of prayer;" and
here he said to the Jews, "Destroy this temple, and in
three days I will raise it up." There still are seen in the
rock the footsteps of our Lord, when he concealed himself,
and went out from the Temple, as we read in the Gospel,
lest the Jews should throw at him the stones they carried.
Thither the woman taken in adultery was brought before
Jesus by the Jews, that they might find some accusation
against him *. There is the gate of the city on the eastern
side of the Temple, which is called the Golden, where Joachim, the father of the Blessed Mary, by order of the Angel
of the Lord, met his wife Anne. By the same gate the Lord
Jesus, coming from Bethany on the day of olives, sitting on
an ass, entered the city of Jerusalem, while the children sang,
"Hosanna to the son of David." By this gate the emperor
Heraclius entered Jerusalem, when he returned victorious
from Persia, with the cross of our Lord; but the stones first
fell down and closed up the passage, so that the gate became
one mass, until humbling himself at the admonition of an
angel, he descended from his horse, and so the entrance was

* John, ii. 19.

opened to him. In the court of the Temple of the Lord, to the south, is the Temple of Solomon, of wonderful magnitude, on the east side of which is an oratory containing the cradle of Christ, and his bath, and the bed of the Virgin Mary, according to the testimony of the Assyrians*.

From the Temple of the Lord you go to the church of St. Anne, the mother of the Blessed Mary, towards the north, where she lived with her husband, and she was there delivered of her daughter Mary. Near it is the pool called in Hebrew Bethsaida, having five porticoes, of which the Gospel speaks. A little above is the place where the woman was healed by our Lord, by touching the hem of his garment, while he was surrounded by a crowd in the street†.

From St. Anne we pass through the gate which leads to the Valley of Jehoshaphat, to the church of St. Mary in the same valley, where she was honourably buried by the Apostles after her death; her sepulchre, as is just and proper, is revered with the greatest honours by the faithful, and monks perform service there day and night. Here is the brook Cedron; here also is Gethsemane, where our Lord came with his disciples from Mount Sion, over the brook Cedron, before the hour of his betrayal; there is a certain oratory where he dismissed Peter, James, and John, saying, "Tarry ye here, and watch with me;"‡ and going forward, he fell on his face and prayed, and came to his disciples, and found them sleeping: the places are still visible where the disciples slept, apart from each other. Gethsemane is at the foot of Mount Olivet, and the brook Cedron below, between Mount Sion and Mount Olivet, as it were the division of the mountains; and the low ground between the mountains is the Valley of Jehoshaphat. A little above, in Mount Olivet, is an

* It may be necessary to remind the reader that the building of which Sæwulf is here talking was the Mosque of Omar, which, during the long period that Jerusalem had remained in the hands of the Saracens, had been entirely closed from the examination of Christians. Now that the Holy City had fallen under the power of the Crusaders, it was thrown open to public inspection, and the monks appear to have laboured industriously to identify every part of the Saracenic edifice with the events of Scripture. Probably some portions of the ancient building were worked up into the Mohammedan mosque; but Sæwulf's description will show us how cautious we ought to be in receiving these traditionary identifications of the localities of Scripture history.

† Matth. ix. 20.   ‡ Matth. xxvi. 38.

oratory in the place where our Lord prayed, as we read in
the Passion, "And he was withdrawn from them about a
stone's cast, and being in an agony, he prayed more earnestly,
and his sweat was, as it were, great drops of blood falling
down to the ground."* Next we come to Aceldama, the
field bought with the price of the Lord, also at the foot of
Mount Olivet, near a valley about three or four arbalist-
shots to the south of Gethsemane, where are seen innumerable monuments. That field is near the sepulchres of the
holy fathers Simeon the Just and Joseph the foster-father of
our Lord. These two sepulchres are ancient structures, in
the manner of towers, cut into the foot of the mountain itself.
We next descend, by Aceldama, to the fountain which is
called the Pool of Siloah, where, by our Lord's command, the
man born blind washed his eyes, after the Lord had anointed
them with clay and spittle.

From the church of St. Mary before mentioned, we go up
by a very steep path nearly to the summit of Mount Olivet,
towards the east, to the place whence our Lord ascended to
heaven in the sight of his disciples. The place is surrounded by a little tower, and honourably adorned, with an
altar raised on the spot within, and also surrounded on all
sides with a wall. On the spot where the Apostles stood with
his mother, wondering at his ascension, is an altar of St. Mary;
there the two men in white garments stood by them, saying,
"Ye men of Galilee, why stand ye gazing into heaven?"
About a stone's throw from that place is the spot where, according to the Assyrians, our Lord wrote the Lord's Prayer
in Hebrew, with his own fingers, on marble; and there a
very beautiful church was built, but it has since been entirely
destroyed by the Pagans, as are all the churches outside the
walls, except the church of the Holy Ghost on Mount Sion,
about an arrow-shot from the wall to the north, where the
Apostles received the promise of the Father, namely, the
Paraclete Spirit, on the day of Pentecost; there they made
the Creed. In that church is a chapel in the place where
the Blessed Mary died. On the other side of the church is
the chapel where our Lord Jesus Christ first appeared to the
Apostles after his resurrection, and it is called Galilee, as he
said to the Apostles, "After I am risen again, I will go be-

---

* Luke, xxii. 41–44.

fore you unto Galilee."* That place was called Galilee, because the Apostles, who were called Galileans, frequently rested there.

The great city of Galilee is by Mount Tabor, a journey of three days from Jerusalem. On the other side of Mount Tabor is the city called Tiberias, and after it Capernaum and Nazareth, on the sea of Galilee or sea of Tiberias, whither Peter and the other Apostles, after the resurrection, returned to their fishing, and where the Lord afterwards showed himself to them on the sea. Near the city of Tiberias is the field where the Lord Jesus blessed the five loaves and two fishes, and afterwards fed four thousand men with them, as we read in the Gospel. But I will return to my immediate subject.

In the Galilee of Mount Sion, where the Apostles were concealed in an inner chamber, with closed doors, for fear of the Jews, Jesus stood in the middle of them and said, " Peace be unto you;"† and he again appeared there when Thomas put his finger into his side and into the place of the nails. There he supped with his disciples before the Passion, and washed their feet; and the marble table is still preserved there on which he supped. There the relics of St. Stephen, Nicodemus, Gamaliel, and Abido, were honourably deposited by St. John the Patriarch after they were found. The stoning of St. Stephen took place about two or three arbalist-shots without the wall, to the north, where a very handsome church was built, which has been entirely destroyed by the Pagans. The church of the Holy Cross, about a mile to the west of Jerusalem, in the place where the holy cross was cut out, and which was also a very handsome one, has been similarly laid waste by the Pagans ; but the destruction here fell chiefly on the surrounding buildings and the cells of the monks, the church itself not having suffered so much. Under the wall of the city, outside, on the declivity of Mount Sion, is the church of St. Peter, which is called the Gallican, where, after having denied his Lord, he hid himself in a very deep crypt, as may still be seen there, and there wept bitterly for his offence. About three miles to the west of the church of the Holy

---

* Matth. xxvi. 32. It is hardly necessary to state that the giving the name of Galilee to this church was a mere legendary blunder, originating in the desire to crowd several holy places in one spot.

† John, xx. 19.

Cross is a very fine and large monastery in honour of St. Saba, who was one of the seventy-two disciples of our Lord Jesus Christ. There were above three hundred Greek monks living there, in the service of the Lord and of the Saint, of whom the greater part have been slain by the Saracens, and the few who remain have taken up their abode in another monastery of the same Saint, within the walls of the city, near the tower of David, their other monastery being left entirely desolate.

The city of Bethlehem in Judea is six miles to the north of Jerusalem. The Saracens have left nothing there habitable, but every thing is destroyed (as in the other holy places without the walls of the city of Jerusalem) except the monastery of the blessed Virgin Mary, which is a large and noble building. In the church there is a crypt under the choir, about the middle, in which is seen the place of our Lord's nativity, as it were to the left. A little lower, to the right, near the place of the nativity, is the manger where the ox and ass stood when the child was placed before them in it; and the stone which supported the head of our Saviour in the sepulchre, which was brought hither from Jerusalem by St. Jerome the Presbyter, may be seen in the manger. St. Jerome himself rests in the same church, under the altar, to the north-east; and the innocents who were slain for the infant Christ, by Herod, lie under the altar on the north part of the church, as well as the two most holy women, Paula and her daughter Eustochium, the virgin. There is the marble table on which the blessed Virgin Mary eat with the three Magians, after they had given their offerings. There is a cistern in the church, near the crypt of our Lord's nativity, into which the star is said to have fallen. There, also, is said to be the bath of the blessed Virgin Mary.

Bethany, where Lazarus was raised by our Lord from the dead, is distant from the city about two miles to the east, on the other side of Mount Olivet, and contains the church of St. Lazarus, in which is seen his sepulchre, as well as those of many bishops of Jerusalem. Under the altar is the place where Mary Magdalene washed the feet of our Lord Jesus with her tears, and wiped them with her hair, and kissed his feet and anointed them with ointment. Bethphage, where our Lord sent forward his disciples to the city, is on Mount Olivet, but nearly all traces of it have disappeared. Jericho, where is the garden of Abraham, is ten leagues from Jerusalem, in a land covered with trees, and producing all kinds of palms and other fruits.   There is the well of the prophet Elisha, the water of which was most bitter to drink and productive of sterility, until he blessed it and threw salt into it, when it became sweet. This place is surrounded on every side by a beautiful plain.   From thence we ascend a lofty mountain, to the spot where our Lord fasted forty days, and where he was afterwards tempted by Satan, about three miles from Jericho.

The river Jordan is four leagues to the east of Jericho. On this side Jordan is the region called Judea, as far as the Adriatic Sea, that is, to the port which is called Joppa; on the other side Jordan is Arabia, most hostile to Christians, and hateful to all who worship God, in which is the mountain whence Elijah was carried into heaven in a fiery chariot. It is eighteen days' journey from Jordan to Mount Sinai, where the Lord appeared to Moses in the burning bush, and where, afterwards, Moses ascended by God's command, and was there fasting forty days and as many nights, and there received from the Lord the two stone tables, written by the finger of God, to teach the Children of Israel the law and the commandments, which were contained in the same tables.

Hebron, where the holy patriarchs, Abraham, Isaac, and Jacob repose, each with his wife, and where Adam, the first of mankind, is also buried, is distant from Bethlehem four leagues to the south.   Here king David reigned seven years, before he obtained possession of the city of Jerusalem from the family of king Saul.   The city of Hebron, which was large and very handsome, is destroyed by the Saracens.   On the eastern side of it the monuments of the holy patriarchs, of ancient workmanship, are surrounded by a very strong castle, each of the three monuments being like a great church, with two sarcophagi placed in a very honourable manner within, that is, one for the man and one for the woman ; and, even at the present day, the smell of the balsam and precious aromatics with which the bodies were anointed, rising sweetly from the sepulchre, fills the nostrils of those who stand round them.   But the bones of Joseph, which the Children of Israel, as he had charged them, brought with them out of Egypt, are buried, more humbly than the rest, as it were, at the extremity of the castle.   The holm-oak, under the shade of which Abraham stood when he saw the three youths descending by the road, still flourishes and bears leaves, according to the statement of the inhabitants of the place, not far distant from the aforesaid castle.

The city of Nazareth of Galilee, where the blessed Virgin Mary received the salutation of our Lord's nativity from the angel, is about four days' journey from Jerusalem, the road lying through Sichem, a city of Samaria, which is now called Neapolis, where St. John the Baptist received sentence of decollation from Herod. There, also, is the well of Jacob, where Jesus, weary with his journey, thirsty, and sitting upon the well, condescended to ask water of the Samaritan woman who came thither to draw it, as we read in the Gospel. From Sichem we come to Cæsarea of Palestine, from Cæsarea to Cayphas *, and from Cayphas to Accaron †. Nazareth is about eight miles to the east of Accaron. The city of Nazareth is entirely laid waste and overthrown by the Saracens ; but the place of the annunciation of our Lord is indicated by a very noble monastery. A most limpid fountain bubbles out near the city, still surrounded, as formerly, with marble columns and blocks, from which the child Jesus, with other children, often drew water for the use of his mother.

From Nazareth we proceed about four miles to the east, to Mount Tabor, the scene of our Lord's transfiguration, which is covered in an extraordinary manner with grass and flowers, and rises in the middle of the green plain of Galilee so as to exceed in altitude all the mountains which, though at a distance, surround it. On the summit still remain three ancient monasteries ; one in honour of our Lord Jesus Christ ; another in honour of Moses ; and a third, at some distance from the others, in honour of Elias, according to the words of Peter, " Lord, it is good for us to be here ; if thou wilt, let us make here three tabernacles, one for thee, and one for Moses, and one for Elias." ‡

The sea of Galilee is about six miles from Mount Tabor to the east and north-east, and is about ten miles long by five in breadth. The city of Tiberias stands on the sea-shore on one side, and on the other side are Corozaim and Bethsaida, the city of Andrew and Peter. About four miles to the north-east of the city of Tiberias is the castle of Gennesareth, where the Lord appeared to the disciples when fishing, as we learn

* Kaiffa. † Acre. ‡ Matth. xvii. 4.

from the Gospel. About two miles to the east of Gennesareth is the mount on which our Lord Jesus fed five thousand men with five loaves and two fishes. This mount is called by the inhabitants our Lord's table; and at its foot stands a very beautiful church of St. Peter, but deserted. Six miles to the north-east of Nazareth, on a hill, is Cana of Galilee, where our Lord converted water into wine at the marriage feast. There nothing is left standing except the monastery called that of Architriclinius *. About half way between Nazareth and Galilee is a castle which is called Roma, where all travellers from Accaron to Tiberias are lodged, having Nazareth on the right, and Galilee to the left.

A day's journey to the north-east of Tiberias is Mount Libanus, at the foot of which the river Jordan boils out from two foundations, of which one is called Jor, and the other Dan; the streams of which, joining in one, become a very rapid river, and take the name of Jordan. Its origin is near Cæsarea, the city of Philip the Tetrarch, in the district where Jesus, as is related in the Gospel, interrogated his disciples, saying, "Whom do men say that I, the Son of Man, am?"† Now the river Jordan, flowing from its spring with a very rapid course, falls into the sea of Galilee on one side, and passing out of it on the opposite side, by the violence of its current, makes itself a bed, through which it runs a distance of eight days' journey, and then falls into the Dead Sea. The water of the Jordan is whiter and more of a milky colour than any other water, and it may be distinguished by its colour a long distance into the Dead Sea.

Having, to the best of our power, visited and paid our devotion at all the holy places in the city of Jerusalem and the surrounding country, we took ship at Joppa on the day of Pentecost‡, on our return; but, fearing to meet the fleet of the Saracens, we did not venture out into the open sea by the same course we came, but sailed along the coast by several cities, some of which have fallen into the hands of the Franks, while

---

* The medieval theologians made a proper name of Architriclinius, or, as they called him popularly, St. Architriclin, whom they looked upon as the lord of the feast on the occasion alluded to, and the person in whose especial favour Christ performed the miracle. It is hardly necessary to say that *architriclinus* is the Latin word which, in the Vulgate, translates what the English text terms "the ruler of the feast."

† Matth. xvi. 13.   ‡ May 17, 1103.

others still remain in the power of the Saracens. Their names are as follows :—First, after Joppa, is the town called popularly Atsuph, but in Latin, Azotum ; next, Cæsarea of Palestine ; and then Cayphas. Baldwin, the flower of kings, has possession of these cities. Next after these is the very strong city of Acre, which is called Accaron ; then Sur and Sagete, which are Tyre and Sidon ; then Jubelet ; then Baruth ; and then Tartusa, which is in possession of duke Raimund. Next Gibel, where are the mountains of Gilboa ; and then Tripolis and Lice. We passed by all these cities*.

On the Wednesday of Pentecost, as we were sailing between Cayphas and Accaron†, twenty-six ships of the Saracens suddenly came in sight, the forces of the admiral of Tyre and Sidon, which were carrying an army to Babylonia to assist the Chaldeans in making war on the king of Jerusalem ; upon which two of our ships, which had come with us from Joppa full of palmers, leaving our ship behind because they were lighter, fled in all haste to Cæsarea. The Saracens, encircling our ship on all sides, at the distance of about an arrow's shot, rejoiced in the prospect of such a rich prey ; but our men, ready to meet death in the cause of Christ, took to their arms, and stationed themselves as quickly as possible on the castle of the ship ; for our dromund carried about two hundred soldiers. After the space of about an hour, the commander of the hostile fleet held a council, and sent a sailor up the mast of his ship, which was the largest, that he might give information of our condition and preparations ; and as soon as he understood from him the bold countenance we showed, they hoisted their sails and put out to sea, and so that day the Lord by his grace snatched us from our enemies.

---

* The names of these cities, in the modern nomenclature, are Arsouph, Kaisariyah, Kaiffa, Akre, Sour, Sayd, Gjobayl, Beyrout, Tortus, Gebely, Tripoli, and Laodicea, the latter of which was the place named by Sæwulf Lice. Jacobus de Vitriaco (Hist. Hierosol., cap. 44) says, " Laodicia Syriæ nuncupata, vulgariter autem Liche nominatur." Our traveller, however, perhaps by a confusion of his memory, having no map before him, has given these places out of their right order. Perhaps, as M. D'Avezac suggests, the fear of the Saracen cruisers drove him sometimes out of his right course.

Baldwin had been made king of Jerusalem on Christmas-day, in the year 1100. Tortosa was captured by Raymond, duke of Toulouse, on the 12th of March, 1102.

† Acre was not taken by the crusaders till the 15th of May, 1104, the year after our traveller's return.

Some of our people from Joppa afterwards took three of the ships we had seen, and enriched themselves with their spoils.

Thus making our way as well as we could along the coast of Syria, in eight days we reached the port of St. Andrew, in the isle of Cyprus*; and thence, next day, we sailed towards Romania, passing the port of St. Simon, and the port of St. Mary, and after many days reached Little Antioch†. In this part of the voyage we were several times attacked by pirates; but, under the Divine protection, we escaped unhurt from the attacks of enemies and the shocks of tempests. Then directing our course along the coast of Romania, and passing the towns of Stamirra‡ and Patras of St. Nicholas, we with difficulty reached the island of Rhodes on the eve of St. John the Baptist§, after a narrow escape from wreck in the bay of Satalia. At Rhodes we hired a smaller ship; that we might proceed more rapidly, and then returned to the coast of Romania. We then came to Stromlo‖, a very fair city, but entirely laid waste by the Turks, and there we were detained many days by a strong contrary wind. Then we came to the island of Samos, and having bought provisions there, as we did in all the islands, we arrived at length at the island of Scio, where we parted with our ship and company, and undertook the journey to Constantinople, to perform our devotions there. After leaving Scio, we passed by the great town of Smyrna, and came to the island of Meteline, and then to Tenit¶, near which, on the coast of Romania, was the very ancient and famous city of Troy, the ruins of the buildings of which, as the Greeks say, are still apparent over a space of many miles.

After leaving this place, we came to the narrow sea which is called the arm of St. George, which divides the two lands, Romania and Macedonia, through which we sailed to St. Phemius, having Greece to the right, and Macedonia to the left. The city of St. Phemius the bishop is on one side of

---

* Cape St. Andrea is the north-eastern point of the island of Cyprus.

† i. e. Antiochetta.

‡ Stamirra is the same place which Sæwulf has before called Myra. M. D'Avezac points out documents of the fourteenth and fifteenth centuries, in which it is named Astamirle, Stamire, and Stamir.

§ June 23.

‖ Stromlo, as M. D'Avezac observes, is evidently the ancient Astypalæa, now called Stampali.

¶ Tenit is the island of Tenedos.

the arm, in Macedonia, and another city, which is called
Samthe, stands on the other side in Greece, so that two or
three arbalist-shots would reach from one city to the other *.
They are said to be the keys of Constantinople.   Then we
sailed by Callipolis, and Agios Georgios, and Paniados, and
other notable castles of Macedonia, and came to the city of
Rothostoca, after Michaelmas.   We came next to the noble
city of Raclea, whence, according to the Greeks, Helen was
ravished by Paris Alexander†.

THE SAGA OF SIGURD THE CRUSADER.
A.D. 1107—1111.

(FROM THE HEIMSKRINGLA, OR CHRONICLE OF THE KINGS OF NORWAY,
BY SAMUEL LAING, ESQ.)

AFTER king Magnus Barefoot's fall, his sons, Eystein, Sigurd,
and Olaf ‡, took the kingdom of Norway.   Eystein got the
northern, and Sigurd the southern parts of the country.   King
Olaf was then four or five years old, and the third part of the
country which he had was under the management of his two
brothers.   King Sigurd was chosen king when he was thirteen
or fourteen years old, and Eystein was a year older.   When
king Magnus's sons were chosen kings, the men who had followed Skopte Ogmundsson returned home.   Some had been
to Jerusalem, some to Constantinople; and there they had
made themselves renowned, and they had many kinds of novelties to talk about.   By these extraordinary tidings many
men in Norway were incited to the same expedition; and it
was also told that the Northmen who liked to go into the
military service at Constantinople found many opportunities
of getting property.   Then these Northmen desired much
that one of the two kings, either Eystein or Sigurd, should
go as commander of the troop which was preparing for this

* M. D'Avezac suggests that perhaps St. Euphemius and Samthe represent
the ancient Eleonta on one coast, and the ancient Æantium, near the mouth of
the Xanthus, on the other.

† Sæwulf's relation seems to break off abruptly here, probably by the
fault of the scribe; but, unfortunately, we know of no other manuscript that
might furnish us with an account of his adventures at Constantinople on his
return home.

‡ They reigned from about 1103 to about 1130.

expedition. The kings agreed to this, and carried on the
equipment at their common expense. Many great men, both
of the lendermen and bonders, took part in this enterprize;
and when all was ready for the journey, it was determined
that Sigurd should go, and Eystein, in the mean time, should
rule the kingdom upon their joint account.

A year or two after king Magnus's fall, Hakon, a son of
earl Paul, came from Orkney. The kings gave him the earl-
dom and government of the Orkney Islands, as the earls
before him, his father Paul or his uncle Erlend, had possessed it; and earl Hakon then sailed back immediately to
Orkney.

Four years after the fall of king Magnus, king Sigurd sailed
with his fleet of sixty ships from Norway. So says Thorarin
Stutfeld :—

> " A young king just and kind,
> People of loyal mind :
> Such brave men soon agree,—
> To distant lands they sail with glee.
> To the distant Holy Land
> A brave and pious band,
> Magnificent and gay,
> In sixty long ships glide away."

King Sigurd sailed in autumn to England, where Henry,
son of William the Bastard, was then king, and Sigurd remained with him all winter. So says Einar Skuleson :—

> " The king is on the waves !
> The storm he boldly braves.
>   His ocean steed,
>   With winged speed,
> O'er the white-flashing surges,
> To England's coast he urges ;
> And there he stays the winter o'er :
> More gallant king ne'er trod that shore."

In spring * king Sigurd and his fleet sailed westward to Valland †, and in autumn came to Galicia ‡, where he staid the
second winter. So says Einar Skuleson :—

> " Our king, whose land so wide
> No kingdom stands beside,
> In Jacob's land § next winter spent,
> On holy things intent ;

---

* A.D. 1108.   † Valland, the west of France.
‡ Galizo land, the province of Galicia, in the north-west of Spain.
§ Jacob's land.   Galicia is called Jacob's land by the scald, from St. James
of Compostella : the apostle James, whose relics are held in veneration at

> And I have heard the royal youth
> Cut off an earl who swerved from truth.
> Our brave king will endure no ill, —
> The hawks with him will get their fill."

It went thus:—The earl who ruled over the land made an
agreement with king Sigurd, that he should provide king
Sigurd and his men a market at which they could purchase
victuals all the winter; but this he did not fulfil longer than
to about Yule. It began then to be difficult to get food and
necessaries, for it is a poor barren land. Then king Sigurd
with a great body of men went against a castle which belonged
to the earl; and the earl fled from it, having but few people.
King Sigurd took there a great deal of victuals and of other
booty, which he put on board of his ships, and then made
ready and proceeded westward to Spain. It so fell out, as
the king was sailing past Spain, that some pirates who were
cruising for plunder met him with a fleet of galleys, and king
Sigurd attacked them. This was his first battle with heathen
men; and he won it, and took eight galleys from them. So
says Halldor Skualldre:—

> "Bold vikings, not slow
> To the death-fray to go,
> Meet our Norse king by chance,
> And their galleys advance.
> The bold vikings lost
> Many a man of their host,
> And eight galleys too,
> With cargo and crew."

Thereafter king Sigurd sailed against a castle called
Sintre*, and fought another battle. This castle is in Spain,
and was occupied by many heathens, who from thence plundered Christian people. King Sigurd took the castle, and
killed every man in it, because they refused to be baptized; and
he got there an immense booty. So sings Halldor Skualldre:—

> "From Spain I have much news to tell
> Of what our generous king befell.
> And first he routs the viking crew,
> At Cintra next the heathens slew;
> The men he treated as God's foes,
> Who dared the true faith to oppose.
> No man he spared who would not take
> The Christian faith for Jesus' sake."

Compostella in Spain.   Portugal appears to have been reckoned part of Spain,
and Galicia a distinct country.
    * Sintre, now Cintra, in Portugal; then reckoned part of Spain.

After this king Sigurd sailed with his fleet to Lisbon, which
is a great city in Spain, half Christian and half heathen; for
there lies the division between Christian Spain and heathen
Spain*, and all the districts which lie west of the city are
occupied by heathens.   There king Sigurd had his third battle with the heathens, and gained the victory, and with it a
great booty.   So says Halldor Skualldre :—

> " The son of kings on Lisbon's plains
> A third and bloody battle gains.
> He and his Norsemen boldly land,
> Running their stout ships on the strand."

Then king Sigurd sailed westwards along heathen Spain,
and brought up at a town called Alkassi†; and here he had
his fourth battle with the heathens, and took the town, and
killed so many people that the town was left empty.   They
got there also immense booty.   So says Halldor Skualldre :—

> " A fourth great battle, I am told,
> Our Norse king and his people hold
> At Alkassi; and here again
> The victory fell to our Norsemen."

And also this verse :—

> " I heard that through the town he went,
> And heathen widows' wild lament
> Resounded in the empty halls;
> For every townsman flies or falls."

King Sigurd then proceeded on his voyage, and came to
Nörfa Sound‡; and in the Sound he was met by a large
viking force, and the king gave them battle : and this was his
fifth engagement with heathens since the time he left Norway.
So says Halldor Skualldre :—

> " Ye moistened your dry swords with blood,
> As through Niorfa Sound ye stood :
> The screaming raven got a feast,
> As ye sailed onward to the East."

---

* The heathen Spain would be the parts of the Peninsula occupied by the
Moors.

† There is some difficulty in finding a town corresponding to this Alkassi.
It cannot be Alkassir in Fez, in Africa, as some have supposed, as the context
does not agree with it; nor with Algesiras, which is within the Straits of
Gibraltar (Nörfasund), and it would have been so described.   Alcasser de Sal
lies too far inland to have been the place.   Lady Grosvenor, in her Yacht
Voyage, 1841, speaks of a Moorish palace near Seville, called Alcasir, which
would correspond best with the Saga account.

‡ Nörfa Sound, the Straits of Gibraltar; so called from Nörfa, the first
Norse viking who passed through it.

King Sigurd then sailed eastward along the coast of Serkland *, and came to an island there called Formentara. There
a great many heathen Moors had taken up their dwelling in
a cave, and had built a strong stone-wall before its mouth. It
was high up to the wall, so that whoever attempted
to ascend was driven back with stones or missile weapons.
They harried the country all round, and carried all their booty
to their cave. King Sigurd landed on this island, and went
to the cave; but it lay in a precipice, and there was a high
winding path to the stone-wall, and the precipice above projected over it. The heathens defended the stone-wall, and
were not afraid of the Northmen's arms; for they could
throw stones, or shoot down upon the Northmen under their
feet: neither did the Northmen, under such circumstances,
dare to mount up. The heathens took their clothes and
other valuable things, carried them out upon the wall, spread
them out before the Northmen, shouted, and defied them,
and upbraided them as cowards. Then Sigurd fell upon this
plan: he had two ship's boats, such as we call barks, drawn
up the precipice right above the mouth of the cave; and had
thick ropes fastened round the stem, stern, and hull of each.
In these boats as many men went as could find room, and then
the boats were lowered by the ropes down in front of the
mouth of the cave; and the men in the boats shot with stones
and missiles into the cave, and the heathens were thus driven
from the stone-wall. Then Sigurd with his troops climbed up
the precipice to the foot of the stone-wall, which they succeeded in breaking down, so that they came into the cave.
Now the heathens fled within the stone-wall that was built
across the cave; on which the king ordered large trees to be
brought to the cave, made a great pile in the mouth of it, and
set fire to the wood. When the fire and smoke got the upper
hand, some of the heathens lost their lives in it; some fled;
some fell by the hands of the Northmen; and part were killed,
part burned; and the Northmen made the greatest booty
they had got on all their expeditions. So says Halldor
Skualldre:—

> " Formentara lay
> In the victor's way;

---

* Serkland is the Saracen's land, the north of Africa; and the inhabitants
bluemen, the Moors.

> His ships' stems fly
> To victory.
> The bluemen there
> Must fire bear,
> And Norsemen's steel
> At their hearts feel."

And also thus :—

> " 'Twas a feat of renown,—
> The boat lowered down,
> With a boat's crew brave,
> In front of the cave ;
> While up the rock scaling,
> And comrades up trailing,
> The Norsemen gain,
> And the bluemen are slain."

And also Thorarin Stuttfeld says :—

> " The king's men up the mountain's side
> Drag two boats from the ocean's tide :
> The two boats lay,
> Like hill-wolves gray.
> Now o'er the rock in ropes they 're swinging,
> Well manned, and death to bluemen bringing :
> They hang before
> The robbers' door."

Thereafter king Sigurd proceeded on his expedition, and came to an island called Ivitsa (Ivica), and had there his seventh battle, and gained a victory. So says Halldor Skualldre :—

> " His ships at Ivica now ride,
> The king's, whose fame spreads far and wide ;
> And here the bearers of the shield
> Their arms again in battle wield."

Thereafter king Sigurd came to an island called Minorca, and held there his eighth battle with heathen men, and gained the victory. So says Halldor Skualldre :—

> " On green Minorca's plains
> The eighth battle now he gains :
> Again the heathen foe
> Falls at the Norse king's blow."

In spring king Sigurd came to Sicily, and remained a long time there. There was then a duke Roger in Sicily, who received the king kindly, and invited him to a feast. King Sigurd came to it with a great retinue, and was splendidly entertained. Every day duke Roger stood at the company's table, doing service to the king ; but the seventh day of the

feast, when the people had come to table, and had wiped their
hands, king Sigurd took the duke by the hand, led him up to
the high seat, and saluted him with the title of king ; and
gave the right that there should be always a king over the
dominion of Sicily, although before there had only been earls
or dukes over that country*.

It is written in the chronicles, that earl Roger let himself
first be called the king of Sicily in the year of our Lord 1102,
having before contented himself with the title of earl only
of Sicily, although he was duke of Calabria and Apulia, and
was called Roger the Great; and when he afterwards made
the king of Tunet or Tunis tributary to him, he had these
words engraved on his sword,—

"Apulus et Calaber, Siculus mihi servit et Afer."

King Roger of Sicily was a very great king.   He won and
subdued all Apulia, and many large islands besides in the
Greek sea ; and therefore he was called Roger the Great.
His son was William, king of Sicily, who for a long time had
great hostility with the emperor of Constantinople.   King
William had three daughters, but no son.   One of his daughters he married to the emperor Henry, a son of the emperor
Frederic ; and their son was Frederic, who for a short time
after was emperor of Rome.   His second daughter was married
to the duke of Kypur†.   The third daughter, Margaret, was
married to the chief of the corsairs ; but the emperor Henry
killed both these brothers-in-law.   The daughter of Roger the
Great, king of Sicily, was married to the emperor Manuel of
Constantinople; and their son was the emperor Kirialax‡.

In summer king Sigurd sailed across the Greek sea to
Palestine§, and came to Acre‖, where he landed, and went by
land to Jerusalem ¶.   Now when Baldwin, king of Palestine,
heard that king Sigurd would visit the city, he let valuable
clothes be brought and spread upon the road, and the nearer

* It appears to have been the feudal idea of the times, that a title or dignity must be conferred by a superior in title or dignity ; and thus a wandering
king from the north could raise Roger of Sicily to the kingly title.   [The
Norseman's account is a fable : the dignity of king of Sicily was given to
count Roger, in 1129, by the pope.]

† Kypur, Cyprus.
‡ Kirialax.   Kuriou Alexou, the emperor Alexius Comnenus.
§ Jorsalaland, Palestine ; the land of Jerusalem.
‖ Akersborg, Acre.   ¶ Jorsalaborg, Jerusalem.

to the city the more valuable ; and said, "Now ye must know
that a celebrated king from the northern part of the earth is
come to visit us; and many are the gallant deeds and celebrated actions told of him, therefore we shall receive him
well; and in doing so we shall also know his magnificence
and power. If he ride straight on to the city, taking little
notice of these splendid preparations, I will conclude that he
has enough of such things in his own kingdom; but, on the
other hand, if he rides off the road, I shall not think so
highly of his royal dignity at home."   Now king Sigurd rides
to the city with great state ; and when he saw this magnificence, he rode straight forward over the clothes, and told all
his men to do the same.   King Baldwin received him particularly well, and rode with him all the way to the river Jordan, and then back to the city of Jerusalem.   Einar Skuleson
speaks thus of it :—

> " Good reason has the scald to sing
> The generous temper of the king,
> Whose sea-cold keel from Northern waves
> Ploughs the blue sea that green isles laves.
> At Acre scarce were we made fast,
> In holy ground our anchors cast,
> When the king made a joyful morn
> To all who toil with him had borne."

And again he sang :—

> " To Jerusalem he came,
> He who loves war's noble game,
> (The scald no greater monarch finds
> Beneath the heaven's wide hall of winds)
> All sin and evil from him flings
> In Jordan's wave : for all his sins
> (Which all must praise) he pardon wins."

King Sigurd staid a long time in the land of Jerusalem in
autumn, and in the beginning of winter.

King Baldwin made a magnificent feast for king Sigurd
and many of his people, and gave him many holy relics. By
the orders of king Baldwin and the patriarch, there was taken
a splinter off the holy cross ; and on this holy relic both made
oath, that this wood was of the holy cross upon which God
himself had been tortured.   Then this holy relic was given
to king Sigurd ; with the condition that he, and twelve other
men with him, should swear to promote Christianity with all
his power, and erect an archbishop's seat in Norway if he
could ; and also that the cross should be kept where the holy

king Olaf reposed, and that he should introduce tithes, and
also pay them himself. After this king Sigurd returned to
his ships at Acre; and then king Baldwin prepared to go to
Syria, to a town called Saet, which some think had been Sidon.
This castle, which belonged to the heathens, he wished to
conquer, and lay under the Christians. On this expedition
king Sigurd accompanied him with all his men, and sixty
ships; and after the kings had besieged the town some time
it surrendered*, and they took possession of it, and of a great
treasure of money; and their men found other booty. King
Sigurd made a present of his share to king Baldwin. So says
Halldor Skualldre:—

> " He who for wolves provides the feast
> Seized on the city in the east,
> The heathen nest; and honour drew,
> And gold to give, from those he slew."

Einar Skuleson also tells of it:—

> " The Norsemen's king, the scalds relate,
> Has ta'en the heathen town of Saet:
> The slinging engine, with dread noise,
> Gables and roofs with stones destroys.
> The town wall totters too,—it falls;
> The Norsemen mount the blackened walls.
> He who stains red the raven's bill
> Has won,—the town lies at his will."

Thereafter king Sigurd went to his ships, and made ready
to leave Palestine. They sailed north to the island of Cyprus;
and king Sigurd staid there awhile, and then went to the
Greek country, and came to the land with all his fleet at
Engilsness†. Here he lay still for a fortnight, although
every day it blew a breeze for going before the wind to the
north; but Sigurd would wait a side wind, so that the sails
might stretch fore and aft in the ship; for in all his sails
there was silk joined in, before and behind in the sail, and
neither those before nor those behind the ships could see the
slightest appearance of this, if the vessel was before the
wind; so they would rather wait a side wind.

When king Sigurd sailed into Constantinople, he steered

---

* Saide, or Sidon, was taken in December, 1110.

† Engilsness, supposed to be the ness at the river Ægos, called Ægisnes
in the Orkneyinga Saga, within the Dardanelles; not Cape Saint Angelo in
the Morea.

near the land.   Over all the land there are burghs, castles,
country towns, the one upon the other without interval.
There from the land one could see into the bights of the
sails; and the sails stood so close beside each other, that they
seemed to form one inclosure.   All the people turned out to
see king Sigurd sailing past.   The emperor Alexius had also
heard of king Sigurd's expedition, and ordered the city port
of Constantinople to be opened, which is called the Gold
Tower, through which the emperor rides when he has been
long absent from Constantinople, or has made a campaign in
which he has been victorious.   The emperor had precious
cloths spread out from the Gold Tower to Loktiar, which is
the name of the emperor's most splendid hall.   King Sigurd
ordered his men to ride in great state into the city, and not
to regard all the new things they might see; and this they
did.   The emperor sent singers and stringed instruments to
meet them; and with this great splendour king Sigurd and
his followers were received into Constantinople.   It is told
that king Sigurd had his horse shod with golden shoes before
he rode into the city, and managed so that one of the shoes
came off in the street, but that none of his men should regard
it.   When king Sigurd came to the magnificent hall, every
thing was in the grandest style; and when king Sigurd's men
had come to their seats, and were ready to drink, the emperor's messengers came into the hall, bearing between them
purses of gold and silver, which they said the emperor had
sent to king Sigurd; but the king did not look upon it, but
told his men to divide it among themselves.   When the messengers returned to the emperor, and told him this, he said,
"This king must be very powerful and rich not to care for
such things, or even give a word of thanks for them;" and
ordered them to return with great chests filled with gold.
They come again to king Sigurd, and say, "These gifts and
presents are sent thee from the emperor."   King Sigurd said,
"This is a great and handsome treasure, my men; divide it
among you."   The messengers return and tell this to the
emperor.   He replies, "This king must either exceed other
kings in power and wealth, or he has not so much understanding as a king ought to have.   Go thou now the third time,
and carry him the costliest purple, and these chests with ornaments of gold:" to which he added two gold rings.   Now
the messengers went again to king Sigurd, and told him the

emperor had sent him this great treasure. Then he stood up, and took the rings, and put them on his hand; and the king made a beautiful oration in Greek, in which he thanked the emperor in many fine expressions for all this honour and magnificence, but divided the treasure again very equitably among his men. King Sigurd remained here some time. The emperor Alexius sent his men to him to ask if he would rather accept from the emperor six skifpound [one ton] of gold, or would have the emperor give the games in his honour which the emperor was used to have played at the Padreimr*. King Sigurd preferred the games, and the messengers said the spectacle would not cost the emperor less than the money offered. Then the emperor prepared for the games, which were held in the usual way: but this day every thing went on better for the king than for the queen; for the queen has always the half part in the games, and their men, therefore, always strive against each other in all games. The Greeks accordingly think that when the king's men win more games at the Padreimr than the queen's, the king will gain the victory when he goes into battle. People who have been in Constantinople tell that the Padreimr is thus constructed:—A high wall surrounds a flat plain, which may be compared to a round bare Thing-place†, with earthen banks all around at the stone-wall, on which banks the spectators sit; but the games themselves are in the flat plain. There are many sorts of old events represented concerning the Asers, Volsungers, and Giukungers, in these games‡; and all the figures are cast in copper, or metal, with so great art that they appear to be living things; and to the people it appears as if they were really present in the games. The games themselves are so artfully and carefully managed, that people appear to be riding in the air; and at them also are used shot-fire §, and all kinds of harp-playing, singing, and music instruments.

---

* Padreimr, or Padrennir, the Hippodrome where the great spectacles were given.

† Place of public assembly.

‡ It is not likely that the feats of the Asers, Volsungers, and Giukungers, were represented in the games of the Hippodrome at Constantinople; but very likely that the Væringers, and other northmen there, would apply the names of their own mythology to the representations taken from the Greek mythology.

§ Fire-works, or the Greek fire, were probably used.

It is related that king Sigurd one day was to give the emperor a feast, and he ordered his men to provide sumptuously all that was necessary for the entertainment; and when all things were provided which are suitable for an entertainment given by a great personage to persons of high dignity, king Sigurd ordered his men to go to the street in the city where fire-wood was sold, as they would require a great quantity to prepare the feast. They said the king need not be afraid of wanting fire-wood, for every day many loads were brought into the town. When it was necessary, however, to have fire-wood, it was found that it was all sold, which they told the king. He replied, " Go and try if you can get walnuts. They will answer as well as wood for fuel." They went and got as many as they needed. Now came the emperor, and his grandees and court, and sat down to table. All was very splendid; and king Sigurd received the emperor with great state, and entertained him magnificently. When the queen and the emperor found that nothing was wanting, she sent some persons to inquire what they had used for firewood; and they came to a house filled with walnuts, and they came back and told the queen. " Truly," said she, " this is a magnificent king, who spares no expense where his honour is concerned." She had contrived this to try what they would do when they could get no firewood to dress their feast with.

King Sigurd soon after prepared for his return home. He gave the emperor all his ships; and the valuable figure-heads which were on the king's ships were set up in Peter's church, where they have since been to be seen. The emperor gave the king many horses and guides to conduct him through all his dominions, and appointed markets for him in his territories at which he could buy food and drink. Then king Sigurd left Constantinople; but many Northmen remained, and went into the emperor's pay. Then king Sigurd travelled from Bulgaria, and through Hungary, Pannonia, Suabia, and Bavaria. In Suabia he met the Roman emperor Lotharius, who received him in the most friendly way, gave him guides through his dominions, and had markets established for him at which he could purchase all he required. When king Sigurd came to Sleswick in Denmark, earl Eilif made a sumptuous feast for him; and it was then midsummer. In Heidaby he met the Danish king Nicolaus, who received him in the most friendly way, made a great entertainment for him, accompanied him north to Jutland, and gave him a ship provided with every thing needful. From thence the king returned to Norway, and was joyfully welcomed on his return to his kingdom. It was the common talk among the people, that none had ever made so honourable a journey from Norway as this of king Sigurd. He was twenty years of age, and had been three years on these travels. His brother Olaf was then twelve years old.

[William of Tyre, book xi., gives the following account of the arrival of the Northmen in Syria:—

" The town of Bereyth was taken in the year 1111 [1110] from the incarnation of our Saviour, and on the 27th of the month of April. That same year people from the isles of the west, and principally from the western country called Norway, having heard that the faithful Christians had taken possession of the holy city of Jerusalem, resolved to repair thither and pay their devotions; and they prepared a fleet accordingly. They embarked, and being favoured by the winds, they traversed the British Sea, passed the strait of Calpe and Assos, by which the Mediterranean Sea is formed, and having coasted along its whole length, they landed at Joppa. The supreme chief of this expedition was a stout, handsome young man, brother of the king of Norway. As soon as he had disembarked at Joppa, with all his followers, they proceeded to Jerusalem, the object of their wishes and vows. The king, on being informed of the arrival of the noble prince of Norway, made all haste to meet him, received him with much kindness, conversed familiarly with him, and tried to discover if the prince would be disposed to stop some time in the kingdom with his naval force, and to consecrate to Christ the fruit of his labour by giving his aid to extend the dominion of the faithful, and by taking possession of some other towns. The Norwegians, after holding a council among themselves, replied that they were come with the express intention of employing themselves usefully in the service of Christ, and that consequently they were quite disposed to proceed, without the least delay, by sea, towards any of the maritime towns which the king was disposed to attack with his army, and would demand no other pay than the victuals necessary for their support. The king accepted these terms with the greatest ardour; and immediately assembling all the forces of his kingdom, and all the knights he could collect, he began his march to Sidon. The fleet left the port of Acre, and proceeded also to Sidon, where the land and sea forces arrived simultaneously. * * * * The people of the fleet received presents from the king, took leave of him, and returned to their country loaded with the blessings of all Christians. The town of Sidon was taken in the year of grace 1111 [1110], and on the 19th of December."

This account of Sigurd the Crusader's expedition to the holy land, by a nearly contemporary historian, native of the country, corroborates Snorro Sturleson's account of it even in the minute details, but he makes him arrive at Joppa, instead of Acre, as the Norse account has it.]

THE TRAVELS OF RABBI BENJAMIN OF TUDELA.

A.D. 1160—1173.

HEBREW PREFACE.

THIS book contains the reports of Rabbi Benjamin, the son of Jonah, of blessed memory*, of Tudela, in the kingdom of Navarre. This man travelled through many and distant countries, as related in the following account, and took down in writing in each place what he saw or what was told him by men of integrity, whose names were known in Spain. Rabbi Benjamin also mentions some of the principal men in the places he visited; and when he returned, he brought this report along with him to the country of Castile in the year 933 (A.D. 1173). The above-mentioned Rabbi Benjamin was a man of wisdom and understanding, and of much information; and after strict inquiry his words were found to be true and correct, for he was a true man.

TRAVELS OF RABBI BENJAMIN OF BLESSED MEMORY.

THUS says Rabbi Benjamin, son of Jonah, of blessed memory. I first set out from the city of Saragossa, and proceeded down the river Ebro to Tortosa. Two days' journey brought me to the ancient city of Tarragona, which contains many cyclopean and pelasgic remains†, and similar buildings are found nowhere else in the whole kingdom of Spain. This city stands on the coast. Two days thence is Barcelona, in which place there is

---

* The expression "of blessed memory" is generally added by Jews when mentioning the "honoured dead," (see Proverbs x. 7,) and recurs frequently in the following narrative.

† This city was one of great antiquity; and at this time the remains of its ancient walls appear to have been very remarkable. Destroyed at an earlier period by the Saracens, Tarragona was rebuilt in the twelfth century.

a congregation of wise, learned, and princely men, such as
R. Shesheth, R. Shealthiel, and R. Solomon, son of R.
Abraham, son of Chisdai of blessed memory. The city is
handsome, though small, and is situated on the sea-shore. Its
trade attracts merchants from all parts of the world: from
Greece, from Pisa, Genoa, and Sicily, from Alexandria in
Egypt, from Palestine and the adjacent countries.

A day's journey and a half brings you to Gerona, which city
contains a small congregation of Jews. From thence it is
three days to Narbonne, eminent for its university, from which
the study of the law spreads over all countries. The city
contains many wise and noble men, especially R. Calonymos,
son of the great and noble R. Theodoros of blessed memory,
a descendant of the house of David, as proved by his pedigree.
This man holds landed property from the sovereigns of the
country, and nobody can deprive him of it by force. There
is also R. Abraham, the president of the university, R. Makhir,
R. Juda, and others of much merit and learning. Altogether the number of Jews amounts to about three hundred.
It is four parasangs thence to the city of Beziers, which contains a congregation of learned men, the principals of which
are R. Solomon Chalaphtha and R. Joseph, son of R. Nathaniel
of blessed memory.

From thence it is two days to Har Gáash, or Montpellier, a
city conveniently situated for trade, being within two parasangs
from the coast. You here meet with Christian and Mohammedan merchants from all parts: from Algarve (Portugal),
Lombardy, the Roman empire, Egypt, Palestine, Greece,
France, Spain, and England. People of all tongues meet
here, chiefly in consequence of the traffic of the Genoese and
Pisans. The Jews of this city are among the wisest and most
esteemed of the present generation. R. Reuben, son of
Theodoros, R. Nathan, son of Zacharias, R. Samuel, their
rabbi, R. Shelemiah, and R. Mordecai of blessed memory,
are the principal among them. Others are very rich, and
benevolent towards all who apply to them for assistance. It
is four parasangs hence to Lunel, a city containing also a holy
congregation of Jews, who employ all their time upon the
study of the law. This town is the place of residence of the
celebrated rabbi R. Meshullam and his five sons (R. Joseph,
R. Isaac, R. Jacob, R. Aaron, and R. Asher), all of whom are
eminent scholars and rich men. The latter is an ascetic,

who does not attend to any worldly business, but studies day and night, keeps fasts, and never eats meat.   He possesses an extraordinary degree of knowledge of every thing relating to Talmudic learning.   R. Moses, his brother-in-law, R. Samuel, the minister, R. Solomon Cohen, and the physician R. Juda, son of Thibbon, of Spanish origin, are also inhabitants of Lunel.   All foreign students who resort hither to study the law, are supplied with food and raiment at the public expense during the whole time of their stay in the university.   The Jews of this city, amounting to about three hundred, are wise, holy, and benevolent men, who support their poor brethren near and far.   The town stands within two parasangs of the coast.   It is two parasangs hence to Beaucaire, a large town, containing about four hundred Jews, and a great university under the presidency of the great rabbi, R. Abraham, son of David of blessed memory, a scholar of the first eminence in scriptural and talmudic learning.   He attracts students from distant countries, who are lodged in his own house and are taught by him; he, moreover, provides them with all necessaries of life from his own means and private property, which is very considerable.   R. Joseph, son of R. Menachem, R. Benbenast, R. Benjamin, R. Abraham, and R. Isaac, son of R. Moses of blessed memory of this city, are also very great scholars and wise men.   It is three parasangs further to Nogres or Bourg de St. Gilles.   The chief of the Jewish inhabitants, of which there are about one hundred, are R. Isaac, son of R. Jacob, R. Abraham, son of R. Juda, R. Eliasar, R. Isaac, R. Moses, and R. Jacob, son of the late rabbi R. Levi of blessed memory.   This town is a place of pilgrimage *, visited by the inhabitants of distant countries and islands.   It is situated within three parasangs of the sea, on the very banks of the large river Rhone, which traverses the whole of Provence.   It is the place of residence of R. Abba Mari, son of R. Isaac of blessed memory, who holds the office of steward to count Raymond.

---

  * The church of St. Egidius, or Giles, in this town, was a celebrated place of pilgrimage in the middle ages.   It was the birthplace and first appanage of the celebrated Raymond, count of St.Gilles and Toulouse, duke of Narbonne, and marquis of Provence, whose family were so active in the crusades.   The count Raymond here mentioned, in whose household R. Abba Mari held office, was Raymond V., son of Alphonso, who had the title of count of St. Gilles during his father's life.

To Arles, three parasangs. The chief of its two hundred Israelites are R. Moses, R. Tobi, R. Isaiah, R. Solomon the rabbi, R. Nathan, and R. Abba Mari of blessed memory. It is three days hence to Marseilles, a city containing many eminent and wise men. Its three hundred Jews form two congregations, one of which resides in the lower town on the shore of the Mediterranean, and the other in the upper part, near the fortress. The latter supports a great university and boasts of many learned scholars. R. Simeon, son of R. Antoli, his brother, R. Jacob, and R. Levaro, are the chief of the upper synagogue, R. Jacob Perpiano, a rich man, R. Abraham, and his son-in-law, R. Meir, R. Isaac, and another Meir, preside over the lower congregation. An extensive trade is carried on in this city, which stands immediately on the coast. And here people take ship for Genoa, which also stands on the coast, and is reached in about four days. Two Jews from Ceuta, R. Samuel, son of Khilam, and his brother, reside there. The city is surrounded by a wall; no king governs over it, but senators chosen by the citizens out of their own body. Every house is provided with a tower, and in times of civil commotion war is carried on from the tops of these towers. The Genoese are masters of the sea, and build vessels called galleys, by means of which they carry on war in many places and bring home much plunder and booty. They are now at war with the Pisans.

From their city it is a distance of two days' journey to Pisa, which is a place of very great extent, containing about ten thousand fortified houses, from which war is carried on in times of civil commotion. All the inhabitants are brave; no king or prince governs over them, the supreme authority being vested in senators chosen by the people. The principal of the twenty Jews resident at Pisa are R. Moses, R. Chaim, and R. Joseph. The city has no walls, and stands about four miles from the sea, the navigation being carried on by means of vessels which ply upon the Arno, a river that runs through the city. Hence it is four parasangs to Lucca, a large city, which contains about forty Jews, the principal of whom are R. David, R. Samuel, and R. Jacob.

A journey of six days from thence brings you to the large city of Rome, the metropolis of all Christendom. Two hundred Jews live there, who are very much respected, and pay tribute to no one. Some of them are officers in the service of pope Alexander *, who is the chief ecclesiastic and head of the Christian church. The principal of the many eminent Jews resident here are R. Daniel and R. Jechiel. The latter is one of the pope's officers, a handsome, prudent, and wise man, who frequents the pope's palace, being the steward of his household and minister of his private property. R. Jechiel is a descendant of R. Nathan, the author of the book Aruch and its comments†. There are likewise at Rome, R. Joab, son of the rabbi R. Solomon, R. Menachem, the president of the university, R. Jechiel, who resides in Trastevere, and R. Benjamin, son of R. Shabthai of blessed memory.

The city of Rome is divided into two parts by the river Tiber, which runs through it. In the first of these divisions you see the large place of worship called St. Peter of Rome, on the site of the extensive palace of Julius Cæsar. The city contains numerous buildings and structures entirely different from all other buildings upon the face of the earth. The extent of ground covered by the ruined and inhabited parts of Rome amounts to four-and-twenty miles. You there find eighty halls of the eighty eminent kings who were all called Imperator, from king Tarquin to king Pepin, the father of Charles (Charlemagne), who first conquered Spain and wrested it from the Mohammedans ‡. In the outskirts of Rome is the palace of Titus, who was rejected by three hundred senators in consequence of his having wasted three years in the conquest of Jerusalem, which, according to their will, he ought to have accomplished in two years. There is likewise the hall of the palace of king Vespasianus, a very large and strong building; also the hall of king Galba, containing 360 windows, equal in number to the days of the year. The circumference of this palace is nearly three miles. A battle was fought here in times of yore, and in the palace fell more than a hundred thousand, whose bones are hung up there even to the present day. The king caused a representation of the battle to be drawn, army against army, the men, the horses, and all their

* Alexander III., who held the papacy from 1159 to 1181. The employment of Jews in the service of the pope is a circumstance worthy of remark.

† The book Aruch was a celebrated dictionary, completed by rabbi Nathan at Rome, in A.D. 1101.

‡ These singular legends relating to the ancient buildings in Rome are chiefly taken from the writings of Josephus Ben Gorion. Some of them may be compared with similar tales which are found in Christian writers, and of which several examples are inserted in William of Malmesbury's History.

accoutrements being sculptured in marble, in order to preserve a memorial of the wars of antiquity. You there find also a cave under ground containing the king and his queen upon their thrones, surrounded by about one hundred nobles of their court, all embalmed by physicians and in good preservation to this day.

Another remarkable object is St. Giovanni *in porta Latina*, in which place of worship there are two copper pillars constructed by king Solomon of blessed memory, whose name, "Solomon, son of David," is engraved upon each. The Jews in Rome told Benjamin, that every year, about the time of the 9th of Ab*, these pillars sweat so much that the water runs down from them. You there see also the cave in which Titus, the son of Vespasian, hid the vessels of the temple, which he brought from Jerusalem; and in another cave on the banks of the Tiber, you find the sepulchres of those holy men of blessed memory, the ten martyrs of the kingdom†. Opposite St. Giovanni de Laterano, there is a statue of Samson, with a lance of stone in his hand; also that of Absalom, the son of David, and of king Constantine, who built Constantinople, which city is called after his name; his statue is cast in copper, the man and horse being gilt. Rome contains many other remarkable buildings and works, the whole of which nobody can enumerate.

Four days from Rome is Capua, a large city, built by king Capys. The town is elegant, but the water is bad, and the country unhealthy. Among the three hundred Jews who reside at Capua are many very wise men of universal fame, such as R. Konpasso and his brother, R. Samuel, R. Saken, and the rabbi R. David, who bears the title of Principalo.

From thence to Puzzuolo, or Sorrento, a large city built by

* The time of the destruction of both temples at Jerusalem. The day is still one of fast and mourning to all Jews, and is celebrated as such by all synagogues.

† These were ten ancient teachers of the Mishna, who suffered violent death in the period between Vespasian and Hadrian. A late legend not only connected these persecutions as one event, but assigned to the victims a common sepulchre at Rome. The legend contains a conversation of the ten martyrs with the emperor. Several of the ten were certainly not buried in Rome; the sepulchres of three, Akiba, Ishmael, and Juda Ben Thema, were shown in Palestine in the thirteenth and sixteenth centuries. Antipatris is said by others to be the place of the sepulchre of R. Akiba. A more recent catalogue notices, as known in Palestine, the sepulchres of R. Juda, son of Baba, and Simon, son of Gamaliel, two others of the "ten martyrs."

Tsintsan Hadareser, who fled in fear of king David of blessed
memory. This city has been inundated in two spots by the sea ;
and even to this day you may see the streets and towers of the
submerged city. A hot spring, which issues forth from under
ground, produces the oil called Petroleum, which is collected
upon the surface of the water and used in medicine. There are
likewise hot baths, proceeding from hot subterranean springs,
which here issue from under ground. Two of these baths are
situated on the sea-shore, and whoever is afflicted with any
disease generally experiences great relief, if not certain cure,
from the use of these waters. During the summer season all
persons afflicted with diseases crowd hither from the whole of
Lombardy *.

From this place a man may travel fifteen miles by a causeway under the mountains, constructed by king Romulus, the
founder of Rome, who feared David, king of Israel, and Joab,
his general, and constructed buildings both upon and under
the mountains. The city of Naples is very strongly fortified ;
it is situated on the coast, and was originally built by the
Greeks. The principal of the five hundred Jews who live here
are R. Chiskiah, R. Shalom, R. Eliah Cohen, and R. Isaac,
from Mount Hor. One day's journey brings you to Salerno,
the chief medical university of Christendom. The number of
Jews living here amounts to about six hundred, among whom
R. Juda, son of R. Isaac, R. Melchisedek, the grand rabbi,
originally from Siponte, R. Solomon Cohen, R. Elija Hajevani (i.e. the Greek), R. Abraham Narboni, and R. Thamon,
deserve particular notice as wise and learned men. The city
is surrounded by a wall towards the land; one part of it however stands on the shore of the sea. The fort on the summit
of the hill is very strong. Half a day to Amalfi, among the
inhabitants of which city are twenty Jews, the chief being R.
Chananel, the physician, R. Elisha, and the benevolent (or
noble) Abu-al-Gid. The Christian population of this country
is chiefly occupied with trade ; they do not till the ground,
but buy every thing for money, because they reside on high
mountains and upon rocky hills ; fruit, however, abounds ; the
land being covered with vineyards, olive-groves, gardens, and
orchards. Nobody ventures to make war upon them.

* This account of Puzzuolo is also chiefly taken from Josephus Gorionides.
Modern researches prove that some Roman villas on the sea-coast are now
covered by the sea ; and this led to the story of the submerged city.

One day to Bavento, a large city between the coast and a high mountain. The congregation of Jews is about two hundred, of which the principals are R. Calonymos, R. Sarach, and R. Abraham of blessed memory. From hence two. days to Melfi in Apulia, the Pul * of scripture, with about two hundred Jews, of which R. Achimaats, R. Nathan, and R. Sadok are the principal. One day's journey hence to Ascoli ; the principal of the forty Jews who live there are R. Kontilo, R. Semach, his son-in-law, and R. Joseph. Two days to Trani, on the coast. All the pilgrims who travel to Jerusalem assemble here, on account of the convenience of its port. This city contains about two hundred Israelites, the chief of whom are R. Elijah, R. Nathan the lecturer †, and R. Jacob. Trani is a large and elegant town. One day's journey to St. Nicholas di Bari ‡, formerly a large city, but it was destroyed by William king of Sicily. It still lies in ruins, and contains neither Jewish nor Christian inhabitants. One day's journey and a half to Taranto, the frontier town of Calabria, the inhabitants of which are Greeks. It is a large city, and the principal of the three hundred Jews who live there are R. Mali, R. Nathan, and R. Israel. One day's journey to Brindisi, on the sea-coast, containing about ten Jews, who are dyers. Two days to Otranto, on the coast of the Grecian sea ; the principal of its five hundred Jewish inhabitants are R. Menachem, R. Khaleb, R. Meier, and R. Mali.

From thence you cross over in two days to the island of Corfu, containing but one Jew, a dyer, of the name of R. Joseph. Unto this place reaches the kingdom of Sicily §.

* See Isaiah, lxvi. 19. This, it need hardly be observed, is one of the erroneous identifications of Scriptural names which have so frequently arisen from a false importance given to their similarity of sound.

† This title was given to a man conversant with the Hagada, or ancient manner of expounding the holy scripture. The Hebrew appellation is "darschan."

‡ Bari, which was taken and almost destroyed by the Greeks during the reign of William of Sicily, was called St. Nicholas, in honour of the celebrated church and priory of that saint, which are its most remarkable ornaments. They were built in 1098, and richly endowed by Roger, duke of Apulia ; and they escaped the great and general destruction with which the city was visited.

§ This island, though for some time subject to Roger and William, kings of Sicily, was reconquered by the emperor Manuel in 1149 ; and the words of our author are probably intended to express that this was the first spot at which he touched after leaving the kingdom of Sicily.

Two days' voyage by sea brings you to the coast of Arta, the confines of the empire of Manuel, king of Greece. On this coast lies a village with about a hundred Jewish inhabitants, the principal of whom are R. Shelachiah, and R. Hercules. Two days to Achelous, containing ten Jews, of whom the principal is R. Shabthai. Half a day to Anatolica on the gulf. One day by sea to Patras. This is the city of Anti-patros, king of Greece, one of the four kings who rose after king Alexander*. It contains large and ancient build-ings, and about fifty Jews reside there, of whom R. Isaac, R. Jacob, and R. Samuel are the principal. Half a day by sea to Lepanto, on the coast. The principal of the hundred Jews who reside there are R. Gisri, R. Shalom, and R. Abra-ham. One day's journey and a half to Crissa. Two hun-dred Jews live there by themselves on mount Parnassus, and carry on agriculture upon their own land and property; of these, R. Solomon, R. Chaim, and R. Jedaiah are the prin-cipal. Three days to the city of Corinth, which contains about three hundred Jews, of whom the chief are R. Leon, R. Jacob, and R. Ezekias.

Three days to the large city of Thebes, containing about two thousand Jewish inhabitants. These are the most emi-nent manufacturers of silk and purple cloth in all Greece †. Among them are many eminent Talmudic scholars and men as famous as any of the present generation. The principal of them are, the great rabbi R. Aaron Koti, his brother, R. Moses, R. Chija, R. Elijah Tareteno, and R. Joktan. No scholars like them are to be found in the whole Grecian empire, except at Constantinople. A journey of three days brings you to Negropont, a large city on the coast, to which merchants resort from all parts. Of the two hundred Jews

---

* This erroneous account of the foundation of Patras is taken from Josephus Gorionides.

† Thebes contained, at this time, the greatest number of Jews of any city in Greece, some of whom are stated to have been eminent manufacturers, prin-cipally of silk and purple cloths. Gibbon states that artists employed upon these trades enjoyed exemption from personal taxes. "These arts, which were exercised at Corinth, Thebes, and Argos, afforded food and occupation to a numerous people : the men, women, and children were distributed according to their age and strength ; and if many of these were domestic slaves, their masters, who directed the work and enjoyed the profits, were of a free and honourable condition." At present the whole population of Thebes does not amount to above 3500 individuals.

who reside there, the principal are R. Elijah Psalteri, R. Emanuel, and R. Khaleb. From thence to Jabustrisa * is one day's journey. This city stands on the coast, and contains about one hundred Jews, the principal of whom are R. Joseph, R. Samuel, and R. Nethaniah. Rabenica † is distant one day's journey, and contains about one hundred Jews, of whom R. Joseph, R. Eleasar, and R. Isaac are the principal. Sinon Potamo, or Zeitun, is one day's journey further; R. Solomon and R. Jacob are the principal of its fifty Jewish inhabitants.

Here we reach the confines of Wallachia, the inhabitants of which country are called Vlachi. They are as nimble as deer, and descend from their mountains into the plains of Greece, committing robberies and making booty. Nobody ventures to make war upon them, nor can any king bring them to submission, and they do not profess the Christian faith. Their names are of Jewish origin, and some even say that they have been Jews, which nation they call brethren. Whenever they meet an Israelite, they rob, but never kill him, as they do the Greeks. They profess no religious creed.

From thence it is two days to Gardiki ‡, a ruined place, containing but few Jewish or Grecian inhabitants. Two days further, on the coast, stands the large commercial city of Ar miro §, which is frequented by the Venetians, the Pisans, the Genoese, and many other merchants. It is a large city, and contains about four hundred Jewish inhabitants; of whom the chief are R. Shiloh, R. Joseph the elder, and R. Solomon, the president. One day to Bissina ‖; the principal of

---

* No place of this name is now known. Mr. Asher conjectures, from the Sclavonic sound of the word, that it was a town of the Wallachians, and that it has been destroyed in the perpetual wars of which this part of Greece was the scene.

† Rabenica is mentioned by several medieval writers, though its exact situation is not now known. Henri de Valencienne, Chronique, edited by Buchon, p. 259, says " Ensi comme jou devant vous dys, fut li parlemens ou val de Ravenique."

‡ Gardiki, or Cardiki, a small town on the coast of the gulf of Volo, and the seat of a bishop. The time at which it was ruined, or the occasion upon which its destruction took place, cannot be ascertained.

§ Armyro, also on the coast of the gulf of Volo. By the writers of the middle ages it was called Amire, Amiro, and Almyro. Poucqueville (iii. 72) mentions it as the principal town of a district which bears its name.

‖ This place is not now known, but it is mentioned by medieval writers

the hundred Jews who reside here are the rabbi R. Shab-
tha, R. Solomon, and R. Jacob. The town of Salunki* is
distant two days by sea ; it was built by king Seleucus, one
of the four Greek nobles who rose after Alexander, is a very
large city, and contains about five hundred Jewish inhabitants. The rabbi R. Samuel and his sons are eminent
scholars, and he is appointed provost of the resident Jews by
the king's command. His son-in-law R. Shabthai, R. Elijah,
and R. Michael, also reside there. The Jews are much
oppressed in this place, and live by the exercise of handi-
craft. Mitrizzi †, distant two days' journey, contains about
twenty Jews. R. Isaiah, R. Makhir, and R. Eliab are the
principal of them. Drama ‡, distance from hence two days'
journey, contains about one hundred and forty Jews, of whom
the chief are R. Michael and R. Joseph. From thence one
day's journey to Christopoli §, which contains about twenty
Jewish inhabitants. Three days from thence by sea stands
Abydos, on the coast.

It is hence five days' journey through the mountains to the

under the name of Vissena, Vessena, and Bezena. As our author embarked
at or near this station, it cannot have been Velestino, which we meet with by
following his route on a map of Greece, because, although in the vicinity of
Armyro, and on the road to Saloniki, it is an inland town.

* The ancient Thessalonica, the modern Saloniki, contained, at our author's
time, more Jewish inhabitants than any town in Greece, Thebes alone ex-
cepted. It is stated by good authorities to contain at present 20,000
Israelites, a large proportion of the whole population, amounting altogether to
but 70,000 souls. Some popular tradition probably induced our author to
ascribe the origin of the city to Seleucus. The favourable situation of
Saloniki, which has made it one of the most commercial towns of the
Turkish empire, was probably the cause of its considerable Jewish population.

† This place, which has vanished from the modern maps of Greece, was called
correctly Dimitritzi, and was situated near Amphipolis, on the Cercinian Sea.

‡ Villehardouin mentions this place as belonging to the king of Thessalonica, and calls it "Dramine el val de Phelippe." Another MS. reads
Draimes, which is more in conformity with the appellation given to it by
Nicephorus Gregoras, who, like our author, frequently calls it Drama. It
stands in a valley, near the site of the ancient city of Philippi, the ruins of
which are still to be seen.

§ The original word is קנישתולי ; but there can hardly be any doubt that
our author wrote it so only because he did not like to mention the name
of Christ. We observe this in several other instances in the course of this
work. Christopoli was on the direct road from Thessalonica to Constantinople.
It was situated on the frontiers of Macedonia and Thracia, on the European
shore of the Propontis, opposite the island of Thaso ; and here travellers from
Macedonia to Constantinople generally embarked.

large city of Constantinople, the metropolis of the whole
Grecian empire, and the residence of the emperor, king
Manuel *. Twelve princely officers govern the whole empire
by his command, each of them inhabiting a palace at Constantinople, and possessing fortresses and cities of his own.
The first of these nobles bears the title of Præpositus magnus; the second is called Megas Domesticus, the third Dominus, the fourth Megas Ducas, the fifth Œconomus magnus, and
the names of the others are similar to these †.

The circumference of the city of Constantinople is eighteen
miles; one half of the city being bounded by the continent,
the other by the sea, two arms of which meet here; the one
a branch or outlet of the Russian, the other of the Spanish
sea. Great stir and bustle prevails at Constantinople in
consequence of the conflux of many merchants, who resort
thither, both by land and by sea, from all parts of the world
for purposes of trade, including merchants, from Babylon and
from Mesopotamia, from Media and Persia, from Egypt and
Palestine, as well as from Russia, Hungary, Patzinakia,
Budia, Lombardy, and Spain. In this respect the city is
equalled only by Bagdad, the metropolis of the Mohammedans.
At Constantinople is the place of worship called St. Sophia,
and the metropolitan seat of the pope of the Greeks, who
are at variance with the pope of Rome. It contains as
many altars as there are days of the year, and possesses
innumerable riches, which are augmented every year by the
contributions of the two islands and of the adjacent towns
and villages. All the other places of worship in the whole
world do not equal St. Sophia in riches. It is ornamented
with pillars of gold and silver, and with innumerable lamps
of the same precious materials. The Hippodrome is a public
place near the wall of the palace, set aside for the king's
sports. Every year the birthday of Jesus the Nazarene is
celebrated there with public rejoicings. On these occasions
you may see there representations of all the nations who

* Manuel Comnenus, emperor from 1143 to 1180.

† The best account of the imperial officers of state will be found in Gibbon,
"Decline and Fall," chap. liii. The Præpositus magnus was one of the principal officers, governor of the city and of the forces stationed in it; the Megas
Domesticus was the commander in chief of the army; the Dominus, court
marshal, lord steward of the household; Megas Ducas, the commander of the
naval forces, or lord high admiral of the empire; Œconomos magnus, a
clerical officer of high rank.

inhabit the different parts of the world, with surprising feats
of jugglery. Lions, bears, leopards, and wild asses, as well
as birds, which have been trained to fight each other, are
also exhibited. All this sport, the equal of which is nowhere
to be met with, is carried on in the presence of the king and
the queen *.

King Manuel has built a large palace for his residence on
the sea-shore, near the palace built by his predecessors; and
to this edifice is given the name of Blachernes. The pillars
and walls are covered with pure gold, and all the wars of
the ancients, as well as his own wars, are represented in pictures. The throne in this palace is of gold, and ornamented
with precious stones; a golden crown hangs over it, suspended on a chain of the same material, the length of which
exactly admits the emperor to sit under it. This crown is
ornamented with precious stones of inestimable value. Such
is the lustre of these diamonds, that, even without any other
light, they illumine the room in which they are kept. Other
objects of curiosity are met with here which it would be
impossible to describe adequately.

The tribute, which is brought to Constantinople every
year from all parts of Greece, consisting of silks, and purple
cloths, and gold, fills many towers. These riches and buildings are equalled nowhere in the world. They say that the
tribute of the city alone amounts every day to twenty thousand florins, arising from rents of hostelries and bazaars, and
from the duties paid by merchants who arrive by sea and by
land. The Greeks who inhabit the country are extremely
rich, and possess great wealth in gold and precious stones.
They dress in garments of silk, ornamented with gold and
other valuable materials. They ride upon horses, and in
their appearance they are like princes. The country is rich,
producing all sorts of delicacies, as well as abundance of

---

* The Hippodrome is now known by the Turkish paraphrased name of
the At-Meidan, *i. e.* the horse-market. It was the site chosen for the display
of the games by which the emperor Manuel entertained the sultan Azeddin
Kilidscharslan, on his visit to Constantinople in 1159; and Mr. Asher observes that Benjamin was probably an eyewitness of the public rejoicings
and games which took place in honour of the celebration of the marriage
of the emperor Manuel with Maria, daughter of the prince of Antiochia, on
"the birth-day of Jesus," A.D. 1161, which he seems to describe here. Compare the account of the games at Constantinople exhibited to the Northmen,
pp. 60, 61.

bread, meat, and wine. They are well skilled in the Greek sciences, and live comfortably, "every man under his vine and his fig tree."* The Greeks hire soldiers of all nations, whom they call barbarians, for the purpose of carrying on their wars with the sultan of the Thogarmim, who are called Turks. They have no martial spirit themselves, and, like women, are unfit for warlike enterprises.

No Jews dwell in the city with them; they are obliged to reside beyond the one arm of the sea, where they are shut in by the channel of Sophia on one side, and they can reach the city by water only, when they want to visit it for purposes of trade. The number of Jews at Constantinople amounts to two thousand Rabbanites and five hundred Caraites †, who live on one spot, but divided by a wall. The principal of the Rabbanites, who are learned in the law, are the rabbi R. Abtalion, R. Obadiah, R. Aaron Khuspo, R. Joseph Sargeno, and R. Eliakim the elder. Many of them are manufacturers of silk cloth, many others are merchants, some being extremely rich; but no Jew is allowed to ride upon a horse, except R. Solomon Hamitsri, who is the king's physician, and by whose influence the Jews enjoy many advantages even in their state of oppression, which is very severely felt by them; and the hatred against them is increased by the practice of the tanners, who pour out their filthy water in the streets and even before the very doors of the Jews, who, being thus defiled, become objects of contempt to the Greeks. Their yoke is severely felt by the Jews, both good and bad; for they are exposed to be beaten in the streets, and must submit to all sorts of bad treatment. Still the Jews are rich, good, benevolent, and religious men, who bear the misfortunes of their exile with humility. The quarter inhabited by the Jews is called Pera.

Two days from Constantinople stands Rodosto, containing a congregation of about four hundred Jews, the principal of whom are R. Moses, R. Abijah, and R. Jacob. From hence it is two days to Gallipoli. Of the two hundred Jews of this city the principal are R. Elijah Kapid, R. Shabthai the little, and R. Isaac Megas; this latter term in the Greek language

---

* Micah, iv. 4.

† The former respect and conform with the authority of the rabbinic explanations, which are rejected by the latter.

means tall. To (Kales, or) Kilia *, two days. The principal of the fifty Jews who inhabit this place are R. Juda, R. Jacob, and R. Shemaiah. It is hence two days to Mitilene, one of the islands of the sea. Ten places in this island contain Jewish congregations. Three days from thence is situated the island of Chio, containing about four hundred Jews, the principal of whom are R. Elijah, R. Theman, and R. Shabthai. The trees which yield mastic are found here †. Two days bring us to the island of Samos, which contains about three hundred Jews, the chief of whom are R. Shemaria, R. Obadiah, and R. Joel. These islands contain many congregations of Jews. It is three days hence by sea to Rhodes. The principal of the four hundred Jews who reside here are R. Aba, R. Chananel, and R. Elijah. Hence it is four days to Cyprus. Besides the rabbanitic Jews in this island, there is a community of heretic Jews called Kaphrosein, or Cyprians. They are epicureans, and the orthodox Jews excommunicate them. These sectarians profane the evening of the Sabbath and keep holy that of the Sunday. We next come in two days to Corycus, the frontier of Aram, which is called Armenia. Here are the confines of the empire of Toros, king of the mountains ‡, sovereign of Armenia, whose rule extends to the city of Dhuchia and the country of the Togarmim, or Turks. Two days further is Malmistras §, which is Thersoos, situated

* This is the Cœla of Ptolemy, and the Celus of Pliny and Mela, a sea-port-town on the eastern coast of the peninsula of Gallipoli, still bearing the Turkish name of Kilia.

† The island of Chio is still celebrated for its mastic; and the population of twenty villages are employed exclusively in cultivating the tree and gathering its produce. These villages are situated in the mountainous parts; and the Christian cultivators of the mastic not only paid no tithe nor tribute, but enjoyed certain privileges.

‡ This prince first resided with the emperor Johannes Porphyrogenitus, with whom he was a great favourite; but on his death, and the succession of Manuel Comnenus to the throne, Thoros left Constantinople, disguised as a merchant, and proceeded by water to Antioch, from whence he went to Cilicia, and with the assistance of the priests and nobles found himself at the head of a formidable army, and soon established himself on the throne of his ancestors. When these news reached Constantinople, Manuel became highly incensed; and, raising a numerous force, he sent Andronicus Cæsar into Cilicia with the command to extirpate all Armenians; but the imperial general was defeated, and Thoros was subsequently reconciled with the emperor. He died in 1167.

§ Malmistras is the ancient Mopsuestia, on the Pyramus, at present Messis on the Jeihan. Under the former name it appears in William of Tyre and his contemporaries.

on the coast. Thus far reaches the empire of the Javanites, who are called Greeks.

The large city of Antioch is distant two days hence. It stands on the banks of the Makloub, which river flows down from Mount Lebanon, from the country of Hamah. The city was founded by king Antiochus, and is overlooked by a very high mountain. A wall surrounds this height, on the summit of which is situated a well. The inspector of the well distributes the water by subterranean aqueducts, and thus provides the houses of the principal inhabitants of the city. The other side of the city is surrounded by the river. This place is very strongly fortified, and in the possession of prince Boemond Poitevin, surnamed le Baube*. It contains about ten Jews, who are glass manufacturers, and the principal of whom are R. Mordecai, R. Chaiim, and R. Ishmael.

Two days bring us from thence to Lega, which is Latachia, and contains about two hundred Jews, the principal of whom are R. Chiia and R. Joseph. Hence it is two days to Jebilee, the Baal Gad of Scripture, under Mount Lebanon.

In this vicinity reside the people called Assassins, who do not believe in the tenets of Mohammedanism, but in those of one whom they consider like unto the prophet Kharmath†. They fulfil whatever he commands them, whether it be a matter of life or death. He goes by the name of Sheikh-al-Hashishin, or their old man, by whose commands all the acts of these mountaineers are regulated. His residence is in the city of Kadmus‡, the Kedemoth of Scripture, in the land of Sichon. The Assassins are faithful to one another by the command of their old man, and make themselves the dread of every one, because their devotion leads them gladly to risk their lives, and to kill even kings when commanded. The extent of their country is eight days' journey. They are at war with the Christians, called Franks, and with the count of

---

* Boemond III., prince of Antioch, surnamed le Baube (or the Stammerer), succeeded his mother in the principality of Antioch in 1163, and died in 1200.

† Kharmath was a famous impostor, founder of a sect called Carmathians, very similar to that of the Assassins. One of the tenets of this sect was, that the soul of the founder transmigrates into the body of his successor, and that the person who held the office of chief among them was the personification of the original founder of the sect.

‡ Kadmus is enumerated by Burckhardt in a list of old castles, on the mountains of Szaffyta, in the territory of the Anzeiry.

Tripoli, which is Tarablous el Sham.   Some time ago **Tripoli** was visited by an earthquake, which destroyed many Jews and Gentiles, numbers of the inhabitants being killed by the falling houses and walls, under the ruins of which they were buried.   More than twenty thousand persons were killed in Palestine by this earthquake.

One day's journey to the other Jebail, which was the Gebal of the children of Ammon *; it contains about one hundred and fifty Jews, and is governed by seven Genoese, the supreme command being vested in one of them named Julianus Embriaco †.   You there find the ancient place of worship of the children of Ammon.   The idol of this people is seated on a cathedral or throne, constructed of stone and richly gilt; two female figures occupy the seats on his side, one being on the right, the other on the left, and before it stands an altar, upon which the children of Ammon anciently offered sacrifices and burned incense.   The city contains about two hundred Jews, the principal of whom are R. Meir, R. Jacob, and R. Szimchah.   It stands on the coast of the sea of the Holy Land.   Two days hence is Beyrut, which is Beeroth ‡.   The principal of its fifty Jewish inhabitants are R. Solomon, R. Obadiah, and R. Joseph.   It is hence one day's journey to Saida, which is Sidon of Scripture, a large city, with about twenty Jewish inhabitants.

Within twenty miles of this place reside a people who are at war with the inhabitants of Sidon, and who are called

* Joshua, xiii. 5.   1 Kings, v. 32.

† This passage was entirely misunderstood by the earlier translators. The family of the Embriaci was one of the most ancient of the patricians of Genoa; and one of its members, Guillelmus Embriacus, was named commander of the fleet which was sent to aid the Christian princes of Syria, and which, in 1109, took Byblus, of which he became the feudal lord.   The jealousy of the other patrician families was subsequently roused, but the family of the Embriaci succeeded in retaining their feudal tenure.   The supreme government of the city, however, at this time, appears to have been vested in a committee of seven persons, six of whom were delegated by the republic, the place of president being always filled by one of the Embriaci.   William of Tyre (xi. 9) relates the conquest of Byblus by the Genoese, and informs us that the Christian name of the Embriacus who governed when he wrote (about 1180) was Hugo, "a grandson of the Hugo who conquered it;" but all other historians call the conqueror Guillelmus, and Mr. Asher thinks that we ought to read, in Benjamin's text, גוילײמו, which stands for William, instead of Julianus.

‡ Joshua, xviii. 25.

Druses. They are called heathens and unbelievers, because they confess no religion. Their dwellings are on the summits of the mountains and in the ridges of the rocks, and they are subject to no king or prince. Mount Hermon, a distance of three days' journey, is the boundary of their territory. This people live incestuously; a father cohabits with his own daughter, and once every year all men and women assemble to celebrate a festival, upon which occasion, after eating and drinking, they hold promiscuous intercourse. They say that the soul of a virtuous man is transferred to the body of a new-born child; whereas that of the wicked transmigrates into a dog or some other animal. This their way is their folly. Jews have no permanent residence among them, although some tradesmen and a few dyers travel through the country occasionally, to carry on their trades or sell goods, and return home when their business is done. The Druses are friendly towards the Jews; they are so nimble in climbing hills and mountains, that nobody can successfully carry on war against them.

One day's journey to New Sur, a very beautiful city, the port of which is in the town itself, and is guarded by two towers, within which the vessels ride at anchor. The officers of the customs draw an iron chain from tower to tower every night, thus effectually preventing any thieves or robbers from escape by boats or by other means. There is no port in the world equal to this. About four hundred Jews reside here, the principal of whom are the judge R. Ephraim Mitsri, R. Meier of Carcasson, and R. Abraham, the elder of the community. The Jews of Sur are ship-owners and manufacturers of the celebrated Tyrian glass*; the purple dye is also found in this vicinity. If you mount the walls of New Sur, you may see the remains of "Tyre the crowning,"† which was inundated by the sea; it is about the distance of a stone's throw from the new town, and whoever embarks may observe the towers, the markets, the streets, and the halls at the bottom of the sea. The city of New Sur is very commercial, and one to which traders resort from all parts.

It is one day hence to Acre, the Acco of Scripture, on the confines of the tribe of Asher. It is the frontier town of Palestine; and, in consequence of its situation on the shore of

---

* It is well known from other sources that Tyre was celebrated in the middle ages for the manufacture of glass.

† Isaiah, xxiii. 8.

the Mediterranean and of its large port, it is the principal
place of disembarkation of all pilgrims who visit Jerusalem by
sea. A river called Kishon* runs near the city. There are
here about two hundred Jewish inhabitants, of whom R.
Zadok, R. Jepheth, and R. Jona are the principal. Three
parasangs further is Kaiffa, which is Gath Hachepher†. One
side of this city is situated on the coast, on the other it is
overlooked by Mount Carmel. Under the mountain are many
Jewish sepulchres, and near the summit is the cavern of
Elija, upon whom be peace. Two Christians have built a
place of worship near this site, which they call St. Elias. On
the summit of the hill you may still trace the site of the altar
which was rebuilt by Elija of blessed memory, in the time of
king Ahab‡, and the circumference of which is about four
yards. The river Mukattua runs down the mountain and
along its base. It is four parasangs hence to Khephar Than-
chum, which is Capernaum, identical with Meon, the place of
abode of Nabal the Carmelite. Six parasangs brings us to
Cesarea, the Gath of the Philistines of Scripture, inhabited by
about ten Jews and two hundred Cutheans. The latter are
Samaritan Jews, commonly called Samaritans. This city is
very elegant and beautiful, situated on the sea-shore, and was
built by king Herod, who called it Cesarea in honour of the
emperor, or Cæsar. To Kakun, the Keilah of Scripture§,
half a day's journey; in this place are no Jews. To St.
George, the ancient Luz‖, half a day's journey. One Jew
only, a dyer, lives here. To Sebaste, one day's journey. This
is the ancient Shomron, where you may still trace the site of
the palace of Ahab, king of Israel. It was formerly a very
strong city, and is situated on a mount, in a fine country,
richly watered, and surrounded with gardens, orchards, vineyards, and olive-groves. No Jews live here.

It is two parasangs further to Nablous, the ancient Sichem,
on Mount Ephraim. This place contains no Jewish inhabitants, and is situated in the valley between Mount Gerizim
and Mount Ebal. It is the abode of about one hundred
Cutheans, who observe the Mosaic law only, and are called
Samaritans. They have priests, descendants of Aaron the

---

* The modern Nahr-el-Mukattua. See Judges, v. 21.
† Joshua, xix. 13. Modern writers identify Kaiffa with the ancient
Ephah, and not with Gath.
‡ 1 Kings, xviii. 30.   § Joshua, xv. 44.   ‖ Judges, i. 26.

priest of blessed memory, whom they call Aaronim. These do not intermarry with any other but priestly families; but they are priests only of their own law, who offer sacrifices and burnt-offerings in their synagogue on Mount Gerizim. They do this in accordance with the words of Scripture*, "Thou shalt put the blessing on Mount Gerizim," and they pretend that this is the holy temple†. On passover and holidays they offer burnt-offerings on the altar which they have erected on Mount Gerizim, from the stones put up by the children of Israel after they had crossed the Jordan. They pretend to be of the tribe of Ephraim, and are in possession of the tomb of Joseph the righteous, the son of our father Jacob, upon whom be peace, as is proved by the following passage of Scripture‡, "The bones of Joseph, which the children of Israel brought up with them from Egypt, they buried in Sichem." The Samaritans do not possess the three letters He, Cheth, and Ain; the He of the name of our father Abraham, and they have no glory; the Cheth of the name of our father Isaac, in consequence of which they are devoid of piety; the Ain of the name of Jacob, for they want humility. Instead of these letters, they always put an Aleph, by which you may know that they are not of Jewish origin, because, in their knowledge of the law of Moses, they are deficient in three letters §. This sect carefully avoid being defiled by touching corpses, bones, those killed by accident, or graves; and they change their daily garments whenever they visit their synagogue, upon which occasion they wash their body and put on other clothes. These are their daily habits.

Mount Gerizim is rich in wells and orchards, whereas Mount Ebal is dry like stone and rock. The city of Nablous lies in the valley between these two hills. Four parasangs from thence is situated Mount Gilboa, which Christians call Monto Jelbon. The country in this part is very barren. Five parasangs further is the valley of Ajalon‖, called by the Christians Val de Luna. One parasang to Gran David, for

---

* Deut. xi. 29.

† To which place, according to the tenets of the Talmudic Jews, the offerings are confined, and since the destruction of which they have been discontinued.

‡ Joshua, xxiv. 32.

§ Modern critics and travellers appear to confirm this statement relating to the peculiar pronunciation of the three letters by the Samaritans.

‖ At present Yâlo.

merly the large city of Gibeon.   It contains no Jewish inhabitants.

From thence it is three parasangs to Jerusalem, a small city strongly fortified with three walls. It contains a numerous population, composed of Jacobites, Armenians, Greeks, Georgians, Franks, and indeed of people of all tongues. The dyeing-house is rented by the year, and the exclusive privilege of dyeing is purchased from the king by the Jews of Jerusalem, two hundred of whom dwell in one corner of the city, under the tower of David. About ten yards of the base of this building are very ancient, having been constructed by our ancestors; the remaining part was added by the Mohammedans. The city contains no building stronger than the tower of David. There are at Jerusalem two hospitals, which support four hundred knights, and afford shelter to the sick; these are provided with every thing they may want, both during life and in death; the second is called the hospital of Solomon, being the palace originally built by king Solomon. This hospital also harbours and furnishes four hundred knights*, who are ever ready to wage war, over and above those knights who arrive from the country of the Franks and other parts of Christendom. These generally have taken a vow upon themselves to stay a year or two, and they remain until the period of their vow is expired. The large place of worship, called Sepulchre, and containing the sepulchre of that man †, is visited by all pilgrims.

Jerusalem has four gates, called the gates of Abraham, David, Sion, and Jehoshaphat. The latter stands opposite the place of the holy temple, which is occupied at present by a building called Templo Domino. Omar Ben Al-Khataab erected a large and handsome cupola over it, and nobody is allowed to introduce any image or painting into this place, it being set aside for prayers only. In front of it you see the western wall, one of the walls which formed the Holy of Holies of the ancient temple; it is called the Gate of Mercy, and all Jews resort thither to say their prayers near the wall of the court-yard. At Jerusalem you also see the stables erected by Solomon ‡, and which formed part of his house. Immense stones have been employed in this fabric, the like of which are nowhere else to be met with. You further see to this day

---

* The knights templars.   † Jesus is thus called in the Talmud.
‡ 1 Kings, iv. 26.

vestiges of the canal near which the sacrifices were slaughtered in ancient times; and all Jews inscribe their name upon an adjacent wall. If you leave the city by the gate of Jehoshaphat, you may see the pillar erected on Absalom's place *, and the sepulchre of king Uzziah †, and the great spring of Shiloah, which runs into the brook Kedron. Over this spring is a large building erected in the times of our forefathers. Very little water is found at Jerusalem; the inhabitants generally drink rain water, which they collect in their houses.

From the Valley of Jehoshaphat the traveller immediately ascends the Mount of Olives, as this valley only intervenes between the city and the mount. From hence the Dead Sea is distinctly visible. Two parasangs from the sea stands the salt pillar into which Lot's wife was metamorphosed; and although the sheep continually lick it, the pillar grows again, and retains its original state. You also have a prospect over the whole valley of the Dead Sea, and of the brook of Shittim, even as far as Mount Nebo. Mount Sion is also near Jerusalem, upon the acclivity of which stands no building except a place of worship of the Nazarenes (Christians). The traveller further sees there three Jewish cemeteries, where formerly the dead were buried; some of the sepulchres had stones with inscriptions upon them, but the Christians destroy these monuments, and use the stones in building their houses.

Jerusalem is surrounded by high mountains. On Mount Sion are the sepulchres of the house of David, and those of the kings who reigned after him. In consequence of the following circumstance, however, this place is at present hardly to be recognised. Fifteen years ago, one of the walls of the place of worship on Mount Sion fell down, and the patriarch commanded the priest to repair it. He ordered stones to be taken from the original wall of Sion for that purpose, and twenty workmen were hired at stated wages, who broke stones from the very foundation of the walls of Sion. Two of these labourers, who were intimate friends, upon a certain day treated one another, and repaired to their work after their friendly meal. The overseer accused them of dilatoriness, but they answered that they would still perform their day's work, and would employ thereupon the time while their fellow labourers were at meals. They then continued to break out

* 2 Sam. xviii. 18.   † 2 Kings, xv. 1—7.

stones, until, happening to meet with one which formed the
mouth of a cavern, they agreed to enter it in search of
treasure, and they proceeded until they reached a large
hall, supported by pillars of marble, encrusted with gold and
silver, and before which stood a table, with a golden sceptre
and crown.   This was the sepulchre of David, king of Israel,
to the left of which they saw that of Solomon in a similar
state, and so on the sepulchres of all the kings of Juda, who were
buried there.   They further saw chests locked up, the contents of which nobody knew, and were on the point of entering
the hall, when a blast of wind like a storm issued forth from
the mouth of the cavern so strong that it threw them down
almost lifeless on the ground.   There they lay until evening,
when another wind rushed forth, from which they heard a
voice like that of a man calling aloud, "Get up, and go forth
from this place."   The men rushed out full of fear, and proceeded to the patriarch to report what had happened to them.
This ecclesiastic summoned into his presence R. Abraham el
Constantini, a pious ascetic, one of the mourners of the downfall of Jerusalem*, and caused the two labourers to repeat what
they had previously reported.   R. Abraham thereupon informed
the patriarch that they had discovered the sepulchres of the
house of David and of the kings of Juda.   The following
morning the labourers were sent for again, but they were
found stretched on their beds and still full of fear; they
declared that they would not attempt to go again to the cave,
as it was not God's will to discover it to any one.   The patriarch ordered the place to be walled up, so as to hide it
effectually from every one unto the present day.   The above-
mentioned R. Abraham told me all this.

Two parasangs from Jerusalem is Bethlehem of Judea,
called Beth-lehem; and within half a mile of it, where several

---

* After the slaughter of the Jews of Jerusalem by the crusaders, the few
that were saved from destruction were dispersed in all directions.   Those
persons who mourned over these unhappy circumstances were called
"mourners of Jerusalem," and are mentioned under that title more than once
by Benjamin.   We find these mourners even among the Caraites about 1147.
We read in several ancient Jewish writers of the danger incurred by the
Jews who visited Jerusalem while it remained in the power of the Christians.
Pethachia found only one Jew at Jerusalem, whereas Benjamin speaks of
200.   A numerous congregation was again to be met with there about 1190;
but about 1216 great discord prevailed among them in consequence of the
pretensions of the different congregations.

roads meet *, stands the monument which points out the grave
of Rachel. This monument is constructed of eleven stones,
equal to the number of the children of Jacob. It is covered
by a cupola, which rests upon four pillars; and every Jew who
passes there inscribes his name on the stones of the monument. Twelve Jews, dyers by profession †, live at Bethlehem.
The country abounds with rivulets, wells, and springs of water.
Six parasangs further is Hebron. The ancient city of that
name was situated on the hill, and lies in ruins at present;
whereas the modern town stands in the valley, even in the
field of Machpelah ‡. Here is the large place of worship
called St. Abraham, which during the time of the Mohammedans was a synagogue. The Gentiles have erected six sepulchres in this place, which they pretend to be those of
Abraham and Sarah, of Isaac and Rebecca, and of Jacob and
Leah; the pilgrims are told that they are the sepulchres of
the fathers, and money is extorted from them. But if any
Jew come, who gives an additional fee to the keeper of the
cave, an iron door is opened, which dates from the times of
our forefathers who rest in peace, and with a burning candle
in his hands, the visitor descends into a first cave, which is
empty, traverses a second in the same state, and at last
reaches a third, which contains six sepulchres, those of Abraham, Isaac, and Jacob, and of Sarah, Rebecca, and Leah, one
opposite the other. All these sepulchres bear inscriptions,
the letters being engraved: thus, upon that of Abraham, we
read, "This is the sepulchre of our father Abraham, upon
whom be peace;" and so on that of Isaac and upon all the
other sepulchres. A lamp burns in the cave and upon the
sepulchres continually, both night and day; and you there see
tubs filled with the bones of Israelites, for unto this day it is
a custom of the house of Israel to bring thither the bones of
their relicts and of their forefathers, and to leave them there.
On the confines of the field of Machpelah stands the house
of our father Abraham §, who rests in peace; before which

* Gen. xxxv. 19, 20.
† It may be observed that most of the richer stuffs, the siclatons, &c.,
used. in the west of Europe during the middle ages, came from the east,
which accounts for the number of dyers mentioned by the traveller.
‡ Gen. xxiii. 19.
§ The "House of Abraham" is still shown to travellers, about an hour's
ride from Hebron, the site being occupied by the ruins of a small convent.

house there is a spring, and, out of respect to Abraham, no-body is allowed to construct any building on that site.

It is five parasangs hence to Beit Jaberim, the ancient Ma-reshah *, where there are but three Jewish inhabitants. Five parasangs further bring us to Toron de los Caballeros, which is Shunem†, inhabited by three hundred Jews. We then proceed three parasangs to St. Samuel of Shiloh, the ancient Shiloh, within two parasangs of Jerusalem. When the Chris-tians took Ramleh, which is Ramah, from the Mohammedans, they discovered the sepulchre of Samuel the Ramathi‡ near the Jewish synagogue, and removed his remains to Shiloh, where they erected a large place of worship over them, called St. Samuel of Shiloh to the present day. Hence it is three parasangs to Pesipua, which is Gibeah of Saul, or Geba of Benjamin; it contains no Jews. Three parasangs to Beith Nubi, which is Nob, the city of the priests. In the middle of the road are the two rocks of Jonathan§, the name of one of which is Botsets, and of the other Séné. The two Jews who live here are dyers.

It is three parasangs hence to Ramleh, which is Harama, where you still find walls erected by our forefathers, as is evident from the inscriptions upon the stones. The city con-tains about three Jews; but it was formerly very considerable, for a Jewish cemetery in its vicinity is two miles in extent. Five parasangs hence to Jaffa, the Japho of Scripture, on the coast; one Jew only, a dyer by profession, lives here. Three parasangs to Ibelin, the ancient Jabneh‖, where the site of the schools may still be traced; it contains no Jews. Here was the frontier of the tribe of Ephraim. Two parasangs to Pal-mis, or Asdoud¶, formerly a city of the Philistines, at present in ruins, and containing no Jews. Two parasangs to Ascalon,

---

* Joshua, xv. 44. It is the Bethogabris of the Greek and Latin writers, and supposed to be the Eleutheropolis of the early Christian fathers.

† Joshua, xix. 18.

‡ 1 Sam. i. 1.

§ The rocks of Jonathan, mentioned (1 Sam. xiv. 5) as being between Gibeah and Michmash, and which formed a narrow path between the two places, were also seen by Robinson and Smith. "Directly between Jeba and Mukhmâs are two conical hills, not very high, which are probably the scene of Jonathan's romantic adventure against the Philistines, recorded in 1 Sam. xiv."

‖ 2 Chron. xxvi. 6.

¶ The Azotus of the ancient geographers.

which is in fact the New Ascalon, built on the coast by Esra
the priest, of blessed memory, and originally called Benebra,
distant about four parasangs from ancient Ascalon, which lies
in ruins. This city is very large and handsome; and merchants from all parts resort to it, on account of its convenient
situation on the confines of Egypt. There are here about two
hundred rabbanite Jews, of whom the principal are R. Tsemach, R. Aaron, and R. Solomon, besides about forty Caraites,
and about three hundred Cutheans or Samaritans. In the
city is a fountain called Bir Ibrahim-al-Khahil, which was
dug in the time of the Philistines. From hence back to St.
George, which is Lydda, and in one day and a half to Serain,
the Jezreel of Scripture *, a city containing a remarkably
large fountain. It has one Jewish inhabitant, a dyer. Three
parasangs to Sufurieh, the Tsippori of antiquity †. The sepulchres of Rabenu Hakkadosh, of R. Chija, who came back from
Babylon, and of Jonah the son of Amittai the prophet, are
shown here; they are buried in the mountain, which also
contains numerous other sepulchres.

From hence it is five parasangs to Tiberias, a city situated
on the Jordan, which here bears the name of the Sea of Chin-
nereth ‡, or Lake of Tiberias. Here are the falls of the Jordan, in consequence of which the place bears also the name
of Ashdoth-Pisga §, which means " the place where the rapid
rivers have their fall:" the Jordan afterwards empties itself
into Lake Asphaltes, or the Dead Sea. Tiberias contains
about fifty Jews, the principal of whom are R. Abraham the
astronomer ||, R. Muchthar, and R. Isaac. The hot waters,
which spout forth from under ground, are called the warm
baths of Tiberias. In the vicinity is the synagogue of Kha

---

* The Esdraela of the Greeks, called by the historians of the crusades
Gerinum and Zarain.

† Now called Sephoury.

‡ Numbers, xxxiv. 11.

§ Deut. iii. 17.

|| During the middle ages Jews were not unfrequently employed as astro-
logers by the Arabian princes. R. Isaac, the son of Baruch (A.D. 1080),
appears, among others, to have rendered services of this kind to Almohammad.
King Alphonso of Castile also entertained Jews who were proficients in
astrology. The surname חוזה, astrologer, was borne by Abraham in Tiberias.
Eliezer, author of an astrological book of chances, lived in 1559. We also
find mention of Joseph, astrologer of Seifeddin, sultan of Mosul; R. Isaac,
an astronomer of the twelfth century in France; and Salomon, an astronomer in Nineveh.

leb, son of Jepuneh; and among numerous other Jewish
sepulchres are those of R. Jochanan, son of Zakhai*, and of
R. Jonathan, son of Levi. These are all in Lower Galilee.
Two parasangs bring us to Tebnin, the Thimnatha of Scrip-
ture†, where you find the sepulchre of Samuel (Simeon) the
Just, and many other sepulchres of Israelites. It is hence one
day to Gish, which is Gush Chaleb, and contains about twenty
Jewish inhabitants. We go hence six parasangs to Meroon,
which is Maron‡; in a cave near this place are the sepulchres of
Hillel and Shamai, and of twenty of their disciples, as well as
those of R. Benjamin, son of Jephet, and of R. Juda, son of
Bethera. Six parasangs to Alma, which contains fifty Jewish
inhabitants, and a large cemetery of the Israelites. Half a
day brings you to Kades, which is Kadesh Naphthali, on the
banks of the Jordan. Here are the sepulchres of R. Eleasar,
son of Arach, of R. Eleasar, son of Asariah, of Chuni Hama-
agal, of R. Simeon, son of Gamaliel, of R. Jose Hagelili, and
of Barak the son of Abinoam§. This place contains no Jews.
A day's journey brings us to Belinas‖, the ancient Dan ¶,

* Jochanan, son of Zakhai, was a celebrated teacher of the Mishna in the
time of Vespasian ; later catalogues mention his sepulchre in Tiberias. The
Jews have a legend relating to him full of extraordinary fables. Some persons have supposed him to be the "John" mentioned in Acts iv. 6.

† This identification is evidently an error, as Thimnatha was in Judea,
far to the south of Tiberias, and could not be Tebnin. Benjamin falls into
another error in placing here the sepulchre of Samuel, who was buried in
Ramah. Mr. Asher proposes to read Simeon.

‡ Meirûn is still a place of pilgrimage to the Jews of the vicinity, who
resort thither on certain days to say prayers on the sepulchres of some rabbis ;
and this corroborates our text, according to which Hillel and Shamai, the two
most celebrated teachers of the Talmud, who flourished before the birth of
our Saviour, are interred in a cave near Merûn. This legend must have been
very prevalent at our author's time, as it is also reported by Pethachia, who
adds that a large stone vase, situated in the cave of the sepulchre, filled itself
spontaneously with water whenever a worthy man entered it for the purpose
of devotion, but remained empty if the visitor was a man of doubtful
character. The two other persons whose sepulchres are mentioned here
were celebrated teachers of the law, who flourished in the third and second
centuries; but Jewish writers appear to differ as to the places of their burial.
The second of them is said to have traced his descent from one of the skele-
tons restored to life by the prophet Ezekiel.

§ All the persons mentioned here were celebrated rabbis of the first century before, and the three centuries after Christ, except Barak, who is well
known by the fourth chapter of the book of Judges.

‖ This is Paneas, or Baneas, the ancient Cæsarea Philippi.

¶ This identification is not quite correct, the ancient Dan having been

where the traveller may see a cave, from which the Jordan issues, and three miles hence this river unites its waters with those of the Arnon, a rivulet of the ancient land of Moab. In front of the cave you may still trace vestiges of the altar of the image of Micha, which was adored by the children of Dan in ancient times. Here also is the site of the altar erected by Jeroboam, son of Nebat, in honour of the golden calf; and here were the confines of the land of Israel toward the uttermost sea*

Two days from this place brings you to Damascus, a large city and the frontier town of the empire of Noureddin†, king of the Thogarmim, or Turks. This city is very large and handsome, and is inclosed with a wall and surrounded by a beautiful country, which in a circuit of fifteen miles presents the richest gardens and orchards, in such numbers and beauty as to be without equal upon earth. The rivers Amana‡ and Parpar§, the sources of which are on Mount Hermon (on which the city leans), run down here; the Amana follows its course through Damascus, and its waters are carried by means of pipes into the houses of the principal inhabitants, as well as into the streets and markets. A considerable trade is carried on here by merchants of all countries. The Parpar runs between the gardens and orchards in the outskirts, and supplies them copiously with water. Damascus contains a Mohammedan mosque, called "the Synagogue of Damascus," a building of unequalled magnificence. They say that it was the palace of Ben-Hadad‖, and that one wall of it is framed of glass by enchantment. This wall contains as many openings as there are days in the solar year, and the sun in gra-

situated on another small rivulet, still called Dan, and distant about four Roman miles west of Paneas on the way to Tyre. William òf Tyre also identifies Dan with Cæsarea. The apparent source of the Jordan flows from under a cave at the foot of a precipice, in the sides of which are several niches with Greek inscriptions, which Benjamin has mistaken for the altar of Micha.

* This is a mistake of rabbi Benjamin, as this term, used in Deut. xi. 24, means the Mediterranean.

† It is hardly necessary to state that this was the celebrated sultan of Damascus, Aleppo, and Egypt, so well known in the history of the crusades. He reigned from 1145 to 1173.

‡ 2 Kings, v. 12. The ancient Greek name of the river was Chrysorrhoas; in modern Arabic it is called the Barady.

§ 2 Kings v. 12. It is now called Ēl Faige.

‖ Jerem. xlix. 27; Amos, i. 4.

dual succession throws its light into the openings, which are divided into twelve degrees, equal to the number of the hours of the day, so that by this contrivance every body may know what time it is. The palace contains vessels richly ornamented with gold and silver, formed like tubs, and of a size to allow three persons to bathe in them at once. In this building is also preserved the rib of a giant, which measures nine spans in length, and two in breadth, and which belonged to an ancient giant king named Abchamas, whose name was found engraved upon a stone of his tomb, and it was further stated in the inscription that he reigned over the whole world.

This city contains three thousand Jews, many of whom are learned and rich men; it is the residence of the president of the university of Palestine, named R. Esra, whose brother, Sar Shalom, is the principal of the Jewish court of law. The other distinguished Jews are R. Joseph, who ranges fifth in the university, R. Matsliach, the lecturer and master of the schools, R. Meir, a flower of the learned, R. Joseph Ibn Pilath, who may be called the prop of the university, R. Heman the elder, and R. Zadok the physician. The city contains also two hundred Caraites and about four hundred Samaritans, sects which here live upon friendly terms, but they do not intermarry.

It is one day's journey thence to Jelaad, which is Gilead; it contains about sixty Jews, the principal of whom is R. Zadok. The city is large, well watered, and surrounded by gardens and orchards. Half a day's journey further stands Salkhat, the city of Salcah of Scripture. From thence to Baalbec is half a day's journey. This is the city mentioned in Scripture as Baalath in the valley of Lebanon, which Solomon built for the daughter of Pharaoh. The palace is constructed of stones of enormous size, measuring twenty spans in length and twelve in breadth; no binding material holds these stones together, and people pretend that the building could have been erected only by the help of Ashmodai. A copious spring takes its rise at the upper side of the city, through which its waters rush like those of a considerable river. They are employed in the working of several mills within the city, which also incloses numerous gardens and orchards.

Tadmor in the desert was also built by Solomon of equally

large stones ; this city is surrounded by a wall, and stands in
the desert, far from any inhabited place, being four days'
journey distant from the above-mentioned Baalath. It contains two thousand warlike Jews, who are at war with the
Christians and with the Arabian subjects of Noureddin, and
assist their neighbours the Mohammedans. Their chiefs are
R. Isaac Hajevani, R. Nathan, and R. Usiel. Half a day
brings us to Cariyatin, which is Kirjathaim ; one Jew only,
a dyer by profession, lives there. One day hence is Hamah,
the Hamath of Scripture, on the Orontes, under Mount
Lebanon. Some time ago this city was visited by an earthquake, in consequence of which fifteen thousand men died in
one day, leaving only seventy survivors *. The principals of
the Jews here are R. Ulah Hacohen, the sheikh Abu al Galeb,
and Muktar. Half a day to Reiha, which is Hazor. Three
parasangs to Lamdin, from whence it is a journey of two days
to Aleppo, the Aram Zoba of Scripture. This city is the residence of king Noureddin, and contains his palace, a building fortified by an extraordinarily high wall. There being
neither spring nor river, the inhabitants are obliged to drink
rain-water, which is collected in every house in a cistern
called in Arabic, Algub. The principal of the fifteen hundred
Jews who live in Aleppo are R. Moses el-Constandini, R.
Israel, and R. Seth.

To Bales, which is Pethor † on the Euphrates, two days.
Even at this day you there still find remains of the tower of
Balaam the son of Beor (may the name of the wicked rot!)
which he built in accordance with the hours of the day. This
place contains about ten Jews. Half a day hence we come
to Kala Jiaber ‡, which is Sela Midbarah. This city remained

* The earthquake alluded to visited this part of Syria in 1157, at which
period Hamah, Antiochia, Emessa, Apamea, Laodicea, and many other cities,
were laid in ruins. R. Benjamin calls the river Orontes Jabbok; the
Arabians call it Oroad, or Asi. Rieha, or Rieha, is a name still borne by a
place and mountain in this part of the road from Damascus to Aleppo.
Burckhardt mentions ruins of numerous towns still visible on the mountain,
among which we must look for Lamdin, mentioned in our text, but by no
other traveller or geographer. The road between Damascus and Aleppo, pursued even by all modern travellers, goes by Homs and Tadmor. Burckhardt
was the first to deviate from this route.

† Numb. xxii. 5. Deut. xxiii. 4. It is the Barbarissus of the Romans.
Bales was taken by the crusaders under Tancred in 1111.

‡ The Dauses, or Davana, of the Greeks. In the history of the crusades,
Kalat (or fort) Jiaber is often mentioned ; and the circumstances alluded to

in the power of the Arabs even at the time when the Thogarmim (or Turks) took their country and dispersed them in the desert. It contains about two thousand Jews, of whom R. Zedekiah, R. Chia, and R. Solomon are the principal. One day brings us to Racca, which is Calneh of Scripture *, on the confines of Mesopotamia, being the frontier town between that country and the empire of the Thogarmim (or Turks); it contains about seven hundred Jewish inhabitants, the principal of whom are R. Sakhai, R. Nadib, who is blind, and R. Joseph. One of the synagogues was built by Esra the scribe, when he returned to Jerusalem from Babylon. It is one day hence to the ancient place of Haran †, which contains twenty Jewish inhabitants, who also possess a synagogue erected by Esra. Nobody is allowed to construct any building on the spot where the house of our father Abraham was situated ; even the Mohammedans pay respect to the place, and resort thither to pray. Two days' journey from thence is . . . . . . ‡ at the mouth of the El-Khabur, the Habor of Scripture. This river takes its course through Media, and loses itself in the Kizil Ozein. About two hundred Jews dwell near this place. Two days to Nisibin, a large city plentifully watered, and containing about one thousand Jews. Two days to Jezireh Ben Omar, an island in the Tigris, at the foot of Mount Ararat §, and four miles distant from the spot where the ark of Noah rested ; Omar Ben al-Khatab removed the ark from the summit of the two mountains and made a mosque of it. There still exists in the vicinity of the ark a synagogue of Esra the

by our author are told at length by Desguignes. In Abulfeda's time this place was a deserted ruin ; but the castle, built on a mound of marl and gypsum, still stands, thirty-five miles below Bir, on the left bank of the Euphrates.

* The Callinicus of the Greeks, afterwards called Nicephorium.

† The Carrhæ of the ancients. The site of the house of Abraham is still pointed out as an object of veneration. Mr. Asher observes that, from Aleppo to Racca, our author, like most modern and ancient travellers, followed the course of the Euphrates ; but being probably attracted, like Marco Polo, by the considerable trade then carried on at Mosul, he proceeded thither from Racca, by way of Haran, Nisibis, and Jezireh, a route pointed out as probably used by Alexander on Rennel's map of the retreat of the Ten Thousand.

‡ It appears that the name of a city is omitted here. Our author probably wrote "from thence to Ras-el-Ain," at which place the Khabur becomes a formidable river.

§ This is of course not the true Ararat. It is called Jebel Judi. The island is the ancient Bezebde.

scribe, which is visited by the Jews of the city on the 9th of
Ab *. The city of Jezireh Omar Ben al-Khatab contains
about four thousand Jews, the principals of whom are R. Mub-
char, R. Joseph, and R. Chiia.

Two days from thence stands Mosul, mentioned in Scripture
as Ashur the great, which contains about seven thousand Jews,
the principal of whom are R. Sakhai, the prince, a descendant
of King David, and R. Joseph, surnamed Borhan-al-Phulkh,
who is astronomer of Seifeddin, the brother of Noureddin,
king of Damascus. This city, situated on the confines of
Persia, is of great extent and very ancient; it stands on the
banks of the Tigris, and is joined by a bridge to Nineveh.
Although the latter lies in ruins, there are numerous inhabited
villages and small towns on its site. Nineveh is on the
Tigris, distant one parasang from the town of Arbil†. Mosul
contains the synagogues of Obadiah, of Jonah, son of Amittai,
and of Nahum the Elkoshite. It is three days hence to
Rahabah, which is Rehoboth, by the river Euphrates, and contains about two thousand Jews, the principal of whom are R.
Ezekiah, R. Ehud, and R. Isaac. The city is surrounded by
a wall, it is very handsome, large, and well fortified; and the
environs abound with gardens and orchards. One day to
Karkisia ‡, the Carchemish of Scripture, on the banks of the
Euphrates, containing about five hundred Jewish inhabitants,
of whom the principal are R. Isaac and R. Elchanan. Two
days to Juba, which is Pumbeditha, in Nehardea; it contains
about two thousand Jews, some of them eminent scholars.
The rabbi R. Chen, R. Moses, and R. Eliakim are the principal. Here the traveller may see the sepulchres of R. Juda
and R. Samuel, opposite two synagogues which they erected
during their lives; as well as the sepulchres of R. Bosthenai,
the prince of the captivity, of R. Nathan, and of R. Nach-
man, the son of Papa §. Five days to Hardah (or Hadrah),
containing fifteen thousand Jews, of whom R. Saken, R.
Joseph, and R. Nathaniel are the principal. Two days to
Akbara, the city which was built by Jeconiah, king of Juda;
it contains about ten thousand Jews, the principal of whom
are R. Joshua and R. Nathan.

---

* See p. 68, note.   † The ancient Erbela.   ‡ The ancient Cercusium.
§ All these were celebrated Jewish rabbis in the earlier centuries of the
Christian era.

Two days from thence stands Bagdad, the large metropolis of the khalif Emir-al-Mumenin al Abassi, of the family of their prophet, who is the chief of the Mohammedan religion *. All Mohammedan kings acknowledge him, and he holds the same dignity over them which the pope enjoys over the Christians. The palace of the khalif at Bagdad is three miles in extent. It contains a large park filled with all sorts of trees, both useful and ornamental, and all kinds of beasts, as well as a pond of water carried thither from the river Tigris ; and whenever the khalif desires to enjoy himself and to sport and carouse, birds, beasts, and fishes are prepared for him and for his courtiers, whom he invites to his palace. This great Abasside is extremely friendly towards the Jews, many of his officers being of that nation ; he understands all languages, is well versed in the Mosaic law, and reads and writes the Hebrew tongue. He enjoys nothing but what he earns by the labour of his own hands, and therefore manufactures coverlets, which he stamps with his seal, and which his officers sell in the public market ; these articles are purchased by the nobles of the land, and from their produce his neces saries are provided. The khalif is an excellent man, trustworthy and kind-hearted towards every one, but generally invisible to the Mohammedans. The pilgrims, who come hither from distant countries on their way to Mecca in Yemen, desire to be presented to him, and thus address him from the palace : " Our lord, light of the Mohammedans and splendour of our religion, show us the brightness of thy countenance ; " but he heeds not their words. His servants and officers then approach and pray : " O lord, manifest thy peace to these men who come from distant lands and desire shelter in the shadow of thy glory." After this petition, he rises and puts one corner of his garment out of the window, which the pilgrims eagerly kiss. One of the lords then addresses them thus : " Go in peace, for our lord, the light of the Mohammedans, is well pleased and gives you his blessing." This prince being esteemed by them equal to their prophet, they proceed on their way, full of joy at the words addressed to them by the lord who communicated the message of peace. All the brothers and other members of the khalif's family

* The khalif alluded to by Benjamin was either Moktafi, who died in 1160, or Mostanjeh-abul-Modhaffer, who reigned from his death to 1170. It is probable that Benjamin was at Bagdad in 1164.

are accustomed to kiss his garments. Every one of them
possesses a palace within that of the khalif, but they are all
bound with chains of iron, and a special officer is appointed over
each household to prevent their rising in rebellion against
the great king. These measures are taken in consequence of what occurred some time ago, when the brothers
rebelled and elected a king among themselves·; to prevent
which in future it was decreed, that all the members of the
khalif's family should be chained, in order to prevent their
rebellious intentions. Every one of them, however, resides in
his palace, and is there much honoured; and they possess
villages and towns, the rents of which are collected for them
by their stewards. They eat and drink, and lead a merry
life. The palace of the great king contains large buildings,
pillars of gold and silver, and treasures of precious stones.

The khalif leaves his palace but once every year, viz. at
the time of the feast called Ramadan; on which occasion
many visitors assemble from distant parts, in order to have
an opportunity of beholding his countenance. He then be-
strides the royal mule, dressed in kingly robes, which are
composed of gold and silver cloth. On his head he wears a
turban, ornamented with precious stones of inestimable value;
but over this turban is thrown a black veil, as a sign of humility, and as much as to say: " See all this worldly honour
will be converted into darkness on the day of death." He is
accompanied by a numerous retinue of Mohammedan nobles,
arrayed in rich dresses and riding upon horses, princes of
Arabia, of Media, of Persia, and even of Tibet, a country distant three months' journey from Arabia. The procession goes
from the palace to the mosque at the Bozra gate, which is
the metropolitan mosque. All who walk in procession, both
men and women, are dressed in silk and purple. The streets
and squares are enlivened with singing and rejoicing, and by
parties who dance before the great king, called khalif. He is
saluted loudly by the assembled crowd, who cry: " Blessed
art thou, our lord and king." He thereupon kisses his
garment, and by holding it in his hand, acknowledges and returns the compliment. The procession moves on into the
court of the mosque, where the khalif mounts a wooden
pulpit and expounds their law unto them. The learned
Mohammedans rise, pray for him, and praise his great kindness and piety; upon which the whole assembly answer,

" Amen ! " The khalif then pronounces his blessing, and kills a camel, which is led thither for that purpose, and this is their offering. It is distributed to the nobles, who send portions of it to their friends, who are eager to taste of the meat killed by the hands of their holy king, and are much rejoiced therewith. The khalif, after this ceremony, leaves the mosque, and returns alone, along the banks of the Tigris, to his palace, the noble Mohammedans accompanying him in boats, until he enters this building. He never returns by the way he came ; and the path on the bank of the river is carefully guarded all the year round, so as to prevent any one treading in his footsteps. The khalif never leaves his palace again for a whole year. He is a pious and benevolent man, and has erected buildings on the other side of the river, on the banks of an arm of the Euphrates, which runs on one side of the city. These buildings include many large houses, streets, and hostelries for the sick poor, who resort thither in order to be cured. There are about sixty medical warehouses here, all well provided from the king's stores with spices and other necessaries ; and every patient who claims assistance is fed at the king's expense, until his cure is completed.

There is further a large building, called Dar-al-Maraphtan *, in which are confined all the insane persons who are met with, particularly during the hot season, every one of whom is secured by iron chains until his reason returns, when he is allowed to return to his home. For this purpose they are regularly examined once a month by officers appointed by the king for that purpose; and when they are found to be possessed of reason they are immediately liberated. All this is done by the king in pure charity towards all who come to Bagdad, either ill or insane ; for the king is a pious man, and his intention is excellent in this respect.

Bagdad contains about one thousand Jews, who enjoy peace, comfort, and much honour under the government of the great king. Among them are very wise men and presidents of the colleges, whose occupation is the study of the Mosaic law. The city contains ten colleges. The principal of the great college is the rabbi R. Samuel, the son of Eli, principal of the college Geon Jacob ; the provost of the Levites is the president of the second ; R. Daniel, the master of the third

* Dar-al-Morabittan in Arabic; literally, abode of those who require being chained, *i. e.* of the raving mad.

college; R. Eleasar, the fellow, presides over the fourth; R.
Eleasar, the son of Tsemach, is chief of the fifth college; he
is master of the studies, and possesses a pedigree of his descent from the prophet Samuel, who rests in peace, and he
and his brothers know the melodies that were sung in the
temple during its existence; R. Chasadiah, principal fellow,
is the master of the sixth, R. Chagai, the prince, the principal
of the seventh, and R. Esra, the president of the eighth college; R. Abraham, called Abu Tahir, presides over the ninth,
and R. Zakhai, son of Bosthenai, master of the studies, is president of the tenth college. All these are called Batlanim,
i. e. the Idle: because their sole occupation consists in the
discharge of public business. During every day of the week
they dispense justice to all the Jewish inhabitants of the
country, except Monday, which is set aside for assemblies
under the presidency of the rabbi Samuel, master of the college Geon Jacob, who on that day dispenses justice to every
applicant, and is assisted therein by the other Batlanim, presidents of the colleges.

The principal of all these, however, is R. Daniel, the son of
Chisdai, who bears the titles of Prince of the Captivity and
Lord, and who possesses a pedigree which proves his descent
from king David. The Jews call him "Lord, Prince of the
Captivity," and the Mohammedans entitle him Saidna Ben
Daoud, noble descendant of David. He holds great command over all Jewish congregations under the authority of
the Emir-al-Mumenin, the lord of the Mohammedans, who
has commanded that he shall be respected, and has confirmed
his power by granting him a seal of office. Every one of his
subjects, whether he be Jew or Mohammedan or of any other
faith, is commanded to rise in the presence of the prince of
the captivity, and to salute him respectfully, under a penalty
of one hundred stripes. Whenever he pays a visit to the
king, he is escorted by numerous horsemen, both Jews and
Gentiles, and a crier proclaims aloud: "Make way before our
lord the son of David, as becomes his dignity;" in Arabic,
Amilu tarik la-saidna ben-Daud. Upon these occasions
he rides upon a horse, and his dress is composed of embroidered silk; on his head he wears a large turban
covered with a white cloth, and surmounted by a chain (or
diadem). The authority of the prince of the captivity extends
over the countries of Mesopotamia, Persia, Khorassan, Seba,

which is Yemen, Diarbekh, all Armenia and the land of Kota
near Mount Ararat, over the country of the Alanians, which
is shut in by mountains, and has no outlet except by the iron
gates which were made by Alexander, over Sikbia and all the
provinces of the Turkmans unto the Aspisian mountains, over
the country of the Georgians unto the river Oxus (these are
the Girgasim of Scripture, and believe in Christianity), and
as far as the frontiers of the provinces and cities of Tibet and
India. All the Jewish congregations of these different countries receive authority from the prince of captivity to elect
rabbis and ministers, all of whom appear before him in order
to receive consecration * and the permission to officiate, upon
which occasions presents and valuable gifts are offered to him,
even from the remotest countries. The prince of the captivity possesses hostelries, gardens, and orchards in Babylonia,
and extensive landed property inherited from his forefathers,
of which nobody can deprive him. He enjoys a certain yearly
income from the Jewish hostelries, the markets, and the merchandise of the country, which is levied in form of a tax, over
and above what is presented to him from foreign countries.
He is very rich, an excellent scholar, and so hospitable, that
numerous Israelites dine at his table every day. At the time
of the installation of the prince of the captivity he expends
considerable sums in presents to the king (or khalif), and to
his princes and nobles. This ceremony is performed by the
king or khalif, who lays his hands on the prince, after which
the latter rides home from the king's abode to his own house,
seated in a royal state carriage, and accompanied with the
sound of various musical instruments; he afterwards lays his
hands on the gentlemen of the university, to reinstal them.
Many of the Jews of Bagdad are good scholars and very rich.
The city contains twenty-eight Jewish synagogues, situated
partly in Bagdad and partly in Al-Khorkh, on the other side
of the river Tigris, which runs through and divides the city.
The metropolitan synagogue of the prince of the captivity is
ornamented with pillars of richly coloured marble, plated with
gold and silver; on the pillars are inscribed verses of the
Psalms in letters of gold. The ascent to the holy ark † is

---

* The ceremony of consecration, performed by the prince of captivity,
consisted in his laying his hands on the heads of the candidates.

† The place where the rolls of the Pentateuch are deposited. It is generally elevated above the seats of the congregation.

composed of ten marble steps, on the uppermost of which are the stalls set apart for the prince of the captivity and the other princes of the house of David.

The city of Bagdad is three miles in circumference; the country in which it is situated is rich in palm-trees, gardens, and orchards, so that nothing equals it in Mesopotamia. Merchants of all countries resort thither for purposes of trade, and it contains many wise philosophers, well skilled in sciences, and magicians proficient in all sorts of enchantment.

Two days from hence stands Gihiagin, or Ras-al-Ain, which is Resen, "the great city;"* it contains about five thousand Jews and a large synagogue. In a house near the synagogue is the sepulchre of† . . . . .; and, in a cave below it, that of his twelve disciples. From hence it is one day to Babylon. This is the ancient Babel, and now lies in ruins; but the streets still extend thirty miles. The ruins of the palace of Nebuchadnezzar are still to be seen; but people are afraid to venture among them on account of the serpents and scorpions with which they are infested. Twenty thousand Jews live within about twenty miles from this place, and perform their worship in the synagogue of Daniel, who rests in peace. This synagogue is of remote antiquity, having been built by Daniel himself; it is constructed of solid stones and bricks. Here the traveller may also behold the palace of Nebuchadnezzar, with the burning fiery furnace into which were thrown Hananiah, Mishael, and Azariah; it is a valley well known to every one ‡. Hillah, which is at a distance of five miles, contains about ten thousand Jews and four synagogues, one of which is that of R. Meier, whose sepulchre is in front of it; another is that of R. Seiri, son of Hama, and R. Miri §. Public worship is performed daily in these synagogues. Four miles from hence is the tower built by the dispersed generation ‖ It is constructed of bricks called al-ajurr; the base measures two miles, the breadth two hundred and forty yards,

---

* Gen. x. 12. Ras-al-Ain is the Ressaina of the Romans; it is erroneously identified with Resen.

† The name is omitted in all editions.

‡ This tradition of the burning furnace is mentioned by the Arabian geographers, by whom we are further informed that the ashes still remained.

§ These are also some of the early rabbis concerning whom the Jews possess many legends; the places of burial of others are mentioned further on.

‖ Benjamin here alludes to the Birs Nimrud, which is, however, more than four miles from Hillah. *Al-ajurr* is the Persian word for these bricks.

and the height about one hundred canna. A spiral passage,
built into the tower (in stages of ten yards each), leads up to
the summit, from which we have a prospect of twenty miles,
the country being one wide plain and quite level. The heavenly
fire, which struck the tower, split it to its very foundation.

Half a day from hence, at Napacha *, which contains two
hundred Jews, is the synagogue of R. Isaac Napacha, in
front of which is his sepulchre. Three parasangs hence, on
the banks of the Euphrates, stands the synagogue of the
prophet Ezekiel, who rests in peace †. The place of the synagogue is fronted by sixty towers, the space between every
two of which is also occupied by a synagogue ; in the court of
the largest stands the ark, and behind it is the sepulchre of
Ezekiel, the son of Buzi the priest. This monument is
covered with a large cupola, and the building is very handsome ; it was erected by Jechoniah, king of Juda, and the
thirty five thousand Jews who went along with him, when
Evil-Merodach released him from the prison ‡, which was
situated between the river Chaboras and another river. The
names of Jechoniah and of all those who came with him are
inscribed on the wall, the king's name first, that of Ezekiel
last. This place is considered holy even to the present day,
and is one of those to which people resort from remote countries in order to pray, particularly at the season of new year
and atonement day §. There are great rejoicings here at
that time, which are attended even by the prince of the captivity and the presidents of the colleges of Bagdad. The
assembly is so large, that their temporary abodes cover twenty-
two miles of open ground, and attract many Arabian merchants, who keep a market or fair. On the day of atonement
the proper lesson of the day is read from a very large manuscript Pentateuch in Ezekiel's own handwriting. A lamp
burns night and day on the sepulchre of the prophet, and has
always been kept burning since the day he lighted it himself;
the oil and wicks are renewed as often as necessary. A large
house belonging to the sanctuary contains a very numerous
collection of books, some of them as ancient as the second,

---

* Perhaps the Nachaba of Ptolemy. It is not found in modern maps.
† This celebrated sepulchre is still a place of pilgrimage to the Jews and
Mohammedans in the east.
‡ 2 Kings, xxv. 27. Jerem. lii. 31.
§ Celebrated on the first and tenth of Thishri (about the end of September
or the beginning of October).

some even coeval with the first temple, it being the custom
that whoever dies childless bequeaths his books to this sanctuary. The inhabitants of the country lead to the sepulchre
all foreign Jews, who come from Media and Persia to visit it
in fulfilment of vows. The noble Mohammedans also resort
thither to pray, because they hold the prophet Ezekiel, on
whom be peace! in great veneration, and they call this place
Dar Melicha (the agreeable abode); the sepulchre is also
visited by all devout Arabs. Within half a mile of the synagogue are the sepulchres of Hananiah, Mishael, and Azariah,
each covered with a large cupola. Even in times of war,
neither Jew nor Mohammedan ventures to despoil and profane
the sepulchre of Ezekiel.

Three miles from hence stands the city of Al-Kotsonaath,
containing three hundred Jewish inhabitants and the sepulchres of R. Papa, R. Huna, R. Joseph Sinai, and R. Joseph,
the son of Hama, in front of each of which is a synagogue in
which Jews daily pray. Three parasangs to Ain Japhata,
which contains the sepulchre of the prophet Nahum the Elkoshite, who rests in peace. In a Persian village, a day from
thence, are the sepulchres of R. Chisdai, R. Akiba, and R.
Dossa; and in another village, half a day's distance in the
desert, are those of R. David, R. Juda, R. Kubreh, R. Se-
chora, and R. Aba; and on the river Lega, a distance of one
day, that of king Zedekiah*, who rests in peace; the latter is
ornamented by a large cupola †. It is one day hence to the
city of Kufa, which contains about seventy thousand Jews; and
in it is the sepulchre of king Jechoniah, which consists of a
large building with a synagogue in front. One day and a half
to Sura, the place called in the Talmud Matha-Mechasia,
formerly the residence of the princes of the captivity and of
the principals of the colleges. At Sura are the sepulchres of
R. Shrira and his son Rabenu Hai, Rabenu Sadiah-al-Fajumi,
R. Samuel, the son of Chophni the priest, and Zephaniah, the
son of Khushi, the son of Gedaliah the prophet, and of many
other princes of the captivity, descendants of the house of
David, who formerly resided there before the city was ruined.

---

* 2 Kings, xxiv. 17.

† The sites of Ain Japhata, and the other places mentioned here, have not
yet been traced by modern travellers. Colonel Shiel ('Journal of the Geog.
Soc.,' vol. viii. p. 93) found a tomb near Elkoth, east of the Tigris, at the foot
of the mountains which border Kurdistan, which the natives described as
that of Nahum.

Two days from thence is Shafjathib, where there is a synagogue, which the Israelites erected with earth and stones
brought from Jerusalem, and which they called "the transplanted of Nehardea." One day and a half from thence is El
Jubar, or Pombeditha, on the river Euphrates, containing about
three thousand Jews, and the synagogues, sepulchres, and colleges of Rab and Samuel.

At twenty-one days' journey through the desert of Sheba,
or Al-Yemen, from which Mesopotamia lies in a northerly
direction, are the abodes of the Jews who are called Beni
(children of) Rechab, men of Thema. The seat of their
government is at Thema (or Tehama), where their prince and
governor rabbi Chanan resides. This city is large, and the
extent of their country is sixteen days' journey towards the
northern mountain range. They possess large and strong
cities and are not subject to any of the Gentiles, but undertake
warlike expeditions into distant provinces with the Arabians, their neighbours and allies, to take the spoil and the
prey. These Arabians are Bedouins, who live in tents in the
deserts and have no fixed abode, and who are in the habit of
undertaking marauding expeditions into the province of
Yemen. The Jews are a terror to their neighbours. Their
country being very extensive, some of them cultivate the land
and rear cattle. A number of studious and learned men,
who spend their lives in the study of the law, are maintained
by the tithes of all produce, part of which is also employed
towards sustaining the poor and the ascetics, called "Mourners
of Sion" and "Mourners of Jerusalem." These eat no meat
and abstain from wine, dress always in black, and live in
caves or in low houses, and keep fasts all their lives except
on Sabbaths and holy-days *. They continually implore the
mercy of God for the Jews in exile, and devoutly pray that
he may have compassion on them for the sake of his own
great name; and they also include in their prayers all the
Jews of Tehama and of Telmas. The latter contains about
one hundred thousand Jews, who are governed by prince
Salomon, who, as well as his brother, prince Chanan, are descendants of the royal house of David, who rests in peace,
which is proved by their pedigrees. In doubtful cases they
solicit the decisions of the prince of the captivity, and set

---

* Fasting being prohibited on these days by the Talmud. This proves
Niebuhr's supposition, that they were Talmudists, to be correct.

aside forty days of every year, during which they go in rent clothes, and keep fasts, and pray for all the Jews who live in exile.

The province of which Thanaejm is the metropolis contains forty cities, two hundred villages, and one hundred small towns, and is inhabited by about three hundred thousand Jews. Thanaejm is a very strong city, fifteen square miles in extent, and large enough to allow agriculture to be carried on within its boundaries; within which are also situated the palace of prince Salomon, and many gardens and orchards. Telmas is also a city of considerable magnitude; it contains about one hundred thousand Jews, is strongly fortified, and situated between two very high mountains. Many of its inhabitants are well informed, wise, and rich. The distance from Telmas to Chaibar is three days' journey. It is reported that these Jews are of the tribes of Reuben, Gad, and half the tribe of Manasseh, who were led away captives by Shalmaneser, king of Ashur, and who repaired into these mountainous regions, where they erected the above-named large and strong cities. They carry on war with many kingdoms, and are not easily to be reached because of their situation, which requires a march of eighteen days through uninhabited deserts, and thus renders them difficult of access.

Chaibar is also a very large city, and contains among its fifty thousand Jewish inhabitants many learned scholars. The people of this city are valiant, and engaged in wars with the inhabitants of Mesopotamia, with those of the northern districts, and with those of Yemen, who live near them; the latter province borders on India. It is a distance of twenty-five days' journey from the country of these Jews to . . . . * on the river Virah, in Yemen, which place contains about three thousand Jews. Waset † is distant seven days, and contains about ten thousand Jews, among whom is R. Nedain. Five days hence bring us to Bassora on the Tigris, which contains two thousand Israelites, many of whom are learned and wealthy. From hence it is two days to . . . . . ‡ on

---

* The name of a city appears to be omitted here.

† Waset is the ancient Cybate. The Hebrew text reads Naset, which Mr. Asher has rightly corrected.

‡ The name of a city is omitted here; no doubt Kornah, on the Samarra, or ancient Delos. The sepulchre of Ezra is described by various modern travellers; it is still an object of pilgrimage to the Jews of the east.

the river Samarra, or Shat-el-Arab. This is the frontier of Persia, and contains fifteen hundred Jews. The sepulchre of Ezra the priest and scribe is in this place, where he died on his journey from Jerusalem to king Artaxerxes. In front of the sepulchre a large synagogue and a Mohammedan mosque have been erected, the latter as a mark of the veneration in which Ezra is held by the Mohammedans, who are very friendly towards the Jews, and resort thither to pray.

Four miles from thence begins Khuzistan, the Elam of Scripture, a large province, which, however, is but partially inhabited, a portion of it lying in ruins. Among the latter are the remains of Shushan*, the metropolis and palace of king Ahasuerus, which still contains very large and handsome buildings of ancient date. It has seven thousand Jewish inhabitants, with fourteen synagogues; in front of one of which is the sepulchre of Daniel, who rests in peace. The river Ulai divides the city into two parts, which are connected by a bridge; that portion of it which is inhabited by the Jews contains the markets, to which all trade is confined, and there all the rich dwell; on the other side of the river they are poor, because they are deprived of the above-named advantages, and have even no gardens or orchards. These circumstances gave rise to jealousy, which was fostered by the belief that all honour and riches originated in the possession of the remains of the prophet Daniel, who rests in peace, and who was buried on the favoured side of the river. A request was made by the poor for permission to remove the sepulchre to the other side, but it was rejected; upon which a war arose, and was carried on between the two parties for a length of time; this strife lasted until " their souls become loath," and they came to a mutual agreement, by which it was arranged that the coffin which contained Daniel's bones should be deposited alternately every year on either side. Both parties faithfully adhered to this arrangement, until it was interrupted by the interference of Sanjar Shah ben Shah†, who governs all Persia, and holds supreme power over forty-five of its

---

* The exact site of Shushan (Susa) is a subject of some doubt among modern geographers. The old Arabian writers give a variety of legends relating to Daniel's tomb.

† Sanjar was a very celebrated and powerful prince. He conquered Samarkand in 1140, and died in 1157, shortly before Benjamin visited the east.

kings. This prince is called in Arabic Sultan-al-Fars-al-Khabir (Supreme Commander of Persia), and his empire extends from the banks of the Shat-el-Arab to the city of Samarkand and the Kizil Ozein, inclosing the city of Nishapur, the cities of Media, and the Chaphton mountains, and reaches as far as Thibet, in the forests of which country that quadruped is found which yields the musk. The extent of his empire is four months and four days' journey. When this great emperor, Sanjar king of Persia, came to Shushan and saw that the coffin of Daniel was removed from one side to the other, he crossed the bridge with a very numerous retinue, accompanied by Jews and Mohammedans, and inquired into the reason of those proceedings. Upon being told what we have related, he declared it to be derogatory to the honour of Daniel, and commanded that the distance between the two banks should be exactly measured, that Daniel's coffin should be deposited in another coffin, made of glass, and that it should be suspended from the centre of the bridge by chains of iron. A place of public worship was erected on the spot, open to every one who desired to say his prayers, whether he be Jew or Gentile; and the coffin of Daniel is suspended from the bridge unto this very day. The king commanded that, in honour of Daniel, nobody should be allowed to fish in the river one mile on each side of the coffin.

It is three days hence to Rudbar, which contains twenty thousand Jews, among whom are many scholars and rich men, but they generally live under great oppression. Two days hence bring us to the river Holwan, near which you find the abodes of about four thousand Jews. Four days to the district of Mulehet *, possessed by a sect who do not believe in the tenets of Mohammed, but live on the summit of high mountains, and pay obedience to the commands of the Old Man in the country of the Assassins. Four congregations of Jews dwell among them, and combine with them in their wars. They do not acknowledge the authority of the kings of Persia, but live on their mountains, whence they occasionally descend to make booty and to take spoil, with which they retire to their mountain fortresses, beyond the reach of their assailants.

---

* Benjamin's account of the Assassins, and their residence at Mulehet, coincides very closely with that given by Marco Polo. It has been supposed that the sect of the Assassins originated in this district of Persia.

Some of the Jews who live in this country are excellent scholars, and all acknowledge the authority of the prince of the captivity, who resides at Bagdad in Babylonia.

Five days from hence is Amaria, which contains five-and-twenty thousand Jews. This congregation forms part of those who live in the mountains of Chaphton, and which amount to more than a hundred, extending to the frontiers of Media These Jews are descendants of those who were originally led into captivity by king Shalmaneser; they speak the Syriac language, and among them are many excellent Talmudic scholars; they are neighbours to those of the city of Amaria, which is situated within one day's journey of the empire of Persia, to the king of which they are tributary. This tribute is collected by a deputy, and amounts here, as well as in all Mohammedan countries, to one amiri of gold, equal to one golden maravedi and one-third, for each male inhabitant of the age of fifteen and upwards.

Ten years ago * there rose a man of the name of David El-Roy, of the city of Amaria, who had studied under the prince of the captivity, Chisdai, and under Eli, the president of the college of Geon Jacob in the city of Bagdad, and who became an excellent scholar, being well versed in the Mosaic law, in the decisions of the rabbins, and in the Talmud; understanding also the profane sciences, the language and the writings of the Mohammedans, and the scriptures of the magicians and enchanters. He made up his mind to rise in rebellion against the king of Persia, to unite and collect the Jews who live in the mountains of Chaphton, and with them to engage in war with all Gentiles, making the conquest of Jerusalem his final object. He gave signs to the Jews by false miracles, and assured them, "the Lord has sent me to conquer Jerusalem, and to deliver you from the yoke of the Gentiles." Some of the Jews did believe in him, and called him Messiah. When the king of Persia became acquainted with these circumstances, he sent and summoned David into his presence. The latter went without fear, and when brought before the court he was asked, "Art thou the king of the Jews?" to which

---

* That is, probably, in A.D. 1155; for 1165 appears to be about the year in which Benjamin of Tudela visited Persia. The history of David El-Roy, and the scene of his imposture, have been illustrated by Major Rawlinson in a memoir communicated to the Geographical Society of London, and printed in its Transactions.

he made answer and said, " I am." Upon this the king immediately commanded that he should be secured and put into the prison where the captives are kept who are imprisoned for life, situated in the city of Dabaristan, on the banks of the Kizil Ozein, which is a broad river. After a lapse of three days, when the king sat in council to take the advice of his nobles and officers respecting the Jews who had rebelled against his authority, David appeared among them, having liberated himself from prison without human aid. When the king beheld him he inquired, "Who has brought thee hither, or who has set thee at liberty?" To which David made answer, "My own wisdom and subtility; for verily I fear neither thee nor thy servants." The king immediately commanded that he should be seized, but his servants answered and said, " We see him not, and are aware of his presence only by hearing the sound of his voice." The king was very much astonished at David's exceeding subtility, who thus addressed him: " I now go my own way;" and he went out, followed by the king and all his nobles and servants to the banks of the river, where he took his shawl, spread it upon the water, and crossed it thereupon. At that moment he became visible, and all the servants of the king saw him cross the river on his shawl. He was pursued by them in boats, but without success, and they all confessed that no magician upon earth could equal him. He that very day travelled to Amaria, a distance of ten days' journey, by the help of the Shem Hamphorash*, and related to the astonished Jews all that had happened to him. The king of Persia afterwards sent to the Emir-el-Mumenin, the khalif of Bagdad, principal of the Mohammedans, to solicit the influence of the prince of the captivity, and of the presidents of the colleges, in order to check the proceedings of David El-Roy, and threatening to put to death all Jews who inhabited his empire. The congregations of Persia were very severely dealt with about that time, and sent letters to the prince of the captivity and the presidents of the colleges at Bagdad to the following purpose: "Why will you allow us to die, and all the congregations of this empire? Restrain the deeds of this man,

---

* Shem Hamphorash, literally, the explained name, the letters of the word Jehovah in their full explanation, a mystery known but to very few, and by which it is believed wonders may be executed. The wonders performed by Jesus are ascribed in the Talmud to his knowledge of this mystery.

and prevent thereby the shedding of innocent blood." The
prince of the captivity and the president of the colleges here-
upon addressed David in letters which run thus : " Be it
known unto thee that the time of our redemption has not yet
arrived, and that we have not yet seen the signs by which it
is to manifest itself, and that by strength no man shall prevail. We therefore command thee to discontinue the course
thou hast adopted, on pain of being excommunicated from all
Israel." Copies of these letters were sent to Sakhai, the
prince of the Jews in Mosul, and to R. Joseph the astronomer,
who is called Borhan-al-Fulkh, and also resides there, with
the request to forward them to David El-Roy. The last mentioned prince and the astronomer added letters of their own,
in which they advised and exhorted him; but he nevertheless
continued in his criminal career. This he carried on until a
certain prince of the name of Sin-el-Din, a vassal of the king
of Persia, and a Turk by birth, cut it short by sending for
the father-in-law of David El-Roy, to whom he offered ten
thousand florins if he would secretly kill David El-Roy. This
agreement being concluded, he went to David's house while
he slept, and killed him on his bed, thus destroying his plans
and evil designs. Notwithstanding this, the wrath of the
king of Persia still continued against the Jews who lived in
the mountains and in his country, who in their turn craved
the influence of the prince of the captivity with the king of
Persia. Their petitions and humble prayers were supported
by a present of one hundred talents of gold, in consideration
of which the anger of the king of Persia was subdued, and
the land was tranquillized.

From that mountain to Hamadan * is a journey of ten days;
this was the metropolis of Media, and contains about fifty
thousand Jews. In front of one of the synagogues is the
sepulchre of Mordecai and Esther. Four days from thence
stands Dabaristan†, on the river Kizil Ozein; it contains
about four thousand Jewish inhabitants. The city of Ispahan
is distant seven days' journey; it is the metropolis of Persia,
and residence of the king, being twelve miles in extent, and
containing about fifteen thousand Jews. Sar Shalom, the rabbi

* Hamadan, which is now in a state of ruin, is said to stand on or near
the site of the ancient Ecbatana. The sepulchre of Mordecai and Esther is
still shown there.
† This town is conjectured to be Farahabad.

of this city and of all other towns of the Persian empire, has been promoted to the dignity by the prince of the captivity.

Four days distant stands Shiraz, or Fars, a large city, containing about ten thousand Jews. It is seven days thence to Giva*, a large city on the banks of the Oxus, containing about eight thousand Jews. Very extensive commerce is carried on in this place, to which traders of all countries and languages resort; the country about it is very flat. Five days from thence, on the frontiers of the kingdom, stands Samarkand, a city of considerable magnitude, which contains about fifty thousand Jews. The prince rabbi Obadiah is the governor of the community, which includes many wise and learned men. Four days from thence is the province of Tibet, in the forests of which country that beast is found which yields the musk. To the mountains of Khazvin, on the river Kizil Ozein, it is a journey of eight-and-twenty days. Jews of those parts, who live in Persia at present, report that the cities of Nisapour are inhabited by four tribes of Israel, viz., the tribe of Dan, that of Zebulon, and that of Naphthali, being part of the first exiles who were carried into captivity by Shalmaneser, king of Ashur, as reported in Scripture†. He banished them to Halah and Habor, the mountains of Gozan, and the mountains of Media. The extent of their country is twenty days' journey, and they possess many towns and cities in the mountains. The river Kizil Ozein forms their boundary on one side, and they are subject to no nation, but are governed by their own prince, who bears the name of rabbi Joseph Amarkhela Halevi‡. Some of these Jews are excellent scholars; others carry on agriculture; and many of them are engaged in war with the country of Cuth, by way of the desert. They are in alliance with the Caphar Tarac, or infidel Turks §, who adore the wind and live in the desert.

---

* The city of Khiva.

† 2 Kings, xvii. 6, and xviii. 11. And the king of Assyria did carry away Israel unto Assyria, and put them in Halah and in Habor, by the river Gozan, and in the cities of the Medes.

‡ Of the tribe of Levi, the descendants of which are divided into Leviim and Khohanim, and are the only Jews who to this day claim the descent from a certain tribe, all others having mixed and become extinct in the course of time.

§ These were the Ghuzes, a Turkish tribe who emigrated in the twelfth century from the country to the north of the Oxus. The events mentioned

This is a people who eat no bread and drink no wine, but devour the meat raw and quite unprepared; they have no noses, but draw breath through two small holes, and eat all sorts of meat, whether from clean or unclean beasts. They are on very friendly terms with the Jews.

About eighteen years ago this nation invaded Persia with a numerous host, and took the city of Rai, which they smote with the edge of the sword, carrying off the spoil to their deserts. Nothing similar had been seen before in the kingdom of Persia; and when the king of that country was made acquainted with this occurrence, his wrath was kindled, for, said he, "in the time of my predecessors no host like this ever issued from the desert; I will go and will extinguish their name from the earth." He raised the war-cry in the whole empire, collected all his troops, and made inquiry whether he could find any guide that would show him the place where his enemies pitched their tents. A man was met with, who spoke thus to the king: "I will show thee the place of their retreat, for I am one of them." The king promised to enrich him if he would fulfil his promise, and show him the way. Upon inquiry how many provisions would be necessary for this long march through the desert, the spy answered: "take with you bread and water for fifteen days, as you will find no provisions whatever before you reach their country." This advice being acted upon, they travelled fifteen days in the desert, and as they met with nothing that could serve for sustenance, they became extremely short of provisions, and men and beasts began to die. The king sent for the spy, and thus spoke to him : " What is become of thy promise to show us our enemy?" No other reply being made than "I have mistaken my way," the head of the spy was cut off by the king's command. Orders were issued that every one who had any provisions left should share them with his companion; but every thing eatable was consumed, even the beasts, and after travelling thirteen additional days in the desert, they at last reached the mountains of Khazvin, where the Jews dwell. They encamped in the gardens and orchards, and near the springs, which are in the vicinity of the river Kizil Ozein. It

in the text seem to have occurred in 1153, when the Ghuzes revolted against the Persians, defeated the sultan, and plundered Mero and Nishabour. The sultan was made a prisoner, and only escaped and returned to his own country in 1156.

being the fruit season, they made free with it and destroyed much, but no living being came forward. They saw, however, cities and many towers on the mountains, and the king commanded two of his servants to go and inquire the name of the nation which inhabited these mountains, and to cross over to them, either in boats or by swimming the river. They at last discovered a large bridge, fortified by towers, and secured by a gate which was locked, and on the other side of the bridge a considerable city. They shouted on their side of the bridge until at last a man came forth to inquire what they wanted or to whom they belonged. They could not, however, make themselves understood, but brought an interpreter who spoke both languages ; the questions being repeated, they replied : "We are the servants of the king of Persia, and have come to inquire who you are and whose subjects." The answer was : " We are Jews, we acknowledge no king or prince of the Gentiles, but are subjects of a Jewish prince." Upon inquiries after the Ghuzi, the Caphar Tarac or infidel Turks, the Jews made answer : " Verily they are our allies, and whoever seeks to harm them we consider our own enemy." The two men returned and reported this to the king of Persia, who became much afraid, and particularly so when, after a lapse of two days, the Jews sent a herald to offer him battle. The king said, " I am not come to make war against you, but against the Caphar Tarac, or infidel Turks, who are my enemies ; and if you attack me I will certainly take my vengeance, and will destroy all the Jews in my own kingdom, for I am well aware of your superiority over me in my present position ; but I entreat you to act kindly and not to harass me, but allow me to fight with the Caphar Tarac, my enemy, and also to sell me as much provision as I want for the maintenance of my host." The Jews took counsel among themselves, and determined to comply with the request of the king of Persia for the sake of his Jewish subjects. The king and all his host were consequently admitted into the country of the Jews, and during his stay of fifteen days he was treated with most honourable distinction and respect. The Jews, however, meanwhile sent information to their allies, the Caphar Tarac, and made them acquainted with the abovementioned circumstances ; these took possession of all the mountain passes, and assembled a considerable host, consisting of all the inhabitants of that desert and when the king of Persia went forth to give them battle, the Caphar Tarac conquered, killing and slaying so many of the Persians, that the king escaped to his country with only very few followers. One of the horsemen of the retinue of the king enticed a Jew of that country, named R. Moses, to go along with him; he carried this man with him into Persia, and there made him a slave. Upon a certain day, when the king was the spectator of sports carried on for his amusement, and consisting principally of the exercise of handling the bow, among all competitors none excelled this R. Moses. The king thereupon inquired after this man by means of an interpreter, and was told what had happened to him, and how he had been forcibly carried away from his country by the horseman; upon learning which the king not only immediately granted him his liberty, but gave him a dress of honour, composed of silk and fine linen, and many other presents. A proposal was also made to R. Moses, that if he would renounce his religion for that of the Persians, he should be treated with the utmost kindness, should gain considerable riches, and be made the king's steward; but he refused, and said, " I cannot make up my mind to any such step." The king, however, placed him in the house of the rabbi Sar Shalom, of the Ispahan congregation, who in the course of time became his father-in-law. This very R. Moses related all these things unto me.

From thence I returned to the country of Khuzistan, which lies on the Tigris. This river runs downward and falls into the Indian Sea (Persian Gulf), in the vicinity of an island called Kish. The extent of this island is six miles, and the inhabitants do not carry on any agriculture, for they have no rivers, nor more than one spring in the whole island, and are consequently obliged to drink rain water. It is, however, a considerable market, being the spot to which the Indian merchants and those of the islands bring their commodities. While the traders of Mesopotamia, Yemen, and Persia import all silk and purple cloths, flax, cotton, hemp, mash *, wheat, barley, millet, rye, and all other sorts of comestibles and pulse, which articles form objects of exchange, those from India import great quantities of spices, and the inhabitants of the island live by what they gain in their capacity of brokers to both parties. The island contains about five hundred Jews. It is ten days

* A sort of pea. See Lee's Ibn-Batuta, p. 106.

passage by sea to El-Katif, a city with about five thousand Israelites. In this vicinity the pearls are found : about the twenty-fourth of the month of Nisan * large drops of rain are observed upon the surface of the water, which are swallowed by the reptiles, which thereupon close their shells and fall to the bottom of the sea; about the middle of the month of Thishri † people dive with the assistance of ropes, collect these reptiles from the bottom, and bring them up, after which they are opened and the pearls taken out.

Seven days from thence is Chulam ‡, on the confines of the country of the sun-worshippers, who are descendants of Kush §, are addicted to astrology, and are all black. This nation is very trustworthy in matters of trade; and whenever foreign merchants enter their port, three secretaries of the king immediately repair on board their vessels, write down their names, and report them to him. The king thereupon grants them security for their property, which they may even leave in the open fields without any guard. One of the king's officers sits in the market, and receives goods that may have been found any where, and which he returns to those applicants who can minutely describe them. This custom is observed in the whole empire of the king. From Easter to new year ‖, during the whole of the summer, the heat is extreme. From the third hour of the day ¶ people shut themselves up in their houses until the evening, at which time every body goes out. The streets and markets are lighted up, and the inhabitants employ all the night upon their business, which they are prevented from doing in the daytime by the excessive heat.

Pepper grows in this country ; the trees which bear this fruit are planted in the fields, which surround the towns, and every one knows his plantation. The trees are small, and the pepper is originally white, but when they collect it they put it into basons and pour hot water upon it; it is then exposed to the heat of the sun, and dried, in order to make it

---

* In April.
† In October.
‡ Chulam, the Koulam of Marco Polo and Ibn-Batuta, was an important place on the coast of Malabar, but is much reduced in modern times.
§ Negroes.
‖ *i. e.* From April to October.
¶ Nine o' clock in the morning.

hard and more substantial, in the course of which process it
becomes of a black colour. Cinnamon, ginger, and many
other kinds of spices also grow in this country. The inhabitants do not bury their dead, but embalm them with certain
spices, put them upon stools, and cover them with cloths,
every family keeping apart. The flesh dries upon the bones;
and as these corpses resemble living beings, every body re-
cognises his parents and all the members of his family for
many years to come. These people worship the sun *. About
half a mile from every town they have large places of worship,
and every morning they run towards the rising sun; every
place of worship contains a representation of that luminary,
so constructed by enchantment that upon the rising of the sun
it turns round with a great noise, at which moment both men
and women take up their censors and burn incense in honour
of this their deity. "This their way is their folly." † All
the cities and countries inhabited by these people contain only
about one hundred Jews, who are of black colour, as well as
the other inhabitants. The Jews are good men, observers of
the law, and possess the Pentateuch, the prophets, and some
little knowledge of the Talmud and its decisions.

The island of Khandy ‡ is distant twenty two days' journey
The inhabitants are fire worshippers called Druzes, and
twenty three thousand Jews live among them. These Druzes

---

* Mr. Asher observes, upon this passage, "Our author states the ancient
inhabitants of Chulam to be fire worshippers. Edrisi, however, (i. 176,)
says of the king, 'he adores the idol of Boudha,' and Ibn-Batuta reports him
to be 'an infidel.' Although the latter appellation was applied by the Mohammedans to the fire worshippers, we have no sufficient proof to show that
Edrisi's information is wrong, or that the majority of the population adored
the sun as a deity. There is no doubt, however, that Malabar became the
asylum of this ancient sect after it had been vanquished by the Mohammedans,
and had been forced by persecution, not only to seek refuge in the mountainous and less accessible parts of Persia (Kerman and Herat), but to toil
on to distant regions. They found a resting place beyond the Indus, which
they crossed in fear of their unrelenting pursuers; and here we still find
their descendants, the Parsees, who form 'a numerous and highly respectable
class of the population.' Very able papers on the history, religion, and worship of the Guebres, will be found in vols. i. and iii. of Ouseley's 'Travels,'
and in Ritter's 'Erdkunde,' v. 615."
† Psalms, xlix. 14.
‡ The modern Ceylon. Benjamin appears to call the inhabitants Druzes
because he had been told that, like the Druzes of Syria, they believed in the
metempsychosis. We learn from the Arabian geographer, Edrisi, that there
was a large population of Jews in Ceylon at this time.

have priests everywhere in the houses consecrated to their idols, and these priests are expert necromancers, the like of whom are to be met with nowhere. In front of the altar of their house of prayer is a deep ditch, in which a large fire is continually kept burning ; this they call Elahuta, Deity. They pass their children through it, and into this ditch they also throw their dead. Some of the great of this country take a vow to burn themselves alive; and if any such devotee declares to his children and kindred his intention to do so, they all applaud him and say, "Happy shalt thou be, and it shall be well with thee." When the appointed day arrives, they prepare a sumptuous feast, place the devotee upon his horse, if he be rich, or lead him on foot, if he be poor, to the brink of the ditch. He then throws himself into the fire, and all his kindred manifest their joy by the playing of instruments until he is entirely consumed. Within three days of this ceremony two of the principal priests repair to his house, and thus address his children : "Prepare the house, for to-day you will be visited by your father, who will manifest his wishes unto you." Witnesses are selected among the inhabitants of the town, and lo! the devil appears in the image of the dead. The wife and children inquire after his state in the other world, and he answers : "I have met my companions, but they will not admit me into their company, before I have discharged my debts to my friends and neighbours ; " he then makes a will, divides his goods among his children, and commands them to discharge all debts he owes and to receive what people owe him ; this will is written down by the witnesses . . . * to go his way, and he is not seen any more. In consequence of this falsehood and deceit, which the priests pass off by magic, they retain a strong hold upon the people, and make them believe that their equal is not to be met with upon earth.

From hence the passage to China † is effected in forty days. This country lies eastward, and some say that the star Orion predominates in the sea which bounds it, and which is called the Sea of Nikpha. Sometimes this sea is so stormy that no mariner can conduct his vessel ; and whenever a storm throws a ship into this sea, it is impossible to govern it; the

---

* A blank occurs here in the two early editions.
† Our author is the first European who mentions China by this name.

crew and the passengers consume their provisions, and then die miserably. Many vessels have been lost in this way; but people have learned how to save themselves from this fate by the following contrivance : they take bullocks' hides along with them, and whenever this storm arises and throws them into the Sea of Nikpha, they sow themselves up in the hides, taking care to have a knife in their hand, and being secured against the sea-water, they throw themselves into the ocean ; here they are soon perceived by a large eagle called a griffin, which takes them for cattle, darts down, seizes them in his gripe, and carries them upon dry land, where he deposits his burden on a hill or in a dale, there to consume his prey. The man, however, now makes use of his knife to kill the bird, creeps forth from the hide, and tries to reach an inhabited country. Many people have been saved by this stratagem.

Gingaleh is but three days distant by land, whereas it requires a journey of fifteen days to reach it by sea; this place contains about one thousand Israelites. To Khulan, seven days by sea; no Jews live there. Twelve days from thence to Sebid, which contains but few Jews. Eight days from thence is Middle India*, which is called Aden, and in Scripture Eden in Thelasar †. This country is very mountainous, and contains many independent Jews, who are not subject to the power of the Gentiles, but possess cities and fortresses on the summits of the mountains, from whence they descend into the country of Maatum, with which they are at war. Maatum, also called Nubia, is a Christian kingdom, and the inhabitants are called Nubians. The Jews generally take spoil and plunder from them, which they carry into their mountain fastnesses, the possession of which makes them almost unconquerable. Many of the Jews of Aden visit Egypt and Persia.

To the country of Assuan twenty days' journey, through the desert of Sheba, on the banks of the Nile (Pison), which comes down here from the country of the blacks. This country is governed by a king, whom they call Sultan-al-Habash, and some of the inhabitants resemble beasts in every respect. They eat the herbs which grow on the banks of the Nile, go naked in the fields, and have no notions like other men; for instance, they cohabit with their own sisters and

* Literally, continental India.   † 2 Kings, xix. 12.

with any body they find. The country is excessively hot; and when the people of Assuan invade their country, they carry wheat, raisins, and figs, which they throw out like bait, thereby alluring the natives. These are made captive, and sold in Egypt and in the adjoining countries, where they are known as black slaves, being the descendants of Ham.

From Assuan to Chaluah it is twelve days. This place contains about three hundred Jews, and is the starting point of the caravans which traverse the desert Al-Zahara in fifty days on their way to Zavila, the Havilah of Scripture *, which is in the country of Ganah †. This desert contains mountains of sand; and, whenever a storm arises, the caravans are exposed to the imminent danger of being buried alive by the sand; those which escape, however, carry iron, copper, different sorts of fruits, pulse, and salt. Gold and precious stones are brought from thence in exchange. This country lies westward of Kush, or Abyssinia. Thirteen days' journey from Chaluah stands Kuts, a city on the frontiers of Egypt, containing thirty thousand Jewish inhabitants. To Fayuhm five days; this is Pithom ‡; it contains about twenty Jews, and has some remains of the buildings erected by our forefathers even to this day. Four days from thence brings us to Mizraim, or Memphis, commonly called Old Cairo. This large city stands on the banks of the Nile, called Al-Nil, and contains about two thousand Jews. Here are two synagogues, one of the congregation of Palestine, called the Syrian, the other of the Babylonian Jews (or those of Irac). They follow different customs regarding the division of the Pentateuch into Parashioth and Sedarim §. The Babylonians read one Parasha every week, as is the custom throughout Spain, and finish the whole of the Pentateuch every year, whereas the Syrians have

---

* Gen. x. 7; 1 Chron. i. 9.

† Chalua or Aloua, the Ghalua of Edrisi (i. 33), is mentioned by the Arabian writers as the starting point for the caravans which traversed the desert of Saharah, and carried on the trade with northern Africa. Zavila, Zuila, Zuela of our maps, Zavila of Edrisi (i. 258-9), was remarkable for the splendour of its bazaars and buildings, as well as for its beautiful streets and thoroughfares. From Zuila the caravans proceeded almost due south to Ganah, in the interior of Africa.

‡ Exod. i. 11.

§ The Pentateuch is divided into fifty-four Parashioth, of seven portions each; and the custom of the Babylonians, as described in the text, is practised at present almost universally.

the custom of dividing every Parasha into three Sedarim, and concluding the lecture of the whole once in three years. They keep, however, the long-established custom of assembling both congregations to perform public service together, as well on the day of the joy of the law as on that of the dispensation of the law *. Rabbi Nathaniel, the lord of lords, is the president of the Jewish university, and, in his capacity of primate of all the Jewish congregations of Egypt, exercises the right of electing Rabanim and ministers. He is one of the officers of the great king, who resides in the fortress of Zoan in the city of Mizraim, which is the metropolis of all those Arabians who obey the Emir-al-Mumenin † of the sect of Ali ben Abitaleb. All the inhabitants of his country are called rebels, because they rebelled against the Emir-al-Mumenin al-Abassi who resides at Bagdad, and there is continual hatred between them.

The residence of Zoan was selected for its convenience. The prince appears in public twice every year; once at the time of their great holiday, and the second time at the moment of the inundation of the Nile. Zoan is inclosed by a wall, whereas Mizraim is open, and the Nile washes one portion of it. The city is large, containing many markets and bazaars, and very wealthy Jewish inhabitants.

Rain, frost, and snow are almost unknown here, the climate being very warm. The river overflows once every year, in the month of Elul ‡, and, inundating the whole country, irrigates it to the extent of fifteen days' journey. The water remains standing on the land during that and the following month, whereby it is moistened and made fit for agriculture. A marble pillar, constructed with great skill, has been erected in front of an island; twelve yards of this pillar protrude above the level of the river; and whenever the water rises to a height sufficient to cover the pillar, people know that it has inundated the whole land of Egypt to the extent of fifteen

* The former is celebrated on the last day of the feast of tabernacles, (Deut. xvi. 13—15,) the latter with the feast of weeks (ibid. 9).

† Benjamin of Tudela does not mention the name of the Fatimite khalif of Egypt who reigned at the time of his visit; but as that dynasty was overthrown in 1171, and as the authority of the last khalif of that family had previously been annihilated by the conquests of the armies of Noureddin, to which Benjamin makes no allusion, it is probable that his visit to Egypt may be placed as early as 1168 or 1169.

‡ August.

days' journey, whereas if one-half only of the pillar be covered, it shows that one-half of the country is yet dry. A certain officer measures the rise of the river every day, and makes proclamation in Zoan and in Mizraim in these words: "Praise God, for the river has risen so and so much!" The measurement and the proclamation is repeated every day. Whenever the water submerges the whole pillar, it produces great plenty in the whole land of Egypt. The river rises by degrees until the whole country is inundated to the extent of fifteen days' journey. The proprietors of land cause ditches to be dug along their fields, into which the fishes are swept with the rising waters; and when the river retires into its bed, the fish remaining in the trenches are collected by the proprietors and used for food. Others sell them to merchants, by whom they are cured, and sold in this state all over the country. The fat of these fishes, with which they abound, is used by the rich of the land instead of oil, and they light their lamps therewith. Those who eat of the fish, and drink Nile water after it, need not fear any bad consequences, the water being an excellent preventive. Persons who inquire the reason of the rise of the Nile are told by the Egyptians that it is caused by the heavy rains which fall in the country of Abyssinia, the Havilah of Scripture, which is elevated above the level of Egypt. This forces the river out of its bed, and inundates the whole country. Whenever the overflowing of the Nile is suspended, they can neither sow nor reap, "and the famine is sore in the land."* The time for sowing in Egypt is the month of Marcheshvan†, after the river has retired into its usual bed; in Adar‡ they cut barley, and in Nissan§ the wheat. In the same month the following fruits are ripe: a kind of acid plum called cherry, nuts, cucumbers, gourds, St. John's bread‖, beans, spelt-corn, chick-pease, as well as all sorts of herbs, such as purslain, asparagus (or fennel), grapes, lettuce, coriander, succory, cabbage, and wine. Upon the whole the country abounds with good things. The gardens and orchards are watered partly from wells and partly from the Nile.

* A phrase taken from Gen. xliii. 1.
† November.   ‡ March.   § April.
‖ "Carob-Siliqua in Latin; Caroube, or Carouge, French. This translation is traditional among Jews, and it has been employed, although Abdol-
latif does not mention this fruit as one indigenous in Egypt."—ASHER.

Above Mizraim the Nile is divided into four arms, one of which proceeds to Damietta, which is Caphtor of Scripture, and there falls into the sea; a second flows towards Rashid (or Rosetta), which is near Alexandria, and there falls into the sea; the third takes the direction of Ashmun, the large city on the frontier of Egypt. The banks of these four arms are lined on both sides with cities, towns, and villages; and are enlivened by numerous travellers who journey both by river and by land. In fact, upon the whole earth there is no country so populous and well cultivated as Egypt, which is of ample territory and full of all sorts of good things.

From New to Old Mizraim is a distance of two parasangs. The latter lies in ruins, but the sites of the walls and the houses may still be traced at this day, as also the granaries of Joseph, of which there is a large number. The pyramids, which are seen here, are constructed by magic; and in no other country or other place is any thing equal to them. They are composed of stones and cement, and are very substantial. In the outskirts of the city is the very ancient synagogue of our great master Moses, upon whom be peace. An old and very learned man is the overseer and clerk of this place of public worship; he is called Al-Sheikh Abunasar. Old Mizraim is three miles in extent. From thence to the land of Goshen, eight parasangs. It is called Belbeis, is a large city, and contains about three thousand Jewish inhabitants. Half a day to Iskiil Ain-al-Shems, the ancient Raamses, which is in ruins. Here are remains of the buildings erected by our forefathers, and tower-like buildings constructed of bricks. One day's journey to Al-Boutidg; about two hundred Jews live here. Half a day to Sefita, which contains about two hundred Jews. To Damira, four parasangs; this place contains about seven hundred Jews. Five days to Mahaleh, which contains about five hundred Israelites*. Two days from thence stands Alexandria, which Alexander the Macedonian, who built, this extremely strong and handsome city, called after his own name. In the outskirts of the city was the school of Aristotle, the preceptor of Alexander. The building is still very handsome and large, and is divided into many apartments by marble pillars. There are about twenty schools, to which people

---

* It may be observed that Benjamin's object appears to have been only to mention those towns in Egypt which contained Jews, and he follows no direct course.

flocked from all parts of the world in order to study the Aristotelian philosophy. The city is built upon arches, which are hollow below. The streets are straight, and some of them are of such extent that the eye cannot overlook them at once; that which runs from the Rosetta to the sea-gate is a full mile in length. The port of Alexandria is formed partly by a pier, which extends a mile into the sea. Here is also a high tower, called lighthouse, in Arabic, Minar of Alexandria, on the summit of which was placed a glass mirror. All vessels which approached with hostile intentions, from Greece and from the western side, could be observed at fifty days' distance by means of this glass mirror, and precautions were taken against them. Many years after the death of Alexander there arrived a Grecian vessel commanded by a man of the name of Theodoros, who was extremely cunning. The Grecians were subject to the Egyptians at the time, and the above-named shipper brought a valuable present to the king of Egypt, consisting of silver, gold, and silk garments. He rode at anchor in view of the mirror, the customary station of all merchantmen who arrived, and the keeper of the light-house, as well as his servants, were invited every day by him, until they became very intimate and paid one another frequent visits. Upon a certain day the keeper and all his servants were invited to a sumptuous meal, and were plied so much with wine that both he and his servants became drunk and fell into a sound sleep. This opportunity was seized by the shipper and his crew to break the mirror, after which exploit they left the port the same night. From that time the Christians began to visit Alexandria with small and large vessels, and took the large island of Crete, as well as Cyprus, which are in possession of the Greeks unto this day; and the Egyptians have not been able to withstand the Greeks ever since *. The lighthouse is still a mark to all seafaring men. It is observed at the distance of one hundred miles by day, and at night bears a light which serves as a guide to all mariners.

The city is very mercantile, and affords an excellent market

---

* This story is one version of a popular tradition which is mentioned by the Arabian writers; and a story similar to it, though not applied to the Pharos of Alexandria, is found among the collections current in the west of Europe during the middle ages, but no doubt brought from the east. See the old English poem of the Seven Sages.

to all nations. People from all Christian kingdoms resort
to Alexandria, from Valentia, Tuscany, Lombardy, Apulia,
Amalfi, Sicilia, Rakuvia, Catalonia, Spain, Roussillon, Germany, Saxony, Denmark, England, Flandres, Hainault, Nor-
mandy, France, Poitou, Anjou, Burgundy, Mediana, Provence,
Genoa, Pisa, Gascony, Arragon, and Navarre. From the west
you meet Mohammedans from Andalusia, Algarve, Africa, and
Arabia, as well as from the countries towards India, Savila,
Abyssinia, Nubia, Yemen, Mesopotamia, and Syria, besides
Greeks and Turks *. From India they import all sorts of
spices, which are bought by Christian merchants. The city
is full of bustle, and every nation has its own fonteccho (or
hostelry) there.

On the sea-shore is a marble sepulchre, upon which are
depicted all sorts of birds and beasts, all in very ancient
characters, which nobody can decipher; but it is supposed
that it is the tomb of a king of very ancient date, who reigned
even before the flood. The length of the tomb is fifteen spans
by six in breadth.

Alexandria contains about three thousand Jews.

From hence we reach Damietta, which is Caphtor †, in two
days; this place contains about two hundred Jews. Half a
day from thence to Sunbat, the inhabitants of which sow flax
and weave fine linen, which forms a very considerable article
of exportation. Four days to Ailah, which is Elim of Scripture; it belongs to the Bedouin Arabs. Two days to Re-
phidim, which is inhabited by Arabians, and contains no Jews.
One day to Mount Sinai, on the summit of which the Syrian
monks possess a place of worship. At the base of the mountain is a large village; the inhabitants, who speak the Chaldean
language, call it Tour Sinai. The mountain is small, is in
possession of the Egyptians, and is distant five days from
Mizraim. The Red Sea is one day's journey from Mount
Sinai; this sea is an arm of the Indian Sea.

Back to Damietta, from whence by sea to Tennis, the
Chanes of Scripture, an island of the sea, containing about

* Mr. Asher has first given a clear and intelligible translation of the
names of the different countries who traded to Alexandria; and he observes
that, in drawing it up, Benjamin probably follows some list of the fontecchi,
or hostelries of the merchants of different nations, made for the use of captains
arriving there.

† This appears to be an error of our traveller.

forty Israelites; here is the boundary of the empire of Egypt.
From thence we go, in twenty days, by sea to Messina,
on the coast of the island of Sicily, situated on the strait
called Lunir, an arm of the sea which divides Calabria from
Sicily. This city, contains about two hundred Jews, and is
beautifully situated in a country abounding with gardens and
orchards, and full of good things. Most of the pilgrims who
embark for Jerusalem assemble here, because this city affords
the best opportunity for a good passage.

Two days from thence stands Palermo, a large city, two
square miles in extent. It contains the extensive palace
of king William*, and is inhabited by about fifteen hundred
Jews and many Christians and Mohammedans. The country
is rich in wells and springs, grows wheat and barley, and is
covered with gardens and orchards; it is, in fact, the best in
the whole island of Sicily. This city is the seat of the viceroy, whose palace is called Al-Hacina, and contains all sorts of
fruit trees, as also a great spring, surrounded by a wall, and a
reservoir called Al-Behira, in which abundance of fish are
preserved. The king's vessels are ornamented with silver
and gold, and are ever ready for the amusement of himself and
his women. There is also a large palace, the walls of which
are richly ornamented with paintings and with gold and silver.
The pavement is of marble and rich mosaic, representing all
sorts of figures; in the whole country there is no building
equal to this.

The island begins at Messina, where many pilgrims meet,
and extends to Catania, Syracuse. Masara, Pantaleone, and
Trapani, being six days in circumference. Near Trapani is
found the stone called coral, in Arabic, al-murgan†. From

---

* William II. king of Sicily, who reigned from 1166 to 1189. On his
accession he was only twelve years of age; and during his minority Stephen,
archbishop of Palermo, governed Sicily as chancellor under the queen
dowager. It is to him that Benjamin alludes under the title of viceroy; in
1169 the viceroy was driven from Sicily by a revolt of the inhabitants of
Palermo, and it was therefore probably early in that year that Benjamin was
in the island.

† Coral (Arabic, bessed; Persian, merjan). The Sicilian coral is mentioned
by several old writers. The produce of the fishery at Messina is stated by
Spallanzani ("Travels in the Two Sicilies," vol. iv. p. 308, &c.) to amount to
twelve quintals of 250 lbs. each. Edrisi mentions the fishery of this production to have been carried on by the Sicilians, and states that it was inferior
to the species found on the African coast.

thence you cross over and reach Rome in three days ; from
Rome by land in five days to Lucca, from whence you get in
twelve days to Bardin, by Mount Maurienne, and over the
passes of Italy.

Here are the confines of Germany, a country full of hills
and mountains. The Jewish congregations of Germany
inhabit the banks of the great river Rhine, from Cologne,
where the empire commences, unto Cassanburg, the frontier
of Germany, which is fifteen days' journey, and is called
Ashkenas by the Jews. These are the cities of Germany
which contain congregations of Israelites, all situated on the
river Moselle—Coblence, Andernach, Kaub, Kartania, Bingen,
Worms, and Mistran. In fact, the Jews are dispersed over
all countries, and whoever hinders Israel from being collected,
shall never see any good sign, and shall not live with Israel.
And at the time which the Lord has appointed to be a limit
of our captivity and to exalt the horn of his anointed, every
one shall come forth and shall say, " I will lead the Jews
and I will assemble them."

These cities contain many eminent scholars; the congregations are on the best terms with one another, and are
friendly towards strangers. Whenever a traveller visits them
they are rejoiced thereat and hospitably receive him. They
are full of hopes, and say—" Be of good spirit, dear brethren,
for the salvation of the Lord will be quick, like the twinkling
of an eye ; and, indeed, were it not that we had doubted
hitherto that the end of our captivity had not yet arrived, we
should have assembled long ago; but this is impossible before
the time of song arrive, and the sound of the cooing turtle
gives warning*; then will the message arrive, and we will
say, The name of the Lord be exalted !"† They send letters
to one another, by which they exhort to hold firm in the
Mosaic law. Those that spend their time as mourners of the
downfall of Sion and the destruction of Jerusalem, are always
dressed in black clothes, and pray for mercy before the Lord,
for the sake of their brethren.

Beside the cities which we have already mentioned as being
in Germany, there are, further, Astransburg, Duidisburg,
Mantern, Pisingas, Bamberg, Zor, and Regensburg, on the
confines of the empire ; all these cities contain many rich and

---

* Solom. Song, ii. 12.   † Psalms, xxxv. 27.

learned Jews. Further on is the country of Bohemia, called Prague. Here begins Sclavonia, called by the Jews who inhabit it Khenaan, because the inhabitants sell their children to all nations, which is also applicable to the people of Russia. The latter country is very extensive, reaching from the gates of Prague to those of Kiev, a large city on the confines of the empire. The country is very mountainous and full of forests; in the latter the beasts called vaiverges * are met, which yield the sable fur or ermine. In winter the cold is so intense that nobody ventures to leave his house. So far the kingdom of Russia.

The kingdom of France, called by the Jews Tsarphat, reaches from the town of Alsodo to Paris, the metropolis, and is six days in extent. This city, situated on the river Seine, belongs to king Louis †, and contains many learned men, the equal of which are to be met with at present nowhere upon earth : they employ all their time upon the study of the law, are hospitable to all travellers, and on friendly terms with all their Jewish brethren.

May the Lord in his mercy be full of compassion towards them and us, and may he fulfil towards both the words of his Holy Scripture (Deut. xxx. 3), "Then the Lord thy God will turn thy captivity, and have compassion upon thee, and will return and gather thee from all the nations, whither the Lord thy God hath scattered thee."—Amen, Amen, Amen.

* Vaiverges, Polish wiewiórka, the white squirrel, a quadruped, the skins of which were considered to be of great value.
† Louis le Jeune, who reigned from 1137 to 1185.

THE BOOK OF SIR JOHN MAUNDEVILLE.
A.D. 1322—1356.

THE PROLOGUE.

FORASMUCH as the land beyond the sea, that is to say, the
Holy Land, which men call the land of promise or of behest,
passing all other lands, is the most worthy land, most excellent, and lady and sovereign of all other lands, and is blessed
and hallowed with the precious body and blood of our Lord Jesus
Christ; in the which land it pleased him to take flesh and
blood of the Virgin Mary, to environ that holy land with his
blessed feet; and there he would of his blessedness shadow
him in the said blessed and glorious Virgin Mary, and become
man, and work many miracles, and preach and teach the faith
and the law of Christian men unto his children; and there
it pleased him to suffer many reprovings and scorns for us;
and he that was king of heaven, of air, of earth, of sea, and
of all things that are contained in them, would only be called
king of that land, when he said, "Rex sum Judeorum," that is
to say, I am king of the Jews; and that land he chose before
all other lands, as the best and most worthy land, and the most
virtuous land of all the world; for it is the heart and the
middle of all the world; by witness of the philosopher, who
saith thus "Virtus rerum in medio consistit :" that is to say,
The virtue of things is in the middle; and in that land he
would lead his life, and suffer passion and death from the
Jews for us, to redeem and deliver us from the pains of
hell and from death without end, which was ordained for us
for the sin of our first father Adam, and for our own sins also;
for, as for himself, he had deserved no evil: for he thought
never evil nor did evil, and he that was king of glory and
of joy might best in that place suffer death, because he
chose in that land, rather than in any other, to suffer his
passion and his death : for he that will publish any thing to
make it openly known, he will cause it to be cried and proclaimed in the middle place of a town; so that the thing that
is proclaimed and pronounced may equally reach to all parts :
right so, he that was creator of all the world would suffer for
us at Jerusalem, that is the middle of the world, to the end and
intent that his passion and his death, which was published

there, might be known equally to all parts of the world. See,
now, how dearly he bought man, that he made after his own
image, and how dearly he redeemed us for the great love that
he had to us, and we never deserved it of him. For more
precious goods or greater ransom might he not put for us,
than his blessed body, his precious blood, and his holy life,
which he enthralled for us; and he offered all for us, that never
did sin. Oh! dear God! what love had he to us his subjects,
when he that never trespassed would for trespassers suffer
death! Right well ought we to love and worship, to dread
and serve such a Lord, and to worship and praise such a holy
land, that brought forth such fruit, through which every man
is saved, unless it be his own fault. Well may that land be
called delectable and a fruitful land, that was made moist
with the precious blood of our Lord Jesus Christ; which is
the same land that our Lord promised us in heritage. And
in that land he would die, as seised * to leave it to us, his
children. Wherefore every good Christian man, that is of
power, and hath whereof, should labour with all his strength
to conquer our right heritage, and drive out all the unbelieving men. For we are called Christian men, after Christ
our father. And if we be right children of Christ, we ought
to claim the heritage that our father left us, and take it out
of heathen men's hands. But now pride, covetousness, and
envy have so inflamed the hearts of worldly lords, that they
are busier to disinherit their neighbours than to claim or
conquer their right heritage aforesaid. And the common
people, that would put their bodies and their goods to conquer our heritage, may not do it without the lords. For an
assembly of people without a chieftain, or a chief lord, is as
a flock of sheep without a shepherd; the which departeth and
disperseth, and know never whither to go. But would God, that
the temporal lords and all worldly lords were at good accord,
and with the common people would take this holy voyage over
the sea! Then I believe confidently, that, within a little time,
our right heritage aforesaid should be recovered and put in
the hands of the right heirs of Jesus Christ..

And forasmuch as it is long time past that there was no
general passage or voyage over the sea, and many men de-
siring to hear speak of the Holy Land, and have thereof great

* An allusion to the legal forms of conveying and bequeathing property in
the middle ages.

solace and comfort, I, John Maundeville, knight, albeit I be not worthy, who was born in England, in the town of Saint Albans, passed the sea in the year of our Lord Jesus Christ 1322, on the day of St. Michael; and hitherto have been a long time over the sea, and have seen and gone through many divers lands, and many provinces, and kingdoms, and isles, and have passed through Tartary, Persia, Ermony, (Armenia) the Little and the Great; through Lybia, Chaldea, and a great part of Ethiopia; through Amazonia, India the Less, and the Greater, a great part; and throughout many other isles that are about India; where dwell many divers folks, and of divers manners and laws, and of divers shapes of men. Of which lands and isles I shall speak more plainly hereafter. And I shall devise you some part of things that are there, when time shall be as it may best come to my mind; and especially for them that will and are in purpose to visit the holy city of Jerusalem, and the holy places that are thereabout. And I shall tell the way that they shall hold thither; for I have oftimes passed and ridden the way, with good company of many lords : God be thanked!

And ye shall understand that I have put this book out of Latin into French, and translated it again out of French into English, that every man of my nation may understand it; and that lords and knights and other noble and worthy men that know Latin but little, and have been beyond the sea, may know and understand, if I err from defect of memory, and may redress it and amend it. For things passed out of long time from a man's mind or from his sight turn soon into forgetting : because a man's mind may not be comprehended or withheld, on account of the frailty of mankind.

***

Chapter. I.

TO TEACH YOU THE WAY OUT OF ENGLAND TO CONSTANTINOPLE.

In the name of God, glorious and Almighty. He that will pass over the sea to go to the city of Jerusalem may go many ways, both by sea and land, according to the country that he cometh from : many ways come to one end. But you must not expect that I will tell you all the towns, and cities, and castles, that men shall go by; for then should I make too long a tale : but only some countries and the principal places that men shall go through to go the right way. First, if a man come from the west side of the world, as England, Ireland, Wales, Scotland, or Norway, he may, if he will, go through Almaine (Germany) and through the kingdom of Hungary, which borders on the land of Polaine (Poland), and to the land of Pannonia, and so to Silesia. And the king of Hungary is a great and mighty lord, and possesses great lordships and much land. For he holds the kingdom of Hungary, Sclavonia, and a great part of Comania and Bulgaria, which men call the land of Bougres, and the realm of Russia a great part, whereof he hath made a duchy, that extendeth unto the land of Nyflan, and borders on Prussia. And we go through the land of this lord, through a city that is called Cypron, and by the castle of Neaseborough, and by the evil town, which is situated towards the end of Hungary. And there men pass the river Danube, which is a very great river, and it goeth into Almaine, under the hills of Lombardy; and it receives forty other rivers, and runs through Hungary and through Greece and through Thrace, and entereth into the sea, towards the east, so roughly and so sharply, that the water of the sea is fresh and keeps its sweetness twenty miles from shore.

And after, men go to Belgrave, and enter the land of Bougres; and there men pass a bridge of stone, which is upon the river Marrok. And men pass through the land of Pyncemartz, and come to Greece to the city of Nye, and to the city of Fynepape, and after to the city of Adrianople, and then to Constantinople, which was formerly called Byzantium, where the emperor of Greece usually dwells. And there is the fairest and noblest church in the world, that of St. Sophia. And before the church is the image of the emperor Justinian, covered with gold, and he sits crowned upon a horse; and he formerly held a round apple of gold in his hand, but it is fallen down; and they say there, that it is a token that the emperor hath lost a great part of his lands and lordships. For he was emperor of Romania and of Greece, of all Asia the Less, and of the land of Syria, of the land of Judea, in which is Jerusalem, and of the land of Egypt, of Persia, and of Arabia; but he hath lost all but Greece; and men would many times restore the apple to the hand of the image, but it will not hold it. This apple betokens the lordship which he had over all the world, which is round; and the other hand he lifts up towards the east, in token to menace the misdoers. This image stands upon a pillar of marble at Constantinople.

CHAPTER II.

OF THE CROSS AND CROWN OF OUR LORD JESUS CHRIST.

AT Constantinople is the cross of our Lord Jesus Christ, and his coat without seams, and the sponge and the reed with which the Jews gave our Lord vinegar and gall on the cross; and there is one of the nails with which Christ was nailed on the cross. And some men believe that half the cross of our Lord is in Cyprus, in an abbey of monks called the Hill of the Holy Cross. But it is not so ; for the cross which is in Cyprus is that on which Dismas *, the good thief, was crucified: But all men know not that, and it is an evil act ; because, for profit of the offering, they say that it is the cross of our Lord Jesus Christ. And you shall understand that the cross of our Lord was made of four kinds of trees, as is contained in this verse—

"In cruce fit palma, cedrus, cypressus, oliva."

For the piece that went upright from the earth to the head was of cypress ; and the piece that went across, to which his hands were nailed, was of palm ; and the stock, that stood within the earth, in which was made the mortise, was of cedar ; and the tablet above his head, which was a foot and a half long, on which the title was written in Hebrew, Greek, and Latin, was of olive. And the Jews made the cross of these four kinds of trees, because they believed that our Lord Jesus Christ should have hanged on the cross as long as the cross might last ; and therefore they made the foot of the cross of cedar, because cedar may not rot in earth or water ; and they thought that it should have lasted long. And because they believed that the body of Christ should have stunk, therefore they made the piece that went from the earth upwards of cypress, for it is well smelling, so that the smell of his body should not grieve men that passed by. And the cross piece was of palm, because in the Old Testament it was ordained that when any one conquered, he should be crowned with palm ; and because they believed that they had the victory of Christ Jesus, therefore made they the cross-piece of

---

* Dismas and Jestes, or Jesmas, were, according to the vulgar legend, the names of the two thieves who were crucified at the same time with the Saviour, Dismas being the one who reproved his companion for his unbelief. Maundeville has introduced more of the popular superstitious and religious legends of the middle ages than the previous travellers.

palm. And the tablet of the title they made of olive, because olive betokens peace ; and the story of Noah witnesseth that when the dove brought the branch of olive, it betokened peace made between God and man ; and so the Jews expected to have peace when Christ was dead ; for they said that he made discord and strife amongst them. And you shall under-stand that our Lord was nailed on the cross in a recum-bent position, and therefore he suffered the more pain. And the Christians that dwell beyond the sea, in Greece, say that the tree of the cross that we call cypress was of that tree of which Adam ate the apple, and that they find written. And they say also, that their Scripture saith* that Adam was sick, and told his son Seth to go to the angel that kept Para-dise, to pray that he would send him oil of mercy to anoint his members with, that he might have health. And Seth went, but the angel would not let him come in, telling him that he might not have of the oil of mercy; but he gave him three grains of the same tree of which his father ate the apple, and bade him, as soon as his father was dead, that he should put these three grains under his tongue, and bury him so: and he did. And of these three grains sprung a tree, as the angel said that it should, and bore a fruit, through which fruit Adam should be saved. And when Seth came again, he found his father near dead. And when he was dead, he did with the grains as the angel bade him; of which sprung three trees, whereof the cross was made, that bare good fruit and blessed, namely, our Lord Jesus Christ, through whom Adam, and all that come of him, should be saved and de-livered from dread of death without end, unless it be by their own fault. The Jews had concealed this holy cross in the earth, under a rock of Mount Calvary; and it lay there two hundred years and more, till the time of St. Helena, the mother of Constantine, emperor of Rome. She was the daughter of king Coel, born in Colchester, who was king of England, which was then called Britain the Greater; the emperor Constantius took her to wife for her beauty, and had by her Constantine, who was afterwards emperor of Rome.

And you shall understand that the cross of our Lord was eight cubits long, and the cross-piece was three cubits and a

* See, on this popular legend, the editor's note on the "Chester Plays" (or Mysteries), vol. i. p. 239. It was derived from one of the apocryphal books of the eastern church.

half in length. And one part of the crown of our Lord,
wherewith he was crowned, and one of the nails, and the
spear-head, and many other relics, are in France, in the
king's chapel*, the crown being placed in a vessel of crystal
richly worked. For a king of France bought these relics
of the Jews, to whom the emperor had given them in pledge
for a great sum of silver. And if it be so, as men say, that
this crown is of thorns, you shall understand that it was of
rushes of the sea, which prick as sharply as thorns ; for I
have seen and beheld many times that of Paris and that
of Constantinople ; for they were both one, made of rushes
of the sea. But men had divided them in two parts ;
of which one part is at Paris, and the other part is at Constantinople. And I have one of these precious thorns, which
seems like a white thorn ; and it was given to me as a great
favour ; for there are many of them broken and fallen into
the vessel that the crown lieth in ; they break for dryness,
when men move it, to show it to great lords that come thither.

And you shall understand that our Lord Jesus, on the
night he was taken, was led into a garden, where he was first
examined very sharply ; and there the Jews scorned him, and
made him a crown of the branches of aubespine, or white
thorn, which grew in the same garden, and set it on his head,
so fast and so sore, that the blood ran down on many parts
of his face, neck, and shoulders. And therefore hath white
thorn many virtues ; for he that beareth a branch thereof
upon him, no thunder nor tempest may hurt him ; and no
evil spirit may enter in the house in which it is, or come to
the place that it is in. And in that same garden St. Peter
denied our Lord thrice. Afterward our Lord was led forth
before the bishops and the masters of the law, into another
garden belonging to Annas ; and there also he was examined,
reproved, and scorned, and crowned again with a white thorn,
which is called barbarines, which grew in that garden, and
which hath also many virtues. And afterward he was led
into a garden of Caiphas, and there he was crowned with
eglantine. And after he was led into the chamber of Pilate,
and there he was examined and crowned. And the Jews
set him in a chair, and clad him in a mantle ; and there they
made the crown of rushes of the sea ; and there they knelt

* The beautiful chapel built by St Louis, and now known as the Sainte
Chapelle.

to him, and scorned him, saying, "Hail, king of the Jews!"
Half of this crown is at Paris, and the other half at Constantinople. And Christ had this crown on his head when
he was placed on the cross; and therefore ought men to worship it, and hold it more worthy than any of the others. And
the emperor of Almaine possesses the spear-shaft, but the head
of the spear is at Paris. Yet the emperor of Constantinople
'saith that he hath the spear-head, and I have often seen it;
but it is greater than that at Paris.

CHAPTER III.

OF THE CITY OF CONSTANTINOPLE, AND OF THE FAITH OF THE GREEKS.

AT Constantinople lieth St. Anne, our Lady's mother, whom
St. Helena caused to be brought from Jerusalem. And there
lieth also the body of John Chrysostom, who was archbishop
of Constantinople. There lieth also St. Luke the Evangelist,
whose bones were brought from Bethany, where he was
buried. And many other relics are there. And there is the
vessel of stone, as it were of marble, which men call Enydros,
and which continually drops water, and fills itself every year,
till it run over, besides what men take from within. Constantinople is a very fair and good city, and well walled, and it is
three-cornered. There is an arm of the sea of Hellespont,
which some men call the mouth of Constantinople, and some
men call it the Brace (or arm) of St. George; and that arm
incloses two parts of the city. And upward to the sea, upon
the water, was wont to be the great city of Troy, in a very
fair plain; but that city was destroyed by the people of Greece,
and little thereof now appears, because it is so long since it
was destroyed.

About Greece there are many isles, as Calliste, Calcas,
Cetige, Tesbria, Mynea, Flaxon, Melo, Carpate, and Lemne.
In this latter isle is Mount Athos, that passeth the clouds.
And there are divers languages and many countries obedient
to the emperor, namely, Turcople, Pyneynard, Cornagne, and
many others, as 'Thrace and Macedonia, of which Alexander
was king. In this country was Aristotle born, in a city called
Stagyra, a little from the city of Thrace. And at Stagyra
Aristotle lieth; and there is an altar upon his tomb. And
they make great feasts for him ever year, as though he were
a saint. And at his altar they hold their great councils and

their assemblies, expecting that through inspiration of God and of him they shall have the better council. In this country are very high hills, toward the extremity of Macedonia. And there is a great hill, called Olympus, which divides Macedonia and Thrace, so high that it passeth the clouds. And there is another hill, called Athos, so high that the shadow of it reaches to Lemne*, which is an island seventy-six miles distant. At the summit of this hill the air is so clear, that no wind is found there, and therefore no animal may live there; and the air is dry. And men say in those countries, that philosophers once went upon those hills, and held to their nose a sponge moistened with water, to have air, because the air above was so dry; and at the summit, in the dust of those hills, they wrote letters and figures with their fingers, and at the year's end they came again, and found the same letters and figures which they had written the year before, without any change. And therefore it appears evident that these hills pass the clouds and join to the pure air.

At Constantinople is the palace of the emperor, very handsome and well built; and therein is a fair place for joustings, or for other plays and sports. And it is made with stages, and hath steps about, that every man may see well, and not intercept the view of those behind. And under these stages are stables well vaulted for the emperor's horses; and all the pillars are of marble. And within the church of St. Sophia, an emperor once would have buried the body of his father when he was dead; and, as they made the grave, they found a body in the earth, and upon the body lay a fine plate of gold, on which was written in Hebrew, Greek, and Latin, letters that said thus, "Jesus Christ shall be born of the Virgin Mary, and I believe in him." And the date when it was laid in the earth was two thousand years before our Lord was born. The plate of gold is still preserved in the treasury of the church. And they say that it was Hermogenes, the wise man.

Although the men of Greece are Christians, yet they vary from our faith; for they say that the Holy Ghost may not come of the Son, but only of the Father. And they are not obedient to the Church of Rome, nor to the pope; for they say that their patriarch hath as much power over the sea as the pope hath on this side the sea. And therefore pope

---

* There is an old Greek iambic to this effect:—" Ἄθως καλύπτει πλευρά Λιμνίας βοός.

John XXII. sent letters to them, how Christian faith should
be all one, and that they should be obedient to the pope, who
is God's vicar on earth, to whom God gave his full power to
bind and to assoil, and therefore they should be obedient to
him. But they sent back divers answers, amongst others
saying thus: " We believe well that thy power is great upon
thy subjects. We may not suffer thy great pride. We are
not in purpose to fulfil thy great covetousness. The Lord
be with thee; for our Lord is with us.—Farewell." And no
other answer might he have of them. They make their sacrament of the altar of unleavened bread, because our Lord
made it of such bread when he made his Maundy*. And on
Shere-Thursday they make their unleavened bread, in token
of the Maundy, and dry it in the sun, and keep it all the
year, and give it to sick men instead of God's body. And they
make but one unction when they christen children. They
anoint not the sick. And they say that there is no purga-
tory, and that the souls shall have neither joy nor pain till
the day of doom. They say, moreover, that fornication is not
a deadly sin, but a thing that is according to nature ; and that
men and women should wed but once ; and whosoever weddeth
oftener than once, their children are bastards, and begotten
in sin. Their priests also are wedded. They say, also, that
usury is no deadly sin; and they sell benefices of holy
church; and so do men in other places, (God amend it when
his will is!) and that is a great scandal ; for now is simony
king crowned in holy church: God amend it for his mercy!
And they say that in Lent men shall not fast, or sing mass,
except on the Saturday and on the Sunday. And they fast
not on the Saturdays, except it be Christmas Eve, or Easter
Eve. They suffer not the Latins to sing at their altars; and
if they do by any chance, they immediately wash the altar
with holy water. And they say, that there should be but one
mass said at one altar upon one day. They say also that our
Lord never ate, but that he made sign of eating. They
say, moreover, that we sin deadly in shaving our beards ; for
the beard is token of a man, and the gift of our Lord. And
they say that we sin deadly in eating of animals that were

* Maundy-Thursday is the day of Christ's commandment on instituting
the Lord's Supper, the Thursday before Easter. It was also called Shere-
Thursday. The ceremony observed on the day was called holding or making
the Maundy.

forbidden in the Old Testament and by the old law, as swine, hares, and other beasts that chew not their cud. And they say that we sin in eating flesh on the days before Ash Wednesday, and in eating flesh on the Wednesday, and eggs and cheese on the Fridays. And they curse all those who abstain from eating flesh on the Saturday. The emperor of Constantinople appoints the patriarch, the archbishops, and the bishops, and gives the dignities and the benefices of churches, and deprives those who deserve it, when he finds any cause; and so is he lord both temporal and spiritual in his country*.

And although these things touch not to our way, nevertheless they touch to that that I have promised you, to show you a part of the customs, and manners, and diversities of countries. And because this is the first country that is discordant in faith and in belief, and varies from our faith on this side the sea, therefore I have set it here, that you may know the diversity that is between our faith and theirs. For many men have great liking to hear of strange things of diverse countries.

CHAPTER IV.

OF THE WAY FROM CONSTANTINOPLE TO JERUSALEM.—OF ST. JOHN THE EVANGELIST, AND OF THE DAUGHTER OF YPOCRAS, TRANSFORMED FROM A WOMAN TO A DRAGON.

Now return I again to explain to you the way from Constantinople to Jerusalem. He that will proceed through Turkey, goes towards the city of Nice, and passes through the gate of Chienetout, and men see constantly before them the hill of Chienetout, which is very lofty: it is a mile and a half from Nice. And if you will go by water, by the Brace of St. George, and by the sea where St. Nicholas lieth, and towards many other places, first, you go to an isle that is called Sylo, in which mastic grows on small trees, out of which comes gum, as it were of plum-trees, or of cherry-trees. And after men go by the isle of Patmos, where St. John the Evangelist wrote the Apocalypse. And you shall understand that St. John was thirty-two years of age when our Lord suffered his passion, and after his

* The period during which Maundeville was in the east was that when the question of reuniting the Greek and Latin churches was in agitation, which is probably the cause he enters so largely into their differences of belief.

passion he lived sixty-seven years, and in the hundredth year of his age he died. From Patmos men go to Ephesus, a fair city, and nigh to the sea. And there died St. John, and was buried in a tomb behind the high altar. And there is a fair church, for the Christians were always wont to hold that place. And in the tomb of St. John is nothing but manna, which is called angels' meat, for his body was translated into Paradise. And the Turks now hold all that place, with the city, and the church; and all Asia the Less is called Turkey. And you shall understand that St. John caused his grave to be made there in his life, and laid himself therein, all alive; and, therefore, some men say that he did not die, but that he rests there till the day of doom*. And, in truth, there is a great marvel, for men may see there the earth of the tomb many times openly stir and move, as though there were living things under.

And from Ephesus we go through many islands in the sea to the city of Patera, where St. Nicholas was born, and so to Myra, where he was chosen to be bishop; and there grows very good and strong wine, which they call wine of Myra. And from thence men go to the isle of Crete, which the emperor once gave to the Genoese. And then we pass through the isles of Colos and of Lango†, of the which isles Ypocras was lord; and some men say, that in the isle of Lango is still the daughter of Ypocras, in form and likeness of a great dragon, which is a hundred fathoms in length, as they say, for I have not seen her. And they of the isles call her lady of the land. And she lies in an old castle, in a cave, and appears twice or thrice in the year; and she doth no harm to any man unless he do her harm. She was thus changed and transformed from a fair damsel into the likeness of a dragon by a goddess named Diana; and they say that she shall remain in that form until the time that a knight come, who shall be so bold that he dare come to her and kiss her on the mouth; and then she shall turn again

---

* Long before our author's time, the text, in John xxi. 22, 23, in the vulgar Latin, happened to be changed in favour of this notion; for Jesus' answer to Peter's question about John, "Lord, and what shall this man do?" is there, "Sic eum volo manere donec veniam," the conjunction *si* being dropped, by means of *sic* following.

† Lango is but another name of the isle of Cos, where Hippocrates, (commonly called by the medieval writers Ypocras,) the famous physician, was born. See before, p. 33.

to her own nature, and be a woman again, but after that she
shall not live long.   And it is not long since a knight of
Rhodes, who was bold and doughty in arms, said that he
would kiss her; when he was upon his courser and went to
the castle, and entered into the cave, the dragon lifted up
her head towards him, and when the knight saw her in that
form, so hideous and horrible, he fled away.   But the dragon
carried the knight upon a rock, and from thence she cast
him into the sea, and so was lost both horse and man.   A
young man that knew not of the dragon, went out of a ship,
and proceeded through the isle until he came to the castle
and entered the cave, and went so far that he found a
chamber; and there he saw a damsel who was combing her
head and looking in a mirror, and she had much treasure
about her, and he believed that she had been a common
woman, who dwelled there to receive men to folly; and he
abode till the damsel saw the shadow of him in the mirror,
and she turned her towards him and asked him, what he
would?   And he said, he would be her paramour.   And she
asked him if he were a knight?   And he said, nay.   And
then she said, that he might not be her leman; but she
bid him go again unto his fellows and get him knighted, and
come again upon the morrow, and she would come out of the
cave before him; and then he should come and kiss her on
the mouth, and have no fear, "for I shall do thee no harm,
although thou see me in likeness of a dragon; for though
thou see me hideous and horrible to look upon, know that it
is made by enchantment.   For without doubt I am no other
than thou seest now, a woman, and therefore fear not; and
if thou kiss me, thou shalt have all this treasure, and be my
lord, and lord also of all the isle."   And he departed from
her and went to his fellows, in the ship, and was made a
knight, and returned on the morrow to kiss this damsel.
But when he saw her come out of the cave, in form of a
dragon, so hideous and so horrible, he had so great fear that
he fled again to the ship; and she followed him.   And when
she saw that he turned not again, she began to cry as a thing
that had much sorrow, and then she returned to her cave;
and anon the knight died.   And from that time to this
might no knight see her, but he died anon.   But when there
shall come a knight who is bold enough to kiss her, he shall
not die; but he shall turn the damsel into her right form

and natural shape, and he shall be lord of all the countries and isles abovesaid.

And from thence men come to the isle of Rhodes, which isle the Hospitalers* hold and govern, having on a time taken it from the emperor. It was formerly called Collos, and so the Turks call it still; and St. Paul, in his Epistles, writes to the people of this isle, *ad Colossenses*†. This isle is nearly eight hundred miles from Constantinople.

From this isle of Rhodes we go to Cyprus, where are many vines, which first produce red wine, and after one year they become white; and those wines that are most white are the clearest and best of smell. And men pass that way by a place which was a great city and a great land; and the city was called Sathalie. This city and the land were lost through the folly of a young man, who had a fair damsel whom he loved well for his paramour, and she died suddenly and was placed in a tomb of marble; and for the great love that he had to her, he went in the night to her tomb, and opened it and went in. And when it came to the end of nine months, there came a voice to him, and said, "Go to the tomb of that woman, and open it, and behold what thou hast begotten on her; and if thou omittest to go, thou shalt have a great harm. And he went and opened the tomb; and there came out a snake, very hideous to behold, which immediately flew about the city and the country, and soon after the city was swallowed up‡. And there are many perilous passages.

From Rhodes to Cyprus are five hundred miles and more; but we may go to Cyprus without touching at Rhodes. Cyprus

---

* The two orders, the Templars and Hospitalers, having been expelled from Palestine by the Mohammedans, on the capture of Acre in 1291, the first retired to Cyprus; but in 1310 the Hospitalers made themselves masters of the isle of Rhodes, which became the chief place of the order until it was taken by the Turks, on the 1st of January, 1523, when they removed to Malta.

† See before, p. 33 of the present volume, where the same blunder is made by Sæwulf.

‡ This story, or one very similar to it, is found in the chronicle of John of Brompton. The bay of Satalia was notoriously dangerous to navigators, who attempted to account for it by legends like these. We have already seen an earlier traveller, Sæwulf, narrowly escape shipwreck in passing it (p. 49). John of Brompton gives two legends to account for the stormy character of the bay, according to one of which the head of the monster alluded to in the text lay at the bottom; and when it was turned with the face upwards, this position caused a perilous tempest.

is a very good, fair, and great island, and it hath four principal cities, with an archbishop at Nicosia, and four other bishops; and at Famagosta is one of the first harbours of the sea in the world; and there arrive Christians, Saracens, and men of all nations. In Cyprus is the hill of the Holy Cross, where there is an abbey of black monks, and there is the cross of Dismas, the good thief, as I have said before. And some men believe that there is half of the cross of our Lord; but it is not so, and they do wrong who make people believe so. In Cyprus lies St. Zenomyne, of whom men of that country make great solemnity; and in the castle of Amours lies the body of St. Hilary, which they keep very worshipfully. Near Famagosta St. Barnabas the apostle was born. In Cyprus they hunt with papyons *, which resemble leopards, and they take wild beasts right well, and they are somewhat larger than lions, and take more sharply and more cleverly than hounds do. In Cyprus it is the custom for lords and all other men to eat on the earth; for they make trenches in the earth about in the hall, deep to the knee, and pave them; and when they will eat, they go therein and sit there. And the reason is that they may be cooler; for that land is much hotter than it is here. And at great feasts, and for strangers, they set forms and tables as men do in this country; but they themselves prefer sitting on the earth.

From Cyprus they go to the land of Jerusalem by sea, and in a day and night he that hath good wind may come to the haven of Tyre, which is now called Sur. Here was once a great and good city of the Christians; but the Saracens have destroyed it in great part; and they guard that haven carefully for fear of the Christians. Men might go more direct to that haven, without touching at Cyprus; but they go gladly to Cyprus, to rest them in the land, or to buy things that they need for their living. On the sea-side many rubies are found. There is the well of which Holy Writ speaketh, saying, " A fountain of gardens, and a well of living waters."† It was in this city of Tyre that the woman said to our Lord, " Blessed is the womb that bare thee, and the paps which thou hast

---

* These were a kind of large wild dogs. Jacobus de Vitriaco ("Hist. Orient.," lib. iii.), speaking of the animals of Judea, says, " Sunt ibi cameli et bubali abundanter, et *papiones* quos appellant, canes silvestres, acriores quam lupi."

† Song of Solomon, iv. 15.

sucked."* And there our Lord forgave the woman of Canaan
her sins. And before Tyre stood formerly the stone on which
our Lord sat and preached, and over which was built the
church of St. Saviour.

Eight miles from Tyre, towards the east, upon the sea, is
the city of Sarphen, in Sarept of the Sidonians. There dwelt
Elijah the prophet, and he raised there Jonas, the widow's
son, from death to life. And five miles from Sarphen is the
city of Sidon, of which Dido was lady, who was wife of Eneas,
after the destruction of Troy, and who founded the city of
Carthage in Africa, and now it is called Didon Sayete. And in
the city of Tyre reigned Agenor, the father of Dido. Sixteen
miles from Sidon is Beruthe (Beirut); and from Beruthe to
Sardenare is three days. And from Sardenare it is five miles
to Damascus.

And those who are willing to go a long time on the sea, and
come nearer to Jerusalem, may proceed from Cyprus by sea
to the port of Jaffa, for that is the nearest port to Jerusalem,
the distance being only one day and a half. The town is called
Jaffa, because one of the sons of Noah, named Japhet, founded
it, and now it is called Joppa. And you shall understand that
it is one of the oldest towns of the world, for it was founded
before Noah's flood. And there may still be seen in the rock
there the place where the iron chains were fastened, wherewith Andromeda, a great giant, was bound and put in prison,
before Noah's flood; a rib of whose side, which is forty feet
long, is still shown †.

And those who go to the port of Tyre or Sur, before
mentioned, may proceed by land, if they will, to Jerusalem.
They go from Sur in a day to the city of Akoun (Acre), which
was called formerly Ptolemais, and it was once a very fine city of
Christians ; but it is now destroyed. It stands upon the sea.
From Venice to Akoun, by sea, is two thousand and eighty
Lombard miles. From Calabria, or from Sicily to Akoun,
by sea, is thirteen hundred Lombard miles. And the Isle
of Crete is just midway. Near the city of Akoun, toward
the sea, one hundred and twenty furlongs on the right,
toward the south, is the hill of Carmel, where Elijah the

---

* Luke, xi. 27.

† Our author has picked up a strange version of the classic story of Perseus
and Andromeda, and has even mistaken Andromeda for the monster that was
to have devoured her. The mark of the chain is mentioned by Solinus.

prophet dwelt, and where the order of friars Carmelites was first founded.   This hill is not very great, nor very high.   At the foot of this hill was formerly a good city of the Christians called Caiphas, because Caiaphas first founded it; but it is now all waste.   And on the left side of the hill of Carmel is a town called Saffre, which is situated on another hill.   There St. James and St. John were born, and there is a fair church in honour of them.   And from Ptolemais, which is now called Akoun, it is one hundred furlongs to a great hill, called the scale (or ladder) of Tyre.   And near the city of Akoun runs a little river called Belon ; and there nigh is the foss of Memnon, which is all round; and it is one hundred cubits broad, and all full of gravel, shining bright, of which men make fair and clear glasses *.   Men come from far, by water with ships, and by land with carts, to fetch of that gravel ; and though ever so much be taken away thereof one day, on the morrow it is as full again as ever it was.   And that is a great wonder. And there is always great wind in that foss, that continually stirs the gravel and makes it troubled ; and if any man put therein any kind of metal, it turns to glass, and the glass made of that gravel, if it be thrown back into the gravel, turns to gravel as it was first ; and therefore some men say that it is a whirlpool of the gravelly sea.

From Akoun, above mentioned, it is four days' journey to the city of Palestine, which was of the Philistines, now called Gaza, which is a gay and rich city; and it is very fair, and full of people, and is at a little distance from the sea.   From this city Samson the strong brought the gates upon a high land, when he was taken in that city : and there he slew, in a palace, the king and himself, and great numbers of the best of the Philistines, who had put out his eyes, and shaved his head, and imprisoned him, by treason of Delilah, his paramour. And therefore he caused a great hall to fall upon them when they were at meat.   From thence we go to the city of Cesarea, and so to the Castle of Pilgrims, and so to Ascalon, and then to Jaffa, and so to Jerusalem.

* A similar description is found in Geoffrey de Vinsauf (Itin. Reg. Ric. I. lib. i. c. 32), who, however, states that it is a mere story taken from So-linus, and he does not assert that there was such a foss in his time.   It may be further observed that Maundeville has fallen into another blunder in confounding the foss alluded to with the pretended sepulchre of Memnon.

CHAPTER V.

OF MANY NAMES OF SULTANS, AND OF THE TOWER OF BABYLON.

AND he who will go by land through the land of Babylonia, where the sultan dwells commonly, he must get leave and grace of him, to go more safely through the lands and countries. And to go to the Mount of Sinai, before men go to Jerusalem, they shall go from Gaza to the castle of Daire. And after that, they come out of Syria and enter a wilderness where the way is sandy; and that wilderness and desert lasts eight days. But men always find good inns and all they need of victuals. And that wilderness is called Athylec. And when a man comes out of that desert, he enters into Egypt, which is called Egypt Canopac: and after other language, men call it Morsyn. And there men first find a good town, called Belethe, which is at the end of the kingdom of Aleppo; and from thence men go to Babylon and to Cairo.

At Babylon there is a fair church of our Lady, where she dwelt seven years, when she fled out of the land of Judea for dread of king Herod. And there lieth the body of St. Barbara, the virgin and martyr. And there dwelt Joseph after he was sold by his brethren. And there * Nebuchadnezzar, the king, caused the three children to be thrown into the furnace of fire because they were in the true belief; which children were called Hananiah, Azariah, Mishael, as the psalm of *Benedicite* says. But Nebuchadnezzar called them otherwise, Shadrach, Meshach, and Abednego, that is to say, God glorious, God victorious, and God over all things and realms, on account of the miracle, that he saw God's Son go with the children through the fire, as he said. The sultan dwells in his Calahelyke (for there is commonly his residence), in a fair castle, strong and great, and well set upon a rock. In that castle dwell always, to keep it and to serve the sultan, more than 6000 persons, who receive here all necessaries from the sultan's court. I ought to know it well, for I dwelt a great while with him as soldier in his wars against the Bedouins; and he would have married me full highly to a great prince's daughter if I would have forsaken my law and my belief. But I thank God I had no will to do it for anything that he promised me. And you shall understand that the

---

* It is curious that Maundeville should thus confound Babylon of Chaldea with Babylon of Egypt.

sultan is lord of five kingdoms, that he hath conquered and
taken possession of by strength; and these are their names:
the kingdom of Canopac, that is Egypt; and the kingdom of
Jerusalem, where David and Solomon were kings; and the
kingdom of Syria, of which the city of Damascus was chief;
and the kingdom of Aleppo, in the land of Mathe; and the
kingdom of Arabia, that belonged to one of the three kings
who made offering to our Lord when he was born. And he holds
many other lands in his hand. And therewithal he holds
khalifs, which is a full great thing in their language, being as
much as to say, kings. And there were wont to be five sultans,
but now there is no more but he of Egypt.   The first sultan
was Sarocon *, who was of Media (the father of Saladin), who
took the khalif of Egypt and slew him, and was made sultan
by strength.   After him was sultan Saladin, in whose time
the king of England, Richard I., with many others, kept the
passage, that Saladin might not pass. After Saladin, reigned
his son Boradin; and after him his nephew.   After that the
Comanians, who were in slavery in Egypt, feeling themselves
of great power, chose them a sultan amongst them, who took
the name of Melechesalan, in whose time St. Louis, king of
France, entered into the country and fought with him; and
the sultan took him prisoner.   This sultan was slain by his
own servants.   And after, they chose another to be sultan,
who was called Tympieman: he delivered St. Louis out of
prison for a certain ransom.   After him one of the Comanians
reigned, named Cachas, and slew Tympieman, in order to be
sultan; he took the name of Melechemes.   He was succeeded
by one named Bendochdare, who slew Melechemes to be
sultan, and called himself Melechdare.   In his time the good
king Edward of England entered into Syria, and did great
harm to the Saracens. This sultan was poisoned at Damascus;
and his son thought to reign after him by heritage, and took
the name of Melechsache; but another, named Elphy, drove
him out of the country, and made himself sultan.   This man
took the city of Tripoli, and destroyed many of the Christian

---

* Sirkouk, or Siracon, was the vizir of Noureddin, sultan of Aleppo, and
was uncle, not father, of Saladin.   He dethroned the last Fatimite khalif of
Egypt, and brought that country under the power of the sultans, which was
soon after usurped by Saladin, who reigned from 1173 to 1193.   The other
sultans mentioned by Maundeville may easily be identified by a reference to
the ordinary histories.

men, in the year of Grace 1289; but he was soon after slain. Elphy's son succeeded as sultan, and took the name of Melechasseraff; he took the city of Acre, and expelled the Christians; and he also was poisoned, upon which his brother was made sultan, and called Melechnasser. And after, one who was called Guytoga took him and threw him into prison in the castle of Mount Royal, and usurped the sovereignty by force, and took the name of Melechcadelle; and he was a Tartar. But the Comanians drove him out of the country, and caused him much sorrow; and made one of themselves sultan, named Lachyn, who assumed the name of Melechmanser. One day he was playing at chess, and his sword lay beside him, and it befel that one angered him, and he was slain with his own sword. After that there was great discord before they could choose a sultan, and finally they agreed to take Melechnasser, whom Guytoga had put in prison at Mount Royal. He reigned long and governed wisely; so that his eldest son, Melechemader, was chosen after him; he was secretly put to death by his brother, who succeeded him, and was called Melechmadabron. And he was sultan when I departed from that country *.

Now you must know that the sultan can lead out of Egypt more than 20,000 men of arms; and out of Syria, and Turkey, and other countries that he holds, he may raise more than 50,000. And all these are at his wages; and they are always ready, besides the people of his country, who are without number. And each of them has six score florins by the year; but he is expected to keep three horses and a camel. And in the cities and towns are admirals, that have the government of the people. One has four to govern, another five, another more, and another a much greater number. And the admiral, himself alone, receives as much as all the other soldiers under him. And therefore, when the sultan will advance any worthy knight, he makes him an admiral. When there is dearth, the knights are very poor, and then they sell both their horses and their harness. The sultan has four wives, one Christian, and three Saracens; of whom one dwells at Jerusalem, another at Damascus, and another at Ascalon.

* This was the sultan Koutchouc-Ascraf, who was chosen successor to his brother in 1341, and, after reigning about six months, was deposed on the 11th of January, 1342. This fixes Maundeville's departure from Egypt to the latter months of the year 1341.

And when they please they remove to other cities ; and when the sultan will he may go and visit them. And he has as many paramours as he pleases ; for he causes to be brought before him the fairest and noblest damsels of his country, who are kept and served full honourably, and when he will have one to lie with him, he makes them all come before him, and looks at them all to see which is most to his liking, and to her anon he sends or throws a ring from his finger ; and then anon she shall be bathed and richly attired, and anointed with delicate things of sweet smell, and then led to the sultan's chamber.   And thus he acts as often as he likes, when he will have any of them.   No stranger comes before the sultan without being clothed in cloth of gold, or of Tartary, or of Camaka, in the Saracens' guise, and according to the usage of the Saracens.   And when men see the sultan for the first time, be it at the window, or in any other place, they must kneel to him and kiss the earth, for that is the manner for those who speak with the sultan to do reverence to him.   When messengers of foreign countries come before him, the sultan's people, when the strangers speak to him, stand round the sultan with drawn swords and gysarmes and axes, their arms raised up on high with their weapons, to smite them, if they say any word that is displeasing to the sultan.   Neither does any stranger come before him without receiving a promise and grant of what he asks reasonably, if it be not against his law ; and so do other princes beyond. For they say that no man should come before a prince without being the better, and departing from his presence in greater gladness than when he came before him.

You must understand that the Babylon of which I have spoken, where the sultan dwells, is not that great Babylon where the diversity of languages was first made by the miracle of God when the great tower of Babel was begun, of which the walls were sixty-four furlongs high; for that is in the great deserts of Arabia, on the way as men go toward the kingdom of Chaldea.   But it is full long since any man dare approach to the tower; for it is all desert and full of dragons and great serpents, and infested by divers venomous beasts. That tower, with the city, was twenty-five miles in the circuit of the walls, as they of the country say, and as men may judge by estimation, according to what men of the country tell.   And though it is called the tower of Babylon, yet there were ordained within it many mansions and great dwelling-places, in length and breadth; and it included an extensive district, for the tower alone was ten miles square. That tower was founded by king Nimrod, who was king of that country, and he was the first king in the world. He caused an image to be made in the likeness of his father, and obliged all his subjects to worship it, in imitation of which other lords begun to do the same, and this was the commencement of idols and simulacres * The town and city were situated in a fair country on a plain, which they call the country of Samar: the walls of the city were two hundred cubits in height, and fifty cubits in breadth. The river Euphrates ran through the city and about the tower; but Cyrus, king of Persia, took from them the river, and destroyed all the city and the tower also, for he divided the river into three hundred and sixty small rivers, because he had sworn that he would put the river in such point that a woman might easily pass it without taking up her clothes; because he had lost many worthy men that tried to pass the river by swimming †. And from Babylon, where the sultan dwells, to go right between the east and the north, towards the great Babylon, it is forty days across the desert. But the great Babylon is not in the land and power of the said sultan, but in the power and lordship of the king of Persia, who holds it of the great chan, who is the greatest emperor and the most sovereign lord of all the parts beyond; and he is lord of the isles of Cathay and of many other isles, and of a great part of India. His land borders unto Prester John's land; and he possesses so much land, that he knoweth not the end of it. And he is a mightier and greater lord without comparison than the sultan. I shall speak more fully of his royal estate and of his might when I treat of India.

The city of Mechon (Mecca), where Mohammed is buried, is also in the great desert of Arabia. His body lies there very honourably in their temple, which the Saracens call mosque. It is from Babylon the Less, where the sultan dwells, to Mechon, about thirty-two days. The realm of Arabia is a very great country; but therein is over much desert, and no man may dwell there in that desert, for want of water, because the land is all gravelly and full of sand. And it is

---

* See Maundeville's explanation of this word in a subsequent chapter.

† This account of Babylon is taken chiefly from Pliny and the ancient geographers.

dry and entirely barren, because it hath no moisture, and
therefore is there so much desert.   And if it had rivers and
wells, and the land were as in other parts, it would be as full
of people and as well inhabited as in other places.   For
there is a great multitude of people wherever the land is
inhabited.   Arabia reaches from the borders of Chaldea to
the extremity of Africa, and borders on the land of Idumea,
towards the end of Botron.   And in Chaldea the chief city is
Baldak *.   The chief city of Africa is Carthage, which Dido,
who was Eneas's wife, founded.   Mesopotamia stretches also
unto the deserts of Arabia; it is an extensive country, and in
it is the city of Haran, where Abraham's father dwelt, and
from whence Abraham departed by command of the angel †.
And of that city was Ephraem ‡, who was a celebrated scholar.
Theophilus was also of that city, whom our Lady saved from
the evil one §.   Mesopotamia reaches from the river Euphrates to the river Tigris, lying between those two rivers;
and beyond the Tigris is Chaldea, which is a very extensive
kingdom.   In that realm, at Baldak abovesaid, the khalifs
formerly dwelt, who were both as emperors and popes of
the Arabians, lords spiritual and temporal.   They were the
successors of Mohammed, from whom they were descended.
The city of Baldak was formerly called Sutis ||, and was
founded by Nebuchadnezzar.   There dwelt the holy prophet
Daniel, and there he saw visions öf heaven, and there he
made the exposition of dreams ¶.   There were formerly three
khalifs, and they dwelt in the city of Baldak abovesaid.

The khalif of Egypt dwelt at Cairo, beside Babylon; and at
Marrok, on the west sea, dwelt the khalif of the Barbarians **
and Africans.   But there are now none of the khalifs, nor
have there been any since the time of the sultan Saladin,
since which the sultan calls himself the khalif, and thus the
khalifs have lost their name.   You must know that Babylon
the Less, where the sultan dwells, and the city of Cairo, which

* Bagdad.   † Gen. xii. 1.   ‡ Ephraem Cyrus.
§ The legend of Theophilus, who sold himself to the evil one, and then
repented, and was saved from the devil by the Virgin Mary, was a popular
one in the Middle Ages.   See Jubinal's Rutebeuf, vol. ii. pages 79 and 260.
He is commonly said to have lived at Adana, in Cilicia.
|| Susa.
¶ A spurious book, purporting to be the exposition of dreams compiled by
the prophet Daniel, was very popular in the middle ages, and is the work
here alluded to.
** i. e. The people of Barbary.

is near it, are great and fair cities, the one nearly adjacent to
the other. Babylon is situated on the river Gyson, sometimes called the Nile, which comes out of terrestrial Paradise,
The river Nile, every year, when the sun enters the sign of
Cancer, begins to increase, and continues increasing as long
as the sun is in Cancer and in Leo. And it increases to
such a degree, that it is sometimes twenty cubits or more
deep, and then it does great harm to the goods that are upon
the land; for then no man can till the earth on account of
its great moistness, and therefore there is dear time in that
country. And also, when it increaseth little, it is dear time
in that country, for want of moisture. And when the sun
is in the sign of Virgo, then begins the river to wane and
decrease gradually, so that when the sun is entered into the
sign of Libra, then they enter between these rivers. This
river comes from terrestrial Paradise, between the deserts of
India; and after it descends on the earth, and runs through
many extensive countries under earth; and after it comes out
under a high hill, which they call Alothe, between India and
Ethiopia, at a distance of five months' journey from the
entrance of Ethiopia; and after it environs all Ethiopia and
Mauritania, and goes all along from the land of Egypt, to the
city of Alexandria, to the end of Egypt, where it falls into the
sea. About this river are many birds and fowls, as storks,
which they call ibes.

Egypt is a long country, but it is narrow, because they
may not enlarge it towards the desert for want of water.
And the country is situated along the river Nile; so that
that river may serve by floods or otherwise, that when it flows
it may spread abroad through the country. For it raineth
but little in that country, and for that cause they have no
water, unless it be by the overflowing of that river. And as it
does not rain, the air is always pure and clear; therefore, in that
country are good astronomers, for they find there no clouds to
obstruct them.

The city of Cairo is very great, more extensive than that
of Babylon the Less; and it is situated above towards the
desert of Syria, a little above the river aforesaid. In Egypt
there are two parts; Upper Egypt, which is towards Ethiopia, and Lower Egypt, which is towards Arabia. In Egypt
is the land of Rameses and the land of Goshen. Egypt is
a strong country, for it has many dangerous havens, because
of the great rocks, that are strong and dangerous to pass by.

Towards the east of Egypt is the Red Sea, which extends to the city of Coston; and towards the west is the country of Lybia, which is a very dry land, and unfruitful, on account of the excess of heat. And that land is called Fusthe. And towards the south is Ethiopia. And towards the north is the desert, which extends to Syria. Thus the country is strong on all sides. And it is full fifteen days' journey in length, and more than twice as much of desert, and it is but two days in breadth. Between Egypt and Nubia there is full twelve days of desert. The men of Nubia are Christians, but they are black, like the Moors, on account of the great heat of the sun.

In Egypt there are five provinces: one is called Sahythe; the other, Demeseer; another, Resithe *, which is an isle in the Nile; another, Alexandria; and another, the land of Damiette. This latter city was once very strong, but it was twice taken by the Christians, and therefore the Saracens have beaten down the walls. And with the walls and the tower thereof the Saracens made another city farther from the sea, and called it New Damiette, so that now the older town of Damiette is uninhabited. That city of Damiette is one of the havens of Egypt, and at Alexandria is the other. This is a very strong city; but it has no water except what is brought by conduit from the Nile, which enters into their cisterns; and if any one stopped that water from them they could not hold out a siege. In Egypt there are but few forts or castles, because the country is so strong of itself.

In Egypt is the city of Heliopolis, that is to say, the city of the Sun, in which there is a temple, made round, after the shape of the temple of Jerusalem. The priests of that temple have all their writings dated by the bird called Phœnix, of which there is but one in the world. It comes to burn itself on the altar of the temple at the end of five hundred years, for so long it lives; and then the priests array their altar, and put thereon spices, and sulphur, and other things that will burn quickly, and the Phœnix comes and burns itself to ashes. The next day they find in the ashes a worm; and the second day after they find a bird, alive and perfect; and the third day it flies away†. This

---

* Rosetta.

† This account of the Phœnix is taken from Pliny's Natural History, x. 2, and xi. 37. The legend of the Phœnix was a very favourite one throughout the middle ages.

bird is often seen flying in those countries; it is somewhat
larger than an eagle, and has a crest of feathers on its
head greater than that of a peacock; its neck is yellow, its beak blue, and its wings of a purple colour, and
the tail is yellow and red. It is a very handsome bird to
look at against the sun, for it shines very gloriously and
nobly.

Also, in Egypt, there are gardens with trees and herbs
which bear fruit seven times in the year. And in that land
abundance of fair emeralds are found, which are on that account
cheaper than elsewhere. When it rains, once in the summer, in the land of Egypt, the country is all full of great
mires. At Cairo they sell commonly in the market, as we
do beasts, both men and women of a different religion. And
there is a common house in that city, which is all full of
small furnaces, to which the townswomen bring their eggs of
hens, geese, and ducks, to be put into the furnaces; and they
that keep that house cover them with horse-dung, without
hen, goose, or duck, or any other fowl, and at the end of
three weeks or a month they come again and take their
chickens, and nourish them and bring them forth, so that
all the country is full of them. And this they do there
both winter and summer.

In that country also, and in some others, are found long
apples in their season, which they call apples of Paradise;
and they are very sweet and of good savour. And though
you cut them in ever so many slices or parts, across or end-
wise, you will always find in the middle the figure of the holy
cross. But they will rot within eight days, for which reason
they cannot be carried to far countries. They have great
leaves, a foot and a half long, and proportionately broad.
They find there also the apple-tree of Adam, the fruit of
which has a bite on one side. And there are also fig-trees
which bear no leaves, but figs grow upon the small branches;
and men call them figs of Pharoah. Also near Cairo is the field
where balm grows: it comes out on small trees, that are no
higher than the girdle of a man's breeches, and resemble the
wood of the wild vine. And in that field are seven wells,
which our Lord Jesus Christ made with one of his feet, when he
went to play with other children *. That field is not so well

* The story is taken from one of the apocryphal books of the Eastern

closed but men may enter at their will; but in the season
when the balm is growing good guards are placed there, that
no man dare enter. This balm grows in no other place but
this; and though men bring of the plants to plant in other
countries, they grow well and fair, but they bring forth no
fruit; and the leaves of balm never fall. They cut the
branches with a sharp flint stone, or with a sharp bone; for if
any one cut them with iron, it would destroy their virtue and
nature. The Saracens call the wood *Enochbalse;* and the
fruit, which resembles cubebs, they call *Abebissam;* and the
liquor that drops from the branches they call *Guybalse.* They
always cause that balm to be cultivated by Christians, or else
it would not fructify, as the Saracens say themselves, for it
hath been oftentimes proved. Men say also that balm
grows in India the Greater, in that desert where the trees of
the sun and moon spake to Alexander*. But I have not
seen it, for I have not been so far upward, because there
are too many perilous passages. And you must know that a
man ought to take great care in buying balm; for, if he does
not know it well, he may very easily be deceived; for they
sell a gum called turpentine instead of balm, putting thereto
a little balm to give a good odour. And some put wax in oil
of the wood of the fruit of balm, and say that it is balm;
and some distil cloves of gilofre and spikenard of Spain, and
other spices that are well smelling, and the liquor from it
they call balm; and they imagine they have balm, but they
are mistaken. For the Saracens counterfeit it to deceive the
Christians, as I have seen many a time; and after them, the
merchants and the apothecaries counterfeit it again, and then
it is less worth, and a great deal worse. But I will show how
you may know and prove it, to the end that you shall not be
deceived. First, you must know that the natural balm is
very clear, of citron colour, and strong smell; and if it be
thick, or red, or black, it is counterfeit. And if you will

sectarians, which had a considerable influence on the legendary literature
of the medieval church.

* The wonderful adventures of Alexander the Great in his Indian expedition, and the marvels he met with, are the subject of a multitude of extraordinary legends in the middle ages, and exerted no little influence on
geography and natural science down to a comparatively recent period. The
hero was made to give an account of them in a supposititious letter to his
preceptor Aristotle, which was published in almost every language in Western
Europe, and is of frequent recurrence in medieval manuscripts.

put a little balm in the palm of your hand towards the sun,
if it be fine and good you will not be able to bear your hand
in the sun's heat. Also, take a little balm with the point of
a knife, and touch it to the fire, and if it burn it is a good
sign. Take also a drop of balm, and put it into a dish, or in
a cup, with milk of a goat, and, if it be natural balm, anon it
will take and curdle the milk. Or put a drop of balm in
clear water, in a cup of silver or in a clean basin, and stir it
well with the clear water; and if the balm be fine and genuine the water will not be troubled; but if the balm be counterfeit the water will become troubled immediately. Also,
if the balm be fine, it will fall to the bottom of the vessel, as
though it were quicksilver; for the fine balm is twice as heavy
as the balm that is counterfeited.

Now I will speak of another thing that is beyond Babylon,
above the Nile, towards the desert, between Africa and Egypt;
that is, of the granaries of Joseph*, that he caused to be
made, to keep the grains against the dear years. They are
made of stone, well made by masons' craft; two of them are
marvellously great and high, the others are not so great.
And each granary has a gate to enter within, a little above
the earth; for the land is wasted and fallen since the granaries were made. Within they are all full of serpents; and
above the granaries without are many writings in divers languages. And some men say that they are sepulchres of great
lords, that were formerly; but that is not true, for all the
common rumour and speech of the people there, both far and
near, is that they are the granaries of Joseph; and so find
they in their writings and chronicles. On the other side, if
they were sepulchres, they would not be empty within; for
you may well know, that tombs and sepulchres are not made
of such magnitude or elevation; wherefore it is not credible
that they are tombs or sepulchres.

Now I will proceed to tell you the other ways that draw
towards Babylon, where the sultan dwells, which is at the
entry of Egypt; because many people go thither first, and
after that to Mount Sinai, and then return to Jerusalem, as I
have told you before. For they perform first the longer
pilgrimage, and return by the nearest ways; because the

* These are, of course, the pyramids. See the slight allusion to them in
Benjamin of Tudela, p. 121.

nearer way is the more worthy, and that is Jerusalem ; for no other pilgrimage is to be compared to it. But to accomplish their pilgrimages more easily and safely, men go first the longer way. But whoever will go to Babylon by another way, and shorter from the countries of the west, he may go by France, Burgundy, and Lombardy. It is not necessary to tell you the names of the cities and towns in that way, for the way is common, and known to every body. There are many ports where men take the sea ; some embark at Genoa ; some at Venice, and pass by the Adriatic Sea, which is called the Gulf of Venice, and divides Italy and Greece on that side ; and some go to Naples ; some to Rome, and from Rome to Brindes *, and embark there, and in many other places. Some go by Tuscia, Campania, Calabria, by Apulia, and by the mountains of Italy Chorisque, by Sardinia, and by Sicily, which is a great and good isle. In that isle of Sicily is a kind of garden, in which are many different fruits ; and the garden is green and flourishing at all seasons of the year, as well in winter as in summer. That isle contains in compass about three hundred and fifty French miles. Between Sicily and Italy there is but a little arm of the sea, which men call the Faro of Messina; and Sicily is between the Adriatic Sea and the Sea of Lombardy. From Sicily to Calabria is but eight Lombard miles. In Sicily there is a kind of serpent by which men assay and prove if their children be bastards or not ; for if they are born in lawful marriage, the serpents go about them, and do them no harm ; but if they are illegitimate, the serpents bite them and kill them with their venom : and thus many wedded men ascertain if the children be their own. Also in that isle is Mount Etna, which men call Mount Gybell, and volcanoes, that are ever burning. And there are seven places which burn and cast out flames of divers colours ; and by the changing of those flames, men of that country know when it will be dearth or good time, or cold or hot, or moist or dry, or in all other manners how the time will vary. From Italy to the volcanoes is but twenty-five miles ; and they say that the volcanoes are ways to hell †.

Also, for those who go by Pisa, there is an arm of the sea, where men go to other havens in those parts, and then they pass by the isle of Greaf, that is at Genoa ; and so they arrive

---

* Brindisi, the ancient Brundusium.　　　† See before, p. 22.

in Greece at the port of the city of Myrok, or at the port of Valone, or at the city of Duras (where there is a duke), or at other ports in those parts ; and so men go to Constantinople. And afterwards they go by water to the isle of Crete, and to the isle of Rhodes, and so to Cyprus, and so to Athens, and from thence to Constantinople.

To hold the more direct way by sea, it is full one thousand eight hundred and eighty Lombard miles. And after, from Cyprus they go by sea, and leave Jerusalem and that country on the left, and proceed to Egypt, and arrive at the city of Damiette, at the entrance of Egypt, whence they go to Alexandria, which is also upon the sea. In that city was St. Catherine beheaded; and there St. Mark the Evangelist was martyred and buried; but the emperor Leo caused his bones to be carried to Venice. There is still at Alexandria a fair church, all white, without pictures ; and so are all the other churches which belonged to the Christians all white within, for the Pagans and the Saracens whitewashed them, to destroy the images of saints that were painted on the walls. The city of Alexandria is full thirty furlongs in length, but it is but ten broad; and it is a noble and fair city. Here the river Nile enters the sea; in which river are found many precious stones, and much also of lignum aloes, a kind of wood that comes out of terrestrial Paradise, and is good for many different medicines; and it is very precious. From Alexandria we go to Babylon, where the sultan dwells, which is situated also on the river Nile; and this is the shortest way to go direct to Babylon.

From Babylon to Mount Sinai, where St. Catherine lieth, you must pass by the desert of Arabia, by which Moses led the people of Israel; and then you pass the well which Moses made with his hand in the desert, when the people murmured because they found nothing to drink. And then you pass the well of Marah, of which the water was first bitter, but the children of Israel put therein a tree, and anon the water was sweet and good to drink. And then you go by the desert to the vale of Elim, in which vale are twelve wells ; and there are seventy-two palm-trees that bear the dates which Moses found with the children of Israel. And from that valley is but a good day's journey to Mount Sinai.

And those who will go by another way from Babylon go by the Red Sea, which is an arm of the ocean. There Moses passed

with the children of Israel across the sea all dry, when
Pharaoh, king of Egypt, pursued him. That sea is about six
miles broad. That sea is not redder than other seas; but in
some places the gravel is red, and therefore they call it the
Red Sea. That sea runs to the borders of Arabia and
Palestine, its extent being more than four days. Then we go
by desert to the vale of Elim, and thence to Mount Sinai.
And you must know that by this desert no man may go on
horseback, because there is neither meat for horses nor water
to drink; wherefore they pass that desert with camels. For
the camel finds always food in trees and on bushes, and he can
abstain from drink two or three days, which no horse can do.

From Babylon to Mount Sinai is twelve good days' journey,
and some make it more; and some haste them, and thus make
it less. And men always find interpreters to go with them in
the countries, and further beyond, until they know the
language. Travellers must carry with them victuals and
other necessaries sufficient to last through those deserts.

Mount Sinai is called the Desert of Sin, that is to say, the
burning bush; because there Moses saw our Lord God many
times in form of fire burning upon that hill, and also in a
burning bush, and spake to him. And that was at the foot of
the hill. There is an abbey of monks, well built and well
closed with gates of iron for fear of wild beasts. The monks
are Arabians or Greeks; and there is a great convent, and
they are all as hermits, and drink no wine except on principal feasts; they are very devout men, and live in poverty
and simplicity on gourds and dates, and perform great ab-
stinence and penance. Here is the church of St. Catherine,
in which are many lamps burning, for they have enough oil of
olives both to burn in their lamps and to eat also, which
plenty they have by God's miracle : for the ravens, crows,
and choughs, and other fowls of that country, assemble there
once every year, and fly thither as in pilgrimage; and each
brings a branch of bays or olive in its beak, instead of offering, and leaves it there; of which the monks make great
plenty of oil; and this is a great marvel. And since fowls
that have no natural knowledge or reason go thither to seek that
glorious Virgin, well more ought men to seek her and worship
her. Behind the altar of that church is the place where
Moses saw our Lord God in a burning bush. When the
monks enter that place they always put off both hose, and

shoes or boots, because our Lord said to Moses, "Put off thy
shoes from off thy feet, for the place whereon thou standest is
holy ground."* And the monks call that place Bezeleel,
that is, the shadow of God. Beside the high altar raised on
three steps, is the chest of alabaster containing the bones of
St. Catherine, and the prelate of the monks shows the
relics to the pilgrims, and rubs the bones with an instrument
of silver, whereupon there issues a little oil, as though it were
a kind of sweating, which is neither like oil nor balm, but is very
sweet of smell; and of that they give a little to the pilgrims,
for there issues but a small quantity of the liquor. They
next show the head of St. Catherine, and the cloth that she
was wrapped in, which is still all bloody. And in that same
cloth, so wrapped, the angels bore her body to Mount Sinai,
and there they buried her with it. They also show the bush
which burnt and was not consumed, in which our Lord spake
to Moses; and they have many other relics. When the
prelate of the abbey is dead, I have been informed that his
lamp becomes extinguished. And when they choose another
prelate, if he be a good man and worthy to be prelate, his
lamp will light by the grace of God, without being touched by
any man. For every one of them has a lamp for himself, and
by their lamps they know well when any of them shall die;
for then the light begins to change and wax dim. And if he
be chosen to be prelate, and is not worthy, his lamp immediately goes out. Other men have told me, that he that sings
the mass for the prelate that is dead finds written upon the
altar the name of him that shall be chosen prelate. One day
I asked several of the monks how this befel. But they would
not tell me, until I said that they ought not to hide the grace
that God did them, but that they should publish it, to make
the people have the more devotion, and that they sinned in
hiding God's miracle, as appeared to me. And then they told
me that it so happened often; but more I might not have of
them. In that abbey no flies, toads, or lizards, or such foul
venomous beasts, nor lice, nor fleas, ever enter, by the miracle
of God and of our Lady; for there were wont to be so many
such kind of pests, that the monks were resolved to leave the
place, and were gone thence to the mountain above, to eschew
that place. But our Lady came to them and bade them return;

* Exod. iii. 5.

and since that time such vermin have never entered in and place amongst them, nor never shall enter hereafter. Before the gate is the well where Moses smote the stone from which the water came out abundantly.

From that abbey you go up the mountain of Moses by many steps; and there is, first, a church of our Lady, where she met the monks when they fled away from the vermin just mentioned; and higher up the mountain is the chapel of Elijah the prophet, which place they call Horeb, whereof holy writ speaks, " And he went in the strength of that meat forty days and forty nights, unto Horeb, the mount of God."*
And close by is the vine that St. John the Evangelist planted ; and a little above is the chapel of Moses, and the rock where Moses fled for dread when he saw our Lord' face to face. And in that rock is imprinted the form of his body ; for he threw himself so strongly and so hard on that rock that all his body was buried into it, through the miracle of God†. And near it is the place where our Lord gave to Moses the ten commandments of the law. And under the rock is the cave where Moses dwelt when he fasted forty days and forty nights. And from that mountain you pass a great valley, to go to another mountain, where St. Catherine was buried by the angels of our Lord ; in which valley is a church of forty martyrs, where the monks of the abbey often sing. That valley is very cold. Next you go up the mountain of St. Catherine, which is higher than the mount of Moses ; and there, where St. Catherine was buried, is neither church nor chapel, nor other dwelling place ; but there is a heap of stones about the place where her body was placed by the angels. There was formerly a chapel there, but it was cast down, and the stones lie still scattered about. And although the collect of St. Catherine says that it is the place where our Lord gave the ten commandments to Moses, and where the blessed virgin St. Catherine was buried, we are to understand this as meaning that it is the same country, or in a place bearing the same name ; for both hills are called the mount of Sinai ; but it is a great way from one to the other, and a great deep valley lies between them.

* 1 Kings, xix. 8.
† This pretended imprint of Moses' body, and some of the other remarkable things described by Maundeville, were still shown to visitors in the earlier part of the last century.

CHAPTER VI.

OF THE DESERT BETWEEN THE CHURCH OF ST. CATHERINE AND JERUSALEM.
—OF THE DRY TREE; AND HOW ROSES FIRST CAME INTO THE WORLD.

AFTER people have visited these holy places, they proceed
towards Jerusalem, having taken leave of the monks and
recommended themselves to their prayers. And then the
monks give the pilgrims victuals to pass the desert towards
Syria, which desert extends full thirteen days' journey. In
that desert dwell many of the Arabians, who are called
Bedouins and Ascopardes, who are people full of all evil conditions, having no houses, but tents, which they make of the
skins of camels and other beasts that they eat; and under
these they sleep and dwell, in places where they can find
water, as on the Red Sea or elsewhere; for in that desert
there is great want of water, and it often happens that where
men find water at one time in a place, there is none at another
time; and for that reason they make no habitations there.
These people do not till the ground nor labour; for they eat
no bread, except it be those who dwell near a good town, who
go thither and eat bread sometimes. They roast their flesh
and fish on the hot stones in the sun; and they are strong
and warlike men, and there is so great a multitude of them
that they are without number. Their only occupation is to
hunt animals for their food. They care not for their lives,
and therefore they fear not the sultan nor any other prince; but
dare to war with all princes who do them any grievance; and
they are often at war with the sultan, as they were at the time
I was with him. They carry but one shield and one spear,
without other arms; they wrap their heads and necks with a
great quantity of white linen cloth; and they are right
felonious and foul, and of a cursed nature.

When you pass this desert, on the way to Jerusalem, you
come to Beersheba, which was formerly a very fair and
pleasant town of the Christians, some of whose churches still
remain. In that town Abraham the Patriarch dwelt a long
time. It was founded by Beersheba (Bathsheba), the wife of
Sir Uriah, the knight, on whom king David begat Solomon the
Wise, who was king, after David, over the twelve tribes of Jerusalem, and reigned forty years. From thence we go to the city
of Hebron, a distance of two good miles; it was formerly called

the Vale of Mamre, and sometimes the Vale of Tears, because Adam wept there a hundred years for the death of
Abel, his son, whom Cain slew.   Hebron was the principal
city of the Philistines, and was inhabited some time by
giants.   And it was a sacerdotal city, that is, a sanctuary,
of the tribe of Judah; and was so free, that all manner of
fugitives from other places, for their evil deeds, were received
there.   In Hebron, Joshua, Calephe, and their company,
came first to espy how they might win the Land of Promise.
Here king David first reigned, seven years and a half; and
in Jerusalem he reigned thirty-three years and a half.   In
Hebron are all the sepulchres of the patriarchs, Adam,
Abraham, Isaac, and Jacob; and their wives, Eve, Sarah,
Rebecca, and Leah: which sepulchres the Saracens keep very
carefully, for they hold the place in great reverence, on account of the holy fathers, the patriarchs, that lie there.   And
they suffer no Christian to enter that place, except by special
grace of the sultan; for they hold Christians and Jews as
dogs, and say that they should not enter into so holy a place.
And they call that place where they lie Double Spelunk,
or Double Cave, or Double Ditch, because the one lies above
the other.   And the Saracens call the place in their language Karicarba, that is, the Place of Patriarchs.   The Jews
call it Arbothe.   And in that same place was Abraham's
house, and there he sat and saw three persons, and worshipped but one: as Holy Writ saith, *He saw three, and
worshipped one:* and at the same place Abraham received the
angels into his house.   Close by that place is a cave in the
rock, where Adam and Eve dwelt when they were put out
of Paradise, and there they begat their children.   And in
that same place was Adam formed and made, as some men
say; for they used to call that place the Field of Damascus,
because it was in the lordship of Damascus.   And from
thence he was translated into Paradise, as they say; and
after he was driven out of Paradise he was left there.   Here
begins the Vale of Hebron, which extends nearly to Jerusalem.   There the angel commanded Adam that he should
dwell with his wife Eve, on whom he begat Seth, of which
tribe Jesus Christ was born.   In that valley is a field where
men draw out of the earth a thing they call cambylle, which
they eat instead of spice, and they carry it to sell.   And
men may not make the hole where it is taken out of the

earth so deep or wide, but at the year's end it is full again up to the sides, through the grace of God.

Two miles from Hebron is the grave of Lot, Abraham's brother. And a little from Hebron is the mount of Mamre, from which the valley takes its name. And there is an oak tree which the Saracens call dirpe, which is of Abraham's time; and people call it the dry tree. They say that it has been there since the beginning of the world, and that it was once green and bore leaves, till the time that our Lord died on the cross, and then it dried; and so did all the trees that were then in the world. And there is a prophecy, that a lord, a prince of the west side of the world, shall win the Land of Promise, that is, the Holy Land, with the help of the Christians; and he shall cause mass to be performed under that dry tree, and then the tree shall become green and bear both fruit and leaves. And through that miracle many Saracens and Jews shall be converted to the Christian faith. And, therefore, they do great worship thereto, and guard it very sedulously. And although it be dry, still it has great virtue; for, certainly, he that hath a little thereof upon him, it heals him of the falling evil, and his horse shall not be afoundered; and many other virtues it hath, on account of which it is highly esteemed.

From Hebron we proceed to Bethlehem, in half a day, for it is but five miles; and it is a very fair way, by pleasant plains and woods. Bethlehem is a little city, long and narrow, and well walled, and on each side inclosed with good ditches. It was formerly called Ephrata, as Holy Writ says, "Lo, we heard it at Ephrata."* And towards the east end of the city is a very fair and handsome church, with many towers, pinnacles, and corners strongly and curiously made ; and within are forty-four great and fair pillars of marble. And between the city and the church is the Field *Floridus*, that is to say, the field flourished; for a fair maiden was blamed with wrong, and slandered, that she had committed fornication, for which cause she was condemned to be burnt in that place ; and as the fire began to burn about her, she made her prayers to our Lord, that as truly as she was not guilty, he would by his merciful grace help her, and make it known to all men. And when she had thus said, she

* Psalms, cxxxii. 6.

entered into the fire, and immediately the fire was extinguished, and the faggots ·that were burning became red rose-bushes, and those that were not kindled became white rose-bushes, full of roses. And these were the first rose-trees and roses, both white and red, that ever any man saw. And thus was this maiden saved by the grace of God. And therefore is that field called the field that God flourished, for it was full of roses. Also near the choir of the church, at the right side, as men go down sixteen steps, is the place where our Lord was born; which is full well made of marble, and full richly painted with gold, silver, azure, and other colours. And three paces from it is the crib of the ox and the ass. And beside that is the place where the star fell, which led the three kings, Jaspar, Melchior, and Balthazar: but the Greeks call them Galgalathe, Malgalathe, and Saraphie: and the Jews call them in Hebrew Appelius, Amerrius, and Damasus. These three kings offered to our Lord gold, incense, and myrrh; and they met together by a miracle of God, for they met together in a city in India called Cassak, which is fifty-three days' from Bethlehem, and yet they arrived at Bethlehem on the thirteenth day, which was the fourth day after they had seen the star, when they met in that city; and thus they were nine days from that city to Bethlehem: and that was a great miracle*. Also, under the cloister of the church, by eighteen steps at the right side, is the charnel-house of the Innocents, where their bones lie. And before the place where our Lord was born is the tomb of St. Jerome, who was a priest and cardinal, and translated the Bible and Psalter from Hebrew into Latin; and without the church is the chair that he sat in when he translated it. And close by that church, at a distance of sixty fathoms, is a church of St. Nicholas, where our Lady rested after she was delivered of our Lord. And forasmuch as she had too much milk in her breasts, which grieved her, she milked them on the red stones of marble; so that the traces may yet be seen all white in the stones. And you must understand that all who dwell in Bethlehem are Christians. And there are fair vineyards about the city, and great plenty of wine, which the

---

* The medieval legendary history of the three kings will be found printed at the end of the first volume of the "Chester Mysteries."

Christians make.   But the Saracens neither cultivate vines
nor drink wine; for their books of their law, that Mohammed
gave them, which they call their Alkoran, (and some call it
Mesaphe, and in another language it is called Harme,) forbids
them to drink wine.   For in that book Mohammed cursed all
who drink wine, and all who sell it.   For some men say
that he slew once a hermit, whom he loved much, in his
drunkenness; and therefore he cursed wine and them that
drink it.   And also, the Saracens breed no pigs and they eat
no swine's flesh, for they say it is brother to man, and it was
forbidden by the old law; and they hold all accursed who eat
thereof.   Also, in the land of Palestine and in the land of
Egypt, they eat but little or no veal or beef, except when
the animal is old, that he may work no more; for it is forbidden; because they have but few of them, and they keep
them to plough their lands.   In this city of Bethlehem was
David the king born, and he had sixty wives; and the first
wife was called Michal: and also he had three hundred
concubines.

From Bethlehem to Jerusalem it is but two miles.   And
in the way to Jerusalem, half a mile from Bethlehem, is a
church, where the angel announced to the shepherds the
birth of Christ.   And in that way is the tomb of Rachel, the
mother of Joseph the patriarch, who died immediately after
she was delivered of her son Benjamin; and there she was
buried by Jacob, her husband, and he caused twelve great
stones to be placed over her, in token that she had borne
twelve * children.   In the same way, half a mile from Jerusalem, the star appeared to the three kings.   In that way
also are many churches of Christians, by which men go
towards the city of Jerusalem.

CHAPTER VII.

OF THE PILGRIMAGES IN JERUSALEM, AND OF THE HOLY PLACES THEREABOUT.

JERUSALEM, the holy city, stands full fair between hills; and
there are no rivers or wells, but water comes by conduit from
Hebron.   And you must know that Jerusalem of old, until
the time of Melchisedek, was called Jebus; and afterwards it
was called Salem, until the time of king David, who put these

* Rachel had but two children, Joseph and Benjamin; but by them she
had twelve grandchildren. Gen. xlvi. 20—22.

two names together, and called it Jebusalem; and after that king Solomon called it Jerosoluma; and after that it was called Jerusalem, and so it is called still.   Around Jerusalem is the kingdom of Syria; and there beside is the land of Palestine; and beside it is Ascalon; and beside that is the land of Maritaine.   But Jerusalem is in the land of Judea; and it is called Judea, because Judas Maccabeus was king of that country.   And it borders eastward on the kingdom of Arabia; to the south, on the land of Egypt; to the west, on the great sea; and to the north, towards Syria, on the sea of Cyprus. In Jerusalem was formerly a patriarch, with archbishops and bishops about in the country.   Around Jerusalem are these cities: Hebron, seven miles; Jericho, six miles; Beersheba, eight miles; Ascalon, seventeen miles; Jaffa, sixteen miles; Ramatha, three miles; and Bethlehem, two miles.   And two miles from Bethlehem, towards the south, is the church of St. Karitot, who was abbot there; for whom they made great lamentation among the monks when he died; and they continue still in mourning in the manner that they made their lamentation for him the first time; and it is very sad to behold.

This country and land of Jerusalem hath been in the hands of many different nations, and often, therefore, hath the country suffered much tribulation for the sin of the people that dwell there.   For that country hath been in the hands of all nations; that is to say, of Jews, Canaanites, Assyrians, Persians, Medes, Macedonians, Greeks, Romans, Christians, Saracens, Barbarians, Turks, Tartars, and of many other different nations; for God will not let it remain long in the hands of traitors or of sinners, be they Christians or others. And now the heathens have held that land in their hands forty years and more*; but they shall not hold it long, if God will.

When men come to Jerusalem, their first pilgrimage is to the church of the holy sepulchre, where our Lord was buried, which is without the city on the north side; but it is now inclosed by the town wall.   And there is a very fair church, round, and open above, and covered in its circuit with lead; and on the west side is a fair and high tower for bells, strongly made; and in the middle of the church is a tabernacle, as it were a little house, made with a little low door; and that

---

* Perhaps Maundeville reckons from the capture of Acre, in 1291, when the Christians lost their last footing in the Holy Land.   Jerusalem was finally taken from the Christians by the Turks in October, 1244.

tabernacle is made in manner of half a compass, right curiously
and richly made of gold and azure and other rich colours.
And in the right side of that tabernacle is the sepulchre of our
Lord; and the tabernacle is eight feet long, and five wide,
and eleven in height; and it is not long since the sepulchre
was all open, that men might kiss it and touch it. But because pilgrims that came thither laboured to break the stone
in pieces or in powder, therefore the sultan has caused a
wall to be made round the sepulchre, that no man may touch
it. In the left side of the wall of the tabernacle, about the
height of a man, is a great stone, the magnitude of a man's
head, that was of the holy sepulchre; and that stone the
pilgrims that come thither kiss. In that tabernacle are no
windows; but it is all made light with lamps which hang
before the sepulchre. And there is one lamp which hangs
before the sepulchre which burns bright; and on Good Friday
it goes out of itself, and lights again by itself at the hour that
our Lord rose from the dead. Also, within the church, at the
right side, near the choir of the church, is Mount Calvary,
where our Lord was placed on the cross. It is a rock of a
white colour, a little mixed with red; and the cross was set in
a mortise in the same rock; and on that rock dropped the
blood from the wounds of our Lord when he was punished on
the cross; and that is called Golgotha. And they go up to
that Golgotha by steps; and in the place of that mortise
Adam's head was found, after Noah's flood, in token that the
sins of Adam should be redeemed in that same place. And
upon that rock Abraham made sacrifice to our Lord. And
there is an altar, before which lie Godfrey de Boulogne and
Baldwin, and other Christian kings of Jerusalem; and near
where our Lord was crucified is this written in Greek:
Ὁ Θεὸς Βασιλεὺς ἡμῶν πρὸ αἰώνων εἰργάσατο σωτηρίαν ἐν μέσῳ τῆς γῆς·
—that is to say, in Latin, "Deus Rex noster ante secula
operatus est salutem in medio terræ;" in English, "God
our king, before the worlds, hath wrought salvation in the
midst of the earth." And also on the rock where the cross
was set is written, within the rock, these words: Ὁ εἶδεις, ἐστὶ
βάσις τῆς πίστεως ὅλης τοῦ κόσμου τούτου·—that is to say, in
Latin, "Quod vides, est fundamentum totius fidei hujus
mundi;" in English, "What thou seest, is the ground of all
the faith of this world." And you shall understand that
when our Lord was placed on the cross he was thirty-three

years and three months old.   Also, within Mount Calvary,
on the right side, is an altar, where the pillar lieth to which
our Lord Jesus was bound when he was scourged; and there,
besides, are four pillars of stone that always drop water; and
some men say that they weep for our Lord's death.   Near
that altar is a place under earth, forty-two steps in depth,
where the holy cross was found by the wisdom of St. Helena,
under a rock, where the Jews had hid it.   And thus was the
true cross assayed; for they found three crosses, one of our
Lord, and two of the two thieves; and St. Helena placed a
dead body on them, which arose from death to life when it was
laid on that on which our Lord died.   And thereby, in the wall,
is the place where the four nails of our Lord were hid; for he
had two in his hands and two in his feet; and of one of these
the emperor of Constantinople made a bridle to his horse, to
carry him in battle; and through virtue thereof he overcame
his enemies, and won all the land of Lesser Asia, that is to
say, Turkey, Armenia the Less and the Greater, and from
Syria to Jerusalem, from Arabia to Persia, from Mesopotamia
to the kingdom of Aleppo, from Upper and Lower Egypt, and
all the other kingdoms, unto the extremity of Ethiopia, and
into India the Less, that was then Christian.   And there were,
in that time, many good holy men, and holy hermits, of whom
the Book of Lives of Fathers* speaks; but they are now in the
hands of Pagans and Saracens.   But when God Almighty will,
as the lands were lost through sin of the Christians, so shall
they be won again by Christians through help of God.   And
in the midst of that church is a compass, in which Joseph of
Arimathea laid the body of our Lord when he had taken him
down from the cross; and there he washed the wounds of our
Lord.   And that compass, men say, is the middle of the
world†.   And in the church of the sepulchre, on the north
side, is the place where our Lord was put in prison (for he
was in prison in many places); and there is a part of the
chain with which he was bound; and there he appeared first
to Mary Magdalene when he was risen, and she thought that
he had been a gardener.   In the church of St. Sepulchre
there were formerly canons of the order of St. Augustin, who
had a prior, but the patriarch was their head.   And outside

* The *Vitas Patrum* was the most popular collection of saints' legends in
the middle ages.

† See before, pp. 4, 38.

the doors of the church, on the right side, as men go upward
eighteen steps, is the spot where our Lord said to his mother,
"Woman, behold thy son!" And after that, he said to John
his disciple, "Behold thy mother!"* And these words he
said on the cross. And on these steps went our Lord when
he bare the cross on his shoulder. And under these steps is
a chapel; and in that chapel sing priests of India, not after
our law, but after theirs; and they always make their sacrament of the altar, saying *Pater noster*, and other prayers
therewith, with which prayers they say the words that the
sacrament is made of; for they know not the additions that
many popes have made; but they sing with good devotion.
And near there is the place where our Lord rested him when
he was weary for bearing of the cross. Before the church of
the sepulchre the city is weaker than in any other part, for
the great plain that is between the church and the city. And
towards the east side, without the walls of the city, is the vale
of Jehoshaphat, which adjoins to the walls as though it were a
large ditch. And over against that vale of Jehoshaphat, out
of the city, is the church of St. Stephen, where he was stoned
to death. And there beside is the golden gate, which may
not be opened, by which gate our Lord entered on Palm Sunday,
upon an ass; and the gate opened to him when he would go
unto the temple; and the marks of the ass's feet are still seen
in three places on the steps, which are of very hard stone.
Before the church of St. Sepulchre, two hundred paces to the
south, is the great hospital of St. John, of which the Hospitallers had their foundation. And within the palace of the
sick men of that hospital are one hundred and twenty-four
pillars of stone; and in the walls of the house, besides the
number aforesaid, there are fifty-four pillars that support the
house. From that hospital, going towards the east, is a very
fair church, which is called Our Lady the Great; and after it
there is another church, very near, called Our Lady the Latin;
and there stood Mary Cleophas and Mary Magdalene, and tore
their hair, when our Lord was executed on the cross.

* John, xix. 26.

CHAPTER VIII.

OF THE TEMPLE OF OUR LORD; THE CRUELTY OF KING HEROD; MOUNT
SION; OF PROBATICA PISCINA, AND NATATORIUM. SILOÆ.

ONE hundred and sixty paces from the church of the Sepulchre, towards the east, is the temple of our Lord. It is a very fair house, circular and lofty, and covered with lead, and well paved with white marble; but the Saracens will not suffer any Christians or Jews to come therein, for they say that no such foul sinful men should come into so holy a place: but I went in there, and in other places where I would, because I had letters of the sultan, with his great seal, and other men have commonly but his signet. In these letters he commanded, of his special grace, to all his subjects, to let me see all the places, and to inform me fully of all the mysteries of every place, and to conduct me from city to city if necessary, and to receive me and my company courteously, and obey all my reasonable requests if they were not contrary to the royal power and dignity of the sultan or of his law. And to others, who have served him and ask him grace, he gives only his signet, which they cause to be borne before them, hanging on a spear, and the people of the country do great worship and reverence to his signet or his seal, and kneel thereto as lowly as we do to the procession of the Host. But they show much greater reverence to his letters, for the admiral, and all other lords to whom they are shown, kneel down before they receive them, and then they take them, and put them on their heads, and after they kiss them, and then they read them, kneeling with great reverence; and then they offer themselves to do all the bearer asks. And in this temple of our Lord were formerly canons regular, who had an abbot to whom they were obedient. And in this temple was Charlemagne, when the angel brought him the prepuce of the circumcision of our Lord Jesus Christ, which king Charles caused to be brought to Paris, to his chapel; and after that he sent it to Poictiers, and after that to Chartres.

You must know that this is not the temple that Solomon made, which lasted only one thousand one hundred and two years. For Titus, the son of Vespasian, emperor of Rome, had laid siege about Jerusalem to overcome the Jews, because they put our Lord to death without the emperor's leave. And when he had won the city, he burnt the temple and beat

it down and all the city, and took the Jews, and put to death
one million one hundred thousand of them; and the others
he put in prison, and sold them to slavery thirty for a penny,
because they said they bought Jesus for thirty pennies; and
he sold them cheaper, giving thirty for one penny.   After
that, Julian the Apostate, when emperor, gave the Jews permission to make the temple of Jerusalem, for he hated the
Christians although he had been christened; but he forsook
his law, and became a renegade.   And when the Jews had
made the temple, an earthquake came and cast it down (as
God would), and destroyed all that they had made.   And
after that, Hadrian, who was emperor of Rome, and of the
lineage of Troy, rebuilt Jerusalem and the temple, in the
same manner as Solomon made it.   And he would not suffer
Jews to dwell there, but only Christians.   For although he
was not christened, yet he loved Christians more than any
other nation, except his own.   This emperor caused the
church of St. Sepulchre to be inclosed within the city walls;
before, it was without the city.   And he would have changed
the name of Jerusalem, and called it Ælia, but that name
lasted not long.   The Saracens continue to show much reverence to that temple, and say that the place is very holy.
And when they go in they go barefooted, and kneel many
times.   And when my fellows and I saw that, when we came
in we took off our shoes, and entered barefooted, and thought
we would do as much worship and reverence there as any of
the misbelieving men, with as great compunction of heart.
This temple is sixty-four cubits wide, and as many in length,
and a hundred and twenty cubits high; and within it has
pillars of marble all round; and in the middle of the temple
are many high stages, fourteen steps high, with good pillars all
about, and this place the Jews call the holy of holies.   No man,
except the prelate of the Saracens, who makes their sacrifice, is
allowed to come in there.   And the people stand all about, in
divers stages, according to their dignity or rank, so that they may
all see the sacrifice.   And in that temple are four entrances,
with gates of cypress, well made and curiously wrought.
Within the east gate is the place where our Lord said
" Here is Jerusalem."   And on the north side of the temple,
within the gate, there is a well, but it does not run; of this
Holy Writ speaks, and says, " I saw water come out of the
temple."   And on the other side of the temple there is a

rock which men call Moriah, but after it was called Bethel, where the ark of God, with relics of Jews, was wont to be put. That ark or hutch, with the relics, Titus carried with him to Rome, when he had overthrown the Jews; it contained the ten commandments, Aaron's rod, and that of Moses, with which he made the Red Sea divide as it had been a wall, on the right side and on the left, while the people of Israel passed the sea dry-foot. And with that rod he smote the rock, and the water came out of it; and with that rod he did many other wonders. And therein was a vessel of gold, full of manna, and clothings, and ornaments, and the tabernacle of Aaron, and a square tabernacle of gold, with twelve precious stones, and a box of green jasper, with four figures, and eight names of our Lord, and seven candlesticks of gold, and twelve pots of gold, and four censers of gold, and an altar of gold, and four lions of gold, which bare cherubim of gold twelve spans long, and the circle of swans of heaven, with a tabernacle of gold, and a table of silver, and two trumpets of silver, and seven barley loaves, and all the other relics that were before the birth of our Lord Jesus Christ. And Jacob was sleeping upon that rock when he saw the angels go up and down by a ladder, and he said, " Surely the Lord is in this place; and I knew it not."* And there an angel held Jacob still, and changed his name, and called him Israel. And in that same place David saw the angel that smote the people with a sword, and put it up bloody in the sheath. And St. Simeon was on that same rock when he received our Lord into the temple. And in this rock he placed himself when the Jews would have stoned him; and a star came down and gave him light. On that rock our Lord preached frequently to the people; and out of that same temple our Lord drove the buyers and sellers. Upon that rock also our Lord set him when the Jews would have stoned him; and the rock clave in two, and in that cleft was our Lord hid; and there came down a star and gave him light; and upon that rock our Lady sat and learned her Psalter; and there our Lord forgave the woman her sins that was found in adultery; and there our Lord was circumcised; and there the angel gave tidings to Zacharias of the birth of St. John the Baptist his son; and there first Melchisedek offered bread and wine to our Lord, in

* Gen. xxviii. 16.

token of the sacrament that was to come; and there David
fell down praying to our Lord, and to the angel that smote the
people, that he would have mercy on him and on the people;
and our Lord heard his prayer, and therefore would he make
the temple in that place; but our Lord forbade him, by an
angel, because he had done treason, when he caused Uriah,
the worthy knight, to be slain, to have Bathsheba, his wife;
and therefore all the materials he had collected for the building of the temple he gave to Solomon, his son, and he built
it.   Without the gate of that temple is an altar, where the
Jews were wont to offer doves and turtles.   And between the
temple and that altar was Zacharias slain.   Upon the pinnacle
of that temple was our Lord brought to be tempted by the fiend.
And on the top of that pinnacle the Jews placed St. James,
who was first bishop of Jerusalem, and cast him down to the
earth.   At the entry of the temple, towards the west, is the
gate that is called the Beautiful Gate.   And near the temple,
on the right, is a church covered with lead, called Solomon's
school.   And near the temple, on the south, is the temple of Solomon, which is very fair and well polished.   And in that temple
dwelt the knights of the temple, that were called Templars;
and that was the foundation of their order; so that knights
dwelt there, and canons regular, in the temple of our Lord.
One hundred and twenty paces from that temple to the east,
in the corner of the city, is the bath of our Lord; and in that
bath water was wont to come from Paradise, and still it drop-
peth.   And there beside is our Lady's bed.   And fast by is
the temple of St. Simeon; and without the cloister of the
temple, toward the north, is a very fair church of St. Anne, our
Lady's mother; and there our Lady was conceived.   And
before that church is a great tree, which began to grow the
same night.   And under that church, in going down by twenty-
two steps, lies Joachim, our Lady's father, in a fair tomb of
stone; and there beside lay sometime St. Anne his wife; but
St. Helena caused her to be translated to Constantinople.
And in that church is a well, in manner of a cistern, which is
called *Probatica Piscina*, which hath five entrances.   Angels
used to come from heaven into that well and bathe them in it,
and the man who first bathed after the moving of the water
was made whole of whatever sickness he had; and there our

---

* Acts, iii. 2.

Lord healed a man of the palsy, with which he had lain thirty-eight years; and our Lord said to him, "Take up thy bed and go."* And near it was Pilate's house. And fast by is king Herod's house, who caused the Innocents to be slain. This Herod was excessively wicked and cruel; for first he caused his wife to be killed, whom he loved well; and for the great love he had to her, when he saw her dead, he fell in a rage, and was out of his mind a great while; and after he recovered, he caused his two sons, whom he had by that wife, to be slain; and after that he killed another of his wives, and a son that he had by her; and after that he put to death his own mother, and he would have slain his brother also, but he died suddenly. And after he fell into sickness, and when he felt that he should die, he sent for his sister, and for all the lords of his land, and sent them to prison; and then he said to his sister, he knew well that people would make no sorrow for his death, and therefore he made his sister swear, that she should cause all the heads of the lords to be struck off when he was dead, that all the land might make sorrow for his death. But his sister fulfilled not his will; for as soon as he was dead she delivered all the lords out of prison, and told them all the purpose of her brother's ordinance; and so this cursed king was never made sorrow for. And you must know that at that time there were three Herods, of great fame for their cruelty. This Herod of which I have spoken was Herod the Ascalonite; and he that caused St. John the Baptist to be beheaded was Herod Antipas; and he that caused St. James to be beheaded was Herod Agrippa; and he put St. Peter in prison.

Furthermore, in the city is the church of St. Saviour, where is preserved the left arm of John Chrysostom, and the greater part of the head of St. Stephen. On the other side of the street, to the south, as men go to Mount Sion, is a church of St. James, where he was beheaded. And one hundred and twenty paces from that church is Mount Sion, where there is a fair church of our Lady, where she dwelt and died. And there was formerly an abbot of canons regular. From thence she was carried by the apostles to the valley of Jehoshaphat, and there is the stone which the angel brought to our Lady from Mount Sinai, which is of the same colour as the rock of St. Catherine. And near there is the gate through which

* Matt. ix. 6.

our Lady passed, when she was with child, on her way to
Bethlehem. Also, at the entrance of Mount Sion is a chapel in which is the great stone with which the sepulchre was
covered, when Joseph of Arimathea had put our Lord therein;
which stone the three Marys saw turned upward when they
came to his sepulchre the day of his resurrection; and there
they found an angel, who told them of our Lord's resurrection
from death to life. There also, in a wall beside the gate, is
a stone of the pillar at which our Lord was scourged; and
there was the house of Annas, who was bishop of the Jews
at that time; and there our Lord was examined in the night,
and scourged, and smitten, and violently treated. In that same
place St. Peter forsook our Lord thrice before the cock crew.
There is a part of the table on which he made his Supper,
when he made his Maundy with his disciples, and gave
them his flesh and his blood, in form of bread and wine. And
under that chapel, by a descent of thirty-two steps, is the place
where our Lord washed his disciples' feet, and the vessel which
contained the water is still preserved; and there, beside that
same vessel, was St. Stephen buried. And there is the altar
where our Lord heard the angels sing mass. And there our
Lord appeared first to his disciples after his resurrection, the
doors being shut, and said to them, "Peace to you!" And on
that mount Christ appeared to St. Thomas the Apostle, and
bade him feel his wounds; and there he first believed, and
said, "My Lord and my God." In the same church, beside
the altar, were all the apostles on Whitsunday, when the Holy
Ghost descended on them in likeness of fire.

Mount Sion is within the city, and is a little higher
than the other side of the city; and the city is strongest on
that side. For at the foot of Mount Sion is a fair and strong
castle made by the sultan. In Mount Sion were buried
king David and king Solomon, and many other Jewish kings
of Jerusalem. And there is the place where the Jews would
have cast up the body of our Lady, when the apostles carried
the body to be buried in the valley of Jehoshaphat. And there
is the place where St. Peter wept bitterly after he had forsaken our Lord. And a stone's cast from that chapel is
another chapel, where our Lord was judged; for at that time
the house of Caiaphas stood there. One hundred and forty
paces from that chapel, to the east, is a deep cave under the
rock, which is called the Galilee of our Lord, where St. Peter

hid himself when he had forsaken our Lord. Between Mount
Sion and the Temple of Solomon is the place where our Lord
raised the maiden in her father's house. Under Mount Sion,
towards the valley of Jehoshaphat, is a well called Natatorium
Siloæ (the pool of Siloah), where our Lord was washed after his
baptism; and there our Lord made the blind man to see.
There was buried Isaiah the prophet. Also straight from
Natatorium Siloæ is an image of stone, and of ancient
work, which Absalom caused to be made, on account of which
they call it the hand of Absalom. And fast by is still the
elder tree on which Judas hanged himself for despair, when he
sold and betrayed our Lord. Near it was the synagogue, where
the bishops of the Jews and the Pharisees came together and
held their council, and where Judas cast the thirty pence
before them, and said that he had sinned in betraying our
Lord. And near it was the house of the apostles Philip and
James the son of Alpheus. On the other side of Mount Sion,
toward the south, a stone's cast beyond the vale, is Aceldama,
that is, the field of blood, which was bought for the thirty
pence for which our Lord was sold; in which field are many
tombs of Christians; for there are many pilgrims' graves.
And there are many oratories, chapels, and hermitages, where
hermits used to dwell. A hundred paces toward the east is
the charnel-house of the hospital of St. John, where they used
to put the bones of dead men.

To the west of Jerusalem is a fair church, where the tree of
the cross grew. And two miles from thence is a handsome
church, where our Lady met with Elizabeth, when they were
both with child; and St. John stirred in his mother's womb,
and made reverence to his Creator, whom he saw not. Under
the altar of that church is the place where St. John was born.
A mile from that church is the castle of Emmaus, where our
Lord showed himself to two of his disciples after his resurrection. Also on the other side, two hundred paces from
Jerusalem, is a church, where was formerly the cave of the
lion; and under that church, at thirty steps deep, were
interred twelve thousand martyrs, in the time of king Cosrhoes,
that the lion met in a night, by the will of God. Two miles
from Jerusalem is Mount Joy, a very fair and delicious place.
There Samuel the prophet lies, in a fair tomb; and it is
called Mount Joy, because it gives joy to pilgrims' hearts, for
from that place men first see Jerusalem. Between Jerusalem

and Mount Olivet is the valley of Jehoshaphat, under the walls
of the city, as I have said before : and in the middle of the
valley is a little river, which is called the brook Cedron ; and
across it lies a tree (of which the cross was made), on which
men passed over; and fast by it is a little pit in the earth,
where the foot of the pillar still remains at which our Lord
was first scourged; for he was scourged and shamefully
treated in many places. Also in the middle of the valley of
Jehoshaphat is the church of our Lady, which is forty-three
steps below the sepulchre of our Lady, who was seventy-two
years of age when she died. Beside the sepulchre of our
Lady is an altar, where our Lord forgave St. Peter all his sins.
From thence, toward the west, under an altar, is a well which
comes out of the river of Paradise. You must know that that
church is very low in the earth, and a part is quite within the
earth. But I imagine that it was not founded so ; but since
Jerusalem has often been destroyed, and the walls beaten down
and tumbled into the valley, and that they have been so filled
again, and the ground raised, for that reason the church is so
low within the earth. Nevertheless, men say there commonly,
that the earth hath so been cloven since the time that our
Lady was buried there ; and men also say there, that it grows
and increases every day, without doubt. In that church were
formerly black monks, who had their abbot. Beside that
church is a chapel, beside the rock called Gethsemane, where
our Lord was kissed by Judas, and where he was taken by the
Jews; and there our Lord left his disciples when he went to
pray before his passion, when he prayed and said, " O, my
Father, if it be possible, let this cup pass from me."* And
when he came again to his disciples, he found them sleeping.
And in the rock within the chapel we still see the mark of the
fingers of our Lord's hand, when he put them on the rock when
the Jews would have taken him. And a stone's cast from
thence, to the south, is another chapel, where our Lord sweat
drops of blood. And close to it is the tomb of king Jehoshaphat,
from whom the valley takes its name. This Jehoshaphat was
king of that country, and was converted by a hermit, who was a
worthy man, and did much good. A bow-shot from thence,
to the south, is the church where St. James and Zachariah the
prophet were buried. Above the vale is Mount Olivet, so

* Matt. xxvi. 39.

called for the abundance of olives that grow there.   That
mount is higher than the city of Jerusalem; and therefore
from that mount we may see many of the streets of the city.
Between that mount and the city is only the valley of Jehoshaphat, which is not wide.   From that mount our Lord Jesus
Christ ascended to heaven on Ascension Day, and yet there
appears the imprint of his left foot in the stone.   And there
is a church where was formerly an abbot and canons regular.
About twenty-eight paces thence is a chapel, in which is the
stone on the which our Lord sat when he preached the eight
blessings.   And there he taught his disciples the pater noster,
and wrote with his finger on a stone.   And near it is a church
of St. Mary, the Egyptian, where she lies in a tomb.   Three
bow-shots thence, to the east, is Bethphage, whither our Lord
sent St. Peter and St. James on Palm Sunday to seek the ass on
which he rode into Jerusalem.   In descending from Mount
Olivet, to the east, is a castle called Bethany, where dwelt
Simon the leper; and there he entertained our Lord; and
afterwards he was baptized by the apostles, and was called
Julian, and was made bishop; and this is the same Julian
to whom men pray for good entertainment, because our Lord
was entertained by him in his house.   In that house our Lord
forgave Mary Magdalene her sins, and there she washed his
feet with her tears, and wiped them with her hair.   And
there St. Martha waited upon our Lord.   There our Lord
raised Lazarus, who was dead four days and stank.   There
also dwelt Mary Cleophas.   That castle is a mile from Jerusalem.   Also in coming down from Mount Olivet is the place
where our Lord wept upon Jerusalem.   And there beside is
the place where our Lady appeared to St. Thomas the apostle
after her assumption, and gave him her girdle.   And very near
it is the stone on which our Lord often sat when he preached;
and upon that same shall he sit at the day of doom, right as
he said himself.

After Mount Olivet is the Mount of Galilee, where the
apostles assembled when Mary Magdalene came and told
them of Christ's ascension.   And there, between Mount
Olivet and the Mount of Galilee, is a church, where the angel
foretold our lady of her death.   We next go from Bethany to
Jericho, which was once a little city, but it is now destroyed,
and is but a little village.   Joshua took that city by miracle
of God, and destroyed it and cursed it, and all them that

should build it again. Of that city was Zaccheus, the dwarf, who climbed up into the sycamore tree to see our Lord, because he was so little he might not see him for the people. And of that city was Rahab, the harlot, who alone escaped with her kinspeople; and she often refreshed and fed the messengers of Israel, and kept them from many great perils of death; and therefore she had good reward; as holy writ saith, " He that receiveth a prophet in the name of a prophet, shall receive a prophet's reward;"* and so had she; for she prophesied to the messengers, saying, " I know that the Lord hath given you the land;"† and so he did. From Bethany you go to the river Jordan, by a mountain, and through a desert; and it is nearly a day's journey from Bethany, toward the east, to a great hill, where our Lord fasted forty days. The devil carried our Lord upon that hill, and tempted him, and said, " Command that these stones be made bread."‡ In that place, upon the hill, there was formerly a fair church, but it is entirely destroyed, so that there is now but a hermitage, occupied by a kind of Christians called Georgians, because St. George converted them §. Upon that hill dwelt Abraham a long while; and therefore they call it Abraham's garden. Between the hill and this garden runs a little brook of water, which was formerly bitter, but, when blessed by the prophet Elisha, it became sweet and good to drink. At the foot of this hill toward the plain is a great well, which flows into the river Jordan. From that hill to Jericho is but a mile, in going toward the river Jordan, which is two miles beyond it; and half a mile nearer is a fair church of St. John the Baptist, where he baptized our Lord ; and there beside is the house of Jeremiah the prophet.

Chapter IX.

OF THE DEAD SEA, AND OF THE RIVER JORDAN.—OF THE HEAD OF ST. JOHN
THE BAPTIST, AND OF THE USAGES OF THE SAMARITANS.

FROM Jericho it is three miles to the Dead Sea. About that sea groweth much alum and alkatran ‖. Between

---

* Matth. x. 41.   † Joshua, ii. 9.   ‡ Matth. iv. 3.

§ This is a very ingenious attempt at derivation, like some others found in the book of Sir John Maundeville, who speaks again of the Georgian Christians at the end of Chapter X.

‖ This word probably means bitumen. The Latin text has *Dalem et*

Jericho and that sea is the land of Dengadda, where formerly
balm grew; but men cause the branches to be drawn up
and carried to Babylon, and still they call them vines of
Gady.   On the coast of that sea, as we go from Arabia, is the
mount of the Moabites, where there is a cave which they call
Karua.   Upon that hill Balak, the son of Boaz, led Balaam
the priest to curse the people of Israel.   The Dead Sea divides
the lands of India and Arabia, and the sea reaches from Soara
to Arabia.   The water of that sea is very bitter and salt, and
if the earth were moistened with that water it would never
bear fruit.   And the earth and land changeth often its colour.
The water casteth out a thing that is called asphalt, in pieces
as large as a horse, every day and on all sides.   From Jerusalem to that sea is two hundred furlongs.   That sea is in
length five hundred and eighty furlongs, and in breadth one
hundred and fifty furlongs, and is called the Dead Sea, because it does not run, but is ever motionless.   Neither man,
beast, nor anything that hath life, may die in that sea; and
that hath been proved many times by men that have been
condemned to death, who have been cast therein, and left
therein three or four days, and they might never die therein,
for it receiveth nothing within him that breatheth life.   And
no man may drink of the water on account of its bitterness.
And if a man cast iron therein, it will float on the surface;
but if men cast a feather therein, it will sink to the bottom;
and these are things contrary to nature.   And there beside
grow trees that bear apples very fair of colour to behold; but
when we break or cut them in two we find within ashes
and cinders, which is a token that by the wrath of God the
cities and the land were burned and sunk into hell.   Some call
that sea the Lake Dasfetidee; some, the River of Devils;
and some the river that is ever stinking.   Into that sea, by
the wrath of God, sunk the five cities, Sodom, Gomorrah,
Aldama, Seboym, and Segor, for the abominable sin that
reigned in them.   But Segor, by the prayer of Lot, was saved
and kept a great while, for it was set upon a hill, and some
part of it still appears above the water; and men may see
the walls when it is fair and clear weather.   In that city Lot
dwelt a little while; and there was he made drunk by his

dalketram; the French, *De alym et d'alketran.*   This would almost lead
us to consider the French as the original text, from which the others were
translated.

daughters, and lay with them, and begat on them Moab and
Amon. The hill above Segor was then called Edom, but
afterwards men called it Seyr, and subsequently Idumea.
At the right side of the Dead Sea the wife of Lot still stands
in likeness of a salt stone, because she looked behind her
when the cities sunk into hell.

And you shall understand that the river Jordan runs into
the Dead Sea, and there it dies, for it runs no further; and
its entrance is a mile from the church of St. John the Baptist, toward the west, a little beneath the place where Christians bathe commonly. ` A mile from the river Jordan is the
river of Jabbok, which Jacob passed over when he came
from Mesopotamia. This river Jordan is no great river, but
it has plenty of good fish; and it cometh out of the hill of
Libanus by two wells, that are called Jor and Dan; and of
those two wells it hath its name. It passes by a lake called
Maron; and after, it passes through the sea of Tiberias and
under the hills of Gilboa; and there is a very fair valley on
both sides of the river. The hills of Libanus reach in length
to the desert of Pharan. And these hills separate the kingdom
of Syria and the country of Phœnicia. Upon these hills grow
cedar trees, that are very high, and bear long apples, as great
as a man's head. This river Jordan also separates the land of
Galilee and the land of Idumea and the land of Betron; and
it runs under the earth a great way, unto a fair and great plain,
which is called Meldan, in the language of Sarmoyz; that is to
say, a fair or market, in their language, because fairs are often
held in that plain. And there becomes the water great and wide.
That plain is the tomb of Job. About the river Jordan are
many churches, where many Christian men dwelt. And near
it is the city of Hay, which Joshua assailed and took. Also
beyond the river Jordan is the valley of Mamre, and that is a
very fair valley. Also upon the hill that I spoke of before,
where our Lord fasted forty days, two miles from Galilee, is
a fair and lofty hill, where the fiend carried our Lord, the
third time, to tempt him, and showed him all the regions of
the world, and said, "All this shall I give thee, if thou fall
down and worship me."

In going eastward from the Dead Sea, out of the borders
of the Holy Land, is a strong and fair castle, on a hill which
is called Carak, in Sarmoyz; that is to say, Royal. That
castle was made by king Baldwin, when he had conquered

that land, who put it into the hands of Christians, to keep
that part of the country; and for that cause it was called the
Mount Royal*; and under it there is a town called Sobache;
and there all about dwell Christians, under tribute. From
thence men go to Nazareth, of which our Lord beareth the
surname. And thence it is three days to Jerusalem : and
men go by the province of Galilee, by Ramoth, by Sodom,
and by the high hill of Ephraim, where Elkanah and Hannah,
the mother of Samuel the prophet, dwelt. There this prophet was born ; and, after his death, he was buried at Mount
Joy, as I have said before. And then men go to Shiloh, where
the ark of God with the relics were long kept under Eli the
prophet. There the people of Hebron sacrificed to our Lord;
and there they yielded up their vows ; and there God first
spake to Samuel, and showed him the change of the order of
priesthood, and the mystery of the sacrament. And right
nigh, on the left side, is Gibeon, and Ramah, and Benjamin,
of which Holy Writ speaketh. And after men go to Shechem,
formerly called Sichar, which is in the province of the Samaritans ; and there is a very fair and fruitful vale, and there is
a fair and good city, called Neapolis, whence it is a day's journey to Jerusalem. And there is the well where our Lord
spake to the woman of Samaria ; and there was wont to be a
church, but it is beaten down. Beside that well king Reho-
boam caused two calves to be made of gold, and made them
to be worshipped, and put the one at Dan and the other at
Bethel. A mile from Sichar is the city of Deluze, in which
Abraham dwelt a certain time. Shechem is ten miles from
Jerusalem, and is called Neapolis, that is to say, the new
city. And near it is the tomb of Joseph, the son of Jacob,
who governed Egypt; for the Jews carried his bones from
Egypt, and buried them there; and thither the Jews go oftentime in pilgrimage, with great devotion. In that city was
Dinah, Jacob's daughter, ravished; for which her brethren
slew many persons, and did many injuries to the city. And
there beside is the hill of Gerizim, where the Samaritans
make their sacrifice : on that hill would Abraham have sacrificed his son Isaac. And there beside is the valley of Dothan;

---

* Mount Royal, which stood in the immediate neighbourhood of the
ancient Petra, was a place of some celebrity in the history of the crusades.
It was said to have been impregnable from the strength of its position ; and
it was only taken by Saladin, in 1187, by starving the garrison.

and there is the cistern wherein Joseph was cast by his
brethren, when they sold him; and that is two miles from
Sichar.　From thence we go to Samaria, which is now called
Sebaste; it is the chief city of that country, and is situated
between the hill of Aygnes in a similar manner to Jerusalem.
In that city was the sittings of the twelve tribes of Israel;
but the city is not now so great as it was formerly.　There
St. John the Baptist was buried, between two prophets, Elisha
and Abdias; but he was beheaded in the castle of Macharyme,
near the Dead Sea; and after he was carried by his disciples,
and buried at Samaria: and there Julian the Apostate caused
him to be dug up, and burned his bones, and cast his ashes to
the wind.　But the finger that showed our Lord, saying, "Behold the Lamb of God!" would never burn, but is all whole;
St. Tecla, the holy virgin, caused that finger to be carried to
the hill of Sebaste, and there men make great feast for it.　In
that place was wont to be a fair church; and many others there
were, but they are all beaten down.　There was wont to be
the head of St. John the Baptist, inclosed in the wall; but
the emperor Theodosius had it drawn out, and found it wrapped in a little cloth, all bloody; and so he carried it to Constantinople; and the hinder part of the head is still at Constantinople; and the fore part of the head, to under the chin,
is at Rome, under the church of St. Silvester, where are
nuns; and it is yet all broiled, as though it were half burnt;
for the emperor Julian above mentioned, of his wickedness
and malice, burnt that part with the other bones, as may still
be seen; and this thing hath been proved both by popes and
emperors.　And the jaws beneath, which hold to the chin,
and a part of the ashes, and the platter on which the head
was laid when it was smitten off, are at Genoa; and the Genoese make a great feast in honour of it, and so do the Saracens also.　And some men say that the head of St. John is
at Amiens, in Picardy; and other men say, that it is the head
of St. John the bishop.　I know not which is correct, but
God knows; but however men worship it, the blessed St.
John is satisfied.

From this city of Sebaste unto Jerusalem it is twelve miles.
And between the hills of that country there is a well that
four times in the year changes its colour; sometimes green,
sometimes red, sometimes clear, and sometimes troubled;
and men call that well Job.　And the people of that country,

who are called Samaritans, were converted and baptized by
the Apostles, but they hold not well their doctrine; and always
they hold laws by themselves, varying from Christian men,
from Saracens, Jews, and Pagans. The Samaritans believe
well in one God; and they say that there is only one God,
who created all things, and judges all things; and they hold
the Bible according to the letter, and use the Psalter as the
Jews do; and they say that they are the right sons of God;
and, among all other folk, they say that they be best beloved
of God, and that to them belongs the heritage that God promised to his beloved children; and they have also a different
clothing and outward appearance from other people, for they
wrap their heads in red linen cloth, as a distinction from others;
and the Saracens wrap their heads in white linen cloth; and
the Christian men that dwell in the country wrap them in
blue of India, and the Jews in yellow cloth.   In that country
dwell many of the Jews, paying tribute as Christians do.

CHAPTER X.

OF THE PROVINCE OF GALILEE, AND WHERE ANTICHRIST SHALL BE BORN.
—OF NAZARETH.—OF THE AGE OF OUR LADY.—OF THE DAY OF DOOM;
; AND OF THE CUSTOMS OF JACOBITES, SYRIANS, AND GEORGIANS.

FROM this country of the Samaritans men go to the plains of
Galilee, and leave the hills on the one side.   Galilee is one
of the provinces of the Holy Land; and in that province are
the cities of Nain, and Capernaum, and Chorazin, and Bethsaida.   In this Bethsaida St. Peter and St. Andrew were born.
And four miles thence is Chorazin; and five miles from Chorazin is the city of Kedar, whereof the Psalter speaketh:
" I dwell in the tents of Kedar*.   In Chorazin shall Anti
christ be born, as some men say; and others say he shall be
born in Babylon; for the prophet saith, " Out of Babylon
shall come a serpent that shall devour all the world."   This
Antichrist shall be nourished in Bethsaida, and he shall reign
in Capernaum; and therefore saith Holy Writ, " Woe unto
thee, Chorazin! woe unto thee, Bethsaida! and thou, Capernaum."†   And all these towns are in the land of Galilee;

* Psalms, cxx. 5.
† Luke, x. 13, 15. This is a curious example of the manner in which
legends were raised on the misapplication of Scripture by the medieval

and also Cana of Galilee is four miles from Nazareth, of
which city was Simon the Canaanite and his wife Cance, of
whom the holy Evangelist speaks : there our Lord performed
the first miracle at the wedding, when he turned water into
wine. And at the extremity of Galilee, on the hills, was the
ark of God taken; and on the other side is Mount Hendor, or
Hermon. And thereabout goeth the brook of Kishon; and
near there Baruch, who was son of Abimelech, with Deborah
the prophetess, overcame the host of Idumea, when Sisera
the king was slain by Jael, the wife of Heber, and Gideon
drove beyond the river Jordan, by strength of the sword, Zeba
and Zalmunna, and there he slew them. Also five miles from
Nain is the city of Jezreel, which was formerly called Zarim,
of which city Jezabel the wicked queen was lady and queen,
who took away the vineyard of Naboth by force. Fast by
that city is the field Mageddo, in which king Joras was
slain by the king of Samaria, and after was carried and buried
in Mount Sion. A mile from Jezreel are the hills of
Gilboa, where Saul and Jonathan, that were so fair, died;
wherefore David cursed them, as Holy Writ saith : "Ye mountains of Gilboa, let there be no dew, neither let there be
rain, upon you."* A mile from the hills of Gilboa, to the
east, is the city of Cyropolis, which was before called Bethsain ;
and upon the walls of that city was the head of Saul hanged.

After men go by the hills, beside the plains of Galilee, unto
Nazareth, which was formerly a great and fair city, but now
there is but a small village, and houses scattered here and
there. It is not walled, but it is situated in a little valley,
with hills all about. Here our Lady was born; but she
was begotten at Jerusalem ; and because our Lady was born
at Nazareth, therefore our Lord bare his surname of that town.
There Joseph took our Lady to wife, when she was fourteen
years of age; and there Gabriel greeted our Lady, saying,
" Hail, thou that art highly favoured, the Lord is with thee†."
And this salutation was made on the site of a great altar of a
fair church that stood there formerly, but it is now all down ;
and they have made a little receptacle, near a pillar of that
church, to receive the offerings of pilgrims. And the Saracens keep that place full dearly, for the profit they have by

theologians, who, in this respect, closely resembled the Talmudists among
the Jews.
* 2 Sam. i. 21.   † Luke, i. 28.

it; and they are very wicked and cruel Saracens, and more spiteful than in any other place, and have destroyed all the churches. Near there is Gabriel's well, where our Lord was wont to bathe, when he was young; and from that well he carried water often to his mother; and in that well she often washed the clothes of her son Jesus Christ; and from Jerusalem thither is three days. Two miles from Nazareth is the city of Sephor, by the way that goes from Nazareth to Acre. And half a mile from Nazareth is the leap of our Lord; for the Jews led him upon a high rock, to make him leap down, and have slain him; but Jesus passed amongst them, and leaped upon another rock; and the steps of his feet are still to be seen in the rock where he alighted. And therefore men say, when in travelling they are in fear of thieves or enemies, "*Jesus autem transiens per medium illorum ibat;*" that is to say, "But Jesus passing through the midst of them, went:" in token and remembrance that as our Lord passed through the Jews' cruelty, and escaped safely from them, so surely may men escape the peril of thieves ; and then men say two verses of the Psalter three times: "*Irruat super eos formido et pavor, in magnitudine brachii tui, Domine, fiant inmobiles, quasi lapis, donec pertranseat populus tuus, Domine; donec pertranseat populus tuus iste, quem possedisti.*" ["May fear and dread fall upon them ; by the greatness of thine arm, O Lord, let them be as still as a stone; till thy people pass over, O Lord, till the people pass over, which thou hast purchased."] And then men may pass without peril *. And you shall understand, that our Lady had child when she was fifteen years old; and she was conversant with her son thirty-three years and three months. And after the passion of our Lord she lived twenty-four years †.

---

* The foregoing passages of Scripture, repeated as directed in Latin, composed, in fact, the common charm against thieves and robbers ; and our forefathers seem to have had the simplicity to believe that, by a proper use of it, they were actually under those circumstances rendered invisible. The quotations are from Luke iv. 30 ; Exod. xv. 16. The latter is wrongly quoted from the Psalter. The misinterpretation of the first passage (it was believed that Jesus became invisible) appears to have arisen at a very early period.

† There was an immense mass of legendary matter of this kind current in the middle ages, with which it is necessary, in a certain degree, to be acquainted, in order to understand the literature and manners of our forefathers. It is to such legends that the old writers frequently allude when we suppose that they are merely misquoting Scripture.

From Nazareth we go four miles to Mount Tabor, which is
a very fair and lofty hill, where was formerly a town and
many churches, but they are all destroyed; but yet there is
a place, which they call the School of God, where he was wont
to teach his disciples, and told them the secrets of Heaven *.
At the foot of that hill Melchisedek, who was king of Salem,
met Abraham in the turning of the hill on his return from
the battle, when he had slain Abimelech; and this Melchisedek was both king and priest of Salem, which is now called
Jerusalem.   On that hill of Tabor our Lord transfigured himself before St. Peter, St. John, and St. James; and there they
saw in spirit Moses and Elias the prophets, and therefore St.
Peter said, "Lord, it is good for us to be here; let us make
here three tabernacles."   On that hill and in that same place,
at Doomsday, four angels shall blow with four trumpets, and
raise all men that have suffered death since the world was
created to life; and they shall come in body and soul in
judgment, before the face of our Lord, in the valley of Jehoshaphat.   And it shall be on Easter-day, the time of our
Lord's resurrection; and the judgment shall begin on the
same hour that our Lord descended to hell and despoiled it;
for at that hour shall he despoil the world, and lead his chosen
to bliss; and the others shall be condemned to perpetual
punishment; and then shall every man have after his desert,
either good or evil, unless the mercy of God exceed his
righteousness.

A mile from Mount Tabor is Mount Hermon, and there
was the city of Nain.   Before the gate of that city our Lord
raised the widow's son.   Three miles from Nazareth is the
castle of Saffra, of which were the sons of Zebedee and the
sons of Alpheus.   Also, seven miles from Nazareth, is Mount
Cain, under which is a well, and beside that well, Lamech,
Noah's father, slew Cain with an arrow.   For this Cain went
through briars and bushes as a wild beast; and he had lived
from the time of Adam, his father, unto the time of Noah;
and so he lived nearly two thousand years.   And Lamech
was blind for old age †.

From Saffra we go to the sea of Galilee, and to the city of

---

* This is of course a little more legend.   The notion that there was a town
on the summit of Mount Tabor is probably a mistake of our traveller.

† This legend arose out of an interpretation given to Gen. iv. 23, 24.   See,
as an illustration, the scene in the "Coventry Mysteries," pp. 44-46.

Tiberias, which is situated upon that sea. And although they call it a sea, it is neither sea, nor arm of the sea; for it is but a stank of fresh water, which is in length one hundred furlongs, and in breadth forty furlongs; and it hath in it great plenty of good fish, and the river Jordan runs through it. The city is not very great, but it has good baths. And where the river Jordan leaves the sea of Galilee is a great bridge, where they pass from the land of promise to the land of Bashan, and the land of Gerrasentz, which are about the river Jordan and the commencement of the sea of Tiberias. And from thence may men go to Damascus in three days, by the kingdom of Traconitis, which kingdom extends from Mount Hermon to the sea of Galilee, or the sea of Tiberias; or the sea of Gennesareth, which are different names of this sea, or rather this stank of which I have spoken, which changes thus its name according to the names of the cities that are situated beside it. On that sea our Lord went dryfoot; and there he took up St. Peter, when he began to sink in the sea, and said to him, "O thou of little faith, wherefore didst thou doubt?" * And after his resurrection our Lord appeared on that sea to his disciples, and bade them fish, and filled the net full of great fishes. In that sea our Lord rowed oftentime; and there he called to him St. Peter, St. Andrew, and St. James and St. John, the sons of Zebedee. In that city of Tiberias is the table on which our Lord ate with his disciples after his resurrection; and they knew him in breaking of bread, as the Gospel saith†. And near the city of Tiberias is the hill where our Lord fed five thousand persons, with five barley loaves and two fishes. In that city a man cast a burning dart in wrath after our Lord, and the head smote into the earth, and waxed green, and it grew to a great tree; and it grows still, and the bark thereof is all like coals. Also in the head of that sea of Galilee, toward the north, is a strong and lofty castle, called Saphor; and close by it is Capernaum: there is not so strong a castle within the land of promise; and there is a good town beneath, also called Saphor. In that castle St. Anne, our Lady's mother, was born. And there, beneath, was the centurion's house. That country is called the Galilee of the Gentiles, who were taken to tribute of Zebulon and Naphthali. And in returning from that castle, at a distance of thirty

---

* Matt. xiv. 31.   † Luke, xxiv. 30.

miles, is the city of Dan, formerly called Belinas, or Cesarea Philippi, situated at the foot of the mountain of Libanus, where the river Jordan arises.   There begins the land of promise, and it extends unto Beersheba, in length from north to south, and contains full one hundred and eighty miles; and in breadth, that is, from Jericho to Jaffa, it contains forty miles of Lombardy, or of our country, which are also little miles. These are not miles of Gascony, or of Germany, where the miles are great miles.

And you must know that the land of promise is in Syria. For the realm of Syria extends from the deserts of Arabia to Cilicia, which is Armenia the Great, that is to say, from south to north; and from east to west it extends from the great deserts of Arabia to the west sea. But in that realm of Syria is the kingdom of Judea, and many other provinces, as Palestine, Galilee, Little Cilicia, and many others.   In that country, and other countries beyond, they have a custom, when they make war, and when men besiege a city or castle, and they within dare not send out messengers with letters from lord to lord to ask succour, of binding their letters to the necks of pigeons, and letting them fly; and the pigeons are so taught, that they fly with those letters to the very place that men would send them to. For they are fed in those places where they are sent to, and they naturally return to where they have been fed.

And you shall understand that amongst the Saracens, in different parts, dwell many Christian men, of many kinds and different names, and all are baptized, and have different laws and different customs; but all believe in God the Father, and the Son, and the Holy Ghost; but they always fail in some articles of our faith.   Some of these are called Jacobites, because St. James converted them, and St. John baptized them.   They say that a man shall make his confession only to God, and not to a man; for only to him should man acknowledge himself guilty of all that he hath misdone; and God ordained not, nor ever devised, nor the prophet either, that one man should confess himself to another (as they say), but only to God; as Moses writeth in the Bible, and as David saith in the Psalter Book, " I will confess to thee, O Lord, in my whole heart:" and " I acknowledge my sin unto thee:"* and " Thou art my God, and I will confess

* Psalms, xxxii. 5.

to thee:" and " Since the thoughts of man shall confess to
thee," &c.   For they know all the Bible and the Psalter, and
therefore allege they so the letter; but they allege not the
authorities thus in Latin, but in their language full openly;
and say well, that David and other prophets say it.   Nevertheless St. Austin, St. Gregory, and St. Hilary say dif-
ferently.   And on such authorities, they say, that only to
God shall a man confess his faults, acknowledging himself
guilty, and crying him mercy, and promising him to amend;
therefore when they will confess them, they take fire, and set
it beside them, and cast therein powder of frankincense; and
in the smoke thereof they confess them to God, and cry him
mercy.   And true it is, that this confession was first and of
nature; but St. Peter the apostle, and they that came after
him, have ordered to make confession to man; and by good
reason, for they perceived well, that no sickness was curable
by good medicine laid thereto, unless men knew the nature
of the malady; and also no man may give fit medicine, unless
he know the quality of the deed.

There are others who are called Syrians, who hold the belief among us and the Greeks; and they all use beards, as
men of Greece do; and they make the sacrament of unleavened bread; and in their language they use the Saracenic
letters, but in their theological mysteries they use Greek letters; and they make their confession as the Jacobites do.

There are others who are called Georgians, who were converted by St. George, and they worship him more than any
other saint, and to him they cry for help; and they came out
of the realm of Georgia.   These people have their crowns
shaven: the clerks have round crowns, and the laity have
their crowns all square; and they hold the same Christian
doctrines as the Greeks, of whom I have spoken before*.

There are others who are called Christians of the girdle,
because they are all girt above†; and there are others called
Nestorians; and some are Arians, some Nubians, some of
Greece, some of India, and some of Prester John's land.
And all these have many articles of our faith, and in others
they differ from us.

* See before, p. 178.

† The khalif Motawakkel had, in A.D. 856, ordered the Christians and
Jews to wear a broad girdle of leather; and they have continued to wear it
in the east till modern times.   From that epoch the Christians of Syria, who
were mostly Jacobites or Nestorians, were called Christians of the girdle.

Chapter XI.

OF THE CITY OF DAMASCUS.—OF THREE WAYS TO JERUSALEM; ONE BY LAND
AND BY SEA; ANOTHER MORE BY LAND THAN BY SEA; AND THE THIRD
WAY TO JERUSALEM ALL BY LAND.

Now that I have told you of some of the people in the countries
before, I will turn again to my way to describe the road back.
From the land of Galilee, of which I have spoken, men come
back to Damascus, which is a very fair and noble city, and full
of all merchandise, and three days from the sea, and five days
from Jerusalem. Men carry merchandise thither upon camels,
mules, horses, dromedaries, and other beasts; and thither
come merchants by sea, from India, Persia, Chaldea, Armenia,
and many other kingdoms. This city was founded by Helizeus
Damascus, who was yeoman and steward to Abraham before
Isaac was born; for he expected to have been Abraham's heir,
and he named the town after his surname, Damascus. And
in that place, where Damascus was founded, Cain slew Abel
his brother. And beside Damascus is Mount Seir. In that
city of Damascus there is great plenty of wells; and within
the city and without are many fair gardens, with diversity of
fruits. No other city can be compared with it for fair gardens
for recreation. The city is great and full of people, and well
walled with double walls, and it contains many physicians;
and St. Paul himself was there a physician, to keep men's
bodies in health, before he was converted; and after that he
was physician of souls. And St. Luke the Evangelist was a
disciple of St. Paul to learn physic, and many others; for St.
Paul held then a school of physic. And near Damascus he
was converted; and after his conversion he dwelt in that city
three days, without sight and without meat or drink. And in
those three days he was raised to heaven, and there he saw
many secrets of our Lord. And close beside Damascus is the
castle of Arkes, which is both fair and strong. From Damascus
we return by our Lady of Sardenak, which is five miles on this
side of Damascus; and it is seated upon a rock, and is a very
fair place, and appears like a castle, which it was formerly;
but it is now a very fair church; and in it are Christian
monks and nuns; and there is a vault under the church where
Christians dwell also; and they have many good vines. In
the church, behind the altar, in the wall, is a table of black
wood, on which formerly was painted an image of our Lady,
which turns into flesh; but now the image appears but little.

But evermore, through the grace of God, that table drops oil, as it were of olive. And there is a vessel of marble under the table, to receive the oil, of which they give to pilgrims; for it healeth many sicknesses. And he that keepeth it cleanly a year, after that year it turneth into flesh and blood.

Between the city of Dark and the city of Raphane is a river, which they call Sabatorye; for on the Saturday * it runs fast, and all the week else it standeth still, and runs nought or little. And there is another river that freezeth wonderfully fast in the night, and by day no frost is seen. And so men go by a city called Beruthe, on the coast of the sea, by which they go to Cyprus; and they arrive at the port of Sur, or Tyre, and then to Cyprus. Or else men may go from the port of Tyre right well, and come not to Cyprus, but arrive at some haven of Greece; and then men come to this country by ways that I have spoken of before.

Now have I told you of ways by the which men go farthest and longest, as by Babylon and Mount Sinai, and many other places, through which lands men turn again to the land of promise. Now I will tell you the direct way to Jerusalem; for some men will not pass it on account of the expense, or because they have no company, or for many other reasonable causes; and therefore I will tell you briefly how a man may go with little expense and in a short time. A man who comes from the lands of the west, goes through France, Burgundy, and Lombardy, and to Venice, and to Genoa, or some other haven of the marshes, and taketh a ship there, and goes by sea to the isle of Gryffle; and so he arrives in Greece, or in Port Moroche, or Valon, or Duras, or at some other haven, and lands to repose himself, and goes again to the sea, and arrives in Cyprus; and comes not to the isle of Rhodes, but arrives at Famagosta, which is the chief haven of Cyprus, or else at Lamatoun, and then embarks again, and passes the haven of Tyre without landing; and so passes by all the havens of that coast till he comes to Jaffa, which is the nearest port to Jerusalem, for it is only seven-and-twenty miles. And from Jaffa men go to the city of Ramla, which is but a short distance thence; and it is a fair city. And beside Ramla is a fair church of our Lady, where our Lord appeared to our Lady in the likeness that betokeneth the Trinity. And there, fast by, is a church of St. George, where his head was smitten off;

---

* It is hardly necessary to remind the reader that *sabbatum*, or *dies sabbati*, is the Latin for Saturday.

and then to the castle of Emmaus; and then to Mount Joy; and from thence pilgrims may first see Jerusalem. And then to Mount Modeyn, and then to Jerusalem. And at Mount Modeyn lies the prophet Maccabeus. And over Ramatha* is the town of Douke, whereof was Amos the good prophet.

Another way. Forasmuch as many men may not bear the sea, but had rather go by land, although it be a more laborious journey, a man shall so go to one of the havens of Lombardy, Venice, or another; and he shall pass into Greece, through Port Moroche or another, and so he shall go to Constantinople. And he shall so pass the water called the Brace of St. George, which is an arm of the sea; and from thence he shall come to Pulveralle, and thence to the castle of Cynople; and from thence he shall go to Cappadocia, which is a great country, where there are many great hills. And he shall go through Turkey, and unto the city of Nice, which the Turks have taken from the emperor of Constantinople. It is a fair city, and wonderfully well walled; and there is a river that is called the Laye; and there men go by the Alps of Aryoprynant, and by the vales of Mallebrynez, and also the vale of Ernax; and so to Antioch the Less, which is situated on the river Riclay. And thereabout are many good and fair hills, and many fair woods, and also wild beasts.

And he that will go by another way, must go by the plains of Romania, coasting the sea. Upon that coast is a wonderfully fair castle, which they call Florathe. And when we are out of those hills, we pass through a city called Maryoche and Arteyse, where there is a great bridge over the river of Ferne, which men call Farfar; and it is a great river, capable of admitting ships. And beside the city of Damascus is a river that comes from the mountain of Libanus, which is called Albane. At the passing of this river St. Eustache lost his two sons, when he had lost his wife. And it goeth through the plain of Arthadoe, and so to the Red Sea; and so men go unto the city of Phenne, and so to the city of Ferne. Antioch is a very fair city, and well walled; it is two miles long, and each pillar of the bridge there has a good tower; and this is the best city of the kingdom of Syria. And from Antioch men may go to the city of Latuche (Latakiyah), and then to Gebel (Jebili), and then to Tourtous (Tortosa); and thereby is the land of Cambre,

---

* Ramah Gibeon, now El Jib. Douke is Ain Duk, the Greek Δωκ (see Robinson, ii. 308, 309). It requires considerable study and research to identify all the names mentioned by Maundeville in the sequel.

where there is a strong castle, which they call Maubeke. And
from Tourtous men go to Tripoli, on the sea; and they go by sea
unto Acre. From this place there are two ways to Jerusalem; on
the left we go first to Damas, by the river Jordan; on the right
we go through the land of Flagam, and so to the city of
Caiphas (Caiffa), of which Caiaphas was lord; and some call
it the Castle of Pilgrims. And from thence it is four days
to Jerusalem, passing through Cesarea Philippi, Jaffa, Ramleh, and Emmaus.

Now I have told you some of the ways by land and water,
how men may go to Jerusalem; but there are many other
ways according to the countries from which they come. There
is one way, all by land, to Jerusalem, without passing any
sea, which is from France or Flanders; but that way is very
long and perilous; and therefore few go that way. It lies
through Germany and Prussia, and so on to Tartary. This
Tartary is held of the great chan, of whom I shall speak more
afterwards; and the lords of Tartary pay the great chan
tribute. This is a very bad land, and sandy, and bears very
little fruit; for there grows little corn, or wine, or beans, or
peas; but there are plenty of cattle; and men eat nothing but
flesh, without bread; and they drink the broth, and also they
drink milk. And they eat all manner of animals, such as
dogs, cats, and rats. And they have little or no wood; and
therefore they warm and boil their meat with horse-dung, and
cow-dung, and that of other beasts, dried by the sun; and
princes and others eat but once a day, and that but little;
and they are very foul people, and of evil nature. And in
summer, in all these countries, fall many tempests, and
dreadful storms of thunder and lightning, which kill many
people, and beasts also. And the temperature passes suddenly from extreme heat to extreme cold. It is the foulest
country, and the most cursed, and the poorest, that men know.
And their prince, whom they call Batho, dwells at the city
of Orda. And truly no good man would dwell in that country;
for it is not worthy for dogs to dwell in. It were a good
country to sow thistles, and briars, and broom, and thorns;
and it is good for no other thing. There is some good land,
but very little, as men say. I have not been in that country;
but I have been in other lands which border on those countries,
and in the land of Russia, and in Nyflan, and in the realm of
Cracow, and Letto (Lithuania), and in Darestan, and in many

other places which border on those parts; but I never went
by that way to Jerusalem, wherefore I cannot describe it from
personal knowledge; for no man may pass by that way well,
except in time of winter, for the perilous waters and difficult
marshes, which no man may pass except it be strong frost, and
snow upon it; for if the snow were not there, men might not
go upon the ice.   And it is full three days of such way to pass
from Prussia to the inhabited land of the Saracens.   And
Christians who shall war against them every year must carry
their victuals with them; for they shall find no good there.
And they must carry their victuals upon the ice, with cars
that have no wheels, which they call sleighs; and as long as
their victuals last they may abide there, but no longer; for
there shall they find no body that will sell them any thing.
And when the spies see any Christian men coming upon them,
they run to the towns, and cry with a loud voice, "Kerra, kerra,
kerra;" and then anon they arm and assemble together.

And you shall understand that it freezeth more strongly in
those countries than in this part of the world; and therefore
hath every man stoves in his house, and on those stoves they
eat and do their occupations all that they may; for that is in
the northern parts, where there is but little sun; and therefore in the very north the land is so cold that no man may
dwell there; and, on the contrary, towards the south it is so
hot that no man may dwell there, because there the sun is
direct over head.

CHAPTER XII.

OF THE CUSTOMS OF THE SARACENS, AND OF THE LAW; AND HOW THE SULTAN DISCOURSED TO ME, THE AUTHOR OF THIS BOOK; AND OF MOHAMMED.

Now since I have spoken of Saracens and of their country,
if you will know a part of their law and belief, I will tell
you, according to their book, which is called Alkoran.   And
some call that book Meshaf; and some call it Harm, according to the different languages of the country.   This
book Mohammed gave them.   In it, among other things, is
written, as I have often seen and read, that the good shall
go to Paradise, and the evil to hell; and that all Saracens
believe.   And if a man ask them what paradise they mean,
they say it is a place of delight, where men shall find all
kinds of fruit, in all seasons, and rivers running with milk

and honey, and wine and sweet water; and they shall have
fair houses and noble,. every man after his desert, made
of precious stones, and of gold and silver ; and every
man shall have eighty wives, all maidens; and he shall
have intercourse every day with them, and still he shall
find them always maidens. Also they believe in and speak
gladly of the Virgin Mary and of the Incarnation. And
they say that Mary was taught of the angel; and that
Gabriel said to her that she was chosen from the beginning of the world ; and that he showed to her the incarnation of Jesus Christ; that she conceived, and bare a
child, remaining a maid; and that witnesseth their book.
And they say also that Jesus Christ spake as soon as he was
born; and that he was a true and holy prophet in word
and deed, and meek, and pious, and righteous, and without
any vice. And they say also that when the angel showed
the incarnation of Christ unto Mary, she was young, and
had great fear. For there was then an enchanter in the
country that dealt with witchcraft, called Taknia, who by
his enchantments could take the likeness of an angel, and
went often and lay with maidens; and therefore Mary feared
lest it had been Taknia, who came to deceive the maidens.
And therefore she conjured the angel that he should tell
her if it were he or no. And the angel answered and said
that she should have no dread of him; for he was a true
messenger of Jesus Christ. Also their book says that when
she had been delivered, under a palm tree, she had great
shame to have a child; and she moaned and said that she
would that she had been dead. And anon the child spake
to her and comforted her, and said, " Mother, have no fear,
for God hath hid in thee his secrets, for the salvation of
the world." And that book saith also that Jesus was sent
from God Almighty to be a mirror and example to all men.
And the Alkoran saith also, of the day of doom, how God
shall come to judge all people ; and the good he shall draw
on his side; and put them into bliss; and the wicked he
shall condemn to the pains of hell. And they say that
among all prophets Jesus was the most excellent and the
most worthy, and that he made the Gospels, in which
is good and healthful doctrine, full of charity and stedfast-
ness, and true preaching to them that believe in God; and
that he was a true prophet, and more than a prophet; and

lived without sin, and gave sight to the blind, and healed the lepers, and raised dead men, and ascended to heaven. They fast a whole month in the year, eating only by night; and they keep from their wives all that month; but the sick are not bound to that fast. Also this book speaks of the Jews, and says they are cursed, because they would not believe that Jesus Christ was come of God; and that they lied falsely on Mary and her son Jesus Christ, saying that they had crucified Jesus the son of Mary; for he was never crucified, as they say, but God made him ascend to him without death; but he transfigured his likeness into Judas Iscariot, and him the Jews crucified, believing that it had been Jesus; and therefore they say that the Christian men err, and have no good knowledge of this, and that they believe falsely that Jesus Christ was crucified. And they say also, that if he had been crucified, God had acted contrary to his righteousness, to suffer Jesus Christ, who was innocent, to be put upon the cross without guilt. And they say that we err in this article, and that the great righteousness of God might not suffer so great a wrong. They acknowledge that the works of Christ are good, and his words and his deeds and his doctrine by his gospels true, and his miracles also true; and the blessed Virgin Mary was a good and holy maiden before and after the birth of Jesus Christ; and that all those that believe perfectly in God shall be saved. And because they go so nigh our faith, they are easily converted to Christian law, when men preach to them and show them distinctly the law of Jesus Christ, and tell them of the prophecies. And also they say that they know well by the prophecies that the law of Mohammed shall fail as the law of the Jews did; and that the law of Christian people shall last to the day of doom. And if any man ask them what is their belief, they answer thus : " We believe in God, creator of heaven and earth, and all other things that he made. And without him is nothing made. And we believe in the day of doom, and that every man shall have his merit according to his desert. And we hold for true all that God hath said by the mouths of his prophets." Also Mohammed commanded, in his Alkoran, that every man should have two wives, or three or four ; but now they take as many as nine, and of lemans as many as a man may support. And if any one of their wives misbehave against her husband, he may cast her out of his house, and part from her and take another; but he shall share with her his goods.   Also when men speak to them of the Father and of the Son and of the Holy Ghost, they say that they be three persons, but not one God.   For their Alkoran speaketh not of the Trinity.   But they say well that God hath speech, and they know well God hath a spirit; for else, they say, he could not be alive.   And when men speak to them of the incarnation, how by the word of the angel God sent his wisdom into earth, and shadowed him in the Virgin Mary; and by the word of God shall the dead be raised at the day of doom; they say that it is true, and that the word of God hath great power.   And they say that whoso knew not the word of God, he should not know God.   And they say also, that Jesus Christ is the word of God, and so saith their Alkoran, where it saith that the angel spake to Mary and said, "Mary, God shall preach the gospel by the word of his mouth, and his name shall be called Jesus Christ." And they say also that Abraham was friend to God, and that Moses spoke familiar with God; and Jesus Christ was the word and the spirit of God; and that Mohammed was the messenger of God.   And they say that of these four Jesus was the most worthy, and the most excellent and the greatest: so that they have many good articles of our faith, although they they have no perfect law and faith as Christian men have, and therefore they are easily converted, especially those that understand the scriptures and the prophecies. For they have the gospels, and the prophecies, and the bible written in their language.   Wherefore they know much of Holy Writ, but they understand it not but after the letter; and so do the Jews, for they understand not the letter spiritually, but carnally, and therefore be they reproved by the wise, who understand it spiritually.

The Saracens say that the Jews are cursed, because they have defiled the law that God sent them by Moses.   And the Christians are cursed also, as they say, for they keep not the commandments and the precepts of the Gospel, which Jesus Christ gave them.   And, therefore, I shall tell you what the sultan said to me one day, in his chamber.   He sent out of his chamber all men, lords and others, because he would speak with me in counsel.   And there he asked me how the Christian men governed themselves in our country?   And

I answered, "Right well; thanked be God." And he said
to me, "Truly, nay; for you Christians care not how un-
truly you serve God. You should set an example to the
common people to do well, and you set them an example of
doing evil. For the commons, upon festival days, when they
should go to church to serve God, go to taverns, and are
there in gluttony all day and night, and eat and drink as
beasts that have no reason, and know not when they have
enough. And also, the Christians encourage one another, in
all ways that they may, to fight, and to deceive one another.
And they are so proud that they know not how to be clothed;
now long, now short, now straight, now large, now with sword,
now with dagger, and in all manner of guises. They should be
simple, meek, and true, and full of alms-deeds, as Jesus was,
in whom they believe; but they are all the contrary, and ever
inclined to evil, and to do evil. And they are so covetous, that
for a little silver they sell their daughters, their sisters, and
their own wives, to put them to lechery. And one seduces
the wife of another, and none of them holdeth faith to
another; but they break their law, that Jesus Christ gave
them to keep for their salvation. And thus, for their sins,
have they lost all this land which we hold. Because, for their
sins here, God hath given them into our hands; not only by
our power, but for their sins. For we know well in very truth,
that when you serve God, God will help you; and when he is
with you, no man may be against you. And that know we well
by our prophecies, that the Christians shall win again this land
out of our hands when they serve God more devoutly. But as
long as they are of foul and unclean living (as they are now),
we have no dread of them, for their God will not help them."*
And then I asked him how he knew the state of the Christians?
And he answered me, "That he knew all the state of the
commons also, by his messengers, whom he sent to all lands,
in guise of merchants of precious stones, cloths of gold, and
other things, to know the manners of every country amongst
Christians. And then he called in all the lords that he had
sent out of his chamber, and he showed me four who were
great lords, who told me of my country, and of many other

---

* We must take this as a little satire of Sir John Maundeville's against the
vices of the day among his own countrymen; and it seems not to have been
without its effect. There is an English metrical version of it in the "Reliquiæ
Antiquæ," ii. 113.

Christian countries, as well as if they had been of the same
country; and they spoke French perfectly well, and the
sultan also, whereof I had great marvel.   Alas! it is great
slander to our faith and to our law, when people that are
without law shall reprove us of our sins.   And they that
should be converted to Christ and to the law of Jesus by
our good examples and by our acceptable life to God, and
so converted to the law of Jesus Christ, are through our
wickedness and evil living, far from us, and strangers from
the holy and true belief shall thus accuse us and hold us
for wicked livers and accursed.   And indeed they say truth.
For the Saracens are good and faithful, and keep entirely
the commandment of the holy book Alkoran, which God
sent them by his messenger Mohammed; to whom, as they
say, St. Gabriel the angel often told the will of God.

And you shall understand that Mohammed was born in
Arabia, and was first a poor boy that kept camels which went
with merchants for merchandise; and so it happened that he
went with the merchants into Egypt.   And in the deserts of
Arabia he went into a chapel where a hermit dwelt; and
when he entered into the chapel, which was but little and
low, and had a small low door, then the entrance became so
great, and so large, and so high, as though it had been of a
great minster, or the gate of a palace.   And this was the
first miracle, the Saracens say, that Mohammed did in his
youth.   Then he began to wax wise and rich; and he was a
great astronomer; and afterwards he was governor and prince
of the land of Cozrodane, which he governed full wisely; in
such manner that, when the prince was dead, he took his
lady, named Gadrige, to wife.   And Mohammed fell often in
the great sickness called the falling evil, wherefore the lady
was sorry that ever she took him to husband.   But Mohammed
made her believe that when he fell so Gabriel the angel
came to speak with him, and for the great brightness of the
angel he might not help falling.   And therefore the Saracens say that Gabriel came often to speak with him.   This
Mohammed reigned in Arabia in the year of our Lord Jesus
Christ 610; and was of the generation of Ishmael, who was
Abraham's son, by Agar, his chambermaid.   And, therefore,
there are Saracens that are called Ishmaelites; and some are
called Agarenes, of Agar; and others are called Saracens, of
Sarah; and some are called Moabites, and some Ammonites,
from the two sons of Lot, Moab and Ammon, whom he begat on

his daughters, and who were afterwards great earthly princes. And also Mohammed loved well a good hermit, who dwelt in the desert a mile from Mount Sinai, in the way from Arabia towards Chaldea and towards India, one day's journey from the sea, where the merchants of Venice come often for merchandise. And so often went Mohammed to this hermit that all his men were angry; for he would gladly hear this hermit preach, and make his men wait all night, and therefore his men thought to put the hermit to death: and so it befel upon a night that Mohammed was drunk with good wine, and he fell asleep; and his men took Mohammed's sword out of his sheath, while he slept, and therewith they slew the hermit, and put his sword, all bloody, in his sheath again. And on the morrow, when he found the hermit dead, he was very wroth, and would have put his men to death; but they all with one accord said that he himself had slain him when he was drunk, and showed him his sword all bloody; and he believed that they said truth. And then he cursed the wine and all those that drink it. And therefore Saracens that be devout never drink wine; but some drink it privately; for if they drank it openly they would be reproved. But they drink good beverage, and sweet and nourishing, which is made of galamelle; and that is what men make sugar of, which is of right good savour, and it is good for the breast. Also it happens sometimes that Christians become Saracens, either from poverty or from ignorance, or else from their own wickedness. And therefore the archiflamen, or the flamen, as our archbishop or bishop, when he receives them, says, *La ellec sila, Machomete rores alla;* that is to say, *There is no God but one, and Mohammed his messenger* *.

Chapter XIII.

OF ALBANIA AND OF LYBIA.—OF THE WISHINGS FOR WATCHING OF THE SPARROW-HAWK; AND OF NOAH'S SHIP.

Now, since I have told you before of the Holy Land, and of that country about, and of many ways to go to that land, and to Mount Sinai, and of Babylon the Greater and the Less,

---

* The foregoing account of Mohammed and his doctrines is of course full of error and prejudice ; but it is curious, as showing the popular notions on the subject in England and France in the fourteenth century, and may be compared with several other popular tracts of that age. The Koran had been translated into Latin as early as the twelfth century. An account very similar to the above is given by Roger of Wendover (Bohn's Antiq. Lib.).

and other places, now is the time, if it please you, to tell you
of the borders and isles, and divers beasts, and of various
peoples beyond these borders. For in the countries beyond
are many divers countries, and many great kingdoms, that
are separated by the four streams that come from terrestrial
Paradise. For Mesopotamia, and the kingdom of Chaldea,
and Arabia, are between the two rivers of Tigris and Euphrates. And Media and Persia are between the rivers of
Nile and Tigris. And Syria, Palestine, and Phœnicia are
between the Euphrates and the Mediterranean Sea, which
sea extends in length from Marok, on the sea of Spain, to
the great sea, so that it lasts beyond Constantinople three
thousand and forty Lombard miles.   Towards the Ocean
Sea, in India, is the kingdom of Scythia, which is inclosed
with mountains ; and after, below Scythia, from the Caspian
Sea to the river Thainy, is Amazonia, or the land of Feminy,
where there is no man, but only women.   And after is
Albania, a full great realm ; so called because the people
are whiter there than in other countries thereabout.   And
in that country are so great and strong dogs, that they assail
lions and slay them.   And then after is Hircania, Bactria,
Iberia, and many other kingdoms.   And between the Red
Sea and the Ocean Sea, towards the south, is the kingdom
of Ethiopia, and Lybia the Higher.   Which land of Lybia
(that is to say, Lower Lybia) commences at the sea of Spain,
from thence where the Pillars of Hercules are, and extends
to Egypt and towards Ethiopia.   In that country of Lybia
the sea is higher than the land, and it seems that it would
cover the earth, and yet it passeth not its bounds.   And
men see in that country a mountain to which no man
cometh.   In this land of Lybia, whoso turneth towards the
east, the shadow of himself is on the right side, and here, in
our country, the shadow is on the left side.   In that sea
of Lybia is no fish, for they may not live for the great heat
of the sun ; because the water is ever boiling for the great
heat.   And many other lands there are that it were too long
to tell or to number ; but of some parts I shall speak more
plainly hereafter.
    Whoever will go towards Tartary, Persia, Chaldea, and
India, must enter the sea at Genoa, or at Venice, or at some
other haven that I have mentioned before, and then pass the
sea and arrive at Trebizond, which is a good city ; and it was

wont to be the haven of Pountz (Pontus). There is the haven
of Persians and of Medians, and of the countries beyond.
In that city lieth St. Athanasius, who was bishop of Alexandria, and made the psalm *Quicunque vult**. This Athanasius was a great doctor of divinity; and because he
preached and spake so deeply of divinity and of the godhead,
he was accused to the pope of Rome of being a heretic;
wherefore the pope sent after him, and put him in prison,
and while he was in prison he made that psalm, and sent it
to the pope, and said, that if he were a heretic that was his
heresy; for that, he said, was his belief. And when the pope
saw it, and had examined it that it was perfect and good, and
verily our faith and our belief, he set him at liberty, and
commanded that psalm to be said every day at prayer; and
so he held Athanasius a good man. But he would never go
to his bishopric again, because he had been accused of heresy.
Trebizond was formerly held by the emperor of Constantinople; but a great man, whom he sent to keep the country
against the Turks, usurped the land and held it to himself,
and called himself emperor of Trebizond†.

And from thence men go through Little Ermony (Armenia),
in which is an old castle, on a rock, called the castle of the
Sparrow-hawk. It is beyond the city of Layays (Lajazzo), beside the town of Pharsipee, which belongs to the lordship of
Cruk, a rich lord and a good Christian. There is found a
sparrow-hawk upon a fair perch, and a fair lady of fairie, who
keeps it; and whoever will watch that sparrow-hawk seven days
and seven nights, and, as some men say, three days and three
nights, without company and without sleep, that fair lady
shall give him, when he hath done, the first wish that he will
wish of earthly things; and that hath been proved oftentimes.
And once a king of Ermony, who was a worthy knight and
brave man, and a noble prince, watched that hawk some time;
and at the end of seven days and seven nights the lady came
to him, and bade him wish, for he had well deserved it; and
he answered that he was a great lord enough, and well in
peace, and had enough of worldly riches; and therefore he
would wish no other thing but the body of that fair lady, to

* *i. e.* The Athanasian Creed.
† A Christian dynasty reigned over the small independent kingdom of
Trebizond from 1204 to 1462, after which it was swallowed up in the
Ottoman empire.

have at his will.   And she answered him, that he knew not
what he asked, and said that he was a fool to desire what he
might not have ; for she said that he should only ask an
earthly thing ; and she was no earthly thing, but a spiritual
thing.   And the king said that he would ask no other thing.
And the lady answered, " Since I may not withdraw you from
your lewd boldness, I shall give you without wishing, and to
all that shall come of you.   Sir king, you shall have war
without peace, and always, to the ninth degree, you shall be
in subjection to your enemies, and you shall be in need of all
goods."   And since that neither the king of Ermony nor the
country were ever in peace or rich ; and they have since been
always under tribute to the Saracens.   At another time the
son of a poor man watched the hawk, and wished that he
might have good success, and be fortunate in merchandise.
And the lady granted it him, and he became the richest and
most famous merchant that might be on sea or on land ; and
he became so rich that he knew not one-thousandth part of
what he had ; and he was wiser in wishing than the king.
Also a knight of the temple watched there, and wished a
purse ever full of gold ; and the lady granted him ; but she
told him that he had asked the destruction of the order ; for
the trust of that purse, and for the great pride that they
should have ; and so it was.   And therefore let him who
watches beware ; for if he sleep he is lost, that never man
shall see him more.   This is not the direct way to go to the
parts that I have mentioned before, but to see the marvel of
which I have spoken.

And, therefore, whoever will go the direct way must proceed
from Trebizond towards Ermony the Great, to a city called Artyroun (Erzeroum), which was formerly a good and populous city,
but the Turks have greatly wasted it.   Thereabout grows little
or no wine or fruit.   In this land the earth is higher than in
any other ; and that makes it very cold.   And there are many
good waters and good wells, that come under earth from the
river of Paradise, which is called Euphrates, which is a day's
journey from this city.   And that river comes towards India,
under earth, and reappears in the land of Altazar.   And so
men pass by this Ermony, and enter the sea of Persia.   From
that city of Artyroun men go to a mountain called Sabissocolle ;
and there beside is another mountain called Ararat, but the
Jews call it Taneez, where Noah's ship rested, and still is upon

that mountain; and men may see it afar in clear weather.
That mountain is full seven miles high; and some men say
that they have seen and touched the ship, and put their
fingers in the parts where the devil went out, when Noah said
"Benedicite."* But they that say so speak without knowledge; for no one can go up the mountain for the great
abundance of snow which is always on that mountain, both
summer and winter, so that no man ever went up since the
time of Noah, except a monk, who, by God's grace, brought
one of the planks down, which is yet in the monastery at the
foot of the mountain. And beside is the city of Dayne, which
was founded by Noah, near which is the city of Any†, in which
were one thousand churches. This monk had great desire to
go up that mountain; and so upon a day he went up; and
when he had ascended the third part of the mountain he was
so weary that he fell asleep; and when he awoke he found
himself lying at the foot of the mountain. Then he prayed
devoutly to God that he would suffer him to go up; and an
angel came to him, and said that he should go up; and so he
did. And since that time no one ever went up; wherefore
men should not believe such words.

From that mountain we go to the city of Thauriso (Tabreez),
which was formerly called Taxis, a very fair and great city,
and one of the best in the world for merchandise; and it is
in the land of the emperor of Persia. And they say that the
emperor receives more in that city for custom of merchandise than the richest Christian king alive from all his realm;
for the toll and custom of his merchants is beyond calculation. Beside that city is a hill of salt, of which every man
taketh what he will. There dwell many Christians under
tribute of Saracens. And from that city men pass by many
towns and castles, on the way towards India to the city of
Sadony, which is ten days from Thauriso; and it is a very
noble and great city. And there the emperor of Persia
dwells in summer, because the climate is temperate. And
there are good rivers capable of bearing ships. Then men
go the way towards India for many days, and by many coun-

* This is an allusion to another medieval religious legend.
† An account of the remarkable ruins, both ecclesiastical and palatial,
that are met with at Anni, which was the capital of the Pakradian branch
of Armenian kings, will be found in the Travels of Sir R. K. Porter, and
those of W. J. Hamilton, vol. i. p. 197.

tries, to the city called Cassak, a full noble city, abounding in corn, wines, and all other goods. This is the city where the three kings met together when they went to seek our Lord in Bethlehem, to worship him, and to present him with gold, essence, and myrrh. And it is from that city to Bethlehem fifty-three days. From that city men go to another city, called Bethe (Beth-Germa? or Old Bagdad), a day from the sea which they call the Sandy Sea. This is the best city which the emperor of Persia has in all his land, and it is called there Chardabago; and others call it Vapa. And the Pagans say that no Christian may remain long alive in that city; but they die within short time, and no man knows the cause. Afterwards men go by many cities and towns and great countries to the city of Cornaa (Kornah?), which was formerly so great that the walls are twenty-five miles about. The walls are still standing, but it is not all inhabited. From Cornaa men go by many lands, and many cities and towns, unto the land of Job; and there ends the land of the emperor of Persia.

Chapter XIV.

OF THE LAND OF JOB, AND OF HIS AGE.——OF THE ARRAY OF MEN OF CHALDEA.
——OF THE LAND WHERE WOMEN DWELL WITHOUT COMPANY OF MEN.——OF
THE KNOWLEDGE AND VIRTUES OF THE TRUE DIAMOND.

AFTER leaving Cornaa, we enter the land of Job, a very fair country, and abounding in all goods; and men call it the land of Sweze (Susiana). In that land is the city of Theman. Job was a pagan, and he was son of Are of Gosre, and held the land as prince of the country; and he was so rich that he knew not the hundredth part of his goods. And, although he was a pagan, still he served God well, after his law; and our Lord took his service in satisfaction. And when he fell in poverty he was seventy-eight years of age. And afterwards, when God had tried his patience, which was so great, he brought him again to riches, and to higher estate than before. And after that he was king of Idumea, after king Esau. And when he was king he was called Jobab. And in that kingdom he lived afterwards one hundred and seventy years*; and so he was of age, when he died, two hundred and forty-eight years. In that land of Job there is no want of any thing needful to

* One hundred and forty years. Job, xlii. 16.

man's body. There are hills, where they get manna in greater abundance than in any other country. This manna is called bread of angels; and it is a white thing, very sweet and delicious, and sweeter than honey or sugar; it comes of the dew of heaven, that falls upon the herbs in that country; and it congeals, and becomes white and sweet; and they put it in medicines for rich men, for it cleanseth the blood, and putteth out melancholy. This land of Job borders on the kingdom of Chaldea. This land of Chaldea is very extensive; and the language of that country is greater in sounding than it is in other parts beyond the sea. We pass it to go to the Tower of Babylon the Great, of which I have spoken, where all the languages were first changed; and that is four days from Chaldea. In that realm are fair men, and they go full nobly arrayed in cloths of gold, orfrayed, and apparelled with great pearls and precious stones full nobly; but the women are very ugly, and vilely arrayed; and they go barefoot, and clothed in evil garments, large and wide, but short to the knees, and long sleeves down to the feet, like a monk's frock, and their sleeves are hanging about their shoulders; and they are black women, foul and hideous; and truly they are as bad as they are foul. In that kingdom of Chaldea, in a city called Ur, dwelt Terah, Abraham's father; and there was Abraham born, which was in the time that Ninus was king of Babylon, of Arabia, and of Egypt. This Ninus made the city of Nineveh, which Noah had begun; and because Ninus completed it, he called it Nineveh, after his own name. There lies Tobit the prophet, of whom Holy Writ speaketh. And from that city of Ur Abraham departed, by the commandment of God, after the death of his father, and led with him Sarah, his wife, and Lot, his brother's son, because he had no child. And they went to dwell in the land of Canaan, in a place called Shechem. And this Lot was he who was saved, when Sodom and Gomorrah and the other cities, where the Dead Sea now is, were burnt and sunk down to hell, as I have told you before.

Beside the land of Chaldea is the land of Amazonia, in which is all women, and no man; not, as some men say, because men may not live there, but because the women will not suffer men amongst them, to be their sovereigns *. This land of Amazonia is an island surrounded by the sea, except

* Here follows, in the original, the common story of the Amazons, taken from the ancient authors, which is not worth reprinting.

in two places, where are two entrances. And beyond the water dwell the men who are their paramours, where they go to solace them when they will. Beside Amazonia is the land of Tarmegyte, a great and very pleasant country, and for the goodness of which king Alexander made there the city of Alexandria: he made twelve cities of the same name, but that city is now called Celsite. And from that other side of Chaldea, toward the south, is Ethiopia, a great country, which extends to the extremity of Egypt. Ethiopia is divided into two principal parts, the east and the south, the latter part being called Mauritania. And the people of that country are blacker than in the other part, and are called Moors. In that country is a well, which in the day is so cold that no man may drink thereof, and in the night it is so hot that no man may suffer his hand therein. Towards the south, to pass by the Ocean Sea, is a great country, but men may not dwell there, for the fervent burning of the sun. In Ethiopia all the rivers and waters are troubled, and somewhat salt, for the great heat that is there. And the people of that country are easily intoxicated, and have but little appetite for meat. And they are afflicted with dysenteries, and live not long. In Ethiopia, the children, when young, are all yellow; and when they grow older that yellowness turns to black. In Ethiopia is the city of Saba and the land where one of the three kings reigned who came to our Lord in Bethlehem.

From Ethiopia they go to India through many different countries; and men call the higher India Emlak. India is divided into three principal parts: the Greater, which is a very hot country; and India the Less, which is a temperate country, extending to the land of Media; and the third part, toward the north, is so cold, that for continual frost the water becomes crystal; and upon those rocks of crystal grow the good diamonds, that are of troubled colour. Yellow crystal draws colour like oil. And they are so hard that no man may polish them; and men call them diamonds in that country, and *hamese* in another country. Other diamonds are found in Arabia, but they are not so good; they are browner and more tender. And other diamonds also are found in the island of Cyprus, which are still more tender, and may easily be polished; and they find diamonds also in Macedonia; but the best and most precious are in India. And they often find hard diamonds in a mass which comes

out of gold, when they break the mass in small pieces, to
purify it and refine it, out of the mine. And it sometimes
happens that they find some as great as a pea, and some less;
and they are as hard as those of India. And although
men find good diamonds in India, yet nevertheless men find
them more commonly upon the rocks in the sea, and upon
hills where the mine of gold is. They grow many together,
one little, another great; and there are some of the greatness
of a bean, and some as great as a hazel nut. They are square
and pointed of their own kind, both above and beneath,
without work of man's hand; and they grow together, male
and female, and are nourished by the dew of heaven; and they
engender commonly and bring forth small children, that multiply and grow all the year. I have oftentimes tried the experiment, that if a man keep them with a little of the rock, and
wet them with May-dew often, they shall grow every year,
and the small will grow great *; for right as the fine pearl
congeals and grows great by the dew of heaven, right so doth
the true diamond ; and right as the pearl of its own nature
takes roundness, so the diamond, by virtue of God, takes
squareness. And a man should carry the diamond on his left
side, for it is of greater virtue than on the right side †; for
the strength of their growing is toward the north, that is the
left side of the world ; and the left part of man is, when he
turns his face towards the east. And if you wish to know the
virtues of the diamond (as men may find in the " Lapidary," ‡
with which many men are not acquainted), I shall tell you,
as they beyond the sea say and affirm, from whom all science
and philosophy comes. He who carries the diamond upon
him, it gives him hardiness and manhood, and it keeps the
limbs of his body whole. It gives him victory over his enemies in court and in war, if his cause be just; and it keeps
him that bears it in good wit; and it keeps him from strife
and riot, from sorrows and from enchantments, and from phan-
tasies and illusions of wicked spirits. And if any cursed
witch or enchanter would bewitch him that bears the diamond,
all that sorrow and mischance shall turn to the offender,

* Maundeville's notions concerning diamonds are somewhat singular; they
are, however, partly taken from Pliny, lib. xxxvii. c. 4.

† Hence the ring was commonly worn on the left hand.

‡ The " Liber Lapidarius " was a popular medieval treatise on the virtues
and properties of precious stones, which was of great importance when
people implicitly believed in the wonderful efficacy of such things.

through virtue of that stone ; and also no wild beast dare assail the man who bears it on him.   Also the diamond should be given freely, without coveting and without buying, and then it is of greater virtue ; and it makes a man stronger and firmer against his enemies ; and heals him that is lunatic, and those whom the fiend pursues or torments.   And if venom or poison be brought in presence of the diamond, anon it begins to grow moist and sweat.   There are also diamonds in India that are called violastres (for their colour is like violet, or more brown than violets), that are very hard and precious, but some men like them not so well as the others.   Also there is another kind of diamonds that are as white as crystal ; but they are a little more troubled ; and they are good and of great virtue, and they are all square and pointed of their own nature ; and some are six-square, some four-square, and some three, as nature shapes them ; and, therefore,. when great lords and knights go to seek honour in arms, they gladly bear the diamond upon them.

I shall speak a little more of the diamonds, that they who know them not may not be deceived by chapmen who go through the country selling them ; for whoever will buy the diamond, it is needful that he know them, because men counterfeit them often with crystal, which is yellow; and with sapphires of citron colour, which is yellow also ; and with the sapphire loupe, and with many other stones.   But these counterfeits are not so hard ; and the points will break easily, and men may easily polish them.   But some workmen, for malice, will not polish them, to that intent, to make men believe that they may not be polished.   But men may assay them in this manner ; first cut with them or write with them in sapphires, in crystal, or in other precious stones.   Also take the adamant *, that is, the shipman's stone, that draws the needle to it, and lay the diamond on it, and lay the needle before the adamant ; and if the diamond be good and virtuous, the adamant draws not the needle, while the diamond is there present.   This is the proof that they beyond the sea use.   Nevertheless it happens often that the good diamond loses its virtue by sin, and for incontinence of him that bears it; and then it is needful to make it recover its virtue again, or else it is of little value.

* *i. e.* The loadstone. The appellation of the " shipman's stone" is curious, as showing that the properties of the mariners' compass were well known before the middle of the fourteenth century. We have other evidence to show that the mariner's compass was known at a much earlier period.

CHAPTER XV.

OF THE CUSTOMS OF ISLES ABOUT INDIA.—OF THE DIFFERENCE BETWEEN
IDOLS AND SIMULACRES.—OF THREE KINDS OF PEPPER GROWING UPON
ONE TREE.—OF THE WELL THAT CHANGES ITS ODOUR EVERY HOUR OF
THE DAY.

IN India are very many different countries; and it is called
India, from a river which runs through the country called
Indus. In that river they find eels thirty feet long and more *
And the people that dwell near that water are of evil colour,
green and yellow. In India, and about India, are more than
five thousand inhabited islands, good and great, besides those
that are uninhabitable, and other small islands. Every island
has great plenty of cities, and towns, and people without
number†. For men of India have this condition of nature,
that they never go out of their own country, and therefore
there is great multitude of people; but they are not stirring
or moveable, because they are in the first climate, that is, of
Saturn. And Saturn is slow, and little moving; for he tar-
rieth thirty years to make his course through the twelve signs;
and the moon passes through the twelve signs in a month.
And because Saturn is so slow of motion, the people of
that country, that are under his climate, have no inclination
or will to move or stir to seek strange places. Our country
is all the contrary; for we are in the seventh climate, which
is of the moon, and the moon moves rapidly, and is a planet of
progression; and for that reason it gives us a natural will to
move lightly, and to go different ways, and to seek strange
things and other diversities of the world; for the moon goes
round the earth more rapidly than any other planet.

Also men go through India by many different countries, to the
great Sea of Ocean. And afterwards men find there an island
that is called Hermes‡; and there come merchants of Venice
and Genoa, and of other parts, to buy merchandise; but there
is great heat in that district. In that country, and in Ethiopia,
and in many other countries, the inhabitants lie all naked in
rivers and waters, men and women together, from undurn§

* This is taken from Pliny's Natural History, lib. ix. c. 3.
† Pliny's Natural History, lib. vi. c. 17.
‡ Ormuz.
§ *Undurn* was nine o'clock in the morning. The Latin text has "*A diei
hora tertia usque ad nonam.*"

of the day till it be past noon. And they lie all in the water, except the face, for the great heat that there is. And the women have no shame of the men, but lie all together, side by side, till the heat is past. There may men see many foul figures assembled, and chiefly near the good towns. In that island are ships without nails of iron or bonds, on account of the rocks of adamants (loadstones *); for they are all abundant thereabout in that sea, that it is marvellous to speak of; and if a ship passed there that had either iron bonds or iron nails, it would perish; for the adamant, by its nature, draws iron to it; and so it would draw to it the ship, because of the iron, that it should never depart from it.

From that island men go by sea to another island called Chana, where is abundance of corn and wine; and it was wont to be a great island, and a great and good haven, but the sea has greatly wasted it and overcome it. The king of that country was formerly so strong and so mighty that he held war against king Alexander. The people of that country differ in their religious belief; for some worship the sun, some the moon, some the fire, some trees, some serpents, or the first thing that they meet in a morning; and some worship simulacres, and some idols. Between simulacres and idols there is a great difference; for simulacres are images made after the likeness of men or of women, or of the sun or of the moon, or of any beast, or of any natural thing; and an idol is an image made by the lewd will of man, which is not to be found among natural things, as an image that has four heads, one of a man, another of a horse, or of an ox, or of some other beast, that no man has seen in nature. And they that worship simulacres worship them for some worthy man who once existed, as Hercules and many others, that did many wonders in their time. For they say well that they are not gods; for they know well that there is a God of nature that made all things, who is in heaven; but they know well that this man may not do the wonders that he did, unless it had been by the special gift of God, and therefore they say that he was well with God, wherefore they worship him. And

---

* This tradition of a mountain of magnetic ore is very general among the Chinese and throughout Asia. The Chinese assign its position to a specific place, which they call Tchang-haï, in the southern sea, between Tonquin and Cochin-China, which is precisely the same geographical region indicated in the adventures of Sinbad the Sailor.

so they say of the sun; because it changes the season and
gives heat and nourishes all things upon earth; and since it
is of so great profit, they know well that that might not be,
unless God loved it more than any other thing. And because God has given it greater virtue in the world, therefore
it is right, as they say, to worship and reverence it. And so
they say of other planets, and of the 'fire also, because it is so
profitable. And of idols, they say also that the ox is the
most holy beast that is on earth, and most patient and more
profitable than any other; and they know well that it may
not be without special grace of God, and therefore make they
their god of an ox the one part, and the other part of a man,
because man is the noblest creature on earth, and also he
hath lordship above all beasts; therefore make they the upper
half of the idol of a man, and the lower half of an ox; and so
of serpents and of other beasts, and different things that they
worship, that they meet first in a morning. And they worship also especially all those that they have good meeting of,
and when they speed well in their journey, after their meeting, and mostly such as they have proved and assayed by experience of long time; for they say, that that good meeting
may not come but by the grace of God; and therefore they
make images like to those things in which they have belief,
to behold them and worship them first in the morning, before
they meet any contrarious thing. And there are also some
Christians who say that it is good to meet some beasts first
in the morning, and bad to meet others; and that they have
often proved that it is very unlucky to meet the hare, and
swine, and many other beasts; and the sparrow-hawk, and
other ravenous birds, when they fly after their prey, and take
it before armed men, is a good sign, and if they fail of taking
their prey it is an evil sign; and also, to such people, it is
unlucky to meet ravens. There are many people that believe
in these things, and in other such, because it happens often so
to fall after their fantasies; and also there are men enough
that disbelieve in them. And since Christians have such belief, who are instructed and taught all day by holy doctrine
wherein they should believe, it is no wonder that the Pagans,
who have no good doctrine, but only of their nature, believe
more largely, on account of their simplicity. And truly I
have seen Pagans and Saracens, whom men call augurs, that
when we ride in arms in different countries against our ene-

mies, they would tell us, by the flight of birds, the prognostications of things that fell after; and so they did full often, and offered to pledge their heads that it would fall as they said. But a man should not, therefore, put his belief in such things, but always have full trust and belief in God our sovereign lord. The Saracens have won and now hold this island of Chana. It contains many lions, and many other wild beasts, with rats as great as dogs, which they take with great mastiffs, for cats cannot take them. In this island, and many others, they do not bury their dead; for the heat is so great, that in a little time the flesh will consume from the bones.

From thence men go by sea towards India the Greater, to a good and fair city called Sarche, where dwell many Christians of good faith: and there are many monks, especially mendicants. Thence men go by sea to the land of Lomb, in which grows the pepper, in the forest called Combar, and it grows nowhere else in all the world; that forest extends full eighteen days in length. In the forest are two good cities, one called Fladrine, and the other Zinglantz, in each of which dwell many Christians and Jews; for it is a good and rich country, but the heat is exceeding. And you shall understand that the pepper grows like a wild vine, which is planted close by the trees of that wood, to sustain it; the fruit hangs like bunches of grapes, with which the tree is so laden that it seems that it would break; and when it is ripe, it is all green like ivy berries; and then men cut them as they do the vines, and put them upon an oven, where they become black and crisp. There are three kinds of pepper all on one tree; long pepper, black pepper, and white pepper. The long pepper is called Sorbotin; the black is called Fulful; and the white is called Bano. The long pepper comes first, when the leaf begins to appear, and is like the catkins of hazel that come before the leaf, and it hangs low. Next comes the black with the leaf, like clusters of grapes, all green; and, when gathered, it becomes the white, which is somewhat less than the black, and of that but little is brought to this country, for they keep it for themselves, because it is better and milder than the black. In that country are many kinds of serpents and other vermin, in consequence of the great heat of the country and of the pepper. And some men say that, when they will gather the pepper, they make fires and burn thereabouts, to make the serpents

and cockodrills to fly; but this is not true   But thus they
do : they anoint their hands and feet with a juice made of
snails and other things, of which the serpents and venomous
beasts hate the savour; and that makes them fly before them,
because of the smell, and then they gather in the pepper in
safety.

Toward the head of that forest is the city of Polombe, above
which is a great mountain, also called Polombe, from which
the city has its name.   And at the foot of that mountain is
a fair and great well, which has the odour and savour of all
spices; and at every hour of the day it changes its odour and
savour diversely; and whoever drinks three times fasting of
the water of that well is whole of all kind of sickness that
he has; and they that dwell there, and drink often of that
well, never have sickness, but appear always young.   I have
drunk thereof three or four times, and methinks I still fare
the better.   Some men call it the Well of Youth; for they
that often drink thereof appear always young, and live without sickness *.   And men say that that well comes out of
Paradise, and therefore it is so virtuous.   All that country
grows good ginger; and therefore merchants go thither for
spicery.   In that land men worship the ox, for his simpleness
and for his meekness, and for the profit that comes of him.
They say that he is the holiest beast on earth; for they consider that whosoever is meek and patient, he is holy and profitable, for then, they say, he hath all virtues in him.   They
make the ox to labour six or seven years, and then they eat
him.   And the king of the country has always an ox with
him; and his keeper has every day great fees, and keeps
every day his dung and urine in two vessels of gold, and
brings it before their prelate, whom they call archiprotopa-
paton, and he carries it before the king, and makes over it a
great blessing; and then the king wets his hands in what
they call gall, and anoints his forehead and breast, and afterwards he rubs himself with the dung and urine with great
reverence, to be filled with the virtues of the ox, and made
holy by the virtue of that holy thing.   And when the king
has done, the lords follow his example; and after them their

* The Well of Youth was a sort of El Dorado of the middle ages, which
most people believed in, and many went in search of; but, in spite of Maundeville's assertion that he had drunk of the water, it appears never to have been
found.

ministers, and other men, if there be any left. In that country they make idols, half man, half ox; and in those idols evil
spirits speak, and even answer to men. Before these idols
men often slay their children, and sprinkle the blood on the
idols, and so they make their sacrifice. And when any man
dies in the country they burn his body in the name of penance, to that intent that he suffer no pain in earth, by being
eaten by worms. And if his wife have no child they burn
her with him, and say that it is right that she accompany him
in the other world as she did in this. But if she have children with him, they let her live with them, to bring them up,
if she will. And if she love more to live with her children then to die with her husband, they hold her for false
and cursed ; and she shall never be loved or trusted by the
people. And if the woman die before the husband, they burn
him with her, if he will; and if he will not, no man con-
straineth him thereto, but he may wed another time without
blame or reproof. In that country grow many strong vines,
and the women drink wine, and men not; and the women
shave their beards, and the men not.

Chapter XVI.

OF THE JUDGMENTS MADE BY SAINT THOMAS.—OF DEVOTION AND SACRIFICE
MADE TO IDOLS THERE, IN THE CITY OF CALAMY ; AND OF THE PROCESSION
ABOUT THE CITY.

FROM that country we pass many districts, towards a country
ten days' journey thence, called Mabaron *, which is a great
kingdom, containing many fair cities and towns. In that
kingdom lies the body of St. Thomas the Apostle, in flesh
and bone, in a fair tomb, in the city of Calamy ; for there he
was martyred and buried. But men of Assyria carried his
body into Mesopotamia, into the city of Edessa; and, afterwards, he was brought thither again. And the arm and the
hand that he put in our Lord's side, when he appeared to
him after his resurrection, is yet lying in a vessel without the
tomb. By that hand they there make all their judgments.
For when there is any dissension between two parties, and
each of them maintains his cause, both parties write their
causes in two bills, and put them in the hand of St. Tho-

* This is the country described by Marco Polo, book iii. c. 20, under the
name of Maabar.

mas; and anon he casts away the bill of the wrong cause,
and holds still the bill with the right cause. And, therefore,
men come from far countries to have judgment of doubtful
causes. The church where St. Thomas lies is both great
and fair, and full of great simulacres, which are great images
that they call their gods, of which the least is as great as two
men. And, amongst the others, there is a great image larger
than any of the others, all covered with fine gold and precious
stones and rich pearls; and that idol is the god of false Christians, who have renounced their faith. It sits in a chair of
gold, very nobly arrayed, and has about the neck large girdles
made of gold and precious stones and pearls. The church is
full richly wrought, and gilt all over within. And to that
idol men go on pilgrimage, as commonly and with as great
devotion as Christian men go to St. James, or other holy pilgrimages. And many people that come from far lands to seek
that idol, for the great devotion that they have, never look
upwards, but evermore down to the earth, for dread to see
any thing about them that should hinder them of their devotion. And some who go on pilgrimage to this idol bear
knives in their hands, that are very keen and sharp, and
continually, as they go, they smite themselves on their arms,
legs, and thighs, with many hideous wounds; and so they
shed their blood for love of that idol. They say that he is
blessed and holy that dieth so for love of his god. And
others there are who carry their children to be slain as a
sacrifice to that idol; and after they have slain them, they
sprinkle the blood upon the idol. And some, who come
from far, in going towards this idol, at every third pass that
they go from their home, they kneel, and so continue till
they come thither; and when they come there, they take
incense and other aromatic things of noble smell, and scent
the idol, as we here do God's precious body. And so people
come to worship this image, some a hundred miles, and
some many more. And before the minster of this idol is a
pool, like a great lake, full of water; and therein pilgrims
cast gold and silver, pearls and precious stones, without
number, instead of offerings. And when the ministers of
that church need to make any reparation of the church
or of any of the idols, they take gold and silver, pearls and
precious stones, out of the pond, to pay the expenses of
such thing as they make or repair. At great feasts and

solemnities of that idol, as the dedication of the church and the
enthroning of the idol, all the country about meet there, and set
the idol upon a chair with great reverence, well arrayed with
cloths of gold, of rich cloths of Tartary, of camaka*, and
other precious cloths; and they lead him about the city with
great solemnity. And before the chair go first in procession
all the maidens of the country, two and two together; and,
after them, the pilgrims. And some of them fall down under
the wheels of the chair, and let the chair go over them, so
that they die immediately. And some have their arms or
their limbs broken. And all this they do for love of their
god, in great devotion. And they think that the more pain
and tribulation they suffer for love of their god, the more
joy they shall have in another world. In a word, they
suffer so great pains and so hard martyrdoms for love of
their idol, that a Christian, I believe, durst not take upon
him the tenth part of the pain for love of our Lord Jesus
Christ. And after them, before the chair, go all the minstrels of the country, with divers instruments, and make all
the melody they can. And when they have all gone about
the city, they return to the minster and put the idol again
into its place. And then, for the love and in worship of
that idol, and for the reverence of the feast, two hundred or
three hundred persons slay themselves with sharp knives,
whose bodies they bring before the idol; and then they
say that those are saints, because they slew themselves
of their own good will, for love of their idol. And as men
here, that had a holy saint of their kin, would think that
it was to them a high worship, right so they think there.
And as men here devoutly would write holy saints' lives and
their miracles, and sue for their canonizations, right so do they
there for them that slay themselves voluntarily for love of
their idol. And they say that they are glorious martyrs and
saints, and put them in their writings and in their litanies,
and boast them greatly one to another of their holy kinsmen,
that so became saints, and say, " I have more holy saints in
my family than thou in thine." And the custom also there
is this, that when any one has such devotion and intent
to slay himself for love of his god, they send for all their
friends, and have numerous minstrels, and they go before the

---

* A rich cloth of silk, mentioned not unfrequently in medieval writers.

idol, leading him that will slay himself for such devotion, between them, with great reverence. And he, all naked, hath a very sharp knife in his hand, and he cuts a great piece of his flesh and casts it in the face of his idol, saying his prayers, recommending himself to his god : and then he smites himself, and makes great wounds and deep here and there, till he falls down dead. And then his friends present his body to the idol; and then they say, singing, " Holy god, behold what thy true servant hath done for thee; he hath forsaken his wife, and his children, and his riches, and all the goods of the world and his own life for the love of thee, and to make for thee sacrifice of his flesh and of his blood. Wherefore, holy god, put him amongst thy best beloved saints in thy bliss of paradise, for he hath well deserved it." Then they make a great fire, and burn the body; and then every one of his friends takes a quantity of the ashes, and keeps them instead of relics, saying that it is a holy thing; and they dread no peril while they have the holy ashes upon them. And they put his name in their litanies as a saint.

Chapter XVII.

OF THE EVIL CUSTOMS IN THE ISLE OF LAMARY; AND HOW THE EARTH AND THE SEA ARE OF ROUND FORM, AS IS PROVED BY THE STAR CALLED ANTAROTIO, WHICH IS FIXED IN THE SOUTH.

FROM that country men go by the Sea of Ocean, and by many divers isles and countries which it would be too long to describe. Fifty-two days from the land I have spoken of there is another extensive land, which they call Lamary, in which the heat is very great; and it is the custom there for men and women to go all naked. And they scorn when they see foreigners going clothed, because they say that God made Adam and Eve all naked, and that no man should be ashamed of what is according to nature. And they say that they that are clothed are people of another world, or people who believe not in God. And they marry there no wives, for all the women are common; and they say they sin if they refuse any man : for God commanded Adam and Eve, and all that come of him, that they should increase and multiply and fill the land, therefore may no man in that country say, " This is my wife;" and no woman may say, " This is my husband." And when they have children, they may give them to what man they will, who has companied with them. And all land and property also is common, nothing being shut up, or kept under lock, one man being as rich as another. But in that country there is a cursed custom, for they eat more gladly man's flesh than any other flesh, although their country abounds in flesh, fish, corn, gold, and silver, and all other goods. Thither merchants go, who bring with them children to sell to them of the country, and they buy them; and if they are fat they eat them anon: and if they are lean they feed them till they are fat, and then eat them; and they say that it is the best and sweetest flesh in the world.

Neither in that land, nor in many others beyond it, may any man see the polar star, which is called the Star of the Sea, which is immoveable, and is towards the north, and which we call the load-star. But they see another star opposite to it, towards the south, which is called antarctic. And right as shipmen here govern themselves by the load-star, so shipmen beyond these parts are guided by the star of the south, which appears not to us. This star, which is towards the north, that we call the load-star, appears not to them. For which cause, we may clearly perceive that the land and sea are of round shape and form, because the part of the firmament appears in one country which is not seen in another country. And men may prove by experience and their understanding, that if a man found passages by ships, he might go by ship all round the world, above and beneath; which I prove thus, after what I have seen. For I have been towards the parts of Brabant, and found by the astrolabe * that the polar star is fifty-three degrees high; and further, in Germany and Bohemia, it has fifty-eight degrees; and still further towards the north it is sixty-two degrees and some minutes; for I myself have measured it by the astrolabe. Now you shall know that opposite the polar star is the other star, called antarctic, as I have said before. These two stars are fixed; and about them all the firmament turns as a wheel that turns on its axle-tree; so that those stars bear the firmament in two equal parts; so that it has as much above as it has beneath. After this I have gone towards the south,

---

* An astronomical instrument used in the middle ages for taking altitudes, &c. Maundeville's notions about the form of the earth, and the possibility of passing round it, are extremely curious, from the circumstance of their having been written and published so long before the time of Columbus.

and have found, that in Lybia we first see the antarctic star;
and I have gone so far in those countries that I have found
that star higher, so that, towards Upper Lybia, it is eighteen
degrees and certain minutes. After going by sea and land
towards the country of which I spoke last, and to other isles
and lands beyond that country, I have found the antarctic
star thirty-three degrees in altitude, and some minutes. And
if I had had company and shipping to go further, I believe
certainly that we should have seen all the roundness of the
firmament all about. For, as I have told you before, the half
of the firmament is between the two stars, which half I have
seen. And the other half I have seen towards the north,
under the polar star, sixty-two degrees and ten minutes; and,
towards the south, I have seen under the antarctic thirty-
three degrees and sixteen minutes; and the half of the firmament in all contains·but one hundred and eighty degrees,
of which I have seen sixty-two on the one part, and thirty-
three on the other, which makes ninety-five degrees, and
nearly the half of a degree; so that I have seen all the
firmament except eighty-four degrees and the half of a degree; and that is not the fourth part of the firmament. By
which I tell you, certainly, that men may go all round the
world, as well under as above, and return to their country,
if they had company, and shipping, and guides; and always
they would find men, lands, and isles, as well as in our part
of the world. For they who are towards the antarctic are
directly feet opposite feet of them who dwell under the polar
star; as well as we and they that dwell under us are feet
opposite feet. For all parts of sea and land have their oppo-
sites, habitable or passable.

And know well that, after what I may perceive and understand, the lands of Prester John, emperor of India, are under
us; for in going from Scotland or from England, towards
Jerusalem, men go always upwards; for our land is in the low
part of the earth, towards the west; and the land of Prester
John is in the low part of the earth, towards the east; and they
have there the day when we have night; and, on the contrary,
they have the night when we have the day; for the earth and
the sea are of a round form, as I have said before; and as
men go upward to one part, they go downward to another.
Also you have heard me say that Jerusalem is in the middle
of the world; and that may be proved and shown there by a

spear which is fixed in the earth at the hour of midday, when
it is equinoxial, which gives no shadow on any side.   They,
therefore, that start from the west to go towards Jerusalem,
as many days as they go upward to go thither, in so many
days may they go from Jerusalem to other confines of the
superficialties of the earth beyond.   And when men go beyond
that distance, towards India and to the foreign isles, they are
proceeding on the roundness of the earth and the sea, under
our country.   And therefore hath it befallen many times of a
thing that I have heard told when I was young, how a worthy
man departed once from our country to go and discover the
world; and so he passed India, and the isles beyond India,
where are more than five thousand isles; and so long he went
by sea and land, and so environed the world by many seasons,
that he found an isle where he heard people speak his own language, calling on oxen in the plough such words as men speak
to beasts in his own country, whereof he had great wonder, for
he knew not how it might be.   But I say that he had gone so
long, by land and sea, that he had gone all round the earth,
that he was come again to his own borders, if he would have
passed forth till he had found his native country.   But he
turned again from thence, from whence he was come; and so
he lost much painful labour, as himself said, a great while
after, when he was coming home; for it befell after, that he
went into Norway. and the tempest of the sea carrried him to
an isle; and when he was in that isle, he knew well that it
was the isle where he had heard his own language spoken
before, and the calling of the oxen at the plough.   But it
seems to simple and unlearned men that men may not go
under the earth, but that they would fall from under towards
the heaven.   But that may not be any more than we fall
towards heaven from the earth where we are; for from what
part of the earth that men dwell, either above or beneath, it
seems always to them that they go more right than any other
people.   And right as it seems to us that they be under
us, so it seems to them that we are under them; for if a
man might fall from the earth unto the firmament, by greater
reason the earth and the sea, that are so great and so heavy,
should fall to the firmament; but that may not be, and therefore saith our Lord God, "He hangeth the earth upon nothing."*   And although it be possible so to go all round the

* Job, xxvi. 7.

world, yet of a thousand persons not one might happen to
return to his country: for, from the greatness of the earth and
sea, men may go by a thousand different ways, that no one
could be sure of returning exactly to the parts he came from,
unless by chance or by the grace of God; for the earth is
very large, and contains in roundness and circuit, above and
beneath, 20,425 miles, after the opinion of the old wise
astronomers; and, after my little wit, it seems to me, saving
their reverence, that it is more; for I say thus: let there be
imagined a figure that has a great compass; and, about the
point of the great compass, which is called the centre, let
there be made another little compass; then, afterwards, let the
great compass be divided by lines in many parts, and all the
lines meet at the centre; so that in as many parts as the
great compass shall be divided, in so many shall the little
one that is about the centre be divided, although the spaces
be less.   Let the great compass be represented for the
firmament, and the little compass for the earth; now the
firmament is divided by astronomers into twelve signs, and
every sign is divided into thirty degrees.   Also let the earth
be divided into as many parts as the firmament, and let every
part answer to a degree of the firmament; and I know well that,
after the authorities in astronomy, seven hundred furlongs of
earth answer to a degree of the firmament, that is eighty-seven
miles and four furlongs.   Now, multiplied by three hundred
and sixty times, it makes 31,500 miles, each of eight furlongs, according to miles of our country.   So much hath the
earth in circuit after my opinion and understanding.

CHAPTER XVIII.

OF THE PALACE OF THE KING OF THE ISLE OF JAVA.—OF THE TREES THAT
BEAR MEAL, HONEY, WINE, AND VENOM; AND OF OTHER WONDERS AND
CUSTOMS IN THE ISLES THEREABOUTS.

BESIDE the isle I have spoken of, there is another great isle
called Sumobor*, the king of which is very mighty.   The
people of that isle make marks in their faces with a hot iron,
both men and women, as a mark of great nobility, to be
known from other people; for they hold themselves most
noble and most worthy of all the world.   They have war

* Perhaps Sumatra.   Maundeville seems to allude to the tattooing practised so generally in the islands of the Pacific.

always with the people that go all naked. Fast beside is
another rich isle called Beteinga. And there are many other
isles thereabout.

Fast beside that isle, to pass by sea, is a great isle and
extensive country, called Java, which is near two thousand
miles in circuit. And the king of that country is a very great
lord, rich and mighty, having under him seven other kings of
seven other surrounding isles. This isle is well inhabited,
and in it grow all kinds of spices more plentifully than in any
other country, as ginger, cloves, canel, sedewalle, nutmegs,
and maces. And know well that the nutmeg bears the maces;
for right as the nut of the hazel hath a husk in which the nut
is inclosed till it be ripe, so it is of the nutmeg and of the
maces. Many other spices and many other goods grow in
that isle; for of all things there is plenty, except wine.
Gold and silver are very plentiful. The king of that country
has a very noble and wonderful palace, and richer than any in
the world; for all the steps leading to halls and chambers are
alternately of gold and silver; and the pavements of halls and
chambers are squares of gold and silver; and all the walls within
are covered with gold and silver in thin plates; in which
plates are inlaid stories and battles of knights, the crowns
and circles about whose heads are made of precious stones
and rich and great pearls. And the halls and the chambers
of the palace are all covered within with gold and silver, so
that no man would believe the richness of that palace unless
he had seen it. And know well that the king of that isle is
so mighty, that he hath many times overcome the great chan
of Cathay in battle, who is the greatest emperor under the
firmament, either beyond the sea or on this side; for they
have often had war between them, because the great chan
would oblige him to hold his land of him; but the other at all
times defendeth himself well against him.

After that isle is another large isle, called Pathan, which is
a great kingdom, full of fair cities and towns. In that land
grow trees that bear meal, of which men make good bread,
white, and of good savour; and it seemeth as it were of wheat,
but it is not quite of such savour. And there are other trees
that bear good and sweet honey; and others that bear
poison*, against which there is no medicine but one; and
that is to take their own leaves, and stamp them and mix

* This seems to be an allusion to the upas tree.

them with water, and then drink it, for no medicine will avail. The Jews had sent for some of this poison by one of their friends, to poison all Christendom, as I have heard them say in their confession before dying; but, thanked be Almighty God, they failed of their purpose, although they caused a great mortality of people *. And there are other trees that bear excellent wine. And if you like to hear how the meal comes out of the trees, men hew the trees with an hatchet, all about the foot, till the bark be separated in many parts; and then comes out a thick liquor, which they receive in vessels, and dry it in the sun; and then carry it to a mill to grind, and it becomes fair and white meal; and the honey, and the wine, and the poison, are drawn out of other trees in the same manner, and put in vessels to keep. In that isle is a dead sea, or lake, that has no bottom; and if any thing fall into it, it will never come up again. In that lake grow reeds, which they call Thaby, that are thirty fathoms long; and of these reeds they make fair houses. And there are other reeds, not so long, that grow near the land, and have roots full a quarter of a furlong or more long, at the knots of which roots precious stones are found that have great virtues; for he who carries any of them upon him may not be hurt by iron or steel; and therefore they who have those stones on them fight very boldly both on sea and land; and, therefore, when their enemies are aware of this, they shoot at them arrows and darts without iron or steel, and so hurt and slay them. And also of those reeds they make houses and ships, and other things, as we here make houses and ships of oak, or of any other trees. And let no man think that I am joking, for I have seen these reeds with my own eyes many times, lying upon the river of that lake, of which twenty of our fellows might not lift up or bear one to the earth.

Beyond this isle men go by sea to another rich isle, called Calonak†, the king of which has as many wives as he will; for he makes search through the country for the fairest maidens that may be found, who are brought before him, and

---

* This accusation was spread against the Jews, as an excuse for persecution and spoliation.

† This may possibly be meant for Ceylon; but it would be vain to attempt to identify the islands mentioned in this and the following chapter. Some of the descriptions may, however, have had their foundation in what was originally correct information, but exaggerated or misunderstood.

he taketh one one night, and another another, and so forth in succession; so that he hath a thousand wives or more. And he lies never but one night with one of them, and another night with another, unless one happens to be more agreeable to him than another. Thus the king gets many children, sometimes a hundred, sometimes two hundred, and sometimes more. He hath also as many as fourteen thousand elephants, or more, which are brought up amongst his serfs in all his towns. And in case he has war with any of the kings around him, he causes certain men of arms to go up into wooden castles, which are set upon the elephants' backs, to fight against their enemies; and so do other kings thereabouts; and they call the elephants *warkes*.

And in that isle there is a great wonder; for all kinds of fish that are there in the sea come once a year, one kind after the other, to the coast of that isle in so great a multitude that a man can see hardly any thing but fish; and there they remain three days; and every man of the country takes as many of them as he likes. And that kind of fish, after the third day, departs and goes into the sea. And after them come another multitude of fish of another kind, and do in the same manner as the first did another three days; and so on with the other kinds, till all the divers kinds of fishes have been there, and men have taken what they like of them. And no man knows the cause; but they of the country say that it is to do reverence to their king, who is the most worthy king in the world, as they say, because he fulfils the commandment of God to Adam and Eve, "Increase and multiply, and fill the earth;" and because he multiplies so the world with children, therefore God sends him the fishes of divers kinds, to take at his will, for him and all his people; and thus all the fishes of the sea come to do him homage as the most noble and excellent king of the world, and that is best beloved of God, as they say.

There are also in that country a kind of snails, so great that many persons may lodge in their shells, as men would do in a little house. And there are other snails that are very great, but not so huge as the other, of which, and of great white serpents with black heads, that are as great as a man's thigh, and some less, they make royal meats for the king and other great lords. And if a man who is married die in that country, they bury his wife alive with him, for they say that it is right that she make him company in the other world, as she did in this.

From that country they go by the Sea of Ocean, by an isle called Caffolos; the natives of which, when their friends are sick, hang them on trees, and say that it is better that birds, which are angels of God, eat them, than the foul worms of the earth. Then we come to another isle, the inhabitants of which are of full cursed kind, for they breed great dogs, and teach them to strangle their friends, when they are sick, for they will not let them die of natural death; for they say that they should suffer great pain if they abide to die by themselves, as nature would; and, when they are thus strangled, they eat their flesh as though it were venison.

Afterwards men go by many isles by sea to an isle called Milk, where are very cursed people; for they delight in nothing more than to fight and slay men; and they drink most gladly man's blood, which they call Dieu. And the more men that a man may slay, the more worship he hath amongst them. And thence they go by sea, from isle to isle, to an isle called Tracoda, the inhabitants of which are as beasts, and unreasonable, and dwell in caves which they make in the earth, for they have not sense to make houses. And when they see any man passing through their countries they hide them in their caves. And they eat flesh of serpents, and they speak nought, but hiss, as serpents do. After that isle, men go by the Sea of Ocean, by many isles, to a great and fair isle called Nacumera, which is in circuit more than a thousand miles. And all the men and women of that isle have dogs' heads; and they are reasonable and of good understanding, except that they worship an ox for their god. And also every man of them beareth an ox of gold or silver on his forehead, in token that they love well their god. And they go all naked, except a little clout, and are large men and warlike, having a great target that covers all the body, and a spear in their hand to fight with. And if they take any man in battle they eat him. The king is rich and powerful, and very devout after his law; and he has about his neck three hundred orient pearls, knotted, as paternosters are here of amber. And as we say our Pater Noster and Ave Maria, counting the paternosters, right so this king says every day devoutly three hundred prayers to his god, before he eats; and he beareth also about his neck an orient ruby, noble and finé, which is a foot in length, and five fingers large. And when they choose their king, they give him that ruby to carry in his hand, and so they lead him riding all about the city. And that ruby he shall bear always about his neck; for if he had not that ruby upon him they would not hold him for king. The chan of Cathay has greatly coveted that ruby, but he might never have it, neither for war, nor for any manner of goods. This king is so righteous and equitable in his judgments, that men may go safely through all his country, and bear with them what they like, and no man shall be bold enough to rob them.

Hence men go to another isle called Silha, which is full eight hundred miles in circuit. In that land is much waste, for it is so full of serpents, dragons, and cockodrills, that no man dare dwell there. These cockodrills are serpents, yellow and rayed above, having four feet, and short thighs, and great nails like claws; and some are five fathoms in length, and some of six, eight, or even ten; and when they go by places that are gravelly, it appears as if men had drawn a great tree through the gravelly place. And there are also many wild beasts, especially elephants. In that isle is a great mountain, in the midst of which is a large lake in a full fair plain, and there is great plenty of water. And they of the country say that Adam and Eve wept on that mount a hundred years *, when they were driven out of Paradise. And that water, they say, is of their tears; for so much water they wept, that made the aforesaid lake. And at the bottom of that lake are found many precious stones and great pearls. In that lake grow many reeds and great canes, and there within are many cockodrills and serpents, and great water leeches. And the king of that country, once every year, gives leave to poor men to go into the lake to gather precious stones and pearls, by way of alms, for the love of God, that made Adam. To guard against the vermin, they anoint their arms, thighs, and legs with an ointment made of a thing called limons, which is a kind of fruit like small pease, and then they have no dread of cockodrills, or other venomous things. This water runs, flowing and ebbing, by a side of the mountain; and in that river men find precious stones

---

* Adam's Peak is in the island of Ceylon, which seems to be the one here alluded to under the name of Silha.

and pearls, in great abundance. And the people of that isle say commonly, that the serpents and wild beasts of the country will do no harm to any foreigner that enters that country, but only to men that are born there.

CHAPTER XIX.

HOW MEN KNOW BY AN IDOL IF THE SICK SHALL DIE OR NOT.—OF PEOPLE OF DIVERS SHAPES, AND MARVELLOUSLY DISFIGURED ; AND OF THE MONKS THAT GIVE THEIR RELIEF TO BABOONS, APES, MONKEYS, AND TO OTHER BEÁSTS.

FROM that isle, in going by sea towards the south, is another great isle, called Dondun, in which are people of wicked kinds, so that the father eats the son, the son the father, the husband the wife, and the wife the husband. And if it so befall that the father or mother or any of their friends are sick, the son goes to the priest of their law, and prays him to ask the idol if his father or mother or friend shall die; and then the priest and the son go before the idol, and kneel full devoutly, and ask of the idol; and if the devil that is within answer that he shall live, they keep him well; and if he say that he shall die, then the priest and the son go with the wife of him that is sick, and they put their hands upon his mouth and stop his breath, and so kill him. And after that, they chop all the body in small pieces, and pray all his friends to come and eat; and they send for all the minstrels of the country and make a solemn feast. And when they have eaten the flesh, they take the bones and bury them, and sing and make great melody. The king of this isle is a great and powerful lord, and has under him fifty-four great isles, which give tribute to him; and in every one of these isles is a king crowned, all obedient to that king. In one of these isles are people of great stature, like giants, hideous to look upon ; and they have but one eye, which is in the middle of the forehead ; and they eat nothing but raw flesh and fish *. And in another isle towards the south dwell people of foul stature and cursed nature, who have no heads, but their eyes are in their shoulders.

In another isle are people who have the face all flat, without nose and without mouth. In another isle are people that

---

* The " marvels " that follow in this paragraph are taken almost entirely from Pliny and Solinus.

have the lip above the mouth so great, that when they sleep
in the sun they cover all the face with that lip. And in
another isle there are dwarfs, which have no mouth, but
instead of their mouth they have a little round hole; and
when they shall eat or drink, they take it through a pipe,
or a pen, or such a thing, and suck it in. And in another
isle are people that have ears so long that they hang down to
their knees. And in another isle are people that have horses'
feet. In another isle are people that go upon their hands
and feet like beasts, and are all skinned and feathered, and
would leap as lightly into trees, and from tree to tree, as
squirrels or apes. In another isle are hermaphrodites. And
in another isle are people that go always upon their knees,
and at every step they go it seems that they would fall;
and they have eight toes on every foot. Many other divers
people of divers natures there are in other isles about, of the
which it were too long to tell.

From these isles, in passing by the Sea of Ocean towards
the east, by many days, men find a great kingdom called
Mancy, which is in India the Greater; and it is the best
land, and one of the fairest in all the world; and the most
delightful and plentiful of all goods. In that land dwell
many Christians and Saracens, for it is a good and great
country. And there are in it more than two thousand great
and rich cities, besides other great towns. And there is
greater plenty of people there than in any other part of India.
In that country is no needy man; and they are very fair
people, but they are all pale. And the men have thin
and long beards, though with few hairs, scarcely any man having
more than fifty hairs in his beard, and one hair set here,
another there, as the beard of a leopard or cat. In that land
are many fairer women than in any other country beyond the
sea; and therefore they call that land Albany, because the
people are white. And the chief city of that country is called
Latoryn; it is a day from the sea, and much larger than
Paris. In that city is a great river, bearing ships, which
go to all the coasts on the sea; for no city of the world is so
well stored of ships. And all the inhabitants of the city and
of the country worship idols. In that country the birds are
twice as large as they are here. There are white geese, red
about the neck, with a great crest like a cock's comb upon
their heads; and they are much greater there than here

And there is great abundance of serpents, of which men
make great feasts, and eat them at great solemnities. And
he that maketh there a feast, be it ever so costly, unless he
have serpents it is not esteemed.
There are many good cities in that country, and men have
great plenty of all wines and victuals cheap. In that country
are many churches of religious men of their law; and in
the churches are idols as great as giants. And to these
idols they give to eat at great festival days, in this manner:
they bring before them meat, hot from the fire, and they let
the smoke go up towards the idols; and then they say
that the idols have eaten, and then the religious men eat the
meat afterwards. In that country are white hens without
feathers, but they bear white wool, as sheep do here. In that
country, women that are unmarried carry tokens on their
heads, like coronets, to be known for unmarried. Also in
that country are beasts taught by men to go into waters,
rivers, and deep ponds, to take fish; which beast is little, and
men call them loyres. And when men cast them into the
water, anon they bring up great fishes, as many as men will.
And from that city, at a distance of many days' journey,
is another city, one of the greatest in the world, called Cansay *,
that is to say, the city of heaven. It is full fifty miles about,
and is so populous that in one house men make ten households.
In that city are twelve principal gates; and before each gate,
three or four miles distant, is a great town or city. That
city is situated upon a great lake on the sea, like Venice.
And in that city are more than twelve thousand bridges; and
upon every bridge are strong and good towers, in which dwell
the wardens, to keep the city from the great chan. And on
the one side of the city runs a great river all along the city.
And there dwell Christians, and many merchants and other
people of divers nations, because the land is so good and
abundant. And there grows very good wine, which they call
bigon, which is very strong and mild in drinking. This is a
royal city, where the king of Mancy formerly resided; and
there dwell many religious men, much resembling the order
of friars, for they are mendicants.
From that city men go by water, solacing and disporting

* This is the city called by Marco Polo (from whom Maundeville appears
to have abridged his description) Kin-sai. It was the capital of Southern
China, under the dynasty of the Song.

them, till they come to an abbey of monks fast by, who are
good religious men, after their faith and law. In that abbey
is a great and fair garden, where are many trees of divers
kinds of fruits; and in this garden is a little hill, full
of pleasant trees. In that hill and garden are various
animals, as apes, monkeys, baboons, and many other divers
beasts; and every day, when the monks have eaten, the
almoner carries what remains to the garden, and strikes on
the garden gate with a silver clicket that he holds in his hand,
and anon all the beasts of the hill, and of divers places of the
garden, come out, to the number of three or four thousand;
and they come in manner of poor men; and men give them the
remnants in fair vessels of silver gilt. And when they have
eaten, the monk strikes again on the garden gate with the
clicket, and all the beasts return to the places they came from.
And they say that these beasts are souls of worthy men, that
resemble in likeness the beasts that are fair; and therefore
they give them meat for the love of God. And the other
beasts, that are foul, they say, are souls of poor men; and
thus they believe, and no man may put them out of this
opinion. These beasts they take when they are young, and
nourish them thus with alms, as many as they may find. And
I asked them if it had not been better to have given that
relief to poor men, rather than to the beasts. And they answered me, and said that they had no poor men amongst them
in that country; and though it had been so that poor men
had been among them, yet were it greater alms to give it to
those souls that here do their penance. Many other marvels
are in that city, and in the country thereabout, that were too
long to tell you.

From that city men go by land six days to another city
called Chilenfo, of which the walls are twenty miles in circumference. In that city are sixty bridges of stone, so fair
that no man may see fairer. In that city was the first seat
of the king of Mancy, for it is a fair city and plentiful in all
goods. Hence we pass across a great river called Dalay,
which is the greatest river of fresh water in the world; for
where it is narrowest it is more than four miles broad. And
then men enter again the land of the great chan. That river
goes through the land of pigmies, where the people are small,
but three spans long*; and they are right fair and gentle,

* Part of this account is taken from Pliny, Hist. Nat., vii. 2.

both the men and the women. They marry when they are half a year of age, and get children; and they live but six or seven years at most; and he that liveth eight years is considered very aged. These men are the best workers of gold, silver, cotton, silk, and of all such things, that are in the world. And they have oftentimes war with the birds of the country, which they take and eat. This little people neither labour in lands nor in vineyards; but they have great men amongst them, of our stature, who till the land and labour amongst the vines for them. And of the men of our stature they have as great scorn and wonder as we should have among us of giants. There is a great and fair city amongst others, with a large population of the little people; and there are great men dwelling amongst them; but when they get children they are as little as the pigmies; and therefore they are for the most part all pigmies, for the nature of the land is such.

From that city men go by land, by many cities and towns, to a city called Jamchay, which is noble and rich, and of great profit to the lord; and thither go men to seek all kinds of merchandise. The lord of the country hath every year, for rent of that city, (as they of the city say,) fifty thousand cumants of florins of gold; for they count there all by cumants, and every cumant is ten thousand florins of gold. The king of that country is very powerful, yet he is under the great chan, who hath under him twelve such provinces. In that country, in the good towns, is a good custom; for whoever will make a feast to any of his friends, there are certain inns in every good town; and he that will make a feast will say to the host, "Array for me, to-morrow, a good dinner for so many people," and tells him the number, and devises him the viands; and he says, also, "Thus much I will spend, and no more." And anon the host arrays for him, so fair, and so well, and so honestly, that there shall lack nothing; and it shall be done sooner, and with less cost, than if it were done in his own house. Five miles from that city, towards the head of the river of Dalay, is another city, called Menke, in which is a strong navy of ships, all white as snow, from the colour of the trees of which they are made; and they are very great and fair ships, and well ordained, and made with halls and chambers, and other easements, as though it were on land. From thence men go by many towns and many cities to a city called Lanterynɛ, eight days from the city last mentioned.

This city is situated upon a fair, great, and broad river, called Caramaron, which passes through Cathay; and it often overflows and does much harm.

CHAPTER XX.

OF THE GREAT CHAN OF CATHAY.—OF THE ROYALTY OF HIS PALACE, AND HOW HE SITS AT MEAT; AND OF THE GREAT NUMBER OF OFFICERS THAT SERVE HIM.

CATHAY is a great country, fair, noble, rich, and full of merchants. Thither merchants go to seek spices and all manner of merchandises, more commonly than in any other part. And you shall understand that merchants who come from Genoa, or from Venice, or from Romania, or other parts of Lombardy, go by sea and by land eleven or twelve months, or more sometimes, before they reach the isle of Cathay, which is the principal region of all parts beyond; and it belongs to the great chan. From Cathay men go towards the east, by many days' journey, to a good city, between these others, called Sugarmago, one of the best stored with silk and other merchandises in the world. Then men come to another old city, towards the east, in the province of Cathay, near which the men of Tartary have made another city, called Caydon, which has twelve gates. And between the two gates there is always a great mile; so that the two cities, that is to say the old and the new, have in circuit more than twenty miles. In this city is the seat of the great chan, in a very great palace, the fairest in the world, the walls of which are in circuit more than two miles; and within the walls it is all full of other palaces. And in the garden of the great palace there is a great hill, upon which there is another palace, the fairest and richest that any man may devise. And all about the palace and the hill are many trees, bearing divers fruits. And all about that hill are great and deep ditches; and beside them are great fish-ponds, on both sides; and there is a very fair bridge to pass over the ditches. And in these fish-ponds are an extraordinary number of wild geese and ganders, and wild ducks, and swans, and herons. And all about these ditches and fish-ponds is the great garden, full of wild beasts, so that, when the great chan will have any sport, to take any of the wild beasts, or of the fowls, he will cause them to be driven, and take them at the windows, without going out of his chamber. Within the palace, in the hall, there are twenty-four pillars of fine gold; and all the walls are covered within with red skins of animals called panthers, fair beasts and well smelling; so that, for the sweet odour of the skins, no evil air may enter into the palace. The skins are as red as blood, and shine so bright against the sun that a man may scarcely look at them. And many people worship the beasts when they meet them first in a morning, for their great virtue and for the good smell that they have; and the skins they value more than if they were plates of fine gold. And in the middle of this palace is the mountour* of the great chan, all wrought of gold, and of precious stones, and great pearls; and at the four corners are four serpents of gold; and all about there are made large nets of silk and gold, and great pearls hanging all about it. And under the mountour are conduits of beverage that they drink in the emperor's court. And beside the conduits are many vessels of gold, with which they that are of the household drink at the conduit. The hall of the palace is full nobly arrayed, and full marvellously attired on all parts, in all things that men apparel any hall with. And first, at the head of tne hall, is the emperor's throne, very high, where he sits at meat. It is of fine precious stones, bordered all about with purified gold, and precious stones, and great pearls. And the steps up to the table are of precious stones, mixed with gold. And at the left side of the emperor's seat is the seat of his first wife, one step lower than the emperor; and it is of jasper, bordered with gold and precious stones. And the seat of his second wife is lower than his first wife; and is also of jasper, bordered with gold, as that other is. And the seat of the third wife is still lower, by a step, than the second wife; for he has always three wives with him, wherever he is. And after his wives, on the same side, sit the ladies of his lineage, still lower, according to their ranks. And all those that are married have a counterfeit, made like a man's foot, upon their heads, a cubit long, all wrought with great, fine, and orient pearls, and above made with peacocks' feathers, and of other shining feathers; and that stands upon their heads like a crest, in token that they are under man's foot, and under subjection of man. And they

---

* This is the word used in the English version. The Latin has *ascensorium*, and the French, *mountaynette*.

that are unmarried have none such.   And after, at the right
side of the emperor, first sits his eldest son, who shall reign
after him, one step lower than the emperor, in such manner
of seats as do the empresses; and after him other great lords
of his lineage, each of them a step lower than the other, according to their rank.   The emperor has his table alone
by himself, which is of gold and precious stones; or of crystal,
bordered with gold and full of precious stones; or of amethysts,
or of lignum aloes, that comes out of Paradise; or of ivory, bound
or bordered with gold.   And each of his wives has also her
table by herself.   And his eldest son, and the other lords
also, and the ladies, and all that sit with the emperor, have
very rich tables, alone by themselves.   And under the emperor's table sit four clerks, who write all that the emperor
says, be it good or evil; for all that he says must be held
good; for he may not change his word nor revoke it.

At great feasts, men bring, before the emperor's table, great
tables of gold, and thereon are peacocks of gold, and many
other kinds of different fowls, all of gold, and richly
wrought and enamelled; and they make them dance and sing,
clapping their wings together, and making great noise; and
whether it be by craft or by necromancy I know not, but it is a
goodly sight to behold.   But I have the less marvel, because
they are the most skilful men in the world in all sciences
and in all crafts; for in subtility, malice, and forethought
they surpass all men under heaven; and therefore they say
themselves that they see with two eyes, and the Christians
see but with one, because they are more subtle than they.   I
busied myself much to learn that craft; but the master told
me that he had made a vow to his god to teach it no creature,
but only to his eldest son.   Also above the emperor's table
and the other tables, and above a great part of the hall, is a
vine made of fine gold, which spreads all about the hall; and
it has many clusters of grapes, some white, some green,
some yellow, some red, and some black, all of precious stones:
the white are of crystal, beryl, and iris; the yellow, of topazes; the red, of rubies, grenaz, and alabraundines; the
green, of emeralds, of perydoz, and of chrysolites *; and the
black, of onyx and garnets.   And they are all so properly

* These are old names of precious stones, which it would not be very easy
now to explain.

made, that it appears a real vine, bearing natural grapes. And before the emperor's table stand great lords, and rich barons, and others, that serve the emperor at meat; and no man is so bold as to speak a word, unless the emperor speak to him, except minstrels, that sing songs and tell jests or other disports to solace the emperor. And all the vessels that men are served with, in the hall or in chambers, are of precious stones, and especially at great tables, either of jasper, or of crystal, or of amethyst, or of fine gold. And the cups are of emeralds, and sapphires, or topazes, of perydoz, and of many other precious stones. Vessel of silver is there none, for they set no value on it, to make vessels of; but they make therewith steps, and pillars, and pavements, to halls and chambers. And before the hall door stand many barons and knights full armed, to hinder any one from entering, unless by the will or command of the emperor, except they be servants or minstrels of the household.

And you shall understand that my fellows and I, with our yeomen, served this emperor, and were his soldiers, fifteen months, against the king of Mancy, who was at war with him, because we had great desire to see his nobleness, and the estate of his court, and all his government, to know if it were such as we heard say. And truly we found it more noble, and more excellent and rich, and more marvellous, than ever we heard, insomuch that we would never have believed it had we not seen it. For it is not there as it is here. For the lords here have a certain number of people as they may suffice; but the great chan hath every day people at his cost and expense without number. But the ordinance, nor the expenses in meat and drink, nor the honesty, nor the cleanliness, is not so arranged there as it is here; for all the commons there eat without cloth upon their knees; and they eat all manner of flesh, and little of bread. And after meat they wipe their hands upon their skirts, and they eat but once a day. But the estate of lords is full great, and rich, and noble. And although some men will not believe me, but hold it for fable, to tell them the nobleness of his person, and of his estate, and of his court, and of the great multitude of people that he has, nevertheless I will tell you a little of him and of his people, according as I have seen the manner and order full many a time; and whoever will may believe me, if he will, and whoever will not, may choose.

CHAPTER XXI.

FIRST I shall tell you why he was called the great chan.
You shall understand that all the world was destroyed by
Noah's flood, except only Noah, and his wife, and his children.
Noah had three sons, Shem, Cham (i. e. Ham), and Japheth.
This Cham was he who saw his father naked when he slept,
and showed him to his brethren in scorn, and therefore he
was cursed of God.   And Japheth turned his face away, and
covered him.   These three brethren shared all the land;
and this Cham, for his cruelty, took the greater and the best
part, toward the east, which is called Asia; and Shem took
Africa; and Japheth took Europe; and therefore is all the
earth parted in these three parts, by these three brethren.
Cham was the greatest and most mighty; and of him came
more generations than of the others.   And of his son Cush
was engendered Nimrod the giant, who was the first king
that ever was in the world, and he began the foundation of
the Tower of Babylon.   And that time the fiends of hell
came many times and lay with the women of his generation,
and engendered on them divers people, as monsters, and people disfigured, some without heads, some with great ears,
some with one eye, some giants, some with horses' feet, and
many other different shapes contrary to nature.   And of that
generation of Cham are come the Pagans, and different people
that are in islands of the sea about India.   And forasmuch as
he was the most mighty, and no man might withstand him,
he called himself the son of God, and sovereign of all the
world.   And on account of this Cham, this emperor called
himself chan and sovereign of all the world.   And of the generation of Shem are come the Saracens.   And of the generation of Japheth came the people of Israel.   And though we
dwell in Europe, this is the opinion that the Syrians and the
Samaritans have amongst them, and that they told me before
I went towards India; but I found it otherwise.   Nevertheless the truth is this—that Tartars, and they that dwell in
Greater Asia, came of Cham.   But the emperor of Cathay
was called not cham, but chan; and I shall tell you how

It is but little more than eight score years since all Tartary was in subjection and servage to other nations about; for they were but herdsmen, and did nothing but keep beasts, and lead them to pastures. But among them they had seven principal nations that were sovereigns of them all, of which the first nation or lineage was called Tartar; and that is the most noble and the most praised. The second lineage is called Tanghot; the third, Eurache; the fourth, Valair; the fifth, Semoche; the sixth, Megly; the seventh, Coboghe. Now it befell that of the first lineage succeeded an old worthy man, that was not rich, who was called Changuys *. This man lay one night in bed, and he saw in a vision that there came before him a knight armed all in white, and he sat upon a white horse, and said to him, "Chan, sleepest thou? The immortal God hath sent me to thee; and it is his will that thou go to the seven lineages, and say to them that thou shalt be their emperor; for thou shalt conquer the lands and the countries that are about; and they that march upon you shall be under your subjection, as you have been under theirs; for that is God's immortal will." Changuys arose, and went to the seven lineages, and told them what the white knight had said. And they scorned him, and said that he was a fool; and so he departed from them all ashamed. And the night following, this white knight came to the seven lineages, and commanded them, on behalf of the immortal God, that they should make this Changuys their emperor, and they should be out of subjection, and they should hold all other regions about them in servage, as they had been to them before. And next day they chose him to be their emperor, and set him upon a black chest, and after that lifted him up with great solemnity, and set him in a chair of gold, and did him all manner of reverence; and they called him chan, as the white knight called him. And when he was thus chosen, he would make trial if he might trust in them or not, and whether they would be obedient to him, and then he made many statutes and ordinances, that they call *Ysya Chan.* The first statute was, that they should believe in and obey immortal God, who is almighty, and who would cast them out of servage, and they should at all times call to him for help in time of need.

* This was the famous Ghengis-khan, who ruled the Moguls from 1176 to 1227, and was the founder of the Tartar empire. It is needless to say that the history Maundeville gives of his accession is a mere fable.

The second statute was, that all manner of men that might
bear arms should be numbered, and to every ten should be a
master, and to every hundred a master, and to every thousand
a master, and to every ten thousand a master. After, he commanded the principals of the seven lineages to leave and forsake all they had in goods and heritage, and from thenceforth
to be satisfied with what he would give them of his grace.
And they did so immediately. After this he commanded the
principals of the seven lineages, that each should bring his
eldest son before him, and with their own hands smite off their
heads without delay. And immediately his command was
performed. And when the chan saw that they made no ob-
stacle to perform his commandment, then he thought that he
might well trust in them, and he commanded them presently to
make them ready, and to follow his banner. And after this,
the chan put in subjection all the lands about him. Afterwards it befell on a day, that the chan rode with a few companies to behold the strength of the country that he had won,
and a great multitude of his enemies met with him, and to
give good example of bravery to his people, he was the first
that fought, and rushed into the midst of his enemies, and
there was thrown from his horse, and his horse slain. And
when his people saw him on the earth, they were all dis-
couraged, and thought he had been dead, and fled every one;
and their enemies pursued them, but they knew not that the
emperor was there. And when they were returned from the
pursuit, they sought the woods, if any of them had been hid
in them ; and many they found and slew. So it happened
that as they went searching toward the place where the emperor was, they saw an owl sitting on a tree above him; and
then they said amongst them that there was no man there,
because they saw the bird there, and so they went their way;
and thus the emperor escaped death. And then he went
secretly by night, till he came to his people, who were very
glad of his coming, and gave great thanks to immortal God,
and to that bird by which their lord was saved; and therefore,
above all fowls of the world, they worship the owl ; and when
they have any of its feathers, they keep them full preciously,
instead of relics, and bear them upon their heads with great
reverence ; and they hold themselves blessed, and safe from
all perils, while they have these feathers on them, and therefore they bear them upon their heads. After all this the chan

assembled his people, and went against those who had assailed him before, and destroyed them, and put them in subjection and servage. And when he had won and put all the lands and countries on this side Mount Belian in subjection, the white knight came to him again in his sleep, and said to him, "Chan, the will of immortal God is, that thou pass Mount Belian; and thou shalt win the land, and thou shalt put many nations in subjection; and because thou shalt find no good passage to go toward that country, go to Mount Belian, which is upon the sea, and kneel there nine times towards the east, in the worship of immortal God, and he shall show the way to pass by." And the chan did so. And soon the sea, that touched and was close to the mountain, began to withdraw itself, and exhibited a fair way of nine feet broad; and so he passed with his people, and won the land of Cathay, which is the greatest kingdom in the world. And on account of the nine kneelings, and the nine feet of way, the chan and all the men of Tartary have the number nine in great reverence *. And, therefore, he that will make the chan any present, be it horses, birds, arrows, bows, or fruit, or any other thing, he must always make it of the number nine; and so the presents are more agreeable to him, and better received, than if he were presented with a hundred or two hundred. Also, when the chan of Cathay had won the country of Cathay, and put in subjection many countries about, he fell sick. And when he felt that he should die, he said to his twelve sons, that each of them should bring him one of his arrows, and so they did anon †. And then he commanded that they should bind them together in three places, and then he gave them to his eldest son, and bade him break them; and he exerted himself with all his might to break them, but he might not. And then the chan bade his second son break them, and so to the others, one after another; but none of them might break them. And then he bade the youngest son separate them from each other, and break every one by itself; and so he did. And then said the chan to his eldest son, and to all

---

* Veneration for peculiar numbers was a very general superstition, and the number three, and its multiple, nine, were, in particular, in universal repute.

† This story of the king and the twelve arrows is told in very nearly the same manner in the Arabian Nights' Entertainments; and the substance of a well-known fable will be easily recognised in it.

the others, "Wherefore might you not break them?" And
they answered that they might not, because they were bound
together. "And wherefore," quoth he, "hath your little
youngest brother broke them?" "Because," quoth they,
"they were separated from each other." Then said the chan,
"My sons, truly thus will it fare with you; for as long as
you are bound together in three places, that is to say, in love,
truth, and good accord, no man shall have power to grieve
you; but if you be divided from these three places, that one
of you help not the other, you shall be destroyed and brought
to nothing; and if each of you love each other, and help each
other, you shall be lords and sovereigns over all other people."
And when he had made his ordinances he died: and then,
after him, reigned Ecchecha* Chan, his eldest son. And his
other brethren went to subdue many countries and kingdoms,
unto the land of Prussia and Russia, and took the name of
chans, but they were all subject to their eldest brother, and
therefore was he called great chan. After Ecchecha reigned
Guyo† Chan, and after him Mango‡ Chan, who was a good
Christian man, and baptized and gave letters of perpetual
peace to all Christian men, and sent his brother Halaon, with
a great multitude of people, to win the Holy Land, and put it
into the hands of the Christians, and destroy the law of Mohammed, and take the khalif of Bagdad, who was emperor
and lord of all the Saracens. And when this khalif was
taken, they found him so rich in treasure, and of so high
worship, that in all the rest of the world no man might find
a man higher in worship. And then Halaon made him come
before him, and said to him, "Why hadst thou not hired
with thee more soldiers for a little quantity of treasure, to
defend thee and thy country, who art so abundant of treasure
and so high in all worship?" And the khalif answered, that
he believed he had enough of his own proper men. And
then said Halaon, "Thou wert as a god of the Saracens; and

* Oktai-khan, who ruled over the Tartars from 1229 (having been absent
in China when his father died) to 1241.

† Gaiouk reigned from 1246 to 1249. The death of his predecessor had
been followed by a regency.

‡ Mango-khan, after another regency, succeeded in 1251; and after conquering Persia and other countries, died in 1259. This monarch was made
known to Europeans by the embassy of William de Rubruquis and others,
and excited interest in the west by the report of his conversion to Christianity.

it is convenient to a god to eat no meat that is mortal; and,
therefore, thou shalt eat only precious stones, rich pearls, and
treasure, that thou lovest so much." And then he ordered
him to prison, and placed all his treasure about him; and so
he died for hunger and thirst. And then after this Halaon
won all the Land of Promise, and put it into the hands of the
Christians. But the great chan, his brother, died, and that
was great sorrow and loss to all Christians. After Mango
Chan reigned Cobyla * Chan, who was also a Christian, and
reigned forty-two years. He founded the great city Igonge
in Cathay, which is much larger than Rome. The other great
chan who came after him, became a pagan, and all the others
since.

The kingdom of Cathay is the greatest realm in the world;
and the great chan is the most powerful emperor and greatest
lord under the firmament; and so he calls himself in his letters right thus : " Chan, son of the high God, emperor of all
who inhabit the earth, and lord of all lords." And the letter of
his great seal has the inscription, " God in heaven, chan upon the
earth, his fortitude; the seal of the emperor of all men." And
the superscription about his little seal is this: " The fortitude
of God; the seal of the emperor of all men." And although
they are not christened, yet the emperor and all the Tartars
believe in immortal God; and when they will threaten any
man, they say, " God knoweth well that I shall do thee such
a thing," and tell their menace

CHAPTER XXII.

OF THE GOVERNMENT OF THE GREAT CHAN'S COURT, AND WHEN HE MAKES
SOLEMN FEASTS.—OF HIS PHILOSOPHERS; AND OF HIS ARRAY WHEN HE
RIDES ABROAD.

Now shall I tell you the government of the court of the great
chan, when he makes solemn feasts, which is principally
four times in the year. The first feast is of his birth; the
second is of his presentation in their temple, such as they call
here moseache (mosque), where they make a kind of circumcision; and the other two feasts are of his idols. The first

---

* Mango's successor was the celebrated Houlagou (1259 to 1265), who
was followed in succession by eight khans between then and the time when
Maundeville wrote. These were followed, in 1360, by the famous Timur-beg,
or Tamerlane.

feast of the idol is, when he is first put into their temple and throned. The other feast is, when the idol begins first to speak or work miracles. There are no more solemn feasts, except when he marries one of his children. At each of these feasts he hath great multitudes of people, well ordained and well arrayed, by thousands, by hundreds, and by tens. Every man knoweth well what service he shall do; and every man gives so good heed and so good attendance to his service, that no man finds any fault. There are first appointed four thousand barons, mighty and rich, to govern and make ordinance for the feast, and to serve the emperor. And these solemn feasts are held in halls and tents made full nobly of cloths of gold and of tartaries. All the barons have crowns of gold upon their heads, very noble and rich, full of precious stones and great orient pearls. And they are all clothed in clothes of gold, or of tartaries, or of camakas, so richly and perfectly, that no man in the world can amend it or devise better; and all these robes are embroidered with gold all about, and dubbed full of precious stones and of great orient pearls, full richly. And they may well do so, for cloths of gold and of silk are cheaper there by much, than are cloths of wool. These four thousand barons are divided into four companies, and every thousand is clothed in cloths all of one colour, and so well arrayed, and so richly, that it is marvel to behold. The first thousand, which is of dukes, earls, marquises, and admirals, all in cloths of gold, with tissues of green silk, and bordered with gold, full of precious stones. The second thousand is all in cloths diapered of red silk, all wrought with gold, and the orfrayes set full of great pearls and precious stones, full nobly wrought. The third thousand is clothed in cloths of silk, of purple, or of India. And the fourth thousand is in clothes of yellow. And all their clothes are so nobly and richly wrought with gold and precious stones and rich pearls, that if a man of this country had but one of their robes, he might well say that he should never be poor. For the gold and the precious stones, and the great orient pearls, are of greater value on this side the sea than in those countries. And when they are thus apparelled, they go two and two together, full orderly, before the emperor, without uttering a word, only bowing to him. And each of them carries a tablet of jasper, or ivory, or crystal; and the minstrels go

before them, sounding their instruments of divers melody.
When the first thousand is thus passed, and hath made its
muster, it withdraws on the one side; and then enters
the second thousand, and proceeds in the same manner of
array and countenance as the first; and so the third, and
then the fourth; and none of them utters a word. And at
one side of the emperor's table sit many philosophers, who
are proved for wise men in many divers sciences, as in
astronomy, necromancy, geomancy, pyromancy, hydromancy,
augury, and many other sciences. And each of them has
before him, some, astrolabes of gold, some, spheres, some, the
skull of a dead man, some, vessels of gold full of gravel or
sand, some, vessels of gold full of burning coals, some, vessels
of gold full of water, wine, and oil, and some, horloges (clocks) of
gold, made full nobly and richly wrought, and many other
sorts of instruments after their sciences. And at certain
hours they say to certain officers who stand before them,
appointed for the time to fulfil their commands, " Make
peace." And then the officers say, " Now peace, listen." And
after that another of the philosophers says, " Every man do
reverence, and bow to the emperor, who is God's son and
sovereign lord of all the world; for now is time." And then
every man bows his head towards the earth. And then the
same philosopher commands again, " Stand up." And they
do so. And at another hour another philosopher says, " Put
your little finger in your ears." And anon they do so. And
at another hour another philosopher says, " Put your hand
before your mouth." And anon they do so. And at another
hour another philosopher says, " Put your hand upon your
head." And after that he biddeth them to take their hand
away, and they do so. And so, from hour to hour, they command certain things. And they say that those things have
divers significations. I asked them privately what those
things betokened. And one of the masters told me that the
bowing of the head at that hour betokened that all those
that bowed their heads should evermore after be obedient and
true to the emperor. And the putting of the little finger in the
ear betokens, as they say, that none of them shall hear any thing
spoken contradictory to the emperor, without telling it anon
to his council, or discovering it to some men that will make
relation to the emperor. And so forth of all other things
done by the philosophers. And no man performs any duty to

the emperor, either clothing, or bread, or wine, or bath, or other thing that belongeth to him, but at certain hours, as his philosophers devise well. And if there fall war, anon the philosophers come and give their advice after their calculations, and counsel the emperor by their sciences; so that the emperor does nothing without their council. And when the philosophers have done and performed their commands, then the minstrels begin to do their minstrelsy on their different instruments, each after the other, with all the melody they can devise. And when they have performed a good while, one of the officers of the emperor goes up on a high stage, wrought full curiously, and cries and says with a loud voice, " Make peace." And then every man is still. And then, anon after, all the lords of the emperor's lineage, nobly arrayed in rich clothes of gold, and royally apparelled on white steeds, as many as may well follow him at that time, are ready to make their presents to the emperor. And then says the steward of the court to the lords, by name, " N. of N.," and names first the most noble and the worthiest by name, and says, " Be ye ready with such a number of white horses to serve the emperor your sovereign lord." And, to another lord, he says, " N. of N. be ye ready with such a number to serve your sovereign lord." And to another, right so. And to all the lords of the emperor's lineage, one after the other, as they are of estate. And when they are all called, they enter one after the other, and present the white horses to the emperor, and then go their way. And then, all the other barons, one by one, give him presents, or jewels, or some other thing, according to their rank. And then, after them, all the prelates of their law, and religious men and others; and every man gives him something. And when all men have thus offered to the emperor, the greatest of dignity of the prelates gives him a blessing, saying an orison of their law. And then begin the minstrels to make their minstrelsy on divers instruments, with all the melody that they can devise. When they have done their craft, then they bring in before the emperor lions, leopards, and other divers beasts, and eagles, and vultures, and other divers fowls, and fishes, and serpents, to do him reverence. And then come jugglers and enchanters that do many marvels; for they cause the sun and the moon to come in the air, apparently, to every man's sight. And afterwards they make the night so dark that no man may see. And after that they make the day to come again, fair and pleasant, with bright sun, to every man's sight. And then they bring in dancers of the fairest damsels in the world, and most richly arrayed. Next they cause to come in other damsels bringing cups of gold full of milk of divers beasts, who give drink to lords and to ladies. And then they make knights to joust in arms full lustily; and they run together and fight full fiercely; and they break their spears so rudely that the fragments fly in pieces all about the hall. And then they cause to come in hunting for the hart and for the boar, with hounds running with open mouth. And many other things they do by craft of their enchantments, which it is marvellous to see. And such plays of sport they make, until the taking up of the boards.

This great chan hath a vast multitude of people to serve him, as I have told you before. For he hath of minstrels the number of thirteen cumants, but they abide not always with him. For all the minstrels that come before him, of whatever nation they are, are retained with him, as of his household, and entered in his books as for his own men. And after that, wherever they go, evermore they rank as minstrels of the great chan; and, under that title, all kings and lords cherish them the more with gifts and all things. And therefore he hath so great multitude of them. And he hath of certain men, as though they were yeomen, that keep birds, as ostriches, gerfaucons, sparrow-hawks, gentle falcons, lanyers, sacres, sacrettes*, well speaking parrots, and singing birds, and also of wild beasts, as of elephants, tame and others, baboons, apes, monkeys, and other divers beasts, to the number of fifteen cumants of yeomen. And of Christian physicians he has two hundred; and of leeches † that are Christians, he has two hundred and ten; and of leeches and physicians that are Saracens, twenty; for he trusts more in the Christian leeches than in the Saracens. And his other common household is without number; all having all neces-

---

* These are the names of different birds used in hawking.

† *Leech* was the old English name for one class of medical practitioners. It is employed here in contradistinction to physicians, and I have not ventured to assign a modern equivalent. The preference given to Christian physicians is somewhat curious when we compare it with a similar feeling existing in the East at the present day.

saries from the emperor's court. And he has in his court
many barons, as servitors, that are Christians and converted
to good faith by the preaching of religious Christian men
who dwell with him, and there are many that will not have it
known that they are Christians.

This emperor may spend as much as he will, without estimation, for his only money is of leather imprinted, or of paper, of
which some is of greater price and some of less, after the
diversity of his statutes *. And when that money has run so
long that it begins to waste, men carry it to the emperor's
treasury, and receive new money for the old. And that
money passes throughout the country. For there, and beyond
them, they make no money of gold or silver. Therefore, he
may spend very largely. And of gold and silver that men
have in this country, he makes ceilings, pillars, and pavements in his palace, and other divers things. This emperor
hath in his chamber, in one of the pillars of gold, a ruby and
a carbuncle of half a foot long, which in the night gives so
great light and shining, that it is as light as day. And he
hath many other precious stones, and many other rubies and
carbuncles, but those are the greatest and most precious.

This emperor dwells in summer in a city towards the
north, called Saduz, where it is cold; and in winter he dwells
in a city called Camaaleche, in a hot country. But the
country where he dwells most commonly is in Gaydo, or in
Jong, a good and temperate country after the weather that
is there; but, to men of our part of the world, it is excessively hot. And when this emperor will ride from one
country to another, he appoints four hosts of his people, of
the which, the first host goes before him a day's journey, for
that host shall be lodged the night where the emperor shall
lie upon the morrow. And there shall every man have all
manner of victuals and necessaries at the emperor's cost
And in this first host the number of people is fifty cumants
of horse and foot, of which every cumant amounts to ten
thousand, as I have told you before. And another host goes
on the right side of the emperor, nigh half a day's journey from
him; and another goes on the left side of him, in the same
manner. And in every host is the same number of people.

* Paper money was in common use among the Tartars and Chinese at an
early period. See, on this curious subject, the travels of Marco Polo.

Then after comes the fourth host, which is much greater than any of the other, and goes behind him, the distance of a bow's draught. And every host has its day's journey ordained in certain places, where they shall be lodged at night, and there they shall have all they need. And if it befall that one of the host die, anon they put another in his place, so that the number shall ever be complete. And you shall understand that the emperor, in person, rides not as other great lords do, unless he choose to go privately with few men, to be unknown. Otherwise, he sits in a chariot with four wheels, upon which is made a fair chamber; and it is made of a certain wood that comes out of terrestrial paradise, which they call lignum aloes. And this chamber is full well smelling, because of the wood it is made of; and it is all covered internally with plates of fine gold, dubbed with precious stones and great pearls. And four elephants and four great steeds, all white and covered with rich coverings, draw the chariot. And four, or five, or six of the greatest lords ride about this chariot, full richly and nobly arrayed, so that no man shall approach the chariot except those lords, unless the emperor call any man to him that he wishes to speak with. And above the chamber of this chariot in which the emperor sits, are set upon a perch four, or five, or six gerfaucons, to that intent, that when the emperor sees any wild fowl, he may take it at his own list, and have the sport, first with one and then with another; and so he takes his sport passing through the country. And no man of his company rides before him, but all after him. And no man dare approach within a bow-shot of the chariot, except those lords only that are about him; and all the host come fairly after him, in great multitude. And also such another chariot, with such hosts, ordained and arrayed, go with the empress upon another side, each by itself, with four hosts, right as the emperor did, but not with so great multitude of people. And his eldest son goes by another way in another chariot, in the same manner. So that there is between them so great multitude of folks that it is marvellous to tell it. And sometimes it happens that when he will not go far, and he chooses to have the empress and his children with him, that they go all together; and then the people are mixed in one company, and divided in four parts only.

The empire of this great chan is divided into twelve pro-

vinces; and every province has more than two thousand
cities, and towns without number.   This country is very extensive, for it has twelve principal kings in twelve provinces;
and each of those kings has many kings under him; and they
are all subject to the great chan.   And his land and lordship
extends so far that a man may not go from one end to the
other, either by sea or land, in less than seven years.   And
through the deserts of his lordship, where are no towns, there
are inns appointed at every day's journey, to receive both man
and horse, in which they shall find plenty of victuals and all
things they need in their way.

And there is a marvellous, but profitable, custom in that
country, that if there happen any contrary thing that should
be prejudicial or grievous to the emperor, in any kind, anon
the emperor has tidings thereof and full knowledge in a day,
though it be three or four days from him, or more.   For his
envoys take their dromedaries, or their horses, and they
ride as fast as they may towards one of the inns; and when
they come there they blow a horn, and anon they of the inn
know that there are tidings to warn the emperor of some
rebellion against him; and they make other men ready, in all
haste that they may, to carry letters, and ride as fast as they
may, till they come to the other inns with their letters; and
then they make fresh men ready, to ride forth with the letters
towards the emperor, while the last bringer rests himself, and
baits his dromedary or horse; and so from inn to inn, till it
comes to the emperor.   And thus anon he has quick tidings
of any thing by his couriers, that run so hastily through all
the country.   And, also, when the emperor sends his couriers
in haste throughout his land, each of them has a large thong
full of small bells; and when they approach the inns of other
couriers, they ring their bells; and anon the other couriers
make them ready, and run their way to another inn; and thus
one runs to another, full speedily and swiftly, till the emperor's
intent be served in all haste.   And these couriers are called
chydydo, after their language, that is to say, a messenger.

Also when the emperor goes from one country to another,
as I have told you before, and he passes through cities and
towns, every man makes a fire before his door, and puts
therein powder of good gums, that are sweet smelling, to make
good savour to the emperor; and all the people kneel down
towards him, and do him great reverence.   And there, where

Christian monks dwell, as they do in many cities in the
land, they go before him in procession, with cross and holy
water; and they sing *Veni creator spiritus*, with a high
voice, and go towards him. And when he hears them, he
commands his lords to ride beside him, that the religious men
may come to him; and when they are nigh him with the cross,
then he puts down his galiot, which is placed on his head in the
manner of a chaplet, made of gold, and precious stones, and
great pearls; and it is so rich that men esteem it the value
of a realm in that country; and then he kneels to the cross.
And then the prelate of the monks says before him certain orisons, and gives him a blessing with the cross; and
he bows to the blessing full devoutly. And then the prelate
gives him some sort of fruit, to the number of nine, in a plate
of silver; and he takes one; and then men give to the other
lords that are about him; for the custom is such that no
stranger shall come before him, unless he give him some
manner of thing, after the old law, that says, *Nemo accedat in
conspectu meo vacuus* *. And then the emperor tells the
monks to withdraw themselves again, that they be not hurt
by the great multitude of horses that come behind him. And
also in the same manner do the monks that dwell there
to the empresses that pass by them, and to his eldest son;
and to all of them they present fruit.

And you shall understand that this multitude of people
dwell not continually with him, but are sent for when he
wants them; and after, when they have done, they return to
their own households, except those that are dwelling with him
in the household to serve him, and his wives, and sons. And
although the others are departed from him after they have
performed their service, yet there remain continually with
him in court fifty thousand horsemen, and twenty thousand
footmen, besides minstrels and those who keep wild beasts
and birds. There is not, under the firmament, so great a
lord, nor so mighty, nor so rich, as the great chan; neither
Prester John, who is emperor of Upper India, nor the
sultan of Babylon, nor the emperor of Persia. All these, in
comparison to the great chan, are neither of might, nobleness,
royalty, nor riches; for in all these he surpasses all earthly
princes. Wherefore it is great harm that he believes not
faithfully in God. And, nevertheless, he will gladly hear

* "And none shall appear before me empty." Exod. xxxiv. 20.

speak of God; and he willingly allows Christian men to dwell in his lordship, and men of his faith to be made Christian men, if they will, throughout all his country; for he forbids no man to hold any faith but what he likes.

In that country some men have one hundred wives, some sixty, some more, and some less. And they take the next of their kin to wife, excepting only their mothers, daughters, and sisters on the mother's side; but their sisters on the father's side, of another woman, they may take; and their brother's wives, also, after their death; and their stepmothers also in the same way.

CHAPTER XXIII.

OF THE LAW AND CUSTOMS OF THE TARTARS IN CATHAY; AND HOW MEN DO WHEN THE EMPEROR SHALL DIE, AND HOW HE SHALL BE CHOSEN.

THE people of that country use all long clothes, without furs; and they are clothed with precious cloths of Tartary, and cloths of gold. And their clothes are slit at the side, and fastened with silk lace: and they clothe them also with pilches*, the hide outside. And they use neither cap nor hood. And the women go in the same dress as the men; so that we can hardly distinguish the men from the women, except only that the women that are married bear upon their heads the token of a man's foot, in sign that they are under man's foot, and under the subjection of man. And their wives dwell not together, but each of them by herself; and the husband may lie with which of them he likes. Each has a separate house, both man and woman; and their houses are made round with staves, with a round window above, which gives them light, and also serves for the escape of smoke. And the roofing of their houses, and the walls, and the doors, are all of wood.

When they go to war, they take their houses with them upon chariots, as men do tents or pavilions. They make their fires in the middle of their houses. And they have a great multitude of all manner of beasts, except swine, which they do not breed. And they believe in one God, who made and formed all things; yet they have idols of gold and silver, and of wood, and of cloth, to which they offer always the first milk

---

* A kind of garment made of skins with the fur on. In the Latin the passage stands, " Habent et pelliceas, quibus utuntur ex transversis ;" in the French, " Et vestent des pellices, le peil dehors."

of their beasts, and also of their meats and drinks before they
eat.   And they frequently offer horses and beasts.   They call
the god of nature Yroga.   Their emperor, whatever name he
has, they add always to it chan; and, when I was there, their
emperor's name was Thiaut, so that he was called Thiaut
Chan; and his eldest son was called Tossúe; and when he
shall be emperor, he shall be called Tossue Chan.   And at
that time the emperor had twelve other sons, named Cuncy,
Ordii, Chahaday, Buryn, Negu, Nocab, Cadu, Siban, Cuten,
Balacy, Babylan, and Garegan.   And of his three wives, the
first and the principal, who was Prester John's daughter, was
named Serioche Chan; and the other Borak Chan; and the
other Karanke Chan.

The people of that country begin all undertakings in the
new moon; and they worship much the moon and the sun,
and often kneel towards them.   All the people of the country
ride commonly without spurs; but they carry always a little
whip in their hands to urge their horses.   And they hold it
for a great sin to cast a knife in the fire, and to draw flesh out
of a pot with a knife, and to smite a horse with the handle of
a whip, or to smite a horse with a bridle, or to break one bone
with another, or to cast milk or any liquor that men may
drink upon the earth, or to take and slay little children; and
the greatest sin that any man may do is to water in their
houses that they dwell in.   And whosoever does so, they slay
him.   And of every one of these sins they must be shriven by
their priests, and pay a great sum of silver for their penance.
The place they have thus defiled must be purified before any
one dare to enter it.   And when they have paid their penance,
men make them pass through a fire, or through two, to cleanse
them of their sins.   And also when any messenger comes and
brings letters, or any present, to the emperor, he must pass,
with the thing that he brings, through two burning fires, to
purge them, that he bring no poison nor venom, nor any
wicked thing, that might be grievance to the lord.   And also,
if any man or woman be taken in adultery or fornication, anon
they slay them.   The people of that country are all good
archers, and shoot right well, both men and women, as well
on horseback, riding, as on foot, running.   And the women do
all things, and exercise all manner of trades and crafts, as of
clothes, boots, and other things; and they drive carts, ploughs,
wagons, and chariots; and make houses, and all manner of

things, except bows and arrows, and armour, which are made
by men. And all the women wear breeches, as well as men.
All the people of that country are very obedient to their
sovereign, and fight not nor chide with one another. And
there are neither thieves nor robbers in that country, but
every man respects the other; but no man there doth reverence to strangers, except they are great princes. And
they eat dogs, lions, leopards, mares and foals, asses, rats,
and mice; and all kinds of beasts, great and small, except
only swine, and beasts that were forbidden by the old law.
They eat but little bread, except in courts of great lords; and
they have not, in many places, either peas or beans, nor any
other pottage but the broth of the flesh; for they eat little
else but flesh and the broth. And when they have eaten they
wipe their hands upon their skirts; for they use no napkins
nor towels, except before great lords. And when they have
eaten, they put their dishes, unwashed, into the pot or cauldron,
with the remnant of the flesh and broth, till they eat again.
The rich men drink milk of mares, or camels, or of asses, or
other beasts. And they are easily made drunk with milk, or
with another drink made of honey and water sodden together;
for in that country is neither wine nor ale. They live full
wretchedly, and eat but once in the day, and that but little,
either in courts or other places. Indeed one man alone, in
our country, will eat more in a day than they will eat in three.
And if any foreign messenger come there to a lord, men make
him to eat but once a day, and that very little.

When they make war they proceed with great prudence,
and always do their best to destroy their enemies. Every
man there bears two or three bows, and great plenty of
arrows, and a great axe; and the gentlemen have short and
large spears, very sharp on the one side; and they have plates
and helmets made of cuirbouilli∗; and their horses' coverings
are of the same. And whoever flies from battle, they slay
him. And when they hold a siege about a castle or town,
which is walled and defensible, they promise them that are
within to do all the profit and good, that it is marvellous to
hear; and they grant also to them that are within all that
they will ask them; and after they have surrendered, they
slay them all, and cut off their ears, and they pickle them in

∗ Leather boiled soft, and then reduced to any required shape and hardened;
a substance very much used for a variety of purposes in the middle ages.

vinegar, and thereof make great service for lords. All their
desire, and all their imagination, is to reduce all countries
under their subjection; and they say that they know well, by
their prophecies, that they shall be overcome by archers;. but
they know not of what nation, nor of what law, they shall be
who shall overcome them.

When they will make their idols, or an image of any one
of their friends, to have remembrance of him, they always
make the image naked, without any kind of clothing; for they
say that in good love there should be no covering, that man
should not love for the fair clothing, nor for the rich array,
but only for the body such as God hath made it.

And you shall understand that it is very perilous to pursue
the Tartars when they fly in battle; for in flying they shoot
behind them, and slay both men and horses. And when they
fight, they close together in a body, so that, if there be twenty
thousand men, you would not think there were ten thousand.
They can conquer land of strangers, but they cannot keep it;
for they like better to lie in tents without, than in castles or
in towns.   They despise all other people.   Amongst them oil
of olives is very dear; for they hold it for a very noble medicine.   All the Tartars have small eyes and little beard, and a
paucity of hair.   They are false and traitorous, never keeping
their promises.   They are a very hardy people, and able to
endure much labour, more than any other people; for they
are accustomed thereto in their own country from youth.

And when any man shall die, they set a spear beside him;
and when he draws towards death, every man flies out of the
house till he is dead; and after that they bury him in the
fields.   And when the emperor dies, they place him in a
chair in the centre of his tent, with a clean table before him,
covered with a cloth, and thereon flesh and divers viands, and
a cup full of mare's milk.   And men put a mare beside him,
with her foal, and a horse saddled and bridled; and they lay
upon the horse great quantities of gold and silver, and they put
about him great plenty of straw, and they make a great and
large pit, and, with the tent and all these other things, they
put him in the earth; and they say that when he shall come
into another world, he shall not be without a house, nor without a horse, nor without gold and silver; and the mare shall
give him milk, and bring him forth more horses, till he be
well stored in the other world; for they believe that, after

their death, they shall be eating and drinking in that other world, and solacing themselves with their wives, as they did here. And after the emperor is thus interred, no man shall be so hardy as to speak of him before his friends. Many cause themselves to be interred privately by night, in wild places, and the grass put again over the pit, to grow; or they cover the pit with gravel and sand, that no man shall perceive where the pit is, to the intent that never after may his friends have mind or remembrance of him. Then they say that he is ravished into another world, where he is a greater lord than he was here. And then, after the death of the emperor, the seven lineages assemble together and choose his eldest son, or the next after him of his blood; and thus they say to him:— "We will, and we pray and ordain, that you be our lord and our emperor." And then he answers, "If you will that I reign over you as lord, each of you do as I shall command him, either to abide or go; and whomsoever I command to be slain, that anon he be slain." And they answer all, with one voice, "Whatsoever you command, it shall be done." Then says the emperor, "Now understand well that my word from henceforth is sharp and biting as a sword." After, they set him upon a black steed, and so bring him to a chair full richly arrayed, and there they crown him. And then all the cities and good towns send him rich presents, so that at that day he shall have more than sixty chariots laden with gold and silver, besides jewels of gold and precious stones, that lords give him, that are beyond estimation; and also horses and cloths of gold, and camakas, and cloth of Tartary, that are innumerable.

CHAPTER XXIV.

OF THE REALM OF THARSE, AND THE LANDS AND KINGDOMS TOWARDS THE
NORTH PARTS, IN COMING DOWN FROM THE LAND OF CATHAY.

THIS land of Cathay is in Central Asia; and after, on this side, is Asia the Greater. The kingdom of Cathay borders towards the west on the kingdom of Tharse, of which was one of the kings that came with presents to our Lord in Bethlehem; and some of those who are of the lineage of that king are Christians. In Tharse they eat no flesh, and drink no wine. And on this side, towards the west, is the kingdom of Turkestan, which extends towards the west to the kingdom of Persia; and toward the north to the kingdom of Chorasm. In the centre of Turkestan are but few good cities; but the best city of that land is called Octorar. There are great pastures, but little corn; and therefore, for the most part, they are all herdsmen; and they lie in tents, and drink a kind of ale made of honey.

And after it, on this side, is the kingdom of Chorasm (Khorasan), which is a good land and a plentiful, but without wine. It has a desert toward the east, which extends more than a hundred days' journey; and the best city of that country is called Chorasm, from which the country takes its name. The people of that country are hardy warriors. And on this side is the kingdom of Comania, whence were driven the Comanians that dwelt in Greece. This is one of the greatest kingdoms of the world, but it is not all inhabited; for in one part there is so great cold, that no man may dwell there; and in another part there is so great heat, that no man can endure it; and also there are so many flies, that no man may know on what side he may turn him. In that country is but little wood or trees bearing fruit, or others. They lie in tents; and they burn the dung of beasts for want of wood.

This kingdom descends on this side towards us, and towards Prussia and Russia. And through that country runs the river Ethille, which is one of the greatest rivers in the world; and it freezes so strongly all year, that many times men have fought upon the ice with great armies, both parties on foot, having quitted their horses for the time; and what on horse and on foot, more than 200,000 persons on every side. And between that river and the great Sea of Ocean, which they call the Maure Sea*, lie all these kingdoms. And towards the head beneath in that realm is the mountain of Chotaz, which is the highest mountain in the world; and it is between the Maure Sea and the Caspian Sea. There is a very narrow and dangerous passage to go towards India; and therefore king Alexander made there a strong city, which they call Alexandria, to guard the country, that no man should pass without his leave; and now men call that city the Gate of Hell. And the principal city of Comania is called Sarak, which is one of the three ways to go into India; but by this way no great multitude of people can pass unless it be in winter; and that passage men call the Derbent. The other way is from the city of Turkestan, by Persia; and by that way are many days'

* The Maure Sea seems to be the Northern Ocean, and the mountains of Chotaz are perhaps the Ourals.

journey by desert; and the third way is from Comania, by
the great sea, and by the kingdom of Abchaz.

And you shall understand that all these kingdoms and
lands above mentioned, unto Prussia and Russia, are all subject to the great chan of Cathay, and many other countries
that border on them.

CHAPTER XXV.

OF THE EMPEROR OF PERSIA, AND OF THE LAND OF DARKNESS, AND OF
OTHER KINGDOMS THAT BELONG TO THE GREAT CHAN OF CATHAY, AND
OTHER LANDS OF HIS, UNTO THE SEA OF GREECE.

Now, since I have spoken of the lands and the kingdoms towards the north part, in coming down from the land of Cathay
unto the lands of the Christians, towards Prussia and Russia,
I will speak of other lands and kingdoms coming down
towards the right side, unto the Sea of Greece, towards the land
of the Christians. And since, after India and Cathay, the
emperor of Persia is the greatest lord, I will tell you of the
kingdom of Persia. He hath two kingdoms; the first begins
towards the east, towards the kingdom of Turkestan, and extends towards the west to the river Pison, which is one
of the four rivers that come out of Paradise. And on another
side it extends toward the north to the Caspian Sea, and toward the south to the desert of India. And this country is
good, and pleasant, and full of people, and contains many
good cities. But the two principal cities are Boycurra and
Seornergant, that some men call Sormagant*. The other
kingdom of Persia extends towards the river Pison, and the
parts of the west, to the kingdom of Media, and from the
Great Armenia toward the north to the Caspian Sea, and
towards the south to the land of India. That is also a good
and rich land, and it hath three great principal cities, Messa-
bor, Caphon, and Sarmassane.

And then after is Armenia, in which were formerly four
kingdoms; it is a noble country, and full of goods. And it
begins at Persia, and extends towards the west in length unto
Turkey, and in breadth it extends to the city of Alexandria†,
that now is called the Gate of Hell, that I spoke of before,
under the kingdom of Media. In this Armenia are many
good cities, but Taurizo‡ is most of name.

---

* These are, no doubt, Bokhara and Samarcand.
† Iskendroon?   ‡ Tabreez.

After this is the kingdom of Media, which is very long, but not broad, beginning, towards the east, with the land of Persia, and India the Less ; and it extends towards the west to the kingdom of Chaldea, and towards the north towards Little Armenia. In that kingdom of Media are many great hills and little of level ground. Saracens dwell there, and another kind of people called Cordines *. The two best cities of that kingdom are Sarras and Karemen.

After that is the kingdom of Georgia, which commences towards the east, at the great mountain called Abzor, and contains many people of different nations. And men call the country Alamo. This kingdom extends towards Turkey, and towards the Great Sea ; and towards the south it borders on the Greater Armenia. And there are two kingdoms in that country, the kingdom of Georgia and the kingdom of Abchaz ; and always in that country are two kings, both Christians ; but the king of Georgia is in subjection to the great chan. And the king of Abchaz has the stronger country, and he always vigorously defends his country against all who assail him, so that no man may reduce him to subjection. In that kingdom of Abchaz is a great marvel ; for a province of the country, that has well in circuit three days, which they call Hanyson, is all covered with darkness, without any brightness or light, so that no man can see there, nor no man dare enter into it. And, nevertheless, they of the country say that sometimes men hear, voices of people, and horses neighing, and cocks crowing ; and men know well that men dwell there, but they know not what men. And they say that the darkness befell by miracle of God ; for a cursed emperor of Persia, named Saures, pursued all the Christians to destroy them, and to compel them to make sacrifice to his idols, and rode with a great host, in all that ever he might, to confound the Christians. And then, in that country, dwelt many good Christians, who left their goods, and would have fled into Greece ; and when they were in a plain, called Megon, anon this cursed emperor met with them with his host, to have slain them and cut them to pieces. And the Christians kneeled to the ground, and made their prayers to God to succour them ; and anon a great thick cloud came, and covered the emperor and all his host ; and so they remain in that manner, that they may go out on no side ; and so shall they

* The Kurds, the Gordynæ of the ancients.

ever more abide in darkness till doomsday, by the miracles of God. And then the Christians went where they liked at their own pleasure, without hindrance of any creature. And you shall understand that out of that land of darkness issues a great river, that shows well there are people dwelling there, by many ready tokens; but no man dare enter into it.

And know well that in the kingdoms of Georgia, Abchaz, and the Little Armenia, are good and devout Christians; for they shrive and housel* themselves always once or twice in the week; and many housel themselves every day.

Also after, on this side, is Turkey, which borders on the Great Armenia. And there are many provinces, as Cappadocia, Saure, Brique, Quesiton, Pytan, and Gemethe; and in each of these are many good cities. This Turkey extends to the city of Sathala, that sitteth upon the Sea of Greece, and so it borders on Syria. Syria is a great and a good country, as I have told you before. And also it has, towards Upper India, the kingdom of Chaldea, extending from the mountains of Chaldea towards the east to the city of Nineveh, on the river Tigris; in breadth it begins towards the north, at the city of Maraga, and extends towards the south to the Sea of Ocean. Chaldea is a level country, with few hills and few rivers.

After is the kingdom of Mesopotamia, which begins towards the east, at the river Tigris, at a city called Moselle†, and extends towards the west to the river Euphrates, to a city called Roianz; and in length it extends from the mountain of Armenia to the desert of India the Less. This is a good and level country; but it has few rivers. There are but two mountains in that country, of which one is called Symar, the other Lyson. This land borders on the kingdom of Chaldea.

There are also, towards the south parts, many countries and regions, as the land of Ethiopia, which borders towards the east on the great deserts, towards the west on the kingdom of Nubia, towards the south on the kingdom of Mauritania, and towards the north on the Red Sea. After is Mauritania, which extends from the mountains of Ethiopia to Upper Lybia. And that country lies along from the Ocean Sea towards the south, and towards the north it borders on Nubia and Upper Lybia. The men of Nubia are Christians. And it extends from the lands above mentioned to the deserts of Egypt, of which I have spoken before. And after is Upper and Lower Lybia, which

* Take the sacrament.   † Mosul.

descends low down, towards the great sea of Spain, in which
country are many kingdoms and different people.

CHAPTER XXVI.

OF THE COUNTRIES AND ISLANDS BEYOND THE LAND OF CATHAY, AND OF
THE FRUITS THERE; AND OF TWENTY-TWO KINGS INCLOSED WITHIN THE
MOUNTAINS.

IN passing by the land of Cathay towards Upper India, and
towards Bucharia, men pass by a kingdom called Caldilhe,
which is a very fair country. And there grows a kind of fruit
like gourds, which, when they are ripe, men cut in two, and
find within a little beast, in flesh, bone, and blood, as though
it were a little lamb, without wool. And men eat both the
fruit and the beast, and that is a great marvel. Of that fruit
I have eaten; and I told them of as great a marvel to them
that is amongst us, and that was of the barnacles. For I
told them that in our country were trees that bear a fruit
that becomes flying birds; and those that fall in the water
live; and those that fall on the earth die anon; and they
are right good for man's meat. And thereof had they also
great marvel, that some of them thought it was an impos-
sibility. In that country are long apples, of good flavour,
whereof there are more than a hundred in a cluster; and
they have great long leaves and large, of two feet long or
more. And in that country, and in other countries thereabout, grow many trees that bear clove-gylofres and nutmegs,
and great nuts of India, and of canelle, and many other
spices. And there are vines which bear grapes so large, that
a strong man would have enough to do to carry one cluster.
In that same region are the mountains of Caspia, which are
called Uber in the country. Between those mountains are
inclosed the Jews of ten lineages, who are called Gog and
Magog; and they may not go out on any side. There were
inclosed twenty-two kings with their people, that dwelt between the mountains of Scythia. King Alexander drove
them between those mountains, and there he thought to inclose them through work of his men. But when he saw that
he might not do it, nor bring it to an end, he prayed to the
God of Nature that he would perform that which he had begun. And although he was a Pagan, and not worthy to be
heard, yet God of his grace closed the mountains together, so

that they dwell there fast locked and inclosed with high
mountains all about, except only on one side, and on that side
is the Caspian Sea. Men say they shall come out in the time
of Antichrist, and that they shall make great slaughter of the
Christians; and therefore all the Jews that dwell in all lands
learn always to speak Hebrew, in hope that when the other
Jews shall go out, that they may understand their speech, and
so lead them into Christendom, to destroy the Christians.
For the Jews say that they know well, by their prophecies,
that they of Caspia shall go out, and spread through all the
world, and that the Christians shall be under subjection as
long as they have been in subjection to them. And if you
will know how they shall find their way, after what I have
heard say I will tell you. In the time of Antichrist, a fox
shall make there his trail, and burrow a hole where king
Alexander made the gates; and so long he shall burrow and
pierce the earth, till he shall pass through, towards that people. And when they see the fox, they shall have great wonder of him, because they never saw such a beast; for of all
other beasts they have some inclosed among them, except
the fox. And then they shall hunt him, and pursue him so
close, till he arrive at the same place he came from; and then
they shall dig and burrow so strongly, till they find the gates
that king Alexander made of immense stones, well cemented
and made strong for the mastery; and those gates they shall
break, and so go out, by finding that issue.

From that land men go towards the land of Bucharia,
where are very evil and cruel people. In that land are trees
that bear wool*, as though it were of sheep, whereof men
make clothes, and all things that may be made of wool. In
that country are many ipotaynes, that dwell sometimes in
the water and sometimes on the land; and they are half man
and half horse, as I have said before; and they eat men,
when they may take them. And there are rivers of water
that are very bitter, three times more than is the water of
the sea. In that country are many griffins, more abundant
than in any other country. Some men say that they have the
body upward of an eagle, and beneath of a lion; and that
is true. But one griffin has a greater body and is stronger
than eight lions, and greater and stronger than a hundred
eagles. For one griffin there will carry, flying to his nest, a

* Cotton.

great horse, or two oxen yoked together as they go at the plough. For he has his talons so long, and so large and great, as though they were horns of great oxen, or of bulls, or of kine, so that men make cups of them to drink out of*; and of their ribs, and of the feathers of their wings, men make bows full strong, to shoot with arrows and darts. From thence men go, by many days, through the land of Prester John, the great emperor of India. And they call his kingdom the isle of Pentexoire.

CHAPTER XXVII.

OF THE ROYAL ESTATE OF PRESTER JOHN; AND OF A RICH MAN THAT MADE A MARVELLOUS CASTLE, AND CALLED IT PARADISE, AND OF HIS CUNNING.

THIS emperor, Prester John†, possesses very extensive territory, and has many very noble cities and good towns in his realm, and many great and large isles. For all the country of India is divided into isles, by the great floods that come from Paradise, that separate all the land into many parts. And also in the sea he has full many isles. And the best city in the isle of Pentexoire is Nyse, a very royal city, noble and very rich. This Prester John has under him many kings, and

* The editor of the edition of our author, printed in 1727, observes, that one four feet long, in the Cotton Library, had a silver hoop about the end, on which is engraved, *Griphi unguis, divo Cuthberto Dunelmensi sacer.* Another, about an ell long, is mentioned by Dr. Grew, in his History of the Rarities of the Royal Society, page 26; though the doctor there supposes it rather the horn of a rock-buck, or of the *ibex mas.*

† Un-khan, or, as he was popularly called, Prester John, and the marvels of his dominions, were for several centuries a subject of great interest to the people of Western Europe, and were an object of anxious inquiry to all travellers in the East. A pretended letter from this monarch to the pope, describing his dominions, was published in Latin, French, and other languages. Much information relating to Prester John is found in Matthew Paris, who wrote before the middle of the thirteenth century. Marco Polo in his travels (book i. ch. xliii.) mentions the former subjection of the Tartars to him. Roger Bacon did not believe the extraordinary tales which were current relative to Prester John—*de quo tanta fama solebat esse, et multa falsa dicta sunt et scripta.* (Opus Majus, edit. Jebb, p. 232.) A most profound and learned dissertation on the personage and history of Prester John, by M. D'Avezac, will be found in the Introduction to his edition of the History of the Tartars, by John du Plan-de-Carpin, (published in the transactions of the Geographical Society of Paris,) 4to, 1838, p. 165-168.

many isles, and many divers people of divers conditions. And this land is full good and rich, but not so rich as the land of the great chan. For the merchants come not thither so commonly to buy merchandise, as they do in the land of the great chan, for it is too far. And on the other side, in the isle of Cathay, men find all things needful to man, cloths of gold, of silk, and spicery. And therefore, although men have them cheap in the isle of Prester John, they dread the long way and the great perils in the sea. For in many places of the sea are great rocks of stone of adamant (loadstone), which of its nature draws iron to it; and therefore there pass no ships that have either bonds or nails of iron in them; and if they do, anon the rocks of adamant draw them to them, that they may never go thence. I myself have seen afar in that sea, as though it had been a great isle full of trees and bushes, full of thorns and briers, in great plenty; and the shipmen told us that all that was of ships that were drawn thither by the adamants, for the iron that was in them. And of the rottenness and other things that were within the ships, grew such bushes, and thorns, and briers, and green grass, and such kinds of things; and of the masts and the sail-yards, it seemed a great wood or a grove. And such rocks are in many places there about. And therefore merchants dare not pass there, except they know well the passages, or unless they have good pilots. And also they dread the long way, and, therefore, they go to Cathay, because it is nearer; and yet it is not so nigh but men must travel by sea and land eleven or twelve months, from Genoa or from Venice, to Cathay. And yet is the land of Prester John more far, by many dreadful days' journey. And the merchants pass by the kingdom of Persia, and go to a city called Hermes *, because Hermes the philosopher founded it. And after that they pass an arm of the sea, and then they go to another city called Golbache; and there they find merchandise, and as great abundance of parrots as men find here of geese. In that country is but little wheat or barley, and therefore they eat rice and honey, milk, cheese, and fruit.

This emperor, Prester John, takes always to wife the daughter of the great chan; and the great chan also in the

* Ormuz.—The derivation is droll enough.

same wise the daughter of Prester John. For they two are the greatest lords under the firmament.

In the land of Prester John are many divers things and many precious stones, so great and so large, that men make of them plates, dishes, cups, &c. And many other marvels are there, that it were too long to put in a book. But I will tell you of his principal isles, and of his estate, and of his law. This emperor Prester John is a Christian, and a great part of his country also; but they have not all the articles of our faith. They believe in the Father, Son, and Holy Ghost, and they are very devout and true to one another. And he has under him seventy-two provinces, and in every province is a king, all which kings are tributary to Prester John. And in his lordships are many great marvels, for in his country is the sea called the Gravelly Sea, which is all gravel and sand, without a drop of water; and it ebbs and flows in great waves, as other seas do, and it is never still. And no man can pass that sea with ships, and, therefore, no man knows what land is beyond that sea. And although it has no water, men find therein, and on the banks, very good fish, of different nature and shape from what is found in any other sea; and they are of very good taste, and delicious to eat.

Three days from that sea are great mountains, out of which runs a great river which comes from Paradise, and it is full of precious stones, without a drop of water, and it runs through the desert, on one side, so that it makes the Gravelly Sea where it ends. And that river runs only three days in the week, and brings with it great stones and the rocks also therewith, and that in great plenty. And when they are entered into the Gravelly Sea they are seen no more. And in those three days that that river runneth, no man dare enter into it, but in the other days men dare enter well enough. Beyond that river, more up towards the deserts, is a great plain all gravelly between the mountains; and in that plain, every day at sun-rise, small trees begin to grow, and they grow till mid-day, bearing fruit; but no man dare take of that fruit, for it is a thing of fairie. And after mid-day they decrease and enter again into the earth, so that at sun-set they appear no more; and so they do every day.

In that desert are many wild men, hideous to look on, and horned; and they speak nought, but grunt like pigs   And there is also great plenty of wild dogs. And there are many parrots, which speak of their own nature, and salute men that go through the deserts, and speak to them as plainly as though it were a man. And they that speak well have a large tongue, and have five toes upon each foot. And there are also others which have but three toes upon each foot, and they speak but little.

This emperor Prester John, when he goes to battle against any other lord, has no banners borne before him; but he has three large crosses of gold full of precious stones; and each cross is set in a chariot full richly arrayed. And to keep each cross are appointed ten thousand men of arms, and more than one hundred thousand footmen. And this number of people is independent of the chief army. And when he has no war, but rides with a private company, he has before him but one plain cross of wood, in remembrance that Jesus Christ suffered death upon a wooden cross. And they carry before him also a platter of gold full of earth, in token that his nobleness, and his might, and his flesh, shall turn to earth. And he has borne before him also a vessel of silver, full of noble jewels of gold and precious stones, in token of his lordship, nobility, and power. He dwells commonly in the city of Susa, and there is his principal palace, which is so rich and noble that no man can conceive it without seeing it. And above the chief tower of the palace are two round pommels of gold, in each of which are two large carbuncles, which shine bright in the night. And the principal gates of his palace are of the precious stones called sardonix; and the border and bars are of ivory; and the windows of the halls and chambers are of crystal; and the tables, on which men eat, some are of emeralds, some of amethyst, and some of gold, full of precious stones; and the pillars that support the tables are of the same precious stones. Of the steps approaching his throne, where he sits at meat, one is of onyx, another crystal, another green jasper, another amethyst, another sardonix, another cornelian, and the seventh, on which he sets his feet, is of crysolite. All these steps are bordered with fine gold, with the other precious stones, set with great orient pearls. The sides of the seat of his throne are of emeralds, and bordered full nobly with gold, and dubbed with other precious stones and great pearls. All the pillars in his chamber are of fine gold with precious stones, and with many carbuncles, which give great light by night to all people. And although the carbuncle gives light enough, nevertheless at all times a vessel of crystal, full of balm, is burning, to give good smell and odour to the emperor, and to expel all wicked airs and corruptions. The frame of his bed is of fine sapphires blended with gold, to make him sleep well, and to refrain him from lechery. For he will not lie with his wives but four times in the year, after the four seasons. He hath also a very fair and noble palace in the city of Nice, where he dwells when he likes; but the air is not so temperate as it is at the city of Susa. And you shall understand that in his country, and in the countries surrounding, men eat but once in the day, as they do in the court of the great chan. And more than thirty thousand persons eat every day in his court, besides goers and comers, but these thirty thousand persons spend not so much as twelve thousand of our country. This emperor Prester John has evermore seven kings with him, to serve him, who share their service by certain months; and with these kings serve always seventy-two dukes and three hundred and sixty earls. And all the days of the year, twelve archbishops and twenty bishops eat in his household and in his court. And the patriarch of St. Thomas is there what the pope is here. And the archbishops, and the bishops, and the abbots in that country, are all kings. And each of these great lords knows well the attendance of his service. One is master of his household, another is his chamberlain, another serveth him with a dish, another with a cup, another is steward, another is marshal, another is prince of his arms; and thus is he full nobly and royally served. And his land extends in extreme breadth four months' journey, and in length out of measure, including all the isles under earth, that we suppose to be under us.

Near the isle of Pentexoire, which is the land of Prester John, is a great isle, long and broad, called Milsterak, which is in the lordship of Prester John. That isle is very rich. There was dwelling not long since a rich man, named Gatholonabes, who was full of tricks and subtle deceits. He had a fair and strong castle in a mountain, so strong and noble that no man could devise a fairer or a stronger. And he had caused the mountain to be all walled about with a strong and fair wall, within which walls he had the fairest garden that might be imagined; and therein were trees bearing all manner of fruits, all kinds of herbs of virtue and of good smell, and all other herbs also that bear fair flowers. And he had also in that garden many fair wells, and by them he had made fair halls and fair chambers, painted all with gold and azure, representing many divers things and many divers stories. There were also beasts and birds which sung full delectably, and moved by craft, that it seemed that they were alive. And he had also in his garden all kinds of birds and beasts, that men might have play or sport to behold them. And he had also in that place the fairest damsels that might be found under the age of fifteen years, and the fairest young striplings that men might get of that same age; and they were all clothed full richly in clothes of gold; and he said they were angels. And he had also caused to be made three fair and noble wells, all surrounded with stone of jasper and crystal, diapered with gold, and set with precious stones and great orient pearls. And he had made a conduit under the earth, so that the three wells, at his will, should run one with milk, another with wine, and another with honey. And that place he called Paradise. And when any good knight, who was hardy and noble, came to see this royalty, he would lead him into Paradise, and show him these wonderful things, for his sport, and the marvellous and delicious song of divers birds, and the fair damsels, and the fair wells of milk, wine, and honey, running plentifully. There he would let divers instruments of music sound in a high tower, so merrily that it was joy to hear, and no man should see the craft thereof; and those he said were angels of God, and that place was Paradise, that God had promised to his friends, saying "I will give you a land flowing with milk and honey." And then he would make them drink of certain drink, whereof anon they should be drunk; after which they seemed to have greater delight than they had before. And then would he say to them, that if they would die for him and for his love, after their death they should come to his paradise; and they should be of the age of the damsels, and they should play with them and yet they would remain maidens. And after that he would put them in a fairer paradise, where they should see the God of Nature visibly, in his majesty and bliss. And then would he show them his intent, and tell them, if they would go and slay such a lord or such a man who was his enemy, or disobedient to his will, they should not fear to do it, or to be slain themselves in doing it;

for after their death he would put them into another paradise
that was a hundred fold fairer than any of the others; and
there should they dwell with the fairest damsels that might
be, and play with them evermore.   And thus went many
divers lusty bachelors to slay great lords in divers countries,
that were his enemies, in hopes to have that paradise.   And
thus he was often revenged of his enemies by his subtle
deceits and false tricks.   But when the worthy men of the
country had perceived this subtle falsehood of this Gatholonabes, they assembled with force, and assailed his castle, and
slew him, and destroyed all the fair places of that paradise.
The place of the wells and of the walls and of many other
things are yet clearly to be seen, but the riches are clean
gone.   And it is not long ago since that place was destroyed.

Chapter XXVIII.

OF THE DEVIL'S HEAD IN THE PERILOUS VALLEY; AND OF THE CUSTOMS OF PEOPLE IN DIVERS ISLES THAT ARE ABOUT, IN THE LORDSHIP OF PRESTER JOHN.

NEAR that isle of Mistorak, upon the left side, nigh to the
river of Pison, is a marvellous thing.   There is a vale between the mountains which extends nearly four miles; and
some call it the Enchanted Vale, some call it the Vale of
Devils, and some the Perilous Vale.   In that vale men hear
oftentimes great tempests and thunders, and great murmurs
and noises, day and night; and great noise, as it were, of
tabors, and nakeres, and trumpets, as though it were of a great
feast.   This vale is all full of devils, and has been always;
and men say there that it is one of the entrances of hell.
In that vale is great plenty of gold and silver; wherefore many
misbelieving men, and many Christians also, oftentimes go in,
to have of the treasure; but few return, especially of the misbelieving men, for they are anon strangled by the devils.
And in the centre of that vale, under a rock, is a head and
the visage of a devil bodily, full horrible and dreadful to
see, and it shows but the head to the shoulders.   But there
is no man in the world so bold, Christian or other, but
he would be in dread to behold it, and he would feel almost
dead with fear, so hideous is it to behold.   For he looks
at every man so sharply with dreadful eyes, that are ever
moving and sparkling like fire, and changes and stirs so often

in divers manners, with so horrible a countenance, that no man dare approach towards him. And from him issues smoke, and stink, and fire, and so much abomination that scarce any man may endure there. But the good Christians, that are stable in their faith, enter without peril; for they will first shrive them, and mark them with the sign of the holy cross, so that the fiends have no power over them. But although they are without peril, yet they are not without dread when they see the devils visibly and bodily all about them, that make full many divers assaults and menaces, in air and on earth, and terrify them with strokes of thunder blasts and of tempests. And the greatest fear is that God will take vengeance then of that which men have misdone against his will.

And you shall understand that when my fellows and I were in this vale, we were in great thought whether we durst put our bodies in aventure, to go in or not, in the protection of God; and some of our fellows agreed to enter, and some not. So there were with us two worthy men, friars minors of Lombardy, who said that if any man would enter they would go in with us; and when they had said so, upon the gracious trust of God and of them, we heard mass, and every man was shriven and housled; and then we entered, fourteen persons, but at our going out we were but nine. And so we never knew whether our fellows were lost, or had turned back for fear; but we never saw them after. They were two men of Greece, and three of Spain. And our other fellows, that would not go in with us, went by another road to be before us; and so they were. And thus we passed that Perilous Vale, and found therein gold and silver, and precious stones, and rich jewels, in great plenty, both here and there, as it seemed; but whether it was as it seemed I know not, for I touched none; because the devils are so subtle to make a thing to seem otherwise than it is, to deceive mankind; and therefore I touched none; and also because that I would not be put out of my devotion, for I was more devout then than ever I was before or after, and all for the dread of fiends that I saw in divers figures; and also for the great multitude of dead bodies that I saw there lying by the way, in all the vale, as though there had been a battle between two kings, and the mightiest of the country, and that the greater party had been discomfited and slain. And I believe that hardly should any country have so many people in it as lay slain in that vale, as it seemed to us, which was a hideous sight to see. And I marvelled much that there were so many, and the bodies all whole, without rotting; but I believe that fiends made them seem to be so fresh, without rotting. And many of them were in habits of Christian men; but I believe they were such as went in for covetousness of the treasure that was there, and had overmuch feebleness in faith; so that their hearts might not endure in the belief for dread. And therefore we were the more devout a great deal; and yet we were cast down and beaten down many times to the hard earth by winds, and thunders, and tempests; but evermore God of his grace helped us. And so we passed that perilous vale without peril and without encumbrance, thanked be almighty God!

After this, beyond the vale, is a great isle, the inhabitants of which are great giants of twenty-eight or thirty feet long, with no clothing but skins of beasts, that they hang upon them; and they eat nothing but raw flesh, and drink milk of beasts. They have no houses to lie in. And they eat more gladly man's flesh than any other flesh. Into that isle dare no man enter; and if they see a ship, and men therein, anon they enter into the sea to take them. And men told us that in an isle beyond that were giants of greater stature, some of forty-five or fifty feet long, and even, as some men say, of fifty cubits long; but I saw none of those, for I had no lust to go to those parts, because that no man comes either into that isle or into the other but he will be devoured anon. And among those giants are sheep as great as oxen here, which bear great rough wool. Of the sheep I have seen many times. And men have said many times those giants take men, in the sea, out of their ships, and bring them to land, two in one hand and two in the other, eating them going, all raw and alive. In another isle, towards the north, in the Sea of Ocean, are very evil women, who have precious stones in their eyes; and if they behold any man with wrath, they slay him with the look. In another isle, which is fair and great, and full of people, the custom is, that the first night that they are married they make another man to lie by their wives, to have their maidenhead, for which they give great hire and much thanks. And there are certain men in every town that serve for no other thing; and they call them cadeberiz, that is to say, the fools of despair, because they believe their occupation is a dangerous one. After that is another isle, where women

make great sorrow when their children are born; and when
they die, they make great feasts, and great joy and revel, and
then they cast them into a great burning fire. And those that
love well their husbands, if their husbands die, they cast
themselves also into the fire, with their children, and burn
them. In that isle they make their king always by election;
and they choose him not for nobleness or riches, but such a
one as is of good manners and condition, and therewithal just;
and also that he be of great age, and that he have no children.

In that isle men are very just, and they do just judgments
in every cause, both of rich and poor, small and great, according to their trespasses. And the king may not judge a
man to death without assent of his barons and other wise men
of council, and unless all the court agree thereto. And if the
king himself do any homicide or crime, as to slay a man, or
any such case, he shall die for it; but he shall not be slain
as another man; but they forbid, on pain of death, that any
man be so bold as to make him company or to speak with
him, or give or sell him meat or drink; and so shall he die
disgracefully. They spare no man that has trespassed, either
for love, or favour, or riches, or nobility; but that he shall
have according to what he has done.

Beyond that isle is another, where is a great multitude of
people, who will not eat flesh of hares, hens, or geese; and
yet they breed them in abundance, to see and behold them
only; but they eat flesh of all other beasts, and drink milk.
In that country they take their daughters and their sisters to
wife, and their other kinswomen. And if there be ten or
twelve men, or more, dwelling in a house, the wife of each of
them shall be common to them all that dwell in that house;
so that every man may lie with whom he will of them on one
night, and with another another night. And if she have any
child, she may give it to what man she list that has kept company with her; so that no man knows there whether the
child be his or another's. And if any man say to them that
they nourish other men's children, they answer that so do
other men theirs. In that country, and in all India, are great
plenty of cockodrills, a sort of long serpent, as I have said
before; and in the night they dwell in the water, and in the
day upon the land, in rocks and caves; and they eat no meat
in winter, but lie as in a dream, as do serpents. These serpents slay men, and they eat them weeping; and when they

eat, they move the upper jaw, and not the lower jaw; and
they have no tongue. In that country, and in many others
beyond, and also in many on this side, men sow the seed
of cotton; and they sow it every year, and then it grows to
small trees, which bear cotton. And so do men every year,
so that there is plenty of cotton at all times. In this isle
also, and in many others, there is a manner of wood, hard and
strong; and whoever covers the coals of that wood under the
ashes thereof, the coals will remain alive a year or more. And
among other trees there are nut trees, that bear nuts as great
as a man's head *. There are also animals called orafles, which
are called, in Arabia, gerfauntz. They are spotted, and a
little higher than a horse, with a neck twenty cubits long;
and the croup and tail are like those of a hart; and one of
them may look over a high house †. And there are also in that
country many cameleons; and there are very great serpents,
some one hundred and twenty feet long, of divers colours, as
rayed, red, green and yellow, blue and black, and all speckled.
And there are others that have crests upon their heads; and
they go upon their feet upright. And there are also wild
swine of many colours, as great as oxen in our country, all
spotted like young fawns. And there are also hedgehogs, as
great as wild swine, which we call porcupines. And there are
many other extraordinary animals.

Chapter XXIX.

OF THE GOODNESS OF THE PEOPLE OF THE ISLE OF BRAGMAN.—OF KING ALEX-
ANDER, AND WHY THE EMPEROR OF INDIA IS CALLED PRESTER JOHN.

AND beyond that isle is another isle, great and rich, where are
good and true people, and of good living after their belief, and
of good faith. And although they are not christened, yet by
natural law they are full of all virtue, and eschew all vices;
for they are not proud, nor covetous, nor envious, nor wrathful,
nor gluttonous, nor lecherous; nor do they to any man otherwise
than they would that other men did to them; and in this
point they fulfil the ten commandments of God. And they
care not for possessions or riches; and they lie not, nor do
they swear, but say simply yea and nay; for they say he that
sweareth will deceive his neighbour; and therefore all that

* Probably cocoa-nuts.
† This is apparently the giraffe.

they do, they do it without oath.   And that isle is called the
isle of Bragman, and some men call it the Land of Faith; and
through it runs a great river called Thebe.   And in general
all the men of those isles, and of all the borders thereabout,
are truer than in any other country thereabout, and more just
than others in all things.   In that isle is no thief, no murderer, no common woman, no poor beggar, and no man was
ever slain in that country.   And they be as chaste, and lead
as good a life, as though they were monks; and they fast all
days.   And because they are so true, and so just, and so full
of all good conditions, they are never grieved with tempests, nor with thunder and lightning, nor with hail, nor with
pestilence, nor with war, nor with famine, nor with any other
tribulation, as we are many times amongst us for our sins;
wherefore it appears evident that God loveth them for their
good deeds.   They believe well in God that made all things,
and worship him; and they prize no earthly riches; and they
live full orderly, and so soberly in meat and drink, that they
live right long.   And the most part of them die without sickness, when nature faileth them for old age.   And it befell, in
king Alexander's time, that he purposed to conquer that isle;
but when they of the country heard it, they sent messengers
to him with letters, that said thus :—" What may we be now
to that man to whom all the world is insufficient?   Thou
shalt find nothing in us to cause thee to war against us; for
we have no riches, nor do we desire any; and all the goods of
our country are in common.   Our meat, with which we sustain
our bodies, is our riches; and instead of treasure of gold and
silver, we make our treasure of acorns and peas, and to love
one another.   And to apparel our bodies we use a simple cloth
to wrap our carcase.   Our wives are not arrayed to make
any man pleased.   When men labour to array the body, to
make it seem fairer than God made it, they do great sin; for
man should not devise nor ask greater beauty than God hath
ordained him to have at his birth.   The earth ministereth to
us two things; our livelihood, that cometh of the earth that
we live by, and our sepulchre after our death.   We have been
in perpetual peace till now that thou art come to disinherit
us; and also we have a king, not to do justice to every man, for
he shall find no forfeit among us; but to keep nobleness, and
to show that we are obedient, we have a king.   For justice
has among us no place; for we do to no man otherwise than

we desire that men do to us, so that righteousness or vengeance have nought to do among us; so that thou mayest
take nothing from us but our good peace, that always hath
endured among us." And when king Alexander had read
these letters, he thought that he should do great sin to trouble
them.

There is another isle called Oxidrate, and another called
Gymnosophe, where there are also good people, and full of good
faith; and they hold, for the most part, the same good conditions and customs, and good manners, as men of the country
above mentioned; but they all go naked. Into that isle entered
king Alexander, to see the customs; and when he saw their
great faith, and the truth that was amongst them, he said
that he would not grieve them, and bade them ask of him
what they would have of him, riches or any thing else, and
they should have it with good will. And they answered that
he was rich enough that had meat and drink to sustain the
body with; for the riches of this world, that is transitory, are
of no worth; but if it were in his power to make them immortal, thereof would they pray him, and thank him. And
Alexander answered them that it was not in his power to do
it, because he was mortal, as they were. And then they asked
him why he was so proud, and so fierce, and so busy, to put all
the world under his subjection, "right as thou wert a God,
and hast no term of this life, neither day nor hour; and
covetest to have all the world at thy command, that shall
leave thee without fail, or thou leave it. And right as it hath
been to other men before thee, right so it shall be to others
after thee, and from hence shalt thou carry nothing; but as
thou wert born naked, right so all naked shall thy body be
turned into earth, that thou wert made of. Wherefore thou
shouldst think, and impress it on thy mind, that nothing is
immortal but only God, that made all things." By which
answer Alexander was greatly astonished and abashed, and all
confused departed from them.

Many other isles* there are in the land of Prester John,
and many great marvels, that were too long to tell, both of
his riches and of his nobleness, and of the great plenty also
of precious stones that he has. I think that you know well
now, and have heard say, why this emperor is called Prester

---

* I have omitted some paragraphs preceding this, which are mere repro-
ductions of the wonderful ethnographic stories of Pliny and Solinus.

John. There was some time an emperor there, who was a
worthy and a full noble prince, that had Christian knights in
his company, as he has that now is. So it befell that he had
great desire to see the service in the church among Christians; and then Christendom extended beyond the sea, including all Turkey, Syria, Tartary, Jerusalem, Palestine, Arabia,
Aleppo, and all the land of Egypt. So it befell that this emperor came, with a Christian knight with him, into a church
in Egypt; and it was the Saturday in Whitsuntide. And
the bishop was conferring orders; and he beheld and listened
to the service full attentively; and he asked the Christian
knight what men of degree they should be that the prelate
had before him; and the knight answered and said that they
were priests. And then the emperor said that he would no
longer be called king nor emperor, but priest; and that he
would have the name of the first priest that went out of the
church; and his name was John. And so, evermore since,
he is called Prester John.

CHAPTER XXX.

OF THE HILLS OF GOLD THAT ANTS KEEP; AND OF THE FOUR STREAMS THAT
COME FROM TERRESTRIAL PARADISE.

TOWARDS the east of Prester John's land is a good and great isle
called Taprobane, and it is very fruitful; and the king thereof is
rich, and is under the obeisance of Prester John. And there
they always make their king by election. In that isle are two
summers and two winters; and men harvest the corn twice a
year; and in all seasons of the year the gardens are in flower.
There dwell good people, and reasonable; and many Christian
men among them, who are so rich that they know not what to
do with their goods. Of old time, when men passed from the
land of Prester John unto that isle, men made ordinance to
pass by ship in twenty-three days or more; but now men pass
by ship in seven days. And men may see the bottom of the
sea in many places; for it is not very deep.

Beside that isle, towards the east, are two other isles, one
called Orille, the other Argyte, of which all the land is mines
of gold and silver. And those isles are just where the
Red Sea separates from the Ocean Sea. And in those isles
men see no stars so clearly as in other places; for there
appears only one clear star called Canopus. And there the

moon is not seen in all the lunation, except in the second quarter. In the isle, also, of this Taprobane are great hills of gold, that ants keep full diligently *.

And beyond the land, and isles, and deserts of Prester John's lordship, in going straight towards the east, men find nothing but mountains and great rocks; and there is the dark region, where no man may see, neither by day nor night, as they of the country say. And that desert, and that place of darkness, lasts from this coast unto Terrestrial Paradise, where Adam, our first father, and Eve were put, who dwelt there but a little while; and that is towards the east, at the beginning of the earth. But this is not that east that we call our east, on this half, where the sun rises to us; for when the sun is east in those parts towards Terrestrial Paradise, it is then midnight in our parts on this half, on account of the roundness of the earth, of which I have told you before; for our Lord God made the earth all round, in the middle of the firmament. And there have mountains and hills been, and valleys, which arose only from Noah's flood, that wasted the soft and tender ground, and fell down into valleys; and the hard earth and the rock remain mountains, when the soft and tender earth was worn away by the water, and fell, and became valleys.

Of Paradise I cannot speak properly, for I was not there. It is far beyond; and I repent not going there, but I was not worthy. But as I have heard say of wise men beyond, I shall tell you with good will. Terrestrial Paradise, as wise men say, is the highest place of the earth; and it is so high that it nearly touches the circle of the moon there, as the moon makes her turn. For it is so high that the flood of Noah might not come to it, that would have covered all the earth of the world all about, and above and beneath, except Paradise. And this Paradise is inclosed all about with a wall, and men know not whereof it is; for the wall is covered all over with moss, as it seems; and it seems not that the wall is natural stone. And that wall stretches from the south to the north; and it has but one entry, which is closed with burning fire, so that no man that is mortal dare enter. And in the highest place of Paradise, exactly in the middle, is a well that casts out the four streams, which run by

* Here follows the story of the ants that keep the gold, taken from Pliny, Hist. Nat. xi. 31, and found in other ancient writers.

divers lands, of which the first is called Pison, or Ganges, that
runs throughout India, or Emlak, in which river are many
precious stones, and much lignum aloes, and much sand of gold.
And the other river is called Nile, or Gyson, which goes through
Ethiopia, and after through Egypt. And the other is called
Tigris, which runs by Assyria, and by Armenia the Great.
And the other is called Euphrates, which runs through
Media, Armenia, and Persia. And men there beyond say
that all the sweet waters of the world, above and beneath,
take their beginning from the well of Paradise; and out of
that well all waters come and go. The first river is called
Pison, that is, in our language, Assembly; for many other
rivers meet there, and go into that river. And some call it
Ganges, from an Indian king, called Gangeres, because it ran
through his land. And its water is in some places clear,
and in some places troubled; in some places hot, and in some
places cold. The second river is called Nile, or Gyson, for it
is always troubled; and Gyson, in the language of Ethiopia,
is to say Trouble, and in the language of Egypt also. The
third river, called Tigris, is as much as to say, Fast Running;
for it runs faster than any of the others. The fourth river
is called Euphrates, that is to say, Well Bearing; for there grow
upon that river corn, fruit, and other goods, in great plenty.

And you shall understand that no man that is mortal may
approach to that Paradise; for by land no man may go for
wild beasts, that are in the deserts, and for the high mountains, and great huge rocks, that no man may pass by for the
dark places that are there; and by the rivers may no man
go, for the water runs so roughly and so sharply, because it
comes down so outrageously from the high places above, that
it runs in so great waves that no ship may row or sail against
it; and the water roars so, and makes so huge a noise, and so
great a tempest, that no man may hear another in the ship,
though he cried with all the might he could. Many great
lords have assayed with great will, many times, to pass by
those rivers towards Paradise, with full great companies; but
they might not speed in their voyage; and many died for
weariness of rowing against the strong waves; and many of
them became blind, and many deaf, for the noise of the water;
and some perished and were lost in the waves; so that no
mortal man may approach to that place without special grace
of God; so that of that place I can tell you no more.

CHAPTER XXXI.

OF THE CUSTOMS OF KINGS AND OTHERS THAT DWELL IN THE ISLES BOR-
DERING ON PRESTER JOHN'S LAND.

FROM those isles that I have spoken of before, in the land of
Prester John, that are under earth as to us, and of other isles
that are further beyond, whoever will pursue them may come
again right to the parts that he came from, and so environ all
the earth; but what for the isles, what for the sea, and what
for strong rowing, few people assay to pass that passage. And
therefore men return from the isles beforesaid by other isles,
coasting, from the land of Prester John. And then come men,
in returning, to an isle called Casson, which is full sixty days
in length, and more than fifty in breadth. This is the best
isle, and the best kingdom, that is in all those parts, except
Cathay; and if the merchants used that country as much as
they do Cathay, it would be better than Cathay in a short
time. This country is well inhabited, and so full of cities
and good towns, and inhabited with people, that when a man
goes out of one city he sees another city before him. In that
isle is great plenty of all goods to live with, and of all manner
of spices; and there are great forests of chestnuts. The king
of that isle is very rich and mighty; and yet he holds his land
of the great chan, and is subject to him; for it is one of the
twelve provinces which the great chan has under him, besides
his own land, and other less isles, of which he has many.

From that kingdom come men, in returning, to another
isle, called Rybothe, which, also, is under the great chan.
It is a full good country, and rich in all goods, and wine
and fruit, and all other riches. And the people of that country
have no houses; but they dwell and lie all under tents made
of black fern. And the principal city, and the most royal, is
all walled with black and white stone; and all the streets,
also, are paved with the same stones. In that city is no man
so hardy as to shed blood of any man, nor of any beast, for
the reverence of an idol that is worshipped there. And in
that isle dwells the pope of their law, whom they call lobassy.
This lobassy gives all the benefices, and other dignities, and
all other things that belong to the idol. In that isle they
have a custom, in all the country, that when any man's father
is dead, and the son wishes to do great honour to his father,

he sends to all his friends, and to all his kin, and for religious
men and priests, and for minstrels also, in great plenty; and
then they bear the dead body unto a great hill, with great
joy and solemnity; and when they have brought it thither,
the chief prelate smites off the head, and lays it upon a great
platter of gold and silver, if he be a rich man; and then he
gives the head to the son; and then the son and his other kin
sing and say many prayers; and then the priests, and the
religious men, smite all the body of the dead man in pieces;
and then they say certain prayers. And the birds of prey of
all the country about know the custom for a long time before,
and come flying above in the air, as eagles, kites, ravens,
and other birds that eat flesh. And then the priests cast the
bits of flesh, and each fowl takes what he may, and goes
a little thence and eats it; and they do so whilst any piece
of the dead body remains. And after that the priests sing with
high voice, in their language, "Behold how worthy a man, and
how good a man this was, that the angels of God came to seek
him, and to bring him into Paradise." And then it seems to
the son that he is highly worshipped when many birds, and
fowls, and ravens, come and eat his father; and he that has
most number of fowls is most worshipped. Then the son
brings home with him all his kin, and his friends, and all the
others, to his house, and makes a great feast; and then all his
friends make their boast how the fowls came thither, here five,
here six, here ten, and there twenty, and so forth; and they
rejoice greatly to speak thereof. And when they are at meat
the son brings forth the head of his father, and thereof he
serves of the flesh to his most special friends, as a dainty.
And of the skull he makes a cup, and drinks out of it with his
other friends in great devotion, in remembrance of the holy
man that the angels of God had eaten. And that cup the
son shall keep to drink out of all his lifetime, in remembrance
of his father.

From that land, in returning by ten days through the land
of the great chan, is another good isle, and a great kingdom,
where the king is full rich and mighty. And amongst the
rich men of his country is a passing rich man, that is neither
prince, nor duke, nor earl; but he has more that hold of him
lands and other lordships; for he has every year, of annual
rent, more than three hundred thousand horses charged with
corn of divers grains and rice; and so he leads a full noble

and delicate life, after the custom of the country; for he has
every day fifty fair damsels, all maidens, that serve him
evermore at his meat, and to lie by him at night, and
to do with them what he pleases. And when he is at the
table, they bring him his meat at every time, five and five
together; and in bringing their service they sing a song.
And after that they cut his meat, and put it in his mouth;
for he touches nothing, nor handles nought, but holds evermore his hands before him upon the table; for he has such
long nails that he may take nothing, nor handle any thing.
For the nobleness of that country is to have long nails, and to
make them grow always to be as long as men may; and there
are many in that country that have their nails so long that
they environ all the hand; and that is a great nobleness.
And the nobleness of the women is to have small feet; and
therefore, as soon as they are born, they bind their feet so
tight that they may not grow half as nature would. And
always these damsels, that I spoke of before, sing all the time
that this rich man eateth; and when he eateth no more
of his first course, then other five and five of fair damsels
bring him his second course, always singing, as they did
before; and so they do continually every day, to the end of
his meat. And in this manner he leads his life; and so they
did before him that were his ancestors; and so shall they that
come after him, without doing of any deeds of arms, but live
evermore thus in ease, as a swine that is fed in a sty to be
made fat. He has a full fair and rich palace, the walls of
which are two miles in circuit; and he has within many fair
gardens, and many fair halls and chambers; and the pavement
of his halls and chambers are of gold and silver. And in the
middle of one of his gardens is a little mountain, where there
is a little meadow; and in that meadow is a little house, with
towers and pinnacles, all of gold; and in that little house will
he sit often to take the air and sport himself.

And you shall understand that of all these countries and
isles, and of all the divers people that I have spoken of before, and of divers laws, and of divers beliefs that they have,
there is none of them all but they have some reason and
understanding in them, and they have certain articles of
our faith, and some good points of our belief; and they
believe in God that created all things and made the world;
but yet they cannot speak perfectly (for there is no man to

teach them), but only what they can devise by their natural
understanding; for they have no knowledge of the Son nor of
the Holy Ghost; but they can all speak of the Bible, namely
of Genesis, of the Prophets' laws, and of the books of Moses.
And they say well that the creatures that they worship are no
gods; but they worship them for the virtue that is in them.
And of simulacres, and of idols, they say that there are no
people but that they have simulacres; and they say that
we Christian men have images, as of our lady, and of other
saints, that we worship; not the images of wood or of stone,
but the saints in whose name they are made; for right as the
books of the Scripture teach the clerks how and in what
manner they shall believe, right so the images and the
paintings teach the ignorant people to worship the saints,
and to have them in their minds, in whose name the images
are made.   They say, also, that the angels of God speak to
them in those idols, and that they do many great miracles.
And they say truth, that there is an angel within them; for
there are two manner of angels, a good and an evil; as the
Greeks say, Cacho and Calo.   This Cacho is the wicked angel,
and Calo is the good angel: but the other is not the good
angel, but the wicked angel, which is within the idols to deceive them and maintain them in their error.
    There are many other divers countries, and many other
marvels beyond, that I have not seen; wherefore I cannot
speak of them properly.   And, also, in the countries where I
have been are many diversities of many wonderful things,
more than I make mention of; for it were too long a thing to
devise you the manner of them all.   And therefore now that
I have devised you of certain countries, which I have spoken
of before, I beseech your worthy and excellent nobleness that
it suffice to you at this time; for if I told you all that is beyond
the sea, another man, perhaps, who would labour to go into
those parts to seek those countries, might be blamed by my
words in rehearsing many strange things; for he might not
say any thing new, in the which the hearers might have either
solace or pleasure.
    And you shall understand that, at my coming home, I came
to Rome, and showed my life to our holy father the pope, and
was absolved of all that lay in my conscience of many divers
grievous points, as men must need that are in company,
dwelling amongst so many divers people, of divers sects and

beliefs, as I have been. And, amongst all, I showed him this
treatise, that I had made after information of men that knew
of things that I had not seen myself; and also of marvels and
customs that I had seen myself, as far as God would give me
grace; and besought his holy fatherhood that my book might
be examined and corrected by advice of his wise and discreet
council. And our holy father, of his special grace, gave my
book to be examined and proved by the advice of his said
council, by the which my book was proved for true, insomuch
that they showed me a book, which my book was examined by,
that comprehended full much more, by an hundredth part, by
the which the *Mappa Mundi* was made. And so my book
(albeit that many men list not to give credence to any thing
but to what they see with their eye, be the author or the person
ever so true) is affirmed and proved by our holy father in
manner and form as I have said.

And I, John Maundeville, knight, abovesaid, (although I be
unworthy,) that went from our countries, and passed the sea,
in the year of Grace 1322, have passed many lands, and many
isles and countries, and searched many full strange places, and
have been in many a full good and honourable company, and
at many a fair deed of arms, (albeit that I did none myself,
for my insufficiency,) now I am come home (in spite of myself)
to rest; for rheumatic gouts, that distress me, fix the end of
my labour, against my will (God knoweth). And thus, taking
comfort in my wretched rest, recording the time passed, I have
fulfilled these things, and written them in this book, as it
would come into my mind, the year of Grace 1356, in the
thirty-fourth year that I departed from our country. Wherefore I pray to all the readers and hearers of this book, if it
please them, that they would pray to God for me, and I shall
pray for them.

THE TRAVELS OF
BERTRANDON DE LA BROCQUIERE.
A.D. 1432, 1433.

To animate and inflame the hearts of such noble men as may
be desirous of seeing the world, and by the order and command of the most high, most powerful, and my most redoubted lord, Philip, by the grace of God duke of Burgundy,
Lorraine, Brabant, and Limbourg, count of Flanders, Artois,
and Burgundy*, palatine of Hainault, Holland, Zealand, and
Namur, marquis of the Holy Empire, lord of Friesland, Sa-
lines, and Mechlin, I, Bertrandon de la Brocquière, a native
of the duchy of Guienne, lord of Vieux-Chateau, counsellor
and first esquire-carver to my aforesaid most redoubted lord,
after bringing to my recollection every event, in addition to
what I had made an abridgment of in a small book by way
of memorandums, have fairly written out this account of my
short travels, in order that if any king or Christian prince
should wish to make the conquest of Jerusalem, and lead
thither an army overland, or if any gentleman should be desirous of travelling thither, they may be made acquainted
with all the towns, cities, regions, countries, rivers, mountains, and passes in the different districts, as well as the lords
to whom they belong, from the duchy of Burgundy to Jerusalem. The route hence to the holy city of Rome is too well
known for me to stop and describe it. I shall pass lightly
over this article, and not say much until I come to Syria. I
have travelled through the whole country from Gaza, which
is the entrance to Egypt, to within a day's journey of Aleppo,
a town situated on the north of the frontier, and which we
pass in going to Persia.

Having formed a resolution to make a devout pilgrimage
to Jerusalem, and being determined to discharge my vow, I

* Burgundy was divided into two parts, the duchy and county. The
last, since known under the name of Franche Comté, began, at this period,
to take that appellation; and this is the reason why our author styles Philip
duke and count of Burgundy.

quitted, in the month of February, 1432, the court of my
most redoubted lord, which was then at Ghent. After traversing Picardy, Champagne, and Burgundy, I entered Savoy,
crossed the Rhone, and arrived at Chambery by the Mont-du-
Chat. Here commences a long chain of mountains, the
highest of which is called Mount Cenis, which forms a dangerous pass for travellers in times of snow. The road is so
difficult to find, that a traveller, unless he wish to lose it,
must take one of the guides of the country, called Marrons.
These people advise you not to make any sort of noise that
may shake the atmosphere round the mountain, for in that
case the snow is detached, and rolls with impetuosity to the
ground. Mount Cenis separates Italy from France.

Having thence descended into Piedmont, a handsome and
pleasant country, surrounded on three sides by mountains, I
passed through Turin, where I crossed the Po, and proceeded
to Asti, which belongs to the duke of Orleans; then to Alexandria, the greater part of the inhabitants of which are said
to be usurers—to Piacenza, belonging to the duke of Milan—
and at last to Bologna la Grassa, which is part of the pope's
dominions. The emperor Sigismund was at Piacenza; he
had come thither from Milan, where he had received his second crown, and was on his road to Rome in search of the
third *. From Bologna I had to pass another chain of mountains (the Appennines) to enter the states of the Florentines.
Florence is a large town, where the commonalty govern.
Every three months they elect for the government magistrates,
called priori, who are taken from different professions; and
as long as they remain in office they are honoured, but on
the expiration of the three months they return to their former
situations. From Florence I went to Monte Pulciano, a
castle built on an eminence, and surrounded on three sides
by a large lake (Lago di Perugia), thence to Spoleto, Monte
Fiascone, and at length to Rome.

Rome is well known. Authors of veracity assure us that
for seven hundred years she was mistress of the world. But
although their writings should not affirm this, would there
not be sufficiency of proof in all the grand edifices now exist-

---

* In 1414, Sigismund, elected emperor, had received the silver crown at
Aix-la-Chapelle. In the month of November, 1431, a little before the passage of our traveller, he had received the iron crown at Milan; but it was
not until 1443 he received at Rome, from the hands of the pope, that of gold.

ing, in those columns of marble, those statues, and those
monuments as marvellous to see as to describe? Add to the
above the immense quantities of relics that are there;
so many things that our Lord has touched, such numbers of
holy bodies of apostles, martyrs, confessors, and virgins; in
short, so many churches where the holy pontiffs have granted
full indulgences for sin. I saw there Eugenius IV., a Venetian, who had just been elected pope*. The prince of Saler-
num had declared war against him; he was of the Colonna
family, and nephew to pope Martin†.

I quitted Rome the 25th of March, and, passing through a
town belonging to count de Thalamoné, a relation to the cardinal des Ursins, arrived at Urbino; thence I proceeded
through the lordships of the Malatestas to Rimini, a part of
the Venetian dominions. I crossed three branches of the
Po, and came to Chiosa, a town of the Venetians, which had
formerly a good harbour; but this was destroyed by themselves when the Genoese came to lay siege to Venice. From
Chiosa, I landed at Venice, distant twenty-five miles

Venice is a large and handsome town, ancient and commercial, and built in the middle of the sea. Its different quarters being separated by water form so many islands, so that a
boat is necessary to go from one to the other. This town
possesses the body of St. Helena, mother of the emperor
Constantine, as well as many others that I have seen, especially several bodies of the Holy Innocents, which are entire.
These last are in an island called Murano, renowned for its
manufactories of glass. The government of Venice is full of
wisdom. No one can be a member of the council, nor hold
any employment, unless he be noble and born in the town.
It has a duke, who is bound to have ever with him, during the
day, six of the most ancient and celebrated members of the
council. When the duke dies, his successor is chosen from

---

* We shall see hereafter, that la Brocquière left Rome on the 25th
March, and Eugenius had been elected on the first days of the month. There
is some doubt whether his election took place on the 3rd, 4th, or 6th of
March; he occupied the papal see till Feb. 23, 1447.

† Martin V., predecessor to Eugenius, was a Colonna; and there was a
declared enmity between his family and that of the Orsini. Eugenius, when
established in the holy chair, took part in this quarrel, and sided with the
Orsini against the Colonnas, who were nephews to Martin. The last took
up arms, and made war on him.

among those who have shown the greatest knowledge and
zeal for the public good.

On the 8th of May I embarked to accomplish my vow, on
board a galley, with some other pilgrims. We sailed along
the coast of Sclavonia, and successively touched at Pola, Zara,
Sebenico, and Corfu. Pola seemed to me to have been formerly a handsome and strong town, with an excellent harbour.
We were shown at Zara the body of St. Simeon, to whom our
Lord was presented in the Temple. The town is surrounded
on three sides by the sea, and its fine port is shut in by an
iron chain. Sebenico belongs to the Venetians, as does Corfu,
which, with a very handsome harbour, has also two castles.

From Corfu we sailed to Modon, a good and fair town in
the Morea, also belonging to the Venetians; thence to Can-
dia, a most fertile island, the inhabitants of which are excellent sailors. The government of Venice nominates a governor, who takes the title of duke, but who holds his place only
three years. Thence to Rhodes, where I had but time to see
the town; to Baffa, a ruined town in the island of Cyprus; and
at length to Jaffa, in the Holy Land of Promise.

At Jaffa, the pardons commence for pilgrims to the Holy
Land. It formerly belonged to the Christians, and was then
strong; at present it is entirely destroyed, having only a few
tents covered with reeds, whither pilgrims retire to shelter
themselves from the heat of the sun. The sea enters the
town, and forms a bad and shallow harbour; it is dangerous
to remain there long for fear of being driven on shore by a
gust of wind. There are two springs of fresh water; but
one is overflowed by the sea when the westerly wind blows a
little strong. When any pilgrims disembark here, interpreters and other officers of the sultan* instantly hasten to ascertain their numbers, to serve them as guides, and to receive,
in the name of their master, the customary tribute.

Ramlé, the first town we came to from Jaffa, is without
walls, but a good and commercial town, seated in an agreeable and fertile district. We went to visit, in the neighbourhood, a village where St. George was martyred; and, on our
return to Ramlé, we continued our route, and arrived, after

* The sultans of Egypt are here meant. Palestine and Syria were at
that time under their power. The sultan will be often mentioned in the
course of the work.

two days, at the holy city of Jerusalem, where our Lord Jesus
Christ suffered death for us. After making the customary
pilgrimages, we performed those to the mountain where Jesus
fasted forty days; to the Jordan, where he was baptized; to
the church of St. John, near to that river; to that of St.
Martha and St. Mary Magdalene, where our Lord raised Lazarus from the dead; to Bethlehem, where he was born; to the
birth-place of St. John the Baptist; to the house of Zachariah; and, lastly, to the holy cross, where the tree grew that
formed the real cross, after which we returned to Jerusalem.

The Cordeliers have a church at Bethlehem, in which they
perform divine service, but they are under great subjection to
the Saracens. The town is only inhabited by Saracens, and
some Christians of the girdle*.

At the birth-place of St. John the Baptist, a rock is shown,
which, during the time of Herod's persecution of the innocents, opened itself miraculously in two, when St. Elizabeth
having therein hid her son, it closed again of itself, and the
child remained shut up, as it is said, two whole days.

Jerusalem is situated in a mountainous and strong country,
and is at this day a considerable town, although it appears to
have been much more so in former times. It is under the
dominion of the sultan, to the shame and grief of Christendom. Among the free Christians, there are but two Cordeliers who inhabit the holy sepulchre, and even they are
oppressed by the Saracens; I can speak of it from my own
knowledge, having been witness of it for two months. In
the church of the Holy Sepulchre reside also many other sorts
of Christians, Jacobites, Armenians, Abyssinians from the
country of Prester John, and Christians of the girdle; but of
these the Franks suffer the greatest hardships.

When all these pilgrimages were accomplished, we undertook another, equally customary, that to St. Catherine's on
Mount Sinai. For this purpose we formed a party of ten
pilgrims, Sir André de Thoulongeon, Sir Michel de Ligne,
Guillaume de Ligne, his brother, Sanson de Lalaing, Pierre
de Vaudrey, Godefroi de Thoisi, Humbert Buffart, Jean de la
Roe, Simonet†, and myself.

---

* See before, p. 189.

† The family name of this person is left blank in the original. These
names, of which the first five are those of great lords in the states of the
duke of Burgundy, show that several persons of the duke's court had formed

For the information of others, who, like myself, may wish
to visit this country, I shall say, that the custom is to treat
with the chief interpreter at Jerusalem, who receives a tax
for the sultan, and one for himself, and then sends to inform
the interpreter at Gaza, who, in his turn, negotiates a passage
with the Arabians of the desert. These Arabs enjoy the
right of conducting pilgrims; and, as they are not always
under due subjection to the sultan, their camels must be used,
which they let to hire at ten ducats a head. The Saracen
who at this time held the office of chief interpreter was called
Nanchardin. Having received the answer from the Arabs,
he called us together before the chapel, which is at the
entrance and on the left of the holy sepulchre; he there took
down in writing our ages, names, surnames, and very particular descriptions of our persons, and sent a duplicate of
this to the chief interpreter at Cairo. These precautions are
taken for the security of travellers, and to prevent the Arabs
from detaining any of them; but I am persuaded that it is
done likewise through mistrust, and through fear of some exchange or substitution that may make them lose the tribute-
money. On the eve of our departure we bought wine for
the journey, and laid in a stock of provision, excepting bis-
cuit, which we were to find at Gaza. Nanchardin having
provided asses and mules to carry us and our provision, with
a particular interpreter, we set off.

The first place we came to was a village formerly more considerable, at present inhabited by Christians of the girdle,
who cultivate vines. The second was a town called St. Abraham, and situated in the valley of Hebron, where our Lord
created our first father Adam. In that place are buried
together Abraham, Isaac, and Jacob, with their wives; but
this sepulchre is now inclosed within a mosque of the Saracens. We were anxious to see it, and even advanced to the
gate; but our guides and interpreter assured us they dared not
suffer us to enter in the day-time, on account of the dangers
they should run, and that any Christian found within a
mosque is instantly put to death, unless he renounces his

---

a company for this pilgrimage to Palestine, and are, probably, those who embarked with our author at Venice, although he has not before named them.
Toulongeon was created this same year, 1432, a knight of the golden fleece,
but was not invested with the order; for he was then a pilgrim, and died on
the road.

religion. After the valley of Hebron, we traversed another
of greater extent, near to which the mountain on which St.
John performed his penitence was pointed out to us. Thence
we crossed a desert country, and lodged in one of those houses
built through charity, and called khan; from this khan we
came to Gaza.

Gaza, situated in a fine country near the sea, and at the
entrance of the desert, is a strong town, although uninclosed.
It is pretended that it formerly belonged to the famous Samson. His palace is still shown, and also the columns of that
which he pulled down; but I dare not affirm that these are
the same. Pilgrims are harshly treated there; and we also
should have suffered, had it not been for the governor, a man
about sixty years of age, and a Circassian, who heard our
complaints and did us justice. Thrice were we obliged to
appear before him; once, on account of the swords we wore,
and the two other times for quarrels which the Saracen
moucres sought to have with us. Many of us wished to purchase asses; for the camel has a very rough movement, which
is extremely fatiguing to those unaccustomed to it. An ass
is sold at Gaza for two ducats; but the moucres not only
wanted to prevent our buying any, but to force us to hire asses
from them, at the price of five ducats, to St. Catherine's.
This conduct was represented to the governor. For myself,
who had hitherto ridden on a camel, and had no intention of
changing, I desired they would tell me how I could ride a
camel and an ass at the same time. The governor decided
in our favour, and ordered that we should not be forced to
hire any asses from the moucres against our inclinations. We
here laid in fresh provisions necessary for the continuance of
our journey; but, on the eve of our departure, four of my
companions fell sick, and returned to Jerusalem. I set off
with the five others, and we came to a village situated at the
entrance of the desert, and the only one to be met with between
Gaza and St. Catherine's. Sir Sanson de Lalaing also there
quitted us, and returned; so that our company consisted of
Sir Andrew de Toulongeon, Pierre de Vaudrei, Godefroi de
Toisi, Jean de la Roe, and myself.

We thus travelled two days in the desert, absolutely without
seeing any thing deserving to be related. Only one morning
I saw, before sunrise, an animal running on four legs, about
three feet long, but scarcely a palm in height. The Ara-

bians fled at the sight of it, and the animal hastened to hide
itself in a bush hard by.   Sir Andrew and Pierre de Vaudrei
dismounted, and pursued it sword in hand, when it began to
cry like a cat on the approach of a dog.   Pierre de Vaudrei
struck it on the back with the point of his sword, but did it
no harm, from its being covered with scales like a sturgeon.
It sprung at Sir Andrew, who, with a blow from his sword,
cut the neck partly through, and flung it on its back, with its
feet in the air, and killed it.   The head resembled that of a
large hare; the feet were like the hands of a young child,
with a pretty long tail, like that of the large green lizard.
Our Arabs and interpreter told us it was very dangerous *.

At the end of the second day's journey I was seized with
such a burning fever that it was impossible for me to proceed.
My four companions, distressed at this accident, made me
mount an ass, and recommended me to one of our Arabs,
whom they charged to reconduct me, if possible, to Gaza.
This man took a great deal of care of me, which is unusual
in respect to Christians.   He faithfully kept me company,
and led me in the evening to pass the night in one of their
camps, which might consist of fourscore and some tents,
pitched in the form of a street.   These tents consist of two
poles stuck in the ground by the bigger end, at a certain
distance from each other, and on them is placed another pole
cross-way, and over this last is laid a thick coverlid of woollen,
or coarse hair.   On my arrival, four or' five Arabs, who were
acquainted with my companion, came to meet us.   They dismounted me from my ass, and laid me on a mattress which I
had with me, and then, treating me according to their
method, kneaded and pinched me so much with their hands †,
that from fatigue and lassitude I slept and reposed for six
hours.   During this time no one did me the least harm, nor
took any thing from me.   It would, however, have been very
easy for them to do so; and I must have been a tempting
prey, for I had with me two hundred ducats, and two camels
laden with provision and wine.

    * From this vague description, it should seem that the animal spoken of
was the great lizard, called *monitor*, because it is pretended that it gives
information of the approach of a crocodile.   The monitor is common in the
Euphrates, where it is sometimes seen four or five feet in length.   The
terror of the Arabs was groundless.

    † This is what is called in French, *masser*, a method used in several
parts of the east for certain disorders.

I set out, on my return to Gaza, before- day; but when I came thither, I found neither my four companions who had remained behind nor Sir Sanson de Lalaing: the whole five had returned to Jerusalem, carrying with them the interpreter. Fortunately I met with a Sicilian Jew to whom I could make myself understood; and he sent me an old Samaritan, who, by some medicines which he gave me, appeased the great heat I endured. Two days after, finding myself a little better, I set off in company with a Moor, who conducted me by a road on the sea-side. We passed near Ascalon, and thence traversed an agreeable and fertile country to Ramlé, where I regained the road to Jerusalem.

On the first day's journey I met on my road the governor of that town returning from a pilgrimage, with a company of fifty horsemen, and one hundred camels, mounted principally by women and children, who had attended him to his place of devotion. I passed the night with them, and the morrow, on my return to Jerusalem, took up my lodgings with the Cordeliers at the church of Mount Sion, where I again met my five comrades.

On my arrival I went to bed, that my disorder might be properly treated; but I was not cured, or in a state to depart, until the 19th of August. During my convalescence I recollected that I had frequently heard it said that it was impossible for a Christian to return overland from Jerusalem to France. I dare not, even now, when I have performed this journey, assert that it is safe. I thought, nevertheless, that nothing was impossible for a man to undertake, who has a constitution strong enough to support fatigue, and has money and health. It is not, however, through vain boasting that I say this; but, with the aid of God and his glorious mother, who never fail to assist those who pray to them heartily, I resolved to attempt the journey. I kept my project secret for some time, without even hinting it to my companions: I was also desirous, before I undertook it, to perform other pilgrimages, especially those to Nazareth and Mount Tabor. I went, in consequence, to make Nanchardin, principal interpreter to the sultan, acquainted with my intentions, who supplied me with a sufficient interpreter for my journey. I thought of making my first pilgrimage to Mount Tabor, and every thing was prepared for it; but when I was on the point of setting out, the head of the convent where I lodged dissuaded me, and opposed my intentions most strongly. The interpreter, on his side, refused to go, saying, that in the present circumstances I should not find any person to attend me; for that the road lay through the territories of towns which were at war with each other, and that very lately a Venetian and his interpreter had been assassinated there. I confined myself, therefore, to the second pilgrimage, in which Sir Sanson de Lalaing and Humbert wished to accompany me. We left Sir Michel de Ligne sick at Mount Sion, and his brother William remained with his servant to attend on him. The rest of us set off on the day of mid-August, with the intention of going to Jaffa by way of Ramlé, and from Jaffa to Nazareth; but, before I departed, I went to the tomb of our Lady, to implore her protection for my grand journey home. I heard divine service at the Cordeliers, and saw there people who call themselves Christians, but some of them are very strange ones, according to our notions.

The principal monk at Jerusalem was so friendly as to accompany us as far as Jaffa, with a Cordelier friar of the convent of Beaune. They there quitted us, and we engaged a bark from the Moors, which carried us to the port of Acre. This is a handsome port, deep and well inclosed. The town itself appears to have been large and strong; but at present there do not exist more than three hundred houses, situated at one of its extremities, and at some distance from the sea. With regard to our pilgrimage, we could not accomplish it. Some Venetian merchants, whom we consulted, dissuaded us, and from what they said we gave it up. They told us, at the same time, that a galley from Narbonne was expected at Baruth; and my comrades being desirous to take that opportunity of returning to France, we consequently followed the road to that town. We saw, on our way thither, Sur, an inclosed town, with a good port, then Seyde, another sea-port tolerably good. Baruth has been more considerable than it is now, but its port is still handsome, deep, and safe for vessels. On one of its points we see the remains of a strong castle which it formerly had, but which is now in ruins *.

---

* Sur is the ancient Tyre—Seyde, Sidon—Baruth, Berytus. What la Brocquière here says is interesting for geography: it proves that all these sea-ports of Syria, formerly so commercial and famous, but at this day so degraded and completely useless, were, in his time, for the greater part, fit for commerce.

As for myself, solely occupied with my grand journey, I employed the time we staid in this town in seeking information concerning it; and to this end addressed myself to a Genoese merchant, called Jacques Pervezin. He advised me to go to Damascus, assuring me that I should find there merchants from Venice, Catalonia, Florence, Genoa, and other places, whose counsels might guide me. He even gave me a letter of recommendation to a countryman of his, named Ottobon Escot. Being resolved to consult Escot before I proceeded farther, I proposed to Sir Sanson to go and see Damascus, without, however, telling him any thing of my project. He accepted my proposal with pleasure, and we set out under the conduct of a moucre. I have before said that the moucres in Syria are the people whose trade is conducting travellers, and hiring out to them asses and mules.

On quitting Baruth, we had to traverse some high mountains to a long plain, called the valley of Noah, because it is said that Noah there built the ark. This valley is not, at the utmost, more than a league wide; but it is pleasant and fertile, watered by two rivers, and peopled by Arabs. As far as Damascus, we continued to travel between mountains, at whose feet are many villages and vineyards. But I warn those who, like me, shall have occasion to make this journey, to take good care of themselves during the night, for in my life I never felt such cold. This excess of cold is caused by the fall of the dew*, and it is thus throughout Syria. The greater the heat during the day, the more abundant the dew and the cold of the night.

It is two days' journey from Baruth to Damascus. The Mohammedans have established a particular custom for Christians all through Syria, in not permitting them to enter the towns on horseback. None that are known to be such dare do it, and, in consequence, our moucre made Sir Sanson and myself dismount before we entered any town. Scarcely had we arrived in Damascus than about a dozen Saracens came round to look at us. I wore a broad beaver hat, which is unusual in that country; and one of them gave me a blow with a staff, which knocked it off my head on the ground†. I own that my first movement was to lift my fist at him; but the

---

* More probably the cold was caused by the ascent of Mount Libanus.

† It is only lately that the people of Damascus have been cured of their bigoted conduct towards black hats.

moucre, throwing himself between us, pushed me aside, and
very fortunately for me he did so, for in an instant we were
surrounded by thirty or forty persons; and if I had given a
blow, I know not what would have become of us. I mention
this circumstance to show that the inhabitants of Damascus
are a wicked race, and, consequently, care should be taken to
avoid any quarrels with them. It is the same in other Mohammedan countries. I know by experience that you must
not joke with them, nor at the same time seem afraid, nor
appear poor, for then they will despise you; nor rich, for
they are very avaricious, as all who have disembarked at Jaffa
know to their cost.

Damascus may contain, as I have heard, one hundred thousand souls. The town is rich, commercial, and, after Cairo,
the most considerable of all in the possession of the sultan.
To the north, south, and east is an extensive plain : to the
west rises a mountain, at the foot of which the suburbs are
built. A river runs through it, which is divided into several
canals. The town only is inclosed by a handsome wall, for the
suburbs are larger than the town. I have nowhere seen such
extensive gardens, better fruits, nor greater plenty of water.
This is said to be so abundant, that there is scarcely a house
without a fountain. The governor is only inferior to the
sultan in all Syria and Egypt; but, as at different times some
governors have revolted, the sultans have taken precautions
to restrain them within proper bounds. Damascus has a
strong castle on the side toward the mountain, with wide and
deep ditches, over which the sultan appoints a captain of his
own friends, who never suffers the governor to enter it. It
was, in 1400, destroyed and reduced to ashes by Tamerlane.
Vestiges of this disaster now remain ; and toward the gate of
St. Paul there is a whole quarter that has never been rebuilt.
There is a khan in the town, appropriated as a deposit and place
of safety to merchants and their goods. It is called Khan Berkot, from its having originally been the residence of a person
of that name. For my part, I believe that Berkot was a
Frenchman* ; and what inclines me to this opinion is, that
on a stone of the house are carved fleur-de-lis, which
appear as ancient as the walls. Whatever may have been

---

* This explanation may possibly admit of a doubt; *bir*, in Arabic, signifies a well; *kut* is also an Arabic word frequently found in names of places,
as Kut-el-Amara, &c.

his origin, he was a very gallant man, and to this day enjoys
a high reputation in that country.   Never during his lifetime,
and while he was in power, could the Persians or Tartars gain
the smallest portion of land in Syria.   The moment he learned
that one of their armies was advancing, he instantly marched
to meet it, as far as the river, beyond Aleppo, that separates
Syria from Persia, and which, from a guess of the situation,
I believe to be the river Jehon, which falls into the Misses in
Turcomania *.   The people of Damascus are persuaded that,
had he lived, Tamerlane would never have carried his arms
thither.   Tamerlane, however, did honour to his memory;
for when he took the town, and ordered it to be set on fire,
he commanded the house of Berkot to be spared, and appointed a guard to prevent its being hurt by the fire, so that
it subsists to this day.

The Christians are hated at Damascus.   Every evening the
merchants are shut up in their houses by persons appointed
for this purpose, who, on the morrow, come to open their
gates when it may please them.   I found there many Genoese,
Venetian, Calabrian, Florentine, and French merchants.   The
last were come thither to purchase several articles, and particularly spiceries, with the intention of taking them to Baruth, and embarking them on board the galley expected from
Narbonne.   Among them was Jacques Cœur†, who has since
acted a great part in France, and was master of the wardrobe
to the king.   He told us the galley was then at Alexandria,
and that probably Sir Andrew and his three companions would
embark on board at Baruth.

I was shown the place, without the walls of Damascus,
where St. Paul had a vision, was struck blind, and thrown
from his horse.   He caused himself to be conducted to Damascus, where he was baptized; but the place of his baptism
is now a mosque.   I saw also the stone from which St. George
mounted his horse when he went to combat the dragon.   It
is two feet square; and they say, that when formerly the Sa-

* De la Brocquière doubtless means the Euphrates.
† Jacques Cœur was an extraordinary character, and a striking instance
of the ingratitude of monarchs.   Although of low origin, he raised himself
by his abilities to high honours, and acquired by his activity immense riches.
He was one of the most celebrated merchants that ever existed; and had it
not been for his superior management of the finances, the generals, able as
they were, of Charles VII. would never have expelled the English from
France.

racens attempted to carry it away, in spite of all the strength
they employed they could not succeed.

Having seen Damascus, Sir Sanson and myself returned
to Baruth, where we found Sir Andrew, Pierre de Vaudrei,
Geoffroi de Toisi, and Jean de la Roe, who had come thither,
as Jacques Cœur had told us. The galley arrived from Alexandria two or three days afterward; and, during this short
interval, we witnessed a feast celebrated by the Moors in their
ancient manner. It began in the evening at sunset. Numerous companies, scattered here and there, were singing and
uttering loud cries. While this was passing, the cannons of
the castle were fired, and the people of the town launched
into the air, very high and to a great distance, a kind of fire,
larger than the greatest lantern that I ever saw lighted.
They told me they sometimes made use of such at sea, to set
fire to the sails of an enemy's vessel. It seems to me, that
as it is a thing easy to be made, and of little expense, it may
be equally well employed to burn a camp or a thatched village,
or in an engagement with cavalry to frighten the horses.
Curious to know its composition, I sent the servant of my
host to the person who made this fire, and requested him to
teach me the method. He returned for answer that he dared
not, for that he should run great danger were it known; but
as there is nothing a Moor will not do for money, I offered
him a ducat, which quieted his fears, and he taught me all
he knew, and even gave me the moulds in wood, with the
other ingredients, which I have brought to France.

The evening before the embarkation, I took Sir Andrew de
Toulongeon aside, and, having made him promise that he
would not make any opposition to what I was about to reveal
to him, I informed him of my design to return home overland. In consequence of his promise, he did not attempt to
hinder me, but represented all the dangers I should have to
encounter, and the risk I should run of being forced to deny
my faith to Jesus Christ. I must own that his representations were well founded; and of all the perils he had menaced
me with, there was not one I did not experience, except de-
nying my religion. He engaged his companions to talk with
me also on this subject; but what they urged was vain: I
suffered them to set sail, and remained at Baruth.

On their departure, I visited a mosque that had originally
been a handsome church, built, as it is said, by St. Barbara.

It is added that, when the Saracens had gained possession, and their criers had, as usual, ascended the tower to announce the time of prayer, they were so beaten that from that day no one has ventured to return thither. There is also another miraculous building that has been changed into a church, which formerly was a house belonging to the Jews. One day these people finding an image of our Lord began to stone it, as their fathers had in times past stoned the Original; but the image having shed blood, they were so frightened with the miracle, that they fled and accused themselves to the bishop, and gave up even their house in reparation for their crime. It was made into a church, which at present is served by the Cordeliers.

I was lodged at the house of a Venetian merchant, named Paul Barberico; and as I had not entirely renounced my two pilgrimages to Nazareth and Mount Tabor, in spite of the obstacles which it had been said I should meet with, I consulted him on this double journey. He procured for me a moucre, who undertook to conduct me, and bound himself before him to carry me safe and sound as far as Damascus, and to bring him back from thence a certificate of having performed his engagement, signed by me. This man made me dress myself like a Saracen. The Franks, for their security in travelling, have obtained permission from the sultan to wear this dress when on a journey.

I departed with my moucre from Baruth on the morrow after the galley had sailed, and we followed the road to Seyde that lies between the sea and the mountains. These frequently run so far into the sea that travellers are forced to go on the sands, and at other times they are three-quarters of a league distant. After an hour's ride, I came to a small wood of lofty pines, which the people of the country preserve with care. It is even forbidden to cut down any of them; but I am ignorant of the reason for such a regulation. Further on was a tolerably deep river, which my moucre said came from the valley of Noah, but the water was not good to drink. It had a stone bridge over it, and hard by was a khan, where we passed the night. On the morrow we arrived at Seyde, a town situated near the sea, and inclosed on the land side by ditches, which are not deep. Sur, called by the Moors Sour, has a similar situation. It is supplied with excellent water from a spring a quarter of a league to the southward of the

town, conducted to it by an aqueduct. I only passed through;
and it seemed to be handsome, though not strong, any more
than Seyde, both having been formerly destroyed, as appears
from their walls, which are not to be compared to those of our
towns. The mountain near Sur forms a crescent, the two
horns advancing as far as the sea: the void between them is
not filled with villages, though there are many on the sides of
the mountain. A league farther we came to a pass which
forced us to travel over a bank, on the summit of which is a
tower. Travellers going to Acre have no other road than
this, and the tower has been erected for their security. From
this defile to Acre the mountains are low, and many habitations are visible, inhabited, for the greater part, by Arabs.
Near the town I met a great lord of the country, called Fan-
cardin: he was encamped on the open plain, carrying his
tents with him.

Acre, though in a plain of about four leagues in extent, is
surrounded on three sides by mountains, and on the fourth
by the sea. I made acquaintance there with a Venetian merchant, called Aubert Franc, who received me well, and procured me much useful information respecting my two pilgrimages, by which I profited. With the aid of his advice, I
took the road to Nazareth, and, having crossed an extensive
plain, came to the fountain, the water of which our Lord
changed into wine at the marriage of Archetriclin*: it is
near a village where St. Peter is said to have been born.

Nazareth is another large village, built between two mountains; but the place where the angel Gabriel came to announce to the Virgin Mary that she would be a mother is in
a pitiful state. The church which had been built there is entirely destroyed; and of the house wherein our lady was when
the angel appeared to her, not the smallest remnant exists.

From Nazareth I went to Mount Tabor, the place where
the transfiguration of our Lord, and many other miracles,
took place. These pasturages attract the Arabs, who come
thither with their beasts; and I was forced to engage four
additional men as an escort, two of whom were Arabs. The
ascent of the mountain is rugged, because there is no road:
I performed it on the back of a mule, but it took me two
hours. The summit is terminated by an almost circular

* See before, p. 47.

plain of about two bow-shots in length, and one in width. It was formerly inclosed within walls, the ruins of which, and the ditches, are still visible : within the wall, and around it, were several churches, and one especially, where, although in ruins, full pardon for vice and sin is gained.

To the east of Mount Tabor, and at the foot of it, we saw the Tiberiade, beyond which the Jordan flows. To the westward is an extensive plain, very agreeable from its gardens, filled with date palm trees, and small tufts of trees planted like vines, on which grows the cotton. At sun-rise these last have a singular effect, and, seeing their green leaves covered with cotton, the traveller would suppose it had snowed on them *. I descended into this plain to dinner, for I had brought with me chickens and wine. My guides conducted me to the house of a man, who, when he saw my wine, took me for a person of consequence, and received me well. He brought me a porringer of milk, another of honey, and a branch loaded with dates. They were the first I had ever seen. I noticed also the manner of manufacturing cotton, in which men and women were employed. Here my guides wanted to extort more money from me, and insisted on making a fresh bargain to reconduct me to Nazareth. It was well I had not my sword with me, for I confess I should have drawn it; and it would have been madness in me, and in all who shall imitate me. The result of the quarrel was, that I was obliged to give them twelve drachms of their money, equivalent to half a ducat. The moment they had received them, the whole four left me, so that I was obliged to return alone with my moucre.

We had not proceeded far on our road when we saw two Arabs, armed in their manner, and mounted on beautiful horses, coming towards us. The moucre was much frightened ; but, fortunately, they passed us without saying a word. He owned that, had they suspected I was a Christian, they would have killed us both without mercy, or, at the least, have stripped us naked. Each of them bore a long and thin pole, shod at the ends with iron ; one of which was pointed, the other round, but having many sharp blades a span long. Their

---

* M. de la Brocquière is here probably mistaken. The cotton tree resembles in its leaves the vine : but the cotton is formed in capsules, and not on the leaves. There are many trees whose leaves are covered externally with a white down, but none that in this manner produce cotton.

buckler was round, according to their custom, convex at the centre, whence came a thick point of iron; and from that point to the bottom it was ornamented with a long silken fringe. They were dressed in robes, the sleeves of which, a foot and a half wide, hung down their arms; and instead of a cap they had a round hat, terminated in a point of rough crimson wool, which, instead of having the linen cloth twisted about it like other Moors, fell down on each side of it, the whole of its breadth.

We went to lodge at Samaria, because I wished to see the lake of Tiberias, where, it is said, St. Peter was accustomed to fish; and, by so doing, some pardons may be gained, for it was the ember week of September. The moucre left me to myself the whole day. Samaria is situated on the extremity of a mountain. We entered it at the close of the day, and left it at midnight to visit the lake. The moucre had proposed this hour to evade the tribute extracted from all who go thither; but the night hindered me from seeing the surrounding country. I went first to Joseph's well, so called from his being cast into it by his brethren. There is a handsome mosque near it, which I entered, with my moucre, pretending to be a Saracen. Further on is a stone bridge over the Jordan, called Jacob's Bridge, on account of a house hard by, said to have been the residence of that patriarch. The river flows from a great lake situated at the foot of a mountain to the north-west, on which Namcardin has a very handsome castle.

From the lake I took the road to Damascus. The country is tolerably pleasant; and, although the road leads between mountains, they are generally from one to two leagues asunder. There is, however, one narrow place, where the road is only wide enough for a horse to pass. The tract all around it, to the right and left for the space of about a league in length and breadth, is covered with immense flint stones, like pebbles in a river, the greater part as big as a wine-tun. Beyond this pass is a handsome khan, surrounded by fountains and rivulets. Four or five miles from Damascus is another, the most magnificent I ever saw, seated near a small river, formed by a junction of springs rising on the spot. The nearer you approach the town, the finer is the country.

I met, near Damascus, a very black Moor, who had ridden a camel from Cairo in eight days, though it is usually sixteen

days' journey.   His camel had run away from him ; but, with
the assistance of my moucre, we recovered it   These couriers
have a singular saddle, on which they sit cross-legged ; but
the rapidity of the camel is so great that, to prevent any bad
effects from the air, they have their heads and bodies tightly
bandaged.   This courier was the bearer of an order from the
sultan.   A galley and two galliots of the prince of Tarentum
had captured, before Tripoli in Syria, a vessel from the Moors ;
and the sultan, by way of reprisal, had sent to arrest all the
Catalonians and Genoese who might be found in Damascus
and throughout Syria.   This news, which my moucre told me,
did not alarm me : I entered the town boldly with other
Saracens, because, dressed like them, I thought I had nothing
to fear.   This expedition had taken up seven days.

On the morrow of my arrival I saw the caravan return
from Mecca.   It was said to be composed of three thousand
camels ; and, in fact, it was two days and as many nights before they had all entered the town.   This event was, according to custom, a great festival.   The governor of Damascus,
attended by the principal persons of the town, went to meet
the caravan out of respect to the Alcoran, which it bore.   This
is the book of law which Mohammed left to his followers.   It
was enveloped in a silken covering, painted over with Moorish
inscriptions ; and the camel that bore it was, in like manner,
decorated all over with silk.   Four musicians, and a great
number of drums and trumpets, preceded the camel, and
made a loud noise.   In front, and around, were about thirty
men—some bearing cross-bows, others drawn swords, others
small harquebuses, which they fired off every now and then *.
Behind this camel followed eight old men, mounted on the
swiftest camels, and near them were led their horses, magnificently caparisoned and ornamented with rich saddles, according to the custom of the country.   After them came a Turkish
lady, a relation of the grand seignior, in a litter borne by two
camels with rich housings.   There were many of these animals covered with cloth of gold.   The caravan was composed
of Moors, Turks, Barbaresques, Tartars, Persians, and other
sectaries of the false prophet Mohammed.   These people pretend that, having once made a pilgrimage to Mecca, they cannot be damned.   Of this I was assured by a renegado slave,

---

* This is an early mention of portable fire-arms in the East : they were
at this time novelties in Europe.

a Bulgarian by birth, who belonged to the lady I have mentioned. He was called Hayauldoula, which signifies, in the
Turkish language, "servant of God," and pretended to have
been three times at Mecca. I formed an acquaintance with
him, because he spoke a little Italian, and often kept me
company in the night as well as in the day. In our conversations I frequently questioned him about Mohammed, and
where his body was interred. He told me he was at Mecca;
that the shrine containing the body was in a circular chapel,
open at the top, and that it was through this opening the
pilgrims saw the shrine; that among them were some who,
having seen it, had their eyes thrust out, because they said,
after what they had just seen, the world could no longer offer
them any thing worth looking at. There were, in fact, in this
caravan two persons, the one of sixteen and the other of
twenty-two or twenty-three years old, who had thus made
themselves blind. Hayauldoula told me also, that it was not
at Mecca where pardons for sin were granted, but at Medina,
where St. Abraham built a house that still remains *. The
building is in the form of a cloister, of which pilgrims make
the circuit.

With regard to the town, it is seated on the sea-shore.
Indians, the inhabitants of Prester John's country, bring
thither, in large ships, spices and other productions of their
country; and thither the Mohammedans go to purchase them.
They load them on camels, and other beasts of burden, for
the markets of Cairo, Damascus, and other places, as is well
known. The distance from Mecca to Damascus is forty
days' journey across the desert. The heat is excessive; and
many of the caravan were suffocated. According to the renegado slave, the annual caravan to Medina should be composed
of seven hundred thousand persons; and when this number
is incomplete, God sends his angels to make it up. At the
great day of judgment Mohammed will admit into Paradise as
many persons as he shall please, where they will enjoy honey,
milk, and women at pleasure. As I was incessantly hearing
Mohammed spoken of, I wished to know something about him;
and, for this purpose, I addressed myself to a priest in Damascus, attached to the Venetian consul, who often said mass in

---

* Our traveller is mistaken. The tomb of Mohammed is at Medina, and
not at Mecca : and the house of Abraham is at Mecca, and not Medina,
where pilgrims gain pardons, and where that great commerce is carried on.

his house, confessed the merchants of that nation, and, when necessary, regulated their affairs. Having confessed myself to him, and settled my worldly concerns, I asked him if he were acquainted with the doctrines of Mohammed. He said he was, and knew all the Alcoran. I then besought him, in the best manner I could, that he would put down in writing all he knew of him, that I might present it to my lord the duke of Burgundy. He did so with pleasure; and I have brought with me his work.

My intention was to go to Bursa*; and, in consequence, I was introduced to a Moor, who engaged to conduct me thither in the track of the caravan on paying him thirty ducats and his expenses; but as I was advised to distrust the Moors, as people of bad faith and accustomed to break their promises, I did not conclude the bargain. I say this for the instruction of those who may have any concerns with them; for I believe them to be such as they were described to me. Hayauldoula, on his part, procured me the acquaintance of some Caramanian merchants; but I took another resolution.

In regard to the pilgrims that go to Mecca, the grand Turk has a custom peculiar to himself—at least, I am ignorant if the other Mohammedan powers do the same—which is, that when the caravan leaves his states he chooses for it a chief, whom they are bound to obey as implicitly as himself. The chief of this caravan was called Hoyarbarach; he was a native of Bursa, and one of its principal inhabitants. I caused myself to be presented to him, by mine host and another person, as a man that wanted to go to that town to see a brother. They entreated him to receive me in his company, and to afford me his security. He asked if I understood Arabic, Turkish, Hebrew, the vulgar tongue, or Greek? When they replied that I did not, he answered, "Well, what can he pretend to do?" However, representations were made to him that, on account of the war, I dared not go thither by sea; and that, if he would condescend to admit me, I would do as well as I could. He then consented; and, having placed his two hands on his head and touched his beard, he told me, in the Turkish language, that I might join his slaves; but he insisted that I should be dressed just like them.

I went, immediately after this interview, with one of my

* Brusa.

friends, to the market, called the Bazaar, and bought two long white robes that reached to my ancles, a complete turban, a linen girdle, a fustian pair of drawers to tuck the ends of my robe in; two small bags, the one for my own use, the other to hang on my horse's head while feeding him with barley and straw; a leathern spoon and salt; a carpet to sleep on; and, lastly, a paletot of a white skin, which I lined with linen cloth, and which was of service to me in the nights. I purchased also a white tarquais (a sort of quiver) complete, to which hung a sword and knives; but as to the tarquais and sword, I could only buy them privately; for if those who have the administration of justice had known of it, the seller and myself would have run great risks.

The Damascus blades are the handsomest and best of all Syria; and it is curious to observe their manner of burnishing them. This operation is performed before tempering; and they have, for this purpose, a small piece of wood, in which is fixed an iron, which they rub up and down the blade, and thus clear off all inequalities, as a plane does to wood. They then temper and polish it. This polish is so highly finished, that, when any one wants to arrange his turban, he uses his sword for a looking-glass. As to its temper, it is perfect; and I have nowhere seen swords that cut so excellently. There are made at Damascus, and in the adjoining country, mirrors of steel, that magnify objects like burning glasses. I have seen some that, when exposed to the sun, have reflected the heat so strongly as to set fire to a plank fifteen or sixteen feet distant.

I bought a small horse that turned out very well. Before my departure I had him shod at Damascus; and thence, as far as Bursa, which is near fifty days' journey, so well do they shoe their horses that I had nothing to do with his feet, excepting one of the fore ones, which was pricked by a nail, and made him lame for three weeks. The shoes are light, thin, lengthened towards the heel, and thinner there than at the toe. They are not turned up, and have but four nail holes, two on each side. The nails are square, with a thick and heavy head. When a shoe is wanted, and it is necessary to work it to make it fit the hoof, it is done cold, without ever putting it in the fire, which can readily be done because it is so thin. To pare the hoof they use a pruning knife, similar to what vine-dressers trim their vines with, both on this as well as on the

other side of the sea. The horses of this country only walk
and gallop; and, when purchased, those which have the best
walk are preferred, as, in Europe, those which trot the best.
They have wide nostrils, gallop well, and are excellent, costing
little on the road; for they eat only at night, and then but a
small quantity of barley with chopped straw. They never
drink but in the afternoon; and their bridles are always left
in their mouths, even when in the stable, like mules. When
there they have the two hinder legs tied; and they are all
intermixed together, horses and mares. All are geldings, excepting a few kept for stallions. Should you have any business with a rich man, and call on him, he will carry you, to
speak with you, to his stables, which are, consequently, kept
always very cool and very clean. We Europeans prefer a
stone-horse of a good breed; but the Moors esteem only
mares. In that country a great man is not ashamed to ride
a mare with its foal running after the dam. I have seen
some, exceedingly beautiful, sold as high as two or three
hundred ducats. They are accustomed to keep their horses
very low, and never to allow them to get fat. The men of
fortune carry with them, when they ride, a small drum, which
they use in battle, or in skirmishes, to rally their men. It is
fastened to the pommel of their saddles, and they beat on it
with a piece of flat leather. I also purchased one, with spurs,
and vermilion coloured boots, which came up to my knees,
according to the custom of the country.

As a mark of my gratitude to Hoyarbarach, I went to offer
him a pot of green ginger; but he refused it, and it was by
dint of prayers and entreaties that I prevailed on him to
accept of it. I had no other pledge for my security than
what I have mentioned; but I found him full of frank-
ness and good will—more, perhaps, than I should have found
in many Christians.

God, who had protected me in the accomplishment of this
journey, brought me acquainted with a Jew of Caiffa, who
spoke the Tartar and Italian languages; and I requested him
to assist me in putting down in writing the names of every
thing I might have occasion to want for myself and my horse
while on the road. On our arrival, the first day's journey, at
Ballec, I drew out my paper to know how to ask for barley
and chopped straw, which I wanted to give my horse. Ten
or twelve Turks near me, observing my action, burst into

laughter; and, coming nearer to examine my paper, seemed
as much surprised at our writing as we are with theirs.   They
took a liking to me, and made every effort to teach me to
speak Turkish.   They were never weary of making me often
repeat the same thing, and pronounced it so many different
ways that I could not fail to retain it; so, when we separated, I
knew how to call for every thing necessary for myself and horse.

During the stay of the caravan at Damascus, I made a pilgrimage, about sixteen miles distant, to our Lady of Serdenay.
To arrive there we traversed a mountain a full quarter of a
mile in length, to which the gardens of Damascus extend.
We then descended into a delightful valley, full of vineyards
and gardens, with a handsome fountain of excellent water.
Here, on a rock, has been erected a small castle, with a
church of green monks, having a portrait of the Virgin
painted on wood, whose head has been carried thither miraculously, but in what manner I am ignorant.   It is added
that it always sweats, and that this sweat is an oil*.   All I
can say is, that when I went thither, I was shown, at the end
of the church, behind the great altar, a niche formed in the
wall, where I saw the image, *which was a flat thing*, and might
be about one foot and a half high by one foot wide.   I cannot
say whether it is of wood or stone, for it was entirely covered
with clothes.   The front was closed with an iron trellis, and
underneath was the vase containing the oil.   A woman accosted me, and with a silver spoon moved aside the clothes,
and wanted to anoint me with the sign of the cross on the
forehead, the temples, and breast.   I believe this was a mere
trick to get money; nevertheless I do not mean to say that
our Lady may not have more power than this image.

I returned to Damascus, and, on the evening of the departure of the caravan, settled my affairs and my conscience
as if I had been at the point of death; for suddenly I found

---

* Many authors of the thirteenth century mention this Virgin of Serdenay,
which was famous during the crusades; and they speak of this oily sweat,
that had the reputation of performing miracles. (See before, p. 190.)   These
fabulous accounts of miraculous sweatings were common in Asia.   Among
others, that which exuded from the tomb of the bishop Nicholas, one of
those saints whose existence is more than doubtful, was much vaunted.   This
pretended liquor of Nicholas was even an object of adoration; and we read
that, in 1651, a clergyman at Paris, having received a phial of it, demanded
and obtained permission from the archbishop to expose it to the veneration
of the faithful.—*Le Bœuf*, " Hist. de Paris," t. i. part 2, p. 557.

myself in great trouble. I have before mentioned the messenger whom the sultan had sent with orders to arrest all the Genoese and Catalonian merchants found within his dominions. By virtue of this order my host, who was a Genoese, was arrested, his effects seized, and a Moor placed in his house to take care of them. I endeavoured to save all I could for him; and, that the Moor might not notice it, I made him drunk. I was arrested in my turn, and carried before one of their cadies, who are considered as somewhat like our bishops, and have the office of administering justice. This cadi turned me over to another cadi, who sent me to prison with the merchants, although he knew I was not one; but this disagreeable affair had been brought on me by an interpreter, who wanted to extort money from me, as he had before attempted on my first journey hither. Had it not been for Antoine Mourrouzin, the Venetian consul, I must have paid a sum of money; but I remained in prison; and, in the mean time, the caravan set off. The consul, to obtain my liberty, was forced to make intercession, conjointly with others, to the governor of Damascus, alleging that I had been arrested without cause, which the interpreter well knew. The governor sent for a Genoese, named Gentil Imperial, a merchant employed by the sultan to purchase slaves for him at Caiffa. He asked me who I was, and my business at Damascus. On my replying that I was a Frenchman returning from a pilgrimage to Jerusalem, he said they had done wrong to detain me, and that I might depart when I pleased.

I set off on the morrow of the sixth of October, accompanied by a moucre, whom I had first charged to carry my Turkish dress out of the town, because a Christian is not permitted to wear a white turban there. At a short distance a mountain rises, on which I was shown a house said to have been that of Cain. During the first day we travelled over mountains, but the road was good. On the second day we entered a fine country, which continued cheerful until we came to Balbeck. My moucre there quitted me, as I had overtaken the caravan. It was encamped near a river, on account of the great heat in these parts; the nights are nevertheless very cold, which will scarcely be believed, and the dews exceedingly heavy. I waited on Hoyarbarach, who confirmed the permission he had granted me to accompany him, and recommended me not to quit the caravan. On the morrow morning, at eleven o'clock, I gave my horse water, with oats and straw, according to the custom of our countries. This time the Turks said nothing to me; but at six o'clock in the evening, when, having given him water, I was about fastening the bag, that he might eat, they opposed it and took off the bag; for they never suffer their horses to eat but during the night, and will not allow one to begin eating before the rest, unless when they are at grass.

The captain of the caravan had with him a mameluke of the sultan, who was a Circassian, and going to Caramania in search of a brother. This man, seeing me alone and ignorant of the language of the country, charitably wished to serve me as a companion, and took me with him; but, as he had no tent, we were often obliged to pass the nights under trees in gardens. It was then that I was obliged to learn to sleep on the ground, to drink nothing but water, and to sit cross-legged. This posture was at first painful, but it was still more so to accustom myself to sit on my horse with such very short stirrups,—and I suffered so much that, when I had dismounted, I could not remount without assistance, so sore were my hams; but after a little time this manner seemed even more convenient than ours. That same evening I supped with the mameluke; but we had only bread, cheese, and milk. I had, when eating, a table-cloth, like the rich men of the country. These cloths are four feet in diameter, and round, having strings attached to them, so that they may be drawn up like a purse. When they are used they are spread out; and, when the meal is over, they are drawn up with all that remains within them, without their losing a crumb of bread or a raisin. But I observed that, whether their repast had been good or bad, they never failed to return thanks aloud to God.

Balbeck is a good town, well inclosed with walls, and tolerably commercial. In the centre is a castle, built with very large stones. At present it contains a mosque, in which, it is said, there is a human skull, with eyes so enormous that a man may pass his head through their openings. I cannot affirm this for fact, as none but Saracens may enter the mosque.

From Balbeck we went to Hamos*, and encamped on the

* Hom3, or Hems, the ancient Emessa.

banks of a river. It was there I observed their manner of
encamping and pitching their tents. The tents are neither
very high nor very large, so that one man can pitch them, and
six persons may with ease repose in them during the heat.
In the course of the day they lay open the lower parts, to give
passage to the air, and close them in the night time. One
camel can carry seven or eight with thin poles; some of them
are very handsome. As my companion, the mameluke, and
myself, had no tent, we fixed our quarters in a garden. There
we were joined by two Turcomans of Satalia, returning from
Mecca, who supped with us. These men, seeing me well
clothed and well mounted, having a handsome sword, and
well furnished tarquais, proposed to the mameluke, as he
afterwards owned when we separated, to make away with me,
considering that I was but a Christian, and unworthy of being
in their company. He answered that, since I had eaten
bread and salt with them, it would be a great crime ; that it was
forbidden by their law; and that, after all, God had created
the Christians as well as the Saracens. They, however, persisted in their design; and as I testified a desire of seeing
Aleppo, the most considerable town in Syria after Damascus,
they pressed me to join them. I was ignorant of their intention, and accepted their offer; but I am now convinced they
only wanted to cut my throat. The mameluke forbade them
to come any more near us, and by this means saved my life.

We set out from Balbeck two hours before day; and our
caravan consisted of from four to five hundred persons, with
six or seven hundred camels and mules; for it had great
quantities of spicery. I will describe the order of its march.
The caravan has a very large drum ; and the moment the
chief orders the departure, three loud strokes are beaten.
Every one then makes himself ready, and, when prepared,
joins the file without uttering a word. Ten of our people
would, in such cases, make more noise than a thousand of
theirs. Thus they march in silence, unless it be at night, or
that any one should sing a song celebrating the heroic deeds
of their ancestors. At the break of day, two or three placed
at a great distance from each other cry out, and answer one
another, as is done from the towers of the mosques at the
usual hours. In short, a little before and after sun-rise,
devout people make their customary prayers and oblations.
To perform these oblations, if they be near a rivulet they dis-

mount, and, with feet naked, they wash their whole bodies.
Should there be no rivulet near, at the usual time for these
ceremonies they pass their hands over their bodies. The last
among them washes his mouth and the opposite part, and
then turns to the south, when all raise two fingers in the air,
prostrate themselves, and kiss the ground thrice; they then
rise up and say their prayers. They have been ordered to
practise these ablutions instead of confessions. Persons of
rank, to avoid failing in their performance, always carry, when
they travel, leathern bottles full of water, which are suspended under the bellies of camels or horses, and are generally very handsome.

Hamos (Hems) is a good town, well inclosed with walls and
ditches " en glacis," situated in a plain on the banks of a
small river. Here terminates one end of the plain of Noah*,
which is said to extend as far as Persia. Tamerlane made
his irruption through this plain when he took and destroyed
so many cities. At the extremity of the town is a handsome
castle, constructed on a height, with glaces as far as the
walls.

From Hems, we went to Hama†. The country is fine, but
I saw few inhabitants excepting Arabs, who were rebuilding
some of the ruined villages. In Hama I met with a merchant
from Venice, named Laurent Souranze. He received me
well, lodged me in his house, and showed me the town and
castle. It has good towers, with strong and thick walls,
built, like the castle of Provins, on a rock, in which deep
ditches have been cut. At one end of the town is the castle,
strongly and well built on an elevation, which is fortified by
ditches, and surmounted by a citadel which commands the
whole; and the sides are washed by a river, said to be one of
the four that flowed out of Paradise‡. I know not if this be
the fact or not; all that I know is, that it runs east-south-east,
and loses itself near Antioch. Here is the greatest wheel§
I ever saw. It is put in motion by the river, and supplies
the inhabitants, although numerous, with the necessary quantity of water. The water falls into a trough cut in the castle-
rock, and thence is conducted to the town, where it flows

* This plain is the ancient Cœlo-Syria.
† Hamath of Scripture, the Epiphania of the Greeks.
‡ The El Asi, or Orontes.
§ These wheels are still common on the Orontes.

through the streets in an aqueduct formed on great square pillars twelve feet high and two wide.   I was in want of several things to be like my fellow-travellers, of which the mameluke having informed me, my host Laurent carried me himself to the bazaar to purchase.   The things wanted were small silken bonnets, in the fashion of the Turcomans, a cap to wear under them, Turkish spoons, knives with their steel, a comb and case, and a leathern cup, all of which are suspended to the sword.   I likewise bought some finger-stalls to draw the bow, another complete tarquais, to save the one I had, which was very handsome, and lastly, a capinat, which is a robe of fine white felt, impenetrable to the rain.

On the road I made acquaintance with some of my fellow-travellers, who, when they found out that I lodged with a Frank, came to ask me to procure them some wine.   This liquor is forbidden them by their religion, and they dare not drink it before their own countrymen; but they hoped to do it without risk at the house of a Frank, and yet they were returning from Mecca!   I spoke of it to my host Laurent, but he said he was afraid to comply, from the great dangers he should run were it known.   I went to carry them this answer, but they had been more fortunate elsewhere, in procuring some at the house of a Greek.   They proposed that I should accompany them to partake, either from pure friendship, or to authorize them to drink wine in the presence of the Greek.   This man conducted us to a small gallery, where we all six seated ourselves in a circle on the floor   He first placed in the midst of us a large and handsome earthen jug, that might contain four gallons at least; he then brought for each of us a pot full of wine, which he poured into the jug, and placed beside it two earthen porringers to serve for glasses.   The first who began drank to his companion, according to their custom; this did the same to the next, and so on the others.   We drank in this manner for a long time without eating; at length, I perceived that I could no longer continue it without suffering, and begged of them, with uplifted hands, to permit me to leave off; but they grew very angry, and complained as if I had been resolved to interrupt their pleasure and do them an injury.   Fortunately there was one among them more acquainted with me than the rest, and who loved me so that he called me *karaays*, that is to say, brother.   He offered to take my place, and to drink for me

when it should be my turn. This appeased them, and, having
accepted the offer, the party continued until evening, when it
was necessary for us to return to the khan.
  The captain of the caravan was at the moment seated on
a bench of stone, and had before him a lighted torch. It was
not difficult for him to guess whence we came, and, consequently, four of our companions slipped away, and one only
remained with me. I mention all this to forewarn any persons that may travel through these countries to avoid drinking
with the natives, unless they shall wish to swallow so much
as will make them fall to the ground. The mameluke, who
was ignorant of my debauch, had, during that time, bought a
goose for us both. He had just boiled it, and for want of
verjuice, had dressed it with the green leaves of the leek; I
ate of it with him, and it lasted us for three days.
  I should have liked to see Aleppo, but the caravan taking
the strait road to Antioch, I was forced to give up all thoughts
of it. As the caravan was not to set out for two days, the
mameluke proposed that we should ride forward, the more
easily to procure lodgings. Four Turkish merchants desired
to be of our party, and we six travelled together. Half a
league from Hama, we came to the river, and crossed it by a
bridge. It had overflowed, although there had not been any
rain. Here I wished to give my horse some water, but as the
bank was steep and the river deep, had not the mameluke
come to my aid I must inevitably have been drowned. On
the opposite side of the river is a long and vast plain, where
we met six or eight Turcomans, accompanied by a woman.
She wore a tarquais like them, and, on inquiring into this, I
was told that the women of this nation are brave, and in time
of war fight like men. It was added, and this seemed to me
very extraordinary, that there are about thirty thousand women
who thus bear the tarquais, and are under the dominion of a
lord, named Turcgadiroly*, who resides among the mountains
of Armenia, on the frontiers of Persia.
  The second day's journey was through a mountainous country, tolerably fertile though ill watered, but we saw nothing
but ruined houses. As we travelled, my mameluke taught
me to shoot with the bow, and made me buy finger-stalls and
rings for this purpose. At length we arrived at a village that

* Tur-Kadir-Oglu.

was rich in woods, vineyards, and corn-fields, but having no other water than what was in cisterns. This district seemed to have been formerly inhabited by Christians, and I own it gave me great pleasure when I was told that it had all belonged to Franks, and the ruins of churches were shown me as a proof of it. We fixed our quarters in this village, and it was then I first saw the habitations of the Turcomans, and women of that nation with uncovered faces. They commonly hide them under a piece of black tammy, to which those who are wealthy attach pieces of money and precious stones. The men are good archers. I saw several draw the bow, which they do sitting, and at a short distance; and this gives to their arrows great rapidity and strength.

On leaving Syria, we entered Turcomania, called by us Armenia. The capital is a very considerable town, named Antequaye (Antakiyah) by them, and by us Antioch. It was very flourishing in former times, and has still handsome walls in good repair, which inclose a large tract of ground, and even some mountains; but its houses are not more than three hundred in number. It is bounded on the south by a mountain, on the north by a great lake, beyond which is an open and fine country. The river that comes from Hama runs alongside the walls. Almost all the inhabitants are Turcomans or Arabs, and their profession is breeding cattle, such as camels, goats, cows, and sheep. The goats are, for the most part, white, and the handsomest I have ever seen, not having, like those of Syria, hanging ears; and their hair is soft, of some length, and curling. Their sheep have thick and broad tails. They also feed wild asses, which they tame; these much resemble stags in their hair, ears, and head, and have, like them, cloven feet. I know not if they have the same cry, for I never heard them. They are large, handsome, and go with other beasts, but I have never seen them mounted* For the carriage of merchandise they use the buffalo and ox, as we do the horse. They also use them to ride on; and I have seen large herds, some carrying goods, and others men.

The lord of this country was Ramedan, a rich, powerful, and brave prince. For some time he was so redoubtable that the

---

* It is not very easy to identify this animal by La Brocquière's description; if he had not described it as "large," we might have supposed it to be a gazelle.

sultan was alarmed, and afraid to anger him; but, wishing to
destroy him, he practised with the karman*, who could more
easily deceive Ramedan than any other, having given him
his sister in marriage. In consequence, one day, as they were
eating together, the karman arrested him and delivered him
to the sultan, who put him to death, and took possession of
Turcomania, giving, however, a portion of it to the karman.
On leaving Antioch, I continued my road with the mameluke,
and we first crossed a mountain called Negre†, on which he
pointed out to me three or four handsome castles in ruins,
that had belonged to the Christians. The road is good, and
incessantly perfumed by the number of laurels with which the
country abounds; but the descent is twice as rapid as the
ascent. It finishes at the gulf of Asacs‡, which we call
Layaste, because, in fact, it takes its name from the town of
Ayas. This gulf extends between two mountains inland for
upwards of fifteen miles; its breadth may be about twelve, but
I refer for this to the sea charts.

At the foot of the mountain, near the road and close to the
sea-shore, are the ruins of a strong castle§, defended on the
land side by a marsh, so that it could only be approached by
sea, or by a narrow causeway across the marsh. It was inhabited, but the Turcomans had posted themselves hard by.
They occupied one hundred and twenty tents, some of felt,
others of white and blue cotton, all very handsome, and
capable of containing, with ease, from fifteen to sixteen persons. These are their houses, and, as we do in ours, they
perform in them all their household business, except making
fires. We halted among them; they placed before us one of
the table-cloths before-mentioned, in which there remained
fragments of bread, cheese, and grapes. They then brought
us a dozen of thin cakes of bread, with a large jug of curdled
milk, called by them yogort‖. The cakes are a foot broad,
round, and thinner than wafers; they fold them up as grocers
do their papers for spices, and eat them filled with the
curdled milk. A league further is a caravansera, where we
lodged. These establishments consist of houses like the
khans of Syria.

* Karaman-oglu, the Seljukian prince of Karamania.
† Ananus, now the Giaour Tagh.   ‡ The Gulf of Ayas, the ancient Ægæ.
§ Probably the one known as Godfrey de Bouillon's castle.
‖ Pronounced yuyurt.

In the course of this day's journey, I overtook on the road an Armenian, who spoke a little Italian. Finding I was a Christian, he entered into conversation with me, and told me many things of the country, its inhabitants, and likewise of the sultan, and Ramedan, lord of Turcomania, whom I have already mentioned. He said that this last was of a large size, very brave, and the most expert of all the Turks in handling a battle-axe and sword. His mother was a Christian, and had caused him to be baptized according to the Greek ritual, to take from him the smell and odour of those who are not baptized*. But he was neither a good Christian nor a good Saracen; and when they spoke to him of the two prophets, Jesus and Mohammed, he said, "For my part, I am for the living prophets; they will be more useful to me than dead ones." His territories on one side joined those of the karman, whose sister he had married, and on the other reached to Syria, which belonged to the sultan. Every time the subjects of the latter passed through his country he exacted tolls from them. But at length the sultan prevailed on the karman, as I have said before, to betray his brother-in-law to him; and at this moment he possesses all Turcomania as far as Tharsis, and even one day's journey further.

That day, accompanied by the Armenian, we once more lodged with the Turcomans, who again served us with milk. It was here I saw women make those thin cakes I spoke of. This is their manner of making them; they have a small round table, very smooth, on which they throw some flour, and mix it with water to a paste, softer than that for bread. This paste they divide into round pieces, which they flatten as much as possible, with a wooden roller of a smaller diameter than an egg, until they make them as thin as I have mentioned. During this operation they have a convex plate of iron placed on a tripod, and heated by a gentle fire underneath, on which they spread the cake and instantly turn it, so that they make two of their cakes sooner than a waferman can make one wafer.

I was two days traversing the country round the gulf. It is handsome, and had formerly many castles belonging to

---

* The Christians of Asia believed implicitly that the infidels had a disagreeable smell which was peculiar to them, and which baptism took away. This superstition will be again noticed. The baptism was, according to the Greek ritual, by immersion.

Christians, at present destroyed. Such was the one seen to
the eastward before we arrived at Ayas. The inhabitants are
Turcomans, who are a handsome race, excellent archers, and
living on little. Their dwellings are round, like pavilions,
covered with felt. They live in the open plain, and have a
chief whom they obey; but they frequently change their situ-
tion, when they carry their houses with them. In this case,
they are accustomed to submit themselves to the lord on whose
lands they fix, and even to assist him with their arms, should
he be at war. But should they quit his domains, and pass
over to those of his enemy, they serve him in his turn against
the other; and they are not thought the worse of for this, as
it is their custom, and they are wanderers. On my road, I
met one of their chiefs hawking with falcons, with which he
took tame geese. I was told that he might have under his
command ten thousand Turcomans. The country is favourable to the chase, but intersected by many small rivers that
fall into the gulf. Wild boars are here abundant.

About the centre of the gulf is a defile formed by a rock*.
under which the road passes; it is not two bow-shots from the
sea; and this passage was formerly defended by a castle,
which made it very strong, but it is now in ruins.

On leaving this strait, we entered a fine extensive plain†,
inhabited by Turcomans; my companion, the Armenian,
pointed out to me a castle on a mountain‡ where were only
people of his nation, and the walls of which were washed by
a river called Jehon§. We travelled along the banks of this
river to a town called Misse on the Jehon||, because it runs
through it.

Misse, situated four days' journey from Antioch, belonged
to the Christians, and was a considerable city. Many churches,
half destroyed, still remain¶; the choir of the great church
is yet entire, but converted into a mosque. The bridge is of
wood, the former stone one having been carried away by the
floods **. One half of the town is completely in ruins; the

* Kara-Kapu, or Temir-Kapu, "the Iron Gates," the ancient Pylæ Ama-
meæ.
† The Campus Aleius of the ancients, now Tchukur Ovah.
‡ Sis, or perhaps Anazarbe.   § Now called Jeihun.
|| Missisah, on the Jeihun.
¶ The churches have now entirely disappeared.
** This bridge is at present constructed of stone.

other half has preserved its walls, and about three hundred houses, filled with Turcomans.

From Misse to Adena* the country continues level and good, inhabited by Turcomans. Adena is two days' journey from Misse, and I there proposed to wait for the caravan. It arrived; I went with the mameluke, together with some others, many of whom were great merchants, to lodge near the bridge, between the river and the walls of the town; and it was there I observed the manner of the Turks saying their prayers and offering sacrifice. They no way hid themselves from my notice, but on the contrary seemed well pleased when I said my paternoster, which seemed to them wonderful. I sometimes heard them chaunt their prayers at the beginning of the night, when they seat themselves in a circle, and shake their bodies and heads while they sing in a very uncouth manner. One day they carried me with them to the stoves and baths of the town; and as I refused to bathe, for I must have undressed myself, and was afraid of showing my money, they gave me their clothes to keep. From this moment we were much connected. The bath-house is very high, and terminated by a dome, in which a circular opening is contrived to light the whole interior. The stoves and baths are handsome, and very clean. When the bathers come out of the water, they seat themselves on small hurdles of thin osiers, dry themselves, and comb their beards. It was at Adena I first saw the two young men who had got their eyes thrust out at Mecca, after having seen the tomb of Mohammed.

The Turks bear well fatigue and a hard life; they are not incommoded, as I have witnessed, during the whole journey, by sleeping on the ground like animals. They are of a gay, cheerful humour, and willingly sing songs of the heroic deeds of their ancestors. Any one, therefore, who wishes to live with them must not be grave or melancholy, but always have a smiling countenance. They are also men of probity, and charitable toward each other. I have often observed, that should a poor person pass by when they are eating, they would invite him to partake of their meal, which is a thing we never do.

In many places I found they did not bake their bread half as much as ours. It is soft, and, unless a person be accus-

* Adanah.

tomed to it, is difficult to be chewed.   In regard to meat,
they eat it raw, dried in the sun.   When any of their beasts,
horse or camel, is so dangerously ill that no hopes remain of
saving its life, they cut its throat, and eat it, not raw, but a
little dressed.   They are very clean in dressing their meat,
but eat it dirtily.   They in like manner keep their beards
very neat and clean, but never wash their hands but when
they bathe, when they are about to say their prayers, or when
they wash their beards and hinder parts.

Adena is a tolerably good commercial town, well inclosed
with walls, situated in a fine country, and sufficiently near the
sea.   The river of Adena*, which is wide, and rises among
the high mountains of Armenia, flows beneath its walls.   It
has over it a long bridge, and the broadest I ever saw.   Its
inhabitants and prince are Turcomans; the prince is brother
to the brave Ramedan, whom the sultan had murdered.   I
was told the sultan had his son in his power, but dared not
suffer him to return into Turcomania.

From Adena I went to Thuro†, which we call Tharsis.
The country continues good, though near the mountains, and
is inhabited by Turcomans, who live in villages or in tents.
The district around Tharsis abounds in corn, wine, wood, and
water.   It was a famous town, and very ancient buildings are
still seen in it.   I believe this was the town‡ besieged by
Baldwin, brother to Godfrey of Bouillon.   At present it has
a governor appointed by the sultan, and many Moors live
within it.   It is defended by a castle with ditches à glacis,
and by a double wall, which in some parts is triple.   A small
river§ runs through it, and there is another at a short dis
tance.   I found there a Cypriot merchant, named Antony,
who had resided in this country a long time, and knew the language well.   He talked to me very pertinently about it; but he
did me another favour, that of giving me some good wine, for
I had not tasted any for several days.   Tharsis is but sixty
miles from Curco‖, a castle built on the sea-shore, belonging
to the king of Cyprus.   In this whole country they speak the
Turkish tongue, which begins even to be spoken at Antioch,
the capital, as I have before said, of Turcomania.   It is a very
fine language, laconic, and easily learned.

* The Seihun, the ancient Surus.   † Tarsus.
‡ La Brocquière is right in his conjecture.   § The ancient Cydnus.
‖ Kurkuss, the ancient Corycus.

As we had to cross the high mountains of Armenia, Hoyarbarach, the chief of our caravan, would have it all assembled;
and for this purpose he waited some days, for those in the
rear to come up. At last we departed, on the eve of All-
Souls'-Day. The mameluke advised me to lay in provision
for four days. I consequently purchased a sufficiency of bread
and cheese for myself, and of oats and barley for my horse.
On quitting Tharsis, we travelled three French leagues over
a fine champaign country, peopled with Turcomans; and then
we entered on the mountains, which are the highest I have
ever seen. They skirt on three sides the country I had travelled over from Antioch; the sea bounds the other on the
south. We first passed through woods during a whole day,
but the road is not bad. We lodged in the evening at a narrow pass, where there seemed to have been formerly a castle.
The second day's journey was not at all disagreeable, and we
passed the night at a caravansera. The third, we followed
the banks of a small river, and saw on the mountains an innumerable quantity of speckled partridges. In the evening,
we halted on a plain, about a league in length and a quarter
wide, where four great valleys meet : the one by which we
had come ; another that runs northward, towards the country
of the lord called Turcgadirony, and towards Persia ; the
third runs eastward, and I know not whether this also does
not lead to Persia; the last extends to the westward, and it is
that which I followed, and which conducted me to the country
of the karman   Each of these four has a river, and the four
rivers run to this last country.

It snowed much during the night. To save my horse from
the weather, I covered him with my capinat, the felt robe
which I used for a cloak; but I myself caught cold, and got
that disagreeable disorder a dysentery. Had it not been for
my mameluke, I should have been in great danger; but he
assisted me, and made me instantly quit the place in which I
was. We both, therefore, set off very early, and ascended the
high mountains where the castle of Cublech * is situated, and is
the highest I am acquainted with. It is seen two days' journey
off ; but sometimes we turned our backs to it, by reason of the
windings of the mountains, sometimes also we lost sight of
it, as it was hidden by their height. No one can penetrate
into the country of the karman but on foot over the moun-

* Kulek Boghaz.

tain on which this castle is built. The pass is narrow, and
in some places has been perforated by the chisel, but it is
every where commanded by Cublech. This castle, the last
which the Armenians lost, belongs at this day to the karman,
who had it in his division after the death of Ramedan. These
mountains are covered with perpetual snow, having only a
road for horses, although there are some plains scattered
among them. They are dangerous on account of the Turcomans who inhabit them; but during the four days I was travelling among them I never perceived a single dwelling.

On leaving the mountains of Armenia, to enter the country
of the karman, there are still others to be crossed. On one
of them is a pass, having a castle called Léve, where a toll is
paid to the karman. This toll was farmed to a Greek, who,
on seeing me, judged from my features that I was a Christian,
and stopped me. If I had been forced to return I should
have been a dead man, for I was afterwards assured, that before I had gone half a league my throat would have been cut,
for the caravan was at a great distance. Fortunately my
mameluke bribed the Greek, and, in consideration of two
ducats that I gave him, he opened the passage. Further on
is the castle of Asers, and beyond that the castle of a town
called Araclie (Eregli).

On descending the mountain, we entered a plain as level
as the sea; then are seen some heights towards the north,
which, scattered here and there, appear like so many islands
in the midst of the waves. It is on this plain that Eregli is
situated, a town formerly inclosed, but now in the greatest
state of ruin. I found there, however, some provision; for
my last four days' journey from Tharsis had afforded me nothing but water. The environs of the town are covered with
villages, inhabited chiefly by Turcomans.

On quitting Eregli, we met two gentlemen of the country,
who appeared to be men of distinction; they showed great
friendship to the mameluke, and carried him to regale at an
adjoining village, the dwellings of which are cut out of the
rock. We passed the night there, but I was forced to stay
the remainder of the time in a cavern, to take care of our
horses. When the mameluke returned, he told me that these
two men had asked who I was, and that in his answer he had
misled them, by saying I was a Circassian, who could not
speak Arabic.

From Eregli to Larande*, whither our route lay, is two days' journey. This town, though not inclosed, is large, commercial, and well situated. There was, in ancient times, a great and strong castle in the centre of the town, the gates of which are now visible; they are of iron, and very handsome, but the walls are destroyed. There is a fine plain between these two towns; and after I left Léve I did not notice a single tree in the open country. There were in Larande two Cypriot gentlemen, the one named Lyachin Castrico, the other Léon Maschero, who both spoke very tolerable French†. They inquired of me my country, and what had brought me thither: I replied that I was a servant of my lord of Burgundy, that I came from Jerusalem to Damascus, and was following the caravan. They appeared astonished that I had been suffered to pass; but when they had asked whither I was going, and I had answered that I was on my return overland through France to my aforesaid lord, they told me it was impossible to be done, and that if I had a thousand lives I should lose them all; they therefore proposed that I should return to Cyprus with them; for there were at that island two galleys that had come thither to convey back the daughter of the king, who had been betrothed in marriage to the son of my lord of Savoy‡; and they doubted not but the king, from the love and respect he bore to the duke of Burgundy, would grant me a passage on board one of them. I replied, that, since God had graciously permitted that I should arrive at Larande, he would probably allow me to go further; but that, at all events, I was determined to finish my journey as I had begun it, or die in the attempt. I asked them, in my turn, whither they were going. They said their king was just dead; that during his life there had always been a truce with the grand karman, and that the young king and his council had sent them to renew this alliance. Being curious to make

---

* Karaman.

† The Lusignans, when kings of Cyprus, towards the end of the twelfth century, had introduced the French language into that island. It was at Cyprus, when St. Louis put in there on his crusade to Egypt, that the code called "the Assizes of Jerusalem" was drawn up and published, and which became the code of laws for the Cypriots. The French language continued long to be that of the court and of well educated persons.

‡ Louis, son to Amadeus VIII., duke of Savoy. He married, in 1432, Anne de Lusignan, daughter to John II., king of Cyprus, deceased in the month of June, and sister to John III., then on the throne.

acquaintance with this great prince, whom his nation reverences as we do our king, I entreated permission to accompany them, to which they consented. I met likewise with another Cypriot at Larande, called Perrin Passerot, a merchant, who had resided some time in the country. He was from Famagusta, and had been banished from that town, because he and one of his brothers had attempted to deliver it up to the king, as it was then in the hands of the Genoese.

My mameluke also met with five or six of his countrymen, young Circassian slaves, who were on their way to the residence of the sultan. He was desirous to regale them on their meeting; and, as he had heard there were Christians at Larande, he guessed they would not be without wine, and begged of me to procure him some. By dint of inquiry, and for half a ducat, I was enabled to purchase the half of a goatskin full, of which I made him a present. He showed great joy on receiving it, and instantly went to his companions, with whom he passed the whole night drinking. He himself swallowed so much, that on the morrow he was near dying on the road, but he cured himself by a method which is peculiar to them. In such cases, they have a very large bottle full of water, and as their stomach becomes empty, they drink water as long as they are able, as if they would rinse a bottle, which they throw up, and then drink of it again. He was thus employed on the road until mid-day, when he was perfectly recovered.

From Larande we went to Qulongue, called by the Greeks Quhonguopoly*. These places are two days' journey distant from each other. The country is fine, and well furnished with villages, but wants water, and has no trees but such as have been planted near houses for their fruit, nor any other river but that which runs near the town. This town is considerable and commercial, defended by ditches *en glacis*, and good walls strengthened with towers, and is the best the karman possesses. There remains a small castle : formerly there was a very strong one in the centre of the town, but it has been pulled down to furnish materials to build the prince's palace.

I staid there four days, that the ambassador from Cyprus

* "The copyist has written it further on *Quohongue* and *Quhongue*. I shall write it henceforward *Couhongue*." (The translator.) It is Koniyeh, the low Greek Koniopolis, the ancient Iconium.

and the caravan might have time to arrive. When the am
bassador came, I asked him when he intended to wait on the
karman, and repeated my request to be present, which he promised to grant. There were, however, among his slaves four
Greek renegadoes, one of whom was his usher-at-arms, who
united in their efforts to dissuade him from it; but he replied
that he saw no inconvenience, and besides, that I had shown
such eagerness to witness the ceremony, that he should take
pleasure in obliging me. He was apprized of the hour when
he might make his obeisance to the prince, inform him of the
object of his mission, and offer his presents; for it is an
established custom in the east never to appear before a superior without bringing presents. His were six pieces of camlet
of Cyprus, I know not how many ells of scarlet, forty sugar
loaves, a peregrine falcon, two cross-bows, and a dozen of
bolts. Some genets were sent him to carry the presents;
and he and his attendants were mounted on horses, which
the great lords, who had come to the palace to attend the
prince during this ceremony, had left at the gate. The ambassador made use of one of them, but dismounted at the
entrance of the palace, when we were ushered into a large
hall where there might be about three hundred persons. The
prince occupied the adjoining apartment, around which were
arranged thirty slaves, standing; he was himself in a corner,
seated on a carpet on the ground, according to the custom of
the country, clad in a crimson and gold cloth, with his elbow
leaning on a cushion of another sort of cloth of gold. Near
him was his sword, his chancellor standing in front, and, at a
little distance, three men seated.

The presents were first laid before him, which he scarcely
deigned to look at; then the ambassador entered, attended
by an interpreter, because he did not understand the Turkish
language. After the usual reverences, the chancellor demanded his credential letters, which he read aloud. The
ambassador then addressed the king by means of his interpreter, and said that the king of Cyprus had sent him to
salute him, and to request that he would accept the presents
now before him, as a mark of his friendship. The prince
made no answer, but caused him to be seated on the ground
after their manner, below the three persons before mentioned,
and at some distance from the prince. He now inquired
after the health of his brother the king of Cyprus, and was

told that he had lost his father, and had commissioned him to renew the alliance that had subsisted between the two countries during the lifetime of the deceased, for which he was very anxious. The prince answered that he desired it as earnestly. He then questioned the ambassador when the late king died, the age of his successor, if he were prudent, if his country was obedient; and, as the answer to these last questions was 'Yes,' he seemed well pleased.

After these words, the ambassador was told to rise, which he did, and took leave of the prince, who did not move more at his departure than at his entrance. On leaving the palace, he found the same horses which had carried him thither; and, having mounted one of them, he was reconducted to his lodgings : but he was scarcely entered, when the ushers of arms presented themselves, for in these ceremonies it is customary to give them money, and the ambassador did not neglect it. He next went to pay his compliments to the son of the prince, to offer him presents and deliver his letters. He was seated like his father, with three persons near him; but when the ambassador made his reverence, he rose up, then reseated himself, and placed the ambassador above these three personages. As for us, who accompanied him, they placed us far behind. Having noticed a bench, I was about to seat myself on it without any ceremony; but I was pulled off, and made to bend my knees and crouch on the ground like the rest. On our return home, an usher of arms to the son visited us, as those of the father had done, who also received some money. These people, however, are satisfied with a little. The prince and his son, in their turn, sent the ambassador a present for his expenses, which is likewise one of their customs. The first sent fifty aspres, the second thirty. An aspre is the money of the country, and fifty are equal in value to a Venetian ducat.

I saw the prince go through the town in procession on a Friday, which is a holiday with them, when he was going to say his prayers. His guards were about fifty horsemen, the greater part his slaves, and about thirty infantry, who surrounded him. He bore a sword in his belt, and had a tabolcan at the pommel of his saddle, according to the custom of the country. He and his son have been baptized in the Greek manner, to take off *the bad smell;* and I was told that the son's mother was a Christian. It is thus all the grandees

get themselves baptized, that they may not stink. His territories are considerable : they begin one day's journey on this
side Tharsis, and extend to the country of Amurath Bey *,
the other karman I spoke of, and whom we call the Grand
Turk. In this line they are, as it is said, twenty leagues in
breadth; but they are sixteen days' journey in length, as I
know well from having travelled them. They extend, as
they assured me, on the north-east, as far as the frontiers of
Persia. The karman possesses also a maritime coast, called
the Farsats. It extends from Tharsis to Courco, which
belongs to the king of Cyprus, and to a port called Zabari.
This district produces the most expert sailors known, but
they have revolted against him.

The karman is a handsome prince, about thirty-two years
old, and married to a sister of Amurath Bey. He is well
obeyed by his subjects, although I have heard people say he
was very cruel, and that few days passed without some noses,
feet, or hands being cut off, or some one put to death.
Should any man be rich, he condemns him to die, that he
may seize his fortune; and it is said that the greater part of
his nobles have thus perished. Eight days before my arrival
he had caused one to be torn to pieces by dogs. Two days
after this execution he had caused one of his wives to be put
to death, even the mother of his eldest son, who, when I saw
him, knew nothing of this murder. The inhabitants of the
country are a bad race—thieves, cheats, and great assassins;
they kill each other, and justice is so relaxed that they are
never arrested for it.

I found at Couhongue Antoine Passerot, brother to Perrin
Passerot, whom I had seen at Larande. They had both been
accused of attempting to deliver Famagusta to the king of
Cyprus, and had been banished. They had retired to the
states of the karman; the one to Larande, the other to Couhongue. Antony had been unfortunate. Vice sometimes
blinds people ; and he had been caught with a Mohammedan
woman, and the king had forced him to deny his religion to
escape death; but he appeared to be still a stanch Catholic.
In our conversations, he told me many particulars of the
country, of the character and government of the prince, and
especially as to the manner in which he had taken and delivered up Ramedan. The karman, he said, had a brother

* Amurath, or Mured, II.

whom he banished from the country, and who took refuge at
the court of the sultan, where he found an asylum. The
sultan did not dare to declare war against him, but gave him
to understand, that, unless he delivered Ramedan into his
hands, he would send his brother with troops so to do. The
karman made no hesitation, and rather than fight with him
committed an infamous treason in regard to his brother-in-
law. Antony added, that he was weak and cowardly, although
his people are the bravest in all Turkey. His real name is
Imbreymbas; but he is called karman, from his being the
lord of the country. Although he is allied to the Grand Turk,
having married his sister, he detests him for having taken
from him a portion of the karman. He is, however, afraid
to make war on him, as he is the stronger; but I am persuaded that if he saw him successfully attacked by the Europeans he would not leave him in peace.

In traversing his country, I passed near the frontiers of
another, called Gasserie*, which is bounded on one side by
the karman, and on the other by the high mountains of Turcomania that extend towards Tharsis and Persia. Its lord is
a valiant warrior, called Gadiroly†, who has under his command thirty thousand Turcoman men-at-arms, and about one
hundred thousand women, as brave and as fit for combat as
men‡. There are four lords continually at war with each
other—Gadiroly, Quharaynich, Quarachust, and the son of
Tamerlane, who is said to govern Persia.

Antony told me, that when I quitted the mountains on the
other side of Eregli, I had passed within half a day's journey
of a celebrated town§ where the body of St. Basil is interred,
and spoke of it in such a manner that I had a wish to see it;
but he so strongly represented that I should lose more by
separating myself from the caravan, and expose myself to
great risks when travelling alone, that I renounced all
thoughts of it. He owned to me that his intentions were to
accompany me to my lord the duke; for that he had no desire
to become a Saracen, and that if he had entered into any
engagements on this head it was solely to escape death. It
had been ordered that he should be circumcised, and he was

---

* Kaisariyeh, or Cæsarea in Cappadocia.   † Kadir-Oglu?
‡ These warlike women probably gave rise to the story of the Amazons.
See Sir John Maundeville, p. 206.
§ Tyana?

expecting the execution of it daily, which gave him many fears. He was a very handsome man, about thirty-six years old. He told me also that the natives offer up public prayers in their mosques, like as we do in our churches on Sundays, in behalf of Christian princes, and for other objects which we ask from God. Now one of the things they pray to God for is, to deliver them from the coming of such a man as Godfrey de Bouillon.

The chief of the caravan making preparations to depart, I went to take leave of the Cypriot ambassadors. They had flattered themselves that I would return with them, and renewed their entreaties, assuring me that I should never complete my journey; but I persisted. It was at Couhongue that the caravan broke up. Hoyarbarach took with him only his own people, his wife, two of his children, whom he had carried with him to Mecca, one or two foreign women, and myself. I bade adieu to my mameluke. This good man, whose name was Mohammed, had done me innumerable services. He was very charitable, and never refused alms when asked in the name of God. It was through charity he had been so kind to me, and I must confess that without his assistance I could not have performed my journey without incurring the greatest danger ; and that, had it not been for his kindness, I should often have been exposed to cold and hunger, and much embarrassed with my horse. On taking leave of him, I was desirous of showing my gratitude ; but he would never accept of any thing except a piece of our fine European cloth to cover his head, which seemed to please him much. He told me all the occasions that had come to his knowledge, on which, if it had not been for him, I should have run risks of being assassinated, and warned me to be very circumspect in my connections with the Saracens, for that there were among them some as wicked as the Franks. I write this to recall to my reader's memory that the person who, from his love to God, did me so many and essential kindnesses, was a man not of our faith.

The country we travelled through, on leaving Couhongue, is handsome, with tolerably good villages, but the inhabitants are wicked. Hoyarbarach forbade me to go out of my quarters when we halted, even in villages, lest I should be assassinated. There is near this place a celebrated bath, to which sick persons come for a cure of their several disorders. There

are the remains of many houses that formerly belonged to
the Knights Hospitallers of Jerusalem, with the cross of Jerusalem on them.

After three days' march, we came to a small town, called
Achsaray *, situated at the foot of a high mountain that shel-
ters it from the south. The country is level, but not populous, and the natives have a bad character; I was consequently
forbidden to leave my house in the evening. I travelled the
ensuing day between two high mountains, whose tops were
crowned with wood. The district is well peopled, partly by
the Turcomans, and consists of pasture and marsh land. I
there crossed a little brook that divides this country of karman from that of the other karman possessed by Amurath
Bey, called by us the Grand Turk. This division resembles
the former, in being a flat country, with mountains here and
there.

On our road we passed a town with a castle, called Acha-
nay, and further on we came to a caravansera, where we intended to pass the night, but we found there twenty-five asses.
Our commander refused to enter, and preferred returning a
league further back to a large village, where we lodged, and
found bread, cheese, and milk.

From this place we went to Carassar †, which took two days.
Carassar, in the Turkish language, signifies "black stone."
It is the capital of the country that Amurath Bey took by
force of arms. Although uninclosed, it is a place of considerable trade, and has one of the finest castles I have seen, but
without any other water than what is collected in cisterns.
It is seated on the summit of a high rock, so round that it
might be thought to be worked with a chisel. Below is the
town, surrounding it on three sides; but both are commanded
by a mountain, from the north-east to the north-west. The
other side opens to a plain, through which runs a river. Not
long ago, the Greeks had gained possession of this place, but
afterwards lost it by their cowardice. They dress sheeps' feet
here with a cleanliness I have nowhere seen. I regaled
myself with them the more eagerly, as I had not eaten any
dressed meat since I had left Couhongue. They cook also a
nice dish with green walnuts. Their manner is to peel them,

---

* Ak-Serai, or Al-Shehr.
† Kara-hissar, which signifies black castle, and not black stone.

cut them into two, and put them on a string; then they are
besprinkled with boiled wine, which attaches itself to them,
and forms a jelly like paste all around them. It is a very
agreeable food, especially when a person is hungry. We
were obliged to lay in a stock of bread and cheese for two
days, as I was disgusted with raw meat.

Two days were employed in journeying from Carassar to
Cotthay*. The country is good, well watered, having no very
high mountains. We traversed one end of a forest, which
seemed to me only remarkable for consisting entirely of oak,
taller and larger than any I had hitherto met with, having
besides, like fir-trees, branches only at the top. We took up
our quarters for the night at a caravansera, distant from any
habitations. We found there barley and straw in plenty, and
we could the more easily have supplied our wants, as there
was but a single servant to take care of them; but the owners
never have any thing to fear of this kind, for at such places
there is no man so bold as to take the smallest article without
paying for it. On our road was a small river renowned for
its water. Hoyarbarach went to drink of it with his women,
and wished me to do the same, he himself offering me some
in his leathern cup. This was the first time on the journey
that he had done me this favour.

Cotthay, although pretty considerable, is without walls;
but it has a handsome and large castle, composed of three
forts rising one above the other, on the declivity of a hill,
which has a double inclosure. This place was the residence
of the son of the Grand Turk. There was a caravansera in
the town, whither we went to lodge. It was already occupied
by a party of Turks, and we were obliged, according to custom, to turn our horses pell-mell. On the next morning,
when making ready to depart, I perceived that one of my
straps had been taken, which served to fasten on my horse's
crupper, my carpets and other things I carried behind me.
At first I began to cry out with much noise and anger; but
there was a Turkish slave present, one belonging to the sultan's son, a man of weight and about fifty years old, who,
hearing me speak the language very incorrectly, took me by
the hand, and conducted me to the gate of the caravansera,
when he asked me in Italian who I was? I was stupified to

* Kutaiyeh, the ancient Cotyæium.

hear him thus speak, and replied that I was a Frank.
"Whence do you come?" "From Damascus, in company
with Hoyarbarach, and I am going to Bursa to meet one of
my brothers." "Indeed! but you are a spy, and come to
make your remarks on this country. If you were not, would
you not have embarked, and returned home by sea?" This
unexpected accusation confounded me. I answered, however,
that the Venetians and Genoese were carrying on so bitter a
war that I was afraid to venture by sea. He asked whence I
came? "From the kingdom of France," was my answer.
"Are you from the neighbourhood of Paris?" I replied I
was not, and, in my turn, asked if he were acquainted with
Paris? He said he had formerly been there with a captain,
named Bernabo. "Take my advice," continued he; "return to the caravansera, seek your horse, and bring him
hither to me, for there are some Albanian slaves, who will
steal from you every thing he carries. While I am taking
care of him, do you go and breakfast, and procure for yourself
and your horse provision for five days, for so long will you be
on the road without meeting with any." I followed his advice, and went to purchase provision. I breakfasted also the
more heartily as I had not tasted meat for two days, and was
told that I must not expect to meet with any for five days
more.

When I quitted the caravansera, I took the road to Bursa*,
leaving that leading to Troy on my left, between the south
and west points. There were many high mountains, several
of which I had to pass over. I had also two days' journey
through forests, after which I traversed a handsome plain, in
which are some villages good enough for the country. Half a
day's journey from Bursa, we came to one that supplied us
with meat and grapes, which last were as fresh as in the time
of vintage; this mode of preserving them is a secret they
have. The Turks offered me some roast meat; but it was
not half dressed, and as the meat was roasting on the spit
we cut off slices. We had also some kaymack, or buffalo cream;
and it was so good and sweet that I ate of it till I almost
burst.

Before we entered this last village, we noticed the arrival
of a Turk from Bursa, who had been sent to the wife of

* Brusa, the ancient Prusa.

Hoyarbarach, to announce to her the death of her father. She showed great grief on the occasion, and I had then, for the first time, an opportunity of seeing her face uncovered. She was a most beautiful woman. There was at this place a renegado slave, a native of Bulgaria, who through affectation of zeal, and to show himself a good Saracen, reproached the Turks of the caravan for having allowed me to be in their company, saying it was sinful in them to do so, who were returning from the holy pilgrimage to Mecca. In consequence, they notified to me that we must separate, and I was obliged to set off for Bursa. I departed, therefore, on the morrow, an hour before day, with the aid of God, who had hitherto conducted me. He now guided me so well, that I never asked my road more than once on the whole way.

On entering the town, I met numbers of people coming out to meet the caravan, for such is the custom. The most considerable look on it as a duty, and it constitutes the festival. Several of them, supposing I was one of the pilgrims, kissed my hands and robe. When I had entered the town, I was greatly embarrassed, for I had come to a square that had four streets opening from it, and I knew not which to take. God again pointed out to me the right one, that which leads to the bazaar, where the merchants reside with their merchandise. I addressed myself to the first Christian I saw, and fortunately he happened to be one of the Espinolis of Genoa, the very person to whom Parvesin of Baruth had given me letters. He was much surprised to see me, and conducted me to the house of a Florentine, where I was lodged, as well as my horse. I remained there ten days, and employed that time in examining the town, being conducted by the merchants, who took great pleasure in so doing.

Of all the towns in the possession of the Turks this is the most considerable. It is of great extent, carries on considerable trade, and is situated at the foot of the north side of Mount Olympus, whence flows a river which, passing through the town, divides itself into several branches, forming, as it were, a number of small towns that make it look larger than it is. It is at Bursa that the Turkish sultans are buried. There are many handsome buildings, and particularly a great number of hospitals, among which there are four, where bread, wine, and meat are frequently distributed to the

poor who will accept of them for the sake of God. At one of
the extremities of the town, towards the west, is a handsome
and vast castle, built on an eminence that may well contain a
thousand houses. There is also the place of the sultan,
which they told me was a very delightful place within side,
having a garden and pretty pond. The prince had at that
time fifty wives; and he often, as they said, amuses himself
in a boat with some of them on this piece of water.

Bursa was also the residence of Camurat, bashaw, or, as we
should say, governor or lieutenant of Turkey. He is a very
brave man, the most active the Turk has, and the most able
to conduct any enterprise, which qualities have been the principal cause of his elevation to this lieutenancy. I asked if
he governed the country well, and if he knew how to make
himself obeyed. I was told that he was obeyed and respected like Amurath himself, and had for his salary fifty
thousand ducats a year; and that, when the Turk went to
war, he brought him, at his own expense, twenty thousand
men; but that he had likewise his pensioners, who in this
case were bound to supply him at their charges, one with a
thousand men, another with two, another with three thousand,
and so on with the rest.

There are in Bursa two bazaars; one where all sorts of
silken stuffs, and rich and brilliant diamonds, are sold, great
quantities of pearls, and cheap cotton cloths, and a variety of
other merchandise, the enumeration of which would be tire-
some. In the other bazaar, cotton and white soap are sold,
and constitute a great article of commerce. I saw also, in a
market-house, a lamentable sight—a public sale of Christians
for slaves, both men and women. The custom is to make
them sit down on benches, and he who comes to buy sees
only the face, the hands, and a little of the arm of the females.
I witnessed at Damascus the sale of a young black girl, of
not more than fifteen or sixteen years of age; she was led
along the streets quite naked, excepting the belly, the hinder
parts, and a little below them.

It was at Bursa that I ate, for the first time, caviare and
olive oil. This food is only fit for Greeks, and when nothing
better can be had. Some days after the return of Hoyarbarach, I went to take leave of him, and to thank him for the
means he had procured me of continuing my journey to this
place. I found him in the bazaar, seated on an elevated

stone bench, with many of the principal inhabitants of the town. The merchants had accompanied me in this visit: some of them, Florentines by nation, interested themselves on behalf of a Spaniard, who, having been a slave to the sultan, found means to escape from Egypt and come to Bursa. They begged I would take him with me. I carried him at my expense as far as Constantinople, where I left him; but I am persuaded he was a renegade, and I have never heard any thing of him since.

Three Genoese had bought spices from the merchants of the caravan, and intended carrying them for sale to Pera, near Constantinople, and on the other side of the straits, which we call the Straits of St. George. Wishing to take the advantage of their company, I waited for their departure, and for this reason stayed at Bursa, for no one can pass this strait unless he be known. With this view, they procured me a letter from the governor, which I carried with me; but it was useless, for I found means to cross with them. We set out together; but they made me, for greater security, buy a high red hat, with a huvette of iron wire*, which I wore as far as Constantinople.

On leaving Bursa, we travelled northward over a plain watered by a deep river, which, about four leagues lower down, falls into the gulf between Constantinople and Gallipoli. We had a day's journey among mountains, which wood and a clayey soil made very disagreeable. There was on the road a small tree bearing a fruit somewhat bigger than our largest cherries, and of the shape and taste of strawberries, but a little acid. It is pleasant to eat; but, if a great quantity be eaten, it mounts to the head, and intoxicates. It is ripe in November and December†.

From the summit of the mountain, the gulf of Gallipoli is visible; and when we had descended it we entered a valley terminated by a very large lake, round which many houses are built. It was there I first saw Turkish carpets made. I passed the night in this valley, which is very fertile in rice. On pursuing our road, we came sometimes to mountains, valleys, pasture-lands, and great forests, which it would be impossible to pass without a guide, and where the horses

---

* The *huvette* was a kind of ornament worn on the hat.
† From the description, it seems to be the arbutus Andrachne.

plunge so deeply in the soil that they can hardly extricate themselves.   I believe, for my part, that is the forest spoken of in the history of Godfrey de Bouillon, which he had such difficulty to traverse.   I passed the night on the further side of it, at a village within four leagues of Nicomedia, which is a large town, with a harbour for shipping.   This harbour is called Lenguo, and commences at the gulf of Constantinople, and extends to the town, where it is a bow-shot in breadth. All this country is difficult to travel; but beyond Nicomedia, towards Constantinople, it is very fine, and tolerably good travelling.   It is more peopled with Greeks than Turks; but these Greeks have a greater aversion to the Latin Christians than the Turks themselves.

I coasted the gulf of Constantinople, and leaving the road to Nicea, a town situated to the southward near the Black Sea, I successively lodged at a village in ruins, inhabited solely by Greeks; then at another near to Scutari; and, lastly, at Scutari itself, on the strait, and opposite to Pera. The Turks guard this passage *, and receive a toll from all who cross it.   It has rocks that would make it easy of defence, if they were fortified.   Men and horses can readily embark and disembark.   My companions and I crossed in two Greek vessels.   The owners of my boat took me for a Turk, and paid me great honours; but when they saw me, after landing, leave my horse at the gate of Pera to be taken care of, and inquire after a Genoese merchant named Christopher Parvesin, to whom I had letters, they suspected I was a Christian.   Two of them waited for me at the gate, and when I returned for my horse they demanded more than I had agreed on for my passage, and wanted to cheat me.   I believe they would even have struck me, had they dared; I had my sword and my good tarquais, but a Genoese shoemaker who lived hard by, coming to my aid, they were forced to retreat.   I mention this as a warning to travellers, who, like me, may have any thing to do with the Greeks.   All those with whom I have had any concerns have only made me more suspicious, for I have found more probity in the Turks.   These people† love not the Christians of the Roman persuasion, and the submis-

* The Turks at this time held Scutari, but they had not obtained posses-sion of Constantinople.

† The Greeks.   It was their hatred to the Latin church which facilitated the fall of Constantinople.

sion which they have since made to this church was more
through self-interest than sincerity*. Therefore I have been
told that, a little before I came to Constantinople, the pope,
in a general council, had declared them schismatics and accursed, and had devoted them to be the slaves of slaves†.

Pera is a large town, inhabited by Greeks, Jews, and
Genoese; the last are masters of it, under the duke of Milan,
who styles himself Lord of Pera. It has a podestat and other
officers, who govern it after their manner. A great commerce
is carried on with the Turks; but the latter have a singular
privilege, namely, that should any of their slaves run away,
and seek an asylum in Pera, they must be given up. The
port is the handsomest of all that I have seen, and I believe
I may add, of any in the possession of the Christians, for the
largest Genoese vessels may lie alongside the quays; but, as
all the world knows this, I shall not say more. It, however,
seems to me, that on the land side and near the church, in
the vicinity of the gate at the extremity of the haven, the
place is weak.

I met at Pera an ambassador from the duke of Milan,
named Sir Benedicto de Fourlino. The duke, wanting the
support of the emperor Sigismond against the Venetians, and
seeing Sigismond embarrassed with the defence of his kingdom of Hungary against the Turks, had sent an embassy to
Amurath, to negotiate a peace between the two princes. Sir
Benedicto, in honour of my lord of Burgundy, gave me a
gracious reception. He even told me, that to do mischief to
the Venetians he had contributed to make them lose Salonica,
taken from them by the Turks; and certainly in this he acted

* In 1438, John Paleologus II. came to Italy to form a union between
the Greek and Latin churches, which took place the ensuing year at the
council of Florence. But this step, as La Brocquière remarks, was, on the
part of the emperor, but a political operation, dictated by interest, and without consequence. His dominions were then in so miserable a state, and
himself so harassed by the Turks, that he was anxious to procure the aid of
the Latins; and it was with this hope that he had come to inveigle the pope.
This epoch, of 1438, is of consequence to our travels; for it proves, since
La Brocquière quotes it, that he published it posterior to that year.

† An error. The general council that took place a little before he came
to Constantinople was that of Basil in 1431, when, far from anathematising
and cursing the Greeks, it was occupied about their reunion. This pretended malediction was undoubtedly a report, which those who were against
this reunion spread abroad in Constantinople; and the traveller seems to
have thought so by the expression "*it was told me.*"

so much the worse, for I have since seen the inhabitants of that town deny Jesus Christ and embrace the Mohammedan religion.

There was also at Pera a Neapolitan, called Peter of Naples, with whom I was acquainted. He said he was married in the country of Prester John, and made many efforts to induce me to go thither with him. I questioned him much respecting this country, and he told me many things which I shall here insert, but I know not whether what he said be the truth, and shall not therefore warrant any part of it *.

Two days after my arrival at Pera, I crossed the haven to Constantinople, to visit that city. It is large and spacious, having the form of a triangle; one side is bounded by the Straits of St. George, another towards the south by the bay, which extends as far as Gallipoli, and on the north side is the port. There are, it is said, three large towns on the earth, each inclosing seven hills,—Rome, Constantinople, and Antioch. Rôme is, I think, larger and more compact than Constantinople. As for Antioch, as I only saw it when passing by, I cannot speak of its size; its hills, however, appeared to me higher than those of the two others.

They estimate the circuit of the city of Constantinople at eighteen miles, a third of which is on the land side towards the west. It is well inclosed with walls, particularly on the land side. This extent, estimated at six miles from one angle to the other, has likewise a deep ditch, *en glacis*, excepting for about two hundred paces at one of its extremities, near the palace called Blaquerne. I was assured that the Turks had failed in their attempt to take the town at this weak part. Fifteen or twenty feet in front of this ditch is a false bray of a good and high wall. At the two extremities of this line were formerly handsome palaces, which, if we may judge from their present ruins, were also very strong. I was told they had been destroyed by an emperor, when taken prisoner by the Turks and in danger of his life. The conqueror insisted

---

* The manner in which our traveller here announces the relation of the Neapolitan shows how little he believed it; and in this his usual good sense does not forsake him. This recital is, in fact, but a tissue of absurd fables and revolting marvels, undeserving to be quoted, although they may generally be found in authors of those times. They are, therefore, here omitted; most of them, however, will be found in the narrative of John de Maundeville.

on his surrendering Constantinople, and, in case of refusal, threatened to put him to death. The other replied, that he preferred death to the disgrace of afflicting Christendom by so great a loss, and that his death would be nothing in comparison. When the Turk saw he could gain nothing by this means, he offered him his liberty on condition that the square in front of St. Sophia should be demolished, with the two palaces. His project was thus to weaken the town, that he might the more easily take it. The emperor accepted his offers, the proof of which exists at this day.

Constantinople is formed of many separate parts, so that it contains several open spaces to a greater extent than those built on. The largest vessels can anchor under its walls, as at Pera; it has, beside, a small harbour in the interior, capable of containing three or four galleys. This is situated to the southward, near a gate, where a hillock is pointed out composed of bones of the Christians, who, after the conquests of Jerusalem and Acre, by Godfrey de Bouillon, were returning by this strait. When the Greeks had ferried them over, they conducted them to this place, which is remote and secret, where they were murdered. The whole, although a very numerous body, would have thus perished, had not a page found means to re-cross to Asia, and inform them of the danger that awaited them. On this, they spread themselves on the shores of the Black Sea; and from them are said to be descended those rude Christians who inhabit that part of the country—Circassians, Mingrelians, Ziques, Gothlans, and Anangats. But, as this is an old story, I know of it no more than what was told me.

The city has many handsome churches, but the most remarkable and principal is that of St. Sophia, where the patriarch resides, with others of the rank of canons. It is of a circular shape, situated near the eastern point, and formed of three different parts; one subterraneous, another above the ground, and a third over that. Formerly it was surrounded by cloisters, and was three miles, as they say, in circumference. It is now of smaller extent, and only three cloisters remain, all paved, and incrusted with squares of white marble, and ornamented with large columns of various colours *. The

---

* Two of these galleries, or porticos, called by our author cloisters, as well as the columns, still exist. These last are formed of different materials,

gates are remarkable for their breadth and height, and are of brass. This church, they say, possesses one of the robes of our Lord, the end of the lance that pierced his side, the sponge that was offered him to drink from, and the reed that was put into his hand. I can only say, that behind the choir, I was shown the gridiron on which St. Laurence was broiled, and a large stone in the shape of a wash-stand, on which they say Abraham gave the angels to eat, when they were going to destroy Sodom and Gomorrah. I was curious to witness the manner of the Greeks' performing divine service, and went to St. Sophia on a day when the patriarch officiated. The emperor was present, accompanied by his wife, his mother, and his brother, the despot of the Morea *. A mystery was represented, the subject of which was the three youths whom Nebuchadnezzar had ordered to be thrown into the fiery furnace †.

The empress, daughter to the emperor of Trebisonde, seemed very handsome, but as I was at a distance I wished to have a nearer view; and I was also desirous to see how she mounted her horse, for it was thus she had come to the church, attended only by two ladies, three old men, ministers of state, and three of that species of men to whose guard the Turks intrust their wives. On coming out of St. Sophia, she went into an adjoining house to dine, which obliged me to wait until she returned to her palace, and consequently to pass the whole day without eating or drinking. At length she appeared. A bench was brought forth and placed near her horse, which was superb, and had a magnificent saddle. When she had mounted the bench, one of the old men took the long mantle she wore, passed to the opposite side of the horse, and held it in his hands extended as high as he could; during this, she put her foot in the stirrup, and bestrode the horse like a man. When she was in her seat, the old man cast the mantle over her shoulders; after which, one of those long hats with a point, so common in Greece, was given to her; it was orna-

porphyry, granite, marble, &c.; and this is the reason why the traveller, not being a naturalist, represents them as being of various colours.

* This emperor was John Paleologus II.; his brother Demetrius, despot or prince of the Peloponnesus; his mother Irene, daughter to Constantine Dragasés, sovereign of a small country in Macedonia; his wife Maria Comnenes, daughter to Alexis, emperor of Trebisonde.

† These devout plays were then as common in the Greek church as in the Latin. They were called "Mysteries" in France; and this is the name given by our traveller to the one he saw in St. Sophia.

mented at one of the extremities with three golden plumes,
and was very becoming. I was so near that I was ordered to
fall back, and, consequently, had a full view of her. She wore
in her ears broad and flat rings, set with several precious
stones, especially rubies. She looked young and fair, and
handsomer than when in church. In one word, I should not
have had a fault to find with her, had she not been painted,
and assuredly she had not any need of it. The two ladies
mounted their horses at the same time that she did; they
were both handsome, and wore, like her, mantles and hats.
The company returned to the palace of Blaquerne.

In the front of St. Sophia is a large and handsome square,
surrounded with walls like a palace, where games were performed in ancient times *. I saw the brother of the emperor,
the despot of the Morea, exercising himself there, with a score
of other horsemen. Each had a bow, and they galloped along
the inclosure, throwing their hats before them, which, when
they had passed, they shot at; and he who with his arrow
pierced his hat, or was nearest to it, was esteemed the most
expert. This exercise they had adopted from the Turks, and it
was one of which they were endeavouring to make themselves
masters.

On this side, near the point of the angle, is the beautiful
church of St. George, which has, fronting Turkey in Asia, a
tower at the narrowest part of the straits. On the other side,
to the westward, is a very high square column, with characters
traced on it, and bearing on the summit an equestrian statue
of Constantine, in bronze. He holds a sceptre in his left
hand, with his right extended towards Turkey in Asia, and
the road to Jerusalem, as if to denote that the whole of that
country was under his government. Near this column are
three others, placed in a line, and of one single piece, bearing
three gilt horses, now at Venice†.

In the pretty church of the Panthéacrator, occupied by
Greek monks, who are what we should call in France Grey
Franciscan Friars, I was shown a stone or table of divers
colours, which Nicodemus had caused to be cut for his own
tomb, and which he made use of to lay out the body of
our Lord, when he took him down from the cross. During this operation the virgin was weeping over the body, but

---

* The Greek hippodrome—the atmeidan of the Turks.
† There are four.

her tears, instead of remaining on it, fell on the stone, and they are all now to be seen upon it. I at first took them for drops of wax, and touched them with my hand, and then bended down to look at them horizontally, and against the light, when they seemed to me like drops of congealed water. This is a thing that may have been seen by many persons as well as myself. In the same church are the tombs of Constantine and of St. Helena, his mother, raised each about eight feet high on a column, having its summit terminated in a point, cut into four sides, in the fashion of a diamond. It is reported that the Venetians, while in power at Constantinople, took the body of St. Helena from its tomb, and carried it to Venice, where they say it is now entire. It is added, that they attempted the same thing in regard to the body of Constantine, but could not succeed; and this is probable enough, for to this day two broken parts are to be seen, where they made the attempt. The two tombs are of red jasper.

In the church of St. Apostola is shown the broken shaft of the column to which our Saviour was fastened when he was beaten with rods, by order of Pilate. This shaft, longer than the height of a man, is of the same stone with the two others that I have seen, at Rome and at Jerusalem; but this exceeds in size the other two put together. There are likewise in the same church, in wooden coffins, many holy bodies, very entire, and any one that chooses may see them. One of them had his head cut off, and that of another saint has been given him. The Greeks, however, have not the like devotion that we have for these relics. It is the same in respect to the stone of Nicodemus and the pillar of our Lord, which last is simply inclosed by planks, and placed upright near one of the columns on the right hand of the great entrance at the front of the church.

Among the fine churches, I shall mention one more as remarkable, namely, that called Blaquerne, from being near the imperial palace, which, although small and badly roofed, has paintings, with a pavement and incrustations of marble. I doubt not but there may be others worthy of notice, but I was unable to visit them all. The Latin merchants have one situated opposite to the passage to Pera, where mass is daily said after the Roman manner.

There are merchants from all nations in this city, but none so powerful as the Venetians, who have a bailiff to regulate all their affairs, independent of the emperor and his officers. This privilege they have enjoyed for a long time *. It is even said, that they have twice by their galleys saved the town from the Turks; but, for my part, I believe that God has spared it, more for the holy relics it contains than for any thing else. The Turks have also an officer to superintend their commerce, who, like the Venetian bailiff, is independent of the emperor; they have even the privilege, that if one of their slaves shall run away, and take refuge within the city, on their demanding him, the emperor is bound to give him up.

This prince must be under great subjection to the Turk, since he pays him, as I am told, a tribute of ten thousand ducats annually; and this sum is only for Constantinople, for beyond that town he possesses nothing but a castle situated three leagues to the north, and in Greece a small city called Salubria.

I was lodged with a Catalonian merchant, who having told one of the officers of the palace that I was attached to my lord of Burgundy, the emperor caused me to be asked if it were true that the duke had taken the Maid of Orleans, which the Greeks would scarcely believe. I told them truly how the matter had passed, at which they were greatly astonished†.

The merchants informed me, that on Candlemas-day there would be a solemn service performed in the afternoon, similar to what we perform on that day, and they conducted me thither. The emperor was at one end of the hall, seated on a cushion. The empress saw the ceremony from a window in an upper apartment. The chaplains who chant the service are strangely ornamented and dressed; they sing the service by heart, "selon leurs dois."

Some days after, they carried me to see a feast given on account of the marriage of one of the emperor's relations. There was a tournament after the manner of the country, but which appeared very strange to me. I will describe it. In the middle of a square they had planted, like a quintain,

---

* Since the conquest of the East by the Latins, in 1204, to which conquest the Venetians greatly contributed.

† The *pucelle* had been made prisoner in 1430, by an officer of Jean de Luxembourg, the duke's general, and, being afterwards sold by Jean to the English, was burnt the following year.

a large pole, to which was fastened a plank three feet wide
and five feet long. Forty cavaliers advanced to the spot,
without any arms or armour whatever but a short stick. They
at first amused themselves by running after each other, which
lasted for about half an hour; then from sixty to fourscore
rods of elder were brought, of the thickness and length of
those we use for thatching. The bridegroom first took one,
and set off full gallop towards the plank, to break it; as it
shook in his hand, he broke it with ease, when shouts of joy
resounded, and the instruments of music, namely, nacaires, like
those of the Turks, began to play. Each of the other cavaliers broke their wands in the same manner. Then the
bridegroom tied two of them together, which in truth were
not too strong, and broke them without being wounded*.
Thus ended the feast, and every one returned to his home
safe and sound. The emperor and empress had been spectators of it from a window.

My intentions were to leave Constantinople with this Sir Benedict de Fourlino, who, as I have said, had been sent ambassador
to the Turk by the duke of Milan. There was a gentleman
named Jean Visconti, and seven other persons in his company,
with ten led horses; for when a traveller passes through
Greece, he must absolutely carry every necessary with him.

I departed from Constantinople the 23rd of January, 1433,
and first came to the pass of Rigory, which was formerly
tolerably strong; it is formed in a valley through which runs
an arm of the sea, twenty miles long. There was a tower,
but the Turks have destroyed it. In this place there remains
a bridge, a causeway, and a Greek village. In the way to
Constantinople by land, there is but this pass, and another
lower down, still more dangerous, on a river which there dis-
charges itself into the sea. From Rigory I went to Thiras,
inhabited also by Greeks; it has been a good town, and a
pass as strong as the preceding one, being formed in like
manner by the sea. At each end of the bridge there was a
large tower; but tower and town have been entirely destroyed
by the Turks.

---

* La Brocquière must have thought these joustings ridiculous, from being
accustomed to our tournaments, where the knights, cased in iron, fought with
swords, lances, and battle-axes, and where, very frequently, men were killed,
wounded, or trodden under foot by the horses. This has made him twice
say, that in this jousting with sticks no one was wounded.

I went from Thiras to Salubria. This town, two days' journey from Constantinople, is situated on the gulf that extends from this place as far as Gallipoli, and has a small harbour. The Turks could never take it, although it is not strong toward the sea. It belongs to the emperor, as well as the whole country hitherto; but this country is completely ruined, and has but poor villages. Thence I came to Chorleu, formerly considerable, destroyed by the Turks, and now inhabited by them and Greeks. Next to Chorleu is Misterio, a small inclosed place, inhabited only by Greeks, with one single Turk, to whom his prince has given it. From Misterio we came to Pirgasy, where there are none but Turks. The walls have been thrown down. Zambry is the next place to Pirgasy, and is equally destroyed.

We next came to Adrianople, a large commercial town, very populous, and situated on a great river called the Mariza, six days' journey from Constantinople. This is the strongest town possessed by the Turk in Greece, and here he chiefly resides. The lieutenant or governor of Greece lives here also; and many merchants from Venice, Catalonia, Genoa, and Florence are likewise residents. The country from Constantinople hither is good and well watered, but thinly peopled, having fertile valleys that produce every thing but wood. The Turk was at Lessère*, a large town in Pyrre, near to Pharsalia, where the decisive battle was fought between Cæsar and Pompey, and Sir Benedict took the road thither to wait on him. We crossed the Mariza in a boat, and shortly after met fifty women of the Turk's seraglio, attended by about sixteen eunuchs, who told us they were escorting them to Adrianople, whither their master proposed soon following them.

We came to Dymodique†, a good town, inclosed with a double wall. It is defended on one side by a river, and on the other by a large and strong castle, constructed on an elevation which is almost round, and which may contain within its extent three hundred houses. In the castle is a dungeon, wherein I was told the Turk keeps his treasure. From Demetica we came to Ypsala‡; it has been a tolerable town, but is totally destroyed. I crossed the Mariza a second time.

---

* Perhaps Larissa (Seres), in Phrygia.   † Demetica?   ‡ Cypsela?

It is two days' journey from Adrianople, and the country
throughout was marshy, and difficult for the horses.

Ayne*, beyond Ypsala, is on the sea-shore, and at the
mouth of the Màriza, which at this place is full two miles
wide.   When Troy flourished this was a powerful city, and
had a king; at present its lord is brother to the lord of
Matelin, and tributary to the Turk.   On the circular hillock
is the tomb of Polydore, the youngest of the sons of Priam.
The father had sent this son during the siege of Troy,
to the king of Eno, with much treasure; but, after the
destruction of Troy, the king, as much through fear of the
Greeks as the wish to possess this treasure, put the young
prince to death.

At Eno, I crossed the Mariza in a large vessel and came to
Macri, another maritime town to the westward of the first,
and inhabited by Turks and Greeks.   It is near to the island
of Samandra†, which belongs to the lord of Eno, and seems
to have been formerly considerable; at present the whole of
it is in ruins excepting a part of the castle.   Caumissin,
whither we came next, after having traversed a mountain, has
good walls, which make it sufficiently strong although it is
small.   It is situated on a brook, in a fine flat country, inclosed by mountains to the westward; and this plain extends
for five or six days' journey, to Lessère.   Missy was equally
strong, and well fortified, but part of its walls are thrown down
and every thing within is destroyed; it is uninhabited.

Peritoq, an ancient town, and formerly considerable, is
seated on a gulf which runs inland about forty miles, beginning at Monte Santo, where are such numbers of monks.
The inhabitants are Greeks, and it is defended by good walls,
which have, however, many breaches in them.   Thence to
Lessère, the road leads over an extensive plain.   It was
near Lessère, they say, that the grand battle of Pharsalia
was fought.

We did not proceed to this last town; for hearing the Turk
was on the road we waited for him at Yamgbatsar, a village
constructed by his subjects.   When he travels, his escort
consists of four or five hundred horse; but, as he is passionately fond of hawking, the greater part of his troop was com-

---

* Eno.   † Samothraki?

posed of falconers and goshawk-trainers, a people that are great favourites with him; and it is said that he keeps more than two thousand of them. Having this passion, he travels very short days' journeys, which are to him more an object of amusement and pleasure. He entered Yamgbatsar in a shower of rain, having only fifty horsemen attending him and a dozen archers, his slaves, walking on foot before him. His dress was a robe of crimson velvet, lined with sable, and on his head he wore, like the Turks, a red hat; to save himself from the rain, he had thrown over this robe another, in the manner of a mantle, after the fashion of the country.

He was encamped in a pavilion which had been brought with him; for lodgings are nowhere to be met with, nor any provision, except in the large towns, so that travellers are obliged to carry all things with them. He had numbers of camels and other beasts of burden. In the afternoon he came out of his pavilion to go to the bath, and I saw him at my ease. He was on horseback, with the same hat and crimson robe, attended by six persons on foot. I heard him speak to his attendants, and he seemed to have a deep-toned voice. He is about twenty-eight or thirty years old, and is already very fat.

The ambassador sent one of his attendants to ask him if he could have an audience, and present him the gifts he had brought. He made answer, that, being now occupied with his pleasures, he would not listen to any matters of business; that, besides, his bashaws were absent; that the ambassador must wait for them, or return to Adrianople. Sir Benedict accepted the latter proposal, and consequently we returned to Caumissin, whence, having repassed the mountain I have spoken of, we entered a road formed between two high rocks, and through them flows a river. A strong castle, called Coloung, had been built on one of these rocks for its defence, but it is now in ruins. The mountain is partly covered with wood, and is inhabited by a wicked race of assassins.

At length we arrived at Trajanopoly, a town built by the emperor Trajan, who did many things worthy of record. He was the son of the founder of Adrianople; and the Saracens say that he had an ear like to that of a sheep*. This town

* Trajanopoly was not so called from having been built by Trajan, but because he died there. It existed before his time, and was named Selinunte. Hadrian was not the father of Trajan, but his adopted son, and, in

was very large, near to the sea and the Mariza; but now nothing is seen but ruins, with a few inhabitants. A mountain
rises to the east of it, and the sea lies on the south. One of
its baths bears the name of Holy Water. Further on is Vyra,
an ancient castle, demolished in many places. A Greek told
me the church had three hundred canons attached to it. The
choir is still remaining, but the Turks have converted it into
a mosque. They have also surrounded the castle with a considerable town, inhabited by them and Greeks. It is seated
on a mountain, near the Mariza.

On leaving Vyra, we met the lieutenant of Greece, whom
the Turk had sent for, and he was on his road to him with a
troop of one hundred and twenty horse. He is a handsome man, a native of Bulgaria, and had been the slave of
his master; but as he has the talent of drinking hard, the
prince gave him the government of Greece, with a revenue
of fifty thousand ducats. Demetica, on my return, appeared
much larger and handsomer than I thought it the first time;
and, if it be true that the Turk has there deposited his treasure, he is certainly in the right to do so.

We were forced to wait eleven days in Adrianople. At
length he arrived, on the first day of Lent. The mufti, who
is with them what the pope is to us, went out to meet him,
accompanied by the principal persons of the town, who formed
a long procession. He was already near the town when they
met him, but had halted to take some refreshment, and had
sent forward part of his attendants. He did not make his
entry until night-fall.

During my stay at Adrianople I had the opportunity of
making acquaintance with several persons who had resided at
his court, and consequently knew him well, and who told me
many particulars about him. In the first place, as I have
seen him frequently, I shall say that he is a little, short, thick
man, with the physiognomy of a Tartar. He has a broad
and brown face, high cheek bones, a round beard, a great and
crooked nose, with little eyes; but they say he is kind, good,
generous, and willingly gives away lands and money. His

---

this right, became his successor. Adrianople was not founded by Hadrian.
An earthquake had ruined it, and he ordered it to be rebuilt, and gave it his
name. Such errors are excusable in an author of the fifteenth century. As
for the sheep's ear, it is spoken of as a Saracenic fable.

revenues are two millions and a half of ducats, including twenty-five thousand received as tribute-money *. Besides, when he raises an army, it not only costs him nothing, but he gains by it; for the troops that are brought him from Turkey in Europe, pay at Gallipoli, the comarch, which is three aspers for each man, and five for each horse. It is the same at the passage of the Danube. Whenever his soldiers go on an expedition, and make a capture of slaves, he has the right of choosing one out of every five. He is, nevertheless, thought not to love war, and this seems to me well founded. He has, in fact, hitherto met with such trifling resistance from Christendom that, were he to employ all his power and wealth on this object, it would be easy for him to conquer great part of it†. His favourite pleasures are hunting and hawking; and he has, as they say, upwards of a thousand hounds, and two thousand trained hawks of different sorts, of which I have seen very many. He loves liquor and those who drink hard; as for himself, he can easily quaff off from ten to twelve gondils of wine, which amount to six or seven quarts‡. When he has drunk much, he becomes generous, and distributes his great gifts; his attendants, therefore, are very happy when they hear him call for wine. Last year, a Moor took it into his head to preach to him on this subject, admonishing him that wine was forbidden by the prophet, and that those who drank it were not good Saracens. The only answer the prince gave was to order him to prison : he then banished him his territories, with orders never again to set his foot on them. He unites to his love for women a taste

* There must be here an error of the copyist, for 25,000 ducats as tribute is too small a sum. We shall see, further on, that the despot of Servia paid annually 50,000 for himself alone.

† The sultan mentioned here under the name of Amourat Bey is Amourath II., one of the most celebrated of the Ottoman princes. History records many of his victories, which are indeed for the most part posterior to the account of our traveller. If he did not conquer more, it was owing to having Huniades, or Scanderberg, opposed to him. But his glory was eclipsed by that of his son, the famous Mohammed II., the terror of Christians, and surnamed by his countrymen "the Great," who twenty years after this period, in 1453, took Constantinople, and destroyed what little remained of the Greek empire.

‡ The *quarte*, so called from being the fourth part of the chenet, which contained four pots and one French pint. The pot held two pints, consequently the quarte made two bottles more than half a septier ; and twelve gondils made twenty-three bottles.

for boys, and has three hundred of the former and about thirty of the latter, which he prefers, and when they are grown up he recompenses them with rich presents and lordships.   One of them he married to a sister of his, with an annual income of 25,000 ducats.   Some persons estimate his treasure at half a million of ducats, others at a million. This is exclusive of his plate, his slaves, the jewels for his women, which last article is estimated alone at a million of gold.   I am convinced that if he would for one year abstain from thus giving away blindly, and hold his hand, he would lay by a million of ducats without wronging any one.

Every now and then he makes great and remarkable examples of justice, which procures him perfect obedience at home and abroad.   He likewise knows how to keep his country in an excellent state of defence, without oppressing his Turkish subjects by taxes or other modes of extortion.   His household is composed of five thousand persons, as well horse as foot; but in war-time he does not augment their pay, so that he does not expend more than in time of peace, contrary to what happens in other nations.   His principal officers are three bashaws, or visir bashaws.   The visir is a counsellor; the bashaw a sort of chief, or lieutenant.   These three have the charge of all that concerns himself or his household, and no one can speak with him but through them.   When he is in Greece, the lieutenant of Greece has the superintendence of the army; and when in Turkey, the lieutenant of Turkey. He has given away great possessions, but he may resume them at pleasure.   Besides, those to whom they have been given are bound to serve him in war, with a certain number of troops, at their own expense.

It is thus that Greece annually supplies him with thirty thousand men, whom he may lead whither he pleases; and Turkey ten thousand, for whom he only finds provisions. Should he want a more considerable army, Greece alone, as they tell me, can then furnish him with one hundred and twenty thousand more; but he is obliged to pay for these. The pay is five aspers for the infantry, and eight for the cavalry.   I have, however, heard, that of these hundred and twenty thousand there was but half, that is to say, the cavalry, that were properly equipped, and well armed with tarquais and sword; the rest were composed of men on foot miserably accoutered; some having swords without bows, others without

swords, bows, or any arms whatever, many having only staves.
It is the same with the infantry supplied by Turkey, one-half
armed with staves.   This Turkish infantry is nevertheless
more esteemed than the Greek, and considered as better
soldiers.

Other persons, whose testimony I regard as authentic, have
since told me, that the troops Turkey is obliged to furnish,
when the prince wants to form an army, amount to thirty
thousand men, and those from Greece to twenty, without including two or three thousand slaves of his own, whom he
arms well.   Among these slaves are many Christians; and
there are likewise numbers of them among the troops from
Greece, Albanians, Bulgarians, and from other countries.   In
the last army from Greece, there were three thousand Servian
horse, which the despot of the province had sent under the
command of one of his sons.   It was with great regret that
these people came to serve him, but they dared not refuse.

The bashaws arrived at Adrianople three days after their
lord, bringing with them part of his people and his baggage.
This baggage consists of about a hundred camels, and two
hundred and fifty mules and sumpter horses, as the nation
does not use wagons.

Sir Benedict was impatient to have an audience, and made
inquiries of the bashaws if he could see the prince : their
answer was a negative.   The reason of this refusal was, that
they had been drinking with him, and were all intoxicated.
They, however, sent on the morrow to the ambassador to let
him know they were visible, when he instantly waited on each
with his presents ; for such is the custom of the country, that
no one can speak to them without bringing something; even
the slaves who guard their gates are not exempted from it.
I accompanied him on this visit.   On the following day, in
the afternoon, he was informed that he might come to the
palace.   He instantly mounted his horse to go thither with
his attendants, and I joined the company ; but we were all
on foot, he alone being on horseback.

In front of the court we found a great number of men and
horses.   The gate was guarded by about thirty slaves, under
the command of a chief, armed with staves.   Should any person offer to enter without permission, they bid him retire : if
he persist, they drive him away with their staves.   What we
call the court of the king, the Turks call " Porte du Seig

neur."* Every time .the prince receives a message or an embassy, which happens almost daily, "il fait porte." "Faire porte," is for him the same as when our kings of France hold royal state and open court, although there is much difference between the two ceremonies, as I shall presently show.

When the ambassador had entered, they made him sit down near the gate, with many other persons who were waiting for the prince to quit his apartment and hold his court. The three bashaws first entered, with the governor of Greece and others of the great lords. His chamber looked into a very large court; the governor went thither to wait for him. At length he appeared. His dress was, as usual, a crimson satin robe, over which he had, by way of mantle, another of green figured satin, lined with sable. His young boys accompanied him, but no further than to the entrance of the apartment, when they returned. There was nobody with him but a small dwarf, and two young persons who acted the part of fools †. He walked across an angle of the court to a gallery, where a seat had been prepared for him. It was a kind of couch covered with velvet, and four or five steps to mount to it. He seated himself on it, like to our tailors when they are. going to work, and the three bashaws took their places a little way from him. The other officers, who on these days make part of the attendants, likewise entered the gallery, and posted themselves along the walls as far from him as they could. Without, but fronting him, were twenty Wallachian gentlemen seated, who had been detained by him as hostages for the good conduct of their countrymen. Within this apartment were placed about a hundred dishes of tin, each containing a piece of mutton and rice. When all were placed, a lord from Bosnia was introduced, who pretended that the crown of that country belonged to him, and came in consequence to do homage for it to the Turk, and ask succour from him against the present king. He was conducted to a seat near the bashaws; and, when his attendants had made their appearance, the ambassador from Milan was sent for. He advanced, followed by his presents, which were set down near the tin dishes. Persons appointed to receive them raised

---

* The origin of the title of "The Sublime Porte."

† Having court fools was a very ancient custom at the eastern courts. It had been introduced by the Crusaders at the courts of Christian princes, and was continued at that of France until the reign of Louis XIV.

them above their heads, as high as they could, that the prince
and his court might see them. While this was passing, sir
Benedict walked slowly toward the gallery. A person of distinction came to introduce him.

On entering, he made a reverence without taking off the
bonnet from his head, and when near the steps of the couch
he made another very low one. The prince then rose, descended two steps to come nearer to the ambassador, and took
him by the hand. The ambassador wished to kiss his hand,
but he refused it; and by means of a Jew interpreter, who
understood the Turkish and Italian languages, asked how his
good brother and neighbour the duke of Milan was in health.
The ambassador having replied to this question, he was conducted to a seat near the Bosnian, but walking backwards,
with his face towards the prince, according to the custom of
the country. The prince waited to reseat himself, until the
ambassador had sat down; then the different officers on
duty who were in the apartment sat down on the floor; and
the person who had introduced the ambassador went to seek
for us his attendants, and placed us near the Bosnians.

In the meantime a silken napkin was attached to the
prince, and a round piece of thin red leather was placed before him, for their usage is to eat only from table-coverings of
leather; then some dressed meat was brought to him in two
gilded dishes. When he was served, his officers went and
took the tin dishes I have spoken of, and distributed them to
the persons in the hall, one dish among four. There was in
each a piece of mutton, and some clear rice, but neither
bread nor any thing to drink. I saw, however, in a corner of
the court a high buffet with shelves, which had some little
plate on them, and at the foot was a large silver vase, in the
shape of a drinking cup, which I perceived many to drink out
of, but whether water or wine I know not. With regard to
the meat on the dishes, some tasted of it, others not; but, before all were served, it was necessary to take away, for the
prince had not been inclined to eat. He never takes any
thing in public, and there are very few persons who can boast
of having heard him speak, or of having seen him eat or
drink. On his going away, the musicians, who were placed
in the court near the buffet, began to play. They played on
instruments, and sung songs that celebrated the heroic actions
of Turkish warriors. When those in the gallery heard any

thing that pleased them, they shouted, after their manner, most horrid cries. Being ignorant on what they were playing, I went into the court, and saw they were stringed instruments, and of a large size. The musicians entered the apartment, and ate whatever they could find. At length the meat was taken away, when every one rose up, and the ambassador retired without having said a word respecting his embassy, which is never customary at a first audience. There is also another custom, that when an ambassador has been presented to the prince, this latter, until he shall have given him his answer, sends him wherewith to pay his daily expenses, and the sum is two hundred aspers. On the morrow, therefore, one of the officers of the treasury, the same who had conducted sir Benedict to the court, came to him with the above sum. Shortly after, the slaves who guarded the gate came for what is usually given them; they are, however, satisfied with a little.

On the third day, the bashaws let the ambassador know, they were ready to learn from him the subject of his embassy. He immediately went to the court, and I accompanied him; but the prince had closed his audience, and was just retired, and only the three bashaws, with the beguelar or governor of Greece, were now remaining. When we had passed the gate, we found these four seated on a piece of wood that happened to be outside of the gallery. They sent to desire the ambassador would come forward, and had a carpet placed on the ground before them, on which they made him seat himself, like to a criminal before his judge, notwithstanding there were present great numbers of people. He explained to them the object of his mission, which was, as I heard, to entreat their lord, on the part of the duke of Milan, to consent to yield up, to the Roman emperor Sigismond, Hungary, Wallachia, Bulgaria, as far as Sophia, Bosnia, and the part of Albania he now possessed, which was dependant on Sclavonia. They replied they could not at that moment inform the prince of his request, as he was occupied; but that within ten days he should have his answer, if they should then have received it from him. There is likewise another custom; that from the time when an ambassador is announced as such, he can never speak with the prince personally. This regulation was made since the grandfather of the present prince was murdered by an ambassador from Servia. That envoy had come to solicit from him some alleviation in favour of his countrymen, whom the prince wanted to reduce to slavery. In despair at not obtaining his object, he stabbed him, and was himself massacred the instant after*.

On the tenth day we went to the court to receive the answer. The prince was there, as at the first time, seated on his couch; but he had with him in the gallery only those that served his table. I saw neither buffet, minstrels, nor the lord of Bosnia, nor the Wallachians, but only Magnoly, brother to the duke of Cephalonia,whose manners to the prince were those of a respectful servant. Even the bashaws were without, and standing at a disfance, as well as the greater part of the persons whom I had before seen in the interior, but their number was much lessened. During the time we were made to wait without, the chief cadi, with his assessors, administered justice at the outward gate of the palace, when I saw some foreign Christians come to plead their cause before him : but, when the prince rose up, the judges ended their sittings and retired to their homes. I saw the prince pass with his attendants to the great court, which I was unable to do the first time. He wore a robe of cloth of gold and green, somewhat rich, and he seemed to me to have a hasty step. When he had re-entered his apartments, the bashaws, seated as on the preceding day on the piece of wood,

---

* The grandfather of Amurath II. was Bajazet I., who died prisoner to Tamerlane, either treated with kindness by the conqueror, as some authors pretend, or confined in an iron cage, according to others. This story of the Servian cannot, therefore, regard him. But we find in the life of Amurath I., father to Bajazet, and, consequently, great-grandfather to Amurath II., a circumstance that may have been the foundation for this story of the assassination. This prince had just gained a complete victory over the despot of Servia, in which he was made prisoner, and was passing over the field of battle near to a Servian soldier, mortally wounded, who, knowing him, exerted his remaining strength and poniarded him. According to others, the despot, named Lazarus, or Eleazer Bulcowitz, finding himself attacked by Amurath, with an irresistible army, and seeing no other chance of opposing him but by treason, gains over one of the great lords of his court, who, feigning discontent, passes over to the party of the sultan, and assassinates him. (Ducange, ' Familiæ Bisant.,' p. 334.) According to another account, Amurath was slain in the combat; and Lazarus, being made prisoner by the Turks, was hewed to pieces on the bleeding corpse of their master. It seems, from the recital of La Brocquière, that the account of the assassination by the Servian is the true one. This, at least, appears probable, from the precautions taken in subsequent times, at the Ottoman Porte, against foreign ambassadors; for, when they were introduced to the sultan, they were held by the sleeves of their coats.

sent for the ambassador. Their answer was that their master charged him to salute, in his name, his brother the duke of Milan; that he was very desirous of doing much for him, but that his present request was unreasonable; that from regard to him their prince had frequently abstained from pushing his conquests further in Hungary, which he might easily have done, and such a sacrifice ought to satisfy him; that it would be too hard for him to surrender all he had won by the sword; and that, in the present circumstances, he and his soldiers had no other theatre to occupy their courage besides the territories of the emperor, and that he should be the more unwilling to renounce them, because hitherto he had never met the emperor's forces without beating them, or putting them to flight, as was well known to all the world.

The ambassador, in fact, knew this personally, for, in the last defeat of Sigismond before Couloubath, he had witnessed his disaster: he had even, the night preceding the battle, quitted his camp, to wait on the Turk. In our conversations, he told me many particulars on this subject. I saw also two Genoese cross-bowmen, who related to me how the emperor and his army had repassed the Danube in his galleys.

The ambassador, having received his answer from the bashaws, returned to his lodgings; but he was scarcely arrived, when he received, on the part of the sultan, five thousand aspers, with a robe of crimson camocas lined with yellow calimanco. Thirty-six aspers are worth a Venetian ducat; but, of the five thousand aspers, the treasurer deducted ten per cent. as fees of office. I saw also, during my stay at Adrianople, a present of another sort, made likewise by the sultan to a bride on her wedding day. This bride was daughter to the Begler Bey, governor of Greece; and the daughter of one of the bashaws, attended by upwards of thirty other women, had been charged to offer it. Her dress was of crimson tissue and gold: her face was covered, according to custom, with a very rich veil ornamented with diamonds. The attendant ladies had magnificent veils, and their dresses were robes of crimson velvet, and robes of cloth of gold without fur. They were all on horseback, riding astride like men, and some of them had superb saddles. In front of the procession marched thirteen or fourteen horsemen, and two minstrels also on horseback, as well as other musicians carrying a trumpet, a very large drum, and about eight pairs of cymbals,

which altogether made a most abominable noise. After the
musicians came the present, and then the ladies.   This present consisted of seventy broad platters of tin loaded with different sorts of sweetmeats, wet and dry, and of twenty other
platters having on them sheep skinned, painted red and
white, and all had a silver ring suspended from the nose, and
two others in the ears.   I had an opportunity of seeing, while
at Adrianople, numbers of Christians chained, who were
brought thither for sale.   They begged for alms in the street;
but my heart bleeds when I think of the shocking hardships
they suffer.

We left that town on the 12th of March, under the escort
of a slave whom the sultan had ordered to accompany the
ambassador.   This man was of great utility to us on the
road, more especially in regard to lodgings—for, wherever he
demanded any thing for us, it was eagerly and instantly
granted.   Our first day's journey was through a beautiful
country ascending the Mariza, which we crossed at a ferry ;
the second, though the roads were good, was employed in
passing through woods.   At length we entered Macedonia,
between two mountains opening to an extensive plain, which
may be forty miles wide, and is watered by the Mariza.   I
there met fifteen men and ten women chained by the neck,
inhabitants of Bosnia, whom the Turks had just carried off in
an excursion which they had made thither.   Two Turks were
leading them for sale to Adrianople.

Shortly after, we arrived at Philopopoli, the capital of
Macedonia, and built by king Philip.   It is situated in a
plain on the Mariza, in an excellent country, where all sorts
of provision are sold very cheap.   It was formerly a considerable town, and indeed is so now.   Within it are three mountains, two of which are at one of its extremities toward the
southward, and the other in the centre.   On this last had
been constructed a large castle, in the form of a crescent, now
destroyed.   I was shown the situation of king Philip's palace,
which has been demolished, but the walls still remain.   Philopopoli is inhabited chiefly by Bulgarians, who follow the
Greek ritual.

I crossed the Mariza by a bridge, on leaving Philopopoli,
and rode a whole day over the plain I mentioned : it terminates at a mountain sixteen or twenty miles in length, covered
with wood.   This place was in former times infested by

robbers, and very dangerous to pass. The Turk has ordered that whoever inhabits these parts shall be free : in consequence, two villages have been erected and inhabited by Bulgarians, in one of which, situated on the confines of Bulgaria and Macedonia, I passed the night. Having crossed the mountain, we came to a plain six miles long by two broad— then to a forest sixteen miles in length—then to another great plain wholly shut in by mountains, well peopled with Bulgarians, and having a river running through it.

After three days' journey, I came at last to a town named Sophia, which had been very considerable, as may be judged from the ruins of its walls, now thrown down; but it is at present the best in Bulgaria. It has a small castle, and is situated near a mountain on the southward, and at the beginning of a great plain sixty miles long by ten wide. The inhabitants are chiefly Bulgarians, as in the adjacent villages. The Turks are few in number, which causes the others to feel the greatest desire to throw off their yoke, if they could find any to assist them. I saw some Turks return from an excursion to Hungary; and a Genoese, named Nicolas Ciba, told me he had also seen those who had crossed the Danube return, and that there was not one in ten that had both bow and sword : for my part, of those I saw there were many more that had neither bow nor sword than those who were armed with both. The best equipped had a small wooden target. In truth, we must confess that it is a great shame for Christendom to suffer itself to be subjugated by such a race, for they are much below what is thought of them.

On quitting Sophia I traversed fifty miles of the plain I spoke of. The country is well inhabited by Bulgarians of the Greek religion. I then passed through a mountainous country, tolerably good for travelling on horseback, and came to a little town in a plain on the Nissave, called Pirotte. It is uninclosed, but has a small castle, defended on one side by the river, on the other by a marsh : to the north is a mountain. It is inhabited by Turks only. Beyond Pirotte the country is again mountainous, when, after a circuit, we came again to the Nissave, which runs through a beautiful valley between two tolerably high hills. At the foot of one of them was the town of Ysvouriere, now totally destroyed, even to the walls. We followed the banks of the river through the valley, and came to another mountain, difficult to pass, al-

though cars and carts do go over it. We then arrived at an
agreeable valley, still watered by the Nissave, which having
crossed by a bridge, we entered Nissa. This town had a
handsome castle that belonged to the despot of Servia. The
Turk took it, five years ago, by storm, and entirely destroyed
it. The situation is in a delightful country, abounding in
rice. I continued to follow the river from Nissa, through a
country equally pleasant, and well filled with villages. I at
last crossed it at a ferry, and saw it no more. The mountains
now commenced, and I had a long miry forest to pass, and,
after ten days' journey from Adrianople, arrived at Corsebech *, a small town situated a mile distant from the Morava.

The Morava is a large river that runs from Bosnia, and divides Bulgaria from La Rascia, or Servia, a province which
indifferently bears these two names, and which the Turk
conquered six years ago. Corsebech had a small castle, now
demolished : it has still a double wall, but the other parts, as
far as the battlements, have been thrown down. I found
there Cénasin Bey, captain or commandant of this vast frontier country, that extends from Wallachia as far as Sclavonia.
He resides part of the year in this town; and they told me
he was originally a Greek, who did not drink wine like other
Turks; that he was prudent and brave, and knew how to
make himself feared and obeyed. The Turk has intrusted
him with the government of this country, of which he possesses the greater part as his own property. He suffers no
one to cross the river, unless they be known to him, or unless
they be bearers of letters from his master, or, in his absence,
from the governor of Greece. We saw there a beautiful
woman, one of the Hungarian nobility, whose situation inspired us with pity. An Hungarian renegado, one of the
lowest rank, had carried her off in an excursion, and treated
her as his wife. On seeing us, she melted into tears, for she
had not as yet renounced her religion.

On leaving Corsebech, we crossed the Morava by a ferry,
and entered the territory of the despot of Servia, a fine and
well-peopled country. All on this side the river belongs to
him—the district on the other to the Turk; but the despot
pays him an annual tribute of fifty thousand ducats. He possesses also, on this river, toward the common boundaries of

* Perhaps Kruzcevaz, or Alagia Hisar.

Bulgaria, Sclavonia, Albania, and Bosnia, a town called Nyeu-
berge, which has a mine producing gold and silver at the same
time.   Each year it pays him more than two hundred thousand ducats, as well-informed people assured me: without
this, he would be soon driven out of his dominions.

I passed on my road near to the castle of Escalache, that
belongs to him.   It has been a strong place, on the point of
a hill, at the foot of which the Nissave forms a junction with
the Morava.   Part of the walls, with a tower in the form of a
dungeon, are all that remain.

At the mouth of these two rivers, the Turk usually keeps
from eighty to a hundred galleys, galliots, and rafts, to convey
over his cavalry and army in time of war.   I could not see
them, as no Christian is allowed to approach them; but a
man, worthy of belief, informed me there was a body of three
hundred men always posted there to guard them, and that
they are relieved every two months.   The distance from Escalache to the Danube is one hundred miles: nevertheless, in
all this distance, there does not subsist any fort, or place of
defence, but a village, and a house erected by Cénasnin-Bey
on the declivity of a mountain, with a mosque.   I followed
the course of the Morava, and with the exception of a very
miry pass, that continues about a mile, caused by a mountain
pressing too close on the river, I had a good road through a
pleasant well-peopled country.   It was not the same the
second day, for I had mountains, wood, and much mud to
travel through.   The country, notwithstanding, was as fine as
a mountainous country can be.   It is full of villages, and all
your wants may be there supplied.

From the time we had entered Macedonia, Bulgaria, and
Servia, I found on our passage that the Turk every where
caused proclamation to be made that whoever was bound to
join the army should hold himself in readiness to march.
They told us that those who, in obedience to this duty, fed a
horse, were exempted from the tax of the comarch; that such
Christians as were desirous of being excused from serving
pay fifty aspers a head; and that some are forced to join the
army, but only when it requires reinforcements.   I learnt
also, at the court of the despot, that the Turk has divided
the guard and defence of these frontier provinces among
three captains; one, called Dysem Bey, has the district from
the confines of Wallachia to the Black Sea; Cénasnin Bey

commands from Wallachia to the borders of Bosnia; and Isaac Bey from these frontiers as far as Sclavonia, that is to say, all beyond the Morava.

To continue the account of my journey, I shall say that I came to a town, or rather a country house, called Nicodem. It is here the despot has fixed his residence because the soil is good, and there are woods and rivers aboundinh with every thing needful for the pleasures of the chase and gawking, of which he is very fond. He was out hawking by the river side, attended by fifty horse, three of his children, and a Turk, who had been sent by the sultan to summon him to send his contingent to the army, under the escort of one of his sons. Independently of his tribute, this is one of the conditions imposed upon him. Every time the sultan sends him his orders, he is obliged to furnish him with eight hundred or a thousand horse, under the command of his second son. He gave the sultan one of his daughters in marriage; nevertheless, there passes not a day that he does not fear being deprived of his dominions. I have even heard say, that some wished to inspire the sultan with this idea, but that he answered, " I draw more from them now than if they were my own, for in this case I should be obliged to give them to one of my slaves, and should not receive any thing." The troops he is now raising are said to be intended against Albania. Ten thousand have already marched thither, which was the reason he had so few with him when I saw him at Lessère; but this first army had been destroyed*.

The prince of Servia is a tall, handsome man, from fifty-eight to sixty years old; he has five children, three boys and two girls†. Of the boys, one is twenty years, another sixteen, and the third fourteen; and all three, like their father, have very agreeable countenances. In respect to the girls, one is married to the sultan, another to the count de Seil; but as I have not seen them I cannot describe them. When we met him hawking, the ambassador and myself took him by

---

* It was in fact this same year, 1433, that the renowned Scanderbeg having, by a stratagem, regained possession of Albania, of which his ancestors were the sovereigns, commenced that sagacious war against Amurath, which covered him with glory, and tarnished the last years of the sultan.

† This prince was named George Brancovitz or Wkovitz. Some account of him and his family is to be found in Ducange. (' Familiæ Bisant.,' page 336.)

the hand, which I kissed, for such is the custom. On the morrow, we went to pay him our respects. He had a tolerably numerous court, composed of very handsome men, who wore the beard and hair long, as they are of the Greek church. There were in the town a bishop, and a doctor in theology, on their road to Constantinople, sent as ambassadors to the emperor, by the holy council of Basil *.

I had employed two days in going from Corsebech to Nicodem, and from Nicodem to Belgrade half a day. There is nothing but forests, mountains, and valleys to this town, but the valleys are crowded with villages, in which provision and good wines are met with.

Belgrade is in Servia, and did belong to the despot; but four years ago he ceded it to the king of Hungary, for fear lest he should suffer it to be taken by the Turk, as he had done Coulumbach. This was a heavy loss to Christendom. The other would be still greater, because the place is stronger, and can contain from five to six thousand horse †. Its walls are washed on one side by a large river that comes from Bosnia, called the Save; and on the other it has a castle, near to which runs the Danube, and into this the Save flows. The town is built on the point formed by these two rivers. Within its walls the ground rises; but on the land side it is so flat that any one may march into the ditch. There is, however, a village on this side that extends from the Save to the Danube, and surrounds the town to the distance of a bowshot. This village is inhabited by Servians, and on Easterday I heard mass there in the Sclavonic tongue. It is under obedience to the church of Rome, and its ceremonies are nothing different from ours.

The place is strong from its situation, and by art, having

---

* This *holy* council concluded its sittings by citing to its tribunal, and deposing the pope, whilst the pope commanded it to dissolve itself, and convoked another at Ferrara. At Florence he had undertaken to form a union of the Greek and Latin churches, and with this design had sent the ambassadors to the emperor. He came actually to Italy, and signed at Florence that political and simulated union before mentioned.

† The reader may perhaps be surprised that our author, when he speaks of the garrison of any strong place, particularizes only cavalry; and that, when he mentions the contingent sent by the despot to the Turkish army, he specifies but horse. The reason is, that, when he wrote, Europe paid no attention but to cavalry; and the infantry, badly armed, formed, and equipped, was not considered of any consequence.

ditches *en glacis*, a double wall, well kept in repair, that
follows exactly the rise and fall of the ground. It has also
five forts, three on the elevated ground I spoke of, and two
on the river, but these last are commanded by the preceding
ones. It has likewise a small harbour, that may hold from
fifteen to twenty galleys, defended by towers constructed at
each extremity. It is shut up by a chain from one tower to
the other, at least so it was told me, for the two shores are so
distant I could not see it. I saw on the Save six galleys and
five galliots, near to the weakest of the five forts. In this are
many Servians, but they are not permitted to enter the other
forts. The whole five are well furnished with artillery. I
particularly noticed three cannons of brass *; two of them were
formed of two pieces, and one of such a size, I never before
saw the like. Its mouth was forty-two inches in diameter,
but it seemed short for its thickness†. The commandant of
the place was Sir Mathico, a knight of Arragon, and he had
for his lieutenant his own brother, styled my lord brother.

The Turk is in possession of the castle of Coulumbach, on
the Danube, two days' journey below Belgrade. He seized it
from the despot, and it is, as they say, a strong place, but
easily attacked with artillery, and all succour may be cut off
from it, which is a great disadvantage. He there keeps a
hundred light galleys having sixteen or eighteen oars on a
side, to pass over to Hungary at his pleasure. The governor
of this place is Cénasnin Bey, before spoken of.

On the Danube, but in Hungary, and opposite to Belgrade,
the despot has a town and castle that were given him by the
emperor‡, with several others, that afford him an income of

---

* From our author thus noticing the brass cannon, it should seem they
were still rare in his time, and looked on as wonders. Louis XI. had a
dozen cast, and gave them the names of the twelve peers of France.

† It was then the fashion to make pieces of artillery of an enormous size.
Mohammed II., at the siege of Constantinople, employed cannon cast on the
spot that threw, as they say, balls of two hundredweight. Monstrelet
speaks of a gun that Louis XI. had cast at Tours, and carried afterwards to
Paris, that flung balls of five hundred pounds. In 1717, prince Eugene,
after his victory over the Turks, found in Belgrade a cannon twenty-five feet
long, that shot balls of one hundred and ten pounds, whose charge was
fifty-two pounds of powder. It was also then customary to make the balls
of marble or stone, worked to fit the mouths of different cannons.

‡ Sigismond, king of Bohemia and Hungary. It is pretended that Sigismond gave them in exchange for Belgrade.

fifty thousand ducats, on condition of his becoming his liege man, but he obeys the Turk more than the emperor.

Two days after my arrival at Belgrade I saw twenty-five men, armed after the manner of the country, enter the town, whom count Mathico the governor had sent for to remain in garrison. They told me they were Germans, although they had Servians and Hungarians so near at hand; but they said the Servians were subjects and tributaries to the Turk: of course they could not trust them; and, as for the Hungarians, they were so much afraid of him, that should he appear they would not dare to defend it, however great its strength. They were obliged therefore to call in strangers, and this measure became the more necessary from its being the only place in the possession of the emperor to enable him to pass and repass the Danube, in case of need. This conversation greatly astonished me, and caused me to make some reflections on the strange subjection in which the Turk keeps Macedonia, Bulgaria, the emperor of Constantinople, the Greeks, the despot of Servia, and his subjects. Such a dependence appeared to me a lamentable thing for Christendom; and, as I lived with the Turks, and became acquainted with their manner of living and fighting, and have frequented the company of sensible persons who have observed them narrowly in their great enterprises, I am emboldened to write something concerning them, according to the best of my abilities, under correction, however, from those better informed, and to show how it may be possible to reconquer the territories they have gained possession of, and to beat them in the field of battle. I shall begin with what regards their persons, and say they are a tolerably handsome race, with long beards, but of moderate size and strength. I know well that it is a common expression to say as strong as a Turk; nevertheless, I have seen an infinity of Christians, when strength was necessary, excel them, and I myself, who am not of the strongest make, have, when circumstances required labour, found very many weaker than me.

They are diligent, willingly rise early, and live on little, being satisfied with bread badly baked, raw flesh dried in the sun, milk curdled or not, honey, cheese, grapes, fruit, herbs, and even a handful of flour, with which they make a potage sufficient to feed six or eight for a day. Should they have a horse or camel sick without hopes of recovery, they cut its throat and eat it. I have witnessed this many and many a time. They are indifferent where they sleep, and lie on the ground. Their dress consists of two or three robes of cotton, thrown one over the other, which fall to their feet. Over these again they wear another of felt, in the manner of a mantle, called a capinat. This, though light, resists rain, and there are some very fine and handsome. Their boots come up to the knees, and they have large drawers, some of crimson velvet, others of silk or fustian and common stuffs. In war, or when travelling, to avoid being embarrassed by their robes, they tuck the ends into their drawers, by which they can move with greater freedom.

Their horses are good, cost little in food, gallop well and for a long time. They keep them very poor, never feeding them but at night, and then only giving them five or six handfuls of barley and double the quantity of chopped straw, the whole put into a bag which hangs from their ears. At break of day, they bridle, clean and curry them, but never allow them to drink before mid-day, then in the afternoon every time that they find water, and in the evening when they lodge or encamp; for they always halt early, and near a river if possible. This last time they leave them bridled for an hour like mules, and then, at a fixed moment, each gives his horse provender. During the night-time, they cover them with felt or other stuffs, and I have seen such coverings very handsome; they have the like also for their hounds, in which they are curious and have a good breed, although with long hanging ears and tufted tails, which, however they carry well. All their horses are geldings; they keep some others for stallions, but so few, that I have never seen a single one. They saddle and bridle them *à la genette.* Their saddles are commonly very rich, but hollow, having pummels before and behind, with short stirrup leathers and wide stirrups.

With regard to their accoutrements and dresses for war, I had twice an opportunity of seeing them, on the occasions of Greek renegadoes, who, renouncing their own, had embraced the Mohammedan religion. The Turks celebrate these events with much festivity. They dress themselves in their best arms, and traverse the town with as numerous a procession as possible. On these occasions I have seen them wear very handsome coats of armour like to ours, except that the links of the mail were smaller; the vambraces were the same. In one word, they resemble those pictures that represent figures of the time of Julius Cæsar. Their armour descends almost half way down the thigh, but a piece of silken stuff is attached circularly to the bottom of it, that falls down to the calf of the leg. On their head they wear a round white cap, half a foot high, terminated in a point. It is ornamented with plates of iron on all sides, to ward off from the face, neck, and cheeks, blows of the sword, and is like the helmets in France, called salades *. Beside this head-piece, they usually wear another over it, namely, a bonnet of iron wire. There are some of these so rich and handsome, that they cost from forty to fifty ducats, whereas the first are bought for one or two; although not so strong as the others, they resist the cut of a sword. I have spoken of their saddles, in which they sit as in an arm-chair, deep sunk in them, their knees very high, and with short stirrups, a position in which they cannot support the smallest blow from a lance without being unhorsed. The arms of those who have any fortune are a bow, a tarquais, a sword, a heavy mace with a short handle, the thick end of which is cut into many angles. This is a dangerous weapon when struck on the shoulders, or on an unguarded arm. I am convinced that a blow given with it on a head armed with a salade would stun a man. Several have small wooden bucklers, with which they cover themselves well on horseback when they draw the bow. I have been assured of this by those who have long used them, as well as from having seen it myself.

Their obedience to superiors is boundless. None dare disobey, even when their lives are at hazard; and it is chiefly owing to this steady submission that such great exploits have been performed, and such vast conquests gained, as render them masters of a more extensive and considerable country than all France. I have been assured that, whenever the Christian powers have taken up arms against them, they have always had timely information of it. In this case the sultan has their march watched by men assigned to this purpose, and he lays wait for them with his army two or three days' march from the spot where he proposes to fight them. Should he think the opportunity favourable, he falls suddenly on them;

---

* A sort of light casque then in use, which, not having vizor nor throat piece, had need of projecting plates of iron to guard the face.

and for these occasions they have a particular kind of march,
beaten on a large drum. When this signal is given, those
who are to lead march quietly off, followed by the others with
the same silence, without the file ever being interrupted, from
the horses and men being trained to this purpose. Ten
thousand Turks, on such an occasion, will make less noise
than one hundred men in the Christian armies. In their
ordinary marches they only walk, but in these they always
gallop; and as they are beside lightly armed, they will thus
advance further, from evening to day-break, than in three
other days; and this is the reason why they cannot wear such
complete armour as the French and Italians. They choose,
also, no horses but such as walk fast, and gallop for a long
time, while we select only those that gallop well and with
ease. It is by these forced marches that they have succeeded
in surprising and completely defeating the Christians in their
different wars. It is thus they conquered Duke John, whose
soul may God pardon*! and, again, the emperor Sigismond,
so recently before Coulumbach, where Sir Advis, a Polish
knight, perished. Their manner of fighting varies according
to circumstances. When they find a favourable opportunity
for it, they divide themselves into different troops, and thus
attack many parts of an army at once. This mode is particularly used when they are among woods or mountains, from the
great facility they have of uniting together again. At other
times they form ambuscades, and send out scouts well mounted
to observe the enemy. If their report be that he is not on his
guard, they instantly form their plan and take advantage of the
circumstance. Should they find the army well drawn up,
they curvet round it within bow-shot, and, while thus prancing,
shoot at the men and horses, and continue this manœuvre so
long, that they at last throw it into disorder. If the army

---

* John, count of Nevers, surnamed *sans peur*, and son to Philippe le
Hardi, duke of Burgundy. Sigismond having formed a league to check the
conquests of Bajazet, Charles VI. sent him a body of troops, in which were
two thousand gentlemen, under the command of the count of Nevers. The
Christian army was defeated at Nicopolis in 1396, and the French slain or
made prisoners. See further particulars in Froissart. When Jean succeeded
his father, as duke of Burgundy, he caused the duke of Orleans, brother to
the king of France, to be assassinated. He was murdered in his turn by
Tannegui du Châtel, an ancient servant of the duke of Orleans. These facts
prove that La Brocquière was in the right, when speaking of John, to pray
that God would pardon him.

attempt to pursue them, they fly, and disperse each separately, even should only a fourth part of their own number be ordered against them; but it is in their flight that they are formidable, and it has been almost always then that they have defeated the Christians. In flying they have the adroitness to shoot their arrows so very true that they scarcely ever fail to hit man or horse. Each cavalier has also on the pummel of his saddle a tabolcan. When the chief, or any of his officers, perceives the enemy who pursues to be in disorder, he gives three strokes on this instrument; the others, on hearing it, do the same, and they are instantly formed round their chief like so many hogs round the old one; and then, according to circumstances, they either receive the charge of the assailants, or fall on them by troops, and attack them in different places at the same time. In pitched battles they employ another stratagem, which consists in throwing fireworks among the cavalry to frighten the horses. They often post in their front a great body of dromedaries and camels, which are bold and vicious; these they drive before them on the enemy's line of horse, and throw it into confusion.

Such are the modes of fighting the Turks have hitherto adopted against the Christians. I would not, most assuredly, wrong or depreciate them; for I must own that I have always found them, in my different connections, frank and loyal, and when it was necessary to show courage they have never failed to do so; but I am not the less convinced that it would be no difficult matter for troops, well mounted and well commanded, to defeat them; and, in regard to myself, I declare that, with one-half of their numbers, I should never hesitate to attack them. Their armies, I know, commonly consist of two hundred thousand men; but the greater part are on foot, and destitute, as I before said, of tarquais, helmets, mallets, or sword; few, indeed, being completely armed. They have, besides, among them a great number of Christians, who serve through force, Greeks, Bulgarians, Macedonians, Albanians, Sclavonians, Wallachians, Servians, and other subjects of the despots of that country. All these people detest the Turk, because he holds them in a severe captivity; and should they see the Christians march in force against him, and above all the French, I have not the smallest doubt but they would turn against him and do him great mischief.

The Turks are not, therefore, so terribly formidable as I

have heard say. I own, however, that it will be necessary, if any attempt be made against them, to have a general well obeyed by his troops, and who would particularly listen to the advice of those acquainted with their mode of warfare. This was the fault, as I am informed, of the emperor Sigismond, when he was defeated by them at Coulumbach. Had he attended to the advice given him, he would not have been forced to raise the siege, since he had from twenty-five to thirty thousand Hungarians. Did not two hundred Genoese and Lombardy cross-bows alone check the enemy, overawe them, and cover his retreat, while he embarked on board the galleys that he had on the Danube; while six thousand Wallachians, under the Polish knight before mentioned, having separated and posted themselves on a small eminence, were all cut to pieces?

I speak nothing here but what I have seen myself, or heard from undoubted authority; therefore, in case any Christian prince or general may wish to attempt the conquest of Turkey in Europe, or even to penetrate further, I think I am able to give much information on this subject. I shall, however, speak according to my abilities; and, should any thing escape me that may be displeasing to some of my readers, I beg they will excuse it, and pass it by, as if I had said nothing.

The monarch who should form such a project ought at first to propose to himself for his object, not glory and renown, but God, religion, and the salvation of so many souls that are in the road to perdition. He must be well assured, beforehand, that the regular payment of his troops is provided for, and that he carries with him none but such as have a fair reputation, with a good will for the purpose, and, above all, that they be not pillagers. With regard to the payment of them, I think it should depend on the holy father to see that it be regularly made; but, until the moment when the army enters the Turkish territory, there should be made a strict law that no one take any thing without paying for it. No person likes to see his property stolen; and I have heard that those who have been guilty of such things have not found themselves the better for it. I, however, refer these things to the prince and the lords of his council; I shall confine myself to speak of the sort of troops I think proper for such an attempt, and whom, if I had the choice, I should like to accompany.

I would, in the first place, select from France men at arms,

archers, and cross-bows, in as great numbers as possible and
of the sort mentioned above.   Secondly, from England, a
thousand men at arms and ten thousand archers.   Thirdly,
from Germany, the greatest number possible of gentlemen,
with their cross-bowmen on horse and foot.   Collect together
from fifteen to twenty thousand archers and cross-bows of these
three nations, adding thereto from two to three hundred light
troops; and I will ask from God the grace to march with them,
and engage they shall advance without difficulty from Belgrade
to Constantinople.   They will require but light armour, as I
have before observed that the Turkish bow has no great
strength.   When near, their archers shoot true and quick;
but they do not shoot nearly so far as we do.   Their bows
are thick and short, and their arrows thin and of no length:
their iron heads are stuck into the wood, which cannot bear a
great blow nor make a deep wound, even on an unarmed
place.   From this it will be seen slight armour only is wanted
for the troops, that is to say, light greaves for the legs and
thighs, thin plate armour for the body, with helmets having
light vizor-pieces.   A Turkish arrow would perhaps pierce a
light coat of mail, but would be turned aside by plate-armour,
however thin.   I shall add that, in case of necessity, our
archers can make use of the arrows of the Turks; but that
they cannot do the same with ours, because the notch is not
sufficiently wide, and the strings of their bows, being made of
sinews, are too thick.

According to my opinion, our cavalry should be armed with
light, sharp-headed lances, and with strong, well-tempered
swords.   It may be also advantageous to have small battle-
axes on the wrist.   The infantry should have double-headed
battle-axes, and a long and sharp spear, both having their
hands defended with gauntlets.   With regard to this last
article, I own I have seen some in Germany, made of boiled
leather, that I consider as effectual as those of iron.

When the army shall come to an open plain, where a combat
may be fought with advantage, it should be done; but then
the whole should be formed into one body; the van and rear
guards should be employed on the wings.   The pikemen to
be intermixed in the line, unless it should be preferred to
post them otherwise to skirmish; but the general will be
careful not thus to post the men at arms.   In front of the
line, and on the wings, the light troops will be scattered; and

every one must be strictly forbidden, under pain of death, to pursue the runaways.

It is the policy of the Turks to have their armies twice as numerous as those of the Christians. This superiority of numbers augments their courage, and allows them to form different corps, and to make their attack on various parts at the same time. Should they once force an opening, they rush through in incredible crowds, and it is then a miracle if all be not lost. To prevent this misfortune, the light troops should be numerously posted on the angles of the line of battle, and, by this means, keep it compact, so as not to suffer it to be broken. This manœuvre seems to me to be the more easily executed from these light troops not being sufficiently armed to form a column capable, by its weight, of any great impulsion. The Turkish lances are worth nothing; their archers are the best troops they have, and these do not shoot so strong nor so far as ours do. They have a more numerous cavalry; and their horses, though inferior in strength to ours, and incapable of bearing such heavy weights, gallop better, and skirmish for a longer time without losing their wind. This is an additional reason for the army always keeping in a close and good order. When this method is constantly followed, they will be forced to combat disadvantageously, and, consequently, to risk every thing or retreat before the army. Should this last be the case, the cavalry must be sent in pursuit; but it must always march in good order, and be ever ready to fight and receive them well should they turn about. With such conduct it is no way doubtful but they must always be defeated; and if a contrary one be followed they will beat us, as has ever happened.

I may, perhaps, be told that it would be disgraceful thus to remain on the defensive when in presence of the enemy; and that, living as they do on little, they would starve us, unless we quitted our intrenchment to fight with them. I shall answer that it is not customary for them to remain long in one place; that to-day they are at this place, to-morrow a day and a half's march off; they reappear again as suddenly as they disappeared; and that, if an army be not continually on its guard, it will run great risks. The important point is, to be ever on the watch from the moment they appear in sight, and ready to mount for the combat. Should there be any difficult passage on the line of march, as many men at arms

and archers must be sent thither as the situation will allow
for a combat, and they must be continually in order of battle
until the whole be passed. No foragers must ever be sent
out, for they would be as so many lost men ; and besides they
would find nothing abroad, for in war-time the Turks transport every thing into towns.

With all these precautions the conquest of Turkey in
Europe would not be a difficult enterprise, provided—I repeat
it—that the army be kept in one body, never divided, and no
detachments ever sent after the enemy. Should I be asked
how I would secure provision, I answer that Turkey and
Servia have navigable rivers, and Bulgaria, Macedonia, and
the Greek provinces are fertile. The army advancing always
thus in a mass, the Turks would be forced to retreat; and
they must of necessity choose one of two extremities, as I
have before said; either to re-cross into Asia, and abandon
their properties, their wives, and their children, since the
country is, as may be seen from my description of it, defence-
less, or risk a battle, as they have always done, when they
have passed the Danube. I conclude, therefore, that with
good troops, composed from the three nations I have named,
French, English, and Germans, success would be certain;
and that, if they were sufficiently numerous, well united, and
commanded, they might march to Jerusalem. But I shall
now return to my travels.

I crossed the Danube at Belgrade. It was at this moment
exceedingly swollen, and may have been twelve miles broad.
Never in the memory of man had such a flood been seen.
Being unable to travel to Buda by the direct road, I went to
a village called Pensey. On leaving Pensey, I came to the
most level plain I ever saw, and, after being ferried over a
river, arrived at the town of Beurquerel, which belongs to the
despot of Servia, and where I crossed two other rivers by a
bridge. From Beurquerel I came to Verchet, belonging also
to the despot; there I crossed the Theis, a wide and deep
river, and at length I arrived at Zegedin, situated upon it.
In the whole length of this road, with the exception of two
small woods inclosed by a rivulet, I did not see a single tree.
The natives use, for firing, straw or reeds, collected from the
banks of rivers, or from their numerous marshes. They eat,
instead of bread, soft cakes ; but they have not much food.

Zegedin is a large country town, of a single street, that seems

about a league in length.   It is in a fertile country, abounding
with all sorts of provision.   Many cranes and bustards are
taken here, and I saw the market-place full of them; but they
dress and eat them in a filthy manner.   The Theis abounds
in fish, and I have nowhere seen a river that produces such
large ones.   Many wild horses are brought thither for sale,
and their manner of conquering and taming them is curious.
I have been told that, should any one want three or four
thousand, they could be procured within the town; and they
are so cheap that a very good road horse may be bought for
ten Hungarian florins.   The emperor, as I heard, had given
Zegedin to a bishop.   I saw this bishop, and he seemed a
man of a broad conscience.   The Cordelier friars have a
handsome church in this town, where I heard service; but it
was performed a little after the Hungarian mode.

From Zegedin I came to Pest, a tolerably good country
town on the Danube, opposite to Buda.   The country, from
one town to the other, was good and level, and full of immense herds of horses, that live wild on these plains like
savage animals; and hence the numbers seen at the markets
of Zegedin.   I crossed the Danube at Pest, and entered Buda
seven days after my departure from Belgrade.   Buda is the
capital of Hungary, situated on an eminence, and longer than
it is broad.   To the east is the Danube, to the west a valley,
to the south a palace, which commands the gate of the town.
It was begun by the present emperor, and, when he shall have
finished it, will be extensive and strong.   On this side, but
without the walls, are very handsome hot baths.   There are
also others along the banks of the Danube to the eastward;
but these are not so good as the preceding ones.   The town
is governed by Germans, as well in respect to police as commerce, and what regards the different professions.   Many
Jews live there who speak French well, several of them being
descendants of those driven formerly from France.   I found,
also, there a merchant from Arras, called Clays Davion.   He
was one of those whom the emperor Sigismond had brought
from France, to establish manufactories in his country.
Clays was a tapestry weaver*.

* Sigismond, in his travels to France, had visited the manufactories, and
particularly those of Flanders, at that time famous for its tapestries.   He
wished to establish similar ones in his capital of Hungary, and for this effect
had engaged different workmen to follow him.

The environs of Buda are agreeable, and its territory fertile
in all sorts of provision, especially in white wines; but they
are somewhat fiery, which is attributed to the adjacent hot
springs, and to the sulphur they emit.   One league from the
town is the body of St. Paul the hermit, which is in a perfect
state of preservation.

I returned to Pest, where I also found six or eight French
families, whom the emperor had sent thither to construct on
the Danube, and opposite to his palace, a large tower.   His
intentions were to shut up the river with a chain, extending
from it; and I should suppose he wanted to imitate what had
been done from the town of Burgundy, that fronts the fort of
L'Ecluse; but I do not believe it is practicable here, for the
river is too broad.   I had the curiosity to visit the tower,
which is about the length of three lances high, and round
about were quantities of hewn stone; but it had remained
some time in this state, because the masons who had begun
the work were dead, and those that had survived them were
said not to have knowledge enough to continue it.   Pest is
inhabited by many horse-dealers; and, whoever may want two
thousand good horses, they can furnish the quantity.   They
sell them by stables full, containing ten horses; and their
price for each stable is two hundred florins.   I looked into
several, where two or three horses alone were worth that
price.   They come for the most part from the mountains of
Transylvania, which bound Hungary to the eastward.   I purchased one that galloped well, as indeed they almost all do.
The country is excellent for breeding them, from the quantity
of grass it produces; but they have the fault of being a little
headstrong, and particularly difficult to shoe; so that I have
sometimes seen them obliged to be cast on the ground to be
shod.

The mountains just spoken of contain mines of gold and
salt, each of which pay annually to the king one hundred
Hungarian florins.   He had given up that of gold to the lord
of Prussia and to count Mathico, on condition that the first
would guard the frontier against the Turk, and the second
Belgrade.   The queen had reserved to her own use the
revenue from salt.   The salt is beautiful.   It is cut out of a
rock like freestone, into pieces of about a foot long, squared,
but a little convex on the upper side.   Whoever should see
them in a cart would take them for stone.   It is afterwards

pounded in a mortar, and turns out tolerably white, but finer and better than any I have elsewhere tasted.

In my road through Hungary I have frequently met wagons with six, seven, or eight persons in them, and drawn by only a single horse; for it is customary with them, when they make long journeys, to use only one. They universally have the hind wheels higher than the fore wheels. There are some covered in their country manner, which are very handsome, and so light that, including wheels, it seemed that a man could carry one of them suspended to his neck. As the country is perfectly smooth and level, there is nothing to prevent the horse from being always on the trot. It is from this great evenness of the ground that, when they plough, they draw furrows of an extraordinary length. Until I came to Pest I had no servant; but there I treated myself with one, and took one of those French masons into my service whom I found at Pest. He was from Brai-sur-Somme.

On my return to Buda I accompanied the Milanese ambassador to pay our compliments to the grand count of Hungary, a title which answers to that of lieutenant of the emperor. The grand count received me with much distinction, because, from my dress, he took me for a Turk; but, when he learnt I was a Christian, he was somewhat colder. I was told that he was a man whose conversation was little to be depended on, and that no great trust must be placed in his promises. This is somewhat generally the reproach made of the Hungarians; and, for my own part, I own that, after the idea given me of them by my acquaintance, I should have less confidence in an Hungarian than in a Turk. The grand count is an old man. It was he, as I heard, who formerly arrested Sigismond, king of Bohemia and Hungary, and afterwards emperor, and threw him into prison, whence he afterwards released him by an amicable agreement. His son was just married to a beautiful Hungarian lady. I saw him at a tournament after their manner, when the combatants were mounted on small horses and low saddles. They were gallantly dressed, and had strong and short lances. It was a pleasing spectacle. Whenever the two champions hit, both perhaps, but certainly one of them, must be unhorsed; and it is then seen who has the firmest seat*.

* The knights in France were mounted for tournaments or battle on large strong horses, called "palefrois." Their saddles were high-piqued before

When they tilt for golden wands, all the horses are of the same size, all the saddles of the same form; and they are drawn for by lot, and the jousters are taken by pairs. Should one of two adversaries fall, the victor is obliged to retire, and is not permitted to tilt again.

I had never quitted the company of the Milanese ambassador until we came to Buda; but he had told me on the road that we must there separate, that he might continue his route to Milan. Soon after my return to Buda I called, in consequence, on Clays Davion, who gave me a letter of recommendation to a merchant of his acquaintance at Vienna. As I had fully opened myself to him, not thinking it right to make a secret of my rank, my name, or the country I had come from, or the honour I had of belonging to my lord duke of Burgundy, he had inserted all this in his letter, and I profited from it.

From Buda I came to Thiat, a country town, where the king is said to be fond of residing; then to Janiz, in German, "Jane,"* a town on the Danube. I afterwards passed by another town, built on an island in that river, which had been given by the emperor to one of the dependants of the duke of Burgundy, whom I believe to be Sir Renier Pot. I also passed through Brut†, situated on a river that divides the kingdom of Hungary from the duchy of Austria. The river runs through a marsh, where a long and narrow causeway has been constructed. This is an important place; and I am convinced that a small body of men could effectually defend it on the Austrian side.

Two leagues further the ambassador took leave of me, and followed another road to return to the duke of Milan, his lord. I took that leading to Vienna, where I arrived after five days' journey. On my entering the town no one would lodge me, supposing I was a Turk. At last, by accident, some one pointed out to me an inn, where I was received. Fortunately my servant, whom I had hired at Pest, knew the Hungarian and high German languages. He desired that the merchant to whom I had a letter might be sent for. On seeking him

---

and behind, which afforded them the greater means of resisting the shock of the lance than the small horses and low saddles of the Hungarians; and this is the reason our author says that, in the tilts of the Hungarians, it may be easily seen which knight has the best seat on his horse.

   * Jane, perhaps Gen.   † Bruck?

he came, and not only offered me every service in his power, but went to inform my lord duke Albert*, cousin-german to my lord, of my arrival, who instantly despatched to me a poursuivant-at-arms, and shortly after Sir Albrech de Potadorf. Not two hours after my arrival I saw Sir Albrech dismount at the gate of my inn, and, hearing him ask for me, I thought myself undone. A little before my departure for the Holy Land, I, with some others, had arrested him between Flanders and Brabant, because we thought him a subject of Frederic of Austria†, who had challenged my lord; and I now doubted not but that he was come, in his turn, to arrest me, and perhaps do worse. He told me, however, that his lord, duke Albert, having learned that I was attached to the duke of Burgundy, had sent him to me to offer, on his part, every service that was in his power; that he desired me to ask whatever I might want as boldly from him as from my own lord; for that he wished to treat his servants in the same manner as he would his own. Sir Albrech then spoke for himself. He presented me with money, and offered me horses or any thing else. In short, he rendered me good for evil; although, after all, I had not done any thing to him but what honour permitted and even obliged me to do.

Two days after duke Albert sent to say he wished to speak with me; and Sir Albrech again came to conduct me to him. I presented myself to him the moment he came from mass, attended by eight or ten old knights of a respectable appearance. Scarcely had I made my reverence when he took me by the hand, and would not suffer me to speak to him on my knees. He asked many questions, particularly about my lord, which induced me to think he had a great affection for him.

He was of a tolerably good size, brown complexion, good-humoured, affable, valiant, and generous, and was said to possess every good quality. Among the persons who accompanied him were some lords from Bohemia, whom the Hussites had expelled from that country because they would not be of their religion. At the same time a great lord of that country, called Paanepot, was presented to him, who had come with several others, on the part of the Hussites, to treat with him and establish peace. These last proposed to march to the

---

* Albert II., duke of Austria, emperor after the death of Sigismond.
† Frederic, duke of Austria, succeeded Albert II. as emperor.

assistance of the king of Poland, against the lords of Prussia, and made, as I heard, great offers to duke Albert, if he would second them; but he replied, according to my information, that, until they submitted themselves to the religion of Jesus Christ, he would never make truce nor peace with them as long as he should live. In fact, at this very time, he had twice beaten them in battle; had conquered from them all Moravia; and, by his conduct and valour, had aggrandized himself at their expense.

On quitting his presence, I was conducted to that of the duchess, a tall, handsome woman, daughter to the emperor, and heiress, after him, to the kingdoms of Hungary and Bohemia and their dependencies. She had just been brought to bed of a daughter, which had occasioned festivals and tournaments, that were the more numerously attended because, hitherto, she had not had any children.

On the morrow the duke sent Sir Albrech to invite me to dinner, and made me sit at his table with an Hungarian lord and another, an Austrian. All his attendants are on board wages, and no one dines with him unless invited by the master of his household. The table was square; and the custom is, for one dish to be brought at a time, and for him who is nearest to eat of it, which supplies the place of a taster*. Fish and flesh were served; and, above all, a quantity of meat, strongly seasoned, but always dish by dish. After the dinner I was carried to see the dancing in the apartments of the duchess. She gave me a bonnet of gold thread and silk, a ring, and a diamond to wear on my head, according to the fashion of the country. There were present many nobles of each sex; and I saw there some very handsome women, with the finest heads of hair that can be conceived. When I had remained in these apartments some time, a gentleman named Payser, who, though but a squire, was a chamberlain and keeper of the jewels of the duke of Austria, came, by his orders, to show them to me. I saw the crown of Bohemia, which has some very fine diamonds, and the largest ruby I ever saw. It seemed bigger than a full-sized date; but it is not clear, and there are some cavities toward the bottom that show a few black spots. The keeper

---

* Formerly there was, at the tables of sovereigns, an officer to taste every dish before it was put on the table. This precaution had originally been taken against poison.

then carried me to see the wague-bonnes *, which the duke of
Austria had constructed to combat the Bohemians. I perceived none that could hold more than twenty men; but he
assured me there was one that would contain three hundred,
and did not require more than eighteen horses to draw it.

I met at this court the lord de Valse, a gallant knight, and
the greatest baron in Austria after the duke. I saw there,
also, Sir Jacques Trousset, a handsome Swabian knight; but
there was another, named Le Chant, hereditary cup-bearer to
the emperor, who having lost his brother and many friends at
the battle of Bar, and hearing that I belonged to my lord of
Burgundy, caused me to be watched, to know the day of my
departure, that he might seize me as I was travelling through
Bavaria. Luckily for me, the duke of Austria was informed
of his intentions, and sent him away, making me stay longer
at Vienna than I intended, to wait for the departure of the
lord de Valse and Sir Jacques Trousset, that I might accompany them.

During my stay I witnessed three of the tournaments I
mentioned, with small horses and low saddles. One took
place at court, the others in the streets; but at the last
several were unhorsed so heavily that they were dangerously
wounded.

The duke of Austria made me, in private, offers of money.
I received similar offers from Sir Albert and Sir Robert
Daurestoff, a great lord in Austria, who, the preceding year,
had travelled in disguise through Flanders, and had there
seen my lord duke, and spoke very handsomely of him. In
short, I received very pressing ones from a poursuivant of lower
Brittany, named Toutseul, who, after having served under
the admiral of Spain, was now in the service of the duke of
Austria. This Breton called on me every day to go to mass,
and attended me wherever I wished to go. Persuaded that I
must have expended on my journey all the money I had, a
little before my departure he presented me with the value of
fifty marcs in enamels, and insisted that I should sell them
for my profit; but, as I equally refused to accept them or to
borrow, he protested that no one should ever know any thing
of it.

* A wague-bonne was a sort of wagon, or moveable tower, used in war.

Vienna is a tolerably large town, well inclosed with deep ditches and high walls, inhabited by rich merchants and all sorts of tradesmen. The Danube washes its wall on the north side. The surrounding country is pleasant and good; and it is a place of amusement and pleasure. The natives are better dressed than those of Hungary, although they all wear coarse doublets, very thick and wide. In war they cover the doublet with an haubergeon, a glaçon *, a large hat of iron, and other armour usual in that country. They have many crennequiniers, for such is the name given in Austria and Bohemia to those called archers in Hungary. Their bows are like those of the Turks, but not so good nor so strong; and they do not use them so well as they do. The Hungarians pull the string with three fingers, and the Turks with the thumb and ring.

When I went to take leave of the duke and duchess of Austria, he recommended me himself to my two travelling companions, sir Jacques Trousset and the lord de Valse, who was setting off for his command on the frontiers of Bohemia. He repeated his question, as to my wanting money; but I answered, as I had before done to all who had offered me some, that my lord of Burgundy had so amply supplied me on my departure, that I had a sufficiency for my return to him, but that I requested he would grant me a safe conduct, which he did.

The Danube, for three days' journey on leaving Vienna, runs eastward; from above Buda to the point of Belgrade, it takes a southerly direction, and then, between Hungary and Bulgaria, it resumes its easterly course, and falls, as they say, into the Black Sea at Mont Castre. I left Vienna in company with the before-mentioned lord of Valse and sir Jacques Trousset. The first was going to his lady at Lintz, and the second to his country-seat. After two days' travelling, we came to St. Polten, where the best knives of the country are made. Thence to Molke on the Danube, where is the best manufacture of cross-bows, having besides a very handsome Carthusian monastery. Thence to Valse, which belongs to the aforesaid lord. The castle is constructed on an elevated rock,

---

* Glaçon, or glachon, a kind of defensive armour. The French called "glaçon," a sort of fine cloth that was doubtless glazed. Glaçon, in German, was perhaps a kind of coat-armour made of many folds of quilted cloth, such as our gambisons. Perhaps it may be only a cuirass.

that commands the Danube.   He himself showed me the ornaments of the altar of the chapel; I never before saw any so rich in embroidery and in pearls.   I there also noticed boats drawn up the Danube by horses.

The morrow of our arrival, a Bavarian gentleman came to pay his respects to the lord of Valse.   Sir Jacques Trousset, informed of his arrival, declared he would hang him on a thorn in the garden.   The lord de Valse hastened to him, and entreated he would not put such an affront on him in his own house.   " Well," replied sir Jacques, " should he come elsewhere within my reach, he shall not escape hanging." The lord de Valse went to the gentleman, and made him a sign to go away, which he complied with.   The cause of this anger of sir Jacques was, that he himself and the greater part of his attendants were of the secret company, and that the gentleman, having been also a member, had misbehaved *.

From Valse we came to Ens, situated on the river Ems; thence to Evresperch, on the same river, and within the domain of the bishop of Passau; and then to Lintz, a very good town, with a castle on the Danube, and not far from the frontiers of Bohemia.   It belongs to the duke of Austria, and the lord of Valse is governor of it.   I saw there madame de Valse, a very handsome lady from Bohemia, who gave me a flattering reception.   She presented me with an excellent trotter for the road, a diamond to put in my hair, after the Austrian fashion, and a bonnet of pearls ornamented with a ring and a ruby †.   The lord of Valse remaining at Lintz with his lady, I continued my journey in company with sir Jacques Trousset, to Erfurt, which belongs to the count de Chambourg.   Here Austria ends, and it had taken us six days to come from Vienna hither.   From Erfurt we came to Riet, a Bavarian town belonging to duke Henry; then to Prenne on the river Sceine; to Bourchaze, a town with a castle on the same river, where we met the duke; thence to Mouldrof, where we crossed the Taing.   In short, having traversed the country of duke Louis of Bavaria, without entering any of its

---

* This relates, probably, to the famous secret tribunal; and the Bavarian, whom Trousset wanted to hang, may have been a false brother, who had revealed the secrets of it.

† These bonnets must not be mistaken for such as ours.   They were only wreaths, or circular crowns.

towns, we arrived at Munich, the prettiest little town I ever saw, and which belongs to duke William of Bavaria.

I quitted Bavaria at Lansperch to enter Swabia, and passed through Mindelheim, that belongs to the duke, through Memingen, an imperial town, and thence to Walporch, one of Sir Jacques's castles. He did not arrivé until three days after me, because he had some friends to visit in the neighbourhood; but he had given orders to his people to treat me as they would do himself. On his return, we set out for Ravensburg, an imperial town, and thence to Martof, and Mersbourg, a town of the bishop of Constance seated on the lake of this name. The lake, in this part, may be about three Italian miles broad. I crossed it and came to Constance, where I passed the Rhine, which there first assumes this name on issuing from the lake.

It was at this town that sir Jacques Trousset left me. This knight, one of the most amiable and valiant in Germany, had done me the honour and pleasure of accompanying me so far from respect to the duke of Austria, and would have escorted me further had he not been engaged at a tournament; but he gave me, in his stead, a poursuivant, whom he charged to escort me as far as I should wish. This tournament had been undertaken by the lord de Valse. They loved each other like brothers, and were to tilt with war lances, bucklers, and helmets of iron, according to the custom of the country, thirteen against thirteen, all friends and relations. Sir Jacques was well furnished with every sort of arms, which he had shown me himself in his castle of Walporch. I took my leave of him, and quitted him with much regret.

From Constance I went to Stein, where I crossed the Rhine; thence to Shaffhousen, a town belonging to the emperor; to Waldshutts, to Lauffembourg, to Rhinfeld, all the property of duke Frederick of Austria; and to Basil, another imperial town, whither, on account of the council then assembled there, the emperor had sent duke William of Bavaria, as his lieutenant.

The duke and duchess were desirous to see me. I assisted at a session of the council, where he represented the emperor; and among the numbers were the lord cardinal of St. Angelo, legate from the holy father pope Eugenius, seven other cardinals, many patriarchs, archbishops and bishops. I met there several on the part of my lord of Burgundy, among whom were sir Guillebert de Lannoy, lord of Villerval, his ambassador, master Jean Germain, and the bishop of Châlons. I had a conversation with the legate, who inquired much about the countries I had seen, especially Turkey. He seemed to have the conquest of this last country much at heart, and recommended me to repeat to my lord of Burgundy certain particulars that I had told to him relative to such conquest.

At Basil I parted with my poursuivant, who returned to Austria; and having travelled through the country of Ferette, belonging to duke Frederick of Austria, and passed by Montbeliart, which is the property of the countess of that name, I entered Franche Compté, which belongs to my lord duke, and arrived at Besançon. I supposed that he was in Flanders, and consequently travelled on the frontiers of Bar and Lorraine to Veson; but at Villeneuve I learnt that he was on the frontier of Burgundy, and had caused Mussi l'Evêque to be besieged. I went then by Auxonne to Dijon, where I found the lord chancellor of Burgundy, in whose company I went to pay my respects to the duke. His people were at the siege, and he himself at the abbey of Poictiers. I appeared in his presence dressed in the same manner as when I left Damascus, and had the horse led before him which I had purchased in that town, and which had brought me to France. My lord received me with much kindness. I presented to him my horse, my dress, with the Koran, and Life of Mohammed, written in Latin, which the chaplain to the Venetian consul at Damascus had given me. He had these books delivered to master John Germain to examine; but I have never heard one word concerning them since that time. This master John was a doctor of divinity; he was bishop of Châlons-sur-Saône, and knight of the Golden Fleece *.

---

* Jean Germain, born at Cluni, and consequently a subject to the duke of Burgundy, had, when a child, pleased the duchess, who sent him to study at the university of Paris, where he distinguished himself. The duke, whose favour he afterwards gained, made him, in 1431, *chancellor* of his order of the Golden Fleece, and not *knight*, as La Brocquière says. The year following he was nominated bishop of Nevers; sent in 1432 ambassador, first to Rome, and then to the council at Basil, as one of his representatives. In 1436, he was translated from the see of Nevers to that of Châlons-sur-Saône. What La Brocquière says of this bishop seems peevish; but if the reader will consider, not hearing any thing of the two interesting manuscripts he had brought from Asia, he had cause for being out of humour. Germain, how-

If I have said little respecting the country between this place and Vienna, it has been because it is well known. With regard to the others I have travelled through, I inform my readers, that the journey was not undertaken through ostentation or vanity, but for the guidance and information of such persons as may have similar desires as I have had to see and be acquainted with these countries, and in obedience to my highly redoubted lord the duke of Burgundy, who commanded me to write these travels. I always carried with me a small book, in which I wrote down my adventures whenever time permitted; and it is from these memorandums that I have composed the history of my journey. If it be not so well composed as others could have done it, I must beg my readers to excuse me.

ever, was employed on them, but he was labouring to refute them. At his death, in 1461, he left two works in manuscript, copies of which are to be found in some libraries; one entitled, "De Conceptione beatæ Mariæ Virginis, adversus Mahometanos et Infideles, Libri duo:" the other, "Adversus Alcoranum, Libri quinque."

A JOURNEY FROM ALEPPO TO JERUSALEM,

AT EASTER, A.D. 1697.

BY HENRY MAUNDRELL.

TO THE RIGHT REVEREND FATHER IN GOD,
THOMAS, LORD BISHOP OF ROCHESTER.

My Lord,

From a large and constant experience of your lordship's favour, I have all reason to believe that you will not think it tedious to hear something of my affairs, though in themselves below your lordship's notice and regard.

It is now more than twelve months since I arrived in this place, during all which time I have had opportunity enough perfectly to observe and discover the genius of the factory among whom my lot is fallen; and upon the result of all my experience of them I am obliged to give them this just commendation, that they are a society highly meriting that excellent character which is given of them in England, and which (besides the general vogue) your lordship has some time received from a most faithful and judicious hand, the excellent bishop Frampton. As he undoubtedly was the great improver of the rare temper of this society, so he may well be esteemed best able to give them their true and deserved character. I need only add, that such they still continue as that incomparable instructor left them; that is, pious, sober, benevolent, devout in the offices of religion, in conversation innocently cheerful, given to no pleasures but such as are honest and manly, to no communications but such as the nicest ears need not be offended at, exhibiting in all their actions those best and truest signs of a Christian spirit, a sincere and cheerful friendship among themselves, a generous charity toward others, and a profound reverence for the liturgy and constitution of the Church of England. It is our first employment, every morning, to solemnize the daily service of the church, at which I am sure to have always a devout, a regular, and full congregation. In a word, I can say no more (and less I am sure I ought not) than this, that in all my experience in the world I have never known a society of young gentlemen, whether in the city or country, (I had almost said the University, too,) so well disposed, in all points, as this.

Your lordship will conclude that, in consequence of all this, my present station cannot but be very agreeable; and though, in leaving England, I was separated from the greatest blessings to me in the world, your lordship's kindness and that of my friends at Richmond, yet I must own I have found here as much recompense as could be made for such a separation.

Among other satisfactions, one great one, which I have had since my arrival, was a voyage to the Holy Land, in company with fourteen others of our factory. We went by way of the coast; and, having visited several places consecrated by the life and death of our blessed Lord, we returned by way of Damascus. If there be any thing, either in these places which I have visited, or elsewhere in these countries, touching which I may be capable of giving your lordship any satisfaction by my poor observations, I should esteem it my great happiness, and my coming thus far would seem completely recompensed.

I entreat your lordship's blessing, as being your lordship's most dutiful, humble servant,

                                        HENRY MAUNDRELL.

Aleppo.

THERE being several gentlemen of our nation (fourteen in number) determined for a visit to the Holy Land at the approaching Easter, I resolved, though but newly come to Aleppo, to make one in the same design, considering that, as it was my purpose to undertake this pilgrimage some time or other before my return to England, so I could never do it either with less prejudice to my cure *, or with greater plea-sure to myself, than at this juncture, having so large a part of my congregation abroad at the same time, and in my company.

Pursuant to this resolution, we set out from Aleppo, Friday, February 26th, 1696 (i. e. Feb. 1697), at three in the afternoon, intending to make only a short step that evening, in order to prove how well we were provided with necessaries for our journey. Our quarters, this first night, we took up at the Honey-khan, a place of but indifferent accommodation, about one hour and a half west of Aleppo.

It must here be noted that, in travelling this country, a man does not meet with a market-town and inns every night, as in England. The best reception you can find here is either under your own tent, if the season permit; or else in certain public lodgments, founded in charity for the use of travellers. These are called by the Turks khani; and are seated sometimes in the towns and villages, sometimes at convenient distances upon the open road. They are built in fashion of a cloister, encompassing a court of thirty or forty yards square, more or less, according to the measure of the

---

* Maundrell was chaplain to the English factory at Aleppo. See the Introduction.

founder's ability or charity. At these places all comers are
free to take shelter, paying only a small fee to the khan-
keeper (khanji), and very often without that acknowledg-
ment; but must expect nothing here but bare walls. As for
other accommodations of meat, drink, bed, fire, provender,
with these it must be every one's care to furnish himself.

Feb. 27.—From the Honey-khan we parted very early the
next morning, and, proceeding westerly as the day before,
arrived in one hour and a half at Oo-rem (Ur-im), an old
village affording nothing remarkable but the ruins of a small
church. From Oo-rem we came, in half an hour, to Kaffre;
and in three quarters more to Essoyn (Es-aïn). At this last
place we entered into the plains of Kefteen (Kaftīn), proceeding in which, we came, in one hour, to another village
called Legene; and in half an hour more, to Hozano; and in
a good hour more, to Kefteen. Our whole stage this day was
about five hours; our course a little southerly of the west.

The plains of Kefteen are of a vast compass, extending to
the southward beyond the reach of the eye, and in most places
very fruitful and well cultivated. At our first descent into
them, at Essoyn, we counted twenty-four villages, or places at
a distance resembling villages, within our view from one
station. The soil is of a reddish colour, very loose and
hollow, and you see hardly a stone in it; whereas, on its
west side, there runs along, for many miles together, a high
ridge of hills, discovering nothing but vast naked rocks, without the least sign of mould or any useful production, which
yields an appearance as if nature had, as it were, in kindness
to the husbandman, purged the whole plain of these stones,
and piled them all up together in that one mountain. Kefteen
itself is a large, plentiful village, on the west side of the
plain; and the adjacent villages, abounding with corn, give
the inhabitants great advantages for breeding pigeons, insomuch that you find here more dove-cots than other houses.
We saw at this place, over the door of a bagnio, a marble
stone, carved with the sign of the cross, and the Δόξα Πατρὶ,
&c., with a date not legible. It was probably the portal of
some church in ancient times; for I was assured by the inhabitants of the village that there are many ruins of churches
and convents still to be seen in the neighbouring rocky
mountains.

Sunday, Feb. 28.—Having a long stage to go this day, we

left Kefteen very early ; and continuing still in the same
fruitful plain, abounding in corn, olives, and vines, we came
in three quarters of an hour to Harbanoose ('Arbanūs), a small
village situated at the extremity of the plain, where, after
crossing a small ascent, we came into a very rich valley called
Rooge. It runs to the south farther than one can discern ;
but in breadth, from east to west, it extends not above an
hour's riding, and is walled in (as it were) on both sides, with
high, rocky mountains. Having travelled in this valley near
four hours, we came to a large water called the lake (or rather,
according to the oriental style, the sea) of Rooge. Through
the skirt of this lake we were obliged to pass, and found it no
small trouble to get our horses, and much more our loaded
mules, through the water and mire ; but all the sea was so
dried up, and the road so perfectly amended at our return,
that we could not then discern so much as where the place
was which had given us so great trouble. From this lake we
arrived, in one hour, at Te-ne-ree, a place where we paid our
first caphar.

These caphars are certain duties which travellers are
obliged to pay, at several passes upon the road, to officers,
who attend in their appointed stations to receive them.
They were at first levied by Christians, to yield a recompense
to the country for maintaining the ways in good repair, and
scouring them from Arabs and robbers. The Turks keep up
so gainful an usage still, pretending the same causes for it ;
but, under that pretence, they take occasion to exact from
passengers, especially Franks, arbitrary and unreasonable
sums, and, instead of being a safeguard, prove the greatest
rogues and robbers themselves.

At a long hour beyond this caphar our road led us over the
mountains on the west side of the valley of Rooge. We were
near an hour in crossing them, after which we descended into
another valley, running parallel to the former, and parted
from it only by the last ridge of hills. At the first descent
into this valley is a village called Bell-Maez*, from which we
came, in two hours, to Shoggle (Jisr Shogher). Our course
was, for the most part of this day, west-south-west. Our
stage, in all, ten hours.

* Bell-Maez, " I don't know," probably an answer to Maundrell's question,
" What is the name of that village ? " and not the name itself.

Shoggle is a pretty large, but exceedingly filthy town,
situated on the river Orontes, over which you pass by a
bridge of thirteen small arches to come at the town. The
river hereabouts is of a good breadth; and yet so rapid that it
turns great wheels, made for lifting up the water, by its
natural swiftness, without any force added to it by confining
its stream. Its waters are turbid and very unwholesome, and
its fish worse, as we found by experience, there being no person of all our company, that had eaten of them over night,
but found himself much indisposed the next morning. We
lodged here in a very handsome khan, far exceeding what is
usually seen in this sort of buildings. It was founded by the
second Kuper-li, and endowed with a competent revenue for
supplying every traveller that takes up his quarters in it with
a competent portion of bread, and broth, and flesh, which is
always ready for those that demand it, as very few people
of the country fail to do. There is annexed to the khan, on
the west side, another quadrangle, containing apartments for
a certain number of alms-men, the charitable donation of the
same Kuper-li. The khan we found, at our arrival, crowded
with a great number of Turkish hadgees, or pilgrims, bound
for Mecca; but, nevertheless, we met with a peaceable reception amongst them, though our faces were set to a different
place.

March 1.—From Shoggle our road led us at first westerly,
in order to our crossing the mountain on that side the valley.
We arrived at the foot of the ascent in half an hour; but met
with such rugged and foul ways in the mountains, that it took
us upwards of two hours to get clear of them, after which we descended into a third valley, resembling the other two which we
had passed before. At the first entrance into it is a village called
Be-da-me, giving the same name also to the valley. Having
travelled about two hours in this valley, we entered into a
woody, mountainous country, which ends the pashalick of
Aleppo and begins that of Tripoli. Our road here was very
rocky and uneven; but yet the variety which it afforded made
some amends for that inconvenience. Sometimes it led us
under the cool shade of thick trees; sometimes through
narrow valleys, watered with fresh, murmuring torrents; and
then, for a good while together, upon the brink of a precipice;
and in all places it treated us with the prospect of plants and
flowers of divers kinds, as myrtles, oleanders, cyclamens,

anemones, tulips, marygolds, and several other sorts of aromatic herbs. Having spent about two hours in this manner, we descended into a low valley, at the bottom of which is a fissure into the earth of a great depth, but withal so narrow that it is not discernible to the eye till you arrive just upon it, though to the ear a notice of it is given at a great distance, by reason of the noise of a stream running down into it from the hills. We could not guess it to be less than thirty yards deep; but it is so narrow that a small arch, not four yards over, lands you on its other side. They call it the Sheikh's Wife, a name given it from a woman of that quality, who fell into it, and, I need not add, perished. The depth of the channel and the noise of the water are so extraordinary, that one cannot pass over it without something of horror. The sides of this fissure are firm and solid rock, perpendicular and smooth, only seeming to lie in a wavy form all down, as it were to comply with the motion of the water, from which observation we were led to conjecture that the stream, by a long and perpetual current, had, as it were, sawn its own channel down into this unusual deepness, to which effect the water being penned up in so narrow a passage, and its hurling down stones along with it by its rapidity, may have not a little contributed*.

From hence, continuing our course through a road resembling that before described, we arrived, in one hour, at a small, even piece of ground, called Hadjar-il-Sultan, or the Sultan's Stone; and here we took up our quarters this night, under our tents. Our road, this day, pointed for the most part south-west; and the whole of our stage was about seven hours and a half.

March 2.—We were glad to part very early this morning from our campagnia lodging, the weather being yet too moist and cold for such discipline. Continuing our journey through woods and mountains, as the day before, we arrived, in about one hour, at the caphar of Crusia (Krusiyeh), which is demanded near a khan of that name. A khan they call it, though it is, in truth, nothing else but a cold, comfortless ruin, on the top of a hill by the way-side.

From hence, in about another hour, we arrived at the foot

---

* Mr. Ainsworth informs me that he verified the account given of this fissure by personal examination, and found it to be perfectly correct in its descriptive details.

of a mountain called Occaby (Akabi), or, as the word denotes, Difficult; and indeed we found its ascent fully answerable to its name.   The moisture and slipperiness of the way at this time, added to the steepness of it, greatly increased our labour in ascending it, insomuch that we were a full hour in gaining the top of the hill.   Here we found no more woods or hills; but a fine country, well cultivated and planted with silk gardens, through which, leaving on the right hand a village called Citte Galle, inhabited solely by Maronites, we came in one hour to Bellulca.   Here we repaired to a place which is both the khan of the village and the aga's house; and resolving, by reason of the rains, which fell very plentifully, to make this our lodging, we went to visit the aga, with a small present in our hands, in order to procure ourselves a civil reception.   But we found little recompense from his Turkish gratitude; for, after all our respect to him, it was not without much importunity that we obtained permission to have the use of a dry part of the house, the place where we were at first lodged lying open to the wind and the beating in of the rain.   Our whole stage, this day, was not much above four hours; our course about south-west.

Being informed that there were several Christian inhabitants in this place, we went to visit their church, which we found so poor and pitiful a structure, that here Christianity seemed to be brought to its humblest state, and Christ to be laid again in a manger.   It was only a room of about four or five yards square, walled with dirt, having nothing but the uneven ground for its pavement; and for its ceiling, only some rude staves laid across it, and covered with bushes to keep out the weather.   On the east side was an altar, built of the same materials with the wall; only it was paved at the top with potsherds and slates, to give it the face of a table. In the middle of the altar stood a small cross, composed of two laths nailed together in the middle, on each side of which ensign were fastened to the wall two or three old prints, representing our blessed Lord and the blessed Virgin, &c., the venerable presents of some itinerant friars that had passed this way.   On the south side was a piece of plank supported by a post, which we understood was the reading desk, just by which was a little hole commodiously broke through the wall to give light to the reader.   A very mean habitation this for the God of heaven! but yet held in great esteem and reverence by the poor people, who not only come

with all devotion hither themselves, but also deposit here
whatever is most valuable to them, in order to derive upon it
a blessing.   When we were there, the whole room was hung
about with bags of silkworms' eggs, to the end that, by
remaining in so holy a place, they might attract a benediction,
and a virtue of increasing.

March 3.—The next morning flattered us with the hopes of
a fair day, after the great rains which had fallen for near eight
hours together.   We therefore ventured to leave Bellulca,
with no great thanks to it for our entertainment.   But we
had not gone far, before we began to wish that we had kept
our former accommodation, bad as it was, for the rains began
to break out afresh with greater fury than before ; nor had we
more comfort under foot, the road being very deep and full of
sloughs.   However, we resolved to go forward, in hopes of a
better time, and in four hours (very long ones in such uncomfortable circumstances) we arrived at Sholfatia, a poor
village situate upon a small river which we were obliged to
pass.   A river we might call it now, it being swollen so high
by the late rains that it was impassable, though at other times
it be but a small brook, and in the summer perfectly dry.

Here, instead of mending our condition, as we expected,
we began to drink more deeply of the bitter cup of pilgrims,
being brought to such a strait that we knew not which way to
turn ourselves.   For (as I said) the stream was not fordable,
so that there was no going forward ; and, as for facing about
and returning to the place from whence we came, that was a
thing we were very averse to, well knowing, by that morning's
experience, the badness of the road, and likewise having
reason to expect but a cold welcome at our journey's end.
As for lodging in the village, that was a thing not to be
endured ; for the houses were all filled with dirt and nasti-
ness, being inhabited promiscuously by the villagers and their
cattle.   As for lying in the campagnia, the rain was so vehe-
ment, we could not do that without an evident danger both to
ourselves and horses.

But whilst we were at this nonplus, not knowing which
course to take, the rain abated, and so we resolved to pitch
in the open field, though thoroughly soaked with the wet,
esteeming this however the least evil.   Accordingly, we betook ourselves to a small ascent by the water-side, intending
there, under our tents, to wait the falling of the stream.

We had not enjoyed this cessation of rain long, when

it began to pour down afresh, with terrible lightning and thunder. And now our care was renewed, and we knew not well which to be most concerned for; whether ourselves, who enjoyed the miserable comfort of a dropping tent over us, or for our servants and horses, which had nothing but their own clothes to protect them. At last, there being a small Sheikh's house, or burying-place hard by, we comforted ourselves with hopes that we might take sanctuary there. The only difficulty was how to get admission into so reverenced a place, the Turks being generally men of greater zeal than mercy. To negotiate this affair, we sent a Turk (whom we had taken with us for such occasions) into the village, ordering him to try first by fair means to gain admittance, and, if that failed, to threaten that we would enter by force. But the religion of this place was of that kind which supersedes instead of improving humanity. The people absolutely denied us the small charity we demanded, and sent us word they would die upon our swords before they would yield to have their faith defiled ; adding, farther, that it was their faith to be true to Hamet and Aly, but to hate and renounce Omar and Abu Beker, and that this principle they were resolved to stand by. We told them we had as bad an opinion of Omar and Abu Beker as they could have; that we desired only a little shelter from the present rain, and had no intention to defile their faith. And thus, with good words, we brought them to consent that we might secure our baggage in the Sheikh's house ; but, as for ourselves and arms, it was our irreversible sentence to be excluded out of hallowed walls. We were glad, however, to get the merciless doors open upon any terms, not doubting but we should be able to make our advantage of it afterwards, according to our desire, which we actually did; for when it grew dark, and the villagers were gone to sleep, we all got into the places of refuge, and there passed a melancholy night among the tombs; thus escaping, however, the greater evil of the rain, which fell all night in great abundance.

Being now crept into the inside of the Sheikh's house, I must not omit, in requital for our lodgings, to give some account of the nature of such structures. They are stone fabrics, generally six or eight yards square (more or less), and roofed with a cupola, erected over the graves of some eminent Sheikhs ; that is, such persons, as by their long beards, prayers of the same standard, and a kind of Pharisaical superciliousness (which are the great virtues of the Mohammedan religion), have purchased to themselves the reputation of learning and saints. Of these buildings there are many scattered up and down the country (for you will find among the Turks far more dead saints than living ones). They are situated commonly, though not always, upon the most eminent and conspicuous ascents. To these oratories the people repair with their vows and prayers, in their several distresses, much after the same manner as the Romanists do to the shrines of their saints. Only in this respect the practice of the Turks seems to be more orthodox, in regard that though they make their saint's shrine the house of prayer, yet they always make God alone, and not the saint, the object of their addresses.

March 4.—To revive us after the heaviness of the last night, we had the consolation to be informed this morning, that the river was fordable at a place a little farther down the stream; and, upon experiment, we found it true as was reported. Glad of this discovery, we made the best despatch we could to get clear of this inhospitable place, and, according to our desires, soon arrived with all our baggage on the other side of the river.

From hence, ascending gently for about half an hour, we came to the foot of a very steep hill, which, when we had reached, its top presented us with the first prospect of the ocean. We had in view, likewise, at about two hours' distance to the westward, the city Latichea (Latakiyah), situate on a flat fruitful ground close by the sea; a city first built by Seleucus Nicator, and by him called in honour of his mother, Λαοδίκεια, which name it retains, with a very little corruption of it, to this day. It was anciently a place of great magnificence, but in the general calamity which befell this country it was reduced to a very low condition, and so remained for a long time. But of late years it has been encouraged to hold up its head again, and is rebuilt, and become one of the most flourishing places upon the coast, being cherished and put in a way of trade by Kaplan Aga, a man of great wealth and authority in these parts, and much addicted to merchandise.

From the hill which we last ascended, we had a small descent into a spacious plain, along which we travelled southward, keeping the sea on the right hand, and a ridge of mountains on the left. Having gone about one hour and a half in this plain, we discerned on the left hand, not far from the road, two ancient tombs. They were chests of stone, each two yards and a half long. Their cavities were covered over with large tables of stone, that had been lifted aside probably in hopes of treasure. The chests were carved on the outside with ox-heads, and wreaths hanging between them, after the manner of adorning heathen altars. They had likewise, at first, inscriptions graven on them; but these were so eaten out, that one could not discover so much as the species of the characters. Here were also several foundations of buildings; but whether there were ever any place of note situated hereabouts, or what it might be, I cannot resolve.

Above an hour from these tombs we came to another stream, which stopped our march again. These mountain rivers are ordinarily very inconsiderable, but they are apt to swell upon sudden rains, to the destruction of many a passenger, who will be so hardy as to venture unadvisedly over them. We took a more successful care at this place; for, marching about an hour higher up by the side of the stream, we found a place where the waters by dilating were become shallower, and there we got a safe passage to the other side. From hence we bent our course to recover our former road again; but we had not got far before there began a very violent storm of hail, followed by a hard and continued rain, which forced us to make the best of our way to Jebilee, leaving our baggage to follow us at leisure.

Our whole stage this day was about six hours, pointing for the first hour west, and for the remaining part near south, having the sea on the right hand, and a ridge of mountains at about two hours' distance on the left. And in this state our road continued for several days after, without any difference, save only that the mountains at some places approach nearer the sea, at other, retire farther off. These mountains go under different names in several places, as they run along upon the coast, and are inhabited by rude people of several denominations. In that part of them above Jebilee, there dwell a people, called by the Turks Neceres*, of a very strange and singular character; for it is their principle to adhere to no certain religion, but, chameleon-like, they put on the colour of religion whatever it be, which is reflected upon them from the persons with whom they happen to converse. With Christians they profess themselves Christians; with Turks they are good Mussulmans; with Jews they pass for

---

* The Nosairi, or Ansarians.

Jews; being such Proteuses in religion, that nobody was ever
able to discover what shape or standard their consciences are
really of. All that is certain concerning them is, that they
make very much and good wine, and are great drinkers.

March 5.—This whole day we spent at Jebilee, to recruit
ourselves after our late fatigues; having the convenience of a
new khan to lodge in, built at the north entrance into the
city, by Ustan, the present pasha of Tripoli.

Jebilee is seated close by the sea, having a vast and very
fruitful plain stretching round about it, on its other sides. It
makes a very mean figure at present; though it still retains
the distinction of a city, and discovers evident footsteps of a
better condition in former times. Its ancient name, from
which also it derives its present, was Gabala, under which
name it occurs in Strabo, and other old geographers. In the
time of the Greek emperors, it was dignified with a bishop's
see, in which sometimes sat Severian the grand adversary and
arch-conspirator against St. Chrysostom.

The most remarkable things that appear here at this day
are a mosque, and an almshouse just by it, both built by sultan Ibrahim. In the former his body is deposited, and we
were admitted to see his tomb, though held by the Turks in
great veneration. We found it only a great wooden chest,
erected over his grave, and covered with a carpet of painted
calico, extending on all sides down to the ground. It was
also tricked up with a great many long ropes of wooden beads
hanging upon it, and somewhat resembling the furniture of a
button-maker's shop. This is the usual way the Turks adorn
the tombs of their holy men, as I have seen in several other
instances; the long strings of beads passing in this country
for marks of great devotion and gravity. In this mosque we
saw several large incense pots, candlesticks for altars, and
other church furniture, being the spoils of Christian churches
at the taking of Cyprus. Close by the mosque is a very beautiful bagnio, and a small grove of orange-trees, under the
shade of which travellers are wont to pitch their tents in the
summer-time.

The Turks that were our conductors into the mosque, entertained us with a long story of this sultan Ibrahim who lies
there interred; especially touching his mortification, and renouncing the world. They reported that, having divested
himself of his royalty, he retired hither, and lived twenty
years in a grotto by the sea-side, dedicating himself wholly to

poverty and devotion; and, in order to confirm the truth of their relation, they pretended to carry us to the very cell where he abode. Being come to the place, we found there a multitude of sepulchres hewn into the rocks by the sea-side, according to the ancient manner of burying in this country. And amongst these they showed one, which they averred to be the very place in which the devout sultan exercised his twenty years' discipline; and, to add a little probability to the story, they showed, at a small distance, another grotto twice as large as any of its fellows, and uncovered at the top, which had three niches or praying places hewn in its south side. This they would have to be sultan Ibrahim's oratory; it being the manner of the Turks always to make such niches in their mosques and other places of devotion, to denote the southern quarter of the world; for that way the Musselmans are obliged to set their faces when they pray, in reverence to the tomb of their prophet. These niches are always formed exactly resembling those usually made for statues, both in their size, fabric, and every circumstance. I have sometimes reflected for what reason the Turks should appoint such marks to direct their faces toward in prayer. And if I may be allowed to conjecture, I believe they did it at first in testimony of their iconoclastic principle, and to express to them both the reality of the divine presence there, and at the same time also its invisibility. The relators of this story of sultan Ibrahim were doubtless fully persuaded of the truth of it themselves. But we could not tell what conjectures to make of it, having never met with any account of such a sultan, but only from this rude tradition.

From these Mahomedan sanctuaries, our guide pretended to carry us to a Christian church, about two furlongs out of the town on the south side. When we came to it, we found it nothing but a small grotto in a rock, by the sea-shore, open on the side towards the sea; and having a rude pile of stones erected in it for an altar. In our return from this poor chapel, we met with the person who was the curate of it. He told us that himself and some few other Christians of the Greek communion were wont to assemble in this humble cell for divine service, not being permitted to have any place of worship within the town.

Jebilee seems to have had anciently some convenience for shipping. There is still to be seen a ridge composed of huge square stones running a little way into the sea, which appears to have been formerly continued farther on, and to have made a mole. Near this place we saw a great many pillars of granite, some by the water-side, others tumbled into the water. There were others in a garden close by, together with capitals of white marble finely carved, which testify in some measure the ancient splendour of this city.

But the most considerable antiquity in Jebilee, and the greatest monument of its former eminence, is the remains of a noble theatre just at the north gate of the city. It passes amongst the Turks for an old castle, which (according to the Asiatic way of enlarging) they report to have been of so prodigious a height, when in its perfect state, that a horseman might have rode, about sun-rising, a full hour in the shade of it.

As for what remains of this mighty Babel, it is no more than twenty feet high. The flat side of it has been blown up with gunpowder by the Turks. And from hence (as they related) was taken a great quantity of marble, which we saw used in adorning their bagnio and mosque before mentioned. All of it that is now standing is the semicircle. It extends from corner to corner just a hundred yards. In this semicircular part is a range of seventeen round windows just above the ground, and between the windows all round were raised, on high pedestals, large massy pillars, standing as buttresses against the wall, both for the strength and ornament of the fabric; but these supporters are at present most of them broken down.

Within is a very large arena; but the just measure of it could not be taken, by reason of the houses with which the Turks have almost filled it up. On the west side the seats of the spectators remain still entire, as likewise do the caves or vaults which run under the subsellia all round the theatre. The outward wall is three yards three quarters thick, and built of very large and firm stones, which great strength has preserved it thus long from the jaws of time, and from that general ruin which the Turks bring with them into most places where they come.

March 6.—Having done with Jebilee, we put forward again early the next morning, with a prospect of much better weather than we had been attended with in our former motions. Our road continued by the sea-side, and in about two hours brought us to a fair deep river, called by the Turks Nahr-il-Melech, or the King's River. Here we saw some heaps of ruins on both sides of the river, with several pillars of granite, and other footsteps of some considerable buildings. About half an hour farther we passed another river called Jobar, showing the remains of a stone bridge over it, once well built, but now broken down.   On the other side of this river, in a large ploughed field, stood a great square tower, and around about, the rubbish of many other buildings.   Likewise, all along this day's journey, we observed many ruins of castles and houses, which testify that this country, however it be neglected at present, was once in the hands of a people that knew how to value it, and thought it worth defending. Strabo calls this whole region, from Jebilee as far as Aradus, the country of the Aradii (of whom in due place), and gives us the names of several places situate anciently along this coast, as Paltus, Balanea, Caranus, Enydra, Marathus, Ximyra. But whether the·ruins which we saw this day, may be the remains of any of those cities, cannot well be determined at this distance of time, seeing all we have of those places is only their names, without any sufficient distinctions by which to discover their situation.   The Balanea of Strabo is indeed said to be still extant, being supposed to be the same place that the Turks (little changing its name) call at this day Baneas. This place is four good hours beyond Jebilee.   It stands upon a small declivity, about a furlong distant from the sea, and has a fine clear stream running swiftly by it on the south side. It is at present uninhabited, but its situation proves it to have been anciently a pleasant, its ruins a well-built, and its bay before it, an advantageous, habitation.   At this place was required another caphar.

Leaving Baneas, we went on by the sea-side, and in about a quarter of an hour passed by an old castle, on the top of a very high mountain.   It is built in the figure of an equilateral triangle, having one of its angles pointing towards the sea.   The Turks call it Merchah *, and enlarge much upon the sieges it has sustained in former times; but, whatever force it may have had anciently, it is at present only a residence for poor country people.   This is probably the same castle mentioned by Adrichomius and others under the name of Margath, to which the bishops of Balanea were forced to translate their see, by reason of the insults of the Saracens.

* Markah, the ancient Marathus.

At about one hour and a half distance from Bancas, we came to a small clear stream, which induced us to take up our lodging near it. We pitched in the campagnia about two or three furlongs up from the sea, having in sight on the mountains above us a village called Sophia, inhabited solely by Maronites; and a little farther Besack, another village possessed by Turks only; and a little farther Merakia, whose inhabitants are a miscellany of Christians and Turks together. Our whole stage, this day, was about six hours.

Sunday, March 7.—From this quarter we removed early the next morning, and in three hours came to a fair deep river called Nahr Hussain, having an old bridge turned over it, consisting of only one arch, but that very large and exceedingly well wrought. In one hour and a half more, travelling still by the sea-side, we reached Tortosa.

The ancient name of this place was Orthosia. It was a bishop's see in the province of Tyre. The writers of the holy wars make frequent mention of it, as a place of great strength. And one may venture to believe them, from what appears of it at this day.

Its situation is on the sea-shore, having a spacious plain extending around about it on its other sides. What remains of it is the castle, which is very large and still inhabited. On one side it is washed by the sea; on the other, it is fortified by a double wall of coarse marble, built after the rustic manner. Between the two walls is a ditch, as likewise is another encompassing the outermost wall. You enter this fortress on the north side, over an old drawbridge, which lands you in a spacious room, now for the most part uncovered, but anciently well arched over, being the church belonging to the castle. On one side it resembles a church, and, in witness of its being such, shows at this day several holy emblems carved upon its walls, as that of a dove descending, over the place where stood the altar, and in another place that of the Holy Lamb. But, on the side which fronts outwards, it has the face of a castle, being built with port-holes for artillery, instead of windows. Round the castle on the south and east sides anciently stood the city. It had a good wall and ditch encompassing it, of which there are still to be seen considerable remains. But for other buildings, there is nothing now left in it, except a church, which stands about a furlong eastward from the castle. It is one hundred and thirty feet in length, in breadth

ninety-three, and in height sixty-one. Its walls, and arches,
and pillars, are of a bastard marble, and all still so entire,
that a small expense would suffice to recover it into the
state of a beautiful church again. But, to the grief of
any Christian beholder, it is now made a stall for cattle, and
we were, when we went to see it, almost up to our knees
in dirt and mire.

From Tortosa we sent our baggage before us, with orders
to advance a few miles farther toward Tripoli, to the intent
that we might shorten our stage to that place the next day.
We followed not long after, and in about a quarter of an hour
came to a river, or rather the channel of a river, for it was
almost dry, though questionless there must have been anciently
no inconsiderable stream, as we might infer both from the
largeness of the channel, and the fragments of a stone bridge
formerly laid over it.

In about half an hour more we came abreast of a small
island, about a league distant from the shore, called by the
Turks Ruad. This is supposed to be the ancient Arvad, Ar-
phad, or Arpad (under which several names it occurs, 2 Kings,
xix. 12; Gen. x. 18; Ezek. xxvii. 11, &c.), and the Aradus of
the Greeks and Romans. It seemed to the eye to be not
above two or three furlongs long, and was wholly filled up
with tall buildings like castles. The ancient inhabitants of
this island were famous for navigation, and had a command
upon the continent as far as Gabala.

About a quarter of an hour farther we came up with our
muleteers, they having pitched our tents, before they had
gone so far as we intended. But this miscarriage they well
recompensed, by the condition of the place where they
stopped, it affording us the entertainment of several notable
antiquities, which we might otherwise perhaps have passed by
unobserved. It was at a green plot lying within one hour of
Tortosa, a little southward of Aradus, and about a quarter of
a mile from the sea, having in it a good fountain (though of a
bad name) called the Serpent Fountain.

The first antiquity that we here observed was a large dyke,
thirty yards over at top, cut in the solid rock. Its sides went
sloping down, with stairs formed out of the natural rock, descending gradually from the top to the bottom. This dyke
stretched in a direct line, east and west, more than a furlong,
bearing still the same figure of stairs running in right lines

all along its sides. It broke off at last at a flat marshy
ground, extending about two furlongs between it and the sea.
It is hard to imagine that the water ever flowed up thus high;
and harder, without supposing that, to resolve for what reason all this pains of cutting the rock in such a fashion was
taken.

This dyke was on the north side of the Serpent Fountain;
and, just on the other side of it, we espied another antiquity,
which took up our next observation. There was a court of
fifty-five yards square, cut in the natural rock; the sides of the
rock standing around it, about three yards high, supplied the
place of walls. On three sides it was thus encompassed, but
to the northward it lay open. In the centre of this area a
square part of the rock was left standing, being three yards
high and five yards and a half square. This served for a
pedestal to a throne erected upon it. The throne was composed of large stones, two at the sides, one at the back, another hanging over all at top, in the manner of a canopy.
The whole structure was about twenty feet high, fronting toward that side where the court was open. The stone that
made the canopy was five yards and three quarters square,
and carved round with a handsome cornice. What all this
might be designed for, we could not imagine, unless, perhaps,
the court may pass for an idol temple, and the pile in the
middle for the throne of the idol; which seems the more probable, in regard that Hercules, *i.e.* the Sun, the great abomination of the Phœnicians, was wont to be adored in an open
temple. At the two innermost angles of the court, and likewise on the open side, were left pillars of the natural rock,
three at each of the former, and two at the latter.

About half a mile to the southward of the aforesaid antiquities, there stood in view two towers. But, it growing dark,
we were forced to defer our examination of them till the next
morning. Our whole stage this day exceeded not six hours.

March 8.—Having passed over a restless night, in a marshy
and unwholesome ground, we got up very early, in order to
take a nearer view of the two towers last mentioned. We
found them to be sepulchral monuments, erected over two
ancient burying-places. They stood at about ten yards' distance from each other.

The first was thirty-three feet high. Its longest stone or
pedestal was ten feet high, and fifteen square. The super-

structure upon which was first a tall stone in form of a cylinder, and then another stone cut in shape of a pyramid. The other tower was thirty feet and two inches high. Its pedestal was in height six feet, and sixteen feet six inches square. It was supported by four lions, carved one at each corner of the pedestal. The carving had been very rude at best, but was now rendered by time much worse. The upper part reared upon the pedestal was all one single stone.

Each of these barbarous monuments had under it several sepulchres, the entrances into which were on the south side. It cost us some time and pains to get into them, the avenues being obstructed, first with briars and weeds, and then with dirt. But, however, we removed both these obstacles, encouraging ourselves with the hopes, or rather making ourselves merry with the fancy, of hidden treasure. But, as soon as we were entered into the vaults, we found that our golden imaginations ended (as all worldly hopes and projects do at last) in dust and putrefaction. But, however, that we might not go away without some reward for our pains, we took as exact a survey as we could of these chambers of darkness, which were disposed in manner as follows.

The chambers under the first tower lie side by side. Going down seven or eight steps, you come to the mouth of the sepulchre, where crawling in you arrive in the first chamber, which is nine feet two inches broad, and eleven feet long. Turning to the right hand, and going through a narrow passage, you come to a room which is eight feet broad and ten long. In this chamber are seven cells for corpses, viz. two over against the entrance, four on the left hand, and one unfinished on the right. These cells were hewn directly into the firm rock. We measured several of them, and found them eight feet and a half in length, and three feet three inches square. I would not infer from hence, that the corpses deposited here were of such a gigantic size as to fill up such large coffins; though, at the same time, why should any men be so prodigal of their labour as to cut these caverns into so hard a rock as this was, much farther than necessity required?

On the other side of the first chamber was a narrow passage, seven feet long, leading into a room whose dimensions were nine feet in breadth and twelve in length. It had eleven cells of somewhat a less size than the former, lying at equal distances all round about it.

Passing out of the first room, you have, right before you, two narrow entrances, each seven feet long, into another room. This apartment was nine feet square. It had no cells in it like the others, nor any thing else remarkable, but only a bench, cut all along its side on the left hand. From the description of this sepulchre, it is easy to conceive the disposition of the other. The height of the rooms in both was about six feet, and the towers were built each over the innermost room of the sepulchres to which it belonged.

At about the distance of a furlong from this place, we discerned another tower, resembling this last described. It was erected likewise over a sepulchre. There was this singularity observable in this last sepulchre, that its cells were cut into the rock eighteen feet in length, possibly to the intent, that two or three corpses might be deposited in each of them, at the feet of one another. But, having a long stage this day to Tripoli, we thought it not seasonable to spend any more time in this place, which might perhaps have afforded us several other antiquities.

And yet, for all our haste, we had not gone a mile, before our curiosity was again arrested by the observation of another tower, which appeared in a thicket not far from the wayside. It was thirty-three feet and a half high, and thirty-one feet square, composed of huge square stones, and adorned with a handsome cornice all around at top. It contained only two rooms, one above the other; into both which there were entrances on the north side, through two square holes in the wall. The separation between both rooms, as also the covering at the top, was made, not of arched work, but of vast flat stones, in thickness four feet, and so great an extent, that two of them in each place, sufficed to spread over the whole fabric. This was a very ancient structure, and probably a place of sepulture.

I must not forget, that around about the Serpent Fountain, and also as far as this last tower, we saw many sepulchres, old foundations, and other remains of antiquity. From all which it may be assuredly concluded, that here must needs have been some famous habitation in ancient times; but whether this might be the Ximyra, laid down by Strabo hereabouts (or, as Pliny calls it, Simyra *), the same, possibly, with the country of the Zemarites, mentioned in conjunction with the Arvadites †, I leave to others to discuss.

Having quitted ourselves of these antiquities, we entered into a spacious plain, extending to a vast breadth, between the sea and the mountains, and in length reaching almost as far as Tripoli. The people of the country call it Junia, that is, the Plain, which name they give it by way of eminency, upon account of its vast extent. We were full seven hours in passing it, and found it all along exceedingly fruitful, by reason of the many rivers and the great plenty of water which it enjoys. Of these rivers the first is about six hours before you come to Tripoli. It has a stone bridge over it of three large arches, and is the largest stream in the whole plain; for which reason it goes by the name of Nahr-el-Kibber, or the Great River. About half an hour farther you come to another river, called Nahr Abrosh, or the Leper's River. In three quarters of an hour more you pass a third river, called Nahr Acchar, having a handsome stone bridge, of one very large arch laid over it. Two good hours more bring you to a fourth river, called . . . . or the Cold Waters, with a bridge of three arches over it. From hence you have two good hours more to Tripoli. I took the more exact account of all these streams to the intent that I might give some light, for the better deciding that difference which is found in geographers about the place of the river Eleutherus. The moderns, all with one consent, give that name to a river between Tyre and Sidon, called by the Turks Casimeer. But this contradicts the universal testimony of the ancients, who place Eleutherus more northward. Strabo will have it somewhere between Orthosia and Tripoli, as a boundary dividing Syria from Phœnicia ‡. Pliny places it near Orthosia, emptying itself into the sea over against Aradus §. The writer of the Maccabees || lays it in the land of Hamath, which country, whatever it were, was certainly without the borders of Israel, as appears from the same author. To this Josephus agrees, placing Eleutherus to the north of Sidon, as may be collected from him ¶, where, speaking of Mark Antony's donation to Cleopatra, he reports how that extravagant gallant gave her

---

* Nat. Hist., lib. v. cap. 20. † Gen. x. 18.
‡ Strabo, p. 518. § Nat. Hist., lib. v. cap. 20.
|| 1 Mac. xii. 25, 30. ¶ Antiq. Jud., lib. 14, cap. 7, 8.

all the cities between Eleutherus and Egypt, except Tyre and
Sidon. Ptolemy, as cited by Terranius, places it yet more
northerly, between Orthosia and Balnea. From all which it
is evident that this cannot be the true ancient Eleutherus,
which the moderns assign for it. But that name is rather to
be ascribed to one of these rivers crossing the plain of Junia;
or else (if Pliny's authority may be relied upon) to that river
(now dry) which I mentioned a little on this side of Tortosa,
and which has its mouth almost opposite to Aradus. But I
will not determine any thing on this point, contenting myself
to have given an account of the several rivers as we passed them.

March 9.—Drawing towards Tripoli, our muleteers were
afraid to advance, lest their beasts might be pressed for
public service; as they were afterwards, in spite of all their
caution, to our vexation. So we left them in the plain of
Junia, and proceeded ourselves to Tripoli, where we arrived
about sunset. Our whole stage this day was ten hours.

At Tripoli we reposed a full week, being very generously
entertained by Mr. Francis Hastings, the consul, and Mr.
John Fisher, merchant; theirs being the only English house
in Tripoli.

Tripoli is seated about half an hour from the sea. The
major part of the city lies between two hills; one on the east,
on which is a castle commanding the place; another on the
west, between the city and the sea. This latter is said to
have been at first raised and to be still increased by the daily
accession of sand, blown to it from the shore, upon which
occasion there goes a prophecy that the whole city shall in
time be buried with this sandy hill. But the Turks seem not
very apprehensive of this prediction; for, instead of preventing the growth of the hill, they suffer it to take its course;
and make it a place of pleasure, which they would have little
inclination to do, did they apprehend it were some time to be
their grave.

March 10.—This day we were all treated by Mr. Fisher in
the Campagnia. The place where we dined was a narrow
pleasant valley, by a river's side, distant from the city about
a mile eastward. Across the valley there runs from hill to
hill a handsome lofty aqueduct, carrying upon it so large a
body of water as suffices the whole city. It was called the
Prince's Bridge, supposed to have been built by Godfrey of
Boulloin.

March 11.—This day we all dined at consul Hastings's house, and after dinner went to wait upon Ustan, the pasha of Tripoli, having first sent our present, as the manner is amongst the Turks, to procure a propitious reception.

It is counted uncivil to visit in this country without an offering in hand. All great men expect it as a kind of tribute due to their character and authority, and look upon themselves as affronted, and, indeed, defrauded, when this compliment is omitted. Even in familiar visits amongst inferior people, you shall seldom have them come without bringing a flower, or an orange, or some other such token of their respect to the person visited; the Turks in this point keeping up the ancient oriental custom hinted in 1 Sam. ix. 7. "If we go," says Saul, "what shall we bring the man of God? there is not a present," &c., which words are questionless to be understood in conformity to this eastern custom, as relating to a token of respect, and not a price of divination.

March 12.—In the afternoon we went to visit Bell-Mount, a convent of Greeks, about two hours to the southward of Tripoli. It was founded by one of the earls of Tripoli, and stands upon a very high rocky mountain, looking over the sea; a place of very difficult ascent, though made as accessible as it was capable by the labour of the poor monks. It was our fortune to arrive there just as they were going to their evening service. Their chapel is large, but obscure, and the altar is inclosed with cancelli, so as not to be approached by any one but the priest, according to the fashion of the Greek churches. They call their congregation together by beating a kind of tune with two mallets on a long pendulous piece of plank at the church door, bells being an abomination to the Turks.

Their service consisted in precipitate and very irreverent chattering of certain prayers and hymns to our blessed Saviour, and to the blessed Virgin, and in some dark ceremonies; the priest that officiated spent at least one-third part of his time in compassing the altar, and perfuming it with a pot of incense, and then going all round the congregation, flinging his incense-pot backwards and forwards, and tendering its smoke with three repeated vibrations to every person present. Towards the end of the service there was brought into the body of the church a small table covered with a fair linen cloth, on which were placed five small cakes of bread cross way, in this form $^o_{oo}$, and in the centre of each cake was fixed a small lighted wax taper, a hole in the cake serving for a·socket.

At this ceremony the priest read the gospel concerning our Lord's feeding the multitude with five loaves. After which the bread was carried into the cancelli, and, being there suddenly broke into bits, was again brought out in a basket, and presented to every one in the assembly, that he might take a little. After this collation the priest pronounced the blessing, and so the service ended. On both sides of the body of the church were seats for the monks, in the nature of the stalls for the fellows of colleges in Oxford; and on each hand of every seat were placed crutches. These you find in like manner in most churches of this country. Their use is for the priest to lean upon, the service being sometimes so long, that they cannot well stay it out without the assistance of such easements, for they are not permitted by their rubric to sit down. The younger monks, who perhaps may have no great occasion for these supporters, do yet delight to use them (as the Spaniards do spectacles), not for any necessity, but in affectation of gravity.

The monks of this convent were, as I remember, forty in all. We found them seemingly a very good-natured, and industrious, but certainly a very ignorant people. For I found upon inquiry they could not give any manner of rationale of their own divine service. And, to show their extreme simplicity, I cannot omit a compliment made to the consul, by the chief of them, viz., that he was as glad to see him as if he had beheld the Messiah himself coming in person to make a visit to him.

Nor is this ignorance to be much wondered at; for what intervals of time they have between their hours of devotion they are forced to spend, not in study, but in managing of their flocks, cultivating their land, pruning their vineyards, and other labours of husbandry, which they accomplish with their own hands. This toil they are obliged to undergo, not only to provide for their own sustenance, but also that they may be able to satisfy the unreasonable exactions which the greedy Turks, upon every pretence they can invent, are ready to impose upon them. But, that it may be the better guessed what sort of men these Greek monks are, I will add this further indication, viz., that the same person whom we saw

officiating at the altar in his embroidered sacerdotal robe
brought us the next day, on his own back, a kid, and a goat's
skin of wine, as a present from the convent.

March 13.—This morning we went again to wait upon
Ustan pasha, by his own appointment, and were entertained
as before with great courtesy. For you must know that the
Turks are not so ignorant of civility and the arts of endear-
ment, but that they can practise them with as much exactness
as any other nation, whenever they have a mind to show
themselves obliging. For the better apprehending of which,
it may not be improper nor unpleasant here to describe the
ceremonies of a Turkish visit, as far as they have ever
fallen under my observation, either upon this or any other
occasion.

When you would make a visit to a person of quality here,
you must send one before with a present to bespeak your
admission, and to know at what hour your coming may be
most seasonable. Being come to the house, the servants
receive you at the outermost gate, and conduct you towards
their lord or master's apartment; other servants (I suppose
of better rank) meeting you in the way, at their several stations, as you draw nearer to the person you visit. Coming
into his room, you find him prepared to receive you, either
standing at the edge of the divan, or else lying down at one
corner of it, according as he thinks it proper to maintain a
greater or less distinction. These divans are a sort of low
stages, seated in the pleasantest part of the room, elevated
about sixteen or eighteen inches or more above the floor.
They are spread with carpets, and furnished all round with
bolsters for leaning upon. Upon these the Turks eat, sleep,
smoke, receive visits, say their prayers, &c. Their whole
delight is in lolling upon them; and in furnishing them richly
out is their greatest luxury.

Being come to the side of the divan, you slip off your
shoes, and stepping up take your place; which you must do
first at some distance, and upon your knees, laying your hand
very formally before you. Thus you must remain till the
man of quality invites you to draw nearer, and to put yourself
in an easier posture, leaning upon the bolster. Being thus
fixed, he discourses with you as the occasion offers, the
servants standing round all the while in a great number, and
with the profoundest respect, silence, and order imaginable.

When you have talked over your business, or the compliments, or whatever other concern brought you thither, he makes a sign to have things served in for the entertainment, which is generally a little sweetmeat, a dish of sherbet, and another of coffee; all which are immediately brought in by the servants, and tendered to all the guests in order, with the greatest care and awfulness imaginable. And they have reason to look well to it; for should any servant make but the least slip or mistake, either in delivering or receiving his dish, it might cost him fifty, perhaps one hundred drubs on his bare feet, to atone for his crime. At last comes the finishing part of your entertainment, which is perfuming the beards of the company, a ceremony which is performed in this manner. They have for this purpose a small silver chafing-dish, covered with a lid full of holes, and fixed upon a handsome plate. In this they put some fresh coals, and upon them a piece of lignum aloes, and then, shutting it up, the smoke immediately ascends with a grateful odour through the holes of the cover. This smoke is held under every one's chin, and offered as it were a sacrifice to his beard. The bristly idol soon perceives the reverence done to it, and so greedily takes in and incorporates the gummy steam, that it retains the savour of it, and may serve for a nosegay a good while after.

This ceremony may perhaps seem ridiculous at first hearing, but it passes among the Turks for a high gratification. And I will say this in its vindication, that its design is very wise and useful. For it is understood to give a civil dismission to the visitants, intimating to them that the master of the house has business to do, or some other avocation, that permits them to go away as soon as they please, and the sooner after this ceremony the better. By this means you may at any time, without offence, deliver yourself from being detained from your affairs by tedious and unseasonable visits, and from being constrained to use that piece of hypocrisy so common in the world, of pressing those to stay longer with you whom perhaps in your heart you wish a great way off for having troubled you so long already. But of this enough.

Having discharged our visit to Ustan pasha, we rode out after dinner to view the marine. It is about half an hour distant from the city. The port is an open sea rather than an inclosed harbour. However it is in part defended from the force of the waves by two small islands about two leagues out from the shore, one of which is called the Bird, the other the Coney Island, being so named from the creatures which they severally produce. For its security from pirates it has several castles, or rather square towers, built all along upon the shore at convenient distances. They are, I think, six in number; but at present void of all manner of force both of men and ammunition.

In the fields near the shore appeared many heaps of ruins and pillars of granite, and several other indications that there must have been anciently some considerable buildings this way, which agrees very well with what Casaubon, in his notes upon Strabo *, quotes out of Diodorus, viz., that the place called Tripoli was anciently a cluster of three cities, standing at a furlong's distance from each other, of which the first was a seat of the Radii, the second of the Sidonians, the third of the Tyrians; and from hence it is probable that Tripoli was a name given at first to three distinct but adjacent places, and not to one city, built, as is usually said, by the mingled interest of Tyre, Sidon, and Aradus; it being hard to conceive how three such independent commonwealths should thus concur in the founding of one city between them; and harder, how they should agree in governing it afterwards.

Sunday, March 14.—We continued still in Tripoli.

March 15.—Resolving to prosecute our journey this day, we had given orders to our muleteers, some time before, to be ready to attend us; but they had been so frightened by the pasha of Sidon's servants, who were abroad in quest of mules for the service of their master, that they were run away, and could not be heard of; a disappointment which gave us much vexation, and left us to no other remedy but only to supply ourselves with fresh beasts where we could find them.

Having, after much trouble, put ourselves in a new posture of travelling, we parted from Tripoli at three o'clock in the afternoon. Proceeding close by the sea, we came, in one hour and a half, to Callemone, a small village just under Bell-Mount. From hence, putting forward till near eight o'clock, we came to a high promontory, which lay directly across our way, and broke off abruptly at the sea-side, with a cape very high and almost perpendicular. In order to pass this barrier we turned up on the left hand into a narrow valley, through

* Page 213.

which our road lay; and, it being now late, we took up our quarters there under some olive-trees, having come, in all, about five hours.

The promontory which terminated our journey seems to be that called by Strabo * τὸ τοῦ Θεοῦ πρόσωπον, or the face of God, assigned by that author for the end of Mount Libanus. Between this place and Tripoli he mentions, likewise, a city called Trieris; but of this we saw no footsteps, unless you will allow for such some sepulchres which we saw cut in the rocks about one hour and a half before we arrived at the promontory.

March 16.—We were no sooner in motion this morning, but we were engaged in the difficult work of crossing over the forementioned cape. The pass over it lies about a mile up from the sea. We found it very deep and rugged; but in an hour or thereabout mastered it, and arrived in a narrow valley on the other side, which brought the sea open to us again. Near the entrance of this valley stands a small fort, erected upon a rock perpendicular on all sides, the walls of the building being just adequate to the sides of the rock, and seeming almost of one continued piece with them. This castle is called Temseida, and commands the passage into the valley.

In about half an hour from this place we came even with Patrone, a place esteemed to be the ancient Botrus. It is situated close by the sea; and, our road lying somewhat higher up in the land, we diverted a little out of the way to see it. We found in it some remains of an old church and a monastery; but these are now perfectly ruined and desolate, as is likewise the whole city; nor is there any thing left in it to testify it has been a place of any great consideration.

In three hours more we came to Gibyle, called by the Greeks Byblus, a place once famous for the birth and temple of Adonis. It is pleasantly situated by the sea-side. At present it contains but a little extent of ground, but yet more than enough for the small number of its inhabitants. It is compassed with a dry ditch and a wall, with square towers in it at about every forty yards' distance. On its south side it has an old castle. Within it is a church exactly of the same figure with that at Tortosa, only not so entire as that. Besides this it has nothing remarkable, though anciently it

---

* Strabo, lib. 16; Pomp. Mela, lib. i. cap. 12.

was a place of no mean extent as well as beauty, as may appear from the many heaps of ruins, and the fine pillars that are scattered up and down in the gardens near the town.

Gibyle is probably the country of the Giblites, mentioned Josh. xiii. 5. King Hiram made use of the people of this place in preparing materials for Solomon's temple, as may be collected from the first of Kings, v. 18, where the word which our translator has rendered stone-squarers, in the Hebrew is גבלים, Giblim, or Giblites, and in the LXXII Interpreters, Βύβλιοι, that is, the Men of Byblus; the former using the Hebrew, the latter the Greek name of this place. The same difference may be observed likewise in Ezekiel, xxvii. 9, where this place is again mentioned; the ancients of Gebal, says our translation, following the Hebrew; instead of which you read in the LXXII. again οἱ πρεσβύτεροι Βυβλίων, the elders of Bybli or Byblus.

Leaving Gibyle, we came in one hour to a fair, large river, with a stone bridge over it, of only one arch, but that exceeding wide and lofty. To this river the Turks give the name of Ibrahim Pasha; but it is doubtless the ancient river Adonis, so famous for the idolatrous rites performed here in lamentation of Adonis. Upon the bank of this stream we took up our quarters for the following night, having come this day about six hours. We had a very tempestuous night both of wind and rain, almost without cessation, and with so great violence that our servants were hardly able to keep up our tents over us. But, however, this accident, which gave us so much trouble in the night, made us amends with a curiosity which it yielded us an opportunity of beholding the next morning.

March 17.—For by this means we had the fortune to see what may be supposed to be the occasion of that opinion which Lucian relates concerning the river, viz., that this stream, at certain seasons of the year, especially about the feast of Adonis, is of a bloody colour, which the heathens looked upon as proceeding from a kind of sympathy in the river for the death of Adonis, who was killed by a wild boar in the mountains out of which this stream rises. Something like this we saw actually come to pass; for the water was stained to a surprising redness, and, as we observed in travelling, had discoloured the sea, a great way, into a reddish hue, occasioned, doubtless, by a sort of minium, or red earth,

washed into the river by the violence of the rain, and not by
any stain from Adonis's blood.

In an hour and a quarter from this river we passed over
the foot of the mountain Climax, where, having gone through
a very rugged and uneven pass, we came into a large bay
called Junia. At the first entrance into the bay is an old
stone bridge, which appoints the limits between the two
pashalicks of Tripoli and Sidon. At the bottom of the bay
are exceeding high and steep mountains, between which and
the sea the road lies. These are the mountains of Castravan,
chiefly inhabited by Maronites, famous for a growth of excellent wine. The Maronite bishop of Aleppo has here his residence in a convent, of which he is the guardian. We saw
many other small convents on the top of these mountains, one
of which, called Oozier, was, as we were here told, in the
hands of ten or twelve Latin friars. Towards the further side
of the bay we came to a square tower, or castle, of which kind
there are many all along upon the coast for several days'
journey from this place. They are said to have been built by
the empress Helena, for the protection of the country from
pirates. At this tower is to be paid a fourth* caphar. It is
received by Maronites, a pack of rogues more exacting and
insolent in their office than the very Turks themselves. A
little beyond this place we came to a road cut through the
rocks, which brought us out of the bay, having been one hour
and a quarter in compassing it. In an hour more, spent upon
a very rugged way, close by the sea, we came to the river
Lycus, called also, sometimes, Canis, and by the Turks, at
this day, Nahr Kelp. It derives its name from an idol in the
form of a dog or wolf, which was worshipped, and is said to
have pronounced oracles, at this place. The image is pretended to be shown to strangers at this day, lying in the sea
with its heels upward. I mean the body of it; for its oracular
head is reported to have been broken off and carried to Venice,
where (if fame be true) it may be seen at this day.

I know not by what mistake several modern geographers
confound this river with Adonis, making them to be one and
the same, whereas the contrary is apparent, both from ex-
perimental observation and from the authority of ancient
geographers.

* Half per Frank, quarter per servant.

This river issues into the sea from between two mountains
excessively steep and high, and so rocky that they seem to
consist each of one entire stone.   For crossing the river you
go up between these mountains about a bow-shot from the
sea, where you have a good bridge of four arches, near the
foot of which is a piece of white marble inlaid in the side of a
rock, with an Arab inscription on it, intimating its founder to
have been the emir Faccardine (of whom I shall have occasion
to speak more when I come to Beirout).   Being passed the
river, you immediately begin to ascend the mountain, or
rather great rock, on the other side.   To accommodate the
passage you have a path of above two yards' breadth cut
along its side, at a great height above the water, being the
work of the emperor Antoninus; for the promontory allowing
no passage between it and the sea, at bottom, that emperor
undertook, with incredible labour, to open this way above,
the memory of which good work is perpetuated by an inscription engraved on a table planed in the side of the natural
rock, not far from the entrance into the way, as follows:—

IMP: CAES: M: AURELIUS
ANTONINUS, PIUS, FELIX, AUGUSTUS
PARTH: MAX: BRIT: GERM: MAXIMUS
PONTIFEX MAXIMUS
MONTIBUS IMMINENTIBUS
LYCO FLUMINI CAESIS VIAM DILATAVIT
PER—(*purposely erased*)—
ANTONINIANAM SUAM

A little higher up in the way are inscribed these words:—

INVICTE IMP: ANTONINE P: FELIX AUG:
MULTIS ANNIS IMPERA!

In passing this way, we observed, in the sides of the rock
above us, several tables of figures carved, which seemed to
promise something of antiquity.   To be satisfied of which,
some of us clambered up to the place, and found there some
signs as if the old way had gone in that region, before Antoninus cut the other more convenient passage a little lower.
In several places thereabouts we saw strange antique figures
of men carved in the natural rock, in mezzo relievo, and in
bigness equal to the life.   Close by each figure was a large

table planed in the side of the rock, and bordered round with mouldings. Both the effigies and the tables appeared to have been anciently inscribed all over, but the characters are now so defaced, that nothing but the footsteps of them were visible. There was only one of the figures that had both its lineaments and its inscriptions entire.

It was our unhappiness to have at this place a very violent storm of thunder and rain, which made our company too much in haste to make any longer stay here. By which misfortune I was prevented, to my great regret, from copying the inscription, and making such an exact scrutiny into this antiquity as it seemed very well to deserve. I hope some curious traveller or other will have better success in passing this way hereafter. The figures seemed to resemble mummies, and were perhaps the representation of some persons buried hereabout, whose sepulchres might probably also be discovered by the diligent observer.

The Antonine way extends about a quarter of an hour's travel. It is at present so broken and uneven, that to repair it would require no less labour than that wherewith it was at first made. After this pass you come upon a smooth sandy shore, which brings you in about one hour and a half to the river Beirout (for I could learn no other name it had). It is a large river, and has over it a stone bridge of six arches. On its other side is a plain field near the sea, which is said to be the stage on which St. George duelled and killed the dragon. In memory of this achievement there is a small chapel built upon the place, dedicated at first to that Christian hero, but now perverted to a mosque. From thence, in an hour, we arrived at Beirout, very wet by reason of the long and severe rain. However, we found here the shelter of a good khan by the sea-side, and there we took up our quarters. Our whole stage, this day, was about six hours and a half.

March 18.—The day following we spent at Beirout, being credibly informed that the river Damer, which lay in our next stage, was so swollen by the late rains that it would be impassable. This place was anciently called Berytus, from which the idol Baal-Berith is supposed to have had its name; and afterwards, being greatly esteemed by Augustus, had many privileges conferred upon it, and together with them a new name, viz. Julia Felix. But at present it retains nothing of its ancient felicity, except the situation, and in that particular

it is indeed very happy. It is seated on the sea-side, in a
soil fertile and delightful, raised only so high above the salt
water as to be secure from its overflowings, and all other
noxious and unwholesome effects of that element. It has the
benefit of good fresh springs flowing down to it from the adjacent hills, and dispensed all over the city, in convenient and
not unhandsome fountains. But, besides these advantages of
its situation, it has at present nothing else to boast of.

The emir Faccardine had his chief residence in this place.
He was in the reign of sultan Morat, the fourth emir, or
prince of the Druses, a people supposed to have descended
from some dispersed remainder of those Christian armies that
engaged in the crusades for the recovery of the Holy Land*,
who afterwards being totally routed, and despairing of a return to their native country again, betook themselves to the
mountains hereabout, in which their descendants have continued ever since. Faccardine, being (as I said) prince of
these people, was not contented to be penned up in the mountains, but by his power and artifice enlarged his dominions
down into the sea-coast, as far from this place to Acre. At
last the Grand Seignior, growing jealous of such a growing
power, drove the wild beast back again to the mountains from
whence he had broke loose; and there his posterity retain
their principality to this day.

We went to view the palace of this prince, which stands
on the north-east part of the city. At the entrance of it is a
marble fountain, of greater beauty than is usually seen in
Turkey. The palace within consists of several courts, all now
run much to ruin, or rather perhaps never finished. The
stables, yards for horses, dens for lions and other savage creatures, gardens, &c., are such as would not be unworthy of the
quality of a prince in Christendom, were they wrought up to
that perfection of which they are capable, and to which they
seem to have been designed by their first contriver.

But the best sight that this palace affords, and the most
worthy to be remembered, is the orange garden. It contains
a large quadrangular plot of ground, divided into sixteen
lesser squares, four in a row, with walks between them. The
walks are shaded with orange-trees, of a large spreading size,

* This is certainly an erroneous notion : the Druses are alluded to by the
rabbi Benjamin in the 12th century. See pp. 79, 80.

and all of so fine a growth both for stem and head, that one
cannot imagine any thing more perfect of this kind. They
were, at the time when we were there, as it were gilded with
fruit, hanging thicker upon them than ever I saw apples in
England. Every one of these sixteen lesser squares in the
garden was bordered with stone, and in the stonework were
troughs very artificially contrived, for conveying the water all
over the garden, there being little outlets cut at every tree,
for the stream, as it passed by, to flow out and water it
Were this place under the cultivation of an English gardener,
it is impossible any thing could be made more delightful.
But these Hesperides were put to no better use, when we
saw them, than to serve as a fold for sheep and goats, insomuch that in many places they were up to the knees in dirt.
So little sense have the Turks of such refined delights as
these, being a people generally of the grossest apprehension,
and knowing few other pleasures but such sensualities as are
equally common both to man and beast. On the east side
of this garden were two terrace-walks, rising one above the
other, each of them having an ascent to it of twelve steps.
They had both several fine spreading orange-trees upon them,
to make shades in proper places. And at the north end they
led into booths, and summer-houses, and other apartments,
very delightful ; this place being designed by Faccardine for
the chief seat of his pleasure.

It may perhaps be wondered how this emir should be able
to contrive any thing so elegant and regular as this garden,
seeing the Turkish gardens are usually nothing else but a
confused miscellany of trees jumbled together, without either
knots, walks, arbours, or any thing of art or design, so that
they seem like thickets rather than gardens. But Faccardine
had been in Italy, where he had seen things of another
nature, and knew well how to copy them in his own country;
for indeed it appears, by these remains of him, that he must
needs have been a man much above the ordinary level of a
Turkish genius.

In another garden we saw several pedestals for statues,
from whence it may be inferred that this emir was no very
zealous Mohammedan. At one corner of the same garden
stood a tower of about sixty feet high, designed to have been
carried to a much greater elevation for a watch-tower, and for
that end built with an extraordinary strength, its walls being

twelve feet thick. From this tower we had a view of the whole city. Amongst other prospects, it yielded us the sight of a large Christian church, said to have been at first consecrated to St. John the Evangelist; but, it being now usurped by the Turks for their chief mosque, we could not be permitted to see it, otherwise than at this distance. Another church there is in the town, which seems to be ancient; but, being a very mean fabric, it is suffered to remain still in the hands of the Greeks. We found it adorned with abundance of old pictures. Amongst the rest I saw one with this little inscription, Κούαρτος πρωτος Αρχιεπίσκοπος Βηρούτου; and just by it was the figure of Nestorius, who commonly makes one amongst the saints painted in the Greek churches, though they do not now profess, nor, I believe, so much as know his heresy. But that which appeared most observable was a very odd figure of a saint, drawn at full length, with a large beard reaching down to his feet. The curate gave us to understand that this was St. Nicephorus; and, perceiving that his beard was the chief object of our admiration, he gratified us with the following relation concerning him; viz., That he was a person of the most eminent virtue in his time; but his great misfortune was, that the endowments of his mind were not set off with the outward ornament of a beard. Upon occasion of which defect he fell into a deep melancholy. The devil, taking advantage of this priest, promised to give him that boon which nature had denied, in case he would comply with his suggestion. The beardless saint, though he was very desirous of the reward proposed, yet he would not purchase it at that rate neither, but rejected the previous bribe with indignation, declaring resolutely that he had rather for ever despair of his wish than obtain it upon such terms; and, at the same time, taking in hand the downy tuft upon his chin, to witness the stability of his resolution (for he had, it seems, beard enough to swear by), behold! as a reward for his constancy, he found the hair immediately stretch with the pluck that he gave it. Whereupon, finding it in so good a humour, he followed the happy omen; and, as young heirs that have been niggardly bred, generally turn prodigals when they come to their estates, so he never desisted from pulling his beard till he had drawn it down to his feet. But enough both of the beard and the story. At the east end of Beirout are to be seen seven or eight beautiful pillars of granite, each . . . .

feet long, and three in diameter. And over another gate, not far distant, we found on a piece of marble the following inscription: Τῆς τοῦ προσίοντος ἀνδρὸς ἐννοίας αἰεὶ σαφὴς ἔληγχος, ἡ πρόσοψις γείνεται δίδου προθυμῶς ὃ παρέχεις ἢ μὴ δίδου παρὰ γὰρ τὸ μειχρὸν γείνεται πτήρης χάρις. It was probably at first an altar inscription, relating to the offertory in the holy communion, for its sense seems to look that way, and it is well known that the comers to the blessed sacrament were called by the ancients by the peculiar name of οἱ προσίοντες, as Valesius proves out of St. Chrysostom *.

On the south side the town wall is still entire, but built out of the ruins of the old city, as appears by pieces of pillars and marble which help to build it. On one piece of marble table we saw these remaining letters of a Latin inscription:—

. . . . VG. ETIA . . . . .
. . . . XI CUM . . . .
. . . . VS PHOEBUS . . . .
All the rest being purposely erased.

A little without this wall we saw many granite pillars and remnants of Mosaic floors, and in a heap of rubbish several pieces of polished marble, fragments of statues, and other poor relics of this city's ancient magnificence. On the sea-shore is an old ruined castle, and some remains of a small mole.

March 19.—Leaving Beirout, we came in one-third of an hour to a large plain extending from the sea to the mountains. At the beginning of the plain is a grove of pine-trees of Faccardine's plantation. We guessed it to be more than half a mile across; and so pleasant and inviting was its shade, that it was not without some regret that we passed it by. Continuing in this plain, we saw at a distance, on our left hand, a small village called Suckfoat. It belongs to the Druses, who possess at this day a long tract of mountains, as far as from Castravan to Carmel. Their present prince is Achmet, grandson to Faccardine, an old man, and one who keeps up the custom of his ancestors of turning day into night, an hereditary practice in his family, proceeding from a traditional persuasion amongst them, that princes can never sleep securely but by day, when men's actions and designs are best observed by their guards, and, if need be, most easily prevented; but

* Vales. Not. in Euseb. Eccl. Hist., lib. vii. cap. 9.

that in the night it concerns them to be always vigilant, lest the darkness, aided by their sleeping, should give traitors both opportunity and encouragement to assault their persons, and by a dagger or a pistol to make them continue their sleep longer than they intended when they lay down.

Two hours from Faccardine's grove brought us to the fifth caphar, and another little hour to the river Damer or Tamyras, the former being its modern, the latter its ancient name. It is a river apt to swell much upon sudden rains; in which case, precipitating itself from the mountains with great rapidity, it has been fatal to many passengers. Amongst the rest, one Monsieur Spon, nephew to Dr. Spon, coming from Jerusalem about four years ago, in company with some English gentlemen, in passing this stream, was hurried down by it, and perished in the sea, which lies about a furlong lower than the passage.

We had the good fortune to find the river in a better temper, its waters being now assuaged since the late rains. However, the country fellows were ready here, according to their trade, to have assisted us in our passage over; in order to which, they had very officiously stripped themselves naked against our coming; and to the end that they might oblige us to make use of their help, for which they would be well paid, they brought us to a place where the water was deepest, pretending there was no other passage besides that, which cheat we saw them actually impose upon some other travellers, who came not long after us. But we had been advised of a place a little higher in the river, where the stream was broader and shallower, and there we easily passed without their assistance. Just by this place are the ruins of a stone bridge, of which one might guess by the firmness of its remains that it might have been still entire, had not these villains broke it down, in order to their making their advantages of passengers, either conducting them over for good pay, or else, if they have opportunity, drowning them for their spoils.

On the other side of the river, the mountains approach closer to the sea, leaving only a narrow rocky way between. From Damer, in two hours, we came to another river of no inconsiderable figure, but not once mentioned by any geographer that I know of. It is within one hour of Sidon. Its channel is deep, contains a good stream, and has a large stone

bridge over it. Speaking of this river to the reverend father
Stephano, Maronite patriarch at Canobine, he told me it was
called Awle, and had its fountain near Berook, a village in
Mount Libanus.

At this river we were met by several of the French merchants from Sidon, they having a factory there the most considerable of all theirs in the Levant. Being arrived at Sidon,
we pitched our tents by a cistern without the city, but were
ourselves conducted by the French gentlemen to the place of
their habitation, which is a large khan close by the sea, where
the consul and all the nation are quartered together. Before
the front of this khan is an old mole running into the sea
with a right angle; it was of no capacity at best, but now is
rendered perfectly useless, having been purposely filled up
with rubbish and earth by Faccardine, to prevent the Turkish
galleys from making their unwelcome visits to this place.
The mole being thus destroyed, all ships that take in their
burden here are forced to ride at anchor under the shelter of
a small ridge of rocks about a mile distant from the shore, on
the north side of the city. Sidon is stocked well enough
with inhabitants, but is very much shrunk from its ancient
extent, and more from its splendour, as appears from a great
many beautiful pillars that lie scattered up and down the gardens without the present walls. Whatever antiquities may at
any time have been hereabout, they are now all perfectly obscured and buried by the Turkish buildings. Upon the south
side of the city, on a hill, stands an old castle, said to have
been the work of Louis IX. of France, surnamed the saint;
and not far from the castle is an old unfinished palace of Faccardine's, serving, however, the pasha for his seraglio, neither
of them worth mentioning, had the city afforded us any thing
else more remarkable. Near about Sidon begin the precincts of the Holy Land, and of that part of it in particular
which was allotted to Asher; the borders of which tribe extended from Carmel as far as Great Zidon, as appears from
Josh. xix. 26, 28. But the people upon the sea-coast were
never actually mastered by the Israelites, being left by the
just judgment of God to be thorns in their sides, for a reason
that may be seen in Judges. ii. 1—3, &c.

The person who is the French consul at Sidon has also
the title of consul of Jerusalem, and is obliged by his master,
the French king, to make a visit to the holy city every Easter,

under pretence of preserving the sanctuary there from the violations, and the friars who have the custody of it from the exactions, of the Turks. But the friars think themselves much safer without this protection. We were desirous to join with Monsieur l'Empereur, the present consul, in this year's pilgrimage, and, accordingly, had sent him a letter from Aleppo on purpose to bespeak that favour, hoping by his protection to pass more securely from the abuses of the Arabs and Turks, who are nowhere so insolent as in Palestine and about Jerusalem. We had his promise to stay for us ; but the remoras and disappointments we met with on the road had put us so backward in our journey, that, fearing to be too late at Jerusalem, he set out from Sidon the day before our arrival there, leaving us, however, some hopes, that if we made the best of our way we might come up with him at Acra, where he promised to expect our coming to the latest moment.

March 20.—Being desirous, therefore, not to lose the convenience of his company, we set out early the next morning from Sidon, and, travelling in a very fruitful plain, came in half an hour to a place where we found a large pillar of granite lying across the high way, and sunk a good part under ground. Observing some letters upon it, we took the pains to dig away the earth, by which means we recovered this fragment of an inscription :—

IMPERATORES

CAESARES

L SEPTIMUS SE

VERUS PIUS PER

TINAX AUG: ARA

BICUS ADIABENICUS

PARTHICUS MAXI

MUS TRIBUNICIA

POTES: VI. IMP: XI. COS [ ]

PRO . COS . P . P

ET M . AUREL: ANTONI

NUS AUG: FILIUS . EJUS

. . . . ET . . . . . ARIA

. . . . EN . . . OIUM . RV

FVM . . . .

. . . . IC PR: PRAET

. . . PROVINC . SYRIAE

[ET PHAE] NIC RENOVAVERUNT

. [　] .

Some gentlemen of our nation, in their journey to Jerusalem this last Easter, anno 1699, found another pillar, about
midway between the one we saw and Sidon, of the same make
and use, from which they took the aforesaid inscription more
perfectly.   As far as *filius ejus* there is no variation, and after
that it goes on thus : —

VIAS ET MILLIARIA

FR . . . O . VENIDIVMRV

FVM . LEG . AUGG .

L . . . PR . PRÆSIDEM

PROVINC . SYRIAEPHOE

NIC . RENOVAVERUNT

. I .

By which we may observe the exactness of the Romans in
measuring out their roads, and marking down upon every pillar the number of miles, as I. II. III., &c.

A little beyond this pillar, we passed in sight of Ko-ri-e, a
large village on the side of the mountains, and in two hours
and a half more came to Sarphan, supposed to be the ancient
Sarephath, or Sarepta, so famous for the residence and
miracles of the prophet Elijah.   The place shown us for this
city consisted of only a few houses on the tops of the mountains, within about half a mile of the sea; but it is more
probable the principal part of the city stood below, in the
space between the hills and the sea, there being ruins still to
be seen in that place of considerable extent.   From thence,
in three hours, we arrived at Casimeer, a river large and
deep, running down to the sea through a plain, in which it
creeps along with various meanders and turnings.   It had
once a good stone bridge laid over it of four arches; but of
that nothing remains at present except the supporters, between which there are laid beams and boards to supply the
room of the arches, and to make a passage over; but so care-
less and loose is the fabric, that it looks like a trap rather
than a bridge.   We had one horse dropped through, notwithstanding our utmost care to prevent such misfortunes; but it
was our good luck to recover him again safe on shore.

This river is assigned by our modern geographers for the old
Eleutherus, but how erroneously has been before mentioned.
Strabo mentions a certain river falling into the sea near Tyre,

on this side *, which can be no other than this, but he omits to acquaint us with its name.   Within a bow-shot of the river Casimeer is a khan of the same name, from which, keeping near the sea-side, you arrive in an hour at Tyre.

This city, standing in the sea upon a peninsula, promises at a distance something very magnificent; but, when you come to it, you find no similitude of that glory for which it was so renowned in ancient times, and which the prophet Ezekiel describes †.   On the north side it has an old Turkish ungarrisoned castle, besides which you see nothing here but a mere Babel of broken walls, pillars, vaults, &c., there being not so much as one entire house left.   Its present inhabitants are only a few poor wretches, harbouring themselves in the vaults, and subsisting chiefly upon fishing, who seem to be preserved in this place by Divine Providence, as a visible argument how God has fulfilled his word concerning Tyre, viz. that it should be as the top of a rock, a place for fishers to dry their nets on ‡.

In the midst of the ruins there stands up one pile, higher than the rest, which is the east end of a great church, probably of the cathedral of Tyre ; and why not the very same that was erected by its bishop Paulinus, and honoured with that famous consecration sermon of Eusebius, recorded by himself §, this having been an archiepiscopal see in the Christian times ?

I cannot, in this place, omit an observation made by most of our company in this journey, viz. that in all the ruins of churches which we saw, though their other parts were totally demolished, yet the east end we always found standing and tolerably entire.   Whether the Christians, when overrun by infidels, redeemed their altars from ruin with money ; or whether even the barbarians, when they demolished the other parts of the churches, might voluntarily spare these out of an awe and veneration ; or whether they have stood thus long by virtue of some peculiar firmness in the nature of their fabric ; or whether some occult providence has preserved them as so many standing monuments of Christianity in these unbelieving regions, and presages of its future restoration, I will not determine.   This only I will say, that we found it, in fact, so as I described in all the ruined churches that came in our

---

* Πρὸς Τύρω Ποταμὸς ἐξίησι, p. 521.   † Ezek. xxvi. 27, 28.
‡ Ezek. xxvi. 14.   § Eccl. Hist., lib. x. cap. 4.

way, being perhaps not fewer than one hundred; nor do I
remember ever to have seen one instance of the contrary.
This might justly seem a trifling observation were it founded
upon a few examples only; but it being a thing so often, and
indeed universally, observed by us, throughout our whole
journey, I thought it must needs proceed from something
more than blind chance, and might very well deserve this
animadversion.

But to return from this digression, there being an old staircase in this ruin last mentioned, I got up to the top of it,
from whence I had an entire prospect of the island, part of
Tyre, of the isthmus, and of the adjacent shore. I thought I
could, from this elevation, discern the isthmus to be a soil of
a different nature from the other two, it lying lower than
either, and being covered all over with sand which the sea
casts upon it as the tokens of its natural right to a passage
there, from which it was, by Alexander the Great, injuriously
excluded. The island of Tyre, in its natural state, seems to
have been of a circular figure, containing not more than forty
acres of ground. It discovers still the foundations of a wall,
which anciently encompassed it round at the utmost margin
of the land. It makes, with the isthmus, two large bays, one
on its north side and the other on its south. These bays are
in part defended from the ocean, each by a long ridge, resembling a mole, stretching directly out, on both sides, from the
head of the island; but these ridges, whether they were walls
or rocks, whether the work of art or nature, I was too far
distant to discern.

Coming out of these ruins, we saw the foundation of a very
strong wall, running across the neck of land, and serving as
a barrier to secure the city on this side. From this place we
were one-third of an hour in passing the sandy isthmus, before
we came to the ground which we apprehended to be the
natural shore. From hence, passing over part of a very fertile
plain, which extends itself to a vast compass before Tyre, we
arrived, in three quarters of an hour, at Ras-el-ayn. Our whole
stage, from Sidon hither, was about eight hours.

Sunday, March 21.—Ras-el-ayn is a place where are the
cisterns called Solomon's, supposed, according to the common
tradition hereabouts, to have been made by that great king, as
a part of his recompense to king Hiram for the supplies of
materials sent by him toward the building of the temple.

They are doubtless very ancient, but yet of a much later date than what this tradition ascribes to them. That they could not be built till since Alexander's time may be conjectured from this, amongst other arguments : because the aqueduct, which conveys the water from hence to Tyre, is carried over the neck of land by which Alexander, in his famous siege of this place, joined the city to the continent; and, as the cisterns cannot well be imagined to be more ancient than the aqueduct, so one may be sure the aqueduct cannot be older than the ground it stands upon. Of these cisterns there are three entire at this day, one about a furlong and a half distant from the sea, the other two a little farther up.

The former is of an octagonal figure, twenty-two yards in diameter. It is elevated above the ground, nine yards on the south side and six on the north ; and, within, is said to be of an unfathomable deepness ; but ten yards of line confuted that opinion. Its wall is of no better a material than gravel and small pebbles; but consolidated with so strong and tenacious a cement, that it seems to be all one entire vessel of rock. Upon the brink of it you have a walk round, eight feet broad, from which, descending by one step on the south side, and by two on the north, you have another walk twenty-one feet broad. All this structure, though so broad at top, is yet made hollow, so that the water comes in underneath the walks, insomuch that I could not, with a long rod, reach the extremity of the cavity. The whole vessel contains a vast body of excellent water, and is so well supplied from its fountain that, though there issues from it a stream like a brook, driving four mills between this place and the sea, yet it is always brim full. On the east side of this cistern was the ancient outlet of the water, by an aqueduct raised about six yards from the ground, and containing a channel one yard wide; but this is now stopped up and dry, the Turks having broke an outlet on the other side, deriving thence a stream for grinding their corn.

The aqueduct (now dry) is carried eastward about one hundred and twenty paces, and then approaches the two other cisterns, of which one is twelve, the other twenty yards square. These have each a little channel, by which they anciently rendered their waters into the aqueduct; and so the united streams of all the three cisterns were carried together to Tyre. You may trace out the aqueduct all along by the

remaining fragments of it. It goes about one hour northward; and then, turning to the west at a small mount, where
anciently stood a fort, but now a mosque, it proceeds over the
isthmus into the city. As we passed by the aqueduct we observed in several places, on its sides and under its arches,
rugged heaps of matter resembling rocks. These were produced by the leakage of the water, which petrified as it
distilled from above, and, by the continual adherence of new
matter, were grown to a large bulk. That which was most
remarkable in them was the frame and configuration of their
parts. They were composed of innumerable tubes of stone,
of different sizes, cleaving to one another like icicles. Each
tube had a small cavity in its centre, from which its parts
were projected, in form of rays, to the circumference, after
the manner of the stones vulgarly called thunder-stones.

The fountain of these waters is as unknown as the contriver
of them. It is certain, from their rising so high, they must
be brought from some part of the mountains, which are about
a league distant; and it is as certain that the work was well
done at first, seeing it performs its office so well at so great a
distance of time.

Leaving this pleasant quarter we came, in an hour and a
half, to the white promontory, so called from the aspect it
yields toward the sea. Over this you pass by a way about
two yards broad, cut along its side, from which the prospect
down is very dreadful, by reason of the extreme depth and
steepness of the mountain, and the raging of the waves at
bottom. This way is about one-third of an hour over, and is
said to have been the work of Alexander the Great. About
one-third of an hour farther you pass by a heap of rubbish,
close by the sea-side, being the ruins of the castle Scandalium,
taking its name from its founder, the same Alexander, whom
the Turks call Scander. The ruin is one hundred and twenty
paces square, having a dry ditch encompassing it; and from
under it, on the side next the sea, there issues a fountain
of very fair water. In an hour from hence you come to the
sixth caphar, called Nachera; and in another hour to the plain
of Acra, over a very deep and rugged mountain, supposed to
be part of Mount Saron. All the way from the white promontory to this plain is exceeding rocky; but here the pleasantness of the road makes you amends for the former labour.

The plain of Acra (Acre) extends itself, in length, from Mount

Saron as far as Carmel, which is at least six good hours ; and in breadth, between the sea and the mountains, it is in most places two hours over. It enjoys good streams of water at convenient distances, and every thing else that might render it both pleasant and fruitful; but this delicious plain is now almost desolate, being suffered, for want of culture, to run up to rank weeds, which were, at the time when we passed it, as high as our horses' backs.

Having travelled about one hour in the plain of Acra, we passed by an old town called Zib, situate on an ascent close by the sea-side. This may probably be the old Achzib*, called afterwards Ecdippa; for St. Jerome places Achzib nine miles distant from Ptolemais toward Tyre, to which account we found the situation of Zib exactly agreeing. This is one of the places out of which the Ashurites could not expel the Canaanitish natives. Two-hours farther we came to a fountain of very good water, called by the French merchants, at Acra, the fountain of the blessed Virgin. In one hour more we arrived at Acra. Our whole stage, from Ras-el-ayn hither, was about eight hours and a half.

Acra had anciently the name of Accho, and is another of the places out of which the children of Israel could not drive the primitive inhabitants†. Being in after times enlarged by Ptolemy the First, it was called by him, from his own name, Ptolemais; but now, since it has been in the possession of the Turks, it has, according to the example of many other cities in Turkey, cast off its Greek‡, and recovered some semblance of its old Hebrew name again, being called Acca, or Acra.

This city was for a long time the theatre of contention between the Christians and infidels, till at last, after having divers times changed its masters, it was, by a long siege, finally taken by the Turks, and ruined by them in such a manner as if they had thought they could never take a full revenge upon it for the blood it had cost them, or sufficiently prevent such slaughters for the future. As to its situation, it enjoys all possible advantages both of sea and land. On its north and east sides it is compassed with a spacious and fertile

---

* Mentioned Josh. xix. 29, and Jud. i. 31.   † Judges, i. 31.

‡ Ammianus Marcellinus says the Greek and Roman names of places never took amongst the natives of this country, which is the reason that most places retain their first oriental names at this day.—Hist. lib. xiv., non longe ab initio.

plain; on the west it is washed by the Mediterranean Sea; and on the south by a large bay, extending from the city as far as Mount Carmel.

But notwithstanding all these advantages, it has never been able to recover itself since its last fatal overthrow; for, besides a large khan, in which the French factors have taken up their quarters, and a mosque, and a few poor cottages, you see nothing here but a vast and spacious ruin. It is such a ruin, however, as sufficiently demonstrates the strength of the place in former times. It appears to have been encompassed, on the land side, by a double wall, defended with towers at small distances; and without the walls are ditches, ramparts, and a kind of bastions faced with hewn stone. In the fields without these works we saw, scattered up and down upon the ground, several large balls of stone, of at least thirteen or fourteen inches diameter, which were part of the ammunition used in battering the city, guns being then unknown. Within the walls there still appear several ruins, which seem to distinguish themselves from the general heaps by some marks of a greater strength and magnificence, as, first, those of the cathedral church, dedicated to St. Andrew, which stands not far from the sea-side, more high and conspicuous than the other ruins; secondly, the church of St. John, the tutelar saint of this city; thirdly, the convent of the Knights Hospitallers, a place whose remaining walls sufficiently testify its ancient strength; and, not far from the convent, the palace of the grand master of that order, the magnificence of which may be guessed from a large staircase and part of a church, still remaining in it; fourthly, some remains of a large church formerly belonging to a nunnery, of which they tell this memorable story. The Turks, having pressed this city with a long and furious siege, at last entered it by storm, May 19, 1291; in which great extremity the abbess of the nunnery, fearing lest she, and those under her care, might be forced to submit to such bestialities as are usual in cases of that deplorable nature, used this cruel but generous means for securing both herself and them. She summoned all her flock together, and exhorted them to cut and mangle their faces as the only way to preserve their virgin purity; and, to show how much she was in earnest, she immediately began, before them all, to make herself an example of her own counsel. The nuns were so animated by this heroical resolution and pattern of the

abbess, that they began instantly to follow her example,
cutting off their noses, and disfiguring their faces with such
terrible gashes as might excite horror, rather than lustful
desires, in the beholders, the consequence of which was, that
the soldiers, breaking into the nunnery, and seeing, instead
of those beautiful ladies they expected, such tragical spectacles, took a revenge for their disappointed lusts by putting
them all to the sword, thus restoring them, as in charity we
may suppose, to a new and inviolable beauty.   But, to go on,
many other ruins here are of churches, palaces, monasteries,
forts, &c., extending for more than half a mile in length, in
all which you may discern marks of so much strength as if
every building in the city had been contrived for war and
defence *.

But that which pleased us most at Acra was to find the
French consul, Monsieur l'Empereur, there, who had been so
generous as to make a halt of two days, in expectation of our
arrival.   But he had stayed to the utmost extent of his time,
and therefore resolved to set forward again the next morning.
Our greatest difficulty was to determine which road to take;
whether that upon the coast by Cæsarea and Joppa, or that by
Nazareth; or a middle way between both the other, over the
plain of Esdraelon.

The cause of this uncertainty was the embroilments and
factions that were then amongst the Arabs, which made us
desirous to keep as far as possible out of the way.   It is the
policy of the Turks always to sow divisions amongst these
wild people, by setting up several heads over their tribes,
often deposing the old and placing new ones in their stead,
by which art they create contrary interests and parties amongst
them, preventing them from ever uniting under any one
prince; which, if they should have the sense to do (being so
numerous and almost the sole inhabitants thereabouts), they
might shake off the Turkish yoke, and make themselves
supreme lords of the country.

But, however useful these discords may be to the Turks in
this respect, yet a stranger is sure to suffer by them, being

---

* Acre has gained a new celebrity by the events of which it has been the
scene in more recent times.   Most of the ruins described by Maundrell have
disappeared to make place for modern buildings; and the population, said to
have been not more than 300 or 400 in the seventeenth century, is now estimated at above 20,000.

made a prey to each party according as he happens to come in
their way; avoiding which abuses, we resolved to take the
middle way, as the most secure at this time.

March 22.—According to which purpose we set out early
the next morning from Acra, having with us a band of
Turkish soldiers for our securer convoy. Our road lay, for
about half an hour, along by the side of the Bay of Acra; and
then, arriving at the bottom of the bay, we turned southward.
Here we passed a small river which we took to be Belus,
famous for its sand, which is said to be an excellent material
for making glass, as also to have ministered the first occasion
and hint of that invention.

Here we began to decline from the sea-coast, upon which
we had travelled so many days before, and to draw off
more easterly, crossing obliquely over the plain, and in two
good hours we arrived at its farthest side, where it is bounded
by Mount Carmel. Here you find a narrow valley letting you
out of the Plain of Acra into that of Esdraelon. Hereabouts
is the end of the tribe of Asher, and the beginning of that of
Zabulon; the borders of these two tribes being thus described
in Joshua, xix. 26.

Passing through the narrow valley which makes a communication between the two plains, we arrived in two hours
at that ancient river, the river Kishon; which cuts its way
down the middle of the Plain of Esdraelon, and then, continuing its course close by the side of Mount Carmel, falls
into the sea at a place called Caypha. In the condition we
saw it, its waters were low and inconsiderable; but, in passing
along the side of the plain, we discerned the tracks of many
lesser torrents falling down into it from the mountains, which
must needs make it swell exceedingly upon sudden rains, as
doubtless it actually did at the destruction of Sisera's host*.
In three hours and a half from Kishon we came to a small
brook, near which was an old village and a good khan called
Legune, not far from which we took up our quarters this
night. From this place we had a large prospect of the Plain
of Esdraelon, which is of a vast extent and very fertile, but
uncultivated; only serving the Arabs for pasturage. At
about six or seven hours' distance eastward stood within view
Nazareth, and the two mounts, Tabor and Hermon. We were
sufficiently instructed by experience, what the holy psalmist

* Judges, v. 21.

means by the dew of Hermon, our tents being as wet with it, as if it had rained all night. At about a mile's distance from us was encamped Chibly, emir of the Arabs, with his people and cattle; and below, upon the brook Kishon, lay encamped another clan of the Arabs, being the adverse party to Chibly. We had much the less satisfaction in this place, for being seated in the midst between two such bad neighbours. Our stage this day was in all eight hours; our course south-east by south, or thereabout.

March 23.—Leaving this lodging, we arrived in one-third of an hour at the emir's tents, who came out in person to take his duties of us. We paid him two caphars *, viz., one of Lagune, and another of Jeneen, and besides the caphars, whatever else he was pleased to demand. He eased us in a very courteous manner of some of our coats, which now (the heat both of the climate and season increasing upon us) began to grow not only superfluous, but burdensome.

Getting quit of Chibly we turned out of the plain of Esdraelon, and entered into the precincts of the half-tribe of Manasses. From hence our road lay for about four hours through narrow valleys, pleasantly wooded on both sides. After which, crossing another small fruitful plain, we came in half an hour to Caphar Arab, where we lodged. Our whole stage exceeded not five hours; our course being nearly as the day before.

March 24.—Having paid our caphar, we set out very early the next morning; and leaving first Arab, and then Rama (two mountain villages), on the right hand, we arrived in one hour at a fair fountain called Selee, taking its name from an adjacent village. In one hour more we came to Sebasta. Here you leave the borders of the half-tribe of Manasses, and enter into those of the tribe of Ephraim.

Sebasta is the ancient Samaria, the imperial city of the ten tribes, after their revolt from the house of David. It lost its former name in the time of Herod the Great, who raised it from a ruined to a most magnificent state, and called it, in honour of Augustus Cæsar, Sebasta. It is situate upon a long mount of an oval figure, having first a fruitful valley, and then a ring of hills running round about it. This great city is now wholly converted into gardens, and all the tokens

---

* For both caphars, eight *per* frank, and three *per* servant.

that remain to testify that there has ever been such a place, are only, on the north side, a large square piazza encompassed with pillars *; and on the east some poor remains of a great church, said to have been built by the empress Helena, over the place where St. John the Baptist was both imprisoned and beheaded. In the body of the church you go down a staircase, into the very dungeon where that holy blood was shed. The Turks (of whom here are a few poor families) hold this prison in great veneration, and over it have erected a small mosque; but for a little piece of money they suffer you to go in and satisfy your curiosity at pleasure.

Leaving Sebasta, we passed in half an hour by Sherack, and in another half hour by Barseba, two villages on the right hand; and then entering into a narrow valley lying east and west, and watered with a fine rivulet, we arrived in one hour at Naplosa.

Naplosa is the ancient Sychem, or Sychar, as it is termed in the New Testament. It stands in a narrow valley between Mount Gerizim on the south and Ebal on the north, being built at the foot of the former; for so the situation both of the city and mountains is laid down by Josephus †. " Gerizim," says he, " hangeth over Sychem;" and " Moses commanded to erect an altar toward the east, not far from Sychem, between Mount Gerizim on the right hand (that is to one looking eastward, on the south), and Hebal on the left ‡ " (that is on the north); which so plainly assigns the position of these two mountains, that it may be wondered, how geographers should come to differ so much about it, or for what reason Adrichomius should place them both on the same side of the valley of Sychem. From Mount Gerizim it was that God commanded the blessings to be pronounced upon the children of Israel, and from Mount Ebal the curses ‖. Upon the former, the Samaritans, whose chief residence is here at Sychem, have a small temple or place of worship, to which they are still wont to repair at certain seasons, for performance of the rites of their religion. What these rites are, I could not certainly learn ; but that their religion consists in the adoration of a

---

* Many of the pillars still remain. According to the accounts of modern travellers, the ruins of Sebaste appear to be more interesting than we might suppose from Maundrell's slight notice.

† Antiq. Jud., lib. v. cap. 9.   ‡ Ibid., lib. iv. cap. ult.

‖ Deut. ii. 29.

calf, as the Jews give out, seems to have more of spite than of truth in it.

Upon one of these mountains also it was that God commanded the children of Israel to set up great stones, plastered over and inscribed with the body of their law; and to erect an altar and to offer sacrifices, feasting and rejoicing before the Lord*. But now, whether Gerizim or Ebal was the place appointed for this solemnity, there is some cause to doubt. The Hebrew Pentateuch, and ours from it, assigns Mount Ebal for the use, but the Samaritan asserts it to be Gerizim.

Our company halting a little while at Naplosa, I had an opportunity to go and visit the chief priest of the Samaritans, in order to discourse with him, about this and some other difficulties occurring in the Pentateuch, which were recommended to me to be inquired about, by the learned Monsieur Job Ludolphus, author of the Æthiopic History, when I visited him at Frankford, in my passage through Germany.

As for the difference between the Hebrew and Samaritan copy, before cited, the priest pretended the Jews had maliciously altered their text, out of odium to the Samaritans; putting for Gerizim Ebal, upon no other account, but only because the Samaritans worshipped in the former mountain, which they would have, for that reason, not to be the true place appointed by God for his worship and sacrifice. To confirm this, he pleaded that Ebal was the mountain of cursing†, and in its own nature an unpleasant place; but on the contrary Gerizim was the mountain of blessing by God's own appointment, and also in itself fertile and delightful, from whence he inferred a probability that this latter must have been the true mountain, appointed for those religious festivals, and not (as the Jews have corruptly written it) Ebal. We observed that to be in some measure true which he pleaded concerning the nature of both mountains; for, though neither of the mountains has much to boast of as to their pleasantness, yet, as one passes between them, Gerizim seems to discover a somewhat more verdant fruitful aspect than Ebal. The reason of which may be, because, fronting towards the north, it is sheltered from the heat of the sun by its own shade; whereas, Ebal looking southward, and receiving the sun that comes directly upon it, must, by consequence, be rendered more scorched and unfruitful. The Samaritan priest

* Deut. xxvii. 4.   † Deut. xi. 29.

could not say that any of those great stones which God directed Joshua to set up were now to be seen in Mount Gerizim, which, were they now extant, would determine the question clearly on his side.

I inquired of him next what sort of animal he thought
those selavæ might be, which the children of Israel were so
long fed with in the wilderness*. He answered they were a
sort of fowls; and, by the description which he gave of them,
I perceived he meant the same kind with our quails. I asked
him what he thought of locusts†, and whether the history
might not be better accounted for, supposing them to be the
winged creatures that fell so thick about the camp of Israel?
But by his answer it appeared he had never heard of any
such hypothesis. Then I demanded of him what sort of
plant or fruit the dudaim or (as we translate it) mandrakes‡
were, which Leah gave to Rachel for the purchase of her
husband's embraces? He said they were plants of a large
leaf, bearing a certain sort of fruit, in shape resembling an
apple growing ripe in harvest, but of an ill savour, and not
wholesome. But the virtue of them was to help conception,
being laid under the genial bed. That the women were often
wont so to apply it at this day, out of an opinion of its prolific
virtue. Of these plants I saw several afterwards in the way
to Jerusalem; and, if they were so common in Mesopotamia
as we saw them hereabout, one must either conclude that
these could not be the true mandrakes (dudaim), or else it
would puzzle a good critic to give a reason why Rachel
should purchase such vulgar things at so beloved and contested a price.

This priest showed me a copy of the Samaritan Pentateuch, but would not be persuaded to part with it upon any
consideration. He had likewise the first volume of the English Polyglot, which he seemed to esteem equally with his
own manuscript.

Naplosa is at present in a very mean condition, in comparison of what it is represented to have been anciently. It
consists chiefly of two streets, lying parallel, under Mount
Gerizim; but it is full of people, and the seat of a pasha.

* Num. xi.   † See before, p. 8.
‡ The mandrake was a very popular object of superstition in the Middle
Ages. The fullest information on the subject will be found in the editor's
Archæological Album, p. 178.

Having paid our caphar here, we set forward again in the evening, and, proceeding in the same narrow valley between Gerizim and Ebal (not above a furlong broad), we saw on our right hand, just without the city, a small mosque, said to have been built over the sepulchre purchased by Jacob of Emmor, the father of Shechem*. It goes by the name of Joseph's Sepulchre, his bones having been here interred after their transportation out of Egypt†.

At about one third of an hour from Naplosa, we came to Jacob's Well, famous not only upon account of its author, but much more for that memorable conference which our blessed Saviour here had with the woman of Samaria‡. If it should be questioned whether this be the very well that it is pretended for, or no, seeing it may be suspected to stand too remote from Sychar for women to come so far to draw water, it is answered, that probably the city extended farther this way in former times than it does now, as may be conjectured from some pieces of a very thick wall, still to be seen not far from hence. Over the well there stood formerly a large church, erected by that great and devout patroness of the Holy Land, the empress Helena. But of this the voracity of time, assisted by the hands of the Turks, has left nothing but a few foundations remaining. The well is covered at present with an old stone vault, into which you are let down through a very straight hole: and, then, removing a broad flat stone, you discover the mouth of the well itself. It is dug in a firm rock, and contains about three yards in diameter, and thirty-five in depth, five of which we found full of water. This confutes a story commonly told to travellers who do not take the pains to examine the well, viz., that it is dry all the year round, except on the anniversary of that day on which our blessed Saviour sat upon it, but then bubbles up with abundance of water.

At this well the narrow valley of Sychem ends, opening itself into a wide field, which is probably part of that parcel of ground given by Jacob to his son Joseph. It is watered with a fresh stream rising between it and Sychem, which makes it so exceeding verdant and fruitful, that it may well be looked upon as a standing token of the tender affection of that good patriarch to the best of sons§.

---

* Gen. xxxiii. 19.   † Josh. xxiv. 32.   ‡ John iv. 5.   § Gen. xlviii. 22.

From Jacob's well our road went southward, along a very spacious and fertile valley. Having passed by two villages on the right hand, one called Howar, the other Sawee, we arrived in four hours at Khan Leban, and lodged there. Our whole stage to-day was about eight hours ; our course variable between east and south.

Khan Leban stands on the east side of a delicious vale, having a village of the same name standing opposite to it on the other side of the vale. One of these places, either the khan or the village, is supposed to have been the Lebonah mentioned in Judges, xi. 19, to which both the name and situation seem to agree.

March 25.—From Khan Leban our road lay through a more mountainous and rocky country, of which we had a specimen as soon as we were mounted the next morning, our first task being to climb a very craggy and difficult mountain. In three quarters of an hour we left, at some distance on the right hand, a village called Cinga, and in one hour more, we entered into a very narrow valley, between two high rocky hills, at the farther end of which we found the ruins of a village and of a monastery. In this very place, or hereabouts, Jacob's Bethel is supposed to have been, where he had his stony couch made easy by that beatifying vision of God, and of the angels ascending and descending, on a ladder reaching from earth to heaven*. Near this place are the limits separating between Ephraim and Benjamin†.

From hence we passed through large olive-yards, and having left first Geeb and then Selwid (two Arab villages) on the right hand, we came in an hour and a half to an old way cut with great labour over a rocky precipice, and in one hour more we arrived at Beer. This is the place to which Jonathan fled from the revenge of his brother Abimelech‡. It is supposed also to be the same with Michmas§.

Beer enjoys a very pleasant situation, on an easy declivity fronting southward. At the bottom of the hill it has a plentiful fountain of excellent water, from which it has its name. At its upper side are the remains of an old church built by the empress Helena in memory of the Blessed Virgin, who, when she was in search of the child Jesus, as it is related ‖,

---

* Gen. xxviii.   † Josh. xviii. 13.   ‡ Judges, ix. 21.
   § 1 Sam. xiv.   ‖ Luke, ii. 24.

came (as tradition adds) to this city, and not finding him
whom her soul loved in the company, she sat down weary and
pensive at so sad a disappointment, in the very place where
the church now stands; but afterwards returning to Jerusalem, she had her maternal fears turned into joy, when "she
found him sitting in the Temple amongst the doctors, both
hearing them, and asking them questions."

All along this day's travel from Khan Leban to Beer, and
also as far as we could see around, the country discovered a
quite different face from what it had before, presenting nothing to the view, in most places, but naked rocks, mountains,
and precipices; at sight of which pilgrims are apt to be much
astonished and baulked in their expectations, finding that
country in such an inhospitable condition, concerning whose
pleasantness and plenty they had before formed in their
minds such high ideas from the description given of it in the
Word of God, insomuch that it almost startles their faith,
when they reflect how it could be possible for a land like
this to supply food for so prodigious a number of inhabitants
as are said to have been polled in the twelve tribes at one
time, the number given in by Joab* amounting to no less
than thirteen hundred thousand fighting men, besides women
and children.   But it is certain that any man who is not a
little biassed to infidelity before, may see, as he passes along,
arguments enough to support his faith against such scruples.
For it is obvious for any one to observe, that these rocks and
hills must have been anciently covered with earth and cultivated, and made to contribute to the maintenance of the inhabitants, no less than if the country had been all plain;
nay, perhaps much more, forasmuch as such a mountainous
and uneven surface affords a larger space of ground for cultivation than this country would amount to if it were all reduced to a perfect level.

For the husbanding of these mountains, their manner was
to gather up the stones, and place them in several lines along
the sides of the hills in form of a wall.   By such borders they
supported the mould from tumbling, or being washed down,
and formed many beds of excellent soil rising gradually one
above another, from the bottom to the top of the mountains.

Of this form of culture you see evident footsteps, where-

* 2 Sam. 24.

ever you go, in all the mountains of Palestine. Thus the very rocks were made fruitful. And perhaps there is no spot of ground in this whole land that was not formerly improved, to the production of something or other administering to the sustenance of human life; for, than the plain countries, nothing can be more fruitful, whether for the production of corn, or cattle and consequently of milk. The hills, though improper for all cattle except goats, yet being disposed into such beds as aforesaid described, served very well to bear corn, melons, gourds, cucumbers, and such like garden stuff, which makes the principal food of these countries for several months in the year. The most rocky parts of all, which could not well be adjusted in that manner for the production of corn, might yet serve for the plantation of vines and olive trees, which delight to extract, the one its fatness, the other its sprightly juice, chiefly out of such dry and flinty places. And the great plain joining to the Dead Sea, which, by reason of its saltness, might be thought unserviceable both for cattle, corn, olives, and vines, had yet its proper usefulness for the nourishment of bees and for the fabric of honey, of which Josephus gives us his testimony *. And I have reason to believe it, because, when I was there, I perceived in many places a smell of honey and wax as strong as if one had been in an apiary. Why, then, might not this country very well maintain the vast number of its inhabitants, being in every part so productive of either milk, corn, wine, oil, or honey, which are the principal food of these eastern nations, the constitution of their bodies, and the nature of their clime, inclining them to a more abstemious diet than we use in England and other colder regions? But I hasten to Jerusalem.

Leaving Beer, we proceeded as before, in a rude stony country, which yet yielded us the sight of several old ruined villages. In two hours and one-third we came to the top of a hill, from whence we had the first prospect of Jerusalem, Rama, anciently called Gibeah of Saul, being within view on the right hand, and the plain of Jericho and the mountains of Gilead on the left. In one hour more we approached the walls of the holy city; but we could not enter immediately, it being necessary first to send a messenger to acquaint the governor of our arrival, and to desire liberty of entrance,

---

* De Bell. Jud., lib. v. c. 4.

without which preceding ceremony no Frank dares come
within the walls. We therefore passed along by the west side
of the city, and coming to the corner above Bethlehem gate,
made a stop there, in order to expect the return of our messenger. We had not waited above half an hour, when he
brought us our permission, and we entered accordingly at
Bethlehem gate. It is required of all Franks, unless they
happen to come in with some public minister, to dismount
at the gate, to deliver their arms, and enter on foot; but we,
coming in company with the French consul, had the privilege
to enter mounted and armed. Just within the gate, we turned
up a street on the left hand, and were conducted by the consul
to his own house, with most friendly and generous invitations
to make that our home as long as we should continue at
Jerusalem. Having taken a little refreshment, we went to
the Latin convent, at which all Frank pilgrims are wont to
be entertained. The guardian and friars received us with
many kind welcomes, and kept us with them at supper, after
which we returned to the French consul's to bed. And thus
we continued to take our lodging at the consul's, and our
board with the friars, during our whole stay at Jerusalem.

March 26.—The next day, being Good-Friday in the Latin
style, the consul was obliged to go into the Church of the Sepulchre, in order to keep his feast, whither we accompanied
him, although our own Easter was not till a week after theirs.
We found the church doors guarded by several Janizaries, and
other Turkish officers, who are placed here to watch that
none enter in but such as have first paid their appointed
caphar. This is more or less according to the country or the
character of the persons that enter. For Franks it is ordinarily fourteen dollars per head, unless they are ecclesiastics,
for in that case it is but half so much.

Having once paid this caphar, you may go in and out gratis
as often as you please during the whole feast, provided you
take the ordinary opportunities in which it is customary to
open the doors; but if you would have them opened at any
time out of the common course, purposely for your own private
occasion, then the first expense must be paid again.

The pilgrims being all admitted this day, the church doors
were locked in the evening, and opened no more till Easter-
day, by which we were kept in a close, but very happy confinement, for three days. We spent our time in viewing the

ceremonies practised by the Latins at this festival, and in
visiting the several holy places, all which we had opportunity
to survey, with as much freedom and deliberation as we
pleased.

And now, being got under the sacred roof, and having the
advantage of so much leisure and freedom, I might expatiate
in a large description of the several holy places which this
church (as a cabinet) contains in it; but this would be a superfluous prolixity, so many pilgrims having discharged this office
with so much exactness already, and especially our learned
sagacious countryman Mr. Sandys, whose descriptions and
draughts, both of this church and also of the other remarkable places in and about Jerusalem, must be acknowledged so
faithful and perfect, that they leave very little to be added by
aftercomers, and nothing to be corrected. I shall content
myself, therefore, to relate only what passed in the church
during this festival, saying no more of the church itself than
just what is necessary to make my account intelligible.

The church of the Holy Sepulchre is founded upon Mount
Calvary, which is a small eminence or hill upon the greater
Mount Moriah. It was anciently appropriated to the execution
of malefactors, and therefore shut out of the walls of the city
as an execrable and polluted place; but since it was made the
altar on which was offered up the precious and all sufficient
sacrifice for the sins of the whole world, it has recovered itself
from that infamy, and has been always reverenced and resorted to with such devotion by all Christians, that it has attracted the city around about it, and stands now in the midst
of Jerusalem, a great part of the hill of Sion being shut out
of the walls to make room for the admission of Calvary.

In order to the fitting of this hill for the foundation of a
church, the first founders were obliged to reduce it to a plain
area, which they did by cutting down several parts of the
rock, and by elevating others; but, in this work, care was
taken that none of those parts of the hill which were reckoned
to be more immediately concerned in our blessed Lord's
passion should be altered or diminished. Thus that very part
of Calvary where they say Christ was fastened to, and lifted
upon, his cross, is left entire, being about ten or twelve yards
square, and standing, at this day, so high above the common
floor of the church, that you have twenty-one steps or stairs
to go up to its top; and the holy sepulchre itself, which was

at first a cave hewn into the rock under ground, having had the rock cut away from it all round, is now, as it were, a grotto above ground.

The church is less than one hundred paces long, and not more than sixty wide; and yet is so contrived that it is supposed to contain under its roof twelve or thirteen sanctuaries, or places consecrated to a more than ordinary veneration, by being reputed to have some particular actions done in them relating to the death and resurrection of Christ. As, first, the place where he was derided by the soldiers; secondly, where the soldiers divided his garments; thirdly, where he was shut up whilst they digged the hole to set the foot of the cross in, and made all ready for his crucifixion; fourthly, where he was nailed to the cross; fifthly, where the cross was erected; sixthly, where the soldier stood that pierced his side; seventhly, where his body was anointed in order to his burial; eighthly, where his body was deposited in the sepulchre; ninthly, where the angels appeared to the women after his resurrection: tenthly, where Christ himself appeared to Mary Magdalen, &c. The places where these and many other things relating to our blessed Lord are said to have been done, are all supposed to be contained within the narrow precincts of this church, and are all distinguished and adorned with so many several altars.

In galleries round about the church, and also in little buildings annexed to it on the outside, are certain apartments for the reception of friars and pilgrims; and in these places almost every Christian nation anciently maintained a small society of monks, each society having its proper quarter assigned to it by the appointment of the Turks, such as the Latins, Greeks, Syrians, Armenians, Abyssinians, Georgians, Nestorians, Cophtites, Maronites, &c., all which had anciently their several apartments in the church; but these have all, except four, forsaken their quarters, not being able to sustain the severe rents and extortions which their Turkish landlords impose upon them. The Latins, Greeks, Armenians, and Cophtites keep their footing still; but of these four the Cophtites have now only one poor representative of their nation left; and the Armenians are run so much in debt that it is supposed they are hastening apace to follow the examples of their brethren, who have deserted before them.

Besides their several apartments, each fraternity have their

altars and sanctuary, properly and distinctly allotted to their
own use, at which places they have a peculiar right to perform
their own divine service, and to exclude other nations from
them.

But that which has always been the great prize contended
for by the several sects is the command and appropriation of
the holy sepulchre, a privilege contested with so much unchristian fury and animosity, especially between the Greeks
and Latins, that, in disputing which party should go into it to
celebrate their mass, they have sometimes proceeded to blows
and wounds even at the very door of the sepulchre, mingling
their own blood with their sacrifices, an evidence of which
fury the father guardian showed us in a great scar upon his
arm, which he told us was the mark of a wound given him by
a sturdy Greek priest in one of these unholy wars. Who can
expect ever to see these holy places rescued from the hands
of infidels? Or, if they should be recovered, what deplorable
contests might be expected to follow about them, seeing,
even in their present state of captivity, they are made the
occasion of such unchristian rage and animosity.

For putting an end to these infamous quarrels, the French
king interposed, by a letter to the grand vizer, about twelve
years since, requesting him to order the holy sepulchre to be
put into the hands of the Latins, according to the tenor of the
capitulation made in the year 1673, the consequence of which
letter, and of other instances made by the French king, was
that the holy sepulchre was appropriated to the Latins. This
was not accomplished till the year 1690, they alone having
the privilege to say mass in it; and though it be permitted to
Christians of all nations to go into it for their private devotions, yet none may solemnize any public office of religion
there but the Latins.

The daily employment of these recluses is to trim the
lamps, and to make devotional visits and processions to the
several sanctuaries in the church. Thus they spend their
time, many of them for four or six years together; nay, so far
are some transported with the pleasing contemplations in
which they here entertain themselves, that they will never
come out to their dying day, burying themselves (as it were)
alive in our Lord's grave.

The Latins, of whom there are always about ten or twelve
residing at the church, with a president over them, make

every day a solemn procession, with tapers and crucifixes, and other processionary solemnities, to the several sanctuaries, singing at every one of them a Latin hymn relating to the subject of each place.   These Latins being more polite and exact in their functions than the other monks here residing, and also our conversation being chiefly with them, I will only describe their ceremonies, without taking notice of what was done by others, which did not so much come under our observation.

Their ceremony begins on Good Friday night, which is called by them the *nox tenebrosa*, and is observed with such an extraordinary solemnity that I cannot omit to give a particular description of it.

As soon as it grew dusk, all the friars and pilgrims were convened in the chapel of the apparition (which is a small oratory on the north side of the holy grave, adjoining to the apartments of the Latins), in order to go in a procession round the church; but, before they set out, one of the friars preached a sermon in Italian in that chapel.   He began his discourse thus : " In questa notte tenebrosa," &c., at which words all the candles were instantly put out, to yield a livelier image of the occasion; and so we were held by the preacher for near half an hour, very much in the dark.   Sermon being ended, every person present had a large lighted taper put into his hand, as if it were to make amends for the former darkness; and the crucifixes and other utensils were disposed in order for beginning the procession.   Amongst the other crucifixes there was one of a very large size, which bore upon it the image of our Lord, as big as the life.   The image was fastened to it with great nails, crowned with thorns, besmeared with blood; and so exquisitely was it formed, that it represented in a very lively manner the lamentable spectacle of our Lord's body as it hung upon the cross.   This figure was carried all along in the head of the procession, after which the company followed to all the sanctuaries in the church, singing their appointed hymn at every one.

The first place they visited was that of the pillar of flagellation, a large piece of which is kept in a little cell just at the door of the chapel of the apparition.   There they sung their proper hymn ; and another friar entertained the company with a sermon in Spanish, touching the scourging of our Lord.

From hence they proceeded in solemn order to the prison

of Christ, where they pretend he was secured whilst the soldiers made things ready for his crucifixion. Here, likewise, they sung their hymn, and a third friar preached in French. From the prison they went to the altar of the division of Christ's garments, where they only sung their hymn, without adding any sermon. Having done here, they advanced to the chapel of the derision, at which, after their hymn, they had a fourth sermon (as I remember) in French.

From this place they went up to Calvary, leaving their shoes at the bottom of the stairs. Here are two altars to be visited, one where our Lord is supposed to have been nailed to his cross, another where his cross was erected. At the former of these they laid down the great crucifix (which I but now described) upon the floor, and acted a kind of a resemblance of Christ's being nailed to the cross; and after the hymn one of the friars preached another sermon, in Spanish, upon the crucifixion.

From hence they removed to the adjoining altar, where the cross is supposed to have been erected, bearing the image of our Lord's body. At this altar is a hole in the natural rock, said to be the very same individual one in which the foot of our Lord's cross stood. Here they set up their cross, with the bloody crucified image upon it; and, leaving it in that posture, they first sung their hymn, and then the father guardian, sitting in a chair before it, preached a passion-sermon in Italian.

At about one yard and a half distance from the hole in which the foot of the cross was fixed, is seen that memorable cleft in the rock, said to have been made by the earthquake which happened at the suffering of the God of Nature, when (as St. Matthew witnesseth*) "the rocks rent, and the very graves were opened." This cleft, as to what now appears of it, is about a span wide at its upper part, and two deep, after which it closes; but it opens again below, as you may see in another chapel contiguous to the side of Calvary, and runs down to an unknown depth in the earth. That this rent was made by the earthquake that happened at our Lord's passion, there is only tradition to prove; but that it is a natural and genuine breach, and not counterfeited by any art, the sense and reason of every one that sees it may convince

* Matt. xxvii. 51.

him ; for the sides of it fit like two tallies to each other, and
yet it runs in such intricate windings as could not well be
counterfeited by art, nor arrived at by any instruments.

The ceremony of the passion being over, and the guardian's
sermon .ended, two friars, personating the one Joseph of
Arimathea, the other Nicodemus, approached the cross, and,
with a most solemn and concerned air, both of aspect and behaviour, drew out the great nails, and took down the feigned
body from the cross.   It was an effigy so contrived that its
limbs were soft and flexible, as if they had been real flesh ;
and nothing could be more surprising than to see the two
pretended mourners bend down the arms, which were before
extended, and dispose them upon the trunk in such a manner
as is usual in corpses.

The body, being taken down from the cross, was received in
a fair, large winding sheet, and carried down from Calvary,
the whole company attending as before, to the stone of
unction.   This is taken for the very place where the precious
body of our Lord was anointed and prepared for the burial *.
Here they laid down their imaginary corpse, and casting over
it several sweet powders and spices, wrapped it up in the
winding sheet.   Whilst this was doing they sung their
proper hymn ; and afterwards one of the friars preached, in
Arabic, a funeral sermon.

These obsequies being finished, they carried off their fancied
corpse and laid it in the sepulchre, shutting up the door till
Easter morning ; and now, after so many sermons and so
long, not to say tedious, a ceremony, it may well be imagined
that the weariness of the congregation, as well as the hour of
the night, made it needful to go to rest.

March 27.—The next morning nothing extraordinary passed,
which gave many of the pilgrims leisure to have their arms
marked with the usual ensigns of Jerusalem.   The artists who
undertake the operation do it in this manner.   They have
stamps in wood of any figure that you desire, which they first
print off upon your arm with powder of charcoal ; then, taking
two very fine needles tied close together, and dipping them
often, like a pen, in certain ink, compounded, as I was informed, of gunpowder and ox-gall, they make with them small
punctures all along the lines of the figure which they have

* John, xix. 39.

printed, and then, washing the part in wine, conclude the work. These punctures they make with great quickness and dexterity, and with scarce any smart, seldom piercing so deep as to draw blood.

In the afternoon of this day, the congregation was assembled in the area before the holy grave, where the friars spent some hours in singing over the lamentations of Jeremiah, which function, with the usual procession to the holy places, was all the ceremony of this day.

Sunday, March 28.—On Easter morning the sepulchre was again set open very early. The clouds of the former morning were cleared up, and the friars put on a face of joy and serenity, as if it had been the real juncture of our Lord's resurrection; nor doubtless was this joy feigned, whatever their mourning might be, this being the day in which their Lenten discipline expired, and they were come to a full belly again.

The mass was celebrated this morning just before the holy sepulchre, being the most eminent place in the church, where the father guardian had a throne erected, and being arrayed in episcopal robes, with a mitre on his head, in the sight of the Turks, he gave the host to all that were disposed to receive it, not refusing children of seven or eight years of age. This office being ended, we made our exit out of the sepulchre, and returning to the convent, dined with the friars.

After dinner, we took an opportunity to go and visit some of the remarkable places without the city walls; we began with those on the north side.

The first place we were conducted to was a large grotto, a little without the Damascus gate, said to have been some time the residence of Jeremiah. On the left side of it is shown the prophet's bed, being a shelf on the rock, about eight feet from the ground; and not far from this is the place where they say he wrote his Lamentations. This place is at present a college of dervises, and is held in great veneration by the Turks and Jews, as well as Christians.

The next place we came to was those famous grottoes called the Sepulchres of the Kings, but for what reason they go by that name is hard to resolve; for it is certain none of the kings, either of Israel or Judah, were buried there, the Holy Scriptures assigning other places for their sepulchres, unless it may be thought, perhaps, that Hezekiah was here interred, and that these were the sepulchres of the sons of David, mentioned in 2 Chron. xxx. 33. Whoever was buried here, this is certain, that the place itself discovers so great an expense, both of labour and treasure, that we may well suppose it to have been the work of kings. You approach to it at the east side, through an entrance cut out of the natural rock, which admits you into an open court of about forty paces square, cut down into the rock with which it is encompassed instead of walls. On the south side of the court is a portico nine paces long and four broad, hewn likewise out of the natural rock. This has a kind of architrave running along its front, adorned with sculpture of fruits and flowers, still discernible, but by time much defaced. At the end of the portico on the left hand you descend to the passage into the sepulchres. The door is now so obstructed with stones and rubbish, that it is a thing of some difficulty to creep through it. But within, you arrive in a large fair room, about seven or eight yards square, cut out of the natural rock. Its sides and ceiling are so exactly square, and its angles so just, that no architect with levels and plummets could build a room more regular; and the whole is so firm and entire, that it may be called a chamber hollowed out of one piece of marble. From this room you pass into (I think) six more, one within another, all of the same fabric with the first. Of these the two innermost are deeper than the rest, having a second descent of about six or seven steps into them.

In every one of these rooms, except the first, were coffins of stone placed in niches in the sides of the chambers. They had been at first covered with handsome lids, and carved with garlands, but now most of them were broke to pieces by sacrilegious hands. The sides and ceiling of the room were always dropping with the moist damps condensing upon them; to remedy which nuisance, and to preserve these chambers of the dead dry and clean, there was in each room a small channel cut in the floor, which served to drain the drops that fall constantly into it.

But the most surprising thing belonging to these subterraneous chambers was their doors, of which there is only one that remains hanging, being left, as it were, on purpose to puzzle the beholders. It consisted of a plank of stone of about six inches in thickness, and in its other dimensions equalling the size of an ordinary door, or somewhat less. It

was carved in such a manner as to resemble a piece of wain-
scot. The stone of which it was made was visibly of the
same kind with the whole rock, and it turned upon two hinges
in the nature of axles. These hinges were of the same
entire piece of stone with the door, and were contained in
two holes of the immoveable rock, one at the top, the other
at the bottom.

From this description it is obvious to start a question,—how
such doors as these were made, whether they were cut out of
the rock in the same place and manner as they now hang, or
whether they were brought and fixed in their station like
other doors? One of these must be supposed to have been
done; and which soever part we choose as most probable, it
seems at first glance to be not without its difficulty. But thus
much I have to say, for the resolving of this riddle (which is
wont to create no small dispute amongst pilgrims), viz., that
the door which was left hanging did not touch its lintel by at
least two inches, so that I believe it might easily have been
lifted up and unhinged; and the doors which had been thrown
down had their hinges at the upper end twice as long as those
at the bottom, which seems to intimate pretty plainly by what
method this work was accomplished.

From these sepulchres we returned toward the city again,
and, just by Herod's gate, were shown a grotto full of filthy
water and mire. This passes for the dungeon in which Jeremiah was kept by Zedekiah, till enlarged by the charity of
Ebed Melech*. At this place we concluded our visits for
that evening.

March 29.—The next day being Easter-Monday, the mosolem, or governor of the city, set out, according to custom, with
several bands of soldiers to convey the pilgrims to Jordan.
Without this guard there is no going thither, by reason of the
multitude and insolence of the Arabs in these parts. The
fee to the mosolem for his company and soldiers upon this
occasion is twelve dollars for each Frank pilgrim, but if they
be ecclesiastics, six, which you must pay whether you are
disposed to go the journey or stay in the city. We went out
at St. Stephen's gate, being in all, of every nation and sex,
about two thousand pilgrims. Having crossed the Valley of
Jehoshaphat, and part of Mount Olivet, we came in half an

* Jer. xxxviii.

hour to Bethany, at present only a small village. At the first entrance into it is an old ruin which they call Lazarus's Castle, supposed to have been the mansion-house of that favourite of our Lord. At the bottom of a small descent, not far from the castle, is shown the sepulchre out of which he was raised to a second mortality, by that enlivening voice of Christ, " Lazarus, come forth." You descend into the sepulchre by twenty-five steep stairs, at the bottom of which you arrive first in a small square room, and from thence you creep down into another lesser room, about a yard and a half deeper, in which the body is said to have been laid. This place is held in great veneration by the Turks, who use it for an oratory, and demand of all Christians a small caphar for their admission into it.

About a bow-shot from thence, you pass by the place which they say was Mary Magdalen's habitation, and then, descending a steep hill, you come to the fountain of the Apostles; so called because, as the tradition goes, those holy persons were wont to refresh themselves here in their frequent travels between Jerusalem and Jericho. And indeed it is a thing very probable, and no more than I believe is done by all that travel this way, the fountain being close by the road-side, and very inviting to the thirsty passenger.

From this place you proceed in an intricate way amongst hills and valleys interchangeably, all of a very barren aspect at present, but discovering evident signs of the labour of the husbandman in ancient times. After some hours' travel in this sort of road, you arrive at the mountainous desert into which our blessed Saviour was led by the Spirit to be tempted by the devil. A most miserable, dry, barren place it is, consisting of high rocky mountains, so torn and disordered, as if the earth had here suffered some great convulsion, in which its very bowels had been turned outwards. On the left hand, looking down in a deep valley as we passed along, we saw some ruins of small cells and cottages, which they told us were formerly the habitations of hermits retiring thither for penance and mortification; and certainly there could not be found in the whole earth a more comfortless and abandoned place for that purpose. From the top of these hills of desolation, we had, however, a delightful prospect of the mountains of Arabia, the Dead Sea, and the Plain of Jericho, into which last place we descended, after about five hours' march from Jerusalem. As soon as we entered the plain, we turned up on the left hand, and going about one hour that way, came to the foot of the Quarantania, which they say is the mountain into which the devil took our blessed Saviour, when he tempted him with that visionary scene of all the kingdoms and glories of the world. It is, as St. Matthew styles it, an exceeding high mountain, and in its ascent not only difficult, but dangerous. It has a small chapel at the top, and another about half way up, founded upon a prominent part of the rock. Near this latter are several caves and holes in the side of the mountain, made use of anciently by hermits, and by some at this day, for places to keep their Lent in, in imitation of that of our blessed Saviour. In most of these grottoes we found certain Arabs quartered, with fire-arms, who obstructed our ascent, demanding two hundred dollars for leave to go up the mountain. So we departed without farther trouble, not a little glad to have so good an excuse for not climbing so dangerous a precipice.

Turning down from thence into the plain, we passed by a ruined aqueduct, and a convent in the same condition, and in about a mile's riding came to the fountain of Elisha, so called because miraculously purged from its brackishness by the prophet, at the request of the men of Jericho*. Its waters are at present received in a basin about nine or ten paces long and five or six broad, and from thence, issuing out in great plenty, divide themselves into several small streams, dispersing their refreshment to all the field between this and Jericho, and rendering it exceedingly fruitful. Close by the fountain grows a large tree spreading into boughs over the water, and here, in the shade, we took a collation with the father guardian, and about thirty or forty friars more, who went this journey with us.

At about one-third of an hour's distance from hence is Jericho, at present only a poor nasty village of the Arabs. We were here carried to see a place where Zaccheus's house is said to have stood, which is only an old square stone building, on the south side of Jericho. About two furlongs from hence, the mosolem, with his people, had encamped; and not far from them we took up our quarters this night.

March 30.—The next morning we set out very early for

---

* 2 Kings, ii. 19.

Jordan, where we arrived in two hours. We found the plain very barren as we passed along it, producing nothing but a kind of samphire, and other such marine plants. I observed in many places of the road, where puddles of water had stood, a whiteness upon the surface of the ground, which upon trial I found to be a crust of salt, caused by the water to rise out of the earth, in the same manner as it does every year in the valley of salt near Aleppo, after the winter's inundation. These saline efflorescences I found at some leagues distance from the Dead Sea, which demonstrates that the whole valley must be all over plentifully impregnated with that mineral.

Within about a furlong of the river, at that place where we visited it, there was an old ruined church and convent, dedicated to St. John, in memory of the baptizing of our blessed Lord. It is founded as near as could be conjectured to the very place where he had the honour to perform that sacred office, and to wash Him who was infinitely purer than the water itself. On the farther side of the aforementioned convent there runs along a small descent, which you may fitly call the first and outermost bank of Jordan; as far as which it may be supposed the river does, or at least did anciently, overflow at some seasons of the year, viz., at the time of harvest * ; or, as it is expressed, Chron. xii. 1., in the first month, that is in March. But at present (whether it be because the river has, by its rapidity of current, worn its channel deeper than it was formerly, or whether because its waters are diverted some other way,) it seems to have forgot its ancient greatness; for we could discern no sign or probability of such overflowings when we were there, which was the thirtieth of March, being the proper time for these inundations. Nay, so far was the river from overflowing, that it ran at least two yards below the brink of its channel.

After having descended the outermost bank, you go about a furlong upon a level strand before you come to the immediate bank of the river. This second bank is so beset with bushes and trees, such as tamarisk, willows, oleanders, &c., that you can see no water till you have made your way through them. In this thicket anciently (and the same is reported of it at this day) several sorts of wild beasts are wont to harbour themselves; whose being washed out of the covert by the

* Josh. iii. 15.

overflowings of the river, gave rise to that allusion, "He shall come up like a lion from the swelling of Jordan."*

No sooner were we arrived at the river, and dismounted, in order to satisfy that curiosity and devotion which brought us hither, but we were alarmed by some troops of Arabs appearing on the other side and firing at us, but at too great a distance to do any execution. This intervening disturbance hindered the friars from performing their service prescribed for this place, and seemed to put them in a terrible fear of their lives, beyond what appeared in the rest of the company; though, considering the sordidness of their present condition, and the extraordinary rewards which they boast to be their due in the world to come, one would think, in reason, they of all men should have the least cause to discover so great a fear of death, and so much fondness of a life like theirs.

But this alarm was soon over, and every one returned to his former purpose; some stripped and bathed themselves in the river, others cut down boughs from the trees, every man was employed one way or other to take a memorial of this famous stream. The water was very turbid, and too rapid to be swam against. For its breadth, it might be about twenty yards over; and in depth it far exceeded my height. On the other side there seemed to be a much larger thicket than on that where we were, but we durst not swim over to take any certain account of that region for fear of the Arabs, there being three guns fired just over against us, and (as we might guess by their reports) very near the river.

Having finished our design here, we were summoned to return by the mosolem, who carried us back to the middle of the plain; and there, sitting under his tent, made us pass before him, man by man, to the end he might take the more exact account of us, and lose nothing of his caphar. We seemed at this place to be near the Dead Sea, and some of us had a great desire to go nearer, and take a view of those prodigious waters. But this could not be attempted without the licence of our commander-in-chief. We therefore sent to request his permission for our going, and a guard to attend us, both which he readily granted, and we immediately prosecuted our purpose.

Coming within about half an hour of the sea, we found the

* Jerem. xlix. 19, and l. 44. See before, p. 21.

ground uneven, and varied into hillocks, much resembling those places in England where there have been anciently lime-kilns. Whether these might be the pits at which the kings of Sodom and Gomorrah were overthrown by the four kings *, I will not determine.

Coming near the sea, we passed through a kind of coppice, of bushes and reeds; in the midst of which our guide, who was an Arab, showed us a fountain of fresh water, rising not above a furlong from the sea; fresh water he called it, but we found it brackish.

The Dead Sea is inclosed on the east and west with exceeding high mountains; on the north it is bounded by the plain of Jericho, on which side also it receives the waters of Jordan. On the south it is open, and extends beyond the reach of the eye. It is said to be twenty-four leagues long, and six or seven broad.

On the shore of the lake we found a black sort of pebble, which being held in the flame of a candle soon burns, and yields a smoke of an intolerable stench. It has this property, that it loses only of its weight, but not of its bulk by burning. The hills bordering upon the lake are said to abound with this sort of sulphureous stone. I saw pieces of it at the convent of St. John, in the wilderness, two feet square. They were carved in basso relievo, and polished to as great a lustre as black marble is capable of, and were designed for the ornament of the new church at the convent.

It is a common tradition, that birds attempting to fly over this sea drop down dead into it; and that no fish, nor other sort of animal, can endure these deadly waters. The former report I saw actually confuted, by several birds flying about and over the sea without any visible harm; the latter also I have some reason to suspect as false, having observed amongst the pebbles on the shore two or three shells of fish resembling oyster-shells. These were cast up by the waves, at two hours' distance from the mouth of Jordan; which I mention, lest it should be suspected that they might be brought into the sea that way.

As for the bitumen, for which the sea had been so famous, there was none at the place where we were. But it is gathered near the mountains on both sides in great plenty. I had several lumps of it brought me from Jerusalem. It

* Gen. xiv. 10.

exactly resembles pitch, and cannot readily be distinguished from it, but by the sulphureousness of its smell and taste.

The water of the lake was very limpid, and salt to the highest degree; and not only salt, but also extremely bitter and nauseous. Being willing to make an experiment of its strength, I went into it, and found it bore up my body in swimming with uncommon force. But as for that relation of some authors, that men wading into it were buoyed up to the top, as soon as they go as deep as the navel, I found it, upon experiment, not true.

Being desirous to see the remains (if there were any) of those cities anciently situate in this place, and made so dreadful an example of the divine vengeance, I diligently surveyed the waters as far as my eye could reach; but neither could I discern any heaps of ruins, nor any smoke ascending above the surface of the water, as is usually described in the writings and maps of geographers. But yet I must not omit what was confidently attested to me by the father guardian and procurator of Jerusalem, both men in years, and seemingly not destitute either of sense or probity; viz., that they had once actually seen one of these ruins; that it was so near the shore, and the waters so shallow at that time, that they, together with some Frenchmen, went to it, and found there several pillars and other fragments of buildings. The cause of our being deprived of this sight was, I suppose, the height of the water.

On the west side of the sea is a small promontory, near which, as our guides told us, stood the monument of Lot's metamorphosed wife; part of which (if they may be credited) is visible at this day. But neither would the present occasion permit us to go and examine the truth of this relation, nor, had the opportunity served, could we give faith enough to their report to induce us to go on such an errand.

As for the apples of Sodom, so much talked of, I neither saw nor heard of any hereabouts; nor was there any tree to be seen near the lake from which one might expect such a kind of fruit*, which induces me to believe that there may be a greater deceit in this fruit than that which is usually reported of it; and that its very being as well as its beauty is a fiction, only kept up, as my Lord Bacon observes many

---

* Tacit. Hist., lib. v.; Joseph. Bell. Jud., lib. v. cap. 5.

other false notions are, because it serves for a good allusion, and helps the poet to a similitude.

In our return from the Dead Sea, at about one hour's distance from it, we came to an old ruined Greek convent. There was good part of the church remaining, with several pieces of painting entire; as the figures of several Greek saints, and over the altar the representation of our Lord's Last Supper, with this text of Holy Writ fairly inscribed Λάβετε Φάγετε, &c. Hereabout, and also in many other places of the plain, I perceived a strong scent of honey and wax (the sun being very hot); and the bees were very industrious about the blossoms of that salt weed which the plain produces. In about an hour and a half more we returned to our tents and company, at the same place where we slept the night before; and there we spent this night also.

Amongst the products of this place I saw a very remarkable fruit, called by the Arabs Za-cho-ne. It grows upon a thorny bush, with small leaves; and both in shape and colour resembles a small unripe walnut. The kernels of this fruit the Arabs bray in a mortar, and then, putting the pulp into scalding water, they skim off an oil which rises to the top. This oil they take inwardly for bruises, and apply it outwardly to green wounds, preferring it before balm of Gilead. I procured a bottle of it, and have found it upon some small trials a very healing medicine. The roses of Jericho were not to be found at this season.

March 31.—This morning we all decamped at half an hour after two, and returning the same way by which we came, arrived in about six hours near the walls of Jerusalem. Our company did not think fit to enter the city, resolving to go immediately to Bethlehem; in order to which we turned down into the valley of Jehoshaphat; and so, passing by the city, instantly took the road to the place intended.

From Jerusalem to Bethlehem is but two hours' travel. The country through which the road lies is the valley of Rephaim, as may be gathered from Josephus*, a valley so famous for being the theatre of David's victories against the Philistines†. In the road you meet with these following remarkable places: first, a place said to be the house of Simeon, that venerable old prophet who, taking our blessed Saviour in his arms, sung his nunc dimittis in the temple;

* Ant., lib. iv. cap. 10.   † 2 Sam. v. 23.

secondly, the famous turpentine tree, in the shade of which the blessed Virgin is said to have reposed when she was carrying Christ in her arms to present him to the Lord at Jerusalem; thirdly, a convent dedicated to St. Elias, the impress of whose body the Greek monks residing here pretend to show in a hard stone, which was wont to serve him for his bed. Near this convent also is a well, where you are told it was that the star appeared to the eastern magi to their exceeding joy. Fourthly, Rachel's tomb. This may probably be the true place of her interment, mentioned in Gen. xxxv. 19; but the present sepulchral monument can be none of that which Jacob erected; for it appears plainly to be a modern and Turkish structure. Near this monument is a little piece of ground, in which are picked up a little sort of small, round stones, exactly resembling peas, concerning which they have a tradition here that they were once truly what they now seem to be; but that the blessed Virgin petrified them by a miracle, in punishment to a surly rustic, who denied her the charity of a handful of them to relieve her hunger.

Being arrived at Bethlehem, we immediately made a circular visit to all the holy places belonging to it, as namely, the place where it is said our blessed Lord was born; the manger in which it is said he was laid; the chapel of St. Joseph, his supposed father; that of the Innocents; those of St. Jerom, of St. Paula and Eustochium, and of Eusebius of Cremona: and lastly, the school of St. Jerom; all which places it shall suffice just to name.

From the top of the church we had a large prospect of the adjacent country. The most remarkable places in view were Tekoah, situate on the side of a hill about nine miles distant to the southward; Engedi, distant about three miles eastward; and somewhat farther off, the same way, a high, sharp hill called the mountain of the Franks, because defended by a party of the crusaders forty years after the loss of Jerusalem.

April 1.—This morning we went to see some remarkable places in the neighbourhood of Bethlehem. The first place that we directed our course to was those famous fountains, pools, and gardens, about one hour and a quarter distant from Bethlehem southward, said to have been the contrivance and delight of king Solomon. To these works and places of pleasure that great prince is supposed to allude* where, amongst the other instances of his magnificence, he reckons up his gardens, and vineyards, and pools.

As for the pools, they are three in number, lying in a row above each other, being so disposed that the waters of the uppermost may descend into the second, and those of the second into the third. Their figure is quadrangular. The breadth is the same in all, amounting to about ninety paces. In their length there is some difference between them, the first being about one hundred and sixty paces long, the second two hundred, the third two hundred and twenty. They are all lined with wall, and plastered, and contain a great depth of water.

Close by the pools is a pleasant castle of a modern structure; and at about the distance of one hundred and forty paces from them is the fountain from which, principally, they derive their waters. This the friars will have to be that "sealed fountain" to which the holy spouse is compared†; and, in confirmation of this opinion, they pretend a tradition that king Solomon shut up these springs, and kept the door of them sealed with his signet, to the end that he might preserve the waters for his own drinking in their natural freshness and purity. Nor was it difficult thus to secure them, they rising under ground, and having no avenue to them but by a little hole like to the mouth of a narrow well. Through this hole you descend directly down, but not without some difficulty, for about four yards, and then arrive in a vaulted room fifteen paces long and eight broad. Joining to this is another room of the same fashion, but somewhat less. Both these rooms are covered with handsome stone arches, very ancient, and perhaps the work of Solomon himself.

You find here four places at which the water rises. From those separate sources it is conveyed, by little rivulets, into a kind of basin; and from thence is carried, by a large subterraneous passage, down into the pools. In the way, before it arrives at the pools, there is an aqueduct of brick pipes, which receives part of the stream, and carries it, by many turnings and windings about the mountains, to Jerusalem.

Below the pools there runs down a narrow, rocky valley, inclosed on both sides with high mountains. This the friars

* Eccl. ii. 5, 6.   † Cant. iv. 12.

will have to be the inclosed garden alluded to in the same place of the Canticles before cited : " A garden inclosed is my sister, my spouse ; a spring shut up, a fountain sealed." What truth there may be in this conjecture I cannot absolutely pronounce. As to the pools, it is probable enough they may be the same with Solomon's, there not being the like store of excellent spring water to be met with any where else throughout all Palestine ; but for the gardens, one may safely affirm that, if Solomon made them in the rocky ground which is now assigned for them, he demonstrated greater power and wealth in finishing his design than he did wisdom in choosing the place for it.

From these memorials of Solomon we returned towards Bethlehem again, in order to visit some places nearer home. The places we saw were, the field where it is said the shepherds were watching their flocks when they received the glad tidings of the birth of Christ ; and, not far from the field, the village where they dwelt ; and a little on the right hand of the village, an old desolate nunnery built by St. Paula, and made the more memorable by her dying in it. These places are all within about half a mile of the convent, eastward ; and with these we finished this morning's work.

Having seen what is usually visited on the south and east of Bethlehem, we walked out after dinner to the westward, to see what was remarkable on that side. The first place we were guided to was the well of David, so called because held to be the same that David so passionately thirsted after*. It is a well (or rather a cistern) supplied only with rain, without any natural excellency in its waters to make them desirable ; but it seems David's spirit had a farther aim.

About two furlongs beyond this well are to be seen some remains of an old aqueduct, which anciently conveyed the waters from Solomon's pools to Jerusalem. This is said to be the genuine work of Solomon, and may well be allowed to be in reality what it is pretended for. It is carried all along upon the surface of the ground, and is composed of stones . . . . feet square, and . . . . thick, perforated with a cavity of . . . . inches diameter, to make the channel. These stones are let into each other, with a fillet framed round about the cavity to prevent leakage, and united to each other with so

* 2 Sam. xxiii. 15.

firm a cement that they will sometimes sooner break (though a kind of coarse marble) than endure a separation.   This train of stones was covered, for its greater security, with a case of smaller stones, laid over it in a very strong mortar.   The whole work seems to be endued with such absolute firmness as if it had been designed for eternity; but the Turks have demonstrated, in this instance, that nothing can be so well wrought but they are able to destroy it; for of this strong aqueduct, which was carried formerly five or six leagues, with so vast expense and labour, you see now only here and there a fragment remaining.

Returning from this place, we went to see the Greek and Armenian convents, which are contiguous to that of the Latins, and have each their several doors opening into the chapel of the holy manger.   The next place we went to see was the grotto of the blessed Virgin.   It is within thirty or forty yards of the convent, and is reverenced upon the account of a tradition that the blessed Virgin here hid herself and her divine babe from the fury of Herod for some time before their departure into Egypt.   The grot is hollowed into a chalky rock; but this whiteness they will have to be not natural, but to have have been occasioned by some miraculous drops of the blessed Virgin's milk, which fell from her breast while she was suckling the holy infant; and so much are they possessed with this opinion, that they believe the chalk of this grotto has a miraculous virtue for increasing women's milk; and I was assured, from many hands, that it is very frequently taken by the women hereabouts, as well Turks and Arabs as Christians, for that purpose, and that with very good effect; which perhaps may be true enough, it being well known how much fancy is wont to do in things of this nature.

April 2.—The next morning, presenting the guardian with two chequeens apiece for his civilities to us, we took our leave of Bethlehem, designing just to visit the wilderness and convent of St. John· the Baptist, and so return to Jerusalem.

In this stage we first crossed part of that famous valley in which it is said that the angel, in one night, did such prodigious execution in the army of Sennacherib.   Having travelled about half an hour, we came to a village called Booteshellah, concerning which they relate this remarkable property, that no Turk can live in it above two years.   By virtue of this report, whether true or false, the Christians keep the village to themselves without molestation, no Turk being willing to stake his life in experimenting the truth of it. In somewhat less than an hour more we came to the fountain where they told us, but falsely, that Philip baptized the Ethiopian eunuch. The passsage here is so rocky and uneven that pilgrims, finding how difficult the road is for a single horseman, are ready to think it impossible that a chariot, such as the eunuch rode in *, should ever have been able to go this way; but it must not be judged what the road was in ancient times by what the negligence of the Turks have now reduced it to; for I observed, not far from the fountain, a place where the rock had been cut away in old time, in order to lay open a good road, by which it may be supposed that the same care was used all along this passage, though now time and negligence have obliterated both the fruit and almost the signs of such labour.

A little beyond this fountain we came to that which they call the village of St. Philip, at which, ascending a very steep hill, we arrived at the wilderness of St. John. A wilderness it is called, as being very rocky and mountainous: but is well cultivated, and produces plenty of corn, and vines, and olive trees. After a good hour's travel in this wilderness, we came to the cave and fountain where, as they say, the Baptist exercised those severe austerities related of him †. Near this cell there still grow some old locust trees, the monuments of the ignorance of the middle times ‡. These the friars aver to be the very same that yielded sustenance to the Baptist; and the Popish pilgrims, who dare not be wiser than such blind guides, gather the fruit of them, and carry it away with great devotion.

Having done with this place, we directed our course towards the convent of St. John, which is about a league distant eastward. In our way we passed along one side of the valley of Elah, where David slew the giant, that defier of the army of Israel §. We had likewise in sight Modon, a village on the

---

* Acts, viii. 28.   † Matt. iii. 4.
‡ See, before, the account of the honey trees, given by Arculf, p. 8. It is curious to compare these traditions of mistaken interpretations, which lasted long, and influenced many good writers.
§ 1 Sam. xvii.

top of a high hill, the burying-place of those heroical defenders of their country, the Maccabees.

Being come near the convent, we were led a little out of the way to visit a place which they call the house of Elizabeth, the mother of the Baptist. This was formerly a convent also, but it is now a heap of ruins, and the only remarkable place left in it is a grotto, in which (you are told) it was that the blessed Virgin saluted Elizabeth, and pronounced her divine magnificat*.

The present convent of St. John, which is now inhabited, stands about three furlongs distance from this house of Elizabeth, and is supposed to be built at the place where St. John was born. If you chance to ask how it came to pass that Elizabeth lived in one house when she was big with the Baptist, and in another when she brought him forth, the answer you are like to receive is, that the former was her country, the latter her city habitation, and that it is no wonder for a wife of one of the priests of better rank, such as she was†, to be provided with such variety.

The convent of St. John has been, within these four years, rebuilt from the ground. It is at present a large square building, uniform and neat all over; but that which is most eminently beautiful in it is its church. It consists of three aisles, and has in the middle a handsome cupola, under which is a pavement of mosaic, equal to, if not exceeding, the finest works of the ancients of that kind. At the upper end of the north aisle you go down seven marble steps, to a very splendid altar, erected over the very place where they say the holy Baptist was born. Here are artificers still employed in adding farther beauty and ornament to this convent, and yet it has been so expensive a work already, that the friars themselves give out that there is not a stone laid in it but has cost them a dollar; which, considering the large sums exacted by the Turks for licence to begin fabrics of this nature, and also their perpetual extortion and avarrias afterwards, besides the necessary charge of building, may be allowed to pass for no extravagant hyperbole.

Returning from St. John's toward Jerusalem, we came in about three quarters of an hour to a convent of the Greeks, taking its name from the holy cross. This convent is very

* Luke i. 46.   † Ibid. i. 6.

neat in its structure, and in its situation delightful. But that
which most deserves to be noted in it, is the reason of its
name and foundation. It is because there is the earth that
nourished the root, that bore the tree, that yielded the timber,
that made the cross. Under the high altar you are shown a
hole in the ground where the stump of the tree stood, and it
meets with not a few visitants so much more very stocks than
itself as to fall down and worship it. This convent is not
above half an hour from Jerusalem; to which place we returned this evening, being the fifth day from our departure
hence.

After our return, we were invited into the convent to have
our feet washed, a ceremony performed to each pilgrim by the
father guardian himself. The whole society stands around,
singing some Latin hymns, all the while the father guardian
is doing his office; and when he has done, every friar comes
in order, and kisses the feet of the pilgrim. All this was
performed with great order and solemnity; and if it served
either to testify a sincere humility and charity in them, or to
improve those excellent graces in others, it might pass for no
unuseful ceremony.

April 3.—We went about mid-day to see the function of the
Holy Fire *. This is a ceremony kept up by the Greeks and
Armenians, upon a persuasion that every Easter-Eve there is
miraculous flame descends from heaven into the holy sepulchre,
and kindles all the lamps and candles there, as the sacrifice
was burnt at the prayers of Elijah†.

Coming to the church of the Holy Sepulchre, we found it
crowded with a numerous and distracted mob, making a
hideous clamour very unfit for that sacred place, and better
becoming Bacchanals than Christians. Getting with some
struggle through the crowd, we went up into the gallery on
that side of the church next the Latin convent, whence we
could discern all that passed in this religious frenzy.

They began their disorders by running round the holy
sepulchre with all their might and swiftness, crying out, as
they went, " Huia!" which signifies "this is he," or "this
is it," an expression by which they assert the verity of the
Christian religion. After they had, by these vertiginous cir-
culations and clamours, turned their heads and inflamed their

---

* See before, p. 27.   † 1 Kings, xviii.

madness, they began to act the most antic tricks and postures, in a thousand shapes of distraction. Sometimes they dragged one another along the floor all round the sepulchre; sometimes they set one man upright on another's shoulders, and in this posture marched round; sometimes they took men with their heels upward, and hurried them about in such an indecent manner as to expose their nudities; sometimes they tumbled round the sepulchre after the manner of tumblers on the stage. In a word, nothing can be imagined more rude or extravagant than what was acted upon this occasion.

In this tumultuous frantic humour they continued from twelve till four o'clock: the reason of which delay was, because of a suit that was then in debate before the cadi, betwixt the Greeks and Armenians, the former endeavouring to exclude the latter from having any share in this miracle. Both parties having expended, as I was informed, five thousand dollars between them in this foolish controversy, the cadi at last gave sentence that they should enter the holy sepulchre together, as had been usual at former times. Sentence being thus given, at four o'clock both nations went on with their ceremony The Greeks first set out, in a procession round the holy sepulchre, and immediately at their heels followed the Armenians. In this order they compassed the holy sepulchre thrice, having produced all their gallantry of standards, streamers, crucifixes, and embroidered habits upon this occasion.

Towards the end of this procession, there was a pigeon came fluttering into the cupola over the sepulchre, at sight of which there was a greater shout and clamour than before. This bird, the Latins told us, was purposely let fly by the Greeks, to deceive the people into an opinion that it was a visible descent of the Holy Ghost.

The procession being over, the suffragan of the Greek patriarch (he being himself at Constantinople), and the principal Armenian bishop, approached to the door of the sepulchre, and, cutting the string with which it is fastened and sealed, entered in, shutting the door after them, all the candles and lamps within having been before extinguished, in the presence of the Turks and other witnesses. The exclamations were doubled as the miracle drew nearer to its accomplishment, and the people pressed with such vehemence towards the door of the sepulchre, that it was not in the power of the

Turks set to guard it, with the severest drubs, to keep them off. The cause of their pressing in this manner is the great desire they have to light their candles at the holy flame as soon as it is first brought out of the sepulchre, it being esteemed the most sacred and pure, as coming immediately from heaven.

The two miracle-mongers had not been above a minute in the holy sepulchre, when the glimmering of the holy fire was seen, or imagined to appear, through some chinks of the door; and certainly Bedlam itself never saw such an unruly transport as was produced in the mob at this sight. Immediately after, out came the two priests with blazing torches in their hands, which they held up at the door of the sepulchre, while the people thronged about with inexpressible ardour, every one striving to obtain a part of the first and purest flame. The Turks, in the meantime, with huge clubs, laid on them without mercy; but all this could not repel them, the excess of their transport making them insensible of pain. Those that got the fire applied it immediately to their beards, faces, and bosoms, pretending that it would not burn like an earthly flame. But I plainly saw none of them could endure this experiment long enough to make good that pretension.

So many hands being employed, you may be sure it could not be long before innumerable tapers were lighted. The whole church, galleries, and every place, seemed instantly to be in a flame, and with this illumination the ceremony ended.

It must be owned, that those two within the sepulchre performed their part with great quickness and dexterity; but the behaviour of the rabble without very much discredited the miracle. The Latins take a great deal of pains to expose this ceremony, as a most shameful imposture, and a scandal to the Christian religion; perhaps out of envy that others should be masters of so gainful a business. But the Greeks and Armenians pin their faith upon it, and make their pilgrimages chiefly upon this motive. And it is the deplorable unhappiness of their priests, that having acted the cheat so long already, they are forced now to stand to it, for fear of endangering the apostasy of their people.

Going out of the church after the rout was over, we saw several people gathered about the stone of unction, who, having got a good store of candles lighted with the holy fire, were

employed in daubing pieces of linen with the wicks of them
and the melting wax, which pieces of linen were designed for
winding-sheets; and it is the opinion of these poor people,
that if they can but have the happiness to be buried in a
shroud smutted with this celestial fire, it will certainly secure
them from the flames of hell.

Sunday, April 4.—This day being our Easter, we did not
go abroad to visit any places, the time requiring an employment of another nature.

April 5.—This morning we went to see some more of the
curiosities which had been yet unvisited by us. The first
place we came to was that which they call St. Peter's prison,
from which he was delivered by the angel*. It is close to the
church of the Holy Sepulchre, and still serves its primitive
use. About the space of a furlong from thence, we came to
an old church, held to have been built by Helena, in the
place where stood the house of Zebedee. This is in the
hands of the Greeks, who tell you, that Zebedee, being a
fisherman, was wont to bring fish from Joppa thither, and to
vend it at this place. Not far from hence we came to the
place where, they say, stood anciently the iron gate, which
opened to Peter of its own accord. A few steps farther is
the small church built over the house of Mark, to which the
apostle directed his course after his miraculous gaol-delivery.
The Syrians, who have this place in their custody, pretend to
show you the very window at which Rhoda looked out, while
Peter knocked at the door. In the church they show a Syriac
manuscript of the New Testament in folio, pretended to be
eight hundred and fifty-two years old, and a little stone font
used by the Apostles themselves in baptizing. About one
hundred and fifty paces farther in the same street, is that
which they call the house of St. Thomas, converted formerly
into a church, but now a mosque. Not many paces farther
is another street crossing the former, which leads you, on the
right hand, to the place where they say our Lord appeared,
after his Resurrection, to the three Marys†. Three Marys,
the friars tell you, though in that place of St. Matthew mention is made but of two. The same street carries you, on the
left hand, to the Armenian convent. The Armenians have
here a very large and delightful space of ground, their con-

* Acts, xii.   † Matt. xxviii. 9.

vent and gardens taking up all that part of Mount Sion which
is within the walls of the city. Their church is built over
the place where they say St. James, the brother of John, was
beheaded*. In a small chapel, on the north side of the
church, is shown the very place of his decollation. In this
church are two altars set out with extraordinary splendour,
being decked with rich mitres, embroidered copes, crosses,
both silver and gold, crowns, chalices, and other church utensils, without number. In the middle of the church is a pulpit
made of tortoise-shell and mother of pearl, with a beautiful
canopy, or cupola over it, of the same fabric. The tortoise-
shell and mother of pearl are so exquisitely mingled and
inlaid in each other, that the work far exceeds the materials.
In a kind of anti-chapel to this church, there are laid up, on
one side of the altar, three large rough stones, esteemed very
precious, as being, one of them, the stone upon which Moses
cast the two Tables, when he broke them, in indignation at
the idolatry of the Israelites; the other two being brought,
one from the place of our Lord's Baptism, the other from that
of his Transfiguration.

Leaving this convent we went a little farther to another
small church, which was likewise in the hands of the Armenians. This is supposed to be founded in the place where
Annas's house stood. Within the church, not far from the
door, is shown a hole in the wall, denoting the place where
one of the officers of the high priest smote our blessed
Saviour†. The officer, by whose impious hand that buffet
was given, the friars will have to be the same Malchus whose
ear our Lord had healed. In the court before this chapel is
an olive tree, of which it is reported, that Christ was chained
to it for some time, by order of Annas, to secure him from
escaping.

From the house of Annas we were conducted out of Sion
Gate, which is near adjoining to that which they call the
house of Caiaphas, which is another small chapel belonging
also to the Armenians. Here, under the altar, they tell us is
deposited that very stone which was laid to secure the door
of our Saviour's sepulchre‡. It was a long time kept in the
church of the sepulchre; but the Armenians, not many years
since, stole it from thence by a stratagem, and conveyed it to

* Acts, xii. 2.   † John, xviii. 22.   ‡ Matt. xxvii. 60.

this place.   The stone is two yards and a quarter long, high one yard, and broad as much.   It is plastered all over, except in five or six little places, where it is left bare to receive the immediate kisses and other devotions of pilgrims.   Here is likewise shown a little cell, said to have been our Lord's prison till the morning when he was carried from hence before Pilate; and also the place where Peter was frightened into a denial of his Master.

A little farther without the gate is the church of the Cœnaculum, where they say Christ instituted his Last Supper. It is now a mosque, and not to be seen by Christians.   Near this is a well, which is said to mark out the place at which the Apostles divided from each other, in order to go every man to his several charge; and close by the well are the ruins of a house in which the blessed Virgin is supposed to have breathed her last.   Going eastward, a little way down the hill, we were shown the place where a Jew arrested the corpse of the blessed Virgin, as she was carried to her interment, for which impious presumption he had his hand withered wherewith he had seized the bier.   About as much lower in the middle of the hill, they show you the grotto in which St. Peter wept so bitterly for his inconstancy to his Lord.

We extended our circuit no farther at this time, but entered the city again at Sion Gate.   Turning down as soon as we had entered, on the right hand, and going about two furlongs close by the city wall, we were taken into a garden lying at the foot of Mount Moriah, on the south side.   Here we were shown several large vaults annexed to the mountain on this side, and running at least fifty yards under ground.   They were built in two isles, arched at top with huge firm stone, and sustained with tall pillars consisting each of one single stone, and two yards in diameter.   This might possibly be some under-ground work made to enlarge the area of the temple, for Josephus seems to describe some such work as this, erected over the valley on this side of the temple*.

From these vaults we returned towards the convent.   In our way we passed through the Turkish bazaars, and took a view of the Beautiful Gate of the Temple.   But we could but just view it in passing, it not being safe to stay here long, by reason of the superstition of the Turks.

* Ant. Jud. lib. xv. cap. ult.

April 6.—The next morning we took another progress about the city. We made our exit at Bethlehem Gate, and turning down on the left hand under the castle of the Pisans, came about a furlong and a half to that which they call Bathsheba's Pool. It lies at the bottom of Mount Sion, and is supposed to be the same in which Bathsheba was washing herself, when David spied her from the terrace of his palace. But others refer this accident to another lesser pool in a garden just within Bethlehem Gate; and perhaps both opinions are equally right.

A little below this pool begins the valley of Hinnom, on the west side of which is the place called anciently the Potter's Field, and afterwards the Field of Blood, from its being purchased with the pieces of silver which were the price of the blood of Christ; but at present, from that veneration which it has obtained among Christians, it is called Campo Sancto. It is a small plot of ground not above thirty yards long, and about half as much broad. One moiety of it is taken up by a square fabric twelve yards high, built for a charnel-house. The corpses are let down into it from the top, there being five holes left open for that purpose. Looking down through these holes we could see many bodies under several degrees of decay, from which it may be conjectured that this grave does not make that quick despatch with the corpses committed to it, which is commonly reported. The Armenians have the command of this burying place, for which they pay the Turks a rent of one seuin a day. The earth is of a chalky substance hereabouts.

A little below the Campo Sancto is shown an intricate cave or sepulchre consisting of several rooms, one within another, in which the apostles are said to have hid themselves, when they forsook their Master, and fled. The entrance of the cave discovers signs of its having been adorned with painting in ancient times.

A little farther, the valley of Hinnom terminates, that of Jehoshaphat running across the mouth of it. Along the bottom of this latter valley runs the brook Cedron; a brook in wintertime, but without the least drop of water in it all the time we were at Jerusalem.

In the valley of Jehoshaphat, the first thing you are carried to is the well of Nehemiah; so called because reputed to be the same place from which the restorer of Israel recovered the fire of the altar, after the Babylonish captivity *. A little higher in the valley, on the left hand, you come to a tree supposed to mark out the place where the Evangelical Prophet was sawn asunder. About one hundred paces higher, on the same side, is the pool of Siloam. It was anciently dignified with a church built over it ; but, when we were there, a tanner made no scruple to dress his hides in it. Going about a furlong farther on the same side, you come to the fountain of the blessed Virgin, so called, because she was wont (as is reported) to resort hither for water ; but at what time and upon what occasions is not yet agreed. Over against this fountain, on the other side of the valley, is a village called Siloe, in which Solomon is said to have kept his strange wives ; and above the village is a hill called the Mountain of Offence, because there Solomon built the high places mentioned in 1 Kings xi. 7, his wives having perverted his wise heart to follow their idolatrous abominations in his declining years. On the same side, and not far distant from Siloe, they show another Aceldama, or Field of Blood ; so called because there it was that Judas, by the just judgment of God, met with his compounded death †. A little farther on the same side of the valley, they showed us several Jewish monuments. Amongst the rest there are two noble antiquities, which they call the sepulchre of Zachary and the pillar of Absolom. Close by the latter is the sepulchre of Jehoshaphat, from which the whole valley takes its name.

Upon the edge of the hill, on the opposite side of the valley, there runs along, in a direct line, the wall of the city, near the corner of which there is a short end of a pillar jutting out of the wall. Upon this pillar, the Turks have a tradition that Mohammed shall sit in judgment at the last day ; and that all the world shall be gathered together in the valley below, to receive their doom from his mouth. A little farther northward is the gate of the Temple. It is at present walled up, because the Turks here have a prophecy that their destruction shall enter at that gate, the completion of which prediction they endeavour by this means to prevent. Below this gate, in the bottom of the valley, is a broad hard stone, discovering several impressions on it, which you may fancy to be footsteps. These, the friars tell you, are prints made by our blessed Saviour's feet, when, after his apprehension, he was

* 2 Mac. i. 19.   † Matt. xxvii. 5. Acts, i. 18, 19.

hurried violently away to the tribunal of his blood-thirsty persecutors.

From hence, keeping still in the bottom of the valley, you come in a few paces to a place which they call the sepulchre of the blessed Virgin.   It has a magnificent descent down into it of forty-seven stairs; on the right hand as you go down is the sepulchre of St. Anna, the mother, and on the left that of St. Joseph, the husband of the blessed Virgin.

Having finished our visit to this place, we went up the hill toward the city.   In the side of the ascent we were shown a broad stone on which they say St. Stephen suffered martyrdom ; and not far from it is a grotto, into which they tell you the outrageous Jewish zealots cast his body, when they had satiated their fury upon him.   From hence we went immediately to St. Stephen's Gate, so called from its vicinity to this place of the protomartyr's suffering, and so returned to our lodging.

April 7.—The next morning we set out again, in order to see the sanctuaries and other visitable places upon Mount Olivet.   We went out at St. Stephen's Gate, and, crossing the Valley of Jehoshaphat, began immediately to ascend the mountains.   Being got about two-thirds of the way up, we came to certain grottos cut with intricate windings and caverns under ground ; these are called the sepulchres of the prophets.   A little higher up are twelve arched vaults under ground, standing side by side ; these were built in memory of the twelve apostles, who are said to have compiled their creed in this place.   Sixty paces higher you come to the place where they say Christ uttered his prophecy concerning the final destruction of Jerusalem *.   And a little on the right hand of this is the place where they say he dictated a second time the Pater Noster to his disciples†.   Somewhat higher is the cave of St. Pelagia ; and as much more above that, a pillar, signifying the place where an angel gave the blessed Virgin three days' warning of her death.   At the top of the hill you come to the place of our blessed Lord's ascension.   Here was anciently a large church, built in honour of that glorious triumph, but all that now remains of it is only an octagonal cupola, about eight yards in diameter, standing, as they say, over the very place where were set the last footsteps of the Son of God here on earth.   Within the cupola there is seen, in a hard stone, as

* Matt. xxiv. 2.   † Luke, xi. 1, 2.

they tell you, the print of one of his feet.　Here was also that of the other foot some time since, but it has been removed from hence by the Turks into the great mosque upon Mount Moria.　This chapel of the Ascension the Turks have the custody of, and use it for a mosque.　There are many other holy places about Jerusalem, which the Turks pretend to have a veneration for, equally with the Christians, and under that pretence they take them into their own hands.　But whether they do this out of real devotion, or for lucre's sake, and to the end that they may exact money from the Christians for admission into them, I will not determine.

About two furlongs from this place, northward, is the highest part of Mount Olivet; and upon that was anciently erected a high tower, in memory of that apparition of the two angels to the apostles after our blessed Lord's ascension *, from which the tower itself had the name given it of Viri Galilæi!　This ancient monument remained till about two years since, when it was demolished by a Turk, who had bought the field in which it stood; but nevertheless you have still, from the natural height of the place, a large prospect of Jerusalem and the adjacent country, and of the Dead Sea, &c.

From this place we descended the mount again by another road.　At about the midway down they show you the place where Christ beheld the city and wept over it†.　Near the bottom of the hill is a great stone, upon which you are told the blessed Virgin let fall her girdle after her assumption, in order to convince St. Thomas, who, they say, was troubled with a fit of his old incredulity upon this occasion.　There is still to be seen a small winding channeɪ upon the stone, which they will have to be the impression made by the girdle when it fell, and to be left for the conviction of all such as shall suspect the truth of their story of the assumption.

About twenty yards lower they show you Gethsemane, an even plot of ground not above fifty-seven yards square, lying between the foot of Mount Olivet and the brook Cedron.　It is well planted with olive trees, and those of so old a growth, that they are believed to be the same that stood here in our blessed Saviour's time, in virtue of which persuasion the olives, and olive stones, and oil, which they produce, became an excellent commodity in Spain; but that these trees cannot be so

---

*　Acts, i. 10, 11.　　　　　　　　† Luke, xix. 41.

ancient as is pretended is evident from what Josephus testifies*, viz. that Titus, in his siege of Jerusalem, cut down all the trees within about one hundred furlongs of Jerusalem; and that the soldiers were forced to fetch wood so far for making their mounts when they assaulted the temple.

At the upper corner of the garden is a flat, naked ledge of rock, reputed to be the place on which the apostles, Peter, James, and John, fell asleep during the agony of our Lord; and a few paces from hence is a grotto, said to be the place in which Christ underwent that bitter part of his passion.

About eight paces from the place where the apostles slept is a small shred of ground, twelve yards long and one broad, supposed to be the very path on which the traitor Judas walked up to Christ, saying "Hail Master, and kissed him." This narrow path is separated by a wall out of the midst of the garden, as a terra damnata, a work the more remarkable as being done by the Turks, who, as well as Christians, detest the very ground on which was acted such an infamous treachery.

From hence we crossed the brook Cedron, close by the reputed sepulchre of the blessed Virgin, and, entering at St. Stephen's Gate, returned again to the convent.

April 8.—We went to see the palace of Pilate, I mean the place where they say it stood; for now an ordinary Turkish house possesses its room. It is not far from the gate of St. Stephen, and borders upon the area of the temple on the north side. From the terrace of this house you have a fair prospect of all the place where the temple stood; indeed the only good prospect that is allowed you of it; for there is no going within the borders of it without forfeiting your life, or, which is worse, your religion. A fitter place for an august building could not be found in the whole world than this area. It lies upon the top of Mount Moriah, over against Mount Olivet, the valley of Jehoshaphat lying between both mountains. It is, as far as I could compute by walking round it without, five hundred and seventy of my paces in length, and three hundred and seventy in breadth; and one may still discern marks of the great labour that it cost to cut away the hard rock, and to level such a spacious area upon so strong a mountain. In the middle of the area stands, at present, a

* Bell. Jud., lib. vii. cap. 15, and other places.

mosque, of an octagonal figure, supposed to be built upon the same ground where anciently stood the sanctum sanctorum. It is neither eminent for its largeness nor its structure; and yet it makes a very stately figure by the sole advantage of its situation.

In this pretended house of Pilate is shown the room in which Christ was mocked with the ensigns of royalty and buffeted by the soldiers. At the coming out of the house is a descent, where was anciently the scala sancta. On the other side of the street (which was anciently part of the palace also) is the room where they say our Lord was scourged. It was once used for a stable by the son of a certain pasha of Jerusalem; but presently, for this profanation, they say there came such a mortality amongst his horses as forced him to resign the place; by which means it was redeemed from that sordid use; but, nevertheless, when we were there, it was no better than a weaver's shop. In our return from Pilate's palace we passed along the Dolorous Way, in which walk we were shown in order, first, the place where Pilate brought our Lord forth, to present to the people, with this mystic saying, "Behold the Man!" secondly, where Christ fainted thrice under the weight of his cross; thirdly, where the blessed Virgin swooned away at so tragical a spectacle; fourthly, where St. Veronica presented to him the handkerchief to wipe his bleeding brows; fifthly, where the soldiers compelled Simon the Cyrenian to bear his cross; all which places I need only to name.

April 9.—We went to take a view of that which they call the pool of Bethesda. It is one hundred and twenty paces long, and forty broad, and at least eight deep, but void of water. At its west end it discovers some old arches, now dammed up. These some will have to be the five porches in which sat that multitude of lame, halt, and blind*; but the mischief is, instead of five, there are but three of them. The pool is contiguous on one side to St. Stephen's Gate, on the other to the area of the temple.

From hence we went to the convent or nunnery of St. Anne. The church here is large and entire, and so are part of the lodgings; but both are desolate and neglected. In a

* John, v.

grotto under the church is shown the place where they say the blessed Virgin was born. Near this church they show the Pharisee's house, where Mary Magdalen exhibited those admirable evidences of a penitent affection towards our Saviour, "washing his feet with her tears, and wiping them with her hair."† This place also has been anciently dignified with holy buildings, but they are now neglected.

This was our morning's work. In the afternoon we went to see Mount Gihon, and the pool of the same name. It lies about two furlongs without Bethlehem Gate, westward. It is a stately pool, one hundred and sixty paces long and sixty-seven broad, and lined with wall and plaster, and was, when we were there, well stored with water.

April 10.—We went to take our leaves of the holy sepulchre, this being the last time it was to be opened this festival.

Upon this finishing day, and the night following, the Turks allow free admittance for all people, without demanding any fee for entrance as at other times, calling it a day of charity. By this promiscuous licence they let in not only the poor, but, as I was told, the lewd and vicious also, who come thither to get convenient opportunity for prostitution, profaning the holy places in such manner (as it is said) that they were not worse defiled even when the heathens here celebrated their aphrodisia.

Sunday, April 11.—Now began the Turks' Byram, that is the feast which they celebrate after their Lent, called by them Ramadan. This being a time of great libertinism among the rabble, we thought it prudent to confine ourselves to our lodgings for some time, to the end that we might avoid such insolences as are usual in such times of public festivity. Our confinement was the less incommodious, because there was hardly any thing, either within or about the city, which we had not already visited.

April 12, 13.—We kept close to our quarters, but, however, not in idleness; the time being now come when we were to contrive and provide things in order for our departure. We had a bad account, from all hands, of the country's being more and more embroiled by the Arabs, which made us somewhat unresolved what way and method to take for our return; but during our suspense it was told us that the mosolem was

† Luke, vii. 38.

likewise upon his return to his master, the pasha of Tripoli, upon which intelligence we resolved, if possible, to join ourselves to his company.

April 14.—We went, with a small present in our hands, to wait upon the mosolem, in order to inquire the time of his departure and acquaint him with our desire to go under his protection. He assured us of his setting out the next morning; so we immediately took our leaves in order to prepare ourselves for accompanying him.

I was willing, before our departure, to measure the circuit of the city; so, taking one of the friars with me, I went out in the afternoon in order to pace the walls round. We went out at Bethlehem Gate; and, proceeding on the right hand, came about to the same gate again. I found the whole city 4630 prces in circumference, which I computed thus:—

	Paces.
From Bethlehem Gate to the corner on the right hand . . .	400
From that corner to Damascus Gate	680
From Damascus Gate to Herod's	380
From Herod's Gate to Jeremiah's prison	150
From Jeremiah's prison to the corner next the valley of Jehoshaphat	225
From that corner to St. Stephen's Gate	385
From St. Stephen's Gate to the Golden Gate	240
From the Golden Gate to the corner of the wall	380
From that corner to the Dung Gate	470
From the Dung Gate to Sion Gate	605
From Sion Gate to the corner of the wall	215
From that corner to Bethlehem Gate	500

In all, paces 4630

The reduction of my paces to yards is by casting away a tenth part, ten of my paces making nine yards; by which reckoning the 4630 paces amount to 4167 yards, which make just two miles and a half.

April 15.—This morning our diplomata were presented us by the father guardian, to certify our having visited all the holy places; and we presented the convent fifty dollars a man as a gratuity for their trouble; which offices having passed betwixt us, we took our leaves.

We set out together with the mosolem, and, proceeding in the same road by which we came, lodged the first night at Khan Leban; but the mosolem left us here, and continued his stage as far as Naplosa; so we saw him no more. The country people were now every where at plough in the fields, in order to sow cotton.   It was observable that, in ploughing, they used goads of an extraordinary size.   Upon measuring of several, I found them about eight feet long, and at the bigger end six inches in circumference.   They were armed at the lesser end with a sharp prickle for driving the oxen, and at the other end with a small spade or paddle of iron, strong and massy, for cleansing the plough from the clay that encumbers it in working.   May we not from hence conjecture that it was with such a goad as one of these that Shamgar made that prodigious slaughter related of him * ?   I am confident that whoever should see one of these instruments would judge it to be a weapon not less fit, perhaps fitter, than a sword for such an execution.   Goads of this sort I saw always used hereabouts, and also in Syria; and the reason is, because the same single person both drives the oxen, and also holds and manages the plough, which makes it necessary to use such a goad as is above described to avoid the encumbrance of two instruments.

April 16.—Leaving Khan Leban, we proceeded still in our former road, and, passing by Naplosa and Samaria, we came to the fountain Selee, and there took up our lodging this night.

April 17.—The next morning we continued on in the same road that we travelled when outward bound, till we came to Caphar Arab.   At this place we left our former way, and, instead of turning off on the left hand to go to Acra, we kept our course strait forwards, resolving to cross directly athwart the plain of Esdraelon, and to visit Nazareth.

Proceeding in this course from Caphar Arab, we came in about half an hour to Jeneen.   This is a large old town, on the skirts of Esdraelon.   It has in it an old castle and two mosques, and is the chief residence of the emir Chibly.   Here we were accosted with a command from the emir not to advance any farther, till he should come in person to receive of us his caphars.   This was very unwelcome news to us, who had met with a trial of his civility before.   But, however, we had no remedy, and therefore thought it best to comply as contentedly as we could.   Having been kept thus in suspense from two in the morning till sun-set, we then received an order from the prince to pay the caphar to an officer, whom he sent to receive it and dismiss us.

* Judg. iii. 31.

Having received this licence, we made all the haste we
could to despatch the caphar, and to get clear of these Arabs.
But, notwithstanding all our diligence, it was near midnight
before we could finish. After which we departed, and, entering immediately into the plain of Esdraelon, travelled over it
all night, and in seven hours reached its other side. Here
we had a very steep and rocky ascent ; but, however, in half
an hour we mastered it, and arrived at Nazareth.

Sunday, April 18.—Nazareth is at present only an inconsiderable village, situated in a kind of round concave valley,
on the top of a high hill. We were entertained at the convent built over the place of the Annunciation. At this place
are, as it were, immured, seven or eight Latin fathers, who
live a life truly mortified, being perpetually in fear of the
Arabs, who are absolute lords of the country.

We went in the afternoon to visit the sanctuary of this
place. The church of Nazareth stands in a cave supposed to
be the place where the blessed Virgin received that joyful
message of the angel, " Hail thou that art highly favoured,"*
&c. It resembles the figure of a cross. That part of it that
stands for the tree of the cross is fourteen paces long and
six over, and runs directly into the grotto, having no other
arch over it at top but that of the natural rock. The traverse
part of the cross is nine paces long and four broad, and is
built athwart the mouth of the grotto. Just at the section of
the cross are erected two granite pillars, each two feet and
one inch diameter, and about three feet distant from each
other. They are supposed to stand on the very places, one
where the angel, the other where the blessed Virgin stood,
at the time of the Annunciation. Of these pillars, the innermost, being that of the blessed Virgin, has been broke away
by the Turks, in expectation of finding treasure under it, so
that eighteen inches length of it is clean gone, between the
pillar and its pedestal. Nevertheless it remains erect, though
by what art it is sustained I could not discern. It touches
the roof above, and is probably hung upon that; unless you
had rather take the friars' account of it, viz. that it is supported by a miracle.

After this we went to see the house of Joseph, being the
same, as they tell you, in which the Son of God lived for near

* Luke, i. 28.

thirty years, in subjection to man*. Not far distant from
hence they show you the synagogue where our blessed Lord
preached that sermon† by which he so exasperated his
countrymen. Both these places lie north-west from the convent, and were anciently dignified each with a handsome
church, but these monuments of queen Helena's piety are
now in ruins.

April 19.—This day we destined for visiting Mount Tabor,
standing by itself in the plain of Esdraelon, about two or
three furlongs within the plain.

Its being situated in such a separate manner, has induced
most authors to conclude that this must needs be that holy
mountain, as St. Peter styles it‡, which was the place of our
blessed Lord's Transfiguration§. You read that Christ "took
with him Peter, James, and John, into a mountain apart,"
from which description they infer that the mountain there
spoken of can be no other than Tabor. The conclusions may
possibly be true, but the argument used to prove it seems in-
competent; because the term κατ' ἰδίαν, or apart, most likely
relates to the withdrawing and retirement of the persons
there spoken of, and not the situation of the mountain.

After a very laborious ascent, which took up near an hour,
we reached the highest part of the mountain. It has a plain
area at top, most fertile and delicious, of an oval figure, extending about one furlong in breadth, and two in length. This
area is inclosed with trees on all parts, except toward the
south. It was anciently environed with walls and trenches,
and other fortifications, of which it exhibits many remains at
this day.

In this area there are in several places cisterns of good
water; but those which are most devoutly visited are three
contiguous grottos, made to represent the three tabernacles
which St. Peter proposed to erect, in the astonishment that
possessed him at the glory of the Transfiguration. "Lord,"
says he, "it is good for us to be here; let us make three
tabernacles, one for thee," &c.

I cannot forbear to mention, in this place, an observation
which is very obvious to all that visit the Holy Land, viz.
that almost all passages and histories related in the Gospel

---

* Luke, ii. 51.   † Luke, iv.
‡ 2 Peter, i. 18.   § Matt. xvii. ; Mark, ix.

are represented by them that undertake to show where every thing was done, as having been done most of them in grottos, and that even in such cases where the condition and the circumstances of the actions themselves seem to require places of another nature.   Thus, if you would see the place where St. Anne was delivered of the blessed Virgin, you are carried to a grotto; if the place of the Annunciation, it is also a grotto; if the place where the blessed Virgin saluted Elizabeth; if that of the Baptist's, or that of our blessed Saviour's Nativity; if that of the Agony, or that of St. Peter's repentance, or that where the Apostles made the Creed, or this of the Transfiguration, all these places are also grottos; and, in a word, wherever you go, you find almost every thing is represented as done under ground.   Certainly grottos were anciently held in great esteem, or else they could never have been assigned, in spite of all probability, for the places in which were done so many various actions.   Perhaps it was the hermits' way of living in grottos from the fifth or sixth century downward, that has brought them ever since to be in so great reputation.

From the top of Tabor you have a prospect which, if nothing else, well rewards the labour of ascending it.   It is impossible for man's eyes to behold a higher gratification of this nature.   On the north-west, you discern at a distance the Mediterranean; and all around you have the spacious and beautiful plains of Esdraelon and Galilee, which present you with the view of so many places memorable for the resort and miracles of the Son of God.   At the bottom of Tabor westward stands Daberah, a small village, supposed by some to take its name from Deborah, that famous judge and deliverer of Israel.   Near this valley is the fountain of Kishon.   Not many leagues distant eastward, you see Mount Hermon, at the foot of which is seated Nain, famous for our Lord's raising the widow's son there*; and Endor, the place where dwelt the witch consulted by Saul.   Turning a little southward, you have in view the high mountains of Gilboa, fatal to Saul and his sons.   Due east, you discover the Sea of Tiberias, distant about one day's journey, and close by that sea they show a steep mountain, down which the swine ran, and perished in the waters†.   A few points towards the north appears that

---

* Luke, vii. 14.   † Matt. viii. 32.

which they call the Mount of the Beatitudes; a small rising,
from which our blessed Saviour delivered his sermon in the
fifth, sixth, and seventh chapters of St. Matthew. Not far
from this little hill is the city of Saphet, supposed to be the
ancient Bethulia. It stands upon a very eminent and conspicuous mountain, and is seen far and near. May we not
suppose that Christ alludes to this city in those words of his
sermon, 'A city set on a hill cannot be hid*? A conjecture
which seems the more probable, because our Lord, in several
places, affects to illustrate his discourse by comparisons taken
from objects that were then present before the eyes of his
auditors; as when he bids them "Behold the fowls of the
air,"† "and the lilies of the field."‡ From Mount Tabor you
have likewise the sight of a place which they will tell you
was Dotham, where Joseph was sold by his brethren; and of
the field where our blessed Saviour fed the multitude with a
few loaves and fewer fishes. But whether it was the place
where he divided the five loaves and two fishes amongst the
five thousand§, or the seven loaves amongst the four thou-
sand‖, I left them to agree among themselves.

Having received great satisfaction in the sight of this
mountain, we returned to the convent the same way that we
came. After dinner we made another small excursion, in
order to see that which they call the Mountain of the Preci-
pitation; that is, the brow of the hill from which the Nazarites
would have thrown down our blessed Saviour, being incensed
at his sermon preached to them ¶. This precipice is at least
half a league distant from Nazareth southward. In going to
it, you cross first over the valley in which Nazareth stands,
and then, going down two or three furlongs in a narrow cleft
between the rocks, you there clamber up a short but difficult
way on the right hand, at the top of which you find a great
stone standing on the brink of a precipice, which is said to
be the very place where our Lord was destined to be thrown
down by his enraged neighbours, had he not made a miraculous escape out of their hands **. There are in the stone
several little holes, resembling the prints of fingers thrust
into it. These, if the friars say truth, are the impresses of

---

* Matt. v. 14.   † Ibid. vi. 16.   ‡ Ibid. v. 28.
§ Matt. xiv. 16, &c.   ‖ Ibid. xv. 32.   ¶ Luke, iv.
** See the account by Sir John de Maundeville, p. 185, and the note.

Christ's fingers, made in the hard stone, while he resisted the violence that was offered to him.   At this place are seen two or three cisterns for saving water, and a few ruins, which are all that now remains of a religious building founded here by the empress Helena.

April 20.—The next morning we took our leave of Nazareth, presenting the guardian five a-piece for his trouble and charge in entertaining us.   We directed our course for Acra, in order to which, going at first northward, we crossed the hills that encompassed the vale of Nazareth on that side; after which we turned to the westward, and passed in view of Cana of Galilee, the place signalized with the beginning of Christ's miracles *.   In an hour and a half more we came to Sepharia, a place reverenced for being the reputed habitation of Joachim and Anna, the parents of the blessed Virgin.   It had once the name of Diocesaria, and was a place of good repute; but at present it is reduced to a poor village, showing only here and there a few ruins to testify its ancient better condition.   On the west side of the town stands good part of a large church, built on the same place where they say stood the house of Joachim and Anna; it is fifty paces long, and in breadth proportionable.

At Sephira begins the delicious plain of Zebulon.   We were an hour and a half in crossing it, and in an hour and a half more passed by a desolate village on the right hand, by name Satyra.   In half an hour more we entered the plains of Acra, and in one hour and a half more arrived at that place.   Our stage, this day, was somewhat less than seven hours.   It lay about west and by north, and through a country very delightful, and fertile beyond imagination.

April 21.—At Acra we were very courteously treated by the French consul and merchants, as we had been when outward-bound.   Having staid only one night, we took our leave, and, returning by the same way of the coast that I have described before, came the first night to our old lodgings at Solomon's cisterns, and the second to Sidon.

April 22.—Three hours distant from Sidon, we were carried by the French consul to see a place which we had passed by unregarded in our journey outward, though it very well deserves a traveller's observation.

---

* John, ii. 11.

At about the distance of a mile from the sea, there runs along a high rocky mountain, in the side of which are hewn a multitude of grottos, all very little differing from each other. They have entrances of about two feet square. On the inside you find, in most, or all of them, a room of about four yards square, on the one side of which is the door, on the other there are as many little cells, elevated about two feet above the floor. There are of these subterraneous caverns, as I was informed by those who had counted them, two hundred in number. They go by the name of the grottos of . . . . . . The great doubt concerning them is, whether they were made for the dead or the living. That which makes me doubt of this is, because, though all the ancient sepulchres in this country very much resemble these grottos, yet they have something peculiar in them, which entices one to believe they might be designed for the reception of the living; for several of the cells within were of a figure not fit for having corpses deposited in them, being some a yard square, some more, and some less, and seeming to be made for family uses. Over the door of every cell there was a channel cut to convey the water away, that it might not annoy the rooms within. And because the cells were cut above each other, some higher, some lower, in the side of the rock, there were convenient stairs cut for the easier communication betwixt the upper and lower regions. At the bottom of the rock were also several old cisterns for storing up water. From all which arguments it may, with probability at least, be concluded, that these places were contrived for the use of the living, and not of the dead. But what sort of people they were that inhabited this subterraneous city, or how long ago they lived, I am not able to resolve. True it is, Strabo describes the habitations of the Troglodytæ to have been somewhat of this kind.

April 23.—We continued this day at Sidon, being treated by our friends of the French nation with great generosity.

April 24.—This morning we took our leave of the worthy French consul, and the rest of our other friends of that nation, in order to go for Damascus.

Damascus lies near due east from Sidon. It is usually esteemed three days' journey distant, the road lying over the mountain Libanus and Anti-Libanus.

Having gone about half an hour through the olive yards of Sidon, we came to the foot of Mount Libanus. In two

hours and a half more we came to a small village called
Caphar Milki. Thus far our ascent was easy; but now it
began to grow more steep and difficult; in which having
laboured one hour and one-third more, we then came to a
fresh fountain called Ambus Lee, where we encamped for this
night. Our whole stage was four hours and one-third; our
course east.

April 25.—The next day we continued ascending for three
good hours, and then arrived at the highest ridge of the
mountain, where the snow lay close to the road. We began
immediately to descend again on the other side, and in two
hours came to a small village called Meshgarah, where there
gushes out at once from the side of the mountain a plentiful
stream, which falling down into a valley below makes a fine
brook, and, after a current of about two leagues, loses itself
in a river called Letane.

At Meshgarah there is a caphar* demanded by the Druses,
who are the possessors of these mountains. We were for a
little while perplexed by the excessive demand made upon
us by the caphar-men, but finding us obstinate they desisted.

Having gone one hour beyond Meshgarah, we got clear of
the mountain, and entered into a valley called Bocat. This
Bocat seems to be the same with Bicath Aven, mentioned in
Amos i. 5, together with Eden and Damascus, for there is
very near it, in Mount Libanus, a place called Eden to this
day. It might also have the name of Aven, that is, Vanity,
given to it, from the idolatrous worship of Baal, practised at
Balbec, or Heliopolis, which is situate in this valley. The
valley is about two hours over, and in length extends several
days' journey, lying near north-east and south-west. It is
inclosed on both sides with two parallel mountains, exactly
resembling each other, the one that which we lately passed
over between this and Sidon, the other opposite against it,
towards Damascus. The former I take to be the true Libanus,
the latter Anti-Libanus, which two mountains are nowhere so
well distinguished as at this valley.

In the bottom of the valley there runs a large river called
Letane. It rises about two days' journey northward, not far
from Balbec, and, keeping its course all down the valley, falls

---

* Half per Frank, quarter per servant.

at last into the river Casimir, or, as it is erroneously called, Eleutherus.

Thus far our course had been due east, but here we inclined some points towards the north. Crossing obliquely over the valley, we came in half an hour to a bridge over the river Letane. It consists of five stone arches, and is called Kor Aren, from a village at a little distance of the same name. At this bridge we crossed the river, and, having travelled about an hour and a half on its bank, pitched our tents there for this night. Our whole stage was eight hours.

April 26.—The next morning we continued our oblique course over the valley Bocat. In an hour we passed close by a small village called Jib Jeneen, and in three quarters of an hour more came to the foot of the mountain Anti-Libanus. Here we had an easy ascent, and in half an hour passed, on our right hand, by a village called Uzzi. In three quarters of an hour more we arrived at Ayta, a village of Christians of the Greek communion. At this last place the road began to grow very rocky and troublesome, in which having travelled an hour we arrived at a small rivulet called Ayn Tentloe. Here we entered into a narrow cleft between two rocky mountains, passing through which we arrived in four hours at Demass, gently descending all the way. At Demass a small caphar * is demanded, which being despatched, we put forward again, but had not gone above an hour and a half when it grew dark, and we were forced to stop at a very inhospitable place, but the best we could find, affording no grass for our horses, nor any water, but just enough to breed frogs, by which we were serenaded all night.

April. 27.—Early the next morning we deserted this uncomfortable lodging, and in about an hour arrived at the river Barrady, our road still descending. This is the river that waters Damascus, and enriches it with all its plenty and pleasure. It is not so much as twenty yards over, but comes pouring down from the mountains with great rapidity, and with so vast a body of water, that it abundantly supplies all the thirsty gardens, and the city of Damascus.

We crossed Barrady at a new bridge over it called Dummar. On the other side our road ascended, and in half an hour

---

* A quarter per head.

brought us to the brink of a high precipice, at the bottom of which the river runs, the mountain being here cleft asunder to give it admission into the plain below.

At the highest part of the precipice is erected a small structure, like a sheikh's sepulchre, concerning which the Turks relate this story:—That their prophet, coming near Damascus, took his station at that place for some time, in order to view the city, and, considering the ravishing beauty and delightfulness of it, he would not tempt his frailty by entering into it, but instantly departed, with this reflection upon it, that there was but one Paradise designed for man, and, for his part, he was resolved not to take his in this world.

You have, indeed, from the precipice, the most perfect prospect of Damascus. And certainly no place in the world can promise the beholder, at a distance, greater voluptuousness. It is situate in an even plain of so great extent, that you can but just discern the mountains that compass it on the farther side. It stands on the west side of the plain, at not above two miles' distance from the place where the river Barrady breaks out from between the mountains, its gardens extending almost to the very place.

The city itself is of a long straight figure, its ends pointing near north-east and south-west. It is very slender in the middle, but swells bigger at each end, especially at that to the north-east. In its length, as far as I could guess by my eye, it may extend near two miles. It is thick-set with mosques and steeples, the usual ornaments of the Turkish cities, and is encompassed with gardens extending no less, according to common estimation, than thirty miles round, which makes it look like a noble city in a vast wood. The gardens are thick-set with fruit-trees of all kinds, kept fresh and verdant by the waters of Barrady. You discover in them many turrets, and steeples, and summer-houses frequently peeping out from among the green boughs, which may be conceived to add no small advantage and beauty to the prospect. On the north side of this vast wood is a place called Solhees, where are the most beautiful summer-houses and gardens.

The greatest part of this pleasantness and fertility proceeds, as I said, from the waters of Barrady, which supply both the gardens and city in great abundance. This river, as soon as it issues out from between the cleft of the moun-

tain before mentioned into the plain, is immediately divided
into three streams, of which the middlemost and biggest runs
directly to Damascus through a large open field called the
Ager Damascenus, and is distributed to all the cisterns and
fountains of the city.   The other two, which I take to be the
work of art, are drawn round, one to the right hand, and the
other to the left, on the borders of the gardens, into which
they are let as they pass by little currents, and so dispersed
all over the vast wood, insomuch that there is not a garden
but has a fine quick stream running through it, which serves
not only for watering the place, but is also improved into fountains and other waterworks very delightful, though not contrived with that variety of exquisite art which is used in
Christendom.

Barrady, being thus described, is almost wholly drunk up
by the city and gardens.   What small part of it escapes is
united, as I was informed, in one channel again, on the south-
east side of the city; and, after about three or four hours'
course, finally loses itself in a bog there without ever arriving
at the sea.

The Greeks, and, from them, the Romans, call this river
Chrysorrhoas; but as for Abana and Pharpar, rivers of Damascus, mentioned in 2 Kings, v. 12, I could find no memory
so much as of the names remaining.   They must doubtless
have been only two branches of the river Barrady; and one
of them was probably the same stream that now runs through
the Ager Damascenus, directly to the city, which seems, by
its serpentine way, to be a natural channel.   The other I
know not well where to find; but it is no wonder, seeing they
may and do turn and alter the courses of this river according
to their own convenience and pleasure.

We continued a good while upon the precipice to take a
view of the city; and indeed it is a hard matter to leave a
station which presents you so charming a landscape.   It exhibits the paradise below as a most fair and delectable place,
and yet will hardly suffer you to stir away to go to it; thus at
once inviting you to the city by the pleasure which it seems
to promise, and detaining you from it by the beauty of the
prospect.

Coming down the hill into the plain, we were there met by
a janissary from the convent, sent to conduct us into the city
He did not think fit to carry us in at the west gate (which was

nearest at hand), and so all across the city to the Latin convent where we were to lodge, for fear the Damascenes, who are
a very bigoted and insolent race, should be offended at so
great a number of Franks as we were ; to avoid which danger
he led us round about the gardens before we arrived at the
gate. The garden walls are of a very singular structure.
They are built of great pieces of earth, made in the fashion
of brick and hardened in the sun. In their dimensions they
are each two yards long, and somewhat more than one broad,
and half a yard thick. Two rows of these, placed edgewise
one upon another, make a cheap, expeditious, and, in this dry
country, a durable wall.

In passing between the gardens we also observed their
method of scouring the channels. They put a great bough
of a tree in the water, and fasten to it a yoke of oxen. Upon
the bough there sits a good weighty fellow, to press it down to
the bottom and to drive the oxen. In this equipage the bough
is dragged all along the channel, and serves at once both to
cleanse the bottom, and also to mud and fatten the water for
the greater benefit of the gardens.

Entering at the east gate, we went immediately to the convent, and were very courteously received by the guardian,
father Raphael, a Majorkine by birth, and a person who,
though he has dedicated himself to the contemplative life, yet
is not unfit for any affairs of the active.

April 28.—This morning we walked out to take a view of
the city. The first place we went to visit was the house of an
eminent Turk. The streets here are narrow, as is usual in
hot countries, and the houses are all built, on the outside, of
no better a material than either sun-burnt brick or Flemish
wall, daubed over in as coarse a manner as can be seen in the
vilest cottages. From this dirty way of building they have
this amongst other inconveniences, that upon any violent rain
the whole city becomes, by the washing of the houses, as it
were a quagmire.

It may be wondered what should induce the people to build
in this base manner when they have, in the adjacent mountains,
such plenty of good stone for noble fabrics. I can give no
reason for it, unless this may pass for such, that those who
first planted here, finding so delicious a situation, were in
haste to come to the enjoyment of it ; and therefore nimbly
set up those extemporary habitations, being unwilling to defer

their pleasures so long as whilst they might erect more magnificent structures, which primitive example their successors have followed ever since.

But, however, in these mud walls you find the gates and doors adorned with marble portals, carved and inlaid with great beauty and variety. It is an object not a little surprising to see mud and marble, state and sordidness, so mingled together.

In the inside the houses discover a very different face from what you see without. Here you find generally a large square court, beautified with a variety of fragrant trees and marble fountains, and compassed round with splendid apartments and divans. The divans are floored and adorned on the sides with variety of marble, mixed in mosaic knots and mazes. The ceilings and traves are, after the Turkish manner, richly painted and gilded. They have generally artificial fountains springing up before them in marble basins; and, as for carpets and cushions, are furnished out to the height of luxury. Of these divans they have generally several on all sides of the court, being placed at such different points that, at one or other of them, you may always have either the shade or the sun, which you please.

Such as I have described was the house we went to see; and I was told the rest resemble the same description.

In the next place we went to see the church of St. John the Baptist, now converted into a mosque, and held too sacred for Christians to enter, or almost to look into. However we had three short views of it, looking in at three several gates. Its gates are vastly large, and covered with brass, stamped all over with Arab characters, and in several places with the figure of a chalice, supposed to be the ancient ensigns or arms of the Mamelukes. On the north side of the church is a spacious court, which I could not conjecture to be less than one hundred and fifty yards long and eighty or one hundred broad. The court is paved all over, and inclosed on the south side by the church, on the other three sides by a double cloister, supported by two rows of granite pillars of the Corinthian order, exceedingly lofty and beautiful.

On the south side the church joins to the bazaars; and there we had an opportunity just to peep into it. It is, within, spacious and lofty, built with three aisles, between which are rows of polished pillars of surpassing beauty, unless, perhaps, we were tempted to overvalue what was so sparingly permitted to our survey.

In this church are kept the head of St. John, and some other relics esteemed so holy that it is death even for a Turk to presume to go into the room where they are kept. We are told here, by a Turk of good fashion, that Christ was to descend into this mosque at the day of judgment, as Mohammed was to do into that of Jerusalem; but the ground and reason of this tradition I could not learn.

From the church we went to the castle, which stands about two furlongs distant towards the west. It is a good building of the rustic manner. In length it is three hundred and forty paces, and in breadth somewhat less. We were admitted but just within the gate, where we saw store of ancient arms and armour, the spoils of the Christians in former times. Amongst the artillery was an old Roman balista; but this was a place not long to be gazed upon by such as we were. At the east end of the castle there hangs down, in the middle of the wall, a short chain cut in stone, of what use I know not, unless to boast the skill of the artificer.

Leaving this place, we went to view the bazaars, which we found crowded with people, but destitute of any thing else worth observing.

April 29.—Very early this morning we went to see the yearly great pomp of the hadgees setting out on their pilgrimage to Mecca*, Ustan, pasha of Tripoli, being appointed their emir or conductor for this year. For our better security from the insolences of the over-zealous votaries, we hired a shop in one of the bazaars through which they were to pass.

In this famous cavalcade there came, first, forty-six dellees, that is religious madmen, carrying each a silk streamer, mixed either of red and green, or of yellow and green; after these came three troops of segmen, an order of soldiers amongst the Turks; and next to them some troops of saphees, another order of soldiery. These were followed by eight companies of Mugrubines (so the Turks call the Barbaroses) on foot. These were fellows of a very formidable aspect, and were designed to be left in a garrison, maintained by the Turks somewhere in the desert of Arabia, and relieved every year with fresh men. In the midst of the Mugrubines there

---

* This account may be compared with De la Brocquière's description of the Mecca caravan, p. 301 of the present volume.

passed six small pieces of ordnance. In the next place came, on foot, the soldiers of the castle of Damascus, fantastically armed with coats of mail, gauntlets, and other pieces of old armour. These were followed by two troops of janissaries and their aga, all mounted. Next were brought the pasha's two horse tails, ushered by the aga of the court; and next after the tails followed six led horses, all of excellent shape and nobly furnished. Over the saddle there was a girth upon each led horse, and a large silver target gilded with gold. After these horses came the mahmal. This is a large pavilion of black silk, pitched upon the back of a very great camel, and spreading its curtains all round about the beast down to the ground. The pavilion is adorned at top with a gold ball, and with gold fringes round about. The camel that carries it wants not also his ornaments of large ropes of beads, fish-shells, fox-tails, and other such fantastical finery, hanged upon his head, neck, and legs. All this is designed for the state of the Alcoran, which is placed with great reverence under the pavilion, where it rides in state both to and from Mecca. The Alcoran is accompanied with a rich new carpet, which the Grand Signor sends every year for the covering of Mohammed's tomb, having the old one brought back in return for it, which is esteemed of an inestimable value after having been so long next neighbour to the prophet's rotten bones. The beast which carries this sacred load has the privilege to be exempted from all other burdens ever after. After the mahmal came another troop, and with them the pasha himself; and, last of all, twenty loaded camels, with which the train ended, having been three quarters of an hour in passing.

Having observed what we could of this show, which perhaps was never seen by Franks before, we went to view some other curiosities. The first place we came to was the Ager Damascenus, a long, beautiful meadow, just without the city on the west side. It is divided in the middle by that branch of the river Barrady which supplies the city, and is taken notice of because of a tradition current here that Adam was made of the earth of this field.

Adjoining the Ager Damascenus is a large hospital. It has within it a pleasant square court, inclosed on the south side by a stately mosque, and on its other sides by cloisters and lodgings of no contemptible structure.

Returning from hence homeward, we were shown, by the

way, a very beautiful bagnio ; and not far from it a coffee
house capable of entertaining four or five hundred people,
shaded over head with trees, and with mats when the boughs
fail.   It had two quarters for the reception of guests, one
proper for the summer, the other for the winter.   That
designed for the summer was a small island, washed all round
with a large, swift stream, and shaded over head with mats
and trees.   We found here a multitude of Turks upon the
divans, regaling themselves in this pleasant place, there being
nothing which they behold with so much delight as greens
and water, to which, if a beautiful face be added, they have a
proverb that all three together make a perfect antidote against
melancholy.

In the afternoon we went to visit the house which, they say,
was some time the house of Ananias, the restorer of sight to
St. Paul*.   The place shown for it is, according to the old
rule, a small grotto or cellar, affording nothing remarkable
but only that there are in it a Christian altar and a Turkish
praying place, seated nearer to each other than well agrees
with the nature of such places.

Our next walk was out of the east gate, in order to see the
place (they say) of St. Paul's vision, and what else is observable
on that side.   The place of the vision is about half a mile
distant from the city eastward.   It is close by the wayside,
and has no building to distinguish it, nor do I believe it ever
had ; only there is a small rock or heap of gravel which serves
to point out the place.

About two furlongs nearer the city is a small timber structure, resembling the cage of a country borough.   Within it is
an altar erected.   There, you are told, the holy apostle rested
for some time in his way to this city after his vision†.

Being returned to the city, we were shown the gate at which
St. Paul was let down in a basket‡.   This gate is at present
walled up by reason of its vicinity to the east gate, which
renders it of little use.

Entering again into the city, we went to see the great
patriarch residing in this city.   He was a person of about
forty years of age.   The place of his residence was mean, and
his person and converse promised not any thing extraordinary.
He told me there were more than one thousand two hundred
souls of the Greek communion in that city.

---

* Acts, ix. 17.   † Acts, ix. 8.   ‡ Acts, ix. 25.

April 30.—The next day we went to visit the gardens, and to spend a day there. The place where we disposed of ourselves was about a mile out of town. It afforded us a very pleasant summer-house, having a plentiful stream of water running through it. The garden was thick-set with fruit trees, but without any art or order. Such as this are all the gardens hereabouts; only with this odds, that some of them have their summer-houses more splendid than others, and their waters improved into greater variety of fountains. In visiting these gardens, Franks are obliged either to walk on foot, or else to ride upon asses, the insolence of the Turks not allowing them to mount on horseback. To serve them upon these occasions here are hackney asses always standing ready equipped for hire. When you are mounted, the master of the ass follows his beast to the place where you are disposed to go, goading him up behind with a sharp-pointed stick, which makes him despatch his stage with great expedition. It is apt sometimes to give a little disgust to the generous traveller to be forced to submit to such marks of scorn; but there is no remedy; and, if the traveller will take my advice, his best way will be to mount his ass contentedly and to turn the affront into a motive of recreation, as we did. Having spent the day in the garden, we returned in the evening to the convent.

May 1.—The next day we spent at another garden, not far distant from the former, but far exceeding it in the beauty of its summer-house and the variety of its fountains.

Sunday, May 2.—We went, as many of us as were disposed, to Sydonaiia, a Greek convent about four hours distant from Damascus to the northward, or north by east. The road, excepting only two steep ascents, is very good. In this stage we passed by two villages, the first called Tall, the second Meneen. At a good distance on the right hand is a very high hill, reported to be the same on which Cain and Abel offered their sacrifices, and where also the former slew his brother, setting the first example of bloodshed to the world.

Sydonaiia is situated at the farther side of a large vale, on the top of a rock. The rock is cut with steps all up, without which it would be inaccessible. It is fenced all round at the top, with a strong wall, which incloses the convent. It is a place of very mean structure, and contains nothing in it extraordinary, but only the wine made here, which is indeed most excellent. This place was at first founded and endowed by the emperor Justinian. It is at present possessed by

twenty Greek monks and forty nuns, who seem to live promiscuously together, without any order or separation.

Here are upon this rock, and within a little compass round
about it, no less than sixteen churches and oratories, dedicated to several names. The first, to St. John; second, to
St. Paul; third, to St. Thomas; fourth, to St. Babylas; fifth,
to St. Barbara; sixth, to St. Christopher; seventh, to St.
Joseph; eighth, to St. Lazarus; ninth, to the blessed Virgin;
tenth, to St. Demetrius; eleventh, to St. Saba; twelfth, to St.
Peter; thirteenth, to St. George; fourteenth, to All Saints;
fifteenth, to the Ascension; sixteenth, to the Transfiguration
of our Lord; from all which, we may well conclude this place was
held anciently in no small repute for sanctity. Many of these
churches I actually visited, but found them so ruined and
desolate, that I had not courage to go to all.

In the chapel made use of by the convent for their daily
services, they pretend to show a great miracle, done here
some years since, of which take this account, as I received it
from them. They had once in the church a little picture of
the blessed Virgin, very much resorted to by supplicants, and
famous for the many cures and blessings granted in return to
their prayers. It happened that a certain sacrilegious rogue
took an opportunity to steal away this miraculous picture; but
he had not kept it long in his custody, when he found it
metamorphosed into a real body of flesh. Being struck with
wonder and remorse at so prodigious an event, he carried
back the prize to its true owners, confessing and imploring
forgiveness for his crime. The monks having recovered so
great a jewel, and being willing to prevent such another
disaster for the future, thought fit to deposit it in a small
chest of stone, and placing it in a little cavity in the wall
behind the high altar, fixed an iron gate before it, in order to
secure it from any fraudulent attempts for the future. Upon
the gates there are hanged abundance of little toys and
trinkets, being the offerings of many votaries in return for
the success given to their prayers at this shrine. Under the
same chest in which the incarnate picture was deposited they
always place a small silver basin, in order to receive the
distillation of a holy oil, which they pretend issues out from
the inclosed image, and does wonderful cures in many dis-
tempers, especially those affecting the eyes.

On the east side of the rock is an ancient sepulchre

hollowed in the firm stone. The room is about eight yards square, and contains in its sides (as I remember) twelve chests for corpses. Over the entrance there are carved six statues as big as the life, standing in three niches, two in each niche. At the pedestals of the statues may be observed a few Greek words, which, as far as I was able to discern them in their present obscurity, are as follows :—

Under the first niche.	Under the second.	Under the third.
ΕΤΟΥϹΙΦ - -	Ι [ΟΥ] Λ . Φ Ι [Λ Ι	ΙΟΥΛ . ΔΗΜΗ
ΙΟΥΛ . ΑΡΤΕ	Π] Π Ι Κ Ο Σ	ΤΡΙΟΣ ΚΑ [Ι] Α [ΡΙ]
ΩΙΔΙΡΟΣ ΚΑΙ	[Κ] ΑΙ ΔΟΜΝϹΙΝΑ	ΑΔΝΗ ΓΥ [ΝΗ]
ΠΡΕΙΓΚΥ ΓΥΝΗ	ΓΥΝΗ	ΠΑΝΤΑΣ ΕΠΟΙΟΤ [Ν]

A gentleman in our company, and myself, have reason to remember this place, for an escape we had in it. A drunken janissary, passing under the window where we were, chanced to have a drop of wine thrown out upon his vest, upon which innocent provocation he presented his pistol at us in at the window; had it gone off, it must have been fatal to one or both of us, who sat next the place. But it pleased God to restrain his fury. This evening we returned again to Damascus.

May 3.—This morning we went to see the street called Straight*. It is about half a mile in length, running from east to west through the city. It being narrow, and the houses jutting out in several places on both sides, you cannot have a clear prospect of its length and straightness. In this street is shown the house of Judas, with whom St. Paul lodged; and in the same house is an old tomb, said to be Ananias's, but how he should come to be buried here they could not tell us, nor could we guess; his own house being shown us in another place. However, the Turks have a reverence for his tomb, and maintain a lamp always burning over it.

In the afternoon, having presented the convent with ten per man for our kind reception, we took our leaves of Damascus, and shaped our course for Tripoli; designing in the way to see Balbec, and the cedars of Libanus. In order to this, we returned the same way by which we came, and, crossing the river Barrady again at the bridge of Dummar, came to a village of the same name a little farther,

* Acts, ix. 11.

and there lodged this night. We travelled this afternoon three hours.

May 4.—This morning we left our old road, and took another more northerly. In an hour and a half we came to a small village called Sinie; just by which is an ancient structure on the top of a high hill, supposed to be the tomb of Abel, and to have given the adjacent country in old times the name of Abilene. The fratricide also is said by some to have been committed in this place. The tomb is thirty yards long, and yet it is here believed to have been but just proportioned to the stature of him who was buried in it. Here we entered into a narrow gut, between two steep rocky mountains, the river Barrady running at the bottom. On the other side of the river were several tall pillars, which excited our curiosity to go and take a nearer view of them. We found them part of the front of some ancient and very magnificent edifice, but of what kind we could not conjecture.

We continued upon the banks of Barrady, and came in three hours to a village called Maday; and in two hours more to a fountain called Ain-il-Hawra, where we lodged. Our whole stage was somewhat less than seven hours; our course nearly north-west.

May 5.—This morning we passed by the fountain of Barrady, and came in an hour and two-thirds to a village called Surgawich. At this place we left the narrow valley, in which we had travelled ever since the morning before, and ascended the mountain on the left hand. Having spent in crossing it two hours, we arrived a second time in the valley of Bocat; here, steering northerly, directly up the valley, we arrived in three hours at Balbec. Our stage this day was near seven hours, and our course near about west.

At Balbec we pitched at a place less than half a mile distant from the town, eastward, near a plentiful and delicious fountain, which grows immediately into a brook; and running down to Balbec, adds no small pleasure and convenience to the place.

In the afternoon we walked out to see the city. But we thought fit before we entered to get licence of the governor, and to proceed with all caution; being taught this necessary care by the example of some worthy English gentlemen of our factory, who, visiting this place in the year 1689, in their return from Jerusalem, and suspecting no mischief, were basely intrigued by the people here, and forced to redeem their lives at a great sum of money.

Balbec is supposed to be the ancient Heliopolis, or City of the Sun; for that the word imports. Its present Arab, which is perhaps its most ancient name, inclines to the same importance. For Baal, though it imports all idols in general, of whatsoever sex or condition, yet it is very often appropriated to the sun, the sovereign idol of this country.

The city enjoys a most delightful and commodious situation, on the east side of the valley of Bocat. It is of a square figure, compassed with a tolerable good wall, in which are towers all round at equal distances. It extends, as far as I could guess by the eye, about two furlongs on a side. Its houses within are all of the meanest structure, such as are usually seen in Turkish villages.

At the south-west side of this city is a noble ruin, being the only curiosity for which this place is wont to be visited. It was anciently a heathen temple, together with some other edifices belonging to it, all truly magnificent; but in latter times these ancient structures have been patched and pieced up with several other buildings, converting the whole into a castle, under which name it goes at this day. The adjectitious buildings are of no mean architecture, but yet easily distinguishable from what is more ancient.

Coming near these ruins, the first thing you meet with is a little round pile of building, all of marble. It is encircled with columns of the Corinthian order, very beautiful, which support a cornice that runs all round the structure, of no ordinary state and beauty. The part of it that remains is at present in a very tottering condition, but yet the Greeks use it for a church; and it were well if the danger of its falling, which perpetually threatens, would excite those people to use a little more fervour in their prayers than they generally do, the Greeks being, seemingly, the most undevout and negligent at their divine service of any sort of people in the Christian world.

From this ruin you come to a large firm pile of building, which, though very lofty and composed of huge square stones, yet, I take to be part of the adjectitious work; for one sees in the inside some fragments of images in the walls and stones, with Roman letters upon them, set the wrong way. In one stone we found graven D I V I S, and in another line,

M O S C. Through this pile, you pass in a stately arched walk
or portico, one hundred and fifty paces long, which leads you
to the temple.

The temple is an oblong square, in breadth thirty-two
yards, and in length sixty-four, of which eighteen were taken
up by the πρόναος or ante-temple, which is now tumbled down,
the pillars being broke that sustained it. The body of the
temple, which now stands, is encompassed with a noble
portico, supported by pillars of the Corinthian order, measuring six feet and three inches in diameter, and about forty-five
feet in height, consisting all of three stones apiece. The
distance of the pillars from each other, and from the wall of
the temple, is nine feet. Of these pillars there are fourteen
on each side of the temple, and eight at the end, counting the
corner pillars in both numbers.

On the capitals of the pillars there runs all round a stately
architrave and cornice, rarely carved. The portico is covered
with large stones hollowed archwise, extending between the
columns and the wall of the temple. In the centre of each
stone is carved the figure of some one or other of the heathen
gods or goddesses, or heroes. I remember amongst the
rest a Ganymede, and the eagle flying away with him, so
lively done that it excellently represented the sense of that
verse in Martial,

" Illæsum timidis unguibus hæsit onus."

The gate of the temple is twenty-one feet wide, but how
high could not be measured, it being in part filled up with
rubbish. It is moulded and beautified all round with exquisite sculpture. On the nethermost side of the portal is
carved a Fame hovering over the head, as you enter, and
extending its wings two-thirds of the breadth of the gate;
and on each side of the eagle is described a Fame, likewise
upon the wing. The eagle carries in its pounces a caduceus.
and in his beak the strings or ribbons coming from the ends
of two festoons, whose other ends are held and supported on
each side by the two Fames. The whole seemed to be a
piece of admirable sculpture.

The measure of the temple within is forty yards in length,
and twenty in breadth. In its walls all round are two rows
of pilasters, one above the other; and between the pilasters
are niches, which seem to have been designed for the recep-

tion of idols.   Of these pilasters there are eight in a row on
each side; and of the niches, nine.

About eight yards' distance from the upper end of the
temple stands part of two fine channelled pillars, which seem
to have made a partition in that place, and to have supported
a canopy over the throne of the chief idol, whose station
appears to have been in a large niche at this end.   On that
part of the partition which remains are to be seen carvings
in rilievo representing Neptune, Tritons, Fishes, Sea-gods,
Arion and his dolphin, and other marine figures.   The covering of the whole fabric is totally broken down; but yet this I
must say of the whole as it now stands, that it strikes the
mind with an air of greatness beyond any thing that I ever
saw before, and is an eminent proof of the magnificence of the
ancient architecture.

About fifty yards distant from the temple is a row of
Corinthian pillars, very great and lofty, with a most stately
architrave and cornice at top.   This speaks itself to have been
part of some very august pile; but what one now sees of it is
but just enough to give a regret that there should be no more
of it remaining.

Here is another curiosity of this place, which a man had
need be well assured of his credit before he ventures to relate,
lest he should be thought to strain the privilege of a traveller
too far.   That which I mean is a large piece of the old wall, or
περίβολος, which encompassed all these structures last described.
A wall made of such monstrous great stones, that the natives
hereabouts (as it is usual in things of this strange nature)
ascribe it to the architecture of the devil.   Three of the
stones, which were larger than the rest, we took the pains to
measure, and found them to extend sixty-one yards in length;
one twenty-one, the other two each twenty yards.   In deepness they were four yards each, and in breadth of the same
dimension.   These three stones lay in one and the same
row, end to end.   The rest of the wall was made also of great
stones, but none, I think, so great as these.   That which
added to the wonder was, that these stones were lifted up into
the wall more than twenty feet from the ground.

In the side of a small ascent, on the east part of the town,
stood an old single column, of the Tuscan order, about
eighteen or nineteen yards high, and one yard and a half in
diameter.   It had a channel cut in its side from the bottom

to the top, from which we judged it might have been erected for the sake of raising water.

At our return to our tents we were a little perplexed by the servants of the mosolem, about our caphar. We were contented at last to judge it at ten per Frank, and five per servant, rather than we would engage in a long dispute at such a place as this.

Near the place where we lodged was an old mosque, and (as I said before) a fine fountain. This latter had been anciently beautified with some handsome stone-work round it, which was now almost ruined; however, it afforded us this imperfect inscription.

ΤΩΝΧΕΙΜΕΡΕΙΩΝ　Π..ΟΝΕΩΚΤΙϹΤΟϹΠΑΝΝ
ΒΛΕΠΕΙΝΔΕΔΩΚΕΝ　ΩΡΡΕϹΤΕΚΛΙΝΕΟΝ
ΧΡΥϹΟΝΠΑΡΑϹΧϹ...ϹΩϹΙΒΙΟϹΤΕΜΕΓΑϹ.
ΥΔΩΡΤΕΝΥΝ-ΡΕΚΤΙΠΗΓΑΙΟΝΠΟΛΥ
ΕΥΧΑΙϹΘΕΟΔΟΤΟΥΤΟΥ　ΟϹΙΟΥΕΠΙϹΚΟΠΟΥ.

May 6. — Early this morning we departed from Balbec, directing our course straight across the valley. As we passed by the walls of the city, we observed many stones inscribed with Roman letters and names, but all confused, and some placed upside down, which demonstrates that the materials of the wall were the ruins of the ancient city. In one place we found these letters, R M I P T I T V E P R; in others these, V A R I ---; in another, N E R I S; in others, L V C I L ---, and S E V E R I, and C E L N A E, and F I R M I; all which serve only to denote the resort which the Romans had to this place in ancient times.

In one hour we passed by a village called Ye-ad; and in an hour more went to see an old monumental pillar, a little on the right hand of the road It was nineteen yards high, and five feet in diameter, of the Corinthian order. It had a table for an inscription on its north side, but the letters are now perfectly erased. In one hour more we reached the other side of the valley, at the foot of Mount Anti-Libanus.

We immediately ascended the mountain, and in two hours came to a large cavity between the hills, at the bottom of which was a lake called by its old Greek name, Limone. It is about three furlongs over, and derives its waters from the melting of the snow. By this lake our guides would have had us stay all night, assuring us that if we went up higher in the mountains we should be forced to lie amongst the snow; but we ventured that, preferring a cold lodging before an unwholesome one. Having ascended one hour, we arrived at the snow, and proceeding amongst it for one hour and a half more, we then chose out as warm a place as we could in so high a region; and there we lodged this night upon the very top of Libanus. Our whole stage this day was seven hours and a half.

Libanus is in this part free from rocks, and only rises and falls with small, easy unevennesses, for several hours' riding; but is perfectly barren and desolate. The ground, where not concealed by the snow, appeared to be covered with a sort of white slates, thin and smooth. The chief benefit it serves for is, that by its exceeding height it proves a conservatory for abundance of snow, which, thawing in the heat of summer, affords supplies of water to the rivers and fountains in the valleys below. We saw in the snow prints of the feet of several wild beasts, which are the sole proprietors of these upper parts of the mountains.

May 7.—The next morning we went four hours almost perpetually upon deep snow, which, being frozen, bore us and our horses; and then descending for about one hour, came to a fountain called, from the name of an adjacent village, Ain-il-Hadede. By this time we were got into a milder and better region.

Here was the place where we were to strike out of the way, in order to go to Canobine and the cedars. And some of us went upon this design, whilst the rest chose rather to go directly for Tripoli, to which we had not now above four hours. We took with us a guide, who pretended to be well acquainted with the way to Canobine, but he proved an ignorant director; and after he had led us about for several hours in intricate and untrodden mazes amongst the mountains, finding him perfectly at a loss, we were forced to forsake our intended visit for the present, and to steer directly for Tripoli, where we arrived late at night, and were again entertained by our worthy friends, Mr. Consul Hastings and Mr. Fisher, with their wonted friendship and generosity.

May 8.—In the afternoon Mr. Consul Hastings carried us to see the castle of Tripoli. It is pleasantly situated on a

hill, commanding the city, but has neither arms nor ammunition in it, and serves rather for a prison than a garrison.
There was shut up in it at this time a poor Christian prisoner,
called Sheikh Eunice, a Maronite. He was one that had formerly renounced his faith, and lived for many years in the
Mohammedan religion, but in his declining age he both re-
tracted his apostacy and died to atone for it, for he was im-
paled by the order of the pasha two days after we left Tripoli.
This punishment of impaling is commonly executed amongst
the Turks for crimes of the greatest degree, and is certainly
one of the greatest indignities and barbarities that can be
offered to human nature. The execution is done in this
manner. They take a post of about the bigness of a man's
leg, and eight or nine feet long, and make it very sharp at
one end. This they lay upon the back of the criminal, and
force him to carry it to the place of execution, imitating
herein the old Roman custom of compelling malefactors to
bear their cross. Being arrived at the fatal place, they thrust
in the stake at the fundament of the person who is the miserable subject of this doom, and then taking him by the legs,
draw on his body upon it, till the point of the stake appears
at his shoulders. After this they erect the stake, and fasten
it in a hole dug in the ground. The criminal, sitting in this
manner upon it, remains not only still alive, but also drinks,
smokes, and talks, as one perfectly sensible, and thus some
have continued for twenty-four hours; but generally, after the
tortured wretch has remained in this deplorable and igno-
minious posture an hour or two, some one of the standers by
is permitted to give him a gracious stab to the heart, so putting an end to his inexpressible misery.

Sunday, May 9.—Despairing of any other opportunity, I
made another attempt this day to see the cedars and Canobine. Having gone for three hours across the plain of Tripoli, I arrived at the foot of Libanus, and from thence, continually ascending, not without great fatigue, came in four
hours and a half to a small village called Eden, and in two
hours and a half more to the cedars. These noble trees
grow amongst the snow near the highest part of Lebanon,
and are remarkable as well for their own age and largeness
as for those frequent allusions made to them in the word of
God. Here are some of them very old, and of a prodigious
bulk, and others younger, of a smaller size. Of the former

I could reckon up only sixteen, and the latter are very numerous. I measured one of the largest, and found it twelve
yards six inches in girth, and yet sound, and thirty-seven
yards in the spread of its boughs. At about five or six yards
from the ground it was divided into five limbs, each of which
was equal to a great tree.

After about half an hour spent in surveying this place, the
clouds began to thicken, and to fly along upon the ground,
which so obscured the road that my guide was very much at
a loss to find our way back again. We rambled about for
seven hours thus bewildered, which gave me no small fear of
being forced one night more at Libanus; but at last, after a
long exercise of pains and patience, we arrived at the way
that goes down to Canobine, where I arrived by the time it
was dark, and found a kind reception, answerable to the great
need I had of it, after so long fatigue.

Canobine is a convent of the Maronites, and the seat of
the patriarch, who is at present F. Stephanus Edenensis, a
person of great learning and humanity. It is a very mean
structure; but its situation is admirably adapted for retirement and devotion, for there is a very deep rupture in the
side of Libanus, running at least seven hours' travel directly
up into the mountain. It is on both sides exceeding steep
and high, clothed with fragrant greens from top to bottom,
and everywhere refreshed with fountains, falling down from
the rocks in pleasant cascades, the ingenious work of nature.
These streams, all uniting at the bottom, make a full and rapid
torrent, whose agreeable murmuring is heard all over the place,
and adds no small pleasure to it. Canobine is seated on the
north side of this chasm, on the steep of the mountain, at
about the midway between the top and the bottom. It stands
at the mouth of a great cave, having a few small rooms
fronting outward that enjoy the light of the sun, the rest are
all under ground. It had for its founder the emperor Theodosius the Great; and though it has been several times rebuilt, yet the patriarch assured me the church was of the
primitive foundation; but, whoever built it, it is a mean
fabric, and no great credit to its founder. It stands in the
grotto, but fronting outwards receives a little light from that
side. In the same side there were also hung in the wall two
small bells to call the monks to their devotions; a privilege
allowed nowhere else in this country, nor would they be suf-

fered here, but that the Turks are far enough off from the hearing of them.

The valley of Canobine was anciently, as it well deserves, very much resorted to for religious retirement. You see here still hermitages, cells, monasteries, almost without number. There is not any little part of rock that jets out upon the side of the mountain, but you generally see some little structure upon it for the reception of monks and hermits, though few or none of them are now inhabited.

May 10.—After dinner I took my leave of the patriarch, and returned to Tripoli. I steered my course down by a narrow oblique path cut in the side of the rupture, and found it three hours before I got clear of the mountains, and three more afterwards before I came to Tripoli.

May 11.—This day we took our leaves of our worthy Tripoli friends, in order to return for Aleppo. We had some debate with ourselves, whether we should take the same way by which we came when outward bound, or a new one by Emissa, Hempse, and Hamal. But we had notice of some disturbances upon this latter road, so we contented ourselves to return by the same way we came; for having had enough by this time both of the pleasure and of the fatigue of travelling, we were willing to put an end to both the nearest and speediest way. All that occurred to us new in these days' travel was a particular way used by the country people in gathering their corn, it being now harvest time. They plucked it up by handfuls from the roots, leaving the most fruitful fields as naked as if nothing had ever grown on them. This was their practice in all places of the east that I have seen; and the reason is that they may lose none of their straw, which is generally very short, and necessary for the sustenance of their cattle, no hay being here made. I mention this, because it seems to give light to that expression of the Psalmist, " which withereth before it be plucked up,"* where there seems to be a manifest allusion to this custom. Our new translation renders this place otherwise; but in so doing it differs from most or all other copies, and here we may truly say the old is the better. There is indeed mention of a mower in the next verse, but then it is such a mower as fills not his hand, which confirms rather than weakens the preceding interpretation.

* Psalms, cxxix. 6.

Returning, therefore, by our former stages without any notable alteration or occurrence, we came in eight days to the Honey Khan, at which place we found many of our Aleppine friends, who, having heard of our drawing homeward, were come out to meet us and welcome us home.   Having dined together, and congratulated each other upon our happy re-union, we went onward the same evening to Aleppo.

Thus, by God's infinite mercy and protection, we were restored all in safety to our respective habitations.   And here, before I conclude, I cannot but take notice of one thing more, which I should earnestly recommend to the devout and grateful remembrance of every person engaged in this pilgrimage, viz., that amongst so great a company as we were, amidst such a multiplicity of dangers and casualties, such variety of food, airs, and lodgings (very often none of the best), there was no one of us that came to any ill accident throughout our whole travels, and only one that fell sick by the consequences of the journey after our return, which I esteem the less diminution to so singular a mercy, in regard that, amongst so many of my dear friends and fellow-travellers, it fell to my own share to be the sufferer.   Δόξα Θεῷ.

Since the book was printed off, the two following letters, relating to the same subject, were communicated by the Rev. Mr. Osborn, Fellow of Exeter College; to whom they were sent by the author, in answer to some questions proposed by him.

Sir,

I RECEIVED yours of June 27, 1698, and returned you an answer to it in brief, about three months since, promising to supply what was then wanting at some other opportunity, which promise I shall now make good.   You desired an account of the Turks, and of our way of living amongst them.   As to the former, it would fill a volume to write my whole thoughts about them.   I shall only tell you at present that I think they are very far from agreeing with that character which is given of them in Christendom, especially for their exact justice, veracity, and other moral virtues, upon account of which I have sometimes heard them mentioned with very extravagant commendations, as though they far exceed Christian nations.   But I must profess myself of another opinion; for the Christian religion, how much soever we live below the true spirit and excellency of it, must still be allowed to discover so much power upon the minds of its professors as to raise them far above the level of a Turkish virtue.   It is a maxim that I have often heard from our merchants, that a Turk will always cheat when he can find an opportunity. Friendship, generosity, and wit (in the English notion), and delightful converse, and all the qualities of a refined and ingenuous spirit, are perfect strangers to their minds, though in traffic and worldly negotiations they are acute enough, and are able to carry the accounts of a large commerce in their heads without the help of books, by a natural arithmetic, improved by custom and necessity. Their religion is framed to keep up great outward gravity and solemnity, without begetting the least good tincture of wisdom or virtue in the mind. You shall have them at their hours of prayer, which are four a day always, addressing themselves to their devotions with the most solemn and critical washings, always in the most public places, where most people are passing, with most lowly and most regular protestations, and a hollow tone, which are amongst them the great excellencies of prayer. I have seen them, in an affected charity, give money to bird-catchers (who make a trade of it), to restore the poor captives to their natural liberty, and at the same time hold their own slaves in the heaviest bondage ; and at other times they will buy flesh to relieve indigent dogs and cats, and yet curse you with famine and pestilence, and all the most hideous execrations, in which way these eastern nations have certainly the most exquisite rhetoric of any people upon earth. They know hardly any pleasure but that of the sixth sense. And yet with all this, they are incredibly conceited of their own religion, and contemptuous of that of others, which I take to be the great artifice of the devil, in order to keep them his own. They are a perfect visible comment upon our blessed Lord's description of the Jewish Pharisees. In a word, lust, arrogance, covetousness, and the most exquisite hypocrisy, complete their character. The only thing that ever I could observe to commend in them is the outward decency of their carriage, the profound respect they pay to religion and to every thing relating to it, and their great temperance and frugality. The dearness of any thing is no motive in Turkey, though it be in England, to bring it into fashion.

As for our living amongst them, it is with all possible quiet and safety ; and that is all we desire, their conversation being not in the least entertaining. Our delights are among ourselves ; and here being more than forty of us, we never want a most friendly and pleasant conversation. Our way of life resembles in some measure the academical. We live in separate squares, shut up every night after the manner of colleges. We begin the day constantly, as you do, with prayers, and have our set times for business, meals, and recreations. In the winter we hunt in the most delightful champaign twice a week ; and in the summer go as often to divert ourselves under our tents, with bowling and other exercises ; so that you see we want not divertisements, and these all innocent and manly. In short, it is my real opinion, that there is not a society out of England that for all good and desirable qualities may be compared to this. But enough of this confusion, which I would have shortened, and put in better order, if I had had time.

March 10, 1698.

_____

SIR,
As for your questions about Gehazi's posterity and the Greek excommunications, I have little to answer ; but yet, I hope, enough to give you and your friend satisfaction. When I was in the Holy Land I saw several that laboured under Gehazi's distemper, but none that could pretend to derive his

pedigree from that person. Some of them were poor enough to be his relations; particularly at Sichem (now Naplosu) there were no less than ten (the same number that were cleansed by our Saviour not far from the same place) that came begging to us at one time. Their manner is to come with small buckets in their hands, to receive the alms of the charitable, their touch being still held infectious, or at least unclean. The distemper, as I saw it in them, was very different from what I have seen it in England; for it not only defiles the whole surface of the body with a foul scurf, but also deforms the joints of the body, particularly those of the wrists and ankles, making them swell with a gouty, scrofulous substance, very loathsome to look upon. I thought their legs resembled those of old, battered horses, such as are often seen in drays in England. The whole distemper, indeed, as it there appeared, was so noisome that it might well pass for the utmost corruption of the human body on this side the grave; and certainly the inspired penmen could not have found out a fitter emblem whereby to express the uncleanness and odiousness of vice. But to return to Gehazi, it is no wonder if the descent from him be by time obscured, seeing the best of the Jews, at this time of day, are at a loss to make out their genealogies. But, besides, I see no necessity in Scripture for his line being perpetuated. The term "for ever" is, you know, often taken in a limited sense in holy writ, of which the designation of Phineas's family to the priesthood * may serve for an instance. His posterity was, you know, cut entirely off from the priesthood, and that transferred to Eli (who was one of another line) about three hundred years after.

I have inquired of a Greek priest, a man not destitute either of sense or probity, about your other question. He positively affirmed it, and produced an instance of his own knowledge in confirmation of it. He said that, about fifteen years ago, a certain Greek departed this life without absolution, being under the guilt of a crime which involved him in the sentence of excommunication, but unknown to the church. He had Christian burial given him; and, about ten years after, a son of his dying, they had occasion to open the ground near where his body was laid, in order to bury his son by him, by which means they discovered his body as entire as when it was first laid in the grave. The shroud was rotted away, and the body naked and black, but perfectly sound. Report of this being brought to the bishop, he immediately suspected the cause of it, and sent several priests (of whom the relator was one) to pray for the soul of the departed, and to absolve him at his grave; which they had no sooner done, but (as the relator goes on) the body instantly dissolved and fell into dust, like slacked lime; and so, well satisfied with the effect of their absolution, they departed. This was delivered to me *verbo sacerdotis.* The man had hard fortune not to die in the Romish communion; for then his body being found so entire would have entitled him to saintship; for the Romanists, as I have both heard and seen, are wont to find out and maintain the relics of saints by this token; and the same sign which proves an *anathema maranatha* amongst the Greeks, demonstrates a saint amongst the Papists. Perhaps both are equally in the right.

    April 12, 1700.

---

    * Numbers, xxv. 13.

AN

ACCOUNT OF THE AUTHOR'S JOURNEY

FROM

ALEPPO TO THE RIVER EUPHRATES, THE CITY BEER, AND TO MESOPOTAMIA.

WE set out from Aleppo, April 17th, 1699, and steering east-north-east, somewhat less, we came in three hours and a half to Surbass.

April 18.—We came in three hours and a half to Bezay, passing by Bab, where is a good aqueduct, Dyn il Daab*, to which you descend by about thirty steps; and Lediff, a pleasant village. Our course thus far was east and by north. In the afternoon we advanced three hours further, course north-east, to an old ruined place, formerly of some consideration, called Acamy. It is situated in the wilderness, on a hill encompassed by a valley; it was large, and had the footsteps of some symmetry, good walls and buildings.

April 19.—We went east and by north, and in four hours arrived at Bambych. This place has no remnants of its ancient greatness† but its walls, which may be traced all round, and cannot be less than three miles in compass. Several fragments of them remain on the east side, especially at the east gate; and another piece of eighty yards long, with towers of large square stone extremely well built. On the north side I found a stone with the busts of a man and woman, large as the life; and, under, two eagles carved on it. Not far from it, on the side of a large well, was fixed a stone with three figures carved on it, in basso relievo. They were two syrens, which, twining their fishy tails together, made a seat, on which was placed, sitting, a naked woman, her arms and the syrens' on each side mutually entwined.

On the west side is a deep pit of about one hundred yards diameter. It was low, and had no water in it, and seemed to have had great buildings all round it, with the pillars and ruins of which it is now in part filled up, but not so much but that there was still water in it. Here are a multitude of subterraneous aqueducts brought to this city, the people attested no fewer than fifty. You can ride nowhere about the city without seeing them.

* The district of Daab. So the note in the original edition, but query if not Aïn-el-Dab, that is, the fountain of Dab.

† It was the ancient Hierapolis.

We pitched by one about a quarter of a mile east of the city, which yields a fine stream, and, emptying itself into a valley, waters it, and makes it extremely fruitful. Here perhaps were the pastures of the beasts designed for sacrifices. Here are now only a few poor inhabitants, though anciently all the north side was well inhabited by Saracens, as may be seen by the remains of a noble mosque and a bagnio, a little without the walls. We were here visited by a company of Begdelies, who were encamped some hours further towards Euphrates, having about a thousand horse there.

April 20.—For avoiding the Begdelies we hired a guide, who conducted us a by-way. We travelled north-north-east, over a desert ground, and came in three hours to a small rivulet called Sejour (Sajur), which falls into the Euphrates about three hours below Jerabolus. In about two hours more we came to a fine fruitful plain, covered with extraordinary corn, lying between the hills and the river Euphrates. In about an hour and a half's travelling through this plain on the banks of the river, we came to Jerabolus. This place is of a semicircular figure. Its flat side lying on the banks of Euphrates, on that side it has a high long mount, close by the water, very steep. It was anciently built upon (and at one end of it I saw fragments of) very large pillars, a yard and a half diameter, and capitals and cornices well carved. At the foot of the mount was carved on a large stone a beast resembling a lion, with a bridle in his mouth, and I believe anciently a person sitting on it, but the stone is in that part now broke away; the tail of the beast was couped[*].

Round about this place are high banks cast up, and there is the traces of walls on them. The gates seem to have been well built. The whole was two thousand two hundred and fifty paces, that is, yards, in circumference. The river is here as large as the Thames in London; a long bullet-gun could not shoot a ball over it, but it dropped into the water. Here is found a large serpent, which has legs and claws, called Woralla[†]. I was told by a Turk that a little below this place, when the river is low, may be seen the ruins of a stone bridge over the river; for my own part I saw it not, nor do I much rely on the Turk's veracity. The river seemed to be lately fallen very suddenly, for the banks were freshly wet two yards and more above the water. It was here north and south.

April 21.—We kept close on the banks of the Euphrates, and in two hours and a half crossed a fine rivulet called Towzad; and in two hours more arrived over against Beer (Bir, or Birijik), and

---

[*] This figure was found on the same spot, but in a more mutilated condition, by the Euphrates Expedition.

[†] The Monitor; the same animal mentioned by La Brocquière. See p. 290.

pitched on a flat, close by the river side.   Observing the latitude
of the place by my quadrant, I found the angle between the sun
and the zenith to be twenty-two degrees; and the declination
this day being fifteen degrees ten minutes, the whole is thirty-
seven degrees ten minutes.

April 22.—We continued at our station, not daring to cross the
river for fear of falling into the hands of the Kaiyah of the Pasha
of Urfa, who was then at Beer, ordering many boats of corn down
to Bagdal. We were supplied in the same time with provisions by
Sheikh Assyne, to whom we made returns.

Sunday, April 23.—The Kaiyah being now departed, Sheikh
Assyne invited us over to Beer; we crossed in a boat of the
country, of which they have a great many, this being the great
pass in,) Mesopotamia.   The boats are of a miserable fabric, flat
and open in the fore part for horses to enter; they are large
enough to carry about four horses each.   Their way to cross is
by drawing up the boat as high as they know to be necessary;
and then with wretched oars striking over, she falls a good way
down by the force of the stream before they arrive at the further
side.

Having saluted Assyne, we were conducted to see the castle,
which is a large old building on the top of a great long rock,
separated by a great gulf, or natural bottom, from the land.   At
first coming within the gates, which are of iron, we saw several
large globes of stone, about twenty inches diameter; and great
axles of iron, with wheels, which were entire blocks of wood two
feet thick in the nave, and cut somewhat to an edge toward the
periphery; and screws to bend bows or engines; as also several
brass field pieces.

Ascending up the sides of the rock by a way cut obliquely, you
come to the castle.   At first entrance, you find a way cut under
ground down to the river.   In the castle, the principal things we
saw were, first, a large room full of old arms; I saw there glass
bottles to be shot at the end of arrows; one of them was stuck at
the end of an arrow, with four pieces of tin by its sides, to keep it
firm.   Vast large cross-bows and beams, seemingly designed for
battering-rams; and Roman saddles and head-pieces of a large
size, some of which were painted; and some large thongs for bow-
strings, and bags for slinging stones.   But the jealousy of the
Turks would not permit us to stay so long as would have been
requisite for a perfect examination of these antiquities.

From the castle we returned to Assyne, and were civilly treated.
In the evening we went up into the country of Mesopotamia.
The hills are chalky and steep, and come close to the water side
without a plain intervening, as it is upon the side of Syria; so
that Beer stands on the side of a hill.   However, it has a couple
of fine streams that run over the top of the hill, one of which
drives two mills, and so runs down to the city, which is well walled.

In the side of the hill there is a khan under ground cut into the rock, with fifteen large pillars left to support its roof.

April 24.—We left Beer, and, travelling west, came in three hours to Nizib, a place well situated at the head of the Towzad. Here is an old small church, very strong and entire, only the cupola in the middle of the cross is broken down, and its space covered with leaves, to fit the place of a mosque. I believe the Turks made the places to which they turn in prayers empty niches, to show that they worshipped one invisible God, not to be represented by images. In two hours we came from Nizib to a Christian village called Uwur; and in an hour and a half more to a well in the desert.

April 25.—We travelled west near two hours, and came through a fine country diversified into small hills and valleys, to a village called Adjia, having left Silam and two other villages on the right hand. At Adjia rises the river of Aleppo, from a large fountain, at once; and just above it runs the Sejour, which might be let into it by a short cut of ten yards. From Adjia our course was west-north-west. The banks of the Sejour are well planted with trees and villages. In two little hours we came to Antab (Aïn-tab), having crossed the Sejour at a bridge about three quarters of an hour before. Leaving the city on the right hand, we passed under its walls, and pitched about three quarters of an hour from it, on a plain field on the banks of the Sejour.

Antab stands mostly on a hill, having a castle on a round mount at its north side, exactly resembling that of Aleppo, though much less. It has a very deep ditch round it; and at the foot of the mount, within the ditch, is a gallery cut through the rock all round the castle, with portals for shot; and it is faced with stone walls where the rock was not strong enough. The houses have generally no upper rooms; the bazaars are large. I saw here a fine stone, very much resembling porphyry, being of a red ground, with yellow specks and veins, very glossy. It is dug just by Antab.

Antab is doubtless Antiochia penes Taurum, in the skirts of which it stands; and is not far distant from the highest ridge. It is about two thirds as big as Aleppo.

April 26.—We passed through a fruitful, mountainous country, and came in seven hours and a quarter to Rowant Castle. It stands on the top of a round, steep hill, and has been strong for the times it was built in. It is probably a Saracen fabric, and is now in ruins. At the foot of the hill, westward, runs the river Ephreen: its course is south-south-west. Our course from Antab to Rowant was north-west and by north.

April 27.—We continued travelling through the mountains, which were now somewhat more uneven and precipitous, but watered every where with fine springs and rivulets. In about six hours we came to Corus. Our course was south-west, having

crossed the Ephreen about two-thirds of an hour before. Just by
Corus is the river Sabon, that is Chor or Char, which encompasses
most part of the city.

Corus stands on a hill, consisting of the city and castle. The
city stands northerly; and from its north end, ascending, you
come at last to a higher hill to the southward, on which stands
the castle. The whole is now in ruins, which seems to have been
very large, walled very strongly with huge square stones. Within
are observable the ruins, pillars, &c., of many noble buildings. On
the west side there is a square inclosure of great capacity, compassed with good walls and five gates, which admitted into it, as
one may discern by the ruins of them. I conjectured they might
be the cathedral. Over the castle gate were written three inscriptions, the middle inscription being over the middle of the portal,
the other two on the top of the pilasters on the right and left-hand.

Below the castle hill, to the southward, stands a noble old monument. It is six square, and opens at six windows above, and is
covered with a pyramidical cupola. In each angle within is a
pillar of the Corinthian order, of one stone; and there is a fine
architrave all round just under the cupola, having had heads of
oxen carved on it. And it ends a top with a large capital of the
Corinthian order. Near this are several sepulchral altars, of which
only one has a legible inscription.

April 28.—We left Corus; and without the town, about half a
mile south-east, we descended through a way cut obliquely on the
side of a precipice, which leads to a bridge of seven arches, of a very
old structure, over the river Sabon; and about a quarter of a mile
further we came to another bridge of three very large arches, over
the river Ephreen. These bridges are very ancient, and well built
of square stone. Three pillars have an acute angle on the side
against the stream, and a round buttress on the other side; and
on both sides are niches for statues. They were well paved on the
top with large stones; and are doubtless, as well as that on the
other side of the town, the work of the excellent and magnificent
Theodorit*.

From this bridge, in about three hours, with a course south-
south-east, or south-east and by south, we arrived at Fan-Bolads.
From Fan-Bolads to Chillis is one hour and two-thirds, course
north-north-east. Chillis is a large, populous town, and has fifteen
mosques that may be counted without the town; and it has large
bazaars. Many medals are found here, which seem to argue it to
be ancient; but under what name I know not.

Aleppo bears from Fan-Bolads south and by east; Seck-Berukel
south-south-west. An hour from Fan-Bolads is Azass; and two

---

* Few European travellers, either before or since Maundrell's time, have
visited the ruins of Cyrrhus in Cyrrhestica, above described; a circumstance
which gives especial interest to Maundrell's account of them.

hours further we lodged in the plain, which, about Chillis and Azass, is very wide and no less fruitful. This country is always given to the Validea, or Grand Signor's mother.

April 28.—We arrived, by God's blessing, safe in Aleppo, having travelled about five hours with a course south and by east. Δόξα Θεῷ.

OF THE VALLEY OF SALT,

WHICH IS ABOUT FOUR HOURS FROM ALEPPO.

THIS valley is of two or three hours extent. We were three quarters of an hour in crossing one corner of it. It is of an exact level, and appears at a distance like a lake of water. There is a kind of dry crust of salt all over the top of it, which sounds, when the horses go upon it, like frozen snow when it is walked upon. There are three or four small rivulets which empty themselves into this place, and wash it all over, about autumn, or when the rains fall.

In the heat of the summer the water is dried off; and, when the sun has scorched the ground, there is found remaining the crust of salt aforesaid, which they gather and separate into several heaps, according to the degrees of fineness, some being exquisitely white, others alloyed with dirt. It being soft in some places, our horses' hoofs struck in deep; and there I found, in one part, a soft, brown clay; in another a very black one; which to the taste was very salt, though deep in the earth. Along, on one side of the valley, viz. that towards Gibul, there is a small precipice, about two men's lengths, occasioned by the continual taking away the salt; and in this you may see how the veins of it lie. I broke a piece of it, of which that part of it that was exposed to the rain, sun, and air, though it had the sparks and particles of salt, yet it had perfectly lost its savour, as in St. Matthew, chap. v. The inner part, which was connected to the rock, retained its savour, as I found by proof.

In several places of the valley we found that the thin crust of salt upon the surface bulged up, as if some insect working under it had raised it; and, taking off the part, we found under it efflorescences of pure salt, shot out according to its proper figure.

At the neighbouring village of Gibul are kept the magazines of salt, where you find great mountains, as I may say, of that mineral ready for sale. The valley is farmed of the Grand Signor at twelve hundred dollars per annum.

INDEX.

A CATALOG OF SELECTED
DOVER BOOKS
IN ALL FIELDS OF INTEREST

A CATALOG OF SELECTED DOVER
BOOKS IN ALL FIELDS OF INTEREST

CONCERNING THE SPIRITUAL IN ART, Wassily Kandinsky. Pioneering work by father of abstract art. Thoughts on color theory, nature of art. Analysis of earlier masters. 12 illustrations. 80pp. of text. 5⅜ x 8½.   23411-8

ANIMALS: 1,419 Copyright-Free Illustrations of Mammals, Birds, Fish, Insects, etc., Jim Harter (ed.). Clear wood engravings present, in extremely lifelike poses, over 1,000 species of animals. One of the most extensive pictorial sourcebooks of its kind. Captions. Index. 284pp. 9 x 12.   23766-4

CELTIC ART: The Methods of Construction, George Bain. Simple geometric techniques for making Celtic interlacements, spirals, Kells-type initials, animals, humans, etc. Over 500 illustrations. 160pp. 9 x 12. (Available in U.S. only.)   22923-8

AN ATLAS OF ANATOMY FOR ARTISTS, Fritz Schider. Most thorough reference work on art anatomy in the world. Hundreds of illustrations, including selections from works by Vesalius, Leonardo, Goya, Ingres, Michelangelo, others. 593 illustrations. 192pp. 7⅛ x 10¼.   20241-0

CELTIC HAND STROKE-BY-STROKE (Irish Half-Uncial from "The Book of Kells"): An Arthur Baker Calligraphy Manual, Arthur Baker. Complete guide to creating each letter of the alphabet in distinctive Celtic manner. Covers hand position, strokes, pens, inks, paper, more. Illustrated. 48pp. 8¼ x 11.   24336-2

EASY ORIGAMI, John Montroll. Charming collection of 32 projects (hat, cup, pelican, piano, swan, many more) specially designed for the novice origami hobbyist. Clearly illustrated easy-to-follow instructions insure that even beginning papercrafters will achieve successful results. 48pp. 8¼ x 11.   27298-2

THE COMPLETE BOOK OF BIRDHOUSE CONSTRUCTION FOR WOODWORKERS, Scott D. Campbell. Detailed instructions, illustrations, tables. Also data on bird habitat and instinct patterns. Bibliography. 3 tables. 63 illustrations in 15 figures. 48pp. 5¼ x 8½.   24407-5

BLOOMINGDALE'S ILLUSTRATED 1886 CATALOG: Fashions, Dry Goods and Housewares, Bloomingdale Brothers. Famed merchants' extremely rare catalog depicting about 1,700 products: clothing, housewares, firearms, dry goods, jewelry, more. Invaluable for dating, identifying vintage items. Also, copyright-free graphics for artists, designers. Co-published with Henry Ford Museum & Greenfield Village. 160pp. 8¼ x 11.   25780-0

HISTORIC COSTUME IN PICTURES, Braun & Schneider. Over 1,450 costumed figures in clearly detailed engravings—from dawn of civilization to end of 19th century. Captions. Many folk costumes. 256pp. 8⅜ x 11¾.   23150-X

CATALOG OF DOVER BOOKS

THE STORY OF THE TITANIC AS TOLD BY ITS SURVIVORS, Jack Winocour (ed.). What it was really like. Panic, despair, shocking inefficiency, and a little heroism. More thrilling than any fictional account. 26 illustrations. 320pp. 5⅜ x 8½.
20610-6

FAIRY AND FOLK TALES OF THE IRISH PEASANTRY, William Butler Yeats (ed.). Treasury of 64 tales from the twilight world of Celtic myth and legend: "The Soul Cages," "The Kildare Pooka," "King O'Toole and his Goose," many more. Introduction and Notes by W. B. Yeats. 352pp. 5⅜ x 8½.
26941-8

BUDDHIST MAHAYANA TEXTS, E. B. Cowell and others (eds.). Superb, accurate translations of basic documents in Mahayana Buddhism, highly important in history of religions. The Buddha-karita of Asvaghosha, Larger Sukhavativyuha, more. 448pp. 5⅜ x 8½.
25552-2

ONE TWO THREE . . . INFINITY: Facts and Speculations of Science, George Gamow. Great physicist's fascinating, readable overview of contemporary science: number theory, relativity, fourth dimension, entropy, genes, atomic structure, much more. 128 illustrations. Index. 352pp. 5⅜ x 8½.
25664-2

EXPERIMENTATION AND MEASUREMENT, W. J. Youden. Introductory manual explains laws of measurement in simple terms and offers tips for achieving accuracy and minimizing errors. Mathematics of measurement, use of instruments, experimenting with machines. 1994 edition. Foreword. Preface. Introduction. Epilogue. Selected Readings. Glossary. Index. Tables and figures. 128pp. 5⅜ x 8½.
40451-X

DALÍ ON MODERN ART: The Cuckolds of Antiquated Modern Art, Salvador Dalí. Influential painter skewers modern art and its practitioners. Outrageous evaluations of Picasso, Cézanne, Turner, more. 15 renderings of paintings discussed. 44 calligraphic decorations by Dalí. 96pp. 5⅜ x 8½. (Available in U.S. only.)
29220-7

ANTIQUE PLAYING CARDS: A Pictorial History, Henry René D'Allemagne. Over 900 elaborate, decorative images from rare playing cards (14th–20th centuries): Bacchus, death, dancing dogs, hunting scenes, royal coats of arms, players cheating, much more. 96pp. 9¼ x 12¼.
29265-7

MAKING FURNITURE MASTERPIECES: 30 Projects with Measured Drawings, Franklin H. Gottshall. Step-by-step instructions, illustrations for constructing handsome, useful pieces, among them a Sheraton desk, Chippendale chair, Spanish desk, Queen Anne table and a William and Mary dressing mirror. 224pp. 8⅛ x 11¼.
29338-6

THE FOSSIL BOOK: A Record of Prehistoric Life, Patricia V. Rich et al. Profusely illustrated definitive guide covers everything from single-celled organisms and dinosaurs to birds and mammals and the interplay between climate and man. Over 1,500 illustrations. 760pp. 7½ x 10⅛.
29371-8